United Nations University Series on Regionalism

Volume 26

This book series offers a platform for innovative work on (supra-national) regionalism from a global and inter-disciplinary perspective. It started with the World Reports on Regional Integration, published in collaboration with other UN agencies, and now publishes theoretical, methodological and empirical contributions related to various themes on interregionalism from academics and policy-makers worldwide. All book proposals are reviewed by an International Editorial Board and final approval on manuscripts also comes from the board.

The series editors are particularly interested in book proposals dealing with:

- comparative regionalism;
- comparative work on regional organizations;
- interregionalism
- the role of regions in a multi-level governance contex;
- the interactions between the UN and the regions;
- the regional dimensions of the reform processes of multilateral institutions;
- the dynamics of cross-border micro-regions and their interactions with supra-national regions;
- methodological issues in regionalism studies.

Accepted book proposals can receive editorial support from UNU-CRIS for the preparation of manuscripts.

Please send book proposals to: pdelombaerde@cris.unu.edu and lvanlangenhove@cris.unu.edu.

Céline C. Cocq

Mutual Trust in Regional and Interregional Cooperation on Counterterrorism

EU and ASEAN Approaches

Springer

Céline C. Cocq
Université libre de Bruxelles
Brussels, Belgium

ISSN 2214-9848 ISSN 2214-9856 (electronic)
United Nations University Series on Regionalism
ISBN 978-3-031-36611-6 ISBN 978-3-031-36612-3 (eBook)
https://doi.org/10.1007/978-3-031-36612-3

This Springer imprint is published by the registered company Springer Nature Switzerland AG
The registered company address is: Gewerbestrasse 11, 6330 Cham, Switzerland

Dr. Cocq provides a rich, rigorous, and in-depth comparative legal analysis of EU and ASEAN counter-terrorism approaches, the legal framework, information sharing, judicial and police cooperation, including context, history, and philosophy. Through the crucial lens of trust, the book explores commonalities, differences, and increased engagement between both organizations. It provides very useful reading and insights for scholars and policy makers.
Dr. Christiane Höhn Council of the European Union Principal Adviser to the EU Counter-terrorism Coordinator.
The views expressed in this endorsement are those of the author alone and in no way reflect the positions of the Council of the European Union or the European Council.

When you are surrounded by people who share the same commitment around a common purpose, anything is possible.

Foreword

The question of why and how states cooperate in national security matters is complex and the role of regional arrangements is particularly under-studied. Two decades after the September 11 attacks, the threat of terrorism may appear to have receded, but regional cooperation to contain and combat it has increased. This depends on, among other things, shared goals and definitions, shared information and shared activities. Some of this can be achieved through fear, but lasting arrangements depend on trust.

In this book, Céline Cocq examines how mutual trust has been developed and operationalised to facilitate cooperation between competent national authorities within regions and between regions, focusing on the shared problem of terrorism.

The relationship between trust and cooperation is also complex, posing a "chicken and egg" problem of which came first. Yet, among the interesting conclusions reached in this book is the finding that trust and cooperation are better thought of as existing in a virtuous circle, reinforcing one another.

To analyse these phenomena, Dr. Cocq proposes an analytical matrix focusing on the methods used to build mutual trust amongst stakeholders at different levels. The first is the development of regional architectures facilitating intra-regional cooperation in criminal matters. Secondly, specific channels for interregional relations in counterterrorism can strengthen and deepen those ties.

The concept of trust itself, vital to the thesis advanced, is examined in three dimensions. Initial stages of cooperation may be premised on interpersonal or social trust, but that will necessarily be limited to the individuals involved—diplomats and other actors who will come and go. More structural possibilities depend on shared interests that go beyond individuals, described here as the political dimension of trust. Further instantiation is possible through legal formalities that are binding on both parties, a reciprocity that reflects the willingness to give up certain aspects of sovereignty to those whom we believe will not abuse that trust.

The choice of case studies is interesting and, helpfully, Dr. Cocq does not gloss over the difficulty of comparing apples and oranges. The European Union may be regarded by some as a model for other regional organizations, but not by the

Association of Southeast Asian Nations (ASEAN). Nonetheless, the challenges each institution has faced and the manner in which those challenges have been overcome (or not) are illuminating in understanding the possibilities and limitations of regional and multilateral approaches to counterterrorism, as well as enriching the field of comparative regionalism and inter-regionalism more generally.

The book, which I had the pleasure of examining in its doctoral form, is structured in three parts. It begins by setting the stage, outlining the terms, introducing key concepts and constructing a data analysis matrix for the examination of trust. Part two brings in the key actors—the EU and ASEAN, as well as national and regional institutions that have played key roles in counterterrorism activities. A central question is whether the formalisation and legalisation of those intra-regional entities, more common in the EU, offers a more effective framework for cross-border cooperation than the looser model adopted in ASEAN. The third and final part looks at the relationship between those actors, tracking the many levels of dialogue with an eye to determining what role (if any) trust plays in such inter-regional relationships.

Any kind of international institution-building faces the dilemma of how to balance legitimacy and effectiveness. ASEAN's gradualist, consensus-bound approach has necessarily meant that it takes more time or acts more hesitantly. The EU, by contrast, is seen by some as a kind of super-state, with greater centralised powers that enable it to act more swiftly—albeit at the expense of the comfort of some of its members (see Brexit). A key finding of the study is that trust is a dynamic concept, rarely of value in the abstract, but cultivated and developed (and lost) through shared practices. Those practices include capability building, capacity building, and knowledge and experience sharing.

Trust and cooperation are, in the end, interdependent. Trust drives, supports and emerges from cooperation. This is true within nations but especially between them. At the interregional level, the abstraction from quotidian interactions makes trust more difficult—even as the need for it in facing shared threats becomes more important.

National University of Singapore, Singapore

Pr. Simon Chesterman

Acknowledgements

This monograph is the product of a 4-year extremely enriching journey. I am very grateful to all the people who helped me, shared their knowledge with me and inspired me. I have crossed path with so many people that listing everyone is not possible. Yet, I would like to specifically thank some people who shared this journey with me and offered me new perspectives, in-depth insights, the benefit of their expertise and experience, as well as their humanity.

Firstly, I am very grateful to Pr. Anne Weyembergh (Université libre de Bruxelles) and Pr. Robert Roth (Université de Genève) who have been absolutely invaluable to the completion of my PhD thesis, and thus to this monograph. I am particularly grateful for their sharp and brilliant comments on my research and for their endless support. Alongside them, I also would like to thank the members of the jury of my PhD thesis: Pr. Pierre Klein, Pr. Nicolas Levrat and Pr. Simon Chesterman.

I also would like to thank the academic community I belong who challenged my hypothesis and arguments.

This research was shaped by the GEM-STONES programme[1] fostering excellence in interdisciplinary research in social sciences which would not have been possible without the dedication of Pr. Mario Telò and Pr. Anne Weyembergh. The interactions with the other fellows and professors taking part in this programme have broadened my intellectual horizons and triggered my curiosity in other disciplines.

As a member of the ECLAN family, I would like to thank the professors who brought me valuable food for thoughts. I also would like to thank my fellow researchers, especially Pr. Chloé Brière et Dr. Julia Burchett who, besides academic discussions, provided moral support and fun during this journey and beyond.

[1] This research has received funding from the European Union's Horizon 2020 research and innovation programme under the Marie Sklodowska-Curie Grant Agreement No 722826.

Secondly, I would like to thank the persons I met in Europe and Southeast Asia. This monograph was nourished by the scholars and professionals from whom I had the opportunity to learn during my travels.

While working in Southeast Asia, I would like to thank the programme officers at the UNODC-ROSEAP who shared with me their experience and guided me within the region, especially those at the Terrorism Prevention Office. The interviewees fascinating insights and incredible experiences have livened up the pages of this book. Scholars and professionals have enlightened me on the actual situation in Southeast Asia.

While being in Europe, I benefitted from EU officials and national experts who kindly accepted to share their knowledge. I would particularly like to express my gratitude to Dr. Christiane Höhn, Principal Advisor to the EU Counterterrorism Coordinator, who encouraged me, supported my project and provided invaluable inputs. I also have a particular thought to the officers and specialists at Europol, at the Data Protection Office and law enforcement officers, with whom I had invaluable exchanges on issues related to EU cooperation.

Thirdly, I would like to thank old and new friends scattered around the world with whom I shared memorable cheerful moments: Frederik, Stéphanie, Johann, Ulla, Aurélie, Nelly, Magali, Florent, Francesca, to name just a few. Your humour, laughs and intelligence have been a constant source of happiness. Finally, I would like to thank my family who supported me until the end of this journey.

Contents

About the Author

Céline C. Cocq is a legal expert in justice and home affairs. Her expertise covers security and criminal matters at the national, regional (e.g. the European Union and Association of South East Asian Nations) and international levels: counterterrorism, cooperation mechanisms, data sharing, human rights law, armed conflicts and humanitarian law.

She holds a PhD in law delivered jointly by the Université libre de Bruxelles (ULB) and the University of Geneva in April 2021, in which she analyses regional and interregional cooperation in counterterrorism-related matters, with a specific focus on the EU and ASEAN. She also holds several graduate degrees in law and criminology from both Belgium (ULB) and France (Lille II, University of Aix-Marseille).

Besides her research and continued membership of the European Criminal Law Academic Network (ECLAN), she has acted as a legal and political analyst for several EU and UN funded actors such as: Europol, European research consortia, or the Terrorism Prevention Office of UNODC-ROSEAP. Recently, she worked at the specialised prosecutor's office in Fort-de-France dealing with complex and serious (transnational) offences. She is presently working for the prosecutor's office in Avignon as a specialised assistant for the prevention of terrorist acts.

Abbreviations

ACCT	ASEAN Convention on Counter Terrorism
ACOT	ASEAN Centre on Transnational Crime
AD	Action Directe
AEC	ASEAN Economic Community
AFSJ	Area of Freedom Security and Justice (EU)
AHRC	Asian Human Rights Commission
AHRD	ASEAN Human Rights Declaration
AICHR	ASEAN Intergovernmental Commission on Human Rights
ALAWMM	ASEAN Law Ministers Meeting
APSC	ASEAN Political and Security Community
AQ	Al-Qaeda
ARF	ASEAN Regional Forum
ASA	Association of Southeast Asia
ASCC	ASEAN Socio-Cultural Community
ASEAN	Association of Southeast Asian Nations
ASG	Abu Sayyaf Group
ATC	Anti-Terrorism Council (Philippines)
ATC-PMC	Anti-Terrorism Council Program Management Council (Philippines)
AU	African Union
CC	Criminal Code
CCC	Cellules Communistes Combattantes
CCP	Code of Criminal Procedure
CEPOL	European Police College
CFD	Council Framework Decision
CISA	Convention implementing the Schengen Agreement
CJEU	Court of Justice of the European Union
CLMV countries	Cambodia, Lao PDR, Myanmar and Vietnam
CoE	Council of Europe
COSI	Standing Committee on Internal Security
CTC	Counter Terrorism Coordinator

CTED	Counter-Terrorism Committee Executive Directorate
CTG	Counter Terrorism Group
CTR	Counter Terrorism Register (Eurojust)
DCRI	Direction Centrale du Renseignement Intérieur
EAEC	European Atomic Energy Community
EAW	European Arrest Warrant
ECHR	European Convention on Human Rights
ECJ	European Court of Justice
ECRIS-TCN	European Criminal Records Information System for Third Country Nationals
ECTC	European Counter Terrorism Centre (Europol)
ECtHR	European Court on Human Rights
EEAS	European External Action Service
EES	Entry/Exist System
EPPO	European Public Prosecutor's Office
ESCAP	Economic and Social Commission for Asia and Pacific
ESDP	European Security and Defence Policy
ETA	Euskadi ta Askatasuna
ETIAS	European Travel Information and Authorisation System
EU CFR	EU Charter of Fundamental Rights
EU	European Union
eu-LISA	European Union Agency for the Operational Management of Large-Scale IT Systems in the Area of Freedom, Security and Justice
FAO	Food and Agriculture Organization
FTF	Foreign Terrorist Fighter
GAM	Free Aceh Movement
HRC	Human Rights Council
ICCPR	International Covenant on Civil and Political Rights
ICESCR	International Covenant on Economic, Social and Cultural Rights
IGC	Inter-Governmental Conference (on the adoption of the 2000 EU Convention and Charter)
IGCI	Interpol Global Complex for Innovation
ILEA	International Law Enforcement Academy
IntCen	Intelligence Analysis Centre
IRA	Irish Republican Army
ISIS	Islamic State of Iraq and the Levant
ISS	Internal Security Strategy
JCLEC	Jakarta Centre for Law Enforcement Cooperation
JHA	Justice and Home Affairs
JI	Jemaah Islamiyah
MB	Moniteur Belge
MILF	Moro Islamic Liberation Front

MNLF	Moro National Liberation Front
MoU	Memorandum of Understanding
NTU	Nanyang Technological University
OEI	Our Eyes Initiative
OHCHR	Office of the United Nations Commissioner for Human Rights
OLAF	European Anti-Fraud Office
OMC	Open Method of Coordination
OSCE	Organisation for Security and Co-operation in Europe
PDPA	Personal Data Protection Act (Malaysia)
RAF	Red Army Faction
RSIS	S. Rajaratnam School of International Studies
SC	Security Council
SEARCCT	Southeast Asia Regional Centre for Counter Terrorism
SIS	Schengen Information System
StGB	Strafgesetzbuch
TREVI	Terrorisme, Radicalisme, Extremisme et Violence Internationale (Terrorism, Radicalisation, Extremism and International Violence)
UDHR	Universal Declaration on Human Rights
UK	United Kingdom
UN	United Nations
UNDP	United Nations Development Programme
UNGA	United Nations General Assembly
UNICRI	United Nations Interregional Crime and Justice Research Institute
UNO	United Nations Organisation
UNOCT	United Nations Office of Counter-Terrorism
UNSC	United Nations Security Council
UNSCR	United Nations Security Council Resolution
UNTOC	United Nations Convention on Transnational Organized Crime
VIS	Visa Information System

List of Diagrams

List of Tables

Chapter 1
Introduction

> *Where the stakes are the highest, in the war on terror, we cannot possibly succeed without extraordinary international cooperation. Effective international police actions require the highest degree of intelligence sharing, planning and collaborative enforcement.*
> *Barack Obama,*
> *Speech to the Chicago Council on Foreign Relations, 12 July 2004*

In a world where crossing borders has become easier, especially in certain regions of the world, transnational cooperation has also become essential. Yet, the salient question remains: which path should one take to reach this 'extraordinary international cooperation'? Then, what could act as the glue binding partners together and consolidating their relations? The best answer is: *trust.*

This chapter presents the *raison d'être* of this book. It briefly introduces the various issues surrounding terrorism, from the nature of the threat to the methods adopted to counter it (Section 1). Then, it designs the contours and purpose of this study (Section 2).

Section 1: Looking for an Effective Response to International Terrorism—The Opportunity to Work at the Regional Level

While the international community has agreed upon some main axes of action against terrorism, implementing them at the international level is not particularly easy (I). For this reason, an intermediary solution has been looked for through regional organisations (II).

I. Benefits of and Obstacles to the Implementation of the Comprehensive Counterterrorism Strategy

C. C. Cocq, *Mutual Trust in Regional and Interregional Cooperation on Counterterrorism*, United Nations University Series on Regionalism 26,
https://doi.org/10.1007/978-3-031-36612-3_1

Terrorism has had an impact on every country in the world, even those that have not suffered from a direct attack (thus far). Countries can be victims of terrorism in various ways: by experiencing attacks on their soil, by involuntarily or voluntarily hosting terrorists, by serving as transit countries, by having their citizens recruited for terrorist purposes, etc. Moreover, the terrorist threat has evolved over time in its form, motives and means, using all available technologies and technical tools. (A)

As asserted in its Charter, the United Nations strives to maintaining international peace and security by taking collective measures for the prevention and removal of threats to peace. In this respect, the attacks on the World Trade Center and the Pentagon on 11 September 2001 followed by other attacks around the world have shown that countering this threat requires collective efforts with respect to international law.[1] (B)

A. The Terrorist Threat: Evolving in Motives, Form and Means

Terrorism has known various motives, sometimes simultaneously, and has taken different forms over time (1). Moreover, terrorist groups and individuals have made the most profitable use of the development of technologies and techniques to perpetrate their crimes (2).

1. A multi-motive and multi-morph terrorist threat creating confusion among States

The United Nations (UN) qualified terrorism as 'a threat to international peace and security'[2] making the notion of 'security' more inclusive and comprehensive. To traditional security, comprising the military dimension of conflicts, has been added the range of non-traditional security threats, including terrorism and other forms of serious transnational crime. These two dimensions of 'security' are reflected in Southeast Asia and Europe. The Association of Southeast Asian Nations (ASEAN) follows the international qualification 'traditional security' and 'non-traditional security', while the European Union (EU) distinguishes between the 'Common Foreign Security Policy' (defence) and the 'Area of Freedom, Security and Justice' (criminal justice).

As part of the non-traditional security threats, the numerous terrorist groups may be roughly categorised on the basis of their motive(s) as follows: separatist, ethno-centric, nationalistic, revolutionary, political, religious and/or social. The motives of terrorist groups often overlap to some extent. The degree of overlap gives an

[1] A/CONF.222/L.6, 13th UN Congress on Crime Prevention and Criminal Justice, *Doha Declaration on integrating crime prevention and criminal justice into the wider United Nations agenda to address social and economic challenges and to promote the rule of law at the national and international levels, and public participation*, Doha, 12–19 April 2015; United Nations Security Council, S/RES/2395(2017), *Threats to international peace and security caused by terrorist acts*, 8146th meeting, 21 December 2017; United Nations General Assembly, A/RES/71/291, *Strengthening the capability of the United Nations system to assist Member States in implementing the United Nations Global Counter-Terrorism Strategy*, 87th plenary meeting, 15 June 2017.

[2] See, e.g., S/RES/1368(2001), *Threats to international peace and security caused by terrorist acts*, 4370th meeting, 12 September 2001.

indication of the multiplicity and complexity of pathways to terrorism.[3] Moreover, these groups may remain domestic or operate beyond borders. Those trends are not specific to a country or a region, but they may appear worldwide. Europe and Southeast Asia have been the theatre of similar terrorist trends as well as interesting developments in counterterrorism.

Extensively written about by many scholars, it may be briefly mentioned some key movements that existed or still existing in the EU. Some European countries, such as the United Kingdom (UK), Spain, Germany, Italy, France and Portugal, have a strong experience in countering terrorism. Some of them faced nationalistic terrorist threats in the past, such as the Irish Republican Army (IRA) in Ireland or *Euskadi ta Askatasuna* (ETA) in Spain mostly and a bit in the Southwest of France. Besides, the concept of 'euro-terrorism' appeared and became popular in the 1980s to designate the activities of transnational terrorist groups, especially some left or ultra-left groups, namely the *Rote Armee Fraktion*, the *Brigate Rosse* and *Action Directe*. Differences in history and terrorist experience have formatted the respective States' approaches. Some countries may have been more protective of human rights due to their authoritarian past but, due to recent attacks, this fierce opposition against restrictions of human rights may not be so strict anymore. Other countries may have never suffered from terrorist attacks, which may explain the absence of eagerness in developing counterterrorism laws and mechanisms to cooperate with other countries. Notably, the EU action was particularly fostered by the 9/11 attacks but also by the European countries' own experience, especially the 2004 train bombings in Madrid, the 2005 attacks on London's public transport system, the 2015 attacks against Charlie Hebdo and in the Bataclan concert hall in Paris and the 2016 Brussels bombings.

While some have considered that terrorism has become more prominent in Southeast Asia in the aftermath of the 9/11 attacks, not everyone agrees with this view.[4] The region has long been exploited by international terrorist groups for its loose borders and limited government control to establish cells and train terrorist candidates.

During the Cold War period, one of the most potent security threats was for long the Communist Party, especially in the Philippines where it emerged in the 1960s, that co-existed or was mixed with armed separatist movements involving indigenous ethnic or religious minorities.[5] In Southern Thailand, the separatist movement remains active.[6]

---

[3]Daniel Masters, 'The Origin of Terrorist Threats: Religious, Separatists, or Something Else?' *Terrorism and Political Violence,* vol. 20, no. 3 (2008).

[4]Aurel Croissant and Daniel Barlow, 'Following the Money Trail: Terrorist Financing and Government Responses in Southeast Asia' *Studies in Conflict & Terrorism,* vol. 30, no. 2 (2007): 133.

[5]See, e.g., MILF and ASG in the Philippines, both of which have links with Indonesian and Malaysian jihadist forces; or also the Free Aceh Movement (GAM) in Indonesia, which aimed to create an Islamic State in Aceh.

[6]Aurel Croissant, 'Unrest in South Thailand: Contours, Causes and Consequences Since 2001' *Contemporary Southeast Asia,* vol. 27, no. 1 (2005): 27.

Among the religious groups, Islamist terrorism was already threatening some Southeast Asian countries in the 1990s.[7] For instance, groups as *Jemaah Islamiyah* (JI) and Abu Sayyaf Group (ASG) were already present throughout the region. Pr. Gunaratna estimated that before 9/11 about 20% of Al Qaeda's organisational strength was in Asia, concentrated in Indonesia, Malaysia, the Philippines and Singapore.[8] Yet, many terrorist organisations in Southeast Asia are motivated by local agendas. While they may benefit from logistical and financial support from international terrorist groups, such as Al Qaeda and Da'esh, when their agendas coincide,[9] organisations such as ASG, Moro Islamic Liberation Front (MILF) and JI have also developed and funded their own agendas regardless of Al Qaeda or Da'esh involvement.

For instance, JI, undoubtedly inspired by Al Qaeda and working in conjunction with this group on occasion to achieve common goals, could not be described as its Southeast Asian branch. By contrast, *Jamaah Ansharut Daulah* (JAD) that emerged in 2015 as a jihadi group pledged allegiance to Islamic State of Iraq and Sham (ISIS) leader Abu Bakr al-Baghdadi. This group became the primary Islamic State-aligned group in Indonesia. Today, the greatest terrorist threat is posed by the Philippine-based ASG and the Indonesia-based JAD, both aligned with ISIS.[10]

Although Southeast Asia has been the theatre of active terrorist groups before 2001, the Bali bombings in 2002 and the pressure from the United States of America (USA) that considered Southeast Asia as the 'second front' in the 'global war on terrorism'[11] have made Southeast Asian governments realise the need to work together against this threat for their population's security and economic well-being.[12] Actions against terrorism have focused on radical Islamist groups present in countries with large Muslim populations, such as Indonesia, Malaysia, the

[7]Ralph Emmers, 'Comprehensive security and resilience in Southeast Asia: ASEAN's approach to terrorism and Piracy' Working Paper no. 132 (S. Rajaratnam School of International Studies: Singapore).

[8]Rohan Gunaratna, *Inside Al Qaeda: Global Network of Terror* (New York: Columbia University Press, 2002).

[9]Croissant and Barlow (2007): 134.

[10]Marc Alphonse Vierstraete-Verlinde, 'EU ACTIONPLAN on CT and P/CVE, South-East Asia PRIORITIES', EU Delegation to Indonesia and Brunei Darussalam and Mission to ASEAN (Jakarta, December 2019).

[11]Gunaratna (2002); John Gershman, 'Is Southeast Asia the Second Front?' *Foreign Affairs,* vol. 81, no. 4 (2002); Woodrow Wilson, 'Fighting Terrorism on the Southeast Asian Front' *Asia Program Special Report,* vol. 112, (2003); Diane K. Mauzy and Brian L. Job, 'U.S. policy in Southeast Asia. Limited Re-engagement after Years of Benign Neglect' *Asian Survey,* vol. 47, no. 4 (2007); Andrew T. H. Tan, 'Terrorism and insurgency in Southeast Asia' in *A Handbook of Terrorism and Insurgency in Southeast Asia*, ed., Andrew T. H. Tan (Cheltenham: Edward Elgar Publishing, 2007): 3–5; Yeo Lay Hwee, 'The EU as a Security Actor in Southeast Asia' in *Security Politics in Asia and Europe*, Panorama: Insights into Asian and European Affairs (Singapore: Konrad Adenauer Stiftung, 2009): 12.

[12]Dong-Yoon Lee, 'Politics of Anti-Terrorism Policy in Southeast Asia: A comparative study of the Philippines and Indonesia' *Pacific Focus,* vol. 24, no. 2 (2009).

Philippines, Singapore and Thailand.[13] However, addressing terrorism is problematic for some Southeast Asian States with significant Muslim populations. Yet, such situation did not prevent these governments from becoming more active to cooperate over time.

Particularly, both Europe and Southeast Asia have suffered from a similar terrorist threat, namely the so-called foreign terrorist fighters (FTFs).[14] The return of citizens from Iraq and Syria is a very topical issue and worries States concerned.[15] The large number of Southeast Asian foreign fighters joining ISIS is reminiscent of the flow of volunteers who joined the Afghan jihad against the Soviet occupation in the 1980s.[16] By contrast, this phenomenon appeared in Europe only recently with ISIS returnees. This recent flow is far more serious than the one of Afghan returnees though. By 2015, approximately 40.000 individuals from 120 countries had travelled to Iraq and Syria. In this number, around 5.000 originating from Europe[17] and around 1.500 originating from Southeast Asia[18] have travelled to join the terrorist organisation ISIS, also called the Islamic State in Iraq and the Levant (ISIL), and al-Nusra Front (ANF), or other affiliated groups. However, despite the Islamic State's (IS) defeat in Iraq and Syria, the terrorist threat remains, due to a radical Islamist jihadist ideology, sleeper cells, lone wolves and skillful exploitation of modern technology.

While these past years show an increase in jihadist extremism, attacks by separatist and left-wing extremist movements have been on a steady decline. Interestingly, there has also been an increase in the number of right-wing terrorist incidents in the past 5 years.

---

[13] Kanita Sapphaisal, *Fighting Terrorism in Southeast Asia* (Harvard University, Law School: PhD degree, dissertation, 2004): 2; Croissant and Barlow (2007): 132; Anna Cornelia Beyer, 'ASEAN Counterterrorism: Participation and Causes' in *Counterterrorism and International Power Relations: The EU, ASEAN and Hegemonic Global Governance*, ed., Anna Cornelia Beyer (London: I.B. Tauris, 2010): 99.

[14] UNSC, S/RES/2178(2014), *Condemning Violent Extremism, Underscoring Need to Prevent Travel, Support for Foreign Terrorist Fighters*, 7272nd meeting, 24 September 2014: FTFs are defined as 'individuals who travel to a State other than their States of residence or nationality for the purpose of the perpetration, planning, or preparation of, or participation in, terrorist acts or the providing or receiving of terrorist training, including in connection with armed conflict'. And, S/RES/2396(2017), *Foreign Terrorist Fighters (Returnees and Relocators)*, 8184th meeting, 21 December 2017.

[15] 'Terrorism Risks Rising in Malaysia as Islamic State Militants Return' *Thailand Business News*, 26 December 2017: available at https://www.thailand-business-news.com/politics/65320-terrorism-risks-rising-in-malaysia-as-islamic-state-militants-return.html (accessed on 1 January 2018).

[16] Jasminder Singh, 'Danger of Southeast Asian Jihadi Returnees: Need for an ASEAN-wide Policy' RSIS Commentary no. 7, 18 January 2016: available at https://www.rsis.edu.sg/wp-content/uploads/2016/01/CO16007.pdf (accessed on 18 July 2017).

[17] Europol, 'European Union Terrorism Situation and Trend Report (TE-SAT) 2019', *report*, 27 June 2019.

[18] Croissant and Barlow (2007): 134.

2. Everyday technologies and other technical means used for terrorist purposes

Our world has experienced enormous and unprecedented technological progress in recent years. Although it may be limited in some countries with strict control and censorship, people have gained access to a large amount of information and can communicate more easily and quicker than before. In parallel, the flow of people has increased and has become smoother. The traditional barriers have been alleviated between some countries (no visa required, formalities diminished) or are not very effective due to political and/or geographical constraints.

Terrorists abuse these communication means, especially Internet, to disseminate propaganda, training manuals, practical advices on how to obtain and import weapons, on how to make bombs and how to select targets, plan and carry out attacks.[19] These means have facilitated the emergence of self-radicalised terrorists. Securing their communications, terrorists have also been using the various methods of privacy protection that have emerged these past years.[20] These methods make the task of law enforcement authorities difficult.[21] The latter are confronted to strong practical and legal obstacles when trying to gain access to data for criminal justice purposes and even more for the prevention of criminal activities.

Confronted with multi-morph, multi-motive and sometimes multiheaded terrorist threats, States have increasingly adapted their response, including through cross-border cooperation.

B. Channelling States' Actions to Facilitate a Transnational Response

Playing an important role in countries' counterterrorism responses, countries' respective experience of this threat has framed their political and legal national frameworks. States have used various sets of military (within and beyond their borders), legal (e.g. anti-terrorism laws) and administrative (e.g. blacklisting, freezing of assets) measures, giving more importance to one measure over another.

In this diversity, the UN has aimed to foster a more comprehensive international response along two main axes: (1) the criminalisation of terrorist offences, which has

---

[19] Edgar Pang (representative of Singapore) qualified terrorism as the 'dark side of globalization', UNGA 6th Committee (4th Meeting) (7 October 2005) UN Doc GA/L/3276. On radicalisation leading to terrorism, see, e.g., S/RES/2178(2014); UNSC, Implementation of Security Council Resolution 2178(2014) by States affected by foreign terrorist fighters; S/RES/2396(2017). A compilation of three reports (S/2015/338, S/2015/683, S/2015/975): available at https://www.un.org/sc/ctc/wp-content/uploads/2016/09/FTF-Report-1-3_English.pdf (accessed on 4 August 2017).

[20] UNSC, 'Letter dated 2 September 2015 from the Chair of the Security Council Committee established pursuant to resolution 1373 (2001) concerning counter-terrorism addressed to the President of the Security Council, Annex Implementation of Security Council Resolution 2178 (2014) by States affected by foreign terrorist fighters' S/2015/683 second report (2 September 2015); Jamie Bartlett & Alex Krasodomski-Jones, 'Online Anonymity Islamic State and Surveillance' (Demos, 2015), 3.

[21] See, e.g., Céline C. Cocq, 'Encryption and anonymisation online: Challenges for law enforcement authorities within the EU' in *Data Protection, Privacy and European Regulation in the Digital Age*, eds., Tobias Bräutigam and Samuli Miettinen (Helsinki: Forum Iuris, 2016).

emerged at different times depending on the countries and which has varied from one country to another, has led to discrepancies hindering the second axis, and the development of cross-border cooperation (2) in order to eliminate any safe haven to perpetrators.[22]

On the one hand, the UN requires States to criminalise terrorist offences and to produce normative standards in order to ensure that terrorists would be prosecuted in every country.[23] Yet, the international community has been confronted with challenges, including the difficulties of establishing common definitions of terrorist offences and of their components. In this context, some countries already had anti-terrorism arsenals in place (e.g. France, Spain or Malaysia, the Philippines, Singapore and Vietnam), while others adopted anti-terrorism norms after the 9/11 attacks or after more local terrorist attacks, and potentially under the pressure of international or, where applicable, European norms and policies. However, national anti-terrorism legislations still vary from one country to another despite international instruments.

Beside criminal laws, human rights are also part of the common normative standards of the legal anti-terrorism package. Governments have been criticised for the radical path they themselves have taken, often allowing security to prevail above people's liberties and rights. They did so despite the UN's request to adopt and implement counterterrorism measures while respecting human rights and fundamental freedoms.[24] Yet, the protection of human rights and the rule of law greatly contribute to the countering of terrorism.[25]

Yet, establishing common legal standards would facilitate further cross-border cooperation and provide for a joint response against terrorism.

On the one hand, the United Nations has boosted international cooperation, identifying it as an essential means for preventing and countering terrorism. However, States tend to struggle between protecting their national sovereignty and using it on the international scene to cooperate with others. They eventually cooperate when it benefits them and to avoid the high costs of non-cooperation.[26]

Traditionally, cross-border cooperation, such as extradition and mutual legal assistance, developed through diplomatic channels. The response time and heavy procedure did not meet the requirements to address criminal dynamics though. Therefore, quicker and more direct, horizontal cooperation mechanisms have developed between competent national authorities.

Considered to be the most crucial means, authorities have particularly focused on acquiring data. States have aimed at gathering the highest number and the most

---

[22] See, e.g., A/CONF.222/L.6, *Doha Declaration* (2015).

[23] Valsamis Mitsilegas, "The European Union and the Global Governance of Crime" in *Globalisation, Criminal Law and Criminal Justice. Theoretical, Comparative and Transnational Perspectives*, ed. Valsamis Mitsilegas, Peter Alldridge, and Leonidas Cheliotis (Oxford: Hart Publishing, 2015); Ramraj, 45.

[24] S/RES/2396(2017), *Foreign Terrorist Fighters (Returnees and Relocators)*, 21 December 2017.

[25] Office of the United Nations High Commissioner for Human Rights (OHCHR), 'Human Rights, Terrorism and Counter-Terrorism', Fact Sheet no. 32, Geneva, July 2008.

[26] Paul Evans, 'Searching for Cooperative Security 2.0. From Security Architecture to Security Order in the Asia Pacific' *China Quarterly of International Strategic Studies*, vol. 1, no. 4 (2015).

accurate data, using all technical and technological means at their disposal. Information is indeed power. However, this endeavour has often led to tragic human rights violations.

Other than or after collecting data, various mechanisms of data sharing were created to facilitate the respective tasks of competent national authorities. Information and intelligence sharing is one of the methods considered to be a prerequisite to combat transnational crime, including terrorism.[27] Competent national authorities share data on (1) the actions and movements of people and networks; (2) the manufacture, transfer and use of goods, such as forged or falsified travel documents, arms, explosives, weapons of mass destruction, sensitive materials or technologies and (3) financial transfers.[28]

While improvements must be noted, information and intelligence sharing is still confronted with numerous obstacles. Among them, the two following elements can be highlighted.

Firstly, the main obstacle in sharing information and intelligence is the compatibility between criminal justice procedures. One's requirements could be incompatible with their partner's legislation. In this very situation, States have to agree on the terms and conditions of the exchange.

A certain degree of trust is thus required for competent national authorities to cooperate. In an international legal framework where the principles of national sovereignty and territorial integrity govern interstate relations, historical tensions and political and legal divergences might hinder trust and, consequently,

---

[27] *International Convention for the Suppression of the Financing of Terrorism*, New York, 9 December 1999, UNTS, vol. 2178, No. 38349; *United Nations Convention against Transnational Organized Crime* (hereafter referred to as 'UNTOC'), A/RES/55/25, New York, 15 November 2000, UNTS, vol. 2225, No. 39574; S/RES/2396(2017). In ASEAN, *ASEAN Convention on Counter-Terrorism*, 12th ASEAN Summit, Cebu, Heads of State/Government, 13 April 2007 (hereafter referred to as 'ACCT'); *ASEAN Comprehensive Plan of Action on Counter Terrorism*, Nay Pyi Taw, 30 June 2009. In the EU, e.g. *Regulation (EU) 2016/794 of the European Parliament and of the Council of 11 May 2016 on the European Union Agency for Law Enforcement Cooperation (Europol) and replacing and repealing Council Decisions 2009/371/JHA, 2009/934/JHA, 2009/935/JHA, 2009/936/JHA and 2009/968/JHA*, O.J.E.U. L135/53, 24 May 2016 (hereafter referred to as 'Europol Regulation'); *Regulation (EU) 2018/1862 of the European Parliament and of the Council of 28 November 2018 on the establishment, operation and use of the Schengen Information System (SIS) in the field of police cooperation and judicial cooperation in criminal matters, amending and repealing Council Decision 2007/533/JHA, and repealing Regulation (EC) No 1986/2006 of the European Parliament and of the Council and Commission Decisions 2010/261/EU*, O.J.E.U. L312/56, 7 December 2018; *Regulation (EU) 2019/818 of the European Parliament and of the Council of 20 May 2019 on establishing a framework for interoperability between EU information systems in the field of police and judicial cooperation, asylum and migration and amending Regulations (EU) 2018/1726, (EU) 2018/1862 and (EU) 2019/816*, O.J.E.U. L135/85, 22 May 2019.

[28] A/CONF.222/L.6, *Doha Declaration* (2015). Regarding the terrorist threat, *International Convention for the Suppression of the Financing of Terrorism* (1999); Art. 3(a), S/RES/1373(2001), *Threats to international peace and security caused by terrorist acts*, 4385th meeting, 28 September 2001.

transnational cooperation. For these reasons, trust is more difficult to establish and maintain on an international level.

In practice, members of a regional organisation or countries which previously belonged to the same colonial empire, for instance, are more likely to have a common historical and cultural ground allowing the development of mutual trust. For example, cooperation between the USA, Australia, Canada, New Zealand and the UK is considered an effective and sustainable alliance in the exchange of information and intelligence.[29] It was criticised though for its general and untargeted surveillance programme over people's telecommunications worldwide as well as for its intrusion into other States' national sovereignty.

Secondly, sharing is an intermediary phase leading to the use of information and intelligence. Countries need to ensure that the data will be protected and lawfully used for the purposes agreed upon. The transfer of data in criminal matters usually encompasses personal data, which creates concerns for the right to privacy and the protection of one's (personal) data.

Not many international instruments protect the right to privacy,[30] and even less guarantee the protection of personal data.[31] Moreover, their impact is still limited by

---

[29] The Five Eyes Alliance, comprised of the US National Security Agency (NSA), the UK's Government Communications Headquarters (GCHQ), Canada's Communications Security Establishment Canada (CSEC), the Australian Signals Directorate (ASD) and New Zealand's Government Communications Security Bureau (GCSB), is the continuation of an intelligence partnership formed in the aftermath of the Second World War. This spying programme and intelligence-sharing agreement constitutes an integrated global surveillance arrangement that covers the majority of the world's communications. See, Carly Nyst and Anna Crowe, 'Unmasking the Five Eyes' global surveillance practices' *Global Information Society Watch. Communications surveillance in the digital age*, ed. Alan Finlay, Privacy International (APC and Hivos, 2014): available at https://giswatch.org/sites/default/files/unmasking_the_five_eyes.pdf (accessed on 29 April 2015); Luke Harding, *The Snowden Files. The Inside Story of the World's Most Wanted Man* (New York: Vintage Books, 2014).

[30] See, e.g., Art. 12, *Universal Declaration of Human Rights*, 10 December 1948, A/RES/217A(III), 183rd plenary meeting, UN Doc A/810; Art. 8, *European Convention for the Protection of Human Rights and Fundamental Freedoms*, ETS No. 5, Rome, 4 November 1950; Art. 17, *International Covenant on Civil and Political Rights* (hereafter referred to as 'ICCPR'), New York, 16 December 1966, UNTS, vol. 999, No. 14668. The right to privacy may be defined in today's context as 'the claim of an individual to determine for him- or herself when, how, and to what extend information about him of her is communicated to others'. This right has changed from a 'right to be left alone' to a right to have the control over one's personal information: see Valeria Santori, 'The UN Security Council's (Broad) Interpretation of the Notion of Threat to Peace in Counter-Terrorism' in *International Cooperation in Counter-terrorism. The United Nations and Regional Organizations in the Fight Against Terrorism*, ed., Giuseppe Nesi (Aldershot: Ashgate Publishing, 2006); Fionnuala Ní Aoláin, 'The Massive Perils of the Latest U.N. Resolution on Terrorism' *Just Security* (8 July 2019): available at https://www.justsecurity.org/64840/the-massive-perils-of-the-latest-u-n-resolution-on-terrorism/ (accessed on 1 January 2021).

[31] A/RES/49/95, *Guidelines for the regulation of computerized personal data files,* 68th meeting, 14 December 1989; Council of Europe (CoE), *Convention for the Protection of Individuals with regard to Automatic Processing of Personal Data*, ETS No. 108, Strasbourg, 28 January 1981; Organisation for Economic Cooperation and Development (OECD), *Guidelines on the Protection of Privacy and Transborder Flows of Personal Data*, 23 September 1980; A/RES/68/167, *The right*

the willingness of States to implement them. The protection of the right to privacy and data protection is in fact far from being comparable between countries. On the one hand, some may consider that the fluidity and success of interactions might be endangered by the lack of common data protection standards. On the other, some might consider data protection standards, control, oversight and review mechanisms to be limiting cooperation.[32]

These challenges can be overcome by building mutual trust. In this respect, progress has been more significant, or at least more promising, between members of regional organisations.

II. Regional Organisations: An Adequate Intermediary Solution

This section briefly mentions reasons why the regional level is most appropriate for dealing with international terrorism (A). It then introduces the two regional organisations identified as amongst the most developed and most active in this endeavour, namely the European Union (EU) and Association of Southeast Asian Nations (ASEAN) (B). The benefits that a regional framework represent for a more effective response against terrorism is further elaborated upon throughout this book.

A. Identifying the Most Effective Level to Handle Transnational Issues

Due to the political, institutional and legal advantages they present, regional organisations have been increasingly considered to be the most effective frameworks for implementing concrete mechanisms of cooperation against serious transnational crime, including terrorism.[33] The advantages of starting a regional project are plural. Among them, the reduced number of States facilitates reaching an agreement.

---

to privacy in the digital age, 68th plenary meeting, 21 January 2014. Interestingly, the Directive 95/46/EC (on *the protection of individuals with regard to the processing of personal data and on the free movement of such data*, O.J.E.C. L281/31, 23 November 1995) is considered a valuable standard at the international level.

[32] For the States of the Maghreb, '[d]ata protection laws introduced to safeguard the right to privacy create additional challenges and may hamper such cooperation'. Pt. 58, S/2015/683, Letter dated 2 September 2015 from the Chair of the Security Council Committee established pursuant to resolution 1373(2001) concerning counter-terrorism addressed to the President of the Security Council, Annex 'Implementation of Security Council Resolution 2178(2014) by States affected by foreign fighters', Second report, 2 September 2015.

[33] See, e.g., S/RES/1631(2005), *Cooperation between the United Nations and regional organizations in maintaining international peace and security*, 5282nd meeting, 17 October 2005; A/RES/60/288(2006), *United Nations Global Counter-Terrorism Strategy*, 99th plenary meeting, 8 September 2006; S/RES/2129(2013), *Threats to international peace and security caused by terrorist acts*, 7086th meeting, 17 December 2013; GA/11639, 'Strengthened Cooperation between United Nations, Regional Organizations Vital to International Peace, Security, Speakers Stress at General Assembly', 69th General Assembly meeting, Meeting coverage, 4 May 2015; Human Rights Council, A/HRC/43/46, *Promotion and protection of all human rights, civil, political, economic, social and cultural rights, including the right to development*, 'Human rights impact of policies and practices aimed at preventing and countering violent extremism' Report of the Special Rapporteur on the promotion and protection of human rights and fundamental freedoms while countering terrorism, 43rd session, 21 February 2020.

However, not all regional groupings are alike. Member States of certain regional organisations have more in common than others.

Although the UN Charter does not define it, a regional organisation may be referred to as an international organisation defined by and with the rights and obligations attributed to it from its constitutive members. In 1968, Pr. Nye was the first to define an 'international region' as 'a limited number of states linked by a geographical relationship and by a degree of mutual interdependence'.[34]

Regional organisations are the theatre of new and evolving political and legal endeavours, such as regionalisation and regionalism. The phenomenon of regionalism represents an increase in the cross-border flow of capital, goods and people within this area. Moreover, the establishment of a formal arrangement among States constitutes the phenomenon of regionalism. Nye defined (international) regionalism as 'the formation of interstate associations or groupings on the basis of regions'.[35] As such, it may lead to the emergence of an acting international subject with a distinct identity, capability, legitimacy and decision-making structure. Historically, the paradigm of regionalism emerged through the establishment of the European Coal and Steel Community in 1951 and evolved over time. Jean Monnet regarded integration as an inevitable process in Europe.[36] Later, regionalism was reinforced by both decolonisation and other attempts at political and economic integration.

Undertaking a regional project is supposed to provide Member States, all together, with a stronger place on the international scene. Members of regional gatherings, whatever their form, have recognised the benefit of such projects and have organised them in various ways.

B. Establishing Regional Ties to Cope with Transnational Non-traditional Security Issues

The establishment and development of each regional organisation and their own particular form of regional cooperation (2) have been influenced by a combination of elements which have fostered or restricted these processes (1).

1. <u>The geopolitical circumstances leading to different regional organisations</u>

The geopolitical elements surrounding the establishment of regional organisations can be placed into two categories: those allowing and facilitating the establishment of regional organisations and regional cooperation, and those limiting and/or retarding the process (Table 1.1).

A combination of similarities and diverging variables between the European and Southeast Asian regional projects make this comparative analysis interesting.

---

[34] Joseph S. Jr. Nye, *International regionalism. Readings* (Boston: Little, Brown & Company, 1968); Christopher B. Roberts, *ASEAN Regionalism. Cooperation, values and institutionalization*, Routledge Security in Asia Pacific (London: Routledge, 2012): 180.

[35] Nye (1968), vii.

[36] Jean Monnet, *Mémoires* (Paris: Libraire Générale Française, 2007).

Table 1.1 Factors related to the establishment of regional organisations and the development of cooperation

Incentive factors	Disincentive factors
• Acknowledgement of the need to ensure security (objective) • Willingness and eagerness to tackle transnational threats and interact with partners • Trust between partners • Capabilities and capacities of the partners	• Failure on the part of some partners to acknowledge that threats affect them or to consider cooperation to be necessary • Limited or lack of willingness to engage in such a project • Limited or lack of trust amongst partners • Weak or absent capabilities and capacities of the partners

Among the similarities, a few relevant elements may be highlighted. The EU and ASEAN's origins are situated in the post-Second World War/Cold War era. Although their regional projects were designed to ensure peaceful relationships between members, interstate tensions are difficult to overcome and the protection of national sovereignty is still a significant factor in their relations. Both regions have also suffered from similar terrorist threats from separatist, political and religious groups.

Specific differences are worth mentioning at this preliminary stage. For instance, except for Thailand, all ASEAN Member States were historically European colonies. As the borders imposed by colonial powers do not necessarily represent the Southeast Asian natural and ethnic borders, most of the security problems manifest from ethnic secessionist demands and from groups whose motives might transcend borders.[37] In fact, the ethnic origins, religions and traditions of the population are more diverse in Southeast Asia[38] than in Europe.

Moreover, Southeast Asia encompasses some of the poorest countries in the world, namely Cambodia, Myanmar, Laos and Vietnam, and two of the ten richest, namely Singapore and Brunei. By contrast, several EU Member States can be found among the wealthiest countries in terms of both nominal GDP and GDP per capita (PPP). In terms of nominal GDP and PPP, Malta and Bulgaria are, respectively, the poorest of the EU members. Yet, they still rank 122nd and 87th out of 211 States in 2020.[39]

The various historical and geopolitical aspects have led to divergent approaches to regional integration and cooperation in European and Southeast Asia.

[37] Alan Collins, *Security and Southeast Asia: Domestic, Regional, and Global Issues* (Boulder: Lynne Rienner Publishers, 2003): 129.

[38] Counter-Terrorism Committee Executive Directorate (CTED), *Implementation of Security Council 2178(2014) by States affected by foreign terrorist fighters: A compilation of three reports (S/2015/338; S/2015/683; S/2015/975)*, New York, 31 August 2016: 26.

[39] 'World Population Review': available at https://worldpopulationreview.com/countries/countries-by-gdp (accessed on 23 January 2021).

2. Different forms of regionalism in Europe and Southeast Asia?

A brief overview of the emergence and evolution of these two regional integration projects demonstrates the key reasons for their selection.

Established first, the European Community/Union's history has not been a long and calm river. This European river as it flows today is the fruit of many currents that crossed over the past centuries. European people have been part of different kingdoms, governed by different kings or emperors (e.g. Habsburg Empire, Austria-Hungary Empire, the two French Empires), changing over the centuries. Europe has been the theatre of many armed conflicts and tensions in various times and for various reasons. In the aftermath of World War II, some European States undertook to build a new order for peace, freedom and prosperity. Despite its predominantly economic content, the European integration project was an eminently political construct. This process started from the Schuman Declaration of the 9th of May 1950 without determined destination. Since then, the integration process has evolved from the European Communities to the Union.[40] To date, the EU Member States have repeatedly given more competence to the EU, making this organisation an increasingly supranational organisation.

Later on, the Association of Southeast Asian Nations emerged as a regional actor after several attempts, such as the Association of Southeast Asia (ASA) created in 1961 and encompassing Thailand, the Philippines and the Federation of Malaya or MAPHILINDO created in 1963 encompassing Malaya, the Philippines and Indonesia.

ASEAN was established on 8 August 1967 by Indonesia, Malaysia, the Philippines, Singapore and Thailand to promote political and economic cooperation and regional stability. Brunei joined the Association in 1984, shortly after its independence from the United Kingdom, and Vietnam joined ASEAN as its seventh member in 1995. Lao PDR and Burma were admitted into full membership in July 1997 as ASEAN celebrated its 30th anniversary. Cambodia became ASEAN's tenth and most recent member in 1999.

Internally, the regional project aimed primarily at preventing conflicts. Thanks to ASEAN's role, the region has not suffered from war since 1967. Externally, the Member States sought to create a counterbalance (economic, diplomatic, security-wise) to major actors in the region: the United States and Russia, two of the most powerful nations in the world, as well as the main regional powers, namely China, Japan and Australia.[41] Importantly, at the time of its formation, States of Southeast

[40]Tampere European Council, Conclusions of the European Council, Annex: 'Composition, Method of Work and Practical Arrangements for the Body to Elaborate a Draft EU Charter of Fundamental Rights, as Set out in the Cologne Conclusions' 15–16 October 1999.

[41]Yoshiyuki Hagiwara, 'Formation and Development of the Association of Southeast Asian Nations' *The Developing Economies,* vol. 11, no. 4 (1973).

Asia did not have any integration project in mind.[42] ASEAN members realised afterwards that they require higher levels of collaboration.[43]

Intra-regional tensions have long undermined cooperation between ASEAN Member States and the development of the regional organisation. Notably, Indonesia-Malaysia's *Konfrontasi* in the 1960s, the Sabah's dispute between the Philippines and Malaysia and Vietnam's invasion of Cambodia in 1978 illustrate the climate of tension which characterised ASEAN during its first decade of existence.

This geopolitical context explains ASEAN's particular approach, namely the 'ASEAN Way' as a law-making process. This 'ASEAN Way' was initially necessary as there was no alternative basis for collaboration given that the differences between the Southeast Asian States far outweighed the similarities.[44] Over the past 50 years, the Association has made tremendous efforts towards the realisation of the ASEAN Community. Its integration process is slow as it pays due attention to States' interests and regional characteristics. Nonetheless, ASEAN can claim to be one of the most successful regional groupings in the 'developing world'[45] thus far.

3. Interregionalism: an interest leading to an opportunity?

The EU and ASEAN share common interests in many areas; not only in trade and investment, but they also share similar traditional as well as non-traditional security threats, including terrorism. While the EU and ASEAN have experienced their own terrorist threats, they have also experienced common cases. In particular, some European foreign terrorist fighters have travelled to Southeast Asia that provides a new avenue to promote radical ideology and fight as foreign fighters.[46]

Growing over time, their region-to-region dialogue has strengthened their respective actions and, where appropriate, coordinated their positioning within wider fora.[47] Notably, the EU has become a normative power trying to export its standards and policies in Southeast Asia.[48]

---

[42] Björn Hettne, 'Globalization, the New Regionalism and East Asia', paper presented at the Global Seminar '96 Shonan Session, *Globalism and Regionalism*, Hayama, 2–6 September 1996 (United Nations University, 1996); Björn Hettne and Fredrik Söderbaum, 'Theorizing the rise of regionness' in *New Regionalisms in the Global Political Economy: Theories and Cases*, eds., Shaun Breslin et al. (London: Routledge, 2002); Björn Hettne, 'The New Regionalism Revisited' in *Theories of New Regionalism*, eds., Fredrik Söderbaum and Timothy M. Shaw, International Political Economy Series (Basingstoke: Palgrave Macmillan, 2003); Roberts (2012): 174.

[43] Roberts (2012): 175.

[44] Ibid.: 178.

[45] Amitav Acharya, *Constructing a Security Community in Southeast Asia. ASEAN and the problem of regional order*, Politics in Asia series (New York: Routledge, 2001): 5; Louise Fawcett, 'Regionalism from an Historical Perspective' in *Global Politics of Regionalism*, eds., Mary Farrell, Björn Hettne, and Luk Van Langenhove (London: Pluto Press, 2005): 25.

[46] Vierstraete-Verlinde (2019).

[47] *Joint Declaration on co-operation to combat terrorism*, 14th EU-ASEAN Ministerial Meeting, No. 5811/03, Brussels, 27–28 January 2003.

[48] See, e.g., Yeo Lay Hwee, 'The EU as a Security Actor in Southeast Asia' Panorama 02/2009 (Singapore: Konrad Adenauer Stiftung, 2009).

Section 2: Conceptual Framework—Building Bridges Between Fields of Research to Cross Rivers Between Regions

This section presents the research question and subsequent hypothesis which are demonstrated throughout this study (I). Then, it explains the methodology used to respond to the research question (II).

I. Purpose: Quid of Mutual Trust in the Fight Against Terrorism?

With all these elements in mind, the central question underpinning this study is: Facing a specific type of serious transnational crime, namely terrorism, how has mutual trust been developed and operationalised to facilitate cooperation between competent national authorities within regions and between regions?

This study submits that there is a strong connection between mutual trust and the development of cross-border cooperation within the EU and ASEAN. The canvas of this comparative regional analysis depicts a three-layer scenery, presenting the situation at different levels of competence, with various landscape elements, representing by the many concepts, that give structure and completeness to the picture.

In a nutshell, this study revolves around the 'chicken and the egg' dilemma. A chapter investigates whether regional integration helps foster mutual trust or whether building trust fosters the establishment of a more integrated regional system. Others investigate whether building trust fosters cross-border cooperation or whether the slow development of cross-border cooperation helps foster mutual trust. It is uncertain whether the answers to these questions can be found more easily than the one answering the chicken and the egg dilemma. Nonetheless, it seems that there is a basic minimum of trust needed to establish regional organisations or to develop cross-border cooperation. Conversely, through the enhancement of regional integration and cross-border relations, mutual trust strengthens. The different elements involved in this process are caught in a virtuous circle which nourishes each other.

An analytical matrix focusing on the methods used to build mutual trust amongst stakeholders enables to identify the place and role of mutual trust along two axes: firstly, and to a large extent, when developing the regional architectures facilitating intra-regional cooperation in criminal matters; and, secondly, when developing channels for interregional relations in counterterrorism.

The respective regional integration processes and development of regional responses against terrorism are among the elements of comparison.

It can be argued that undertaking a regional integration process and developing cross-border cooperation imply a minimum level of trust based on common minimum denominators and the identification of similar objectives. The members of the respective regions have initially started their own regional project with modest objectives due to the low level of trust present at that time. However, this book argues that to evolve further, trust needs to be based on something more tangible than simple interpersonal trust (i.e. social dimension of mutual trust). Trust based on political agreements is already a step towards sustainability but still retains an element uncertainty (i.e. political dimension of mutual trust). Legal engagements ensure more sustainability and accountability in international relations (i.e. legal dimension of mutual trust), but they are hard to reach as they are binding upon the parties.

As such, this book highlights the strong differences between the mostly practice-based approach of ASEAN and the legalistic approach adopted in the EU. Yet, mutual trust is a fundamental yardstick in the establishment of these regional organisations and in the development of cooperation mechanisms.

Based on this comparison, an analysis of interregional challenges and prospects follows. The question was raised whether the EU would be a model transferable to other regions. Some authors, as Pr. Ernst Haas, said that 'whatever assurance may be warranted [. . .] European integration is not readily transferable to other regional contexts'.[49] This might have been true in the 1960s. The situation has changed though. The EU needs to adapt its objectives, priorities and means to the features of other regional organisations while retaining its own standards.

Since 1972, the EU and ASEAN have increasingly engaged with one another on different issues of interest, including terrorism. They have slowly developed channels of dialogue in order to build up trust between competent authorities of the two regions.

II. Methodology and Structure: How to Analyse Mutual Trust in the Fight Against Terrorism?

As Machiavelli would say, this study aims to go beyond the appearances and posturing and deals with 'the effective reality of things'.[50] As such, the research question determines the methodology (A) and the subsequent outline (B).

A. Methodological Considerations: Extending the Legal Literature

The EU is widely regarded as the most successful experiment in regional institution-building. For some, it is a yardstick against which all other regional institutions are compared and their success measured.[51] Consequently, there has

[49] Ernst Haas, 'International Integration: The European and the Universal Process' *International Organisation,* vol. 15, no. 3 (1961): 378.

[50] Niccolò Machiavelli, *The Prince*, translated by Rufus Goodwin (Boston: Dante University Press, 2003): 87.

[51] See e.g. Axel Berkofsky, 'Comparing EU and Asian Integration Processes. The EU a role model for Asia?', European Policy Centre (EPC, 18 January 2005); Sanoussi Bilal, 'Is the EU a Model of Regional Integration? Risks and Challenges' Briefing for ACP-EU Joint Parliamentary Assembly's Committee on Political Affairs, European Centre for Development Policy Management (Bruxelles, 13 September 2007); Nele Marianne Ewers-Peters, "The EU as an Interorganizational Influencer?" *European Foreign Affairs Review* 23, no. 3 (2018): 375.

long been a disproportionate focus on the EU within the field of regionalism, and it is still the case in law.

Other regional organisations have slowly been included in regional studies; mostly in political science and international relations.[52] For a long time, assessments of other regional organisations have been framed in comparison with the EU model. This approach has changed over the years. Today, comparative regionalism suggests that 'regional institutions ought to be judged in terms of their own set goals, rather than some universal standard derived from the European Union model'.[53] Investigations on regional organisations should bring the specifics of each regional context out and not push them out for the sake of generalisability. For example, some studies reveal that ASEAN Member States, to a large degree, see themselves as facing contexts dissimilar to those in Europe, not just in terms of their geographical location, history and culture, but also in terms of their perceptions of security. This has defined their objectives, approaches and practices within regional cooperation.[54]

However, such development in regional studies has not reached legal studies yet, or scarcely. Except the thoroughly analysed EU law, there has only been very few legal regional studies, including comparative regional studies, on other regional organisations.

Therefore, finding the right approach and meeting point that makes this study interesting for both sides of the Ural mountain divide is a difficult task. It is not easy to establish common ground when caught between an abundance of legal literature on EU counterterrorism and scarcity on ASEAN counterterrorism.

Therefore, due to its particularities, this study makes use of the cross-fertilisation between fields of research which has grown over the past 50 years. Adopting a dominant legal approach has the advantage of bringing a steady tool in debates concerning the development of regional responses against terrorism. Adding a touch of interdisciplinarity ensures the most accurate conceptualisation of the geopolitical and normative situation and the concepts, especially mutual trust. Therefore, a legal

[52] See, e.g., Hettne, 'The New Regionalism Revisited' (2003); Edward Best and Thomas Christiansen, 'Regionalism in international affairs' in *The Globalisation of World Politics: An Introduction to International Politics*, eds., John Baylis, Steve Smith and Patricia Owens (Oxford: Oxford University Press, 2008); Warleigh-Lack, Robinson, and Rosamund, (2011); Amitav Acharya, 'Comparative Regionalism: A Field Whose Time has Come?' *The International Spectator,* vol. 47, no. 1 (2012); Jens-Uwe Wunderlich, 'Comparing regional organisations in global multilateral institutions: ASEAN, the EU and the UN' *Asia Europe Journal,* vol. 10, no. 2–3 (2012); Björn Hettne, 'Regional Actorship: A Comparative Approach to Interregionalism' in *Intersecting Interregionalism. Regions, Global Governance and the EU*, eds., Francis Baert, Tiziana Scaramagli, and Fredrik Söderbaum (Dordrecht: Springer, 2014); Frank Mattheis, 'Repositioning Europe in the study of regions: comparative regionalism, interregionalism and decentred regionalism' *Journal of European Integration,* vol. 39, no. 4 (2017).

[53] Acharya, 'Comparative Regionalism' (2012): 495; Amitav Acharya, 'Arguing about ASEAN: what do we disagree about?' *Cambridge Review of International Affairs,* vol. 22, no. 3 (2009).

[54] See, e.g., Nikolas Busse, 'Constructivism and Southeast Asian security' *The Pacific Review,* vol. 12, no. 1 (1999); Amitav Acharya, *Constructing a Security Community in Southeast Asia. ASEAN and the problem of regional order*, 3rd ed. (London: Routledge, 2014).

study inspired by other social and political sciences is beneficial at this stage of the development of the literature on regionalism.

Consequently, this book aims to fill in a gap in the legal literature in comparative regionalism and interregionalism, and it shows that such study is possible despite being confronted with two very different levels of regional institutionalisation.

B. Outline of the Chapters

This book entails that there is a symbiotic relationship between the establishment and enhancement of regional and interregional counterterrorism measures and the different dimensions of mutual trust. The mutually beneficial impact of these interactions on the fight against terrorism is assessed by going through three main successive steps.

The first part of this book, encompassing the two first chapters, is dedicated to clarifying the path taken in this journey.

Analysing anti-terrorism measures implies to navigate through numerous fields of action, actors, and policies and laws. In a context such as this where diversity sets the tone, the key terminology is often not defined or ill-defined. While Chap. 2 discusses and raises the potential issues associated with the terminology used in cross-border cooperation, the principle of mutual trust alone necessitates the whole Chap. 3 to cover its features and for its operationalisation to be unveiled. This process of qualification is the necessary primary step for this research and for any officials aiming at shared objectives. Reaching an understanding of the key terminology constitutes the basic ground for in-depth discussions between officials and practitioners. From Chap. 3, a data analysis matrix related to the building up of mutual trust as a three-dimensional concept and its operationalisation is established and determines the conceptual approach, structure and content of the rest of this monograph.

The second part, encompassing the three chapters dedicated to the comparison between the EU and ASEAN, details the correlation between mutual trust and the development of effective intra-regional cooperation mechanisms. It investigates whether the formalisation and legalisation of mutual trust, as in the EU, provides a better framework for the development of more effective cross-border cooperation, than a looser one, as it exists in ASEAN.

Chapter 4 examines how the EU and ASEAN Member States have engaged in regional integration. Depending on the regional institutional and legal architecture, the Member States receive different degrees of incentives from the regional organisation to behave in a certain way and fulfil certain tasks to reach their shared goal. This chapter highlights the link between the development of regional legal architectures associated with the necessary institutions and the form mutual trust takes or, at least, has the potential to take.

After defining the two regional institutional and legal architectures, the two following chapters focus on the two major counterterrorism axes: criminalising terrorist offences (Chap. 5) and fostering cooperation between competent national authorities (Chap. 6). These chapters verify whether working at the regional level makes it easier to reach these two objectives. In this process, it defines the place and role of mutual trust in fostering a regional criminalisation of terrorist offences and the adoption of common criminal justice standards (i.e. human rights standards and criminal procedure safeguards) within the respective regions as well as in facilitating intra-regional cooperation. In so doing, Chap. 5 discusses the normative effect of the three layers of competence (i.e. international, regional and national) towards enhancing mutual trust or creating preliminary trust development (cf. chicken and the egg dilemma). Following the same dynamic, Chap. 6 examines the causal link between, on the one hand, mutual trust and, on the other, the establishment of cooperation mechanisms and the relevant actors and platforms which facilitate the cross-border flow of data.

The final part of this book shifts to interregionalism and explores the different channels of interactions existing between these two regions. Chapter 7 highlights the challenges posed by the existence of a vast number of channels of dialogue and the role mutual trust—if there is any—plays in fostering the establishment and maintenance of these channels and in streamlining the dialogue and the decision making. It thus describes the complexity of the multiheaded and multifaceted relations between the EU and ASEAN in counterterrorism.

Overall, these eight chapters form a thoroughly researched study on the operationalisation of mutual trust as an essential means for facilitating the development of cross-border cooperation in counterterrorism. This study aims to establish some guidelines to serve future legal studies in comparative regionalism and interregionalism. Most importantly, this study's findings shall serve the exportability, and potential adaptability, of its theoretical framework to other regions.

Chapter 2
Definitions of Key Concepts: In Search of a Common Language to Facilitate Cross-Border Cooperation

Counterterrorism law is a broad field. It contains numerous laws and regulations. Besides criminal law, it includes various other fields, including administrative law, immigration law and military law. With this variety of fields, the array of actors has also increased. In addition to States, it also incorporates international and regional organisations, non-governmental organisations (NGOs) and private actors, and transnational organisations, amongst others. The various stakeholders have adopted diverging or common positions and actions to ensure the effectiveness of the fight against terrorism. In this diversity of fields and actors, this monograph focuses on cooperative approaches in criminal matters, especially in terrorism-related matters, which mainly involve public actors, namely national, regional and international actors.

Before discussing specific counterterrorism cooperation actions, this chapter identifies the ways in which terrorism, as a form of serious transnational crime, has been defined at the global and regional levels (Section 1). When countering terrorism, States implicitly agree to multiple actions at different levels and cross-border cooperation. The concepts which are essential to transnational interaction are discussed and placed into context herein (Section 2).

This chapter provides definitions or, at least, a framework for debates. It investigates the existence of a common language worldwide or region-wide, as a potential guidance to their members. It allows for the identification of similarities and underlining discrepancies within and between the European Union (EU) and Association of Southeast Asian Nations (ASEAN). Having an improved understanding of the concepts involved in interstate cooperation is useful as it aids the respective actors to operate and regulate with a similar or shared legal language.

C. C. Cocq, *Mutual Trust in Regional and Interregional Cooperation on Counterterrorism*, United Nations University Series on Regionalism 26,
https://doi.org/10.1007/978-3-031-36612-3_2

Section 1: Terrorism as a Specific Type of Serious Transnational Crime—Putting an End to a Long-Running Uncertainty?

Historically, the threat of 'terrorism' has long served as a poorly-defined master-key, leading to the adoption of controversial measures, many of which have been criticised for endangering and violating human and constitutional rights. 'Terrorist offences' have been increasingly defined by national legislators to enable States to adopt widespread coercive and intrusive measures. Focusing on terrorism with a transnational dimension, terrorism is deemed one of the top offences within the category of 'serious transnational crime'. After 'serious transnational crime' (I), the notion of terrorism is briefly examined as it pertains to this study (II). Using a 'funnelling approach', this chapter defines the key terminology, beginning with the international framework and moving unto regional ones.

I. Serious Transnational Crime: Qualifying a Broad Category of Offences

No region and no country is completely immune to transnational criminal activities. The fight against serious transnational crime, including terrorism, trafficking in human beings and organised crime, has become a worldwide concern for two primary reasons. Firstly, transnational crime, especially terrorism, constitutes a threat to the collective security.[1] Secondly, some serious transnational crimes, including terrorism and trafficking in human beings, have a wide impact on human lives and political stability in several countries concurrently. After the transnational nature of the crime (A), this section defines its seriousness (B).

A. The Transnational Nature of a Crime

The concept of *transnational* crime is not to be confused with that of *international* crime.

While transnational crime implies that a crime includes links with various countries and thus has to do with the number of countries involved, international crime is that which is committed in contravention of international law. In the latter case, there must be a violation of a criminal norm derived from an international treaty or other international customary law. It is international due to the source of law against which it infringes, but it may concern a single country. The criminalisation of behaviours at the international level can be motivated by the threat it poses to specific higher interests or common fundamental values (e.g. genocide, crime against humanity) and/or by the need to cooperate efficiently in combating them (e.g. transnational crime such as smuggling of human beings, trafficking in human beings, arms, drugs).

---

[1] Arts. 1 and 2(4), United Nations, *Charter of the United Nations* (hereafter referred to as 'UN Charter'), San Francisco, 26 June 1945. The doctrine of collective security is the very foundation upon which the United Nations Organisation is built. Also, Gary Wilson, *The United Nations and Collective Security* Routledge Research in International Law (Oxon: Routledge, 2014).

Unlike States, for which the criminal responsibility does not exist, individuals may become responsible in their personal capacity at the international level as a result of violations of international law. An individual commits an international crime when international law determines that the constitutive elements of an offence are punishable under criminal law. These acts are considered to be international offences or 'treaty crimes'. Chronologically, the oldest international criminalisation is that of the maritime piracy developed by the international custom and then codified in the 1958 Geneva set of conventions on the Law of the Sea.[2] Such criminalisation was followed by that of the slave trade, drugs trafficking, unlawful interference into international civil aviation and acts of terrorism.[3] Presently, genocide, crimes against humanity, war crimes and crimes of aggression are most representative of this category of crime. These crimes are defined as 'the most serious crimes of concern to the international community as a whole'.[4] Interestingly, terrorism and drug trafficking were not specifically added to the list of crimes punished by the International Criminal Court due to the current lack of agreement when defining these crimes.[5] In addition to being covered by the competence of different international jurisdictions, the core international crimes give rise to 'universal jurisdiction'.

Some international crime may be transnational in nature. Transnational crime has increased significantly over the past decade. More than 20 years ago, the UN Secretary-General specifically emphasised the point that with 'the new permeability of frontiers, markets [among other things] had developed in many parts of the world without a State and without the rule of law'.[6] Taking advantage of this situation, criminal organisations continually make profit in different countries, transferring funds across borders by exploiting new technologies and means of communication

---

[2] A/CONF.13/L.58, United Nations Conference on the Law of the Sea, *Final Act*, Off. Rec. vol. II, Geneva, 24 February–27 April 1958. Also, *Convention on the Territorial Sea and the Contiguous Zone*, Geneva, 29 April 1958, UNTS vol. 516, No. 7477; *Convention on the High Sea*, Geneva, 29 April 1958, UNTS vol. 450, No. 6465; *Convention on Fishing and Conservation of the Living Resources of the High Seas*, Geneva, 29 April 1958, UNTS vol. 559, No. 8164; *Convention on the Continental Shelf*, Geneva, 29 April 1958, UNTS vol. 499, No. 7302; and *Optional Protocol of Signature concerning the Compulsory Settlement of Disputes*, Geneva, 29 April 1958, UNTS vol. 450, No. 6466.

[3] See a detailed analysis in Patrick Daillier, Mathias Forteau and Alain Pellet, *Droit international public (Nguyen Quoc Dinh †)*, 8th ed. (Paris: Librairie Générale de Droit et de Jurisprudence, 2009): 780 and ff.

[4] Art. 5(1), *Statute of the International Criminal Court*, Rome, 17 July 1998, A/CONF.183/9, UNTS, vol. 2187, No. 38544.

[5] See, e.g., Fiona Londras, 'Terrorism as an international crime' in *Routledge Handbook of International Criminal Law*, eds., William A. Schabas and Nadia Bernaz (London: Routledge, 2010).

[6] A/49/748, 'Report of the World Ministerial Conference on Organized Transnational Crime' *Crime Prevention and Criminal Justice*, Naples, 2 December 1994. See David McLean, *Transnational Organized Crime. A Commentary on the UN Convention and Its Protocols*, Oxford Commentary on International Law (Oxford: Oxford University Press, 2007): 3.

and penetrating national economies, thereby becoming 'criminal multinationals'. By definition, transnational crime involves a border being crossed and more than one country being affected. Transnational crime encompasses various kinds of offences committed across borders by an organised group, or by individuals acting alone, or acting with others, but who, when combined, do not meet the legal conditions to qualify as an 'organised criminal group'.[7] Due to the nature of its specifications, transnational crime requires tenuous international cooperation.

While identifying transnational crime as an international threat, the UN recognised that defining it is difficult.[8] It was only in 1995 that the UN provided that this type of crime should involve more than one country. Recognising in Article 2 of the report of the Ninth UN Congress on the Prevention of Crime and the Treatment of Offenders that it is 'difficult' to define transnational crime, the UN provided a list of 19 offences which constitute transnational crime. These include (1) money laundering; (2) terrorist activities; (3) theft of art and cultural objects; (4) theft of intellectual property; (5) illicit trafficking in arms; (6) aircraft hijacking; (7) sea piracy; (8) land hijacking; (9) insurance fraud; (10) computer crime; (11) environment crime; (12) trafficking in persons; (13) trade in human body parts; (14) illicit drug trafficking; (15) fraudulent bankruptcy; (16) infiltration of legal business; (17) corruption and bribery of public officials; (18) corruption and bribery of party officials and elected representatives; and (19) other offences committed by organised criminal groups.[9] Importantly, these offences may not inherently be transnational, but most of them often are. Surprisingly, this list did not include smuggling of human beings that is transnational by nature. Currently, there is no other convention that covers the combating of transnational crime, nor any others that provide a definition for transnational crime.

Five years later, the *United Nations Convention on Transnational Organized Crime* (UNTOC), also called the 'Palermo Convention', defined a crime as transnational in nature if:

> (a) It is committed in more than one State;
>
> (b) It is committed in one State but a substantial part of its preparation, planning, direction or control takes place in another State;
>
> (c) It is committed in one State but involves an organised criminal group that engages in criminal activities in more than one State or

---

[7] Both Art. 2, UNTOC (2000); Art. 2(f), *ASEAN Convention against Trafficking in Persons, Especially Women and Children* (27th ASEAN Summit, Kuala Lumpur, 21 November 2015) repeats verbatim the definition of 'organised criminal group' in the UNTOC: 'a structured group of three or more persons existing for a period of time and acting in concert with the aim of committing one or more serious crimes or offences established in accordance with this Convention, in order to obtain, directly or indirectly, a financial or other material benefit'.

[8] Art. 2 'Definition' of the report, A/CONF.169/15/Add.1, Ninth United Nations Congress on the Prevention of Crime and the Treatment of Offenders, 'International Cooperation and Practical Technical Assistance for Strengthening the Rule of Law: Promoting the United Nations Crime Prevention and Criminal Justice Programme', Cairo, 29 April–8 May 1995.

[9] A/CONF.169/15/Add.1, 9th UN Congress on the Prevention of Crime and the Treatment of Offenders (1995).

(d) It is committed in one State but has substantial effects in another State.[10]

This UN Convention deals with transnational organised crime, but no longer provides a list of offences. Nonetheless, it does provide for specific offences such as laundering of proceeds of crime (Article 6), money laundering (Article 7) and corruption (Articles 8 and 9). Three supplementary protocols have further elaborated upon the criminalisation duties of States and the means which are to be implemented. They concern, firstly, the prevention, suppression and punishment of trafficking in persons, especially women and children; secondly, the smuggling of migrants by land, sea and air; and, thirdly, the illicit manufacturing and trafficking in firearms, their parts and components and ammunition. Notably, the *Protocol against the Smuggling of Migrants* has filled the gap left by the aforementioned list from Article 2 of 1995. Smuggling of migrants is now recognised as an inherently transnational crime and has received an international legal definition.[11] The wording of the Convention and the Protocols is clear. States have to criminalise these offences and to take all necessary measures to work together in order to combat these offences in an effective manner.[12]

These UN texts had a strong influence in the EU and ASEAN. The UNTOC was, for instance, referred to in the preamble of the *Council Framework Decision 2008/841/JHA of 24 October 2008 on the fight against organised crime.*[13] The definition of transnational crime is especially interesting in the EU context since, according to the *Treaty on the Functioning of the European Union* (TFEU), the EU's action in criminal matters and, more specifically, the EU competence to approximate substantive criminal law can only focus on 'serious crime with a cross-border dimension resulting from the nature or impact of such offences or from a special need to combat them on a common basis'.[14] Terrorism, organised crime, trafficking in humans and counterfeit payments are only some examples of crimes covered by the EU legislator in its effort to approximate national legislations.[15]

On the other side of the Eurasian continent, it is said that '[t]hough Southeast Asian states have been dealing with transnational crimes—which include not just terrorism, but also illegal drugs, human trafficking, smuggling, money laundering,

---

[10] Art. 3, UNTOC (2000). All ASEAN and EU Member States are parties to this Convention.

[11] Art. 3(a), *Protocol against the Smuggling of Migrants by Land, Sea and Air, supplementing the United Nations Convention against TRansnational Organized Crime*, A/RES/55/25, New York, 15 November 2000, UNTS vol. 2241, No. 39574.

[12] In English, the use of 'shall' makes clear that States parties have the obligation to comply with the requirements of the Convention and the protocols. In French, the use of verbs conjugated in the present simple has the same purpose, requiring States to comply with these requirements. On the normative impact of various norms, see, e.g., Catherine Thibierge and et alii, eds., *La force normative. Naissance d'un concept* (Paris: L.G.D.J., Bruylant, 2009).

[13] *Council Framework Decision 2008/841/JHA of 24 October 2008 on the fight against organised crime*, O.J.E.U. L300/42, 11 November 2008.

[14] Art. 83(1), *Treaty on the Functioning of the European Union* (hereafter referred to as 'TFEU'), O.J.E.U. C326/1, 26 October 2012.

[15] Art. 83(1), TFEU.

piracy, and more recently, intellectual property theft and cybercrime—for decades, regional cooperation really began to take off only in the late 1990s'.[16] In 1997, ASEAN Ministers of Interior and Home Affairs on transnational crime held their inaugural meeting, signed the *ASEAN Declaration on Transnational Crime*, and formed the ASEAN Ministerial Meeting on Transnational Crime (AMMTC), initially to be held every 2 years. And, interestingly, the UN definition of 'transnational crime' was transposed word for word more than 20 years later in Article 2(h) of the 2015 *ASEAN Convention against Trafficking in Persons, Especially Women and Children.*[17]

B. **The Seriousness Element of Some Transnational Offences**

Seriousness is an essential component of terrorist offences. There are different methods to evaluate the seriousness of an offence. The first, and most obvious, method would be to evaluate the harmfulness of an offence, namely the importance of the affected interests (namely, protected rights or any obligation provided by the law) and the gravity of the violation of these interests. However, it is difficult to establish a clear hierarchy between competing interests and to effectively quantify the harm done by an offence to a specific interest. Facing this difficulty, some States have preferred to weigh the seriousness of an offence based on the sentence provided by the law. Penalties are an indicator of the degree of harm caused by a criminal behaviour. The seriousness of the harm and the severity of the punishment should correlate. According to criminal law theory, penalties must be proportionate to the degree of harmfulness caused by the criminal act and to the extent of the actor's guilt.[18] Higher penalties are logically requested for the most harmful offences committed with a high degree of guilt. However, depending on the countries, the seriousness, with regard to the harm done and to the punishment imposed by the law, can be interpreted, defined and framed differently. States may have different values and approaches towards the importance of the affected interests and on the seriousness of the harm done to a person and/or to society. One State may consider a specific offence to be serious, while another State does not. In addition to States' varied sensitivity towards degrees of harmfulness, seriousness can vary according to the punishment provided by each State's law. The sanctions scale can thus differ widely from one country to another.

Importantly, Article 2 of the UNTOC defines 'serious crime' as the 'conduct constituting an offence punishable by a maximum deprivation of liberty of at least 4

[16] 'What did ASEAN's latest transnational crime meeting achieve?' *The Diplomat*, 23 September 2017: available at https://thediplomat.com/2017/09/what-did-aseans-latest-transnational-crime-meeting-achieve/ (accessed on 19 January 2018).

[17] *ASEAN Convention against Trafficking in Persons* (2015).

[18] See, e.g., Art. 49(3), *Charter of fundamental rights of the European Union* (hereafter referred to as 'EU Charter'), O.J.E.C. C364/1, 18 December 2000. By contrast, the ICCPR (1966) does not mention the principle of proportionality of the punishment to the criminal offence. See, Cesare Beccaria, *Of Crimes and Punishments*, originally published in Italian in 1764, Chap. 6: available in English at http://www.constitution.org/cb/crim_pun.htm (accessed on 6 October 2015).

years or a more serious penalty'.[19] In this Convention, serious crime is based on the gravity of the punishment, and not directly on the seriousness of the crime. This is a more objective manner with which to define serious crime. However, other sanctions thresholds can be envisaged. Other defining methods could include a listing of relevant types of serious crimes.

The EU has made good progress in harmonising the definitions of criminal offences. The TFEU offers the possibility for the European Parliament and the Council to approximate the national criminal legislations of the EU Member States 'in the areas of particularly serious crime'.[20] However, it fails to define 'serious crime'. The Treaty includes 'terrorism, trafficking in human beings and sexual exploitation of women and children, illicit drug trafficking, illicit arms trafficking, money laundering, corruption, counterfeiting of means of payment, computer crime and organised crime' into the category of 'serious crime'. However, this list is not exhaustive as Article 83 provides the possibility for States to unanimously decide to approximate other areas of serious transnational crime (pursuant to obtaining the consent of the European Parliament).

The secondary legislation does not provide more detailed guidance than primary EU law does. Some norms target only specific offences including terrorist offences,[21] while others apply to several offences falling into the categories of 'forms of crime'[22] or 'forms of serious crime'[23] or even 'serious crime'.[24] Thus, the scope of police and judicial cooperation may differ depending on the instruments involved. Some instruments may even organise cooperation beyond serious crime, including pettier offences. The European arrest warrant, for instance, applies to offences 'punishable by the law of the issuing Member State by a custodial sentence or a detention order for a maximum period of at least 12 months or, where a sentence has been passed or a detention order has been made, for sentences of at least four months'.[25]

---

[19] Art. 2, UNTOC (2000). The different delegations had different views on the minimal sanction allowing to qualify an offence as a serious crime, which is not unsurprising given the very different sentencing practices in the different States. Interestingly for this analysis on the ASEAN region, this definition is copied *verbatim* in Art. 2(g) of the *ASEAN Convention against Trafficking in Person* (2015).

[20] Art. 83(1), TFEU.

[21] See, e.g., *Council Framework Decision 2008/841/JHA on the fight against organised crime*; *Directive (EU) 2017/541 of the European Parliament and of the Council of 15 March 2017 on combating terrorism and replacing Council Framework Decision 2002/475/JHA and amending Council Decision 2005/671/JHA*, O.J.E.U. L88/6, 31 March 2017.

[22] See, e.g., Art. 3(1) and Annex I, *Europol Regulation.*

[23] See, e.g., Recital 1 and 38, and Art. 20, *Europol Regulation.*

[24] See, e.g., Art. 3(1), *Europol Regulation; Directive (EU) 2016/681 of the European Parliament and of the Council on the use of Passenger Name Record (PNR) data for the prevention, detection, investigation and prosecution of terrorist offences and serious crime*, O.J.E.U. L119/132, 27 April 2016.

[25] Art. 2(1), *Council Framework Decision 2002/584/JHA of 13 June 2002 on the European Arrest Warrant and the Surrender Procedures between Member States*, O.J.E.C. L190/1, 18 July 2002.

Instruments dealing with cooperation help identify the contours of 'serious crime'. This particularly applies to the new Europol and Eurojust Regulations. Europol (the European Police Office) is competent in preventing and combating organised crime, terrorism and other *forms of serious crime* affecting two or more Member States.[26] At the following stage, Eurojust (the European Union Agency for Criminal Justice Cooperation) aims to support and strengthen coordination and cooperation between national investigating and prosecuting authorities in relation to *serious crime*, also, affecting two or more Member States, or requiring a prosecution on common bases, on the basis of operations conducted and information supplied by the Member States' authorities and by Europol, by the European Public Prosecutor Office (EPPO) and by European Anti-Fraud Office (OLAF).[27] Neither of these two instruments defines 'serious crime'. The first Annex of the respective regulations provides for a list of offences qualified as serious crime; the minor discrepancies between them should not present a challenge to the consistency of their common action.[28]

Other potential discrepancies may appear with other instruments that could define 'serious crime' in different ways or would not define it; that could have a list of offences associated to the text or not. For instance, Article 3(9) of the *EU PNR Directive*[29] refers to serious crime as 'the offences under national law referred to in Annex II that are punishable by a custodial sentence of a detention order for a maximum period of at least 3 years under the national law of a Member State'.[30] The

[26] Art. 3(1), *Europol Regulation.*

[27] Art. 2(1), *Regulation (EU) 2018/1727 of the European Parliament and of the Council of 14 November 2018 on the European Union Agency for Criminal Justice Cooperation (Eurojust) and replacing and repealing Council Decision 2002/187/JHA*, O.J.E.U. L295/138, 21 November 2018 (hereafter referred to as 'Eurojust Regulation').

[28] Art. 3(1) and Annex I, *Europol Regulation;* and Art. 3(1) and Annex I, *Eurojust Regulation.* Notably, Eurojust's list includes 'sexual abuse and sexual exploitation, *including child abuse material* [...]' while Europol's list talks about 'sexual abuse and sexual exploitation *of women and children, child pornography* [...]'; also, while Eurojust sees 'robbery and aggravated theft' as part of its competence, Europol focuses on 'organized robbery'. Probably without any specific any consequence, Eurojust Regulation grouped together environment crime and ship source pollution.

[29] *Directive 2016/681 on the use of PNR data for the prevention, detection, investigation and prosecution of terrorist offences and serious crime.*

[30] *Directive 2016/681.* In addition to terrorism, Annex II encompasses participation in a criminal organisation; trafficking in human beings; sexual exploitation of children and child pornography; illicit trafficking in narcotic drugs and psychotropic substances; illicit trafficking in weapons, munitions and explosives; corruption; fraud, including that against the financial interests of the Union; laundering of the proceeds of crime and counterfeiting of currency, including the euro; computer-related crime/cybercrime; environmental, including illicit trafficking in endangered animal species and in endangered plant species and varieties; facilitation of unauthorised entry and residence; murder, grievous bodily injury; illicit trade in human organs and tissue; kidnapping, illegal restraint and hostage-taking; organised and armed robbery; illicit trafficking in cultural goods, including antiques and works of art; counterfeiting and piracy of products; forgery of administrative documents and trafficking therein; illicit trafficking in hormonal substances and other growth promoters; illicit trafficking in nuclear or radioactive materials; rape; crimes within the

definition in the *EU PNR Directive* is narrower than the *European Arrest Warrant Framework Decision.*[31] This means that the scope and lists of offences may diverge between all the instruments of cooperation, including in the Europol and Eurojust Regulations. Moreover, the EU PNR Directive's scope is broader than that of UNTOC (punished by a maximum deprivation of liberty of at least 4 years).

Therefore, the absence of uniformity in the definition of serious crime within EU law may hinder the constituency of its action.

In ASEAN, there is no definition and no uniform list of offences qualified as 'serious crime'. Nonetheless, ASEAN Member States have identified a list of transnational crimes as priorities. This list has grown over the past 20 years. The process began when the 1999 *Plan of Action to Combat Transnational Crime* implemented the 1998 Manila *Declaration on the Prevention and Control of Transnational Crime* which listed terrorism, drug trafficking, arms smuggling, money laundering, trafficking in persons and piracy among the 'serious crime' category.[32] Over time, new additions included economic crimes and cybercrime, followed by illicit trafficking in wildlife, illicit trafficking in timber and people smuggling.[33] Environmental crimes like timber and wildlife trafficking were the most recent additions.[34]

This list is not written within a single binding instrument. Rather, they are amalgamated by an analysis of the different ASEAN instruments. These include the 2007 *ASEAN Convention on Counter-Terrorism* (ACCT),[35] the 2015 *ASEAN*

jurisdiction of the International Criminal Court; unlawful seizure of aircraft/ships; sabotage; trafficking in stolen vehicles; industrial espionage. Some of these offences appear in the list of the Council Framework Decision 2002/584/JHA, namely 'racism and xenophobia', 'swindling', 'racketeering and extortion', 'forgery of means of payment' and 'arson', or in the Europol Regulation, namely 'motor vehicle crime', 'racism and xenophobia', 'swindling', 'insider dealing and financial market manipulation', 'racketeering and extortion' or 'forgery of money and means of payment'.

[31] *Council Framework Decision 2002/584/JHA of 13 June 2002 on the European Arrest Warrant and the Surrender Procedures between Member States*, O.J.E.C. L190/1, 18 July 2002.

[32] Recital 4, *ASEAN Declaration on the Prevention and Control of Transnational Crime*, Manila, 25 March 1998; *ASEAN Plan of Action to Combat Transnational Crime*, Yangon, 23 June 1999.

[33] More specifically, the preambles of the Joint Declarations for cooperation to combat terrorism agreed between ASEAN and external partners, such as China on 4 November 2002; Australia on 1 July 2004; New Zealand on 29 July 2005; Canada on 28 July 2006. See the full list in the bibliography. On drug abuse and trafficking, see the preamble the Joint *Declaration for a Drug-Free ASEAN*, Manila, 25 July 1998. Also, 'What Did ASEAN's Latest Transnational Crime Meeting Achieve?' *The Diplomat*, 23 September 2017: available at https://thediplomat.com/2017/09/what-did-aseans-latest-transnational-crime-meeting-achieve/ (accessed on 23 November 2017).

[34] UNODC Southeast Asia and Pacific, 'ASEAN countries recognize wildlife and timber trafficking as serious transnational crime requiring regional action', Kuala Lumpur, 2 October 2015: available at https://www.unodc.org/southeastasiaandpacific/en/2015/10/asean-wildlife-timber/story.html (accessed on 23 November 2017); also, para. 4, Joint Statement, 11th ASEAN Ministerial Meeting on Transnational Crime, Manila, 20 September 2017.

[35] ASEAN Convention on Counter-Terrorism, 12th ASEAN Summit, Cebu, Heads of State/Government, 13 April 2007.

Convention against Trafficking in Persons, Especially Women and Children and other regional instruments or policy documents.

Moreover, the term 'serious' does not appear in these ASEAN instruments, which might mean that ASEAN Member States are not ready to engage in a broader discussion on the fight against serious crime. They have adopted a more sectorial approach. The UNTOC and its protocols serve as a general reference for ASEAN Member States. Every Member State is party to the UNTOC, but not all have ratified the Protocols.[36] The lack of common definitions or precise list of respective crimes may lead to different interpretations of the notion of 'seriousness'. Some offences may be identified as serious in some countries while not in others, thus potentially hindering their cooperation. Based on an examination of national legislations, differences effectively do exist. Singapore's legislation states that an extraditable offence is an offence punishable with 'a maximum penalty of death or imprisonment of not less than 12 months'.[37] With such a definition, Singapore may extradite in more cases than those stipulated by the UNTOC. By contrast, Indonesia defines extraditable offences as 'serious crimes'[38] listed in the annexes of the law. Indonesia does not define an extraditable offence on the basis of the punishment. Therefore, important differences between ASEAN Member States exist.

ASEAN has clearly avoided the issue of defining 'serious crime', whereas the EU has attempted to define the term, but failed to provide a uniform one. The legal stability in the EU regarding the definition of serious crime is quite uncertain. It may endanger the harmonisation process between Member States and weaken the dialogue between competent national authorities. As ASEAN has not yet engaged in the process of defining the term, the issue of non-uniformity has not been raised.

II. Terrorist Offences: No General Definition at the Global Level Despite Long-Running Debates

Terrorist offences are serious offences. They frequently possess a transnational nature, but are not inherently so. Therefore, defining terrorism has been—and still

---

[36] Brunei Darussalam is the latest country to have recently accessioned the *Protocol to Prevent, Suppress and Punish Trafficking in Persons, Especially Women and Children, supplementing the United Nations Convention against Transnational Organized Crime* (A/RES/55/25, New York, 15 November 2000, UNTS Vol. 2237, No. 39574) on 30 March 2020. And, Brunei Darussalam, Malaysia, Singapore and Vietnam have not ratified the *Protocol against the Smuggling of Migrants by Land, Sea and Air, supplementing the United Nations Convention against Transnational Organized Crime* (A/RES/55/25, New York, 15 November 2000, UNTS Vol. 2241, No. 39574) and Thailand has only signed it for now. Last date of consultation: 25 May 2020.

[37] Art. 2, *Singapore's Extradition Act* (Chap. 103), Act 14 of 1968, revised on 30 December 2000.

[38] See, e.g., Art. 4(1), *Law No. 1/1979 of the Republic of Indonesia concerning Extradition*, State Gazette of the Republic of Indonesia Year 1979 No. 2, Supplement No. 3130, 18 January 1979 with its annexed list of extraditable offences; Art. 4(1), *Extradition (Republic of Indonesia) Regulations 1994 No. 441 transposing the Extradition Treaty of 22 April 1992 between Government of the Republic of Indonesia and Government of Australia*, Statutory Rules, Attorney-General, 24 November 1994.

is—extremely complex. More complex than defining transnational organised crime.[39]

As for serious transnational crime, it hardly seems possible to discuss and develop anti-terrorism measures without defining 'terrorism' or 'terrorist offences'. Yet, such definition is lacking in many jurisdictions. Defining a crime is a step towards the realisation of the law.[40] In fact, '[t]he differences in definitions of terrorism and in social viewpoints have led to many incidents of domestic terrorism being categorised as actions by extremists, anarchists, radicals, and revolutionaries, and even unions. Depending on the time and era, incidents we would now consider terrorism were seen as anti-government or antisocial behaviours or were perceived as improving a way of life for fledgling nation'.[41]

The lack of a consensually agreed-upon definition at the international level can be seen as problematic seeing that several Security Council resolutions require States to adopt counterterrorism measures.[42] For instance, Security Council resolutions 1373(2001) and 1566(2004) pinpoint cooperation in the area of criminal justice as one of the key counterterrorism strategies.[43] Though it does not contain a general and compelling duty to criminalise terrorism. The only UN instrument that comes close enough to establishing a definition of terrorist offences is the 1999

---

[39] States are increasingly aware of the 'growing link between transnational organized crime and terrorist crimes'. See Preamble, UNTOC (2000); also A/55/383/Add.1, Report of the Ad Hoc Committee on the Elaboration of a Convention against Transnational Organized Crime on the work of its first to eleventh sessions, Addendum 'Interpretative notes for the official records (*travaux préparatoires*) of the negotiation of the United Nations Convention against Transnational Organized Crime and the Protocols thereto', 55th session, 3 November 2000.

[40] See Qualification in *Dictionnaire de la culture juridique*, eds., Denis Alland and Stéphane Rials, 1st ed. (Paris: PUF, 2003); Christian Atias, *Epistémologie Juridique*, Droit fondamental, Droit politique et théorique (Paris: PUF, 1985).

[41] Michael R. Ronczkowski, *Terrorism and Organized Hate Crime: intelligence Gathering, Analysis and Investigations*, 2nd ed. (Boca Raton: CRC Press, 2007): 27.

[42] Marco Sassòli, 'La définition du terrorisme et le droit international humanitaire' *Revue québécoise de droit international,* vol. 30, no. 1 (2007).

[43] Providing markers for the definition of terrorism, 18 international instruments currently ask States to criminalise terrorist behaviours and to cooperate in order to eliminate terrorism, from the *Convention on the Prevention and Punishment of Crimes against Internationally Protected Persons, including Diplomatic Agents*, New York, 14 December 1973, UNTS vol. 1035, No. 15410 to the *Convention on the Suppression of Unlawful Acts relating to International Civil Aviation*, Beijing, 10 September 2010, DCAS Doc No. 22. See also *Draft Comprehensive Convention against International Terrorism*: Consolidated text prepared by the Coordinator for discussion contained at Appendix II of Letter dated 3 August 2005 from the Chairman of the Sixth Committee addressed to the President of the General Assembly, UN Doc. A/59/894, 12 August 2005; GA/L/3433, *Legal Committee Urges Conclusion of Draft Comprehensive Convention on International Terrorism*, 67th session, 6th Committee, 8 October 2012 repeated on 7 October 2013, GA/L/3453; and again later. See also, Mariona Llobet Angli, 'What does "terrorism" mean?' in *Counter-Terrorism, Human Rights and the Rule of Law: Crossing Legal Boundaries in Defence of the State*, eds., Aniceto Masferrer and Clive Walker (Cheltenham: Edward Elgar, 2013): 19.

International Convention for the Suppression of the Financing of Terrorism, which was ratified or accessioned by all EU and ASEAN Member States.[44] Indeed, Article 2 Subsection (b) of this Convention defines a terrorist offence as 'any other act intended to cause death or serious bodily injury to a civilian, or to any other person not taking an active part in the hostilities in a situation of armed conflict, when the purpose of such act, by its nature or context, is to intimidate a population, or to compel a government or an international organisation to do or to abstain from doing any act'. Certain elements of Article 2 have been introduced into the 2005 *Draft Comprehensive Convention against International Terrorism.*[45] However, this Draft Comprehensive Convention has never been adopted due to unresolved tensions between and dissent amongst UN Member States.

Immediately after the 9/11 attacks, both the EU and ASEAN affirmed their commitment to prevent and counter terrorism.[46] However, the deployment of counterterrorism means, including the approximation of criminal laws, the adaptation of the criminal justice systems to this specific crime, the adoption of counterterrorism policies, and the development and enhancement of cooperation mechanisms all vary greatly from one region to the other.

In a similar way to the UN's affirmations, ASEAN Member States declared, in 2001, their aim to 'counter, prevent and suppress all forms of terrorist acts in accordance with the charter of the United Nations and other international law, especially taking into account the importance of all United Nations Resolutions'.[47] In 2007, ASEAN Member States adopted a binding instrument, namely the *ASEAN Convention on Counter-Terrorism* (ACCT). With regard to its scope, the ACCT does not mirror one international instrument as such, but rather amalgamates provisions from several instruments such as the 1997 *International Convention for the Suppression of Terrorist Bombings,*[48] the 1999 *International Convention for the Suppression of the Financing of Terrorism,* and other counterterrorism instruments.[49]

The Convention aims to provide a regional framework for intra-regional cooperation.[50] Nonetheless, there is no regional definition of terrorist offences. The Convention refers to 14 international instruments which deal with terrorism.[51] Interestingly, ASEAN's approach is similar to that of the Council of Europe within

---

[44] *International Convention for the Suppression of the Financing of Terrorism* (1999).

[45] Art. 2, *Draft Comprehensive Convention against International Terrorism*, UN Doc. A/59/894 (2005).

[46] Council of the EU, Conclusions and Plan of Action of the Extraordinary European Council Meeting, SN 140/01, 21 September 2001; *ASEAN Declaration on Joint Action to Counter Terrorism*, Bandar Seri Begawan, 5 November 2001.

[47] Preamble, *ASEAN Declaration on Joint Action to Counter Terrorism* (2001).

[48] *International Convention for the Suppression of Terrorist Bombings* (1997).

[49] See the list in Art. II(1) ACCT.

[50] Art. I, ACCT.

[51] Art. II, ACCT.

the *Convention on the Prevention of Terrorism*, which refers to international treaties for the definition of terrorist offences.[52] The scope of the ACCT is, therefore, as broad as it is at the international level.

The ACCT was adopted and ratified by all Member States. Malaysia was the last to ratify the Convention on 11 January 2013, 2 years after it became enforceable; on 13 January 2011. Because of the reference made by the ACCT to the UN instruments, checking the status of ratifications of these instruments by ASEAN Member States is necessary in order to establish potential discrepancies between their national legislations. All ASEAN Member States ratified or later accessioned the 1970 *Convention for the Suppression of Unlawful Seizure of Aircraft*, the 1971 *Convention for the Suppression of Unlawful Acts against the Safety of Civil Aviation*, the 1988 *Protocol for the suppression of Unlawful Acts of Violence at Airports Serving International Civil Aviation, supplementary to the Convention for the Suppression of Unlawful Acts against the Safety of Civil Aviation* (except from Indonesia that just signed it), the 1997 *International Convention for the Suppression of Terrorist Bombings,* and the 1999 *International Convention for the Suppression of the Financing of Terrorism.*[53] Certain international treaties were ratified or accessioned only by some Member States. These treaties include the 1973 *Convention on the Prevention and Punishment of Crimes against Internationally Protected Persons*, the 1979 *International Convention against the Taking of Hostages* and the 1979 *Convention on the Physical Protection of Nuclear Material.*[54]

[52] Art. 1 and Appendix, CoE, *Convention on the Prevention of Terrorism*, ETS No. 196, Warsaw, 16 October 2005.

[53] *Convention for the Suppression of Unlawful Seizure of Aircraft*, 16 December 1970, UNTS vol. 860, No. 12325; *Convention for the Suppression of Unlawful Acts against the Safety of Civil Aviation*, Montreal, 23 September 1971, UNTS vol. 974, No. 14118; *Protocol for the Suppression of Unlawful Acts of Violence at Airports Serving International Civil Aviation, supplementary to the Convention for the suppression of Unlawful Acts against the Safety of Civil Aviation*, Montreal, 24 February 1988, UNTS vol. 1589, No. 14118; *International Convention for the Suppression of Terrorist Bombings* (1997); *International Convention for the suppression of the financing of terrorism* (1999).

[54] *Convention on the Prevention and Punishment of Crimes against Internationally Protected Persons, including Diplomatic Agents* (1973); *Convention on the Physical Protection of Nuclear Material*, Vienna, 26 October 1979, UNTS vol. 1456, No. 24631; *International Convention against the Taking of Hostages*, New York, 17 December 1979, UNTS vol. 1316, No. 21931; *Convention for the Suppression of Unlawful Acts against the Safety of Maritime Navigation*, Rome, 10 March 1988, UNTS vol. 1678, No. 29004; *Protocol for the Suppression of Unlawful Acts against the Safety of Fixed Platforms Located on the Continental Shelf*, Rome, 10 March 1988, UNTS vol. 1678, No. 29004; *International Convention for the Suppression of Acts of Nuclear Terrorism,* New York, 13 April 2005, UNTS vol. 2445, No. 44004; *Protocol of 2005 to the Convention for the Suppression of Unlawful Acts against the Safety of Maritime Navigation*, London, 14 October 2005, IMO Doc. LEG/CONF.15/21; *Amendment to the Convention on the Physical Protection of Nuclear Material*, Vienna, 8 July 2005, GOV/INF/2005/10-GC(49)/INF/6; *Protocol of 2005 to the Convention for the Suppression of Unlawful Acts against the Safety of Maritime Navigation*, London, 14 October 2005, [2005] ATNIF 30; *Protocol of 2005 to the Protocol for the Suppression of Unlawful Acts against the Safety of Fixed Platforms Located on the Continental Shelf*, London, 14 October 2005, IMO DOC.LEG/CONF.15/22. For the ratifications, see Appendix 1.

Since then, the 2009 *ASEAN Comprehensive Plan of Action on Counter Terrorism,* the revised 2017 *ASEAN Comprehensive Plan of Action on Counter Terrorism* and other ASEAN texts have not added further precision in the definition of 'terrorist offences'.[55] As such, ASEAN Member States have not reached a deeper understanding of 'terrorist offences' yet than the one in international law.

Through a process of reduction, the ACCT specifies that terrorism should not be associated with any religion, nationality, civilisation, or ethnic group.[56] The Convention also excludes the possibility for States to consider a terrorist offence as a political offence or related to a political offence.[57] Even though these exclusions are helpful in certain respects, they are not sufficient to provide useful and harmonised guidance.

The EU has developed a much more elaborate counterterrorism legal arsenal. This process had begun before the 9/11 attacks.[58] The EU is not the first regional organisation to engage with defining terrorism.[59] Yet, it adopted a definition of terrorist offences precise enough to approximate all of its Member States' legislations. The EU adopted two consecutive Framework Decisions in 2002 and 2008,[60] followed by a Directive in 2017[61] which replaced these framework decisions.

After recognising the importance of defining terrorist offences,[62] the *2002/475/ JHA Council Framework Decision* defined terrorist offences as 'offences under national law, which, given their nature or context, may seriously damage a country or an international organisation where committed with the aim of seriously intimidating a population, or unduly compelling a Government or international

[55] ASEAN Comprehensive Plan of Action on Counter Terrorism, Nay Pyi Taw, 30 June 2009; Revised ASEAN Comprehensive Plan of Action on Counter Terrorism, 11th AMMTC, Manila, 20 September 2017.

[56] Preamble, ACCT.

[57] Art. XIV, ACCT.

[58] See, e.g., the TREVI (*Terrorisme, Radicalisme, Extrémisme et Violence Internationale*) Group was the forum of the operational cooperation between Ministers of Interior and Justice. This forum was formalised on 29 June 1972 in Luxembourg at a meeting between the European Community Interior Ministers and it functioned till the entering into force of the TEU. Also, the Tampere European Council, Conclusions of the Presidency, SN 200/99, Brussels, 15–16 October 1999; and, further developed in Chap. 5. See, e.g., Anna Cornelia Beyer, *Counter Terrorism and International Power Relations: The EU, ASEAN and Hegemonic Global Governance* (London: I.B.Tauris & Co Ltd., 2010): 68 and ff; Maria O'Neill, *The Evolving EU Counter-Terrosim Legal Framework*, Research in EU Law (Oxon: Routledge, 2012); Cian C. Murphy, *EU Counter-Terrorism Law. Pre-Emption and the Rule of Law*, Modern Studies in European Law (Oxford: Hart Publishing, 2012).

[59] See, e.g., Art. 1(2) and (3), League of Arab States, *The Arab Convention for the Suppression of Terrorism*, Cairo, 22 April 1998.

[60] *Council Framework Decision 2002/475/JHA on combating terrorism*; *Council Framework Decision 2008/919/JHA of 28 November 2008 amending the Council Framework Decision 2002/ 475/JHA on combating terrorism*, O.J.E.U. L330/21, 9 December 2008.

[61] *Directive (EU) 2017/541 on combating terrorism.*

[62] Recital 6, *Council Framework Decision 2002/475/JHA on combating terrorism.*

organisation to perform or abstain from performing any act, or seriously destabilising or destroying the fundamental political, constitutional, economic or social structures of a country or an international organisation'. This was followed by a list of specific offences.[63] This EU definition includes three constitutive elements, namely the material elements, a seriousness or gravity element and the intentional element ('the terrorist intention').[64] These elements need to be met to prosecute the acts committed as being 'terrorist' by nature. Firstly, the material elements are the 'ordinary' offences listed within the Framework Decision. The constitutive elements of those 'ordinary offences' may differ depending on the qualification and characterisation provided in each national legislation. Secondly, these acts must seriously damage a country or an international organisation. This constitutes a restrictive, but imprecise seriousness element. Thirdly, these acts must fulfil one of the following objectives: (a) 'seriously intimidating a population' (b) 'unduly compelling a Government or international organisation to perform or abstain from performing any act' or (c) 'seriously destabilising or destroying the fundamental political, constitutional, economic or social structures of a country or an international organisation'. This definition was almost completely copied into the 2017 Directive.[65]

Unlike in ASEAN, the 2002 Framework Decision obliged Member States to criminalise and define the participation to the activities of a terrorist group. Such provision was then repeated word for word in the Directive, the terrorist group being defined as 'a structured group of more than two persons, established for a period of time and acting in concert to commit terrorist offences'.[66]

The 2002 Framework Decision was later amended to criminalise behaviours at an earlier stage of the perpetration of a criminal act. The 2008 Framework Decision

---

[63] Art. 2, *Council Framework Decision 2002/475/JHA*: Shall be deemed to be terrorist offences: (a) attacks upon a person's life which may cause death; (b) attacks upon the physical integrity of a person; (c) kidnapping or hostage taking; (d) causing extensive destruction to a Government or public facility, a transport system, an infrastructure facility, including an information system, a fixed platform located on the continental shelf, a public place or private property likely to endanger human life or result in major economic loss; (e) seizure of aircraft, ships or other means of public or goods transport; (f) manufacture, possession, acquisition, transport, supply or use of weapons, explosives or of nuclear, biological or chemical weapons, as well as research into, and development of, biological and chemical weapons; (g) release of dangerous substances, or causing fires, floods or explosions the effect of which is to endanger human life; (h) interfering with or disrupting the supply of water, power or any other fundamental natural resource the effect of which is to endanger human life; (i) threatening to commit any of the acts listed in (a) to (h).

[64] For more developments, see Daniel Flore, *Droit pénal européen. Les enjeux d'une justice pénale européenne* (Bruxelles: Larcier, 2009): 140 and ff.

[65] Art. 3, *Directive 2017/541 on combating terrorism*. The list of offences knows an exception regarding the 'manufacture, possession, acquisition, transport, supply or use of explosives and weapons [. . .]' and adds one form of crime to the list of terrorist offences, namely 'illegal system interference, as referred to in Article 4 of Directive 2013/40/EU of the European Parliament and of the Council (1) in cases where Article 9(3) or point (b) or (c) of Article 9(4) of that Directive applies, and illegal data interference, as referred to in Article 5 of that Directive in cases where point (c) of Article 9(4) of that Directive applies'.

[66] Art. 1(1), *Council Framework Decision 2002/475/JHA on combating terrorism.*

added public provocation, recruitment and active training for terrorism to the list of terrorist offences.[67] After the terrorist attacks in Paris, and within the foreign terrorist fighters context, the 2017 Directive integrated new provisions in order to criminalise passive training for terrorism as well as the travelling—and facilitating of travelling—abroad for terrorist purposes.[68]

Of course, this approximation of the definition of terrorist offences has had consequences on the growth of cooperation between EU Member States.

The international legal framework remains broadly defined which leaves States with a large room for manoeuvrability and many gaps for discrepancies between them. Within this context, the EU has gone much further than the ASEAN in defining terrorist offences, thus providing EU Member States' actions with a clearer legal framework. As will be discussed later on, the discrepancies between regions—that result from different approaches when defining terrorist offences—may lead to diverging counterterrorism responses. Moreover, it may also impact interregional relations.

Section 2: Key Notions Concerning Transnational Interactions in Criminal Matters

The UN and certain regional organisations, such as the Council of Europe, the EU or ASEAN, require States to criminalise specific serious transnational acts and implement effective measures to prevent, investigate, detect and prosecute these offences, among which terrorism.[69] Among those measures, cooperation, coordination and collaboration are key notions to help ensure the effectiveness of States' actions. These measures have developed in the last decade, but in various forms, at different levels and through different channels (I).

Dealing with cooperation between competent national authorities, the most topical cooperation mechanism is information and intelligence sharing. Information and intelligence sharing is analysed as a primary mechanism of cooperation that

---

[67] Art. 1(1), *Council Framework Decision 2008/919/JHA on combating terrorism.*

[68] Arts. 9–10, *Directive 2017/541.*

[69] See, e.g., Art. 31, UNTOC (2000); and Art. 9, A/RES/55/25(2000), *Protocol to Prevent, Suppress and Punish Trafficking in Persons*; S/RES/1373 (2001). In the EU, see, e.g., the enactment of Europol (*Council Decision 2009/371/JHA of 6 April 2009 establishing the European Police Office (Europol)*, O.J.E.U. L121/37, 15 May 2009) and Eurojust (*Council Decision 2009/426/JHA of 16 December 2008 on the strengthening of Eurojust and amending Decision 2002/187/JHA setting up Eurojust with a view to reinforcing the fight against serious crime*, O.J.E.U. L138/14, 4 June 2009); *Council Framework Decision 2002/475/JHA on combating terrorism*; *Council Framework Decision 2008/919/JHA on combating terrorism*; *Council Framework Decision 2008/841/JHA on the fight against organised crime*. In the CoE, *Convention on Laundering, Search, Seizure and confiscation of the Proceeds from Crime*, Strasbourg, 8 November 1990; *Convention on Cybercrime*, ETS No. 185, Budapest, 23 November 2001. In ASEAN, *Declaration on Transnational Crime*, Manila, 20 December 1997; *Declaration on the Prevention and Control of Transnational Crime*, Manila, 25 March 1998; and ACCT.

provides an interesting link between the different phases of the procedure, as it is always useful in the phases of prevention, investigation, detection and prosecution. Becoming better informed and knowing the situation and all elements of the offence is essential to prevent and combat serious transnational crime. Mechanisms of cooperation facilitating the flow of data have developed and improved in the past 50 years. It has been increasingly written about and particularly debated, especially due to the concerns that it raises for privacy, data protection and data security (II).

I. Working Together to Prevent and Combat Terrorism but How?

The international community has agreed upon common objectives and States have worked together in order to reach them.[70] However, States have adopted different ways of contributing to a common purpose. International and regional legal instruments and declarations urge States to 'collaborate' and/or to 'cooperate' together and to 'coordinate' their efforts. These terms remain undefined within international and regional instruments and often seem to be used interchangeably. It can be however wondered whether each term implies a specific dynamic and power relation (A).

Whatever the terminology, the period, the context and the framework have played a role in defining and formalising the interactions between competent national authorities. At certain times it is also organised in a transversal manner, for all types of crimes concerned; and at other times in a more sectorial manner (B).

A. The Notions of Cooperation, Collaboration and Coordination: Interchangeable or Distinct Notions?

Properly qualifying the different interactions, namely 'cooperation', 'collaboration' and 'coordination', may help enhance the communications between partners, and thus improve the accuracy of the analysis. Yet, these terms are generally used in instruments dealing with various forms of interactions without any specific meaning and purpose to differentiate them.

1. Starting from the basics: looking at the ordinary meaning of these terms

When glancing at the ordinary meaning of the three terms, it is evident that 'cooperation' and 'collaboration' are rather similarly defined or even identically so—according to certain ordinary dictionaries—as 'the work and activity of a number of persons who individually contribute towards the efficiency of the whole'.[71] Coordination is defined as 'the process of organising people or groups

---

[70] See, e.g., A/RES/49/60, *Measures to eliminate international terrorism*, 84th plenary meeting, 9 December 1994; A/RES/50/6, *Declaration on the Occasion of the Fiftieth Anniversary of the United Nations*, 50th session, 24 October 1995; and other following resolutions and conventions.

[71] Merriam-Webster, definitions of 'cooperation' and 'collaboration'. Also, see 'collaboration' and 'cooperation' are defined similarly, with a different wording though in *Oxford Advanced Learner's Dictionary*, eds., A.S. Hornby et al., 8th ed. (Oxford: Oxford University Press, 1995). 'Collaboration' refers to 'the act of working with another person or group of people to create or produce

so that they work together properly and well'.[72] Thus, one should understand that 'coordinative interactions' aim to ensure the best ordering of tasks in order to enhance the effectiveness of competent authorities' actions.

2. What do international and regional organisations make of them?

Concerning international and regional instruments, there is no specific definition for either of these interaction terms. It can be said that there is a tendency for official documents—and within the doctrine—to use them broadly.[73] This is certainly true for collaboration and cooperation. It is particularly difficult to acknowledge the appropriate application of each type of interaction, especially since both terms are often used interchangeably. This can make the authors' intentions and their implications unclear. When it comes to international relations, a lack of common terminology may weaken reliable communication and collective understanding.[74]

Thankfully, official documents are often associated with specific actions to be fulfilled by States involved in determined interactions.

The international community agreed to take the necessary steps to enhance cooperation against terrorism,[75] especially regional cooperation. According to the Plan of Action annexed to the *UN Global Counter-Terrorism Strategy,* States shall undertake:

> [t]o cooperate fully [. . .], in accordance with [their] obligations under international law, in order to find, deny safe haven and bring to justice, on the basis of the principle of extradite or prosecute, any person who supports, facilitates, participates or attempts to participate in the financing, planning, preparation or perpetration of terrorist acts or provides safe havens.[76]

Coordination is also required to ensure the effectiveness of interstate cooperation.[77]

---

something' and 'cooperation' refers to 'the fact of doing something together or of working together towards a shared aim'.

[72] Merriam-Webster: 'coordination'.

[73] Martin Lundin, 'Explaining cooperation: How resource interdependence, goal congruence, and trust affect joint actions in policy implementation' *Journal of Public Administration Research and Theory* vol. 17, no. 4 (2007): 653; Madeleine McNamara, 'Starting to Untangle the Web of Cooperation, Coordination and Collaboration: A Framework for Public Managers' *International Journal of Public Administration,* vol. 35, no. 6 (2012).

[74] Myrna Mandell and Toddi Steelman, 'Understanding what can be accomplished through interorganizational innovations: The importance of typologies, context, and management strategies' *Public Management Review,* vol. 5, no. 2 (2003); Beyer (2010): 68 and ff.; O'Neill (2012); Murphy (2012); Anne Weyembergh and Veronica Santamaria, 'Lutte contre le terrorisme et droits fondamentaux dans le cadre du troisième pilier. La Décision-cadre du 13 juin 2002 relative à la lutte contre le terrorisme et le principe de la légalité' in *Les droits fondamentaux dans l'Union européenne. Dans le sillage de la Constitution européenne*, ed., Joël Rideau (Bruxelles: Bruylant, 2009); Anne Weyembergh, 'L'Espace Pénal Européen: Entre Coopération Judiciaire et Territoire Pénal Européen' in *La Grande Europe*, ed., Paul Magnette (Bruxelles: Editions de l'Université de Bruxelles, 2004).

[75] Recital, A/RES/60/288(2006), *United Nations Global Counter-Terrorism Strategy.*

[76] Pt. II(13), Plan of Action, Annex of the A/RES/60/288(2006).

[77] Ibid.

There has been no change in vocabulary amongst international instruments over time. Cooperation has always been the type of interaction requested, instead of collaboration; whatever each term may imply.[78] Apart from UN Security Council (UNSC) resolutions 1377(2001) and 2396(2017) which refer to collaboration, cooperation appears in each UN resolution related to terrorism, including the 2014 resolution on foreign terrorist fighters.[79]

In the absence of clear international distinction, collaboration and cooperation are often used together. The ASEAN constitutive Declaration of 1967 requires Member States to collaborate and cooperate together to reach shared objectives. Qualifying the relation between States, collaboration is not used separately, but instead is associated with cooperation.[80] Within the texts of the recently adopted Blueprint 2025, ASEAN mentioned the endeavour of States 'to enhance cooperation against terrorism'.[81] As for coordination, it is associated with cooperation to ensure that the competent authorities combine their efforts to prevent and combat terrorism.[82] As no specific meaning rises from the texts, the basic one applies.

In the EU, 'cooperation' is the official qualifier of the interactions in police and judicial matters. Title V of Part III of the TFEU has a Chap. 4 on 'Judicial Cooperation in Criminal Matters' (Articles 82–86) and a Chap. 5 on 'Police Cooperation' (Articles 87–89). These provisions refer to 'cooperation' as a generic term which covers various types of mechanisms that can be of a different nature. The relevant chapters in the TFEU dealing with police and judicial cooperation in criminal matters elaborate upon the EU agencies' actions in facilitating them. Indeed, the EU has been especially active in implementing effective mechanisms of 'cooperation' through the development of regional agencies, mainly Europol and Eurojust. The TFEU also uses the word coordination when defining the missions of

[78] Collaboration between States is required in UN Security Council, S/RES/2195(2014), *Threats to international peace and security*, 7351st meeting, 19 December 2014; S/RES/2253(2015), 7587th meeting, 17 December 2015; but not in General Assembly resolutions, as A/RES/60/288(2006) or in the Security Council resolutions (taking only the year 2015) S/RES/2220(2015), *Non-proliferation of weapons*, 7447th meeting, 22 May 2015; S/RES/2250(2015), *Maintenance of international peace and security*, 7573rd meeting, 9 December 2015; S/RES/2255(2015) *Threats to international peace and security caused by terrorist acts,* 7590th meeting, 22 December 2015 in which cooperation is required. Similarly, the *Convention for the Suppression of Terrorist Bombings* (1997), *Convention for the Suppression of the Financing of Terrorism* (1999) and *Convention for the Suppression of Acts of Nuclear Terrorism* (2005) only refer to cooperation, but not to collaboration.

[79] S/RES/2178(2014), *Resolution Condemning Violent Extremism, Underscoring Need to Prevent Travel, Support for Foreign Terrorist Fighters*, 7272nd meeting, 24 September 2014.

[80] B3.1.iv), ASEAN Political-Security Community, Blueprint 2025, *ASEAN 2025 Forging Ahead Together* (Jakarta: ASEAN Secretariat, 2015).

[81] B3.2. and B3.2.x), APSC, Blueprint 2025.

[82] See, e.g., B1.2.v), B3.1. iv), B3.2. x) and B3.7. ii), APSC, Blueprint 2025. This association can also be found in the *ASEAN Plan of Action Against Trafficking in Persons, Especially Women and Children*, 27th ASEAN Summit, Kuala Lumpur, 22 November 2015.

Europol and Eurojust. Eurojust is meant to support and strengthen coordination and cooperation between national investigating and prosecuting authorities. Among the tasks of Europol, the Treaty also refers to coordinating investigative and operational actions.[83] 'Collaboration' is not even mentioned in the chapters of the TFEU which deals with police and judicial cooperation. The word is however used when the EU secondary legislation organises the interactions between the different agencies or between the agencies and other EU entities, such as the EPPO and OLAF.

Thus, these three terms have appeared in crime-related policy and legal texts at international and regional levels. However, in the EU particularly, the different forms of interactions end up being slightly more specifically used, but without any precise definition and systematisation.

Currently, 'cooperation' remains the most used concept in official instruments that deal with criminal and security issues. In the field of counterterrorism, 'cooperation' appears to be the main qualifier of the interactions between competent authorities, especially in cross-border cases.

3. Looking elsewhere to find a more precise meaning?

In the absence of official definition for these three terms, it is interesting to take a look at studies carried out in other fields of research that analysed these types of interaction. In particular, political science studies on inter-organisational theory and education literature provide valuable insight. Notably, Thatcher, Keast, Brown and Mandell, and McNamara are among the rare scholars to have conducted empirical analysis on differentiating each type of interaction.[84] From their study, 15 elements were identified to distinguish among the 3 types of interactions: design, formality of the agreement, organisational autonomy, policy authority, key personnel, information sharing, decision making, resolution of turf issues, resource allocation, systems thinking, incentives, commitment, trust, risk taking and willingness to change. Thus, this study provides a useful conceptual basis for exploration into a better qualification of the existing interactions between authorities.

The following table draws distinctions among the interactions.[85] The list of elements is not exhaustive. There are certainly other variables such as representativeness that might play a role (Table 2.1).

Besides the context, some elements carry more weight than others in defining one type of interaction. In the case of interactions in criminal matters, the most significant elements include formality, information sharing, decision-making process and trust.

Firstly, the different types of interactions tend to evolve and to build upon one another. This may lead to overlaps, especially between cooperation and

[83] Arts. 85(1) and 88(2), TFEU.

[84] Robyn Keast, Kerry Brown, and Myrna Mandell, 'Getting the right mix: Unpacking integration meanings and strategies' *International Public Management Journal,* vol. 10, no. 1 (2007); Christine Thatcher, *A study of interorganizational arrangement among three regional campuses of a large land-grant university* (University of Hartford, College of Education, Nursing and Health Professions: doctoral degree, PhD thesis, 2007).

[85] Inspired by McNamara's analysis and definitions of the different elements, McNamara (2012): 392; Thatcher (2007).

Table 2.1 Distinguishing between cooperation, coordination and collaboration

Element	Cooperation	Coordination	Collaboration
Design	Work within existing organisational structures	Centralised control through hierarchical structures	Shared power arrangements
Formality of the agreement	Informal and formal agreements	Formalised agreements	Informal and formal agreements
Organisational autonomy	Fully autonomous; policies to govern the collective arrangement are not necessarily developed but they may be	Semi-autonomous; policies to govern the collective arrangement may be developed by higher authorities	Not autonomous; policies to govern the collective arrangement are developed jointly by participants
Key personnel	Implementation of the partnership occurs at the lowest level(s); leaders are not necessarily involved but they may be	Implementation of the partnership is based on higher authority; a boundary spanner may be used to foster linkages	Implementation of the partnership is based on the participants; a convener may help bring participants together
Information sharing	Basic/raw information and intelligence shared through informal and formal channels	Information is exchanged through more formal channels	Open and frequent communications through formal and informal channels
Decision making	Independent decision making	Centralised decision making	Participative decision making
Resolution of issues	Conflicts avoided through independence	A neutral facilitator may help resolve conflicts	Participants work together to resolve conflicts
Resource allocation	Information is exchanged	Physical and non-physical resources are exchanged to achieve individual goals	Physical and non-physical resources are pooled in support of collective goals
Systems thinking	System integration does not necessarily occur but may exist	System integration may occur to better achieve individual goals	System integration does occur to better achieve collective goals
Trust	Trust relationships are not required but may develop, particularly through interpersonal relations	Leaders work closely to create relationships based on trust, particularly through political and legal agreements	Trust between participants is needed to sustain relationships, as such political and/or legal agreements support it

collaboration. An interaction between participants may be perceived differently depending on the criteria pointed out.

Secondly, trust plays a significant part in the three cases. According to this study, trust is based on the willingness to be vulnerable to the behaviours of others based on the belief that their actions will be consistent with individual interest.[86] The more closely parties decide to work together, the deeper trust needs to be in order to ensure the effectiveness of their common action. The level of trust varying depending on the types of interactions ensures the effectiveness of their counterterrorism actions.

4. The different forms of cooperation in criminal matters based on the ill-defined key terms

Cross-border cooperation in criminal matters may take three forms: cooperation between national administrative authorities; cooperation between national law enforcement authorities and cooperation between national judicial authorities. Such cooperation occurs at successive stages of the criminal proceeding. Furthermore, it usually involves different actors and rules.

Criminal proceedings increasingly involve administrative measures. For prevention purposes, or even as means of repression (sometimes without judicial authorisation), administrative measures, including the freezing of assets, passport revocations, control orders, to name a few, may be decided against terrorist organisations or individuals. Administrative acts may be carried out by law enforcement authorities and be the object of cross-border cooperation.[87]

While police and judicial cooperation is legally dealt with in Title V of the TFEU, it is required but not specifically framed within the ASEAN Political-Security Community. Cross-border cooperation may even be supported by regional agencies, such as Europol and Eurojust, or other bodies such as the European Judicial Network, while it is not the case yet in ASEAN.

The type of mechanisms may be more specific to one or another form of cooperation. But some cooperation mechanisms are similar in the two regions. Among the judicial mechanisms of cooperation, mutual legal assistance, extradition and the transfer of persons exist in both the EU and ASEAN. Meanwhile, police cooperation mainly focuses on data sharing. The latter is in fact an intersectional

---

[86] McNamara (2012): 392.

[87] Among the most recent cases of the ECtHR, see on the deprivation of nationality *Ghoumid and others* v. *France*, App. No. 52273/16, 52285/16, 52290/16 et al., judgement, ECLI:CE:ECHR:2020:0625JUD005227316, 25 June 2020. See, e.g., Anna Oehmichen, *Terrorism and Anti-Terror Legislation. The Terrorised Legislator?* (Antwerp: Intersentia, 2009); Victor V. Ramraj et al., eds., *Global Anti-Terrorism Law and Policy*, 2nd ed. (Cambridge: Cambridge University Press, 2012); Mariane F. H. Hirsch Ballin, *Anticipative criminal investigation. Theory and counterterrorism practice in the Netherlands and the United States* (The Hague: T.M.C. Asser Press, 2012); Francesca Galli and Anne Weyembergh, eds., *Approximation of substantive criminal law in the EU: The way forward*, vol. 10, Etudes européennes (Bruxelles: Editions de l'Université de Bruxelles, 2013); Céline C. Cocq and Francesca Galli, 'The catalysing effect of serious crime on the use of surveillance technologies for prevention and investigation purposes' *N.J.E.C.L.*, vol. 4, no. 3 (2013); Kent Roach, ed., *Comparative Counter-Terrorism Law. The State of the Art* (Cambridge: Cambridge University Press, 2015); Murphy (2012); Céline C. Cocq, 'Transposition de la Résolution 2178 (2014) par la Belgique et la France: Vers une répression des combattants terroristes étrangers toujours plus préventive et fournie' *Les Nouveaux Problèmes Actuels de Sciences Criminelles - Lextenso,* vol. XXVI, no. 3 (2016).

cooperation mechanism used by law enforcement authorities and judicial authorities. For instance, mutual legal assistance in criminal matters is also about exchanging information. It is one of the most significant mechanisms of cooperation where all the actors of the criminal procedure are involved. Crucially, data sharing is better legally framed in judicial—and even administrative—cooperation (more formal) than in police cooperation (less formal than informal).

B. A Mix of 'Sectorial v. Transversal' Approaches Leading to 'Informal v. Formal' Methods of Cooperation in Criminal Matters

Within this unclear terminology, texts promoting cross-border interactions (i.e. generally qualified as 'cooperation') have emerged at different levels, creating various forms of cooperation.

International cooperation has been regulated mainly on a sectorial basis and barely on a transversal basis. Apart from UN model treaties, there is no real transversal cooperation conventions (no UN extradition convention for instance).

Since the 70s, the UN incentive to develop interstate cooperation was mostly framed in sectorial conventions dealing with specific types of offences, such as terrorism[88] and drug trafficking.[89] In particular in the field of terrorism, many Security Council resolutions enshrine precise and specific obligations to cooperate.[90] None of the resolutions focus on transnational crime per se, but rather focus on specific threats which constitute terrorism.[91]

The most general convention where States have formalised their will to cooperate together[92] is the UN Convention against Transnational Organized Crime (UNTOC). This convention presents a 'limited' transversal approach that requires States to criminalise a set of criminal acts under a general category that may encompass

---

[88] See, e.g., the first convention tackling terrorist offences: *Convention on offences and certain other acts committed on board aircraft*, Tokyo, 14 September 1963, *UNTS vol. 704, No. 10106.*

[89] See, e.g., *United Nations Convention against Illicit Traffic in Narcotic Drugs and Psychotropic Substances*, Vienna, 20 December 1988, UNTS vol. 1582, No. 27627.

[90] See, e.g., UNSC resolutions on threats to international peace and security: S/RES/1368(2001), *Threats to international peace and security caused by terrorist acts*, 4370th meeting, 12 September 2001; S/RES/1373(2001); S/RES/1377(2001); S/RES/1378 (2001) and followings.

[91] It is only since 2011 that the Security Council linked terrorist offences to other serious transnational crime such as drug trafficking: S/RES/1988(2011), *Threats to international peace and security caused by terrorist acts,* 6557th meeting, 17 June 2011; then, see, e.g., S/RES/2083 (2012); S/RES/2129(2013); S/RES/2195(2014).

[92] The UNTOC remains restricted to 'transnational organised crime' instead of the broader category of 'transnational crime' (underlined by the author). See also A/RES/49/159, *Naples Political Declaration* and *Global Action Plan against Organized Transnational Crime*, 94th plenary meeting, 23 December 1994; UNTOC (2000); A/RES/59/157, *International cooperation in the fight against transnational organized crime: Assistance to States in capacity-building with a view to facilitating the implementation of the United Nations Convention against Transnational Organized Crime and the Protocols thereto*, 74th plenary meeting, 20 December 2004; UN Economic and Social Council (ECOSOC), E/RES/2005/17, *International cooperation in the fight against transnational organized crime*, 36th plenary meeting, 22 July 2005.

specific offences such as trafficking in persons and drug trafficking. In this sense, the UNTOC is supposed to constitute the legal framework for the criminalisation of and international cooperation in all forms of transnational organised criminal activities.[93] The General Assembly has also proposed a transversal approach meant to foster cooperation at a more global scale.[94] Unfortunately, in general, instruments from the General Assembly remain too vague to be considered a step forward in international cooperation. For this reason, the United Nations has developed a diversity of methods, including commissions,[95] working groups[96] and even research institutes[97] supervised by the General Assembly, and tools with which to address these issues.

ASEAN has no general convention related to cooperation in criminal matters. It adopted a sectorial approach with conventions against specific types of crimes as terrorism or trafficking in persons. Within these sectorial instruments, requirements give objectives for States, including cooperating together. As for the fight against transnational crime, ASEAN has a looser transversal approach, through declarations and general requirements.[98] As such, its approach seems quite similar to the UN one.

In Europe, the Council of Europe (CoE)[99] and of the EU have followed a more transversal approach to cooperation in criminal matters.[100] The CoE and EU norms aim to foster cooperation between competent national authorities through effective

---

[93] Pt. 6, UNTOC.

[94] See, e.g., A/RES/49/159(1994); A/RES/59/157(2005).

[95] See Commission on Narcotic Drugs and the Commission on Crime Prevention and Criminal Justice part of the ECOSOC and are governing bodies of the United Nations Office on Drugs and Crime (UNODC): available at http://www.unodc.org/unodc/en/commissions/index.html?ref=menuside (accessed on 29 April 2015).

[96] See, e.g., Working Group on international cooperation, 1st session, 11–12 October 2006; Working Group of Government Experts on Technical Assistance, 1st session, 16–17 October 2006: available at http://www.unodc.org/unodc/en/treaties/CTOC/working-groups.html (accessed on 29 April 2015).

[97] See, e.g., United Nations Interregional Crime and Justice Research Institute (UNICRI) established in 1967: available at www.unicri.it/institute (accessed on 8 December 2015).

[98] See, e.g., *ASEAN Declaration on Transnational Crime*, Manila, 20 December 1997; *ASEAN Declaration on the Prevention and Control of Transnational Crime* (1998); *ASEAN Plan of Action to Combat Transnational Crime* (1999); *APSC Blueprint*, Jakarta, 1 March 2009; ASEAN, *Joint Statement. ASEAN Ministerial Meeting on Transnational Crime (AMMTC)*, 11th AMMTC, Manila, 20 September 2017.

[99] See, e.g., CoE, Ad Hoc Drafting Group on Transnational Organised Crime (PC-GR-COT), 1st meeting, Paris, 24–26 June 2013; European Committee on Crime Problems, Steering Committee, Terms of reference valid 1 January 2014–31 December 2015. It refers to improving the mechanisms of coordination, instruments for implementation of cooperation between competent authorities.

[100] *Council Framework Decision 2002/584/JHA on the European arrest warrant*; also *Council Framework Decision 2006/960/JHA 18 December 2006 on simplifying the exchange of information and intelligence between law enforcement authorities of the Member States of the European Union* ('Swedish Framework Decision'), O.J.E.U. L386/89, 29 December 2006.

mechanisms, such as extradition, mutual legal assistance or special investigation techniques,[101] which are implemented for a wide range of cross-border offences. However, the EU has supplemented this intersectional approach of cooperation (e.g. European arrest warrant) with more sectorial texts, taking into consideration the specificities of some serious transnational crimes.

Both methods present advantages and disadvantages. A sectorial approach may be relevant to the development of cooperation mechanisms and be potentially more effective in very specific instances, as it is easier to agree on actions in a very specific case than actions for any transnational crime. Nonetheless, maintaining this sectorial approach by multiplying the sectors may end up being less effective in the long run. There is always a risk of one type of crime being excluded from the list of sectors or where the list of offences has become so extensive as to become confusing.

II. Among Key Mechanisms of Cooperation: Sharing Information and Intelligence Between Competent National Authorities

Sharing information and intelligence has become essential in the fight against impunity, especially when cross-border situations occur. For instance, the possibility of gathering information about an individual who committed an offence in country A and who is at that time in country B or gathering information about constitutive acts committed in countries A and B while prosecuting in country C has become crucial as criminals have been using the borders as shields against prosecution for many years. Information gathering and sharing are particularly prominent in preventing crime and thus has become one of the main priorities of decision-makers at the international, regional and national levels. States have pooled their resources to coordinate their policies in the framework of international and—even more—regional organisations in granting top priority to prevention.[102]

States have enhanced their arsenal to respond preventively and pro-actively against terrorist threats. For example, intelligence services and law enforcement agencies have progressively been granted coercive powers or proactive investigative means in order to obtain the necessary information on groups or individuals and to prevent the perpetration of offences.[103]

The mechanisms of information and intelligence sharing involve many different actors and many key elements still subject to discussion. Accordingly, taking a step towards defining the myriad of key terms, actors and objectives shall provide a better understanding of the relevant issues related to cooperation mechanisms.

---

[101] CoE, Committee of Ministers, *Recommendation Rec(2005)10 of the Committee of Ministers to Member States on 'special investigation techniques' in relation to serious crimes including acts of terrorism*, 924th meeting, Ministers' Deputies, 20 April 2005.

[102] See, e.g., S/RES/1368(2001); Security Council Committee, Counter-Terrorism Committee, *Policy guidance on international cooperation*, S/AC.40/2010/PG.3, 14 June 2010.

[103] Hirsch Ballin (2012): 1.

A. **Information and Intelligence: Coping with Diverging Definitions**

There is no unified, and internationally accepted, definition for 'information' or 'intelligence' in criminal matters. The definitions given in common dictionaries provide generic guidance in criminal matters.

Ordinarily speaking, 'information' is defined as the knowledge that a person gets about someone or something, including facts or details about a subject.[104] By contrast, the ordinary dictionary provides two meanings of the term 'intelligence'. On the one side, intelligence may refer to the ability of somebody to learn or understand things or to deal with new or difficult situations (translated into French by '*intelligence*'). On the other side, intelligence may involve the processing of raw data/information for a specific purpose, which is translated into French by '*renseignement*'. *Renseignement* is defined by ordinary dictionaries as 'indication, information, éclaircissement donnés sur quelqu'un ou quelque chose'.[105] Additionally, intelligence may also refer to 'secret information that a government, or a government organisation, collects about an enemy or possible enemy',[106] which is also translated into French by *renseignement.*

An analysis of these terms shows very different understandings depending on, among other things, the countries or regions, the language (e.g. French and English[107]), the authors and their purpose. This variety is partly due to the fact that the definitions are often answering different questions such as: (1) To what kind of material/type of data does it refer (a potential secrecy issue)? (2) Who gathers the data (law enforcement or intelligence agencies)? (3) At what stage of the criminal justice procedure are 'information' and/or 'intelligence' gathered and processed? (4) What method is used to gather 'information' and/or 'intelligence'? (5) For which purpose are they gathered and processed?[108] On the basis of the responses to these questions, this part draws and constructs the definition of 'information' and 'intelligence' in tailored fashion for counterterrorism measures.

1. A general international guidance and confusing regional frameworks for the respective Member States

[104] Merriam-Webster dictionary, definition of 'information': available at http://www.merriam-webster.com/dictionary/information (accessed on 31 August 2015).

[105] Larousse dictionary defines 'renseignement' as clues, information, clarifications given about someone or something (translation by the author): available at: http://www.larousse.fr/dictionnaires/francais/renseignement/68242 (accessed on 7 October 2015).

[106] Merriam-Webster dictionary, definition of 'intelligence': available at: http://www.merriam-webster.com/dictionary/intelligence (accessed on 7 October 2015).

[107] Each language brings particularities and different understandings to these definitions. A/RES/2 (1), *Rules of Procedure Concerning Languages,* 21st plenary meeting, 1 February 1946.

[108] On the differentiation between definitions, Céline C. Cocq, '"Information" and "intelligence". The current divergences between national legal systems and the need for common (European) notions' *New Journal of European Criminal Law,* vol. 8, no. 3 (2017).

Although using these terms extensively, international norms do not specifically define either 'information' or 'intelligence'. It is only recently that relevant documents started providing guidance.

At the international level, the United Nations Office on Drugs and Crime (UNODC) is the organ competent on criminal matters and, in this regard, it aids national stakeholders with sharing knowledge and experience and, reciprocally, it provides an (arguably loose) international framework for cooperation.

The UNODC manuals are valuable tools for law enforcement activities. They are not the result of an international agreement between States, but rather are the product of an international agency that is built upon significant law enforcement experience. They may only be used as guidelines by States wishing to develop legislation on topics which demand a certain understanding of criminal information and intelligence or to develop cooperation mechanisms and/or agreements with other States.

Information is generally defined as a material that has not been processed yet. Thus, it answers the first question (i.e. what kind of material is it?). This approach is clearly adopted by UNODC in the Manual for Front-Line Law Enforcement on Criminal Intelligence defines information as 'knowledge in raw form',[109] while 'intelligence' is data that have been worked on, given added value or significance.[110]

While the use of 'information' in the criminal law area should be understood in the generic sense of the term, the definition of intelligence needs further elaborations. 'Intelligence' may refer to information that is acquired, processed and exploited by intelligence services and/or law enforcement agencies to decide upon and support criminal investigations. More specifically, intelligence is divided into two main areas in the UN documents. Firstly, strategic intelligence focuses on the long-term goals of law enforcement agencies. It typically reviews current and emerging trends plus changes in the crime environment, threats to public safety and order, opportunities for controlling action, and the development of counter-programmes as well as likely avenues for changes to policies, programmes and legislation.[111] Secondly, operational intelligence aims at providing an investigation team with hypotheses and inferences concerning specific elements of operations of any sort, including those not officially and legally regulated. These include hypotheses and inferences about specific criminal networks, groups or individuals involved in unlawful activities.

In both cases, intelligence is the product of analysis of the information gathered or, at the least, held by competent national authorities. The specific purpose of this product is to provide in-depth knowledge of threats in order to prevent and combat crime.

---

[109]UNODC, *Criminal Intelligence. Manual for Front-line Law Enforcement* (Vienna: UNODC Publications, December 2010): 1; *Criminal Intelligence. Manual for Analysts* (Vienna: UNODC Publications, April 2011): 1.

[110]UNODC, *Criminal Intelligence. Manual for Front-Line Law Enforcement* (2010) and *Manual for Analysts* (2011). In these manuals, intelligence is defined as 'information that is capable of being understood; information with added value; and information that has been evaluated in context to its source and reliability'.

[111]UNODC, *Criminal Intelligence* (2010) and (2011): 9.

Within this context, the definition of 'information' answers the first question (i.e. what kind of material is it?) while the definition of 'intelligence' answers the fifth question (i.e. for what purpose are they gathered and processed?).

On a regional level, none of the regional organisations have adopted clear definitions of these terms. Unlike ASEAN, the EU has adopted many instruments related to information and intelligence sharing. It has done this while avoiding to provide clear definitions. This has led to an uncertain regional situation, which may become problematic seeing that the EU is supposed to provide a framework for its members, allowing them to cooperate more effectively.

Before exploring further into the EU's contribution, it is important to note that the EU is not competent in national security matters;[112] matters which generally involve the intelligence community. National security remains the sole competence of the Member States. By contrast, the EU is competent on matters dealing with internal security, including police and judicial cooperation.[113] The distinction between national security and EU internal security is important as it may involve different actors and it may also impact cooperation between EU Member States (in case of a threat to internal security and potentially limiting it in the case of a national security threat). Although qualified as national security threats, certain of these threats, such as terrorism, may impact several Member States and thus, require interstate cooperation. It is even more important to underscore this significant aspect as 'intelligence' is not only part of national security issues but also part of EU internal security.[114]

Despite its lack of competence in the field of national security, the EU has an Intelligence Analysis and Situation Centre (EU IntCen) that provides intelligence analysis to the High Representative of the EU for Foreign Affairs and Security Policy. It is comprised of representatives of the intelligence services of Member States and supplies analytical products based on information provided by Member States' security and intelligence services. In this forum, intelligence is also drawn from open sources (media, websites, blogs, etc.), diplomatic reporting, consular warden networks, international organisations, NGOs, CSDP missions and operations, and EU Satellite Centre visits and field trips.[115] This EU IntCen constitutes a channel of communication between the various intelligence services. Their discussions or written productions are not available to the public.

The lack of a uniform definition has not prevented the EU from adopting binding instruments in criminal matters in which 'information' or 'intelligence' is central. For example, the *Council Framework Decision 2006/960/JHA on simplifying the*

[112] Art. 4(2), *Treaty on the European Union* (hereafter referred to as 'TEU'), O.J.E.U. C326/1, 26 October 2012.

[113] Art. 4 TEU, and Chaps. 4 and 5 TFEU.

[114] See the numerous debates around Snowden's leaks revealing that States were spying on citizens in gathering information then analysing it.

[115] EU IntCen, Intelligence Analysis Centre, Fact Sheet, 5 February 2015: available at: http://eeas.europa.eu/factsheets/docs/20150206_factsheet_eu_intcen_en.pdf (accessed on 4 November 2015).

exchange of information and intelligence between law enforcement authorities[116] or the *Europol Regulation* deal with the exchange of 'information' and 'intelligence'. The former provides a confused definition of 'information and/or intelligence' by stating that it constitutes:

> (i) any type of information or data which is held by law enforcement authorities; and, (ii) any type of information or data which is held by public authorities or by private entities and which is available to law enforcement authorities without the taking of coercive measures [...][117]

The provision includes the word 'information', making it circular in nature. The definition is therefore unclear and does not clarify the difference between the two terms.

However, the same *Council Framework Decision 2006/960/JHA* also defines 'criminal intelligence operation' as:

> a procedural stage, not yet having reached the stage of a criminal investigation, within which a competent law enforcement authority is entitled by national law to collect, process and analyse information about crime or criminal activities with a view to establishing whether concrete criminal acts have been committed or may be committed in the future.[118]

When applying this last definition, 'intelligence' might be defined as information gathered, processed and analysed by competent authorities to prevent criminal activities or as a means to start an investigation surrounding committed criminal activities. It corresponds partially to the definition provided by UNODC, but focuses on the phrase 'not yet having reached the stage of criminal investigation'. Therefore, this definition might answer the third and fifth question (i.e. when are 'information' and/or 'intelligence' gathered and processed?; for which purpose are they gathered and processed?).

The *Europol Regulation*[119] provides that Europol's task is to 'collect, store, process, analyse and exchange information, *including* criminal intelligence'.[120] 'Intelligence' is perceived as a specific category of information, which was not the case in the previous *Europol Council Decision* which required the agency to 'collect, store, process, analyse and exchange information *and intelligence*'.[121] Could this mean that the understanding of 'intelligence' has evolved? The modified wording alters the meaning of the term, yet no explanation for such a change has been provided by any EU institution so far.

Focusing on 'intelligence', the Special Committee on Organised Crime, Corruption and Money Laundering of the European Parliament does not necessarily clarify

---

[116] Art. 1, *Council Framework Decision 2006/960/JHA on simplifying the exchange of information and intelligence between law enforcement authorities of the Member States of the European Union.*

[117] Art. 2(d), *Council Framework Decision 2006/960/JHA.*

[118] Art. 2(c), Council Framework Decision 2006/960/JHA.

[119] Art. 4, *Europol Regulation.*

[120] Art. 4(1), *Europol Regulation.* Italics added by the author.

[121] Art. 5(1)a, *Europol Council Decision.* Italics added by the author.

the situation. It defines criminal intelligence according to a three-dimensional approach: strategic, tactical and operational. Firstly, strategic criminal intelligence (*renseignement criminel stratégique*) provides background context on current and future criminal phenomena and security threats. Any strategic criminal intelligence may come from international organisations such as Interpol, Europol or the UN and national actors such as intelligence services, police and customs agencies. Secondly, tactical criminal intelligence (*renseignement criminel tactique*) gives the opportunity for competent authorities to undertake specific actions against criminal activity or a criminal group. Thirdly, operational criminal intelligence (*renseignement criminel opérationnel*) encompasses precise elements of information that may lead to identification of a fact, a suspect or a specific element of an investigation. These three dimensions may be complementary.[122] As a result of this three-dimensional approach, 'intelligence' is defined by its purpose, answering the fifth question (i.e. for what purpose are they gathered and processed?).

The EU has not yet provided any clear and distinct definition of either 'information' or 'intelligence'. The outlook remains confusing, which might indicate that Member States have not yet succeeded in establishing an agreement on these definitions—or that they do not wish to do for now. However, it is becoming clearer from the evolution of EU documents in criminal matters that 'intelligence' involves an analysis of 'information' gathered before deciding to instigate an investigation, whether it is reactive or proactive.

In ASEAN, the wording of the regional texts remains unclear on the place of 'intelligence' vis-à-vis 'information'.

Both information and intelligence seem to be used interchangeably within the different ASEAN texts relating to transnational crime, including terrorism.[123] This is particularly evident in the ASEAN instruments on transnational crime or terrorism, including the 2001 *ASEAN Declaration on Joint Action to Counter Terrorism.*[124]

Alternatively, other wordings or contexts could bring some specific meanings to 'intelligence'. Firstly, intelligence may appear alone without reference to information in the same paragraph or sentence. For example, States agreed to enhance international cooperation against all forms of terrorism through such modalities as intelligence sharing, coordinated policies and law enforcement training.[125] Would it

[122] European Parliament, Special Committee on Organised Crime, Corruption and Money Laundering (CRIM), 'Approche intégrée du renseignement criminel dans la lutte contre le crime organisé: dynamique locale, nationale et européenne', Hearing on 19 February 2013: available at http://www.europarl.europa.eu/document/activities/cont/201302/20130221ATT61502/20130221ATT61502EN.pdf (accessed on 24 June 2022).

[123] See, e.g., pts. 17 and 18, *ASEAN Plan of Action to Combat Transnational Crime* (1999); *ASEAN Declaration on Joint Action to Counter Terrorism* (2001): 'Enhance information/intelligence exchange to facilitate the flow of information, in particular, on terrorists and terrorist organisations [...]'.

[124] Pt. 5, *ASEAN Declaration on Joint Action to Counter Terrorism* (2001).

[125] Preamble and pt. 4, *ASEAN Declaration on Transnational Crime* (1997); *ASEAN Plan of Action to Combat Transnational Crime* (1999). See also, e.g., *ASEAN-United States of America Joint*

give it a specific meaning from 'information'? The documents do not provide clarity on its precise meaning. Secondly, intelligence may be differentiated from information, without giving it a specific understanding. For instance, the *ASEAN—United States Joint Declaration for Cooperation to Combat International Terrorism* affirms the importance of 'information exchange, intelligence sharing and capacity building'.[126] Here, intelligence does not seem to be a specific form of information, but rather something different. Thirdly, 'intelligence' may also appear as a qualifier of 'information'.[127] This may mean that 'intelligence information' would form part of the global concept of 'information'.

Most notably, the different sequences of words and understandings that may imply within the same document detract from the consistency of the ASEAN position. ASEAN Member States can only rely loosely on the international framework for some guidance.

In this loose international architecture, regional organisations have not provided much assistance to strengthen the architecture. The EU has offered definitions, but those add more confusion than help. Meanwhile, ASEAN has not yet offered any definition.

2. Some serious national discrepancies to overcome

The broad international definitions and confusing regional legal frameworks probably result from strong national discrepancies and difficulties to find compromises. This framework can hardly provide, in return, guidance for the respective Member States.

On a national level, even the term 'information' is marked by discrepancies, dependant on the criminal justice systems considered. States usually use 'information' in a general meaning. For instance, the United Kingdom's Association of Chief Police Officers defines information as 'all forms of information obtained, recorded or processed by the police, including personal data and intelligence'.[128] Information is thus the accumulated outputs from preventative and investigative activities (i.e. what kind of material is it?).

Declaration for Cooperation to Combat International Terrorism, Bandar Seri Begawan, 1 August 2002, 'Scope and Areas of Cooperation' 3.I.; *ASEAN-India Joint Declaration for Cooperation to Combat International Terrorism*, Bali, 8 October 2003; *Memorandum of Understanding between the Governments of the Member Countries of the Association of Southeast Asian Nations (ASEAN) and the Government of the People's Republic of China on Cooperation in the Field of Non-Traditional Security Issues*, Bangkok, 10 January 2004.

[126] *ASEAN-United States of America Joint Declaration for Cooperation to Combat International Terrorism* (2002), pt. 1. See the complete list of joint declarations between ASEAN and external partners in the bibliography. Art. VI(1) h of the ACCT requires States to take the appropriate measures to 'enhance intelligence exchange and sharing of information', which was then relayed in pt. 10, Comprehensive Plan of Action on Counter Terrorism (2009).

[127] See 'Programme of actions/priorities' in *ASEAN Plan of Action to Combat Transnational Crime* (1999), which encourages the 'sharing and analysis of critical intelligence information'.

[128] See the United Kingdom, *Guidance on The National Intelligence Model*, produced on behalf of the Association of chief Police Officers by the National Centre for Policing Excellence (2005), 13.

On a side note, information may also refer to the stage of the criminal justice proceedings when the investigative judge—where such a judge exists—gathers the information necessary to build up a case against a suspect. This stage is referred to in the Belgian and French justice procedures as the *information judiciaire*.

'Intelligence' is the most challenging concept to define; even more at the national level. Criminal intelligence remains generally undefined or, at least, unclearly defined. Interestingly, this issue does not seem to be associated with many debates among officials, but discrepancies and nuances exist and may be highlighted as follows:[129]

Firstly, intelligence may be defined by focusing on the nature of data gathered, which answers to the first question (i.e. what material is it?). In Pr. Kent Roach's analysis, intelligence refers to secret material collected by intelligence agencies and increasingly by the police to provide background information and advance warning about people who are thought to risk committing acts of terrorism or other threats to national security.[130] Instead of this understanding, EU countries rather associate 'information' or 'intelligence' with a qualifier specifying the level of security clearance (e.g. top secret, secret or confidential).[131]

Secondly, intelligence may be defined according to the respective authority who gathers the data. In this case, criminal intelligence mean information gathered by intelligence services. In this case, such distinction between 'information' and 'intelligence' has become blurry over time including in France. However, the distinction remains in some countries as Lithuania, where criminal intelligence information (*Kriminalinės žvalgybos informacija*) refers to data recorded and collected according to the law, by criminal intelligence services during the time of their active duty, and while dealing with criminal intelligence tasks.[132] Some EU countries have also adopted this position in particular contexts, such as Belgium and Germany.

Thirdly, and strongly linked to the issue of who it is that gathers the data, intelligence may be qualified as such because of the phase of the criminal justice procedure when data are gathered. Intelligence services, working at a very early stage of the criminal procedure or even further upstream, gather data which is not supposed to be presented as evidence in court. At this stage, data gathering usually involves methods that might potentially be legally unregulated. These data are usually only gathered for prevention and investigation purposes but not for the prosecution of

[129] François Farcy and Jean-François Gayraud, *Le renseignement criminel* (Paris: CNRS Editions, 2011): 25 and ff.

[130] Kent Roach, 'Secret evidence and its alternatives' in *Post 9/11 and the state of permanent legal emergency. Security and human rights in countering terrorism*, ed., Aniceto Masferrer, Ius Gentium: Comparative Perspectives on Law and Justice (Dordrecht: Springer, 2012): 180.

[131] Cocq, '"Information" and "intelligence"' (2017).

[132] 'kriminalinės žvalgybos subjektų veikla renkant, fiksuojant, vertinant ir panaudojant turimą informaciją apie kriminalinės žvalgybos objektus, vykdoma šio įstatymo nustatyta tvarka' (from Lithuanian to English, Roberta Kuchalsyte, Lithuanian trainee at Europol). Art. 2, Lithuanian Republic Law on Criminal Intelligence (*Lietuvos Respublikos Kriminalines Zvalgybos Istatymas*), Nr. XI-2234, Vilnius, 2 October 2012.

the offences. However, it must be highlighted that the different stages of the procedure are becoming increasingly blurred, which makes the understanding and use of intelligence even more confusing.[133]

Fourthly, some focus on the method used by competent authorities to gather data; answering to the fourth question (i.e. how it is gathered?). Notably, Pr. Chesterman notes that 'secret intelligence' can be defined as 'information obtained covertly—that is, without the consent of the person or entity that controls the information'.[134] Two sub-categories emerge from this. The first is intelligence obtained wittingly or unwittingly from individuals, known as human intelligence. The second is signals intelligence, which comprise communications intercepted and other electronic intelligence. With this perspective, data refers to information obtained from covert human intelligence sources or form technical deployments that would usually attract a general protection in law from disclosure.[135] Thanks to new technologies and technical means, the amount of intelligence gathered has increased exponentially in recent years.

Lastly, intelligence may also have the meaning adopted by the UNODC,[136] namely based on what is the purpose of the data gathered. The two most representative Anglo-Saxon countries, namely the UK and the USA,[137] have adopted this understanding. The UK requires the police 'to consider how and why it collects information and to identify *ways to convert this information into intelligence*'.[138] This document goes further in actually defining intelligence as 'information that has been subject to a define evaluation and risk assessment process in order to assist with police decision-making'.[139] Similarly, some authors refer to intelligence as 'the analytic product of intelligence services, best understood as a risk assessment intended to guide action'.[140] Legal scholars have elaborated on this particular notion in order to propose a functional definition of the term.[141] Intelligence would be the product of a processing and analysis of information for a specific operational and strategic purpose.

---

[133] See, e.g., Cocq and Galli (2013); Galli and Weyembergh, (2013).

[134] Simon Chesterman, *One Nation Under Surveillance. A New Social Contract to Defend Freedom Without Sacrifying Liberty* (New York: Oxford University Press, 2011): 7.

[135] See the UK *Guidance on The National Intelligence Model* (2005): 22.

[136] See, e.g., UNODC, *Criminal Intelligence. Manual for Front-line Law Enforcement* (Vienna: UNODC Publications, December 2010); UNODC, *Criminal Intelligence. Manual for Analysts* (Vienna: UNODC Publications, April 2011).

[137] See on the Federal Bureau of Investigation's website: available at https://www.fbi.gov/about/leadership-and-structure/intelligence-branch (accessed on 1 July 2022).

[138] UK *Guidance on The National Intelligence Model* (2005): 13 (italics by the author).

[139] Ibid.

[140] Chesterman (2011): 7.

[141] On the French debates related to the evolution of the understanding of 'intelligence', see, e.g., Jacques Baud, 'Intelligence' in *Encyclopédie du renseignement et des services secrets*, 2nd ed. (Paris: Lavauzelle, 1998). More specifically on 'criminal intelligence', Frédéric Lemieux (with the participation of Sophie Allard), *Normes et pratiques en matière de renseignement*

Looking at the national approaches in Europe and Southeast Asia, former European colonies' influence on Southeast Asian countries' legislation is very obvious. Colonisation brought common law and civil law systems in Southeast Asia.

On the one hand, the French system has defined as intelligence data gathered by intelligence services to become processed data gathered by competent authority. When 'judiciarised', it represents documentary data with very low value or even no value in court.[142] In practice, it generally does not reach the trial and only nourishes the prevention and investigation of offences. The former French colonies, such as Cambodia, would tend to have the same understanding of this reference to *renseignement.*[143]

On the other hand, the former British colonies as Brunei Darussalam, Malaysia, Singapore, Myanmar would tend to have similar approach vis-à-vis 'intelligence'. For example, Malaysian intelligence services analyse and give advice on the necessary course of action to the different bodies within the police and other related agencies. Worth being noticed, depending on the agency and their purpose, a degree of secrecy or, at least its exclusive use for prevention and investigation purposes, seems to be implied in the *Security Offences Act 2012* that differentiates between evidence and intelligence[144] and in the *Police Act 1967.*[145] Similarly, the Philippines—strongly inspired by the USA—considers intelligence to be the end product resulting from the processing of information (i.e. an unprocessed material of every description including those derived from observations, communications, reports, rumours, imagery and other sources from which intelligence is produced—raw data). In other words, intelligence results from the following activities: collection, collation, evaluation, analysis, integration and interpretation of all available information.[146]

It is therefore clear that there are strong national discrepancies within and between regions. Competent national authorities do not use a similar terminology with the same meaning, which may present an issue for interstate cooperation.

---

criminel. Une comparaison internationale (Saint-Nicolas: Les Presses de l'Université de Laval, 2006): 4–5; Farcy and Gayraud (2011): 30.

[142] Arts. 330(3), 336 and 430, French Code of Criminal Procedure (CCP).

[143] See, e.g., paras. 78 and 82 of the *Code of criminal procedure of Cambodia*: available at https://bit.ly/3bL3aGv (accessed on 1 July 2022).

[144] Para. 3, *Security Offences (Special Measures) Act 2012*, Act 747, Gazette, 22 June 2012 (latest amended by Act A1487) Laws of Malaysia.

[145] Para. 3, *Police Act 1967*, Act 41 (latest amendment made by Act 344 of 6 October 1988) Laws of Malaysia.

[146] Definition adopted by the Philippine Anti-Terrorism Council (ATC). Restricted information gathered during the 'Training for collaborative intelligence, investigation and prosecution of terrorism-related cases', organised by the Philippine ATC Program Management Center (ATC-PMC) with the support of UNODC, General Santos City, 18–22 April 2016.

3. An element of significant importance in the processing of data: the secrecy of data

An element that needs to be taken into account when defining and processing 'information' and 'intelligence' and in giving each term its specific characteristics or purposes, is the degree of secrecy associated with the data.

Secrecy can be either an adjunct to 'information' or an element which would reclassify 'information' as 'intelligence'. For example, information in any kind of field (criminal, military or any other field that may restrict its access) can be qualified as Restricted, Confidential, Secret or Top Secret dependent upon its secrecy and security clearance required. It must be mentioned that, at the national level, the use of information in court depends mainly on whether it is gathered with respect to the rules of the criminal justice procedure including the use of available open sources or special investigative techniques, or whether it is gathered by intelligence services or security agencies outside the criminal justice process. When gathering by means which are unregulated by the law or an unidentifiable source, information is qualified as secret and cannot be used in ways such as evidence in court. Its use must be authorised for criminal justice purposes and be 'judiciarised' in order to be presented in court.[147]

4. Reaching the appropriate definitions of 'information' and 'intelligence'

The previous developments were necessary in order to explain the discrepancies that might hamper or slow down cooperation between States. Additionally, it highlights the most common understanding of these terms in this field of interstate cooperation in criminal matters that shall be used in this study.

On the one hand, *information* refers to *all forms of data obtained, recorded or processed by the competent national authorities* (i.e. *law enforcement authorities, intelligence services and other related authorities), including personal data.* Competent national authorities encompass law enforcement agencies, intelligence services or other public national authorities, as long as they are competent in their national jurisdiction to share information and intelligence and to cooperate together in the fight against terrorism.

On the other hand, after critical analysis of all the definitions and for the sake of this study, *intelligence* shall refer to *information collected, processed and subsequently analysed to be exploitable by the competent national authorities for a specific purpose, namely*—in this case—*for prevention, investigation, detection and prosecution purposes.*

---

[147] For example, in France, Cour de Cassation, Opinion of Ms. Petit, First Advocate-General: available at https://www.courdecassation.fr/jurisprudence_2/assemblee_pleniere_22/petit_premier_18515.html (accessed on 8 December 2015); Philippe Conte and Patrick Maistre du Chambon, *Procédure Pénale* (Paris: Masson, 1995): 29 and ff; Mireille Delmas-Marty, 'La preuve pénale' *Droits. Revue française de théorie juridique* vol. 26, (1996). In Spain, José L. González Cussac, 'El secreto de Estado en el proceso penal: denegación de auxilio y el delito de revelación' *Inteligencia y Seguridad* vol. 12, (2012); José L. González Cussac, 'Intromisión en la Intimidad y CNI. Critica al modelo español de control judicial previó' *Inteligencia y Seguridad* vol. 15, (2014).

Although these definitions generally correspond to the global mainstream definition of the two terms, it must be recognised that they may not always mirror the meaning for which those terms are used by certain Member States or regional organisations.

5. Data and personal data: a generic terminology that tends to be more operational

Gathering, sharing and using 'information' and/or 'intelligence' are particularly sensitive in light of data protection issues.

The two terms 'data' and 'information' are sometimes confused, but a distinction exists.[148] The term 'data' describes the input of words or signs, which have no autonomous significance.[149] By contrast, information refers to the meaning or knowledge, which can be allocated to data.[150] Nonetheless, data gathered in the context of police and judicial proceedings generally result in information on an individual. This differentiation might explain why the data protection instruments do not refer to 'information' and/or 'intelligence', but rather to 'data' or 'personal data'. International and regional instruments dealing with cooperation, especially those related to information and intelligence sharing, usually refer to 'data' or 'personal data' as the general and raw material being transferred.

At the international level, the Organisation for Economic Cooperation and Development (OECD) Guidelines on the Protection of Privacy and Transborder Flows of Personal Data and, at a more regional level, the *Convention for the Protection of Individuals with regard to Automatic Processing of Personal Data* of the Council of Europe provide a general definition of personal data as 'any information relating to an identified or identifiable individual (data subject)'.[151] An identifiable individual is not defined by these conventions.

The EU has adopted binding data protection instruments applying in the territory of the Member States. With a rather more detailed approach, the EU defines 'personal data' as:

> any information related to an identified or identifiable natural person ('data subject'). An identifiable person is one who can be identified, directly or indirectly, in particular by reference to an identifier such as a name, an identification number, location data, an online

[148] See, e.g., Evelien Brouwer, *Digital borders and Real Rights. Effective remedies for third-country nationals in the Schengen Information System* (Leiden: Martinus Nijhoff Publishers, 2008): 8 with further references; Franziska Boehm, *Information Sharing and Data Protection in the Area of Freedom, Security and Justice. Towards Harmonised Data Protection Principles for Information Exchange at EU-level* (Verlag Berlin Heidelberg: Springer, 2012): 14.

[149] Brouwer (2008); Boehm (2012): 14.

[150] Brouwer (2008): 8.

[151] Art. 2, s. 1b), OECD *Guidelines on the Protection of Privacy and Transborder Flows of Personal Data* (1980) and CoE, *Convention for the Protection of Individuals with regard to Automatic Processing of Personal Data* (1981). This definition was repeated in the EU *Directive 95/46/EC* and in texts adopted later.

identifier or to one or more factors specific to the physical, physiological, genetic, mental, economic, cultural or social identity of that natural person.[152]

Both definitions of personal data and identifiable individual are reiterated in the *Council Decision 2009/934/JHA on the rules governing Europol's relations with partners, including the exchange of personal data and classified information* with the Europol Regulation[153] and in the *Directive 2016/680 on the protection of natural persons with regard to the processing of personal data by competent authorities for the purposes of the prevention, investigation, detection or prosecution of criminal offences or the execution of criminal penalties, and on the free movement of such data.*[154]

By contrast, there has been no discussion regarding data protection in ASEAN. No regional data protection instruments have been adopted in order to define 'personal data' or establish common standards in this matter.

In the absence of regional framework, some Member States have enacted legislations on data protection in the commercial area; not in the criminal area. These legislations remain quite different, including those relating to the definition of personal data. For example, the Malaysian *Personal Data Protection Act of 2010*—first data protection law adopted in the region—defines personal data as any information 'that relates directly or indirectly to a data subject who is identified or identifiable from that information or from that and other information in the possession of a data user, including any sensitive personal data and expression of opinion about the data subject'.[155] The *Personal Data Protection Act 2012* of Singapore defines personal data as 'data, whether true or not, about an individual who can be identified (a) from that data; or (b) from that data and other information to which the organisation has or is likely to have access'.[156] In the Philippines, the *Data Privacy Act of 2012* defines personal information as 'any information whether recorded in a material form or not, from which the identity of an individual is apparent or can be reasonably and directly ascertained by the entity holding the information, or when put together with other information would directly and

---

[152] Art. 2(a), *Directive 95/46/EC*; and, more recently, Art. 4(1), *Regulation (EU) 2016/679 of the European Parliament and the Council of 27 April 2016 on the protection of natural persons with regard to the processing of personal data and on the free movement of such data, and repealing Directive 95/46/EC (General Data Protection Regulation)* (hereafter referred to as 'GDPR'), O.J. L119/1, 4 May 2016.

[153] Art. 1(e), *Council Decision 2009/934/JHA of 30 November 2009 adopting the implementing rules governing Europol's relations with partners, including the exchange of personal data and classified information*, O.J.E.U. L325/6, 15 December 2009; see also Art. 2(i), *Europol Regulation.*

[154] Art. 3(1), *Directive (EU) 2016/680 of the European Parliament and the Council of 27 April 2016 on the protection of natural persons with regard to the processing of personal data by competent authorities for the purposes of the prevention, investigation, detection or prosecution of criminal offences or the execution of criminal penalties, and on the free movement of such data, and repealing Council Framework Decision 2008/977/JHA*, O.J.E.U. L119/89, 4 May 2016.

[155] Art. 4, *Personal Data Protection Act 2010*, Laws of Malaysia, Act 709, 10 June 2010.

[156] Art. 2, *Personal Data Protection Act 2012*, Acts Supplement, No. 26 of 2012, Government Gazette, Republic of Singapore, 7 December 2012.

certainly identify an individual'.[157] Comparing this sample, it is noteworthy that Malaysia's definition focuses on identified *or identifiable* data subjects, while the others do not. Differences between Member States' legislations do not facilitate—official of more formal—data sharing, especially in criminal matters where there is no specific legislation.

B. **Sharing or Exchanging Information and Intelligence?**

Sharing or exchanging information and intelligence is among the most useful mechanisms of cooperation.[158] Although the official instruments as well as the doctrine extensively use the term 'sharing' and 'exchanging' interchangeably, they usually remain ill-defined.[159]

Although there are some irrelevant discrepancies between the definitions of these two terms, their characteristics are still worth identifying.

Sharing information provides competent authorities with the capability to simultaneously have and use the same information. When a national authority shares data with another foreign national authority, the initial party can expect that the second authority will also use this data. By contrast, the term 'exchange' should mean that one party gives data and receives something in return; other data or any other form of recompense. According to the original meaning of the term, only the person who receives the object exchanged can use it. Moreover, considering that intangible objects, namely data, are at the core of the cooperation, the term 'sharing' seems to be the most appropriate. A competent authority can share information and/or intelligence and yet be able to use it for their own purposes. The term 'sharing' is therefore more appropriate, especially when it concerns data.

The methods of data sharing are numerous. Both information and intelligence may be shared in the framework of bilateral, regional and international agreements. These methods of cooperation can take several forms, including exchange of data upon request, spontaneous exchanges, data sharing in common databases that the authorised competent authorities may access, automatic exchange of information, and through an electronic interconnection of national and potentially regional databases.

The methods used to share data have an impact on the handling of these data by the competent authorities. For example, sharing data through automated means might involve the application of specific rules, especially those concerning data

---

157 Section 3(g), *Data Privacy Act of 2012*, Republic Act No. 10173, Republic of the Philippines, 25 July 2011.

158 See, e.g., Arts. 13(1) and 20(1)(a), (e) and (f), *ASEAN Convention against Trafficking in Persons* (2015).

159 See, e.g., *International Convention for the Suppression of the Financing of Terrorism* (1999); UNTOC (2000); Council of the EU, Presidency, Working Group on Information Exchange and Data Protection (DAPIX), *Council Framework Decision 2006/960/JHA*—Assessment of compliance pursuant to Article 11(2)—Draft Report, Brussels, 13970/11, 13 September 2011; Eveline R. Hertzberger, 'Counter-Terrorism Intelligence Cooperation in the European Union', *United Nations Interregional Crime and Justice Research Institute (UNICRI)*, 2007: available at https://bit.ly/3xBMaca (accessed on 28 June 2015).

protection as provided by the national, regional or international norms.[160] After being shared, information is processed, analysed and used for specific purposes. The analysis carried out on data depends mainly on the purpose for which these data are gathered.

After the various attacks in the EU, notably in Paris in 2016 and in Brussels in 2017, and in ASEAN, notably in Bali in 2002 and Jakarta in 2009 and 2016, the regional organisations and their members reaffirmed their determination to improve information management and to increase cross-border exchange of information, including interoperability of systems to prevent and combat terrorism. The objective is to support operational counterterrorism investigations and to swiftly provide front-line practitioners, such as law enforcement and judicial authorities with comprehensive, topical and high-quality information to cooperate and act effectively.[161] However, these actions often raise concerns about their impact on human rights.

C. Who Are the Competent National Authorities Involved in Information and Intelligence Sharing?

Countering terrorism involves a large variety of actors in each country, region and at the international level. The most relevant authorities in the prevention, investigation and detection phases are the intelligence services and law enforcement authorities. They play a key role in countering terrorism, especially when gathering and sharing information and intelligence.

Intelligence services usually refer to the government departments that are responsible for collecting and analysing information about enemies. The enemy has traditionally been another State. However, over time the threat has evolved, adding new forms of threats, adding internal threats to the external ones, and adding new actors (e.g. terrorist organisations, mafia and other criminal organisations). For this reason, intelligence services' capacities have also evolved. Each State has its own definition of the threat and can determine the competence, objectives and capacities of its intelligence service(s). Despite differences, some common characteristics are present. They aim to prevent crime or any other threats to national security. The information which they have gathered and the operations that have been carried out to acquire the intelligence are generally associated with a high degree of secrecy. This constitutes an issue when gathering data that is (un-)likely to be presented in court for the prosecution of a suspected criminal.

---

[160] See, e.g., *Directive 2016/680 on the protection of natural persons with regard to the processing of personal data by competent authorities for the purposes of the prevention, investigation, detection or prosecution of criminal offences or the execution of criminal penalties, and on the free movement of such data.*

[161] In the EU, Presidency of the Council of the EU, 'Roadmap to enhance information exchange and information management including interoperability solutions in the Justice and Home Affairs area', Brussels, 6 June 2016; in ASEAN, Comprehensive Plan of Action on Counter Terrorism, Nay Pyi Taw, 30 June 2009 and Revised Comprehensive Plan of Action on Counter Terrorism, 11th AMMTC, Manila, 20 September 2017.

Law enforcement agencies refer to government agencies that are responsible for the enforcement of the laws. Law enforcement agencies aim to prevent and investigate criminal offences. They are competent during the official first phase of the criminal procedure. However, over the past 15 years, there has been a clear tendency to criminalise conduct in the preparatory stage, especially in the field of terrorism. Due to this trend, law enforcement agencies increasingly end up working pro-actively together with or in parallel with intelligence services' actions. Therefore, the competence and tasks of both intelligence services and law enforcement agencies are becoming increasingly blurred.[162] This is particularly true in the case of terrorism.[163]

The TFEU expressly excludes EU competence in the field of national security, namely in intelligence services matters, but shares competence in law enforcement agency's matters.[164] When it comes to those, the EU refers to police agencies, custom agencies or other specialised agencies in charge of enforcing the law.[165] By contrast, with some exceptions, the majority of ASEAN instruments do not specify the national authorities competent to cooperate together, including in sharing information and/or intelligence.[166] Member States are free to decide on the national authorities competent in cross-border cooperation in terrorism-related cases.

Distribution of competences between intelligence services and law enforcement services may differ depending on the country. This might lead to difficulties for interstate cooperation as a threat may fall under the competence of intelligence services in a country and/or under the competence of law enforcement agencies in another. Some States may give such a competence to police officers, some others to intelligence services, or to both law enforcement and intelligence agencies; some others may even give such competence to military authorities or other agencies. In some countries, military agencies may even be partially—with other potentially civilian agencies—or totally in charge of such a task.

An examination of just one example from each region of the different distribution of tasks, particularly France and Malaysia, reveals the complexity of domestic systems.

[162] See, e.g., Francesca Galli and Anne Weyembergh, eds., *Do labels still matter? Blurring boundaries between administrative and criminal law. The influence of the EU*, Études européennes (Bruxelles: Éditions de l'Université de Bruxelles, 2014).

[163] See, e.g., at the international level, S/RES/2178(2014). In the EU, *Council Framework Decision 2002/475/JHA on combating terrorism*; *Council Framework Decision 2008/919/JHA on combating terrorism*. In ASEAN, see the complete list of ASEAN Joint Declarations for cooperation to combat terrorism with external partners in the table of legislations.

[164] Art. 4(2), TEU.

[165] Art. 87(1), TFEU.

[166] See, e.g., *Manila Declaration on Prevention and Control of Transnational Crime* (1998); *ASEAN Declaration on Joint Action to Counter Terrorism* (2001); *ASEAN-USA Joint Declaration for Cooperation to Combat International Terrorism* (2002) and the other Joint Declarations between ASEAN and external partners; also; *Treaty on Mutual Legal Assistance in Criminal Matters* (2004).

In France, the actors and agencies in charge at the different levels of the fight against terrorism have constantly evolved over the past 20 years. Over the years, France has adopted a more centralised system among the governmental, police and judicial authorities. In the executive branch, the first agency coordinating intelligence actions was the *Unité de Coordination de le Lutte Anti-Terroriste* (UCLAT).[167] A *coordonnateur national du renseignement et de la lutte contre le terrorisme* was created later. It is the government authority in charge of the coordination of intelligence and the fight against terrorism, with the help of the *Centre national de contre-terrorisme*.[168] In the judicial branch, France has centralised the terrorist cases in the Public Prosecution Office and the investigating judge in Paris.[169] A similar rationalisation process occurred in the police and intelligence environment, especially with regard to the gathering and centralisation of data. The *Direction Générale de la Sécurité Intérieure* (DGSI)[170] gathering law enforcement and intelligence authorities, and the *Direction Générale de la Sécurité Extérieure* (DGSE)[171]—are, respectively, in charge of internal and external security threats. Their mission is to seek, centralise and exploit any useful data which would help them carry out their mandate. The data is gathered by civil and military intelligence services as well as civil and military law enforcement authorities, respectively, the police and *gendarmerie*.[172] Interestingly, the most recent years have shown a slight move towards decentralisation, with the specialised assistants in the prevention of terrorism (e.g. assistants spécialisés pour la prévention du terrorisme) working in the different jurisdictions within the territory.

Malaysia also possesses a large variety of competent bodies and authorities which are in charge of preventing and combating terrorism. The Royal Malaysia Police is the main agency tasked with law enforcement, but other agencies are also competent in countering terrorism within their own scope, including the Malaysian Maritime Enforcement Agency, the Royal Malaysian Customs and the Immigration

[167] Created by the Ministère de l'Intérieur et de la décentralisation, *Arrêté ministériel*, signed by Pierre Joxe on 8 October 1984. With the development of other agencies, the UCLAT is progressively losing relevance. 'Lutte antiterroriste: que reste-t-il de l'UCLAT?' *Valeurs actuelles*, 7 March 2017: available at https://bit.ly/3eNXIAq (accessed on 6 August 2022).

[168] *Décret No. 2017-1095 du 14 Juin 2017 relative au coordinateur nation du renseignement et de la lutte contre le terrorisme, à la coordination nationale du renseignement et de la lutte contre le terrorisme et au centre national de contre-terrorisme*, J.O.R.F. No. 0139, 15 June 2017.

[169] Arts. 706-16 to 706-22-1, French CCP. For more explanation, see 'Le développement de formes de spécialisation pus souples autour de la notion de pôles de compétences' Sénat: available at https://www.senat.fr/rap/r01-345/r01-34598.html (accessed on 12 December 2017).

[170] Décret 2014-445 du 30 avril 2014 *relatif aux missions et à l'organisation de la direction générale de la sécurité intérieure*, J.O.R.F. No. 0102, 2 May 2014.

[171] DGSE's website: available at https://www.dgse.gouv.fr/fr (accessed on 6 August 2022).

[172] See, e.g., Commandement des Opérations Spéciales, 'DGSE/DGSI: Les Services de Renseignement Français' COS website: available at http://le.cos.free.fr/services%20secret.htm (accessed on 6 August 2022); Association ProECA, 'L'organisation des services de renseigmement français', 18 May 2017: available at https://bit.ly/338MZLr (accessed on 12 December 2017).

Department. The Royal Police is comprised of several divisions, including one on counterterrorism which was created in 2017.[173]

The reality is that the number of relevant actors is multiplying. As such, the notion of 'competent national authorities' may vary from one to another. Therefore, for the purpose of this analysis, *comptent national authorities* shall encompass *all police authorities, and other law enforcement services, intelligence services and other public authorities existing in the Member States, which are responsible under national law for preventing and combating criminal offences, especially terrorism.*[174]

Section 3: Still a Long Road Towards a Shared Language

Counterterrorism is a multifaceted security issue which is difficult to grasp and is subjected to different approaches and responses.

While being used extensively in policy and legal documents, the key terms involved in the development of cooperation remain undefined or ill-defined at the international, regional and sometimes even at the national level. The absence of uniform definitions is particularly evident in ASEAN, whereas attempts to define terms have been made in the EU. While requiring States to cooperate together, the international and regional organisations do not indeed provide clear definitions of the key concepts, including the definitions of the listed offences, actors and types of interactions.

Where several definitions are present, the discrepancies and similarities have been discussed in such a manner as to find a common, yet broad, understanding. This understanding acts as the basis for this study and could potentially be used for intra- and interregional dialogue. The term 'intelligence' is probably one of the most debated terms. This represents the absence of international and regional definitions and indicates the tremendous discrepancies that exist at different levels (i.e. international, regional and national).

Below is a table summarising the major outcomes of this chapter's analysis. It illustrates where definitions do or do not exist as well as where discrepancies are relevant enough to be highlighted (Table 2.2).

Therefore, the EU and its Member States agreed upon a number of definitions, but have not successfully reached a clear agreement on others. In its institutionalised architecture, which facilitates cooperation, there is room for various formal and informal ways of cooperation between competent authorities. With its very loose—or even limited—legal architecture in criminal matters, ASEAN does not

[173] 'Malaysia sets up new federal counter-terrorism department' *The Strait Times*, 7 July 2017: available at https://bit.ly/3aUeTiS (accessed on 12 December 2017).

[174] See Art. 2(a), *Europol Regulation*.

Table 2.2 Summary of the comparative analysis of the key definitions of the research

	Global level	ASEAN	EU
Transnational	Art. 3 UNTOC: '(a) It is committed in more than one State; (b) It is committed in one State but a substantial part of its preparation, planning, direction or control takes place in another State; (c) It is committed in one State but involves an organised criminal group that engages in criminal activities in more than one State: or (d) It is committed in one State but has substantial effects in another State'.	UN definition applying: Art. 2(h), 2015 *ASEAN Convention against Trafficking in Persons, Especially Women and Children*	Broad definition and reference to the UNTOC (cf. *CFD 2008/841/JHA on the fight against organised crime*) Art. 83(1) TFEU: 'cross-border dimension resulting from the nature or impact of such offences or from a special need to combat them on a common basis'
Seriousness	Art. 2 UNTOC: 'conduct constituting an offence punishable by a maximum deprivation of liberty of at least 4 years or a more serious penalty'	No regional definition. Reference to the UNTOC.	No constitutional definition. Definitions in the EU secondary legislation differ from one instrument to another.
Terrorist offences	UN has followed a sectorial approach through the adoption of a series of Conventions. But, Art. 2(b), 1999 *International Convention for the Suppression of the Financing of Terrorism*: 'any other act intended to cause death or serious bodily injury to a civilian, or to any other person not taking an active part in the hostilities in a situation of armed conflict, when the purpose of such act, by its nature or context, is to intimidate a population, or to compel a government or an international organisation to do or to abstain from doing any act'. No criminalisation required.	ASEAN has followed the sectorial approach of the UN. Art. II ACCT refers to a list of international anti-terrorism instruments. Art. IX(1) ACCT: 'The parties shall adopt such measures as may be necessary, including, where appropriate, national legislations to ensure that offences covered in Article II [. . .] especially when it is intended to intimidate a population, or to compel a government or an international organisation to do or to abstain from doing any act, are under no circumstances justifiable by considerations of a political, philosophical, ideological, racial, ethnic, religious or other similar nature'.	Art. 3 of the 2017 Directive gives a transversal definition of terrorist offences: 'offences under national law, which, given their nature or context, may seriously damage a country or an international organisation'. These offences need to be committed with one the following aims: – seriously intimidating a population; – unduly compelling a government or an international organisation to perform or abstain from performing any act; – seriously destabilising or destroying the fundamental political, constitutional, economic or social structures of a

(continued)

Table 2.2 (continued)

	Global level	ASEAN	EU
		No criminalisation required.	country or an international organisation. This Directive requires the criminalisation of terrorist offences and other offence, as for instance those related to a terrorist group.
Cooperation	No clear definition. Generic term.	No specific regional definition. Term used interchangeably with 'collaboration'.	Mostly, common notion used, especially in the TFEU (Part III, Title V, Chaps. 4 and 5). No specific regional definition.
Collaboration	General understanding of the term, usually assimilated to cooperation.	No specific regional definition. Term used interchangeably with 'cooperation'.	No mention in the TFEU (Part III, Title V, Chaps. 4 and 5). Term used in secondary legislations to designate interactions between agencies and/or other EU bodies. No specific regional definition.
Coordination	General understanding of the terms.	No specific regional definition.	No specific regional definition. But especially used in the definition of tasks of EU agencies (Eurojust and Europol).
Information	Generic definition: knowledge in raw form.	No regional definition. Information and intelligence seem to be used interchangeably in the ASEAN texts.	Generic definition used; but, when definitions are provided, they vary. See, e.g., Art. 2(d) *CFD 2006/960/JHA* defines 'information and/or intelligence' as '(i) any type of information or data which is held by law enforcement authorities; and, (ii) any type of information or data which is held by public authorities or by private entities and which is available to law enforcement authorities without the taking of coercive measures [...]'.

(continued)

Table 2.2 (continued)

	Global level	ASEAN	EU
			For this study, information refers to all forms of data obtained, recorded or processed by the competent national authorities, including personal data.
Intelligence	Generic definition: data that have been worked on and given added value or significance.	No regional definition. Information and intelligence seem to be used interchangeably in the ASEAN texts. Yet, sometimes the two terms are listed, leaving the impression of having different meaning. See, e.g., *ASEAN—United States Joint Declaration for Cooperation to Combat International Terrorism*: 'flow of information, intelligence [. . .]' and 'information exchange, intelligence sharing'.	No regional definition. But, 'criminal intelligence operation' referred, in Art. 2 (c) *CFD 2006/960/JHA*, to 'a procedural stage, not yet having reached the stage of a criminal investigation, within which a competent law enforcement authority is entitled by national law to collect, process and analyse information about crime or criminal activities with a view to establishing whether concrete criminal acts have been committed or may be committed in the future'. For this study, intelligence refers to information collected, processed and analysed to be exploitable by the competent national authorities for a specific purpose, namely for prevention, investigation, detection and prosecution purposes.
Personal data	OECD Guidelines: 'any information relating to an identified or identifiable individual (data subject)'	No regional definition.	GDPR definition: 'any information related to an identified or identifiable natural person'.
Law enforcement authorities	Freedom left to States to determine who are the competent authorities. Law enforcement agencies generally refer to government agencies that	No regional definition. Same approach as at the international level.	No regional definition. Same approach as at the international level.

(continued)

Table 2.2 (continued)

	Global level	ASEAN	EU
	are responsible for the enforcement of the laws.		
Intelligence services	Freedom left to States to determine who are the competent authorities.	No regional definition. Same approach as at the international level.	No regional definition. Same approach as at the international level.

provide precise definitions and resembles more the international framework, facilitating more informal ways for cooperation.

There is still a long way to go to reach a precise common terminology with which to facilitate cooperation in criminal matters within each region, including in the most integrated regional framework. This process will take even more time and negotiation to be able to reach a worldwide agreement. Divergences still remain prominent in the various realms.

At first, and in theory, the absence of clear terminology may be seen as an issue when attempting to establish and enhance cooperation. Cooperation may be hampered as the parties must ensure they are discussing the same things, or they may take a more informal format, or these talks will be avoided altogether. In practice, however, this vague framework does not seem to present much of an issue when authorities interact. Competent authorities have found ways to collaborate and cooperate in terrorism-related matters more freely maybe, because of the absence of 'legal' mutual understanding. Competent authorities have thus collaborated and cooperated more freely in matters involving terrorism. Therefore, the very absence of uniformity dangerously provides parties with too much room to manoeuvre.

Due to the freedom that these legal frameworks leave, States need to trust that their partner(s) will act in the most appropriate manner, potentially respecting the steps they agree upon, in order to reach an identified common objective. Competent authorities need mutual trust to work together and implement their agreement. Cooperation cannot happen without trust between relevant authorities and/or without a legal framework to facilitate such interactions.

The next chapter addresses the complicated establishment and further development of mutual trust as a useful concept in facilitating cross-border cooperation in criminal matters within the EU and ASEAN.

Chapter 3
Mutual Trust: A Variable Concept in Facilitating Cross-Border Cooperation in Criminal Matters

Nowadays, trust is on everyone's lips. Trust applies to two different types of relations: horizontal and vertical ones. Currently, one of the most debated types of trust relationship is a vertical one between citizens and their governments. As a result of the global surveillance programmes becoming public knowledge, governments faced strong criticism and the level of public's confidence in governmental actions waned.

Vertical and horizontal relations generally exist on three levels, namely the national, regional and international levels (Table 3.1).

Amongst the different interactions, a differentiation must be made between strategic and operational ones. For instance, the horizontal relations described in the second line tend to be of a more operational nature, while the vertical and horizontal relations described in the last line are predominantly of a strategic or even diplomatic nature.

The volume and depth of interstate interactions have developed in various fields, such as financial, commercial, social, political, or in security matters. Governing international interactions, the principle of good faith as one of the most fundamental principles of international law plays an eminent role. It might manifest into *pacta sunt servanda,*[1] which is an important principle in itself.[2] The principle of *pacta sunt servanda* dictates that States must respect their obligations with each other and refrain from any acts which would hamper the object and purpose of a treaty. Beyond traditional principles, international law aims to foster mutual trust and develop confidence amongst the signatories to each treaty. Good faith and mutual trust underlie the cooperation between national authorities and significantly affect its

[1] Art. 26, *Convention on the Law of Treaties*, Vienna, 23 May 1969, UNTS vol. 1155, No. 18232.

[2] See, e.g., Patrick Daillier, Mathias Forteau, and Alain Pellet, *Droit international public (Nguyen Quoc Dinh †)*, 8th ed. (Paris: Librairie Générale de Droit et de Jurisprudence, 2009): 238 and ff.

C. C. Cocq, *Mutual Trust in Regional and Interregional Cooperation on Counterterrorism*, United Nations University Series on Regionalism 26,
https://doi.org/10.1007/978-3-031-36612-3_3

Table 3.1 Three layers of vertical and horizontal relations

Vertical	Horizontal
Between people and governments	Between competent national authorities within the same country
Between national authorities and regional or international bodies/agencies	**Between national authorities of different countries** (either through direct channels or via regional/international agencies)
Between regional and international organisations	**Between regional organisations**

effectiveness. Originally, these principles facilitate cooperation without having to discuss the seemingly unrealistic task of approximating national legislations.

Mutual trust between States is regarded as a precondition for stable relations, premised on the expectations of other States' behaviour.[3] These interstate interactions are thus only possible because States have decided to trust each other on specific actions which aim to achieve a determined objective. After identifying a shared objective, relations develop based on a certain level of trust in order to ensure the effectiveness of cooperation. Yet, other important elements in international relations have also an influence on the choice of States in cooperating with others in the fight against terrorism, such as the notion of risk, the economic and political incentives.

Mutual trust is the bedrock upon which intra-regional and interregional cooperation are being built. While regional organisations' establishment was motivated by conflict resolution and prevention, they seem to have had greater success than global organisations when developing and implementing interstate cooperation. This is because trust and integration are inherently deeper within a regional setting, where there are fewer States, with similar concerns and sharing common history, cultures and the like.

Taking the EU and ASEAN, they both experienced significant trust issues at their beginning, after the second World Ward in the EU and the decolonisation in Southeast Asia. Notably, the most significant trust problems between European countries were those involving Germany. In ASEAN, the scares of the decolonisation or even the separation of Singapore from Malaysia hindered the trust between the members right from the start. Yet, as Pr. Telò argues, '[a]ssocier des ennemis en tant que membres était déjà une preuve extraordinaire de confiance mutuelle'.[4]

Trust issues remain within the EU, but have drastically diminished because of the increased interactions and interdependence between the Member States. Particularly, the 'legalisation' of interstate interactions has played a significant role in building

[3] Aaron M. Hoffman, 'A Conceptualization of Trust in International Relations', *European Journal of International Relations*, vol. 8, no. 3 (2002).

[4] Associating enemies as members was already an extraordinary proof of mutual trust (translation by the author): Mario Telò, *L'Europe en crise et le monde* (Bruxelles: Editions de l'Université de Bruxelles, 2016): 112.

trust within the region. Knowledge of their mutual interests and their different points of view aids dialogue and understanding. However, it must not be forgotten that 'legalisation' of international cooperation has progressed quite slowly before reaching the level of cooperation which exists today. Member States had developed mutual knowledge and shared best practices prior to reaching the current level of legal obligations. In contrast, cooperation within ASEAN is quite limited and is primarily based on interpersonal skills, mutual understanding and knowledge sharing. This process is usually facilitated by the discussions at workshops, trainings and other fora.

This chapter analyses the different constructs of mutual trust and its impact on cooperation in the EU and ASEAN. It assesses whether cooperation differs in the two regions. It also examines the ways in which 'mutual trust' is defined and used in each region when involved in criminal matters, namely in the EU Area of Freedom, Security and Justice (AFSJ) and in the relevant section of the ASEAN Political-Security Community (APSC) (Section 1). This chapter then highlights the main components of the concept, as identified from some initial observations in the two regions as well as the EU case-law and literature. It begins with the most extensive and detailed understanding of mutual trust found in the EU context and moves unto the most conventional version one found in the ASEAN context. From these elements, a data analysis matrix (hereafter referred to as the matrix) was created. This matrix determines the approach, structure and content of the rest of this study and, hopefully, future research in regional legal studies (Section 2).

Section 1: An Unclear Concept Widely Used to Justify and Foster Cross-Border Cooperation in Criminal Matters

Mutual trust does not have the same meaning, status and implications in the EU as it does in ASEAN.

EU Member States have associated mutual trust with specific cooperation mechanisms. Although it does not appear in the Lisbon Treaty, mutual trust has become a 'buzzword omnipresent'[5] within the EU discourse. Mutual trust is reflected in numerous texts of secondary law as well as in numerous instruments of political nature, especially those related to the AFSJ.[6] Even if it is not a regional 'constitu-

[5]Matthias Weller, 'Mutual trust: in search of the future of European Union private international law', *Journal of Private International Law,* vol. 11, no. 1 (2015): 4.

[6]Roland Genson, 'Une confiance mutuelle qui ne se limite pas au processus de la reconnaissance mutuelle' in *La confiance mutuelle dans l'espace pénal européen—Mutual trust in the European Criminal Area*, eds., Gilles De Kerchove and Anne Weyembergh, Études européennes (Bruxelles: Editions de l'Université de Bruxelles, 2005); Emmanuelle Bribosia and Anne Weyembergh, 'Confiance mutuelle et droits fondamentaux: 'Back to the future', *Cahiers de droit européen,* vol. 52, no. 2 (2016).

tional' principle, 'mutual trust' is widely used by the EU institutions within criminal justice discourse (e.g. in policy documents, legislation and case-law). Notably, the Court of Justice of the EU (CJEU) raised the concept to the level of a principle of 'fundamental importance in EU law, given that it allows an area without internal borders to be created and maintained'.[7] Despite being a central concept in EU cooperation in criminal matters and despite the multiplication of studies dedicated to this concept, mutual trust has not yet been clearly and legally defined.[8] Although the CJEU stated that mutual trust is a 'principle of fundamental importance', this statement does not clarify its status. A 'principle of fundamental importance' has indeed no specific meaning in EU law or in international law. However, in a field as dynamic as cooperation in criminal matters, the existence of this lacuna may be intentional. Such absence of clear definition in the EU has been strongly criticised, in particular due to the legal implications of mutual trust. Some authors consider that associating legal consequences with trust would remove the genuine meaning of 'trust' (i.e. its social construct).[9] Others, such as Pr. Herlin-Karnell, hold that the lack of 'articulation of what mutual trust actually means in the field of criminal law' poses 'a significant lacuna in EU criminal law cooperation'.[10] Similarly, while speaking of

---

[7] Para. 191, Court of Justice of the EU (CJEU), Opinion pursuant to Article 218(11) TFEU, Opinion 2/13 (full court), ECLI:EU:C:2014:2454, 18 December 2014.

[8] See, e.g., Meijers Committee (Hemme Battjes, Evelien Brouwer, Paulien de Morree & Jannemieke Ouwerkerk), *The principle of mutual trust in European Asylum, migration and criminal law* (Utrecht: FORUM, December 2011); Valsamis Mitsilegas, 'The Limits of Mutual Trust in Europe's Area of Freedom, Security and Justice: From Automatic Inter-State Cooperation to the Slow Emergence of the Individual', *Yearbook of European Law,* vol. 31, no. 1 (2012); Dominik Düsterhaus, 'Judicial Coherence in the Area of Freedom, Security and Justice. Squaring Mutual Trust with Effective Judicial Protection', *Review of European Administrative Law,* vol. 8, no. 2 (2015). In civil matters, Weller (2015). In asylum matters, Henri Labayle, 'Droit d'asile et confiance mutuelle: regard critique sur la jurisprudence européenne', *Cahiers de droit européen,* vol. 50, no. 3 (2014). In criminal matters, Gilles De Kerchove and Anne Weyembergh, eds., *La confiance mutuelle dans l'espace pénal européen—Mutual trust in the European Criminal Area,* Études européennes (Bruxelles: Éditions de l'Université de Bruxelles, 2005); Guy Stessens, 'The principle of Mutual Confidence between Judicial Authorities in the Area of Freedom, Security and Justice' in *L'espace pénal européen: enjeux et perspectives*, eds., Gilles De Kerchove and Anne Weyembergh (Bruxelles: Editions de l'Université de Bruxelles, 2005). Also, see, e.g., Luc Leboeuf, *Le droit européen de l'asile au défi de la confiance mutuelle* (Université Catholique de Louvain, Political science: PhD degree, dissertation, 2015); Auke Willems, 'Mutual trust as a term of art in EU criminal law: revealing its hybrid character', *European Journal of Legal Studies,* vol. 9, no. 1 (2016); Auke Willems, *The principle of mutual trust in EU criminal law*, Hart Studies in European Criminal Law (Oxford: Hart Publishing, 2021).

[9] See, e.g., Valsamis Mitsilegas, 'Judicial Concepts of Trust in Europe's Multi-Level Security Governance: From Melloni to Schrems via opinion 2/13', *eucrim*, no. 3 (2015).

[10] Ester Herlin-Karnell, 'Constitutional Principles in the Area of Freedom, Security and Justice' in *EU Security and Justice Law: After Lisbon and Stockholm*, eds., Diego Acosta Arcarazo and Cian C. Murphy, Modern Studies in European Law (Oxford: Hart Publishing, 2014): 42.

the importance of a principle of mutual trust, Dr. Ostropolski recognises that it 'lacks an explicit normative basis'.[11]

In ASEAN, mutual trust is also considered to be a useful concept as it applies to all forms of cooperation in the region. It is implied in its objectives and methods while requiring States to improve the exchange of information and best practices, to develop programmes for joint tactical exercises in the policy and law enforcement, etc.[12] Meanwhile, and in contrast to the EU, regional documents hardly mention it expressly and do not define it.[13]

There is no document setting out a clear and shared understanding of its characteristics and scope in either region.[14] It is therefore necessary to define the concept and its legal implications (I) in order to understand its role in the development of cooperation mechanisms in both regions (II).

I. Providing Contours to a Concept Essential to the Development of More Trustworthy Relations

This chapter provides guidance for a better understanding of mutual trust and describes how it affects transnational cooperation within the EU and ASEAN and between these two regions. Defining and contouring mutual trust would ensure that the concept is interpreted the same way by all partners and then confers the same obligations and rights for all parties engaged in any form of relation. Interestingly, before becoming a political or legal concept in the EU, mutual trust was first and foremost a social construct.[15] The most significant distinction between the use of mutual trust in legal affairs and the social construct of trust is that the former is a normative principle underpinning a distinct model of cooperation, whereas the latter is norm-free. From a social perspective, trusting someone is to lower one's guard and to refrain from taking precautions against a partner, even when the other, for any reason (including opportunism or incompetence), could act in a way that might seem to justify precautions.

As a legal presumption in the EU, it must be clarified that a presumption assumes some facts are accepted as real and true, potentially fictitious though, to achieve a

[11] Tomasz Ostropolski, 'The CJEU as a Defender of Mutual Trust', *New Journal of European Criminal Law* vol. 6, no. 2 (2015).

[12] See, e.g., *ASEAN Plan of Action to Combat Transnational Crime* (1999); *ASEAN Declaration on Joint Action to Counter Terrorism* (2001); *Declaration of ASEAN Concord II*, adopted by the Heads of State/Government, 9th ASEAN Summit, Bali, 7 October 2003; *ASEAN Political-Security Community Blueprint*, Jakarta, 1 March 2009; *ASEAN Comprehensive Plan of Action on Counter Terrorism* (2009); *Revised ASEAN Comprehensive Plan of Action on Counter Terrorism* (2017).

[13] Among the few examples, may be mentioned the Bali Declaration on ASEAN Community in a Global Community of Nations 'Bali Concord III', Plan of Action, 2013–2017, 19th ASEAN Summit, Bali, 17 November 2011, pt. A.1.a.ix.

[14] Willems, 'Mutual trust as a term of art in EU criminal law' (2016): 215.

[15] Ibid.: 234 and ff; Ermioni Xanthopoulou, *Fundamental Rights and Mutual Trust in the Area of Freedom, Security and Justice. A Role for Proportionality?*, Modern Studies in European Law (Oxford: Hart Publishing, 2020): 23.

particular goal in legal matters. In this particular case, equivalent standards and level of protection of human rights are assumed to achieve the particular goal of preventing and combating crime. This key concept is the basis for substantial and durable interactions within a region that is without internal borders, such as in the EU, or within a region where borders are, de facto, increasingly open, such as in ASEAN.

As it legally supports binding obligations for EU Member States, especially those to cooperate against serious transnational crime, mutual trust has been extensively written about and debated in the EU.[16] It has been far less elsewhere, be it at the international and ASEAN levels.

Pr. Flore is one of the first scholars who reflected on the concept of mutual trust in the EU.[17] He recognises the specific nature of mutual trust and underlines its usefulness in interstate relations: 'La confiance mutuelle est un concept positif et simple du genre de ceux que la politique affectionne. Nous avançons ensemble parce que nous nous faisons confiance. Nul besoin d'aller en amont de cette confiance, qui constitue un axiome de notre action en commun en vue d'un monde meilleur'.[18] This remark applies to the development of any interstate relations, especially those where States want to engage in more interdependent or integrated relations.

Discussions and reflections related to mutual trust in the EU will serve as a basis for a wider approach. Whatever the framework, a minimum level of trust is needed to cooperate and to ensure the consistency and effectiveness of members' actions. Mutual trust is therefore a useful concept to be used in various regions, especially when analysing interstate cooperation. It indeed contains interesting aspects and

---

[16] See, e.g., Petter Asp, 'Basic Models of a European Penal Law: Mutual Recognition, Cooperation, Harmonisation', *Europäischer Juristentag,* vol. 4 (2008): 264; Markus Möstl, 'Preconditions and Limits of Mutual Recognition', *Common Market Law Review,* vol. 47, no. 2 (2010): 419; Theodore Konstadinides, 'The Europeanisation of Extradition: How Many Light Years Away to Mutual Confidence?' in *Crime Within the Area of Freedom, Security and Justice: A European Public Order*, eds., Cristina Eckes and Theodore Konstadinides (Cambridge: Cambridge University Press, 2011): 194. Also, Gisèle Vernimmen-Van Tiggelen and Laura Surano, 'Analysis of the future of mutual recognition in criminal matters in the European Union' Final Report to the European Commission from the Institute for European Studies, Université libre de Bruxelles, 20 November 2008: available at http://ec.europa.eu/justice/criminal/files/mutual_recognition_en.pdf (accessed on 3 May 2017).

[17] See, e.g., the different chapters in De Kerchove and Weyembergh, eds. (2005); Valsamis Mitsilegas, *EU Criminal Law after Lisbon. Rights, Trust and the Transformation of Justice in Europe* (Oxford: Hart Publishing, 2016); Saskia Hufnagel and Carole McCartney, eds., *Trust in International Police and Justice Cooperation*, Oñati International Series in Law and Society (Oxford: Hart Publishing, 2017).

[18] Daniel Flore, 'La notion de confiance mutuelle: l''alpha' ou l''oméga' d'une justice pénale européenne' in *La confiance mutuelle dans l'espace pénal européen—Mutual trust in the European Criminal Area*, eds., Gilles De Kerchove and Anne Weyembergh (Bruxelles: Editions de l'Université de Bruxelles, 2005): 17: Mutual trust is a positive and simple concept of the type that politics affectionate. We walk the same path side by side because we trust each other. No need to go further upstream of this trust that constitutes an axiom of our common action for a better world. (translation by the author)

elements which apply to all interstate relations. Keeping in mind that the EU has adopted its own form of mutual trust and other forms may arise elsewhere, mutual trust is a key principle that needs to be contextually clarified due to the potentially divergent understandings and implications in each region.

For a better understanding of the concept, it is interesting to analyse its relation with other notions which play a crucial role in the development of more or less integrated cooperation mechanisms. Establishing a fertile ground, namely a community of values and interests, is essential to each regional project and to intra-regional cooperation, and thus, constitutes a first step in building up mutual trust (A). In this process, traditional interstate relations are generally based on various principles, particularly the principle of reciprocity (B). With their respective approach concerning mutual trust, States aim at forging strong confidence in the relations amongst themselves (C).

A. Establishing a Community of Values and Interests: The Starting Point in Building Up Mutual Trust

There are at least two requirements needed for parties to form a relation which is based upon trust. Firstly, trust involves the willingness to take risks. These risks are mitigated when parties adopt a legal framework which imposes obligations upon them (e.g. the rules applying in the framework of the European arrest warrant). The second requirement is the identification of an existing common interest(s), which might only be reached (or more easily reached) through a process of collaboration. This second element is a powerful motivator for parties to trust one another. All parties need to have an interest in collaborating together to reach their own objective. Regional security is one such objective.

At the beginning of their regional journey, the respective Member States recognised the strong differences that exist between them relating to various subjects (i.e. historical, cultural, political, legal differences), whilst agreeing that they need to adopt common positions on regional and international issues such as preventing and countering terrorism. While agreeing on such a shared objective, the regional requirements might diverge, remaining much less formal in ASEAN than in the EU. Indeed, ASEAN leaves to each of its members broad discretion to decide how to reach common objectives.[19] As will be shown later, this room for discretion has become a bit more limited in the EU due to regional legal obligations.

Despite clear differences, there are some similarities in the foundations of both regional organisations. Symbolically, the motto 'unity in diversity' is the ideological foundation behind both the construction and intra-regional relations in the EU[20] and

[19] Art. VI, ACCT (2007) and *ASEAN Comprehensive plan of action on Counter Terrorism* (2009).

[20] Adopted by the European Parliament, 'Proclamation of this European motto', Brussels, 4 May 2000 after the competition to find 'A Slogan for Europe'; European Parliament, Report on cultural cooperation in the European (2000/2323(INI)), Committee on Culture, Youth, Education, the Media and Sport, Rapporteur: Giorgio Ruffolo, A5-0281/2001, 16 July 2001; reminded in the Declaration by the Kingdom of Belgium, the Republic of Bulgaria, the Federal Republic of Germany, the Hellenic Republic, the Kingdom of Spain, the Italian Republic, the Republic of

ASEAN.[21] Their respective Member States emphasise both their characteristics and common values in the spirit of unity in diversity. The Member States come with their divergent backgrounds to develop unity in certain aspects of their political, economic and socio-cultural affairs.[22] These nations have decided to work for peace and prosperity, while at the same time being enriched by the regions' many different cultures, traditions and languages. Whilst in the EU the expression of 'united in diversity' was directly generalised to all matters of regional competence, it was instead progressively integrated into the different communities in ASEAN. The expression 'unity in diversity' was introduced in the Socio-Cultural Community and then more broadly included in the *ASEAN Charter*. However, it is only in November 2015 that this expression was specifically integrated in the Political-Security Community by the ASEAN 2025 programme.[23]

Presently, diversity is more prominent in ASEAN where the States lack effective and enforceable common standards, especially human rights standards. Although diversity remains significant in the EU, Member States have tried to reduce their differences to an extent and in specific fields. EU Member States tend to have indeed approximated their standards in various domains, particularly those pertaining to criminal law and human rights standards.

The identification of shared objectives and common values has been the driving force behind the establishment of regional organisations. Among other factors, these objectives and values have defined their intra-regional dynamics. These factors are the essential foundation upon which mutual trust might flourish to facilitate cross-border cooperation. The composition of this foundation may determine the features of mutual trust in each regional organisation.

In this respect, the distinct approaches of the EU and ASEAN are interesting case studies as they follow an apparent common objective, yet diverge in many aspects.

Cyprus, the Republic of Lithuania, the Grand-Duchy of Luxembourg, the Republic of Hungary, the Republic of Malta, the Republic of Austria, the Portuguese Republic, Romania, the Republic of Slovenia and the Slovak Republic on the symbols of the European Union, pt. 52, accompanying the *Treaty of Lisbon Amending the Treaty on European Union and the Treaty Establishing the European Community*, 13 December 2007, 2007/C 306/01: available at https://bit.ly/2YZ2Ytp (accessed on 10 February 2021). Notably, it is also written on the big electronic banner installed in front of the European Parliament in Brussels.

[21] Art. 2.2(l), *ASEAN Charter*, 13th ASEAN Summit, Singapore, 20 November 2007; Pts. 42 about building ASEAN identity and 43 about the promotion of ASEAN awareness and sense of community, in Roadmap for an ASEAN Community 2009–2015, ASEAN Secretariat, Jakarta, 2009; Bali Declaration on ASEAN Community in a Global Community of Nations 'Bali Concord III'. The references in these documents only appear in the section on ASEAN Socio-Cultural Community. Pt. 2.1.g., *ASEAN Intergovernmental Commission on Human rights (Terms of reference)*, 15th ASEAN Summit, Cha-Am Hua Hin, 23–25 October 2009 dealing with the principles guiding the AICHR.

[22] See, e.g., Art. 2.2(l), 'AEC: Unity in Diversity', ASEAN Information Center, 19 May 2015: available at http://www.aseanthai.net/english/ewt_news.php?nid=212&filename=index (accessed on 30 May 2017).

[23] Pt. 8.3., *ASEAN 2025: Forging Ahead Together*, Jakarta, ASEAN Secretariat, November 2015.

On the West side of the Ural mountain divide, mutual trust is more than a social construct as it is also based on the approximation of legislations and the identification of common human rights standards. With approximated legislations and common human rights standards, EU Member States have legal expectations, which usually allows for improving the effectiveness of interstate cooperation.[24] Legal expectations are based on 'legal certainty', which entails the knowledge of which laws are applicable to foster confidence in the other States' rules.[25] Approximation and the creation of common standards mitigate the inherent risks of mutual trust when it is viewed as a social construct. The more significant the disparities, the riskier trusting is. On the East side of the Ural, mutual trust seems to lack a normative meaning, but does have a social and political one. Trust fosters cooperation in Southeast Asia, but, from a normative and practical perspective, there is no clarity as to what the principle entails.[26]

B. **Reciprocity: A Tool for Building Trusting Relations and Its Distinct Application in the EU and ASEAN**

It is common to find 'trust' or 'confidence' associated with 'mutual' in many regional and international documents related to the fight against terrorism.[27] This 'mutual' qualification usually implies reciprocity according to the ordinary sense of

---

[24] Xanthopoulou (2020): 36.

[25] Annika Suominen, 'What Role for Legal Certainty in Criminal Law Within the Area of Freedom, Security and Justice in the EU?', *Bergen Journal of Criminal Law and Criminal Justice,* vol. 2, no. 1 (2014); Xanthopoulou (2020).

[26] See, e.g., Benny Teh Cheng Guan, 'ASEAN's Regional Integration Challenge: The ASEAN Process', *The Copenhagen Journal of Asian Studies,* vol. 20 (2004); Chairman of the ASEAN Regional Forum, 'ASEAN Regional Forum (ARF) Statement on Information Sharing and Intelligence Exchange and Document Integrity and Security in Enhancing Cooperation to Combat Terrorism and other Transnational Crimes' (2005); Anna Cornelia Beyer, *Counter Terrorism and International Power Relations: The EU, ASEAN and Hegemonic Global Governance* (London: I.B. Tauris & Co Ltd., 2010): 117.

[27] See, e.g., in ASEAN, recital 2, Joint Declaration of ASEAN and China on Cooperation in the Field of Non-Traditional Security Issues, 6th ASEAN-China Summit, Phnom Penh, Cambodia, 4 November 2002; pt. 7, Chairman's Statement, 1st ASEAN Defence Ministers' Meeting-Plus (ADMM-Plus) (Hanoi: 12 October 2010); pt. A.1.a.ix., Bali Concord III (2011). In the literature, see, e.g., Rodolfo C. Severino, *The ASEAN Regional Forum* (Singapore: Institute of Southeast Asian Studies, 2009): 33 and 64 speaking about 'mutual confidence'; Sartika Soesilowati, 'ASEAN's Response to the Challenge of Terrorism', vol. 24, no. 3 (2011): 231. In the EU, Council of the European Union, 'General orientations', *The Hague Programme: Strengthening Freedom, Security and Justice in the European Union,* O.J.E.U. C53/1, 3 March 2005; European Commission, *Communication from the Commission to the European Parliament and the Council. The EU Counter-Terrorism Policy: main achievements and future challenges,* COM(2010)386 final, Brussels, 20 July 2010. Interestingly, the Council of Europe used the expression of 'mutual confidence' long before the 9/11 attacks, the Explanatory Report to the *European Convention on the Suppression of Terrorism,* ETS No. 90, Strasbourg, 27 January 1977.

the word. Thus, mutual trust is not a one-way street relationship: 'mutual' refers to 'un rapport double et simultané, un échange d'actes, de sentiments'.[28]

It is then interesting to link the concept of mutual trust with the general principle of international law that is reciprocity. Reciprocity is a customary principle with a long history in international law and diplomacy.[29] Reciprocity plays a crucial role in international law as a source of obligations in horizontal relation (e.g. cooperation). Essentially, it is an assurance offered by the Requesting State that it will comply, in kind, with the same type of request and provide similar cooperation to the Requested State in a comparable situation should it arise. The principle of reciprocity is often reflected in domestic laws. As such, assurances of reciprocity (legal or otherwise) are a valuable addition to any type of cooperative agreement. If the Requesting State is asking for a form and/or level of assistance which it would not be able to reciprocate, then this should be stipulated in the request. Such cooperation is still possible, yet not mutual or the Requested State may reciprocate in alternate ways. For example, in situations where there is no pre-existing legal basis for extradition, the Requested State may nonetheless decide to agree to a request, generally on the basis of an assurance of reciprocity. Reciprocity is an inherent aspect of trusting relations.

Reciprocity is not only a source of obligations, but it is also an efficient manner to sanction recalcitrant States who do not respect their international obligations. According to the reciprocity principle, a State will not have to implement the provisions of a treaty if the other contracting party does not respect it. In interstate relations where there are not more specific norms than international law, the reciprocity principle is useful and essential. It is particularly useful when serving as an efficient sanction, depriving a recalcitrant State of the execution of their obligations by its partners.

As it will be shown later on, the relations between ASEAN Member States remain primarily governed by international law principles and norms. ASEAN intra-regional relations are not significantly different from worldwide relations. In this context, reciprocity is presupposed in ASEAN interstate cooperation.[30] If there is no specific mention of 'reciprocity' in the area of law enforcement cooperation, it is probably because norms do not require the implementation of specific mechanisms of cooperation. On the contrary, reciprocity is present in judicial cooperation with the 2004 *ASEAN Treaty on Mutual Legal Assistance in Criminal Matters.*[31] When

---

[28] A double and simultaneous relation, an exchange of acts, of feelings (translation by the author): Leboeuf (2015): para. 1416.

[29] For further explanations, see, e.g., Francesco Paris and Nita Ghei, 'The role of reciprocity in international law', *Cornell International Law Journal,* vol. 31, no. 1 (2003); Daillier, Forteau, and Pellet (2009).

[30] See, e.g., *ASEAN Treaty on Mutual Legal Assistance in Criminal Matters*, Ministers of Justice/ Law Attorneys-General, Kuala Lumpur, 29 November 2004. Reciprocity is also required in different domains such as in the field of investment, see, e.g., Pt. A3.17.i.b., *ASEAN 2025: Forging Ahead Together* (2015).

[31] *ASEAN Treaty on Mutual Legal Assistance in Criminal Matters* (2004); ACCT (2007); ASEAN Comprehensive plan of action on Counter Terrorism (2009).

implementing the Treaty, Indonesian law (*Law 1/2006*)[32] provides that mutual legal assistance may be provided based on a treaty,[33] or on the basis of good relationships under the reciprocity principle.[34] Trust plays a significant role in developing these good relations and, subsequently, fostering cooperation on the basis of interpersonal and political relations.

ASEAN is not a supranational organisation.[35] The ASEAN Member States are in the early stages of adopting a more integrated approach in their Economic Community and are in strong contrast to the objectives of the Political-Security Community in which such an integration project is not even mentioned. Because there is no specific regional infringement proceeding applying when a Member State does not respect its obligations enacted in an ASEAN agreement, trust is even more useful in developing and consolidating their interactions. If an ASEAN State violates a regional norm, ASEAN States may use countermeasures as authorised under international law[36] and/or lodge a request with the International Court of Justice (ICJ).[37]

By comparison, the term 'reciprocity' is decreasingly used in EU instruments related to police and judicial cooperation. Reciprocity is now inherent in the use of the qualifier 'mutual', which is particularly prevalent in the principles of mutual recognition and mutual trust. While working towards regional integration, EU Member States have adopted various legal instruments organising intra-regional mechanisms of cooperation. Consequently, there is a phasing out of reciprocity as a source of cooperation. Reciprocity as a sanction of non-execution of duties, including cooperation duties, has become obsolete in the EU's legal order. The CJEU has rejected the legal status of the principle of reciprocity in the EU legal framework. In *Hedley Lomas*, for example, the CJEU ruled that a Member State could not unilaterally decide to relieve itself of its obligations under EU law because

[32] *Law No.1/2006 concerning mutual legal assistance in criminal matters*, State Gazette Year 2006 No. 18, 3 March 2006.

[33] Art. 5(1), *Indonesian Law 1/2006*.

[34] Art. 5(2), *Indonesian Law 1/2006*.

[35] Supranational organisations have more binding powers on the Member States than a traditional international organisation may have, depending on its constitutive treaty. For further explanations, see Chap. 4.

[36] For further explanations on countermeasures, see the UN Legislative Series, 'Countermeasures' in Book 25: *Materials on the Responsibility of States for Internationally Wrongful Acts* (New York: United Nations, 2012), 304–306; Art. 22, International Law Commission, *Draft Articles on Responsibility of States for Internationally Wrongful Acts*, November 2001, Supplement No. 10 (A/56/10), Chap. IV.E.1.

[37] Art. 92, *UN Charter*; *Statute of the International Court of Justice*, San Francisco, 24 October 1945. See, e.g., the tension between Singapore and Malaysia over the sovereignty of Pedra Branca: International Court of Justice (hereafter referred to as 'ICJ'), *Sovereignty over Pedra Branca/Pulau Batu Puteh, Middle Rocks and South Ledge (Malaysia/Singapore), Judgement of 23 May 2008, I.C.J. Reports 2008*; or the border issue between Malaysian and Indonesian territories on the island of Borneo: ICJ, *Sovereignty over Pulau Ligitan and Pulau Sipadan (Indonesia/Malaysia)*, Judgement of 17 December 2002, I.C.J. Reports 2002.

another Member State has breached its obligation.[38] In the same judgement, the Court emphasised the need for 'trust in each other'.[39] This decision seems appropriate given its attempt to safeguard the EU legal order. Formally allowing reciprocity would consequently mean that if one Member State, for whatever reason, errs in its obligations under EU law, the whole system would be jeopardised.

Amongst the relations between EU Member States or between the EU and the Member States, the obligations have increasingly become more vertical (i.e. obligations of the Member States vis-à-vis the EU) and less horizontal (i.e. obligations between States). The supranational organisation that is the EU, and its institutions, particularly the European Commission, is indeed the 'guardian' of EU law. Within this context, countermeasures are less relevant amongst Member States, especially when the EU intervenes as a legislator and then as a controller of Member States' behaviour. The European Commission can initiate an infringement procedure when it considers that a Member State has failed to fulfil an obligation under the Treaties. If a State does not comply with the opinion delivered by the Commission, the latter may bring the matter before the CJEU, which can impose financial sanctions.[40] With this vertical system, reciprocity has lost its relevance in the implementation of EU regional norms and mechanisms of cooperation. Interestingly, if a State does not share information following the requirements of the *Europol Regulation,*[41] an infringement procedure might be initiated. This is unlikely to occur as there is no viable way to identify and establish a comparison between the information a government has and that which it chose to share. In practice, if one country's national authorities do not share data with their counterparts, it may lead to informal countermeasures from their counterparts who may become reluctant to share data with them or refuse to participate in joint actions. Thus, despite lacking an explicit reference to 'reciprocity', an implicit form of reciprocity may still exist.

Therefore, reciprocity has gradually lost its significance in the EU intra-regional relations. With regard to police cooperation, reciprocity was still expressed in The Hague Programme of 2005 concerning the access to national databases. However, the term 'reciprocity' has been gradually abandoned in judicial cooperation such as

---

[38] Para. 20, *The Queen* v. *Ministry of Agriculture, Fisheries and Food, ex P Hedley Lomas*, C-5/94, judgement, ECLI:EU:C:1996:205, 23 May 1996.

[39] Notably, the Court does not provide with any basis for such trust and does not even talk of 'mutual trust' but 'trust'. Para. 19, *The Queen v Ministry of Agriculture, Fisheries and Food,* C-5/94, 23 May 1996.

[40] Art. 258, TFEU.

[41] *Regulation (EU) 2016/794 of the European Parliament and of the Council of 11 May 2016 on the European Union Agency for Law Enforcement Cooperation (Europol) and replacing and repealing Council Decisions 2009/371/JHA, 2009/934/JHA, 2009/935/JHA, 2009/936/JHA and 2009/968/ JHA*, O.J. L135/53, 24 May 2016; as amended by *Regulation (EU) 2022/991 of the European Parliament and of the Council of 8 June 2022 amending Regulation (EU) 2016/794, as regards Europol's cooperation with private parties, the processing of personal data by Europol in support of criminal investigations, and Europol's role in research and innovation*, O.J.E.U. L169/1, 27 June 2022.

the Swedish Initiative, or other instrument of EU agencies fostering cooperation.[42] Nonetheless, reciprocity remains an underlying principle of the relations between EU agencies as well as between EU agencies and third countries.[43] It is however not very clear the shape such reciprocity—or rather lack of it—would take.

There are thus clear discrepancies between the two regions. In the EU, the principle of reciprocity is losing its traditional meaning along with the regional integration process. By contrast, it remains an important element of intra-regional cooperation in ASEAN.

C. **Building Trust to Reach Confidence**

The EU and ASEAN national and regional documents tend to assimilate 'trust' and 'confidence' when mentioning the relations between their respective members and even the relations with external partners, in all areas.[44] However, one needs to

---

[42] See, e.g., *Council Act of 29 May 2000 establishing in accordance with Article 34 of the Treaty on European Union the Convention on Mutual Assistance in Criminal Matters between the Member States of the European Union,* O.J.E.C. C197/1, 12 July 2000; *Council Framework Decision 2002/465/JHA of 13 June 2002 on Joint Investigation Teams,* O.J.E.C. L162/1, 20 June 2002; *Council Framework Decision 2002/584/JHA on the European arrest warrant*; pt. 2.1., *The Hague Programme* (2005); *Council Framework Decision 2006/960/JHA on simplifying the exchange of information and intelligence between law enforcement authorities of the Member States of the European Union*; *Regulation (EC) No 1986/2006 of the European Parliament and of the Council of 20 December 2006 regarding access to the Second Generation Schengen Information System (SIS II) by the services in the Member States responsible for issuing vehicle registration certificates,* O.J.E.U. L381/1, 28 December 2006; *Regulation (EC) No 1987/2006 of the European Parliament and of the Council of 20 December 2006 on the establishment, operation and use of the second generation Schengen Information System (SIS II)*, O.J.E.U. L381/4, 28 December 2006; *Europol Regulation*; *Regulation (EU) 2016/1624 of the European Parliament and of the Council of 14 September 2016 on the European Border and Coast Guard and amending Regulation (EU) 2016/399 of the European Parliament and of the Council and repealing Regulation (EC) No 863/2007 of the European Parliament and of the Council, Council Regulation (EC) No 2007/2004 and Council Decision 2005/267/EC*, O.J. L251/1, 16 September 2016 (hereafter referred to as 'Frontex Regulation'); *Regulation (EU) 2018/1727 of the European Parliament and of the Council of 14 November 2018 on the European Union Agency for Criminal Justice Cooperation (Eurojust) and replacing and repealing Council Decision 2002/187/JHA*, O.J.E.U. L295/138, 21 November 2018 (hereafter referred to as 'Eurojust Regulation').

[43] See, e.g., Recital 28 of the preamble and Art. 21(2), *Europol Regulation*; Art. 77(2), *Frontex Regulation;* Recital 109, *Council Regulation (EU) 2017/1939 of 12 October 2017 implementing enhanced cooperation on the establishment of the European Public Prosecutor's Office* (hereafter referred to as 'EPPO'), O.J.E.U. L283/1, 31 October 2017.

[44] See, e.g., in the EU, pt. 2.3, *The Hague Programme* (2005); paras. 78, 79, 83, Court of Justice of the European Union (CJEU), *N.S. and others*, Joined Cases C-411/10 and C-493/10, judgement, ECLI:EU:C:2011:865, 21 December 2011; European Parliament, Committee on petitions, Public hearing, 'Restoring citizens' confidence and trust in the European project' (Brussels: 22 June 2017); European Commission, Communication from the Commission to the European Parliament, the European Council and the Council, 'Comprehensive Assessment of EU Security Policy', Commission Staff Working Document, 9th progress report towards an effective and genuine Security Union, COM(2017) 407 final (Brussels: 26 July 2017), 74. In ASEAN, the remarks by H.E. Le Luong Minh, Secretary-General of ASEAN, High-Level International

assess whether there is a real difference between 'trust' and 'confidence'. Pr. Walker argues that '[trust is something] in which we must invest when we do not—or do not yet—have confidence in the workings of institutions or the behaviour of other agents. In other words, while confidence is an accomplished state upon which we can more or less passively rely; trust is an active way of building confidence or otherwise dealing with the absence of confident expectations'.[45] Therefore, confidence would be the final step States would need to take to secure trust.

The wording adopted by policy-makers in both regions is not always precise. In fact, ASEAN Member States declare that they aim to strengthen 'confidence' within the region,[46] while the EU has boasted about achieving a 'high level of confidence between Member States'.[47] 'Trust' and 'confidence' support cooperation between competent national authorities of different countries. For this reason, the concept of 'mutual trust' is central to this study. Meanwhile, the term 'confidence' might appear when it is used by public authorities and the doctrine.

II. A Three-Dimensional Concept Supporting Other Principles and Mechanisms of Cooperation

Explicating the principle of mutual trust helps to clarify its role as a support for regional cooperation mechanisms. All fields of this EU area have been significantly impacted by the importance of mutual trust, but this is particularly well reflected in the EU Area of Freedom, Security and Justice (AFSJ). Mutual trust tends to be narrowly associated with specific cooperation mechanisms in the EU and to a lesser or different degree in ASEAN.

The different levels of regional integration have had an impact on the understanding of mutual trust as well as on the regional respective legal framework and cooperation mechanisms. Consequently, this section discusses the foundational role

---

Workshop 2015: Managing South China Sea Conflict from ASEAN Perspective (Jakarta: 26 June 2015); 'ASEAN, Korea to build trust and confidence in e-commerce', ASEAN-Korea Workshop on Enhancing Consumer Protection in E-Commerce (Da Nang: 5–6 September 2016); 'About the ASEAN Defence Ministers' Meeting (ADMM-Plus)' (6 February 2017): available at https://admm.asean.org/index.php/about-admm/about-admm-plus.html (accessed on 26 December 2022).

[45] Neil Walker, 'The Problem of Trust in an Enlarged Area of Freedom, Security and Justice: A Conceptual Analysis' in *Police and Justice Cooperation and the New European Borders*, eds., Malcolm Anderson and Joanna Apap, European Monographs (The Hague: Kluwer Law International, 2002): 22.

[46] *ASEAN Plan of Action*, 6th ASEAN Summit (Hanoi: 15 December 1998); *ASEAN Political-Security Community Blueprint* (Jakarta: 1 March 2009); pt. 7, Chairman's Statement, 1st ADMM-Plus (Hanoi: 12 October 2010) who stated that the ADMM-Plus aims at enhancing 'friendship, mutual trust and confidence through greater dialogue and concrete cooperation'; Bali Concord III (2011); Chairman's Statement of the 29th ARF, Phnom Penh, 5 August 2022.

[47] See, e.g., Recital 10, *Council Framework Decision 2002/584/JHA on the European arrest warrant*; European Commission, Communication from the Commission to the European Parliament, the European Council and the Council delivering on the European Agenda on security to fight against terrorism and pave the way towards an effective and genuine Security Union, COM(2016) 230 final, Brussels, 20 April 2016.

of mutual trust in EU cooperation mechanisms concerning criminal matters. This section also details the ways in which mutual trust has been developed to foster further cooperation, while maintaining respect for fundamental human rights (A). Due to the lack of institutionalised mechanisms of cooperation within ASEAN, mutual trust has not (as of yet) reached the same level of importance (B).

A. Mutual Trust in the EU: A Three-Dimensional Support to Cooperation Mechanisms with Legal Implications

Norms, case-law and doctrine referring to mutual trust have shown particular growth in the domains of migration and asylum, as a part of the AFSJ.[48] Among the first cooperation mechanisms based on mutual trust, the Schengen area may be used as an example. The *Schengen Agreement*, signed on 14 June 1985, marked the start of the process that abolished the checks at the borders between the Schengen countries (the so-called internal borders). The first borders were opened 10 years later in March 1995. This abolition of checks at internal borders was made possible by a strengthening of controls at external borders. Dimitris Avramopoulos, Commissioner for Migration, Home Affairs and Citizenship, emphasised the importance of mutual trust in the development of the Schengen area:

> Removing the control at the borders between the Member States is one of the most outstanding achievements of European integration visible to every cross-border traveller. It would not have been possible without the mutual trust between the Member States. Mutual trust and close cooperation is something that we need today (...).[49]

Mutual trust is at the core of the entire Dublin System, which determines the State responsible for examining applications for asylum lodged in one of the Member States.[50]

---

[48] Directive 2001/40/EC of 28 May 2001 on the mutual recognition of decisions on the expulsion of third-country nationals, O.J.E.C. L149/34, 2 June 2001; completed by Council Decision 2004/191/EC of 23 February 2004 setting out the criteria and practical arrangements for the compensation of the financial imbalances resulting from the application of Directive 2001/40/EC on the mutual recognition of decisions on the expulsion of third-country nationals, O.J.E.U. L60/55, 27 February 2004.

[49] Quoted in Eimys Ortiz, ed., *Free movement of people: Schengen at risk*, IED Bibliographies (Institute of European Democrats, 2016): 8.

[50] *Convention determining the State responsible for examining applications for asylum lodged in one of the Member States of the European Communities* (hereafter referred to as 'Dublin Convention'), O.J. C254/1, 19 August 1997; *Council Regulation (EC) 343/2003 of 18 February 2003 establishing the criteria and mechanisms for determining the Member State responsible for examining an asylum application lodged in one of the Member States by a third-country national*, O.J L50, 25 February 2003; *Regulation (EU) 604/2013 of the European Parliament and of the Council of 26 June 2013 establishing the criteria and mechanisms for determining the Member State responsible for examining an application for international protection lodged in one of the Member States by a third-country national or a stateless person (recast)*, O.J. L180/31, 29 June 2013. On the development of the Dublin System, see, e.g., Labayle (2014); Leboeuf (2015); Sílvia Morgades-Gil, 'The Discretion of States in the Dublin III System for Determining Responsibility for Examining Applications for Asylum: What Remains of the Sovereignty and Humanitarian

Mutual trust has also become a foundational principle in judicial cooperation, in both civil and criminal matters. It constitutes the underlying principle behind the launch and implementation of the principle of mutual recognition which greatly facilitated intra-regional cooperation.[51] Mutual recognition is a basic principle in EU law and is strongly connected to mutual trust. It was first developed with regard to the European single market. It was particularly successful due to the high level of harmonisation that had already existed in this field.[52] Within the internal market, legal expectations are more prominent and the role of mutual trust, as a social construct, has decreased.

In the AFSJ, mutual trust was first developed in judicial cooperation in civil matters.[53] It was later extended to criminal matter by the initiative of the UK at the Cardiff Summit in 1998 and was subsequently rolled out to the entire AFSJ by way of the 1999 Tampere Council Conclusions.[54,55] Mutual recognition was implemented in criminal matters through the adoption of a series of framework decisions and has subsequently entered into force by way of the Lisbon Treaty via the adoption of directives and regulations.[56] Given the major developmental growth

---

Clauses After the Interpretations of the ECtHR and the CJEU?', *International Journal of Refugee Law,* vol. 27, no. 3 (2015).

[51] See, e.g., Tony Marguery, 'Rebuttal of mutual trust and mutual recognition in criminal matters: Is 'exceptional' enough?' Special section—Mutual recognition and mutual trust: Reinforcing EU integration? (first part), *European papaers,* vol. 1, no. 3 (2016).

[52] Willems, 'Mutual trust as a term of art in EU criminal law' (2016). Also, Massimo Fichera, 'Mutual Trust in European Criminal Law' Working paper, *University of Edinburgh Working Paper Series,* vol. 10 (2009): 19; Helmut Satzger, 'Is mutual recognition a viable general path for cooperation?', *New Journal of European Criminal Law,* vol. 10, no. 1 (2019).

[53] The first instrument using the concept was the *1968 Brussels Convention on jurisdiction and the enforcement of judgments in civil and commercial matters*, O.J.E.C. L299/32, 31 December 1972. For more, Bribosia and Weyembergh (2016).

[54] Tampere European Council, Presidency Conclusions, 'VI: Mutual recognition and judicial decisions', SN 200/99, Brussels, 15–16 October 1999.

[55] John A.E. Vervaele, 'Mutual Trust in Gathering of Evidence at the EU Level. What the Past Learned and the Future Brings?', *Revista de Criminologie, Criminalistica si Penologie,* vol. 1/2 (2014): 219.

[56] See, e.g., *Council Framework Decision 2002/584/JHA on the European arrest warrant*; *Council Framework Decision 2006/783/JHA of 6 October 2006 on the application of the principle of mutual recognition to confiscation orders*, O.J.E.U. L328/59, 24 November 2006; *Council Framework Decision 2008/675/JHA of 24 July 2008 on taking account of convictions in the Member States of the European Union in the course of new criminal proceedings*, O.J.E.U. L220/32, 15 August 2008; *Council Framework Decision 2008/947/JHA of 27 November 2008 on the application of the principle of mutual recognition to judgements and probation decisions with a view to the supervision of probation measures and alternative sanctions*, O.J.E.U. L337/102, 16 December 2008; *Council Framework Decision 2008/909/JHA of 27 November 2008 on the application of the principle of mutual recognition to judgements in criminal matters imposing custodial sentences or measures involving deprivation of liberty for the purposes of their enforcement in the European Union*, O.J.E.U. L327/27, 5 December 2008; *Council Framework Decision 2009/829/JHA of 23 October 2009 on the application, between Member States of the European Union, of the principle of mutual recognition to decisions on supervision measures as an alternative to*

of mutual recognition, mutual trust has become a core element of the EU's criminal justice agenda.[57]

Mutual recognition requires Member States to give full recognition to judicial decisions taken in other jurisdictions across the EU and to execute them.[58] Courts of all Member States do accept that the criminal courts of the other Member States whose orders they are now required to implement can be trusted to deliver an acceptable quality of justice by ensuring, for instance, decent standards of treatment for defendants. Although not appearing as such in the Tampere Council Conclusions, it is clear that a high level of mutual trust is needed for this mechanism of cooperation to be effective.[59] It is the Programme of measures to implement the principle of mutual recognition of decisions in criminal matters[60] that mentioned mutual trust as a prerequisite to the implementation of mutual recognition:

> Implementation of the principle of mutual recognition of decisions in criminal matters presupposes that Member States have trust in each other's criminal justice systems. That trust is grounded, in particular, on their shared commitment to the principles of freedom, democracy and respect for human rights, fundamental freedoms and the rule of law.[61]

Most mutual recognition instruments adopted in criminal matters serve the purpose of strengthening security, by enhancing the efficiency of criminal investigations, prosecutions and execution of convictions. The European arrest warrant is

---

provisional detention, O.J.E.U. L294/20, 11 November 2009. Since the Lisbon Treaty, two new directives were adopted, i.e. the *Directive 2011/99/EU of the European Parliament and of the Council of 13 December 2011 on the European protection order* (O.J. L338/2, 21 December 2011) and *Directive 2014/41/EU of the European Parliament and of the Council of 3 April 2014 regarding the European Investigation Order in criminal matters* (O.J.E.U. L130/1, 1 May 2014) as well as a regulation, i.e. the *Regulation (EU) 2018/1805 of the European Parliament and of the Council of 14 November 2018 on the mutual recognition of freezing orders and confiscation orders*, O.J. L303/1, 28 November 2018. See, Gilles De Kerchove and Anne Weyembergh, eds., *La reconnaissance mutuelle des décisions judiciaires pénales dans l'Union européenne* (Bruxelles: Editions de l'Université de Bruxelles, 2001); Annika Suominen, *The principle of mutual recognition in cooperation in criminal matters* (Bergen: Universitas Bergensis, 2011); Jannemieke Ouwerkerk, Quid Pro Quo*?: A Comparative Law Perspective on the Mutual Recognition of Judicial Decisions in Criminal Matters* (Cambridge: Intersentia, 2011); Guillemine Taupiac-Nouvel, 'The Principle of Mutual Recognition in Criminal Matters: a New Model of Judicial Cooperation Within the European Union', *European Criminal Law Review,* vol. 2, no. 3 (2012).

[57] Willems, 'Mutual trust as a term of art in EU criminal law' (2016): 213.

[58] See, e.g., Christine Janssens, *The Principle of Mutual Recognition in EU Law* (Oxford: Oxford University Press, 2013); Wouter Van Ballegooij, *The Nature of Mutual Recognition in European Law* (Cambridge: Intersentia, 2015).

[59] John R. Spencer, 'The UK and EU Criminal Law: Should we be Leading, Following or Abstaining?' in *Globalisation, Criminal Law and Criminal Justice. Theoretical, Comparative and Transnational Perspectives*, eds., Valsamis Mitsilegas, Peter Alldridge, and Leonidas Cheliotis (Oxford: Hart Publishing, 2015): 140.

[60] European Council, Programme of measures to implement the principle of mutual recognition of recognition of decisions in criminal matters, O.J.E.C. C12/10 (15 January 2001): 10–22.

[61] Ibid.

especially representative of this as it fosters cooperation between competent national authorities in order to fight against impunity. It was the first instrument adopted on the basis of the principle of mutual recognition.[62] It aims at establishing direct cooperation between judicial authorities by facilitating the arrest and surrender of suspects, accused, or convicted persons. With the exception of certain grounds for refusal, this cooperation mechanism requires the mandatory execution of warrants by the Requested State(s). The European arrest warrant is founded upon members' belief that the judicial decisions adopted by all counterparts in the EU are sufficiently accurate. Mutual trust is therefore paramount, given that the judicial authorities have to work in synergy.[63] This mechanism directly effects foreign judicial decisions at national level.

Mutual recognition also facilitated judicial protection of individual's rights and freedoms.[64] This is especially apparent in the *ne bis in idem* principle that aims to avoid double prosecution and punishment and can also be seen as an expression of the mutual recognition principle. The principle of *ne bis in idem*, as enacted in the *Convention implementing the Schengen Agreement* (CISA) and at the level of EU primary law in the EU Charter of Human Rights,[65] is also partially linked to mutual trust.[66] This has been made clear in the CJEU case-law. In the *Gözütok and Brügge* case,[67] for instance, the Court declared about Article 54 CISA that 'there is a necessary implication that the Member States have mutual trust in their criminal justice systems and that each of them recognises the criminal law in force in the other Member States even when the outcome would be different if its own national law

[62] *Council Framework Decision 2002/584/JHA on the European arrest warrant* supported by *Framework Decision 2003/577/ JHA of 22 July 2003 on the execution in the European Union of orders freezing property or evidence*, O.J.E.U. L196/45, 2 August 2005; and other EU instruments adopted later (see, e.g., supra footnote 296 and table of legislation).

[63] See, e.g., Stessens (2005): 94; Anne Weyembergh, Inès Armada, and Chloé Brière, 'European Added Value Assessment: The EU Arrest Warrant. Annex I: Critical Assessment of the existing European Arrest Warrant Framework Decision', Study for the European Parliament (Bruxelles: European Union, January 2014).

[64] European Council, Programme of measures to implement the principle of mutual recognition of recognition of decisions in criminal matters, O.J.E.C. C12/10 (15 January 2001): 1. See also, para. 33, Tampere European Council (1999): 'Enhanced mutual recognition of judicial decisions and judgements and the necessary approximation of legislation would facilitate cooperation between authorities and the judicial protection of individual rights'.

[65] Art. 54, *The Schengen Acquis—Convention implementing the Schengen Agreement of 14 June 1985 between the Governments of the States of the Benelux Economic Union, the Federal Republic of Germany and the French Republic on the gradual abolition of checks at their common borders* (CISA), O.J.E.C. L239/19, 22 September 2000; Art. 50, *Charter of fundamental rights of the European Union* (EU Charter), O.J.E.C. C364/1, 18 December 2000.

[66] See, e.g., Bribosia and Weyembergh (2016): 478 and ff.

[67] CJEU, *Gözütok and Brügge*, Joined Cases C-187/01 and C-385/01, judgement, ECLI:EU:C:2003:87, 11 February 2003. See also, *Miraglia*, C-469/03, judgement, ECLI:EU:C:2005:156, 10 March 2005; *Turansky*, C-491/07, judgement, ECLI:EU:C:2008:768, 22 December 2008.

were applied'.[68] The main idea being that if a Member State considers an internal judicial decision as final, another Member State must accept and trust the assessment on the merits of the case made in another EU country.[69]

Mutual trust, through its political and legal components, seems to be a strong driving force in the development of legalised cooperation mechanisms, especially judicial cooperation mechanisms, within the EU.

B. Mutual Trust in ASEAN: A Vague Concept Without any Legal Dimension

By comparison with the EU, ASEAN Member States have a more protective approach to their national sovereignty. It is even truer when it concerns security and criminal issues. For this reason, they may have agreed on cooperating together, but they have not adopted precise mechanisms of cooperation. There is no specific ASEAN instrument dealing with police cooperation. There are a few ASEAN instruments dealing with judicial cooperation in criminal matters and even fewer organising it. The sole regional instrument meant to foster cross-border cooperation is the ASEAN *Treaty of Mutual Legal Assistance in Criminal Matters* which was adopted in 2004. It highlights the engagement of the Member States in cooperative measures related to certain criminal sectors as terrorism.[70] All ASEAN Member States have signed the Treaty as well as other international conventions, such as the 2000 *UN Convention against Transnational Organized Crime*. They are working to comply with UN Security Council resolutions requiring mutual legal assistance.[71] However, the duties are much looser than in the EU framework. In ASEAN, the parties must 'render to one another the widest *possible* measure of mutual legal assistance in criminal matters'.[72] Additionally, there is a list of actions the States 'may' take in order to provide this assistance. Moreover, the list of refusal grounds of cooperation is considerably long. This list differs, at least in its wording, and is longer compared to the one in the 1959 *European Convention on Mutual Assistance in Criminal Matters* of the Council of Europe[73] or in the 2000 EU *Convention on Mutual Assistance in Criminal Matters.*[74] For instance, a request shall be refused

[68] Para. 33, *Gözütok and Brügge*.

[69] See, e.g., Ibid.; *Van Straaten*, C-150/05, judgement, ECLI:EU:C:2006:614, 28 September 2006; *Gasparini*, C-467/04, judgement, ECLI:EU:C:2006:610, 28 September 2006; *Bourquain*, C-297/07, judgement, ECLI:EU:C:2008:708, 11 December 2008; *Mantello*, C-261/09, judgement, ECLI:EU:C:2010:683, 16 November 2010; *M.*, C-398/12, judgement, ECLI:EU:C:2014:1057, 5 June 2014.

[70] Art. XII, ACCT.

[71] UNTOC. See also the list of ratifications of the most relevant international instruments in Appendix I.

[72] Art. 1 (italics added by the author), *ASEAN Treaty on Mutual Legal Assistance in Criminal Matters* (2004).

[73] Art. 2, Council of Europe, *European Convention on Mutual Assistance in Criminal Matters*, ETS No. 30, Strasbourg, 20 April 1959.

[74] *Council Act of 29 May 2000 establishing the Convention on Mutual Assistance in Criminal Matters between the Member States of the European Union.*

when there are 'substantial grounds for believing that the request was made for the purpose of investigating, prosecuting, punishing or otherwise causing prejudice to a person on account of the person's race, religion, sex, ethnic origin, nationality or political opinions'; or if such assistance 'would impose an excessive burden on the resources of the Requested Party'.[75]

There is a much wider margin of appreciation left to ASEAN Member States than to EU Member States. Moreover, mutual legal assistance has taken a step further with the adoption of the *Directive on the European Investigation Order* (EIO),[76] which associates mutual legal assistance with the principle of mutual recognition. Mutual legal assistance has been understood and applied in different ways by ASEAN countries, mainly because the level of trust may vary depending on the relations between the ASEAN countries and because the combination between the loose requirements and legal systems and national capacities.

Mutual trust has supported the development of cooperation mechanisms within ASEAN; mainly in its social dimension—through the development of interpersonal relations—to which was slowly added a political dimension—through the adoption of shared objectives and the identification of means to reach them. Despite commitments to regional and international norms, cooperation in the ASEAN region has largely taken place on an ad-hoc and informal basis, leading to mixed results.

There is thus no cooperation mechanism similar or comparable to the EU mutual recognition principle in criminal matters in ASEAN. There are however some mutual recognition arrangements in trade,[77] as it started and still exists in the EU. Should we see this similarity as a sign of future adoption of mutual recognition applying to criminal matters?

Mutual trust is a flexible concept with social, political and legal dimensions. It is a concept, elevated to the rank of fundamental principle in the EU, with features, status and degree that vary according to the respective regions. They also have different implications. Regardless of the regional framework, trust (or 'mutual trust') has been a useful tool to foster cooperation between competent national authorities. It is built upon legal and/or non-legal incentives to ensure its purpose, i.e. to make sure that competent national authorities work together against transnational crime. This concept is three-dimensional in the EU in the sense that it presents a social, political and legal dimension, while it is two-dimensional at best in ASEAN meaning presenting a social and—at best—political nature.

---

[75] Art. 3.1 (c) and (k), *ASEAN Treaty on Mutual Legal Assistance in Criminal Matters* (2004).

[76] *Directive 2014/41/EU regarding the European Investigation Order in criminal matters.*

[77] *ASEAN Framework Agreement on Mutual Recognition Arrangements*, Hanoi, 16 December 1998.

Section 2: Finding Ways to Build up Mutual Trust—Tailored-Made Approaches for the Different Regions

Mutual trust is the driving force behind international and regional cooperation. It is only because States have an interest in the outcome and accept risks that they engage in cooperation. This principle of mutual trust is, however, often confronted with scepticism, especially when it concerns judicial or police cooperation. Indeed, real life might witness cases of mistrust, including within the EU. As police officers from a certain city may sometimes have concerns about the method of their colleagues in another part of the country - the way they may handle data, etc. - why would not it be the case vis-à-vis counterparts in other countries who may not have the same status and competences and/or do not apply the same rules and most likely do not speak the same language. Thus, the reluctance of competent authorities, such as judicial or law enforcement authorities, to trust its foreign counterparts may be understandable given that there is no legal guarantee.

Each group of States has developed their unique, and potentially divergent, methods of building up mutual trust to achieve their objective(s), such as combating transnational crime including terrorism. Some shared grounds for the development of mutual trust and for the enhancement of cross-border cooperation shall be highlighted within each region and in the two regions (I). The different understandings of mutual trust, as elaborated in the previous section, and the shared grounds identified by public authorities, scholars and the author thus led to the creation of a matrix that shall serve as a framework for the analysis of the EU and ASEAN's development of cross-border cooperation in the fight against terrorism (II).

I. Seeking Grounds Supporting and Accompanying Mutual Trust: Diverging Approaches

Mutual trust is meant to ensure that partners respect their engagement vis-à-vis each other. Assurances may be considered low in the absence of legally binding norms though.

A cursory overview of the relevant international and regional documents related to cooperation in criminal matters reveals two main elements to be key in building mutual trust within regions. First, the partners agree upon their common objective, namely preventing and combating terrorism, and, gradually, upon the means to reach this objective. Concurrently, the protection of human rights has also developed and become a significant component of cooperation, especially in the EU. Human rights, as guaranteed in the EU law, have become enforceable within the region, even prior to the criminalisation of terrorist acts and the development of cooperation mechanisms. However, this trend has not been mirrored in ASEAN, where authorities do not necessarily link cooperation in criminal matters with the protection of human rights.

This book argues that the identification of the common objective, preventing and combating terrorism, and means to tackle it, such as approximation of the relevant legislations, constitutes the first phase to build up mutual trust, especially in the legal use of the term (A). Then, but not necessarily in chronological order, the establishment of common human rights standards and mechanisms of control of the effective respect of human rights, which has been particularly developed in Europe, may be considered a means of enhancing, guaranteeing and consolidating mutual trust (B). These elements are discussed in further detail in the subsequent chapters.

A. Approximation of Legislations: An Essential Step Towards Mutual Trust or a Way to Avoid Resorting to Trust?

The way(s) to achieve identified objective(s) may diverge between countries and regions. Ideological and cultural differences, or the gap between a State's current practice and the proposed standard(s) are becoming apparent during the negotiation process of agreements.

Mentioned several times already, standards are important pieces in the process of building and consolidating interactions. The International Organization for Standardization (ISO) broadly defines standards as 'the distilled wisdom of people with expertise in their subject matter and who know the needs of the organisations they represent'.[78] Adopted by the appropriate authorities, they constitute points of reference, models or rules for the relevant actors to speak the same language, to share the same expectations, but also to ensure their accountability.

Criminal justice and human rights standards, including data protection standards, provide a reliable (legal) basis for transnational cooperation. Agreeing on minimum standards, minimum legal rules, helps Member States to overcome the discrepancies between their respective norms.

Reducing legal deviation and introducing a certain level of approximation of the key legislative domains, especially procedural rights norms, might constitute the logical next step to facilitate further cooperation. The adoption of minimum standards in criminal procedure would accommodate the lack of trust or strengthen trust.[79] This is what is occurring in the EU context. The EU Member States agreed to approximate some elements of their national legislation, including their procedural laws.[80] Thus, further developing common human rights standards legitimate trust and facilitate cooperation.

The degrees of approximation also differentiate the levels and forms of regional integration of the various regional organisations. Despite their differences, 'harmonisation', 'approximation' and 'unification' may involve adaptations of

---

[78] ISO Standards: available at https://www.iso.org/standards.html (accessed on 4 April 2021). See also, Benoît Géniaut, 'La force normative des standards juridiques. Eléments pour une approche pragmatique' in *La force normative. Naissance d'un concept*, eds., Catherine Thibierge and et alii (Paris: L.G.D.J., Bruylant, 2009).

[79] On the issue related to the European Arrest Warrant, Willems, 'Mutual trust as a term of art in EU criminal law' (2016): 217–18.

[80] Art. 82(2) a) and b) TFEU; in addition to procedural approximation, trust building capacities have been attributed to substantive approximation, see, e.g., Anne Weyembergh, 'Approximation of Criminal Laws, the Constitutional Treaty and the Hague Programme', *Common Market Law Review*, vol. 42, no. 6 (2005): 1575.

national legislations.[81] Harmonising national legislations means establishing analogies or similarities among national laws to achieve a common goal in eliminating the incompatible discrepancies.[82] All forms of harmonisation may imply a modification of national legislations, if these are not already adequate. But, they may do so to varying degrees, ranging from the lowest approximation to the highest, namely a unification.[83] Unification eliminates all disparities between judicial systems by introducing an additional 'uniform' set of rules or, more likely, by substituting pre-existing national legislations for a new and sole unique rule or legislation, rendering the need for a mutual recognition type of cooperation mechanism obsolete.[84] The unification constitutes one of the most significant steps towards integration. Unification of criminal law is not a prospect that may happen any time soon in either the Southeast Asian region or even the European region as Member States regard their national criminal justice system to be at the core of statehood and reflecting a national tradition and culture. At the start of harmonisation, approximation aims at eliminating the most relevant disparities between Member States. It does not lead to a full harmonisation of national systems, but only creates a common minimum standard, so Member States can rely on this 'minimum' standard to be existent in all jurisdictions. It creates the common ground required for cooperation.[85] On this scale, harmonisation might float somewhere in between unification and approximation, but these are not clearly delineated categories. While harmonisation involves changes on procedural and substantial laws without any impact on the form of the texts, unification is a method of integration having an impact on both the

[81] See, e.g., Raymond Vander Elst, 'Les notions de coordination, d'harmonisation, de rapprochement et d'unification du droit dans le cadre juridique de la Communauté économique européenne' in *Les instruments du rapprochement des législations dans la Communauté économique européenne*, eds., Denise de Ripainsel-Landy, Alain Gérard, and Anne Limpens-Meinertzhagen, Thèses et travaux juridiques (Bruxelles: Editions de l'Université de Bruxelles, 1976): 14; Jochen Abr. Frowein, 'Integration and the Federal Experience in Germany and Switzerland' in *Integration Trough Law. Europe and the American Federal Experience*, eds., Mauro Cappelletti, Monica Seccombe, and Joseph H. H. Weiler (Berlin: Walter de Gruyter, 1986): 584; Jean Boulouis, *Droit institutionnel de l'Union européenne*, 5th ed. (Paris: Montchrestien, 1995): 244.

[82] See, e.g., Patrick Deboyser, *Le rapprochement des législations*, 1st ed., updated class notes (Bruxelles: PUB, 1992-1993/1); Edward Best and Thomas Christiansen, 'Regionalism in international affairs' in *The Globalisation of World Politics: An Introduction to International Politics*, eds., John Baylis, Steve Smith, and Patricia Owens (Oxford: Oxford University Press, 2008): 436.

[83] For a more detailed discussion, see Anne Weyembergh, 'Introduction', *Revue internationale de droit pénal,* vol. 77, no. 1 (2006); Carlos Gómez-Jara Diez, 'Models for a System of European Criminal Law: Unifications vs. Harmonisation?', *New Journal of European Criminal Law,* vol. 1, no. 3 (2010).

[84] Weyembergh, 'Introduction' (2006).

[85] Wendy De Bondt and Geert Vermeulen, 'Appreciating Approximation: Using Common Offence Concepts to Facilitate Police and Judicial Cooperation in the EU' in *EU and International Crime Control: Topical Issues*, eds., Marc Cools et al., Governance of Security Research Paper Series (Antwerp: Maklu, 2010): 16.

substance and the form of the laws.[86] The term 'harmonisation' is often used in a broad manner encompassing all efforts that have a 'harmonising effect'. Therefore, the terms 'approximation' and 'harmonisation' are often used interchangeably, and the difference (if any) between the two is rather thin.[87]

1. Strengthening the Legal Dimension of Mutual Trust Through the Approximation of EU National Legislations

When the British government launched the idea of mutual recognition at the Cardiff Summit in 1998, its goal was in fact to use this mechanism, based on mutual trust, as an alternative to the harmonisation of laws. Mutual recognition was selected as a principle to further cooperation without having to harmonise widely national legal systems, which was both unfeasible and undesirable at that time. Rather than being an alternative, mutual recognition actually led to an important rise in the approximation of laws, particularly in the field of criminal procedure (substantive and procedural criminal laws and common human rights standards).[88] Mutual trust may be independent from harmonisation, but harmonisation helps predicting States' action while facing similar cases and circumstances. It gives legal assurance to others; thus, facilitating cooperation.[89]

As emphasised by the European Parliament, the common EU legal culture is not intended to replace national traditions.[90] However, as the EU and its Member States share competence on matters dealing with the EU internal security, including police and judicial cooperation,[91] the regional and national norms need to be at least compatible and nourish one another. For this reason, the EU has developed common norms on what is deemed necessary to facilitate cooperation, which reveals to become wider over time.

[86] See, e.g., Karl Kreuzer, 'La communautarisation du droit international privé: les acquis et les perspectives', *in* Louis Vogel (dir.), *Unifier le droit: le rêve impossible?* (Paris: Panthéon Assas Editions, 2001): 97; Ursula Nelles, 'Definitions of harmonisation' in *Harmonisation and harmonising measures in criminal law*, eds., André Klip and Harmen van der Wilt (Amsterdam: Koninklijke Nederlandse Akad. van Wetenschappen, 2002); Weyembergh, 'Introduction' (2006).

[87] According to Vervaele, the two are even similar: John Vervaele, presentation at Leiden University, 'EU's Criminalisation Policy: Prospects and Challenges', 19 September 2016.

[88] See document submitted by the UK Delegation to the (then) K4 Committee, Doc 7090/99, Brussels, 29 March 1999, paras. 7–8. See also Anne Weyembergh, 'Consequences of Brexit for European Union Criminal Law', *New Journal of European Criminal Law,* vol. 8, no. 3 (2017); Xanthopoulou (2020): 12–15.

[89] See, e.g., Anne Weyembergh, *L'harmonisation des législations: Condition de l'espace pénal européen et révélateur de ses tensions* (Bruxelles: édition de l'Université de Bruxelles, 2004).

[90] European Parliament resolution of 22 May 2012 on an EU approach to criminal law (2010/2310 (INI)), O.J.E.U. C264/02E, 13 September 2013, pt. G: 'whereas the harmonisation of criminal law in the EU should contribute to the development of a common EU legal culture in relation to fighting crime, which adds up to but does not substitute national legal traditions and has a positive impact on mutual trust amongst the legal systems of the Member States'.

[91] Art. 4, TEU; Chaps. 4 and 5 TFEU.

The approximation of substantive and procedural criminal law started within the Third Pillar of the *Treaty on the EU* (TEU) introduced by the Maastricht Treaty. Then, the Amsterdam Treaty introduced a specific legal basis in this Third Pillar, namely Art. 31 e) TEU to progressively establish 'minimum rules related to the constituent elements of criminal acts and to penalties in the fields of organised crime, terrorism and illicit drug trafficking'. It is on that basis that the EU reacted and legislated right after the 9/11 attacks by adopting two consecutive framework decisions in 2002 and 2008[92] to approximate national laws in the field of terrorist offences. So far, there was no explicit legal basis for EU approximation in the criminal procedural field. This changed with the Lisbon Treaty. The current legal basis for the approximation of *substantive* criminal law is Article 83 TFEU. It is on this basis that the 2017 *Directive on combating terrorism*, replacing the former framework decisions, was adopted.[93] Article 82 of the TFEU constitutes the new specific and explicit legal basis for approximation in *procedural* criminal law. It is on that basis that six Directives have been adopted to approximate procedural guarantees for suspects and accused persons. Those were included upon the adoption of the 2009 *Roadmap on Criminal Procedural Rights*.[94]

This 'package' aimed to respond to criticisms, according to which the EU was disregarding the EU human rights standards at the benefit of the security tendency in the counter-terrorist context. It was also directly linked to the purpose of enhancing mutual trust within the region: from this perspective, it was indeed important that, complementary to the *European Convention for the Protection of Human Rights and Fundamental Freedoms* (ECHR)[95] and the *EU Charter for Fundamental Rights*, EU standards in the field of procedural rights were raised.[96]

Such direct link between approximation of procedural guarantees for suspects and accused persons and mutual trust was affirmed in the aforementioned Roadmap and in the 2009 Stockholm Programme, which strongly continued the quest for enhancement of mutual trust and mutual understanding between EU Member States.[97] The protection of the rights of suspected and accused persons in criminal proceedings is deemed a fundamental value in the Union. It is meant to maintain mutual trust

[92] Art. 1, *Council Framework Decision 2008/919/JHA on combating terrorism.*

[93] *Directive (EU) 2017/541 on combating terrorism.*

[94] *Resolution of the Council of 20 November 2009 on a Roadmap for strengthening procedural rights of suspected or accused persons in criminal proceedings*, O.J.E.U. C295/1, 4 December 2009. For more on the Roadmap, Jodie Blackstock, 'Procedural Safeguards in the European Union: a Road well travelled?', *European Criminal Law Review*, vol. 2, no. 1 (2012).

[95] *European Convention for the Protection of Human Rights and Fundamental Freedoms*, ETS No. 5, Rome, 4 November 1950.

[96] *Resolution of the Council of 20 November 2009 on a Roadmap for strengthening procedural rights of suspected or accused persons in criminal proceedings.*

[97] Pt. 1.2.1., Council of the European Union, *The Stockholm Programme: An open and secure Europe serving and protecting the citizens* (hereafter referred to as 'Stockholm Programme'), O.J.E.U. C115/1, 4 May 2010.

between the Member States and public confidence.[98] The Programme highlighted the need to adopt concrete policy targets in this respect:

> to enhance mutual trust in the legal systems of the Member States by establishing minimum rights as necessary for the development of the principle of mutual recognition and by establishing minimum rules concerning the definition of criminal offences and sanctions as defined by the Treaty. The European judicial area must also allow citizens to assert their rights anywhere in the Union by significantly raising overall awareness of rights and by facilitating their access to justice.[99]

This link was subsequently confirmed by the 2010 Commission's Action Plan implementing the Stockholm Programme, which states that '[mutual recognition] can only function effectively on the basis of mutual trust among judges, legal professionals, businesses and citizens'.[100] The Commission's Action Plan further explains that '[m]utual trust requires minimum standards and a reinforced understanding of the different legal traditions and methods'.[101] It implies dual actions: agreeing on common minimum standards and reaching mutual understanding.

The development of such approximation of legislations, particularly in the field of procedural criminal law, has in some ways strengthened the 'legalisation' of the EU criminal justice area and of mutual trust itself. Far from replacing the need for mutual trust, it has aided in the development of its legal dimension. In fact, the Commission guidelines 'The EU Justice Agenda for 2020—Strengthening Trust, Mobility and GRowth within the Union' explains that:

> EU justice policy has sought to develop a European area of justice based on mutual recognition and mutual trust by building bridges between the different justice systems of the Member States. This has required proper legal safeguards to be built in, to make sure that the bridges built between Member States' legal systems are structurally sound. In the area of criminal justice, mutual trust between Member States has been strengthened by progressively establishing, throughout the EU, a set of fair trial rights by means of common, EU-wide, minimum standards to protect persons suspected or accused of a crime. The standing of victims throughout the criminal procedure has also been improved by providing minimum rights, support, advice and protection for victims and their close relatives.[102]

---

[98] Pt. 2.4., Stockholm Programme.

[99] Pt. 3., Stockholm Programme.

[100] European Commission, Communication from the Commission to the European Parliament, the Council, the European Economic and Social Committee and the Committee of the Regions delivering an area of freedom, security and justice for Europe's citizens. Action Plan Implementing the Stockholm Programme, COM(2010) 171 final, Brussels, 20 April 2010.

[101] Section 4, Ibid.

[102] European Commission, Communication from the Commission to the European Parliament, the Council, the European Economic and Social Committee and the Committee of the Regions. The EU Justice Agenda for 2020—Strengthening Trust, Mobility and Growth within the Union, COM (2014)144 final, Strasbourg, 11 March 2014; see also, European Commission, Report from the European Commission to the European Parliament and the Council on the implementation of Council Framework Decision 2008/919/JHA of 28 November 2008 amending Framework Decision 2002/475/JHA on combating terrorism, COM(2014) 554 final, Brussels, 5 September 2014.

With the aim of approximating legislations, while also respecting the national constitutional values and principles, the European Commission introduced the evaluation *ex-ante* and *ex-post* impact assessment. The first procedure analyses the opportunity and feasibility of adopting a new regional norm that would harmonise national legislations, without infringing essential values and principles of the Member States. The second evaluates the good reception of EU norms into national jurisdictions. The *ex-post* procedure specifically assesses the performance of EU action.[103] Concerning adopted terrorism norms, some impact assessments took place leading to the drafting of the 'Report from the European Commission to the European Parliament and the Council on the implementation of Council Framework Decision 2008/919/JHA of 28 November 2008 amending Framework Decision 2002/475/JHA on combating terrorism.' This evaluation served to oversee the implementation of the anti-terrorism norms and was useful in the drafting of the *Directive on combating terrorism.*[104]

2. The absence of approximation of ASEAN national legislations: An avenue worth exploring?

While EU Member States have progressively and at an exponential rate accepted to take steps towards the harmonisation of their legislations, approximating legislations is still generally considered by ASEAN Member States as giving up some degree of sovereignty.[105] Nonetheless, they have decided to take slow, gradual steps in this direction.

Similar to the initial steps of the European Community, Southeast Asia has focused on approximating policies and eventually legislations within the economic community, and less so in the field of the other communities.[106] The normative rules

[103]European Commission, 'Evaluating laws, policies and funding programmes': available at: https://bit.ly/2SgQ221 (accessed on 19 June 2017).

[104]*Directive 2017/541 on combating terrorism.*

[105]See the Bandung principles, Final Communiqué of the Bandung Conference (Afro-Asian Conference), 18–24 April 1955: available at http://franke.uchicago.edu/Final_Communique_Bandung_1955.pdf (accessed on 9 December 2015): 9. And, with a more elaborated and critical approach, see, e.g., Pratap Bhanu Mehta, 'Sovereignty Tradeoffs and Regional Integration. Theoretical and Comparative Reflections' in *International Relations Theory and South Asia: Security Political Economy, Domestic Politics, Identities, and Images*, ed., E. Sridharan (Oxford: Oxford University Press, 2011). See also, Joseph H. H. Weiler and Ulrich R. Haltern, 'The autonomy of the Community Legal Order: Through the Looking Glass', *Harvard International Law Journal,* vol. 37, no. 2 (1996); Walter Mattli, 'Sovereignty Bargains in Regional integration', *Review of international Studies,* vol. 2, no. 2 (2000); Anne Weyembergh, 'L'Espace Pénal Européen: Entre Coopération Judiciaire et Territoire Pénal Européen' in *La Grande Europe* ed., Paul Magnette (Bruxelles: Editions de l'Université de Bruxelles, 2004).

[106]See, e.g., ASEAN, 'Roadmap for an ASEAN Community 2009–2013', ASEAN Secretariat, Public Affairs Office (Jakarta: ASEAN Secretariat); Min-hyung Kim, 'Theorizing ASEAN Integration', *Asian Perspective,* vol. 35 (2011); Clara Portela, 'The Association of Southeast Asian Nations (ASEAN): Integration, Internal Dynamics and External Relations', Study for the European Parliament, Policy Department Directorate-General for External Policies, EXPO/B/AFET/FWC/2009-01/Lot2/13, PE 433.713 (Bruxelles: European Union, September 2013).

governing regional interaction have traditionally been: (1) consensus-based decision-making; (2) a respect for national sovereignty; and (3) the non-interference in the domestic affairs of others.[107] Based on the continued practice of consensus-based decision-making, the lowest common denominator and the implicit right to veto have directed the ASEAN institutional and legal developments.[108] ASEAN is likely to rely on these modes of 'consultation' and 'consensus' principles to approximate national laws, while respecting cultural sensitivities and national sovereignty.

Approximation is more complicated in criminal matters as it involves sensitive issues such as national security. Some ASEAN declarations and plans of action adopted in the 1990s and 2000s mentioned an effort of harmonisation of national laws,[109] but nothing concrete has been implemented. In particular, the adoption of the *ASEAN Convention on Counter Terrorism* in 2007 does not approximate national legislations on the subject. The only slight touch of approximation comes under external pressure, from the influence of international instruments and UN agencies' actions. In fact, the adoption of ASEAN binding instruments is following up on similar UN requirements.[110] ASEAN norms solely transpose the pre-existing international norms; approximation of national criminal laws remains thus extremely limited.

The approximation of the relevant national laws may be seen in two different ways: on the one hand, it may support and complete a more political use of mutual trust or, on the other, and as some would argue, it may replace the political use of mutual trust. In any case, the approximation of laws is viewed in the EU as key to the development of mutual trust, while this view is not shared in Southeast Asia.[111] The approximation of legislations and the legalisation of the concept of

[107] Kusuma Snitwongse, 'Thirty Years of ASEAN: Achievements through Political Cooperation', *The Pacific Review,* vol. 11, no. 2 (1998): 183.

[108] Christopher B. Roberts, *ASEAN Regionalism. Cooperation, values and institutionalization*, Routledge Security in Asia Pacific (London: Routledge, 2012): 70–71. Also, see, e.g., Deborah A. Haas, 'Out of Others' Shadows: ASEAN Moves Toward Greater Regional Cooperation in the Face of the EC and NAFTA', *American University International Law Review,* vol. 9, no. 3 (1994).

[109] See, e.g., Pt. 4, *ASEAN Declaration on Transnational Crime* (1997); Pts. A(b)2 and C7, *ASEAN Plan of Action to Combat Transnational Crime* (1999); Pt. 6.5.d), Work Programme to Implement the ASEAN Plan of Action to Combat Transnational Crime, Kuala Lumpur, 17 May 2002. Further developed in Chap. 5.

[110] *ASEAN Treaty on Mutual Legal Assistance in Criminal Matters* (2004) adopted on the basis of the *UN Model Treaty on Mutual Legal Assistance in criminal Matters*, A/RES/45/117 (68th plenary meeting, 14 December 1990) as amended by General Assembly Resolution A/RES/53/112 (53rd session, 20 January 2000); the ACCT based on the 14 UN anti-terrorism instruments cited in the Convention; *ASEAN Convention against Trafficking in Persons* (2015) based on the UNTOC (2000), and, more specifically, the *Protocol to Prevent, Suppress and Punish Trafficking in Persons*, A/RES/55/25(2000).

[111] Argument nourished by the following interviews: with a professor from the Faculty of Law of the National University of Singapore (NUS), Singapore, 3 June 2016; with an official from Special Branch's Counter-Terrorism Division of the Royal Malaysian Police, Royal Malaysian Police Headquarters, Kuala Lumpur, 7 June 2016; with an official from the Global Programme for Combating Wildlife and Forest Crime, UNODC-ROSEAP, Bangkok, 1 July 2016.

mutual trust improved EU cooperation. In ASEAN, the agreement on shared objectives constitutes the main source of trust-building, facilitating interpersonal cooperative relations between competent national authorities. The existence of interpersonal trust—and potentially the political willingness to reach such mutual trust showed in some recent regional norms—is central to the ASEAN intra-regional relations, taking the central form of reciprocity. This results in less instances of cooperation between competent authorities and weakens implementation of cooperative agreements.

B. Reaching Regional Human Rights Standards: Another Essential Step in Building Up Mutual Trust or a Way to Consolidate It?

There is a clear discrepancy emerging *prima facie* between the EU and ASEAN regarding the place of human rights standards vis-à-vis mutual trust. These standards are an essential component of mutual trust in the EU, while they are not in ASEAN.

It is of the European view that agreeing to set human rights as the lowest common denominator ensures the effectiveness of the cooperation between competent national authorities as it guarantees citizens the minimum standards proclaimed in international and regional instruments.[112] To this end, the EU has gone beyond the simple requirements and has established effective mechanisms of control and enforcement, whereas ASEAN has transposed the international norms without going further in the requirements and has not developed any enforcement mechanisms.

1. Looking *at* the fundamentals of the EU understanding of mutual trust: Common human rights standards

This tension between facilitating interstate cooperation and guaranteeing human rights is not new. Although 'freedom' appears first in the 'Area of Freedom, Security and Justice', the EU does not seem to be a legal space primarily founded on the protection of fundamental rights. Rather, it seems to have security measures prevailing over freedom, especially in recent years. European security has in fact been the driving force behind the establishment and swiftness of cross-border cooperation in criminal matters.[113] This tension has been the object of numerous judicial and doctrinal debates.

The *Treaty on the EU* states that the Union is founded on the 'respect for human dignity, freedom, democracy, equality, the rule of law and respect for human rights, including the rights of persons belonging to minorities'. It then provides that '[t]hese values are common to the Member States in a society in which pluralism, non-discrimination, tolerance, justice, solidarity and equality between women and men prevail'.[114] Besides the international norms related to human rights, two main regional conventions apply in the EU. Firstly, all Member States are bound by the

[112] See, e.g., Xanthopoulou (2020): 85.
[113] Ibid.: 84–85.
[114] Art. 2, TEU.

European Convention of Human Rights and submitted to the jurisdiction of the Court of Strasbourg.[115] Secondly, the *Charter of Fundamental Rights of the European Union* proclaimed in the *Treaty of Nice* on 7 December 2000, as a EU instrument, was integrated into the EU constitutional package with the Lisbon Treaty.[116] The Charter is binding upon EU institutions when adopting norms and measures as well as Member States when implementing them. The respect for the fundamental rights recognised by the Charter is a condition of the lawfulness of EU acts, so that measures incompatible with those rights are not acceptable in the EU.[117] The CJEU ensures its full compliance. It is thus hard to deny that Member States, at least formally, adhere, together, to fundamental values such as democracy, the rule of law and respect for human rights and that the legal systems recognise the basic principles of criminal justice. These values form the foundation of the Union and are direct requirements for membership.[118]

It is those common standards and mechanisms of control and enforcement that have justified and given its special status to mutual trust in the EU. They constitute the main justification for the presupposition according to which all Member States comply with the fundamental rights enshrined in EU law.[119] The Member States are required to presume that fundamental rights have been observed by the other Member States. They shall abstain from checking whether other Member States have observed the fundamental rights guaranteed by the EU.[120] The objective is to avoid duplicate controls and smoothen cross-border cooperation.

While significant role to the developments and interpretation of the EU norms, the CJEU has also played an important role in evaluating the balance between security and human rights. Its judgements may have led to changes in the EU legislation.[121]

---

[115] Art. 6(3), TEU.

[116] EU Charter as integrated into the EU constitutional framework by Art. 6(1) TEU.

[117] Art. 6(1) TEU: 'The Union recognises the rights, freedoms and principles set out in the Charter of Fundamental Rights of the European Union of 7 December 2000, as adapted at Strasbourg, on 12 December 2007, which shall have the same legal value as the Treaties'. See, e.g., CJEU, *Kadi and Al Barakaat International Foundation* v. *Council and Commission*, Joined Cases C-402/05 P and C-415/05 P, judgement, ECLI:EU:C:2008:461, 3 September 2008, paras. 283–284 and the following Kadi judgements. More recently, CJEU, Opinion 2/13, para. 169.

[118] Arts. 2 and 6, TEU.

[119] To that effect, CJEU, *N.S. and others*, Joined Cases C-411/10 and C-493/10, judgement, ECLI: EU:C:2011:865, 21 December 2011, paras. 78–80; and *Melloni* v. *Ministerio Fiscal*, C-399/11, judgement (Grand Chamber), ECLI:EU:C:2013:107, 26 February 2013, paras. 37 and 63; also, CJEU, Opinion 2/13, para. 191. See Sergio Carrera et al., 'Criminal Justice and Police Cooperation between the EU and the UK after Brexit. Towards a principled and trust-based partnership', ed. Peter Hustinx and Michael Kennedy, CEPS & QMUL (Bruxelles: Centre for European Policy Studies, August 2018): v.

[120] CJEU, Opinion 2/13, para. 192. See also, Xanthopoulou (2020): 26–45.

[121] See, e.g., CJEU, *Pupino*, C-105/03, judgement, ECLI:EU:C:2005:386, 16 June 2005; *People's Mojahedin Organization of Iran* v. *Council of the European Union*, T-256/07, judgement, ECLI: EU:T:2008:461, 23 October 2008; *People's Mojahedin Organization of Iran* v. *Council of the European Union*, T-284/08, judgement, ECLI:EU:T:2008:593, 17 December 2008; *Commission*

As it is sometimes debated, it is questionable whether or not the Court has raised the human rights requirements to such a level that might limit cooperation in criminal matters within the EU.

Mutual trust has been discussed by both the Courts of Luxembourg and Strasbourg. Some cases demonstrated that this presumption of respect of fundamental rights is not absolute. In particular, the CJEU ruled in 2011 in the *N.S.* case on asylum that this presumption may be rebutted.[122] Stating this, the Court altered interstate cooperation in the AFSJ. According to Pr. Mitsilegas, this decision puts an end to the 'automaticity in interstate cooperative systems in the fields of criminal law'.[123] Although fundamental rights are still assumed,[124] their protection is not a blank check for Member States to cooperate without respecting fundamental rights *in concreto*.[125]

First developed in the field of immigration, the Advocate General Tanchev to the CJEU defended the effectiveness of the Dublin transfer in the name of the presumption of mutual trust.[126] His opinion was not followed by the Court. While acknowledging that the EU was not bound by ECHR,[127] the CJEU stated that, other than those situations where 'systemic deficiencies' exist in the responsible State against individuals, any transfer of asylum seekers shall be excluded where it gives rise to a real risk for the individual concerned to suffer inhuman or degrading treatment. Finally, the Court concluded that this position 'fully respected the principle of mutual trust since, far from affecting the presumption of respect of fundamental rights by Member States, it ensures that exceptional situations are duly taken into consideration by Member States'.[128] This ruling introduces a crucial change when acknowledging the necessary interdependence of the principle of mutual trust and the protection of individuals against inhuman and degrading treatment.[129]

---

and Others v. *Kadi*, Joined Cases C-584/10 P, C-593/10 P and C-595/10 P, judgement (Grand Chamber), ECLI:EU:C:2013:518, 18 July 2013.

[122] CJEU, *N.S. and others*, Joined Cases C-411/10 and C-493/10, para. 86.

[123] Mitsilegas, 'The Limits of Mutual Trust in Europe's Area of Freedom, Security and Justice' (2012): 358; Xanthopoulou (2020): 25.

[124] CJEU, *Bundesrepublik Deutschland* v. *Puid*, C-4/11, judgement (Grand Chamber), ECLI:EU:C:2013:740, 14 November 2013; *Abdullahi* v. *Bundesasylamt*, C-394/12, judgement (Grand Chamber), ECLI:EU:C:2013:813, 10 December 2013.

[125] CJEU, *Radu*, C-396/11, judgement (Grand Chamber), ECLI:EU:C:2013:39, 29 January 2013; *N.S. and others*, para. 82; Opinion 2/13, para. 191. Cecilia Rizcallah, 'The Dublin system: the ECJ Squares the Circle Between Mutual Trust and Human Rights Protection' *EU Law Analysis*: available at https://bit.ly/2Z7qbtq (accessed on 21 February 2017).

[126] CJEU, *C.K. and others* v. *Republika Slovenija*, C-578/17 PPU, Opinion of Advocate General Tanchev, ECLI:EU:C:2017:108, 9 February 2017, para. 51.

[127] Ibid., para. 52.

[128] Ibid., para. 95.

[129] As Art. 2 TEU specifies '[t]he Union is founded on the values of respect for human dignity, freedom, democracy, equality, the rule of law and respect for human rights, including the rights of persons belonging to minorities. These values are common to the Member States in a society in

The reasoning of the Court was then extended to criminal law. Until recently, the Court seemed very reluctant to acknowledge any exception to the principle of mutual trust in criminal matters, especially in the framework of the European arrest warrant.[130] Notably, the CJEU held, in the *Melloni* case, that Member States must not apply higher fundamental rights protection standards that would jeopardise the primacy, unity or effectiveness of EU law.[131] Yet, the German Constitutional Court did not hesitate, in its decision of 15 December 2015, to make an exception to the principle of mutual trust, as implemented by the European arrest warrant system, in order to protect the right of human dignity, which, according to this ruling, forms part of German constitutional identity.[132] This case led to a tense dialogue between national courts and the CJEU.

It is with the cases of *Aranyosi and Căldăraru* and *Kovalkovas*[133] judged in 2016 that the CJEU rebutted the absolute nature of the presumption of mutual trust in criminal matters.[134] Similar to asylum cases, the Court eventually recognised that 'the principle of mutual trust requires each of those States, save in exceptional circumstances, to consider all the other Member States to be complying with EU law and particularly with the fundamental rights recognised by EU law'.[135] The Court stated that where the authority responsible for the execution of a warrant has in its possession evidence of a real risk of inhuman or degrading treatment of persons detained in the Member State where the warrant was issued that authority must assess that risk before deciding on the surrender of the individual concerned. In practice, such evaluation is not obvious and such a national decision is not easy to take. The Court highlighted that limitations to the principle of mutual trust could be made in 'exceptional circumstances',[136] as proclaimed in Opinion 2/13.[137] Mutual trust no longer means 'blind trust'.[138]

---

which pluralism, non-discrimination, tolerance, justice, solidarity and equality between women and men prevail'. Also, CJEU, Opinion 2/13, para. 168.

[130] See, among other cases, CJEU, *Radu*, C-396/11 and *Melloni*, C-399/11.

[131] *Melloni*, C-399/11, para. 60.

[132] Bundesverfassungsgericht, Headnotes to the order of the Second Senate of 15 December 2015, 2BvR 2735/14: available at https://bit.ly/3ueq3q2 (accessed on 18 October 2017).

[133] CJEU, *Aranyosi and Caldaru*, Joined Cases C-404/15 and C-659/15 PPU, judgement (Grand Chamber), ECLI:EU:C:2016:198, 5 April 2016; *Kovalkovas*, C-477/16 PPU, judgement, ECLI:EU: C:2016:861, 10 November 2016. On the consequences of the case *Aranyosi and Caldaru*, see, e.g., Adam Lazowski, 'The Sky Is Not the Limit: Mutual Trust and Mutual Recognition après Aranyosi and Caldararu', *Croatian Yearbook of European Law and Policy,* vol. 14, no. 1 (2018).

[134] See, e.g., Bribosia and Weyembergh (2016).

[135] CJEU, *Aranyosi and Căldăraru* (2016), C-404/15 and C-659/15 PPU, para. 78; *Kovalkovas* (2016), C-477/16 PPU, para. 27.

[136] *Aranyosi and Căldăraru* (2016), para. 82.

[137] CJEU, Opinion 2/13 (full court), 18 December 2014.

[138] Carrera et al. (2018): vi; Xanthopoulou (2020): 29–36; Tony Marguery, 'Confiance mutuelle, reconnaissance mutuelle et crise de valeurs: la difficile équation entre justice pénale européenne et diversité nationale', *European papers,* vol. 5, no. 3 (2020).

More recently, the operationalisation of mutual trust has taken a new step during the evaluation of the rule of law crisis in Poland. It was feared that Poland breached the principle of judicial independence in light of the recent reforms to the judicial system. The CJEU was consequently asked whether the European arrest warrant might be rejected where there is a reasonable suspicion that the right to a fair trial has been breached in light of reports indicating systematic breaches of the rule of law. In this case, the Court accepted that mutual trust might be challenged where non-absolute rights are under threat, i.e. when there is a real risk of breach of the essence of the right.[139]

It must be highlighted that in this period of huge waves of migration and with some Member States such as Poland and Hungary taking backward steps in fundamental rights protection, the unity of the human rights standards is in serious jeopardy and, with it, the concept mutual trust and its effective implementation within the EU.[140]

Regarding the place of mutual trust in terrorism-related cases, the CJEU has been very active in ensuring a good balance between security and liberties and in framing the role of mutual trust. EU Member States have often used international law to shield enforcement actions from the Union's human rights standards.[141] There were many discussions on the impact of the measures imposed by the Security Council to States (e.g. blacklists) on human rights.[142] In the *Kadi II* case, the Advocate General Bot considered that:

> an effective global fight against terrorism requires confidence and collaboration between the participating international, regional and national institutions, rather than mistrust. The mutual confidence which must exist between the European Union and the United Nations is justified by the fact that the values concerning respect for fundamental rights are shared by those two organisations.[143]

The CJEU did not follow the reasoning of the Advocate General and even advocates for a standard of evidence-based, detailed, substantive judicial review *in concreto*

---

[139] CJEU, *L.M.*, C-216/18 PPU, judgement (Grand Chamber), ECLI:EU:C:2018:586, 28 June 2018. At the national level, see, e.g., the French Cour de Cassation (Criminal Chamber), case No. 20-87.140, 12 January 2021; Xanthopoulou (2020): 39–40.

[140] See, e.g., Cecilia Rizcallah, 'Le principe de confiance mutuelle dans l'Union européenne: un principe en péril', *Les cahiers de la justice,* vol. 2022/3, no. 3 (2022).

[141] Valsamis Mitsilegas, 'The European Union and the Global Governance of Crime' in *Globalisation, Criminal Law and Criminal Justice. Theoretical, Comparative and Transnational Perspectives*, eds., Valsamis Mitsilegas, Peter Alldridge, and Leonidas Cheliotis (Oxford: Hart Publishing, 2015): 198.

[142] See, e.g., CJEU, *Kadi and Al Barakaat International Foundation* v. *Council and Commission*, Joined Cases C-402/05 P and C-415/05 P, judgement, ECLI:EU:C:2008:461, 3 September 2008*;* *Hassan* and *Ayadi*, Joined Cases C-399/06 and C-403/06, judgement, ECLI:EU:C:2009:748, 3 December 2009*;* *EP* v. *Council of the EU,* C-130/10, judgement (action for annulment), ECLI: EU:C:2012:472, 11 March 2010*;* *Commission* v. *Kadi*, Joined Cases C-584/10 P, C-593/10 P, and C-595/10 P.

[143] Opinion of Advocate General Bot, *European Commission* v. *Kadi*, Joined Cases C-584/10P, C-593/10 and C-595/10P, ECLI:EU:C:2013:176, 19 March 2013, para. 85.

and not *in abstracto*.[144] The Court confirmed, as in *Kadi I*,[145] the autonomy of the EU legal order based on the respect for the rule of law and fundamental rights. The interactions between the regional and/or international organisations have also had an impact on the establishment of a consistent regional framework. Any divergence between the international and regional legal frameworks may lead to inconsistency in the Member States approach vis-à-vis these rules. When anti-terrorism and human rights norms confront each other, mutual trust decreases, as Member States may not prioritise the same set of rules.

Within this uncertain space, finding a threshold limiting mutual trust could make the fundamental premise behind the concept collapse.[146] Suggesting a strict threshold of fundamental rights' protection to a legal fiction, that all Member States respect in a similar manner, would be quite a paradox. Legal standards may support mutual trust, but a strict framing of the concept would annihilate its very existence.

After this overview of the judicial debates, a brief mention must be made of the parallel debates between the CJEU and the European Court of Human Rights (ECtHR). Attempting to ensure a harmonised response within the two courts, the European Commission repeatedly proposed (in 1979, 1990 and 1993) the accession of the European Community to the European Convention on Human Rights (ECHR). The CJEU found in its Opinion 2/94[147] that the Treaty did not foresee any competence for the EC to enact rules on human rights or to conclude international conventions in this field, making accession legally impossible. Over time, European discussions have had an impact on the compatibility of EU human rights standards with the ECHR. In 2009, the Treaty of Lisbon remedied the legal incompatibility by introducing Article 6(2) in the TEU, which provides that the EU shall accede to the ECHR. This means that the EU, as is already the case for its Member States, would become subject to external control, as such by the ECtHR. Yet, no accession occurred at that time. In fact, the absence of verification of the effective respect of fundamental rights was heavily criticised and condemned by the Strasbourg Court in 2014.[148] It was even an argument against the accession of the EU to the ECHR.[149] After 4 years of negotiations, the CJEU issued a negative opinion on 18 December 2014 stating that the *Draft Agreement on the Accession of the European Union to the European Convention for the Protection of Human Rights and fundamental Freedoms* was liable to adversely affect the specific characteristics and the autonomy of EU law (Opinion 2/13).[150] Due to the 'systemic deficiencies'

[144] *Kadi* (2013), Joined Cases C-584/10P, C-593/10P and C-595/10P, paras. 121–124.

[145] *Kadi* (2008), Joined Cases C-402/05 P and C-415/05 P.

[146] Mitsilegas, 'The Limits of Mutual Trust in Europe's Area of Freedom, Security and Justice' (2012): 362; Xanthopoulou (2020): 43–44.

[147] European Court of Justice (ECJ), Opinion of the Court pursuant to Article 228 of the EC Treaty on the Accession by the Community to the European Convention for the Protection of Human Rights and Fundamental Freedoms, Opinion 2/94, ECLI:EU:1996:140, 28 March 1996.

[148] European Court of Human Rights (ECtHR), *Tarakhel* v. *Switzerland*, App. No. 29217/12, judgement (Grand Chamber), ECLI:CE:ECHR:2014:1104JUD002921712, 4 November 2014.

[149] CJEU, Opinion 2/13.

[150] Ibid.

test developed in the EU, the ECtHR considered the absence of 'check that another Member State has observed fundamental rights, even though EU law imposes an obligation of mutual trust between those Member States' was incompatible with the ECHR.[151] However, the case-law of the two courts have moved closer together and they recognise each other's case-law in various fields.[152] The ECtHR even recognises that limitations to the principles of mutual recognition and mutual trust can be admitted, but only 'in exceptional circumstances'.[153]

On 31 October 2019, the President and the First Vice-President of the European Commission informed the Secretary General of the Council of Europe that the EU stood ready to resume the negotiations on its accession to the ECHR. Discussions about the conduct of the negotiations resumed.[154] A series of ad hoc meetings composed of representatives of the 47 Member States of the Council of Europe and a representative of the EU have been taking place. The adoption of the legal instruments setting out the modalities of accession of the EU to the ECHR (ETS No. 5), including its participation in the Convention system, and the related issues were identified as a matter of priority on 15 January 2020. Subsequent meetings have followed along the same line but nothing has been decided so far.

Before any case of violation of human rights is brought to court, no particular body carries out any general evaluation of the Member States' human rights records. It must nonetheless be noted that the Venice Commission under the Council of Europe provides legal advice to its members and helps them bring their legal and institutional structures into line with European standards.[155] This type of commission remains consultative, without holding any enforcement powers.

2. Looking *for* regional human rights standards in ASEAN: A slow and difficult political endeavour unrelated to the building up of mutual trust?

In ASEAN, interstate cooperation seems rather devoid of human rights concerns. Preventing and countering terrorism is the priority over any other considerations. States trust each other—up to a certain point—because they have the same objective and agree on certain common measures. However, nowhere in the texts are common human rights standards mentioned as a constructive element in building mutual trust and as a condition for cooperation.

[151] Ibid., para. 194.

[152] CJEU, *Aranyosi and Căldăraru* (2016), para. 78 and 82; ECtHR, *Avotins* v. *Latvia*, app. 17502/07, Grand Chamber, 23 May 2016, paras. 46 and ff., 101 and ff., especially para. 104. The ECtHR recognised the application of a comparable protection between the guarantees of the ECHR and the EU human rights principles applied within the region.

[153] See ECtHR, *Varga and others* v. *Hungary*, App. No. 14097/12, 45135/12, 73712/12, and al., judgement (Grand Chamber), ECLI:CE:ECHR:2015:0310JUD001409712, 5 April 2016, para. 78 and 82; *Avotins* v. *Latvia* (2016). See also e.g. Bribosia and Weyembergh (2016).

[154] See on the Council of Europe Portal, the latest news about the EU accession to the ECHR: available at https://bit.ly/3xP4nDp (accessed on 28 August 2020).

[155] Venice Commission of the Council of Europe, 'For Democracy Through Law': available at http://www.venice.coe.int/webforms/events/default.aspx?lang=en (accessed on 16 February 2018).

The strong national divergences relating to matters of human rights, and the apparent lack of knowledge about each other's legislations, need to be addressed before they are able to state that the protection of human rights is a component of mutual trust. The adoption of the *ASEAN Human Rights Declaration* (AHRD) in 2012 could be seen as Member States overcoming their differences. This step could indeed suggest that the Member States understand that human rights are no longer a domestic issue.[156] However, in practice, evidence suggests that the Declaration has not yet had a notable impact on the protection of human rights in the region.

The ASEAN Intergovernmental Commission on Human Rights (AICHR) is working through soft collaborations and dialogues in order to foster the effective implementation of the AHRD. AICHR organises workshops which are intended to be a platform of exchanging and sharing experiences, best practices and lessons learned amongst participants on the implementation of effective measures on human rights in the region.[157] There is no regional court—and therefore no case-law—ensuring an effective and harmonised protection of human rights proclaimed in the Declaration.

The Declaration seems to be a soft political engagement with objectives to reach instead of a legal binding instrument engaging the Member States on the international plane. The Declaration nonetheless constitutes a common ground for discussions. Moving forward, it may enhance future cooperation in criminal matters thanks to an equivalent protection of human rights within the Southeast Asian region. Although not foreseen, the establishment of regional mechanisms of control would also be a significant step in guaranteeing these rights.

In the current ASEAN's state of the law, the enactment of regional human rights standards does not constitute a common background for fostering mutual trust between Member States.[158] Instead, mutual trust is something that remains to be built upon through diplomacy and interpersonal relations.[159]

---

[156] See, e.g., AICHR 'ASEAN member states reaffirm their commitment to human rights dialogue', Siem Reap, 19 November 2022: available at https://aichr.org/news/asean-member-states-reaffirm-their-commitment-to-human-rights-dialogue/ (accessed on 27 December 2022); 'ASEAN celebrates 10 years of Human Rights Declaration' (ceremony hold in Siem Reap on 18 November 2022), 28 November 2022: available at https://asean.org/asean-celebrates-10-years-of-human-rights-declaration/ (accessed on 26 December 2022).

[157] ASEAN Intergovernmental Commission on Human Rights (AICHR), 'Sharing national experience on human rights implementation in ASEAN', 23 December 2014: available at http://aichr.org/press-release/sharing-national-experience-on-human-rights-implementation-in-asean/ (accessed on 9 December 2015).

[158] See further elaboration in Chap. 5.

[159] See, e.g., Robin Ramcharan, 'ASEAN's Human Rights Commission: Policy Considerations for Enhancing its Capacity to Protect Human Rights', *University College London Human Rights Review,* vol. 3 (2010); Attilio Pisanò, 'Human Rights and Sovereignty in the ASEAN Path Towards a Human Rights Declaration', *Human Rights Review,* vol. 15 (2014); Shahrim Tamrin, 'AICHR: Diplomacy between countries is an important tool to remove death penalty' *Human Rights in ASEAN*, 16 June 2015): available at https://humanrightsinasean.info/article/aichr-diplomacy-between-countries-important-tool-remove-death-penalty.html (accessed on 1 June 2017); Ministry

While building mutual trust, the EU has adopted human rights norms and control mechanisms that go further than the international norms, whereas ASEAN has transposed at the regional level international norms. Those standards and control mechanisms have become a significant element in the enhancement of mutual trust within the EU, whereas mutual trust does not seem to be built upon a regionalisation of human rights in ASEAN.

Taking the experience of the EU and acknowledging the international human rights standards, the protection of human rights should be part of the components of mutual trust. Interestingly, the lack of respect for human rights and for the rule of law is increasingly recognised, including by the UN, as undermining the programmes implemented to prevent and combat terrorism, including violent extremism, and lead to mistrust.[160]

II. Tailoring Regional Methods to Build Up Mutual Trust: Ways to Bolster Cooperation

As shown, one cannot proclaim that mutual trust exists de facto in regional cooperation. It too cannot be said that it is easy to implement. Mutual trust needs to be built and nourished by the relevant stakeholders, dependent upon their willingness to accept risks to reach a shared objective, as well as upon the means at their disposal.

Various measures have been debated, adopted and implemented in order to develop mutual trust between the relevant authorities, while taking each other's characteristics into consideration. The following chapters examine and compare the EU and ASEAN's respective approaches in this respect. In so doing, these chapters focus on the measures and methods adopted that might eventually lead towards the aforementioned two main legal developments: the approximation of the relevant national legislations on the one end of the spectrum, and the establishment of common standards in terms of protection of human rights and enforcement mechanisms on the other. Developing and consolidating common standards and norms constitutes a significant added value in the process of building mutual trust amongst the relevant actors. The measures adopted and implemented upon this process might however diverge in their adaption within the specific context of each region. Taking the specifics of each region, and that of their respective countries, into consideration ensures that the measures to establish mutual trust and to develop cross-border cooperation are effective and respectful of each relevant regional context. Development and enhancement of mutual trust and cooperation have been defined on the basis of regional history, culture and experience. Against their respective background, the EU has adopted a more legalistic approach in building up mutual trust

of Foreign Affairs of the Republic of Indonesia, 'Understanding the Challenges of Human Rights Diplomacy in Indonesia', 1 June 2017): available at http://www.kemlu.go.id/en/berita/Pages/understanding-challenges-human-rights-diplomacy-indonesia.aspx (accessed on 1 June 2017).

[160] See, e.g., A/HRC/43/46(2020), 'Human rights impact of policies and practices aimed at preventing and countering violent extremism' Report of the Special Rapporteur on the promotion and protection of human rights and fundamental freedoms while countering terrorism.

leaving less space to the traditional understanding of trust (A) and ASEAN with a more flexible approach (B).

A. A Trend Towards an Institutionalisation and 'Legal' Accompaniment of Mutual Trust in the EU: Aiming for Legal Expectations?

Defending the EU supranational and integrated approach, the European Commission noted 'the central importance of EU policies to building mutual trust between Member States' law enforcement and judicial authorities as well as towards EU agencies [...which is] especially the case in the fight against terrorism where traditional channels for structured information exchange and operational cooperation have been bilateral, rather than at EU level'.[161]

Although the EU has progressively clearly institutionalised and legalised intra-regional interactions, cooperation has first progressed through informal means. These informal interactions remain very present and critical. The numerous 'non-legal' actions (i.e. interpersonal relations, training and networking fostering mutual learning and understanding) are usually the preliminary steps leading to the development of a norm and/or to its effective implementation and may still sometimes be the only channel of cooperation. It also supports anything else that cannot be erected as law and is essential to favour the good functioning of formal mechanisms of interactions.

Acknowledging and declaring this search for completeness, not only does the TFEU require States to criminalise offences concerned with mutual recognition and provides guidelines to enhance police and judicial cooperation, but it also encourages competent national authorities to organise training activities.[162] The EU has adopted a multilevel (governments, police and judicial actors and other stakeholders) and multi-tasking approach (legal and non-legal measures).

The EU indeed aims to achieve a comprehensive approach which places an increasing focus on legal measures[163] coupling, on the one hand, legalised mechanisms of interstate cooperation and institutionalised regional agencies facilitating such cooperation; and, on the other hand, informal bilateral and multilateral interactions, including through networks.[164] Taking the sharing of data as a core

---

[161] Pt. 2.2., European Commission, 'Comprehensive Assessment of EU Security Policy', COM (2017) 407.

[162] Arts. 82(1) and 87(1), TFEU.

[163] See the numerous EU instruments adopted on the AFSJ, such as *Council Framework Decision 2002/475/JHA on combating terrorism*; *Council Framework Decision 2006/960/JHA on simplifying the exchange of information and intelligence between law enforcement authorities*; *Council Framework Decision 2008/919/JHA on combating terrorism*; *Directive 2016/680 on the protection of natural persons with regard to the processing of personal data by competent authorities for the purposes of the prevention, investigation, detection or prosecution of criminal offences*; *Europol Regulation*.

[164] See, e.g., Art. 4, *Council Decision 2008/976/JHA of 16 December 2008 on the European Judicial Network*, O.J.E.U. L348/130, 24 December 2008; Art. 2(7), *Council Decision 2009/426/JHA on the strengthening of Eurojust and amending Decision 2002/187/JHA setting up Eurojust with a view to reinforcing the fight against serious crime* on the liaison officers and liaison

Table 3.2 EU's action in developing cross-border cooperation

Legal and non-legal/informal measures	Conceptual means	Objective
Implementation of EU-wide human rights norms + Approximation of relevant legislations + Development of interpersonal relations →	Enhancement of mutual trust between the relevant national and regional authorities (worthiness of developing means to enhance cooperation) →	Facilitation and legitimation of an increasingly ambitious cross-border cooperation

mechanism of cooperation, the establishment of Europol and Eurojust, two regional agencies gathering together the respective competent national authorities of the EU Member States, has not only for objective to host EU databases and institutionalised systems of cooperation but it also aims to facilitate the direct dialogue between competent national authorities and to host trainings/meetings on common issues. Similarly, the European Judicial Training Network, which favours formal and informal contacts, has been praised for its positive results in enhancing mutual trust amongst practitioners (Table 3.2).[165]

B. Avoiding any Legal Expectation: A More Flexible Understanding of Mutual Trust in ASEAN

ASEAN, with its less structured architecture, is the scene for fora of strategic discussions between officials as well as informal operational cooperation between field agents.[166] ASEAN provisions which foster cooperation remain broad and their normative force is almost non-existent. This is the primary difference between ASEAN and the EU in their method and aim to build mutual trust between competent national authorities (Table 3.3).

The EU may be considered as a step ahead in comparison with ASEAN in their legal and institutional integration processes and their enactment of enforceable mechanisms of cooperation. Yet, Member States in the two regions have used informal channels to share experiences and knowledge since the creation of their regional organisation. It governed horizontal intra-regional relations in the 1970s up

magistrates; pts. 1.2.6. and 3.2.1., Stockholm Programme. See also the European Judicial Training Network (EJTN): available at http://www.ejtn.eu/ (accessed on 16 February 2018) and Judicial Training Principles: available at https://bit.ly/3a7Pq5l (accessed on 16 February 2018).

[165] For more information, see the EJTN website; also, Carrera et al. (2018): 136.

[166] Rodolfo C. Severino, Secretary-General of the ASEAN, 'The ASEAN Way and the rule of law', International Law Conference on ASEAN Legal Systems and Regional Integration, sponsored by the Asia-Europe Institute and the Faculty of Law, University of Malaya, 3 September 2001: available at https://bit.ly/2OhtTyy (accessed on 18 April 2015).

Table 3.3 ASEAN's action in developing cross-border cooperation

Non-legal (or too broad to have any precise outcome)/informal measures	**Conceptual means**	**Objective**
Mostly soft power, with a focus on interpersonal relations (social component) + Political proclamation of human rights without control (weak political component) + Slight approximation of legislations based on international norms rather than regional ones (weak political component), but agreement on the way forward (i.e. objective and broad means)	Establishment of social trust between competent national authorities Low and/or varying (depending on the regime in place at a 't' moment in a country) political trust Agreement on the means to implement in order to tackle terrorism	Slow and informal facilitation cross-border cooperation

until the end of the '80s in the EU[167] and remains essential to police and judicial cooperation nowadays. Informal channels are the sole actual method of cooperation within ASEAN. Except from the cooperation through the *ASEAN Treaty on MLACM* that slightly formalises cooperation between judicial authorities, interpersonal relations are necessary to make cross-border cooperation effective.[168] Throughout its evolution, the EU has gone from informal interactions only to more formal supranational and intergovernmental channels of interactions and decision-making. At present, ASEAN's approach remains two-fold: (a) informal—operational cooperation—channels of cooperation between foreign authorities of a 'lower level', namely law enforcement authorities, intelligence services (up to a certain point) or immigration authorities; and (b) a combination of formal and informal channels—intergovernmental decision-making and strategic collaboration—between the ASEAN official representatives, namely the head of governments and ministers.

[167] For example, the TREVI Group was based on informal relations between competent authorities. On this group, Tony Bunyan, 'Trevi, Europol and the European State' in *Statewatching the New Europe*, ed., Tony Bunyan (London: Statewatch, 1993).

[168] *ASEAN Treaty on Mutual Legal Assistance in Criminal Matters* (2004); Acharya defines the ASEAN Way as 'a process of regional interactions and cooperation based on discreteness, informality, consensus building and non-confrontational bargaining styles'. Amitav Acharya, *Constructing a Security Community in Southeast Asia. ASEAN and the problem of regional order*, Politics in Asia series (New York: Routledge, 2001): 63.

The characteristics of the 'ASEAN Way'[169] make the regional structure more flexible in comparison with the more integrated approach of the EU.[170] It is also important to recall the diversity of ASEAN's ten member countries. The ASEAN population speak hundreds of languages, belong to all of the major religions of the world, and draw their appearances from numerous ethnic groups. Due to this diversity, ASEAN has much to overcome before it might represent a harmonised voice on an international stage—not that the EU always presents the common voice of its members and certainly not without many negotiations—and before it might potentially reach its own particular form of integrated structure. ASEAN's creation was nonetheless based on the promise that cooperation among nations in the spirit of equality and partnership would bring mutual benefits and stimulate solidarity which contribute to building the foundations for peace, stability and prosperity in the world at large and in the ASEAN region in particular. Accordingly, ASEAN Member States have increased the fora of exchanges by way of training activities, workshops and other means of discussions. At these fora, competent national authorities can exchange experience, information and network to further extend and deepen cooperation as opposed to the development of binding norms and creating institutions. In fact, it has become 'ASEAN practice for Ministers and officials of ASEAN governments to maintain close contacts with each other through ASEAN Meetings and through informal multilateral visits'.[171] The ASEAN architecture serves as a general umbrella to develop bilateral and multilateral relations. When discussing the ASEAN Regional Forum (ARF), H.E. Pr. S. Jayakumar Minister for Foreign Affairs of Singapore declared that '[b]ilateral dialogue and cooperation should of course always continue, but the complexity of our interdependent world calls for us to go beyond bilateral relationships'.[172] The place of multilateralism has become increasingly prominent in the region. However, the regional institutional and legal endeavours that have emerged have been few and limited in nature.

In this region, the UN is a significant actor which fosters discussions on topical subjects considered to be better addressed at the regional level. Many training activities and workshops are organised by the UNODC Regional Office for Southeast Asian and the Pacific (ROSEAP) to ensure that international norms are respected. For instance, the UNODC organised a training programme for collaborative intelligence, investigation and prosecution of terrorism-related cases organised

---

[169] Further developed in Chap. 4.

[170] Céline C. Cocq, 'The EU and ASEAN approaches in fighting terrorism: collaboration or cooperation?' in *Countering Daesh Extremism. European and Asian Responses*, Panorama: Insights into Asian and European Affairs (Singapore: Konrad Adenauer Stiftung, 2016).

[171] H. E. Mr. Lee Kuan Yew, Prime Minister of the Republic of Singapore, Opening Address, 15th ASEAN Ministerial Meeting and Post-Ministerial Meeting with The Dialogue countries, Singapore, 14–18 June 1982.

[172] H. E. Pr. S. Jayakumar, Minister for Foreign Affairs of Singapore, Opening Statement, 27th ASEAN Ministerial Meeting, Bangkok, 22 July 1994; ASEAN Regional Forum and Post-Ministerial Conferences with dialogue partners, Bangkok, 22–28 July 1994.

with the support of the EU in General Santos City on 18–22 April 2016. The objective of this training was to ensure the transposition into the national legislation of international norms. At this workshop, presentations were made on the anti-terrorism legislation and the way to implement it on the field by 'instructors' who were various national authorities, such as a public prosecutor, the head of the anti-terrorism section. Practical cases were then submitted for them to work on together. In addition to their added value regarding international norms implementation, training activities of national authorities[173] are also useful to develop networking and share experiences and knowledge. This meeting was purely national as inter-agency cooperation is not obvious either and it is still based on interpersonal relations and trust. The UN uses every opportunity to help Member States, more specifically the relevant national authorities, to develop channels of cooperation through networking and effective means of cooperation. For example, tablets were given by the border management programme of the UNODC-ROSEAP to border patrols in order to help them communicate and exchange data on cross-border crime.

All of these meetings, especially the close-doors dialogues, which were organised either by external actors or by the ASEAN Member States themselves (e.g. the annual ASEAN Summits organised by the Member State chairing during this period[174]) have helped build mutual understanding and trust between competent national authorities.[175]

An illustration of the development of channels of cooperation between law enforcement authorities within each region is the regional 'bodies' dedicated to this task. Aseanapol,[176] gathering ASEAN Chiefs of Police, is a forum of discussions aiming to harmonise and standardise coordination and communication mechanisms amongst police officers. There is still a long way to go before achieving more systematic interactions between ASEAN police authorities. As a reference for comparison, Aseanapol would better be compared to the former European Police

[173] See, e.g., UNODC, 'Human Rights and Criminal Justice Responses to Terrorism' *Counter-Terrorism Legal Training Curriculum*, Module 4 (Vienna: UNODC Publications, August 2014).

[174] See the ASEAN Summits since the first one organised in Bali on 23–24 February 1976.

[175] See, e.g., recital 2, *Joint Declaration of ASEAN and China on Cooperation in the Field of Non-Traditional Security Issues*, 6th ASEAN-China Summit, Phnom Penh, 4 November 2002; pt. 3, *Joint Declaration on Cooperation to Combat Terrorism*, 14th ASEAN-EU Ministerial Meeting, Brussels, 27–28 January 2003; recital 10, *ASEAN-Russia Joint Declaration for Cooperation to Combat International terrorism*, Jakarta, 2 July 2004; recital 9, *ASEAN-New Zealand Joint Declaration for Cooperation to Combat International Terrorism*, Vientiane, 29 July 2005; recital 12, *ASEAN-Canada Joint Declaration for Cooperation to Combat International Terrorism*, Kuala Lumpur, 28 July 2006; pt. 16, *ASEAN Comprehensive Plan of Action on Counter Terrorism* (2009); pt. 7, *Blueprint on the ASEAN Political-Security Community*, Heads of State/Government, 14th ASEAN Summit, Cha-Am, 1 March 2009. In the literature, see, e.g., Hiro Katsumata, David Martin Jones, and Michael L.R. Smith, 'ASEAN, Regional Integration and State Sovereignty', *International Security*, vol. 33, no. 2 (2008): 183; 'Reviewing the ASEAN Charter: An Opportunity to Reform ASEAN Processes', Singapore Institute of International Affairs, Policy Brief (Singapore, September 2014): 5.

[176] For further information, see www.aseanapol.org (accessed on 15 April 2015).

Chiefs Operational Task Force which was required by the Tampere European Council in 1999 to be replaced with the Lisbon Treaty by the Standing Committee on Internal Security (COSI) and, doing so, losing the representativeness of police forces. Currently, operational cooperation between EU law enforcement authorities has become much more institutionalised (Europol).

Creating networks and sharing good practices, experience and information between competent national authorities is important to develop and guarantee cooperation, especially in a non-legalised context. However, having a legal architecture might provide more insurance that there will be compliance with the agreed objectives.

C. **Drawing a Data Analysis Matrix for Regional Studies**

Drawing from preliminary observations of the EU and ASEAN experiences and of the UN's work,[177] the different methods aiming to develop mutual trust can be classified into three clusters: capability building, capacity building and knowledge and experience sharing.

Notably, capability building aims at developing a framework for members to work together. It features the structure, faculty, process that can be developed by the members and within which their competences and abilities can be applied. Subsequently, capacity building refers to the process of providing the members the sufficient knowledge, strength, skills and tools to reach what is aimed at. In this particular case, the international, regional, national and even local structures are the legal and/or institutional framework (*capability*) providing the formal possibilities and even, in some cases, obligations to develop and enhance specific means (*capacities*). For instance, channels of communications and data sharing between countries (*information and experience sharing*) are meant to be the most significant way to facilitate cooperation in the prevention and combating of terrorism across borders (final objective). The cluster of information and experience sharing is both independent from and cross-cutting the two other clusters. Information and experience sharing may be an end in itself, but also a means to improve the legal capability and capacity in the fight against terrorism.

---

[177] See, e.g., Commission on Crime Prevention and Criminal Justice, CCPCJ/RES/22/8, *Promoting technical assistance and capacity-building to strengthen national measures and international cooperation against cybercrime*, 26 April 2013; UNODC, 'UNODC Services & Tools. Practical solutions to global threats to justice, security and health': available at https://bit.ly/3rKhuBA (accessed on 10 February); UNODC Terrorism Prevention Branch, *Menu of Services. Legislative and Capacity-Building Assistance to Prevent and Combat Terrorism*: available at https://bit.ly/3aX1qFW (accessed on 8 December 2020). In another domain, see A/RES/69/237, 'Building capacity for the evaluation of development activities at the country level', 19 December 2014; UN, 'Report of the Capacity Building Workshop and Expert Group Meeting on Integrated Approaches to Sustainable Development Planning and Implementation' Department of Economic and Social Affairs, Division for Sustainable Development, New York, 27–29 May 2015. See also the EU approach in ASEAN, Marc Alphonse Vierstraete-Verlinde, 'EU ACTIONPLAN on CT and P/CVE, South-East Asia PRIORITIES', EU Delegation to Indonesia and Brunei Darussalam and Mission to ASEAN, Not for public distribution (Jakarta, December 2019).

These clusters include some specific activities that can be briefly described as follows:

Capability Building:

- Adoption of comprehensive international, regional and national 'constitutional' architectures, national legislations and other appropriate norms in compliance with international and regional norms (with a particular focus on harmonisation of norms and policies);
- Improvement of the national legislations and cooperation mechanisms; and
- Mutual learning on each other respective legal framework(s) to improve the national and, potentially, regional criminal justice systems.

Capacity Building:

- Organisation of trainings for competent national authorities, including police and judicial authorities, to ensure that the effective implementation of international standards by the key actors; and
- Enhancement of the operational capacities (providing technologies, techniques, communications tools and other cooperation means) of law enforcement authorities, prosecutors, judges and all other actors, including potentially intelligence services, involved in the field of criminal justice, and development of their tools to fight serious (transnational) crime.

Knowledge and Experience Sharing:

- Organisation of trainings or workshops for competent national authorities where best practices, experiences and knowledge can be shared;
- Development of networks that should serve as channels for communication between various officials and professionals working in the criminal justice field, including through fora;[178] and
- Evaluation of legal systems and their implementation disseminated to the public and/or competent national authorities (e.g. evaluation of the EU legislation on diverse topics[179]) to learn and implement best practices and methods.

These three clusters complement each other and aim to develop and enhance mutual trust, and subsequently, develop and enhance cooperation between competent national authorities. Although there is no specific order to follow when going through these means of mutual trust building, it is quite clear that, without any legal framework, some capacity building activities, such as the trainings of competent

---

[178] Meeting with Aseanapol's Executive Director Brigadier General Yohanes Agus Mulyono (Indonesian National Police), assisted by representatives from the Philippines National Police (Director of Police Services) and the Indonesian National Police (Director of Plans and Programmes), at Aseanapol Headquarters hosted in the Royal Malaysian Police in Kuala Lumpur, 8 June 2016.

[179] See, e.g., European Commission, COM(2014) 554, Report from the Commission to the European Parliament and the Council on the implementation of Council Framework Decision 2008/919/JHA.

Table 3.4 The operationalisation of mutual trust

Methods (legal or non-legal)		**Conceptual mean(s)**		**Objective(s)**
Capability building; capacity building; knowledge/experience sharing	→	Development and enhancement of mutual trust at the regional level (with a legal dimension or not)	→	Facilitation of cooperation

national authorities, may not be fully implemented. Importantly, the actions under capability building and capacity building are cross-fertilising. Establishing a legal framework that could facilitate cooperation without giving officers the legal authority to implement cooperation mechanisms cannot be successful. Conversely, if competent authorities do not have the necessary legal framework to ensure the sustainability of their actions, their actions may not achieve the desired long-term results.

Mutual trust serves as a conceptual link, as a principle, between will and end (s).[180] In this respect, the means detailed in these clusters are important to ensure the development and the implementation of cooperation mechanisms (Table 3.4).

This schema might apply to all regional organisations, including ASEAN and the EU. However, regions—i.e. the regional organisations and their respective Member States—have adapted the activities of mutual trust building to their regional context and States' abilities, which have led to discrepancies. Some activities are more prominent in one region than the other. Following their own path, the EU and ASEAN Member States have engaged in mutual trust building measures taking both legal (mostly within the EU[181]) and non-legal forms.[182]

The elements encompassing these clusters are analysed throughout this monograph to demonstrate the usefulness of this schema and its accuracy. The long-term objective is to use this schema for further comparative regional analysis and interregional studies.

[180]Willems, 'Mutual trust as a term of art in EU criminal law' (2016): 219.

[181]*Resolution of the Council of 20 November 2009 on a Roadmap for strengthening procedural rights of suspected or accused persons in criminal proceedings*, C295/1. Also, Blackstock (2012).

[182]In the EU, Willems, 'Mutual trust as a term of art in EU criminal law' (2016): 213.

Section 3: Mutual Trust—A Three-Dimensional and Adaptable Principle as a Means or Driving Force Behind Cross-Border Cooperation

As initially stated in this chapter, this study focuses on horizontal relations within regions (i.e. between competent national authorities, including through regional bodies) and between regions.

Mutual trust is a relevant and debated concept, with varying statuses, understandings, degrees and occurring at different levels within the respective regions. These discrepancies prevent from providing a precise definition that would be applicable to each case where interactions take place. However, it is a widely used term that has the advantage of being dynamic and flexible enough to foster cooperation between competent national authorities. In a pragmatic perspective, mutual trust bridges the variations.

The question as to whether associating legal characteristics to mutual trust does not deprive the principle of its original meaning and purpose remains debatable. However, the author has adopted the position that incorporating certain elements of law is not incompatible with the essence of the principle of mutual trust.

Mutual trust has a meaning and a function specific to each environment in which it is meant to be used. Yet, the role of this concept remains unclear as to whether it is a necessary ground for cooperation, or whether it is an intermediate support, or even the result of actions adopted and implemented in order to further develop cooperation. Although it is a malleable concept, mutual trust certainly acts as the gold yardstick with which to develop cross-border cooperation. It is indeed inseparable from cooperation, as a driving force, a complementary element or as a consequence.

Moreover, mutual trust does not imply that the two parties will trust each other on all matters. A partner A may trust partner B to do Y, but maybe not to do Z.[183]

Different methods in building mutual trust have been implemented with the final objective being the fostering and enhancing of cross-border cooperation. It is essential in the two regions to create the conditions that enhance trustworthiness while preserving, as far as possible, the specific identities of national criminal justice systems. Although mutual trust was not meant to disturb the legal diversity within the EU AFSJ, it ended up fostering the adoption of minimum standards in the field of EU criminal law as well as enforceable EU human rights standards.[184] In ASEAN, this diversity is wider and approximation almost non-existent. Rather, the focus is on establishing informal interactions.

The concept of mutual trust and the data analysis matrix, as elaborated upon in this chapter, constitute the yardstick used throughout the different stages of this book. The clusters are not examined sequentially but rather transversally across the consecutive chapters. As aforementioned, the various actions carried out—and

[183] Ibid.: 239.

[184] Willems, *The principle of mutual trust in EU criminal law* (2021).

developed in each cluster—may also nourish more than one cluster. A too-linear approach may only support the hypothesis, while approaching it through different angles might ensure that this rationale is indisputable. The perspective adopted to verify the applicability of this schema is a legal comparative analysis between regions and an EU-ASEAN interregional analysis.

Firstly, Chaps. 4 and 5 examine whether the EU and ASEAN legal architectures foster mutual trust and facilitate cooperation in criminal matters. While Chap. 4 examines the development of the respective regional legal architectures and regional organisations' competences and tasks, Chap. 5 details the analysis of the respective counterterrorism regional legal architectures. These chapters mainly, but not only, put forward the clusters related to capability building and capacity building.

Secondly, based on the results of the two previous chapters, Chap. 6 focuses on the actual intra-regional cooperation between competent national authorities through information and intelligence sharing. This chapter involves a detailed analysis of the third cluster based on the two firsts.

Lastly, Chap. 7 examines the interregional interactions between the EU and ASEAN in the field of counterterrorism. When focusing on interregional relations, this chapter makes very little mention of the third cluster between the regions. Rather, it highlights the way in which EU and ASEAN influence one another—concentrating on the EU's influence on ASEAN—when implementing the three clusters within each region.

Chapter 4
Regional Integration: Tailoring One's Institutional and Legal Architecture

Although the international counterterrorism legal framework is developing, countries' political and legal structures diverge and their objectives may widely differ with one another. In the absence of effective international response, the regional level represents an interesting solution, as gathering countries that may share a common history, face similar issues, aim to the same objective(s) and the like. With that in mind, this chapter examines how the EU and ASEAN institutional and legal architectures have been set up and further developed with the purpose of responding to shared issues, including terrorism, and how they have taken into account their own specificities (i.e. potential political and legal restrictions) while doing so.

This chapter is based on the premise that engaging in a regional integration process is not a natural project in itself. The establishment of interdependent and binding relations between States is an endeavour which challenges their place on the international landscape, their sovereignty and autonomy in relation to other States. It explains the intense caution States use when engaging with a significant project of this nature. Initiating an integration process is a decision formed when intergovernmental or supranational solutions are considered to be more appropriate than those at national level.

Addressing the EU and ASEAN institutional frameworks, this chapter mainly highlights components encompassed in the *capability building* category. Some components of the *capacity building* and *knowledge and experience sharing* categories complement the analysis. By developing their own regional 'constitutional' architectures, the EU and ASEAN members have developed their capabilities to interact within their own region as well as those of the regional organisation, depending on the competence and power which were attributed to it. Establishing a common umbrella, i.e. a common regional institutional and legal architecture, shapes the Member States' action(s). A regional system of governance based on shared values and principles represents and/or fosters mutual trust between its members. Member States may need to have a minimum level of trust in each other

C. C. Cocq, *Mutual Trust in Regional and Interregional Cooperation on Counterterrorism*, United Nations University Series on Regionalism 26,
https://doi.org/10.1007/978-3-031-36612-3_4

in order to develop a regional architecture that would link them together; but such a regional framework may also constitute the basis for developing further mutual trust when providing the guidelines of their common action(s) and the limits of what they may do.

Reaching a coherent regional response against terrorism requires the regional organisations, whatever their structure, to have the capability to coordinate their members' actions on topics they identified as being addressed more effectively when done so together. Within each region, Member States engage in interstate interactions whenever they decide that they cannot succeed with the situation independently but, before doing so, they need to overcome their own national political and legal challenges, and to identify a common ground (Section 1). Subsequently, they tailor their respective regional institutional and legal architecture based on their own background, perspectives and limitations (Section 2). More specifically, the second section focuses on the recently established ASEAN legal personality and questions the shift by the EU and ASEAN from practice-based to rules-based regional approaches. This process clearly impacts each regional legal structure and the vertical relations between the regional organisation and its members, especially the regional organisation's ability to influence and/or impose measures on its members. Depending on the regional legal architecture, the Member States receive varying degrees of incentives from the respective regional organisation to behave in a certain way and fulfil certain tasks to reach their shared goal. This includes criminalising terrorist offences in a more harmonised manner as well as adopting certain cooperation mechanisms.

Section 1: Regional Institutional and Legal Designs—What Are States Getting Themselves into?

Engaging in regional integration is a serious challenge which States are willing to undertake when it provides added value. In practice, they often engage in such processes when under pressure from particular circumstances (e.g. a way to avoid future armed conflicts; the geopolitical necessity to challenge more powerful countries). Although transnational crime may not be at the heart of States' motivation when engaging in a regional integration process, it is usually a subject of concern which drives governments towards the strengthening of regional integration and/or leads to a diversification of their objectives.

Bearing this in mind, States have engaged in different forms of collective engagements chosen and defined according to their own requirements and purpose (I). Highlighting the similarities and differences in approaching the challenges between the two regional systems explains the degree and form of integration in the two regions. Consequently, the emergence of each region's own identity is also a means to further develop a more in-depth regional integration (II).

I. The different forms of collective engagements: between challenges to overcome and opportunity to enhance States' response to transnational issues

Any integration process and/or regionalisation process goes through various phases and may take different forms. Defining these different phases and the associated terminology allows the identification of the level of integration and the form of regionalisation the EU and ASEAN have adopted thus far.

In this context, partner States have engaged in a variety of regional projects depending on the regions and on the domain (i.e. economic, political and/or socio-cultural) (A). In each respective endeavour, partner States have faced serious challenges, including the emergence of an apparent schizophrenic dilemma between protecting their sovereignty and exercising it through their regional organisation (B).

This part of the analysis starts with ASEAN as its regional architecture remains closest to the broadest international framework. It then compares it to one of the most integrated regional systems that exists today, namely the EU. Due to its intense experience with regionalism and regionalisation, scholars have paid particular attention to the regional integration process in this region.

A. Regional integration and other transnational interactive designs

States may have engaged in various forms of joint activities. This section starts with the analysis of the regional integration process and what it means for the Member States (1). Then, it explores other forms of collective interactions (2).

1. What does it mean to engage in a regional integration project?

The term integration comes from the Latin *integrare*, which means 'repair'. The etymology of this term brings an interesting perspective to the process concerned as it takes place at the regional level. More specifically, regional integration refers to the process by which States go beyond the removal of obstacles to facilitate their interactions and create a regional space subject to certain distinct common regional rules.[1] However, various levels of integration and various combinations exist. Regional integration may therefore be considered a dynamic and evolving process, with a gradual movement towards increased cooperation; a gradual harmonisation of values; different levels of transfer of authority, with 'supranational' institutions being the extreme; and the establishment of a transnational civil society including, the construction of new forms of transnational political community.[2] Such an integration process includes the economical, political and socio-cultural affairs as well as the traditional (defence) and non-traditional (criminal) security issues. This is the case in the EU and ASEAN.

---

[1] Edward Best and Thomas Christiansen, 'Regionalism in international affairs' in *The Globalisation of World Politics: An Introduction to International Politics*, eds., John Baylis, Steve Smith, and Patricia Owens (Oxford: Oxford University Press, 2008): 436.

[2] Martin Griffiths, Terry O'Callaghan, and Steven C. Roach, *International Relations: The Key Concepts*, 2nd ed. (Oxon: Routledge, 2008): 155.

Although they both mention their aim for some form of integration, there is no definition of 'integration' in any of the EU or ASEAN texts. Thus, the specifics of what 'integration' entails in the two regions are unclear and are difficult to decipher from the various texts. Some similarities may nonetheless be found, such as the finding that regional integration constitutes that which the Member States of each region are willing, and able, to 'put in common'. In the EU, they have 'communautarised' specific areas of common interest to reach their objectives. In many domains, work has been done by the EU Member States and the EU institutions in order to solidify the relations between members. It is noteworthy that ASEAN integration programme only targets the Economic Community, while the EU has aimed for a wider and deeper form of regional integration. In contrast to ASEAN, the EU system goes beyond the principle of international law of *pacta sunt servanda* and is, in fact, akin to the principle of *Bundestreue*.[3] This principle implies that Member States should support each other and the EU institutions by taking common actions.

However, members of regional organisations often have conflicting interests when deciding on common action. These conflicting interests have an impact on the depth of their integration and on the width of the territorial realm of the organisation, as they did in Europe and Southeast Asia. Although they have always existed, such debates have been exacerbated in Europe with Brexit. Since this substantial upheaval, expansion of the EU has been approached more cautiously.[4] Similarly, ASEAN is both attempting to reduce the differences between its members[5] and discussing the additional membership of a new country, namely Timor Leste that very recently obtained the status of observer.[6] Notably, Timor Leste even joined an ASEAN-only meeting for the first time on 3 February 2023 at the 32nd ASEAN Coordinating Council.

---

[3] Art. 35, *Grundgesetz für die Bundesrepublik Deutschland* (German Basic Law), DEU-1949-C-39140, 23 May 1943.

[4] See, e.g., Maja Poznatov, 'Analysts: Brexit will slow EU enlargement in the Western Balkans' *EURACTIV*): available at https://www.euractiv.com/section/global-europe/news/analysts-brexit-will-slow-eu-enlargement-in-the-western-balkans/ (accessed on 4 July 2016). Yet, the EU recently re-opened the discussions: Council of the EU, 'Enlargement and Stabilisation and Association Process. The Republic of North Macedonia and the Republic of Albania—General Conclusions' General Secretariat of the Council to Delegations, 7002/20, Brussels, 25 March 2020.

[5] See below the reference to the 'CLMV countries' (i.e. Cambodia, Lao PDR, Myanmar and Vietnam).

[6] Timor Leste applied in 2011. See, e.g., Angaindrankumar Gnanasagaran, 'Admitting ASEAN's 11th member' *The ASEAN Post* (5 January 2018): available at https://theaseanpost.com/article/admitting-aseans-11th-member (accessed on 10 February 2021); Khoo Ying Hooi, 'What Will It Take to Admit Timor-Leste Into ASEAN?' *The Diplomat* (1 August 2019): available at https://thediplomat.com/2019/08/what-will-it-take-to-admit-timor-leste-into-asean/ (accessed on 1 August 2019); ASEAN leaders, 'ASEAN leaders' statement on the application of Timor-Leste for ASEAN membership', 40th and 41st ASEAN Summits and related Summits, Phnom Penh, 11 November 2022: available at shorturl.at/ezEJ8 (accessed on 28 December 2022).

2. Integration and its relation with other forms of joint activities

Besides the integration project, States engage in various activities, including different types of interactions.

Among them, 'cooperation', 'coordination' and 'collaboration' are the most relevant in dealing with international counterterrorism. Although explained in detail in Chap. 2, it is useful to briefly restate that these interactions deal with the effects of the norms, namely which kinds of action the norms require from States when working together. They do not necessarily lead to any modification of national legislations.

Something should be said about the effects of cooperation and coordination involved in the integration process. Going deeper into their commitment, Member States may establish some coordinative mechanisms to eliminate the contrasts between norms, as dispute resolution mechanisms when confronted with conflicts of laws.[7] While States cooperating together remain independent from each other, coordination implies a stronger commitment from the governments involved and requires more interdependent relations.

The different forms of interaction are actions part of the *capacity building* and *knowledge and experience sharing* clusters. Cooperation and coordination involve the organisation of trainings where best practices, experience and knowledge are shared between competent authorities which may ensure the fluidity of their interactions; the enhancement of operational capacities of the competent national authorities involved in the field of criminal justice; and, the development of networks using different channels for communication to facilitate effective cooperation and the flow of information.

A distinction is often made between integration and cooperation.[8] At first sight, they can represent two different mechanisms. However, they can interact with each other and even be useful to each other. It is worth noticing that it is not easy to determine when integration cease to be mere intergovernmental cooperation. The dividing line may comprise a complex combination and interaction of institutions, structures, processes and effects.[9] Even the establishment of a central authority, and the partial transfer of sovereign powers thereto, are not in themselves sufficient

---

[7] See, e.g., Raymond Vander Elst, 'Les notions de coordination, d'harmonisation, de rapprochement et d'unification du droit dans le cadre juridique de la Communauté économique européenne' in *Les instruments du rapprochement des législations dans la Communauté économique européenne*, eds., Denise de Ripainsel-Landy, Alain Gérard, and Anne Limpens-Meinertzhagen, Thèses et travaux juridiques (Bruxelles: Editions de l'Université de Bruxelles, 1976): 5; Mauro Cappelletti, Monica Seccombe, and Joseph H. H. Weiler, 'A Political, Legal and Economic Overview' in *Integration Through Law: Europe and the American Federal Experience*, eds., Mauro Cappelletti, Monica Seccombe, and Joseph H. H. Weiler (Berlin: de Gruyter, 1985): 24.

[8] See, e.g., Anne Weyembergh, 'Introduction', *Revue internationale de droit pénal,* vol. 77, no. 1 (2006).

[9] Mauro Cappelletti, Monica Seccombe, and Joseph H. H. Weiler, eds., *Integration Through Law: Europe and the American Federal Experience*, vol. 1: Methods, Tools and Institutions, A-Law (Berlin and New York: Walter de Gruyter Inc., 1986).

indications. The quantitative difference may arise when at a certain point in the integration process, competence in so many important or essential sectors may have been transferred to the central authority as to result in a real division in substantive governmental powers. However, it may also be qualitative when the reach of the central authority, its law-making, decision-making, implementation and enforcement powers and possibilities is such as to allow it a direct impact in the government of the whole territory comprised in the Union/Association (or any other qualification a regional organisation may take).[10]

Cooperation has always been one of the main characteristics and purpose of a regional system. However, as previously stated, the type and degree of cooperation vary depending on the organisations concerned. It is more ambitious in the EU than in ASEAN. It manifests according to the degree of integration, and even more so according to the objective or strategy of the cooperation. The deeper the integration is, the more methods of coordination and approximation of national legislations are developed.[11] Moreover, when associated with a deeper integration process, as in the EU, cooperation may exist in two forms: the first is horizontal cooperation involving interstate mechanisms of cooperation; and the second is vertical cooperation between a regional entity and the Member States.

In contrast to these forms of interactions, 'harmonisation', 'approximation' and 'unification' involve different levels of adaptation, or even replacement in the case of unification, of national legislations.[12] These elements are also crucial criteria when defining the level of integration of each regional organisation.

All regional organisations contain distinct mixtures of interactions and approximation of national legislations, leading to various types and degrees of regional integration. These different forms of interaction are also determined by the position each State has regarding its national sovereignty.

B. National sovereignty: the main challenge to regional integration

The twentieth century was characterised by spreading sovereignty claims in an unprecedented manner, quickly followed by a period of relativisation of its meaning.[13] Sovereignty is traditionally defined as the independence of a State, its authority to govern itself and its recognition by the international community. It especially means that no State or group of States has the right to intervene, directly or indirectly, for any reason whatsoever, in the internal and external affairs of any other State.[14]

---

[10] Cappelletti, Seccombe, and Weiler, 'A Political, Legal and Economic Overview' (1985): 24.

[11] Weyembergh (2006). Emanuel Adler and Michael Barnett, eds., *Security Communities* (Cambridge: Cambridge University Press, 1998).

[12] On their definitions, see Chap. 2.

[13] Adrián Tokár, 'Something Happened. Sovereignty and European Integration' *Extraordinary Times, IWM Junior Visiting Fellows Conferences*, Vienna, 2001 (Institut für die Wissenschaften vom Menschen, 2001): 2.

[14] See A/RES/2625 (XXV), *Declaration on Principles of International Law concerning Friendly Relations and Co-operation among States in accordance with the Charter of the United Nations,*

This principle is protected by several key international instruments such as Article 2(1) of the *UN Charter* providing that 'the Organisation is based on the principle of the sovereign equality of all its Members'; the preamble of the Vienna *Convention on the Law of Treaties*;[15] and, the *Declaration on Principles of International Law concerning Friendly Relations and Co-operation among States*.[16,17] It was also restated within the fundamental principles at the 1955 Bandung Conference. Although the first principle stated among the ten Bandung principles includes the respect for fundamental human rights, it is then directly followed by the need to respect the sovereignty of States and their national integrity.[18]

Subsequently, the *Opinion n°1 of the Arbitration Commission on Questions arising from the dissolution of Yugoslavia* defines a State as 'a community which consists of a territory and a population subject to an organised political authority', and it specifies that it 'is characterised by sovereignty'.[19] Sovereignty is thus the basis of the existence of the State and of its power on the international scene. Signing conventions, international contracts and agreements, and even entering in a regional integration process are manifestations of States' sovereignty.

Yet nowadays, sovereignty is increasingly relativised by trends stemming from globalisation. This phenomenon implies an increased economical and cultural interdependence, driven by technological development and economic growth. Moreover, sovereignty is also mitigated by the need to maintain international peace and security, which has been highlighted by the international community. In this respect, legal barriers have been erected to limit certain exercises of sovereignty, such as the prohibition of aggression, or any other attempt of threat to international security, as defined by the United Nations.

In the international context, States usually start building up a minimum level of mutual trust by establishing cooperation mechanisms meant to achieve common goals. Then, they may deepen further and expand their shared goals, set up regional

---

1883rd plenary session, 24 October 1970. Also, Patrick Daillier, Mathias Forteau, and Alain Pellet, *Droit international public (Nguyen Quoc Dinh †)*, 8th ed. (Paris: Librairie Générale de Droit et de Jurisprudence, 2009): 465–81.

[15] *Convention on the Law of Treaties*, Vienna, 23 May 1969, UNTS vol. 1155, No. 18232.

[16] A/RES/2625(XXV), *Declaration on Principles of International Law concerning Friendly Relations and Cooperation among States*.

[17] See also A/CONF.39/26, *Final Act of the United Nations Conference on the Law of Treaties*, Vienna, 23 May 1963; Pt 1(a), A/RES/53/101, *Principles and guidelines for international negotiations*, 83rd plenary meeting, 8 December 1998. In terrorism-related matters, see, e.g., S/RES/1618 (2005), *Condemnation of terrorist attacks in Iraq*, 5246th meeting, 4 August 2005 reaffirming the sovereignty of Iraq; S/RES/2083(2012), *Threats to international peace and security caused by terrorist acts*, 6890th meeting, 17 December 2012. Regarding transnational organised crime, Art. 4, UNTOC (2000).

[18] *Final Communiqué of the Bandung Conference* (Afro-Asian Conference), Bandung, 18–24 April 1955. See also Daillier, Forteau, and Pellet (2009): 642–44.

[19] Robert Badinter (chair), 'Opinion No. 1: Conference on Yugoslavia, Arbitration Commission. 29 November 1991', *International Law Reports*, vol. 92 (Cambridge: Grotius Publications Limited, 1993) 163. For further development, Best and Christiansen (2008): 443.

institutions for the purpose of increasing the prospects of effective compliance, develop stronger mechanisms of cooperation and coordination, and launch an harmonisation of their legislations, for example.[20] Eventually, it is only when they perceive the added value of an integration process that States may accept sharing of sovereignty (i.e. some renunciation of autonomous action), delegation of powers and/or an institutionalisation to the benefit of the regional organisation.[21] Such evolution is happening in the EU, whereas reluctances in embarking on a similar path are much stronger in Southeast Asia.

One may of course consider that granting powers to a supranational organisation is a form of dispossession of a State's attributes.[22] However, two elements may contradict this hypothesis: firstly, the States agree upon such transfer of competence and, secondly, this may actually be considered as a means of exercising and even 'regaining' their sovereignty.[23] This process may also be considered a major sovereignty compromise where States accept to give competence to a regional organisation in exchange for this regional organisation helping its members reach their shared objective. Some scholars refer to this as 'sovereignty trade-off'.[24] An integration process is usually associated with the idea that the Member States voluntarily accepted this situation, which cannot, by definition, limit their sovereignty. Member States are simply exercising their sovereignty in a different way.[25] States do not transfer their sovereignty but may cede certain component(s) of their sovereignty to give a regional or international organisation specific competences.[26] In fact, Member States define in their agreement their positions regarding the role of the respective

[20] Walter Mattli, *The Logic of Regional Integration: Europe and Beyond* (Cambridge: Cambridge University Press, 1999).

[21] Andrew Moravcsik, *The Choice for Europe: Social Purpose and State Power from Messina to Maastricht*, Cornell Studies in Political Economy (Ithaca: Cornell University Press, 1998); Kenneth W. Abbott et al., 'The concept of legalization', *International Organization,* vol. 54, no. 3 (2000).

[22] Stephen Krasner, *Sovereignty: Organized Hypocrisy* (Princeton: Princeton University Press, 1999); Anne Weyembergh, 'L'Espace Pénal Européen: Entre Coopération Judiciaire et Territoire Pénal Européen' in *La Grande Europe* ed., Paul Magnette (Bruxelles: Editions de l'Université de Bruxelles, 2004).

[23] Weyembergh, 'L'Espace Pénal Européen' (2004).

[24] Pratap Bhanu Mehta, 'Sovereignty Tradeoffs and Regional Integration. Theoretical and Comparative Reflections' in *International Relations Theory and South Asia: Security Political Economy, Domestic Politics, Identities, and Images*, ed., E. Sridharan (Oxford: Oxford University Press, 2011): 35. See also, e.g., Jens-Uwe Wunderlich, 'Comparing regional organisations in global multilateral institutions: ASEAN, the EU and the UN', *Asia Europe Journal,* vol. 10, no. 2–3 (2012): 129–30; Jens-Uwe Wunderlich, 'The EU an Actor *Sui Generis*? A Comparison of EU and ASEAN Actorness', *Journal of Common Market Studies,* vol. 50, no. 4 (2012): 663.

[25] Sergio Carrera et al., 'Criminal Justice and Police Cooperation between the EU and the UK after Brexit. Towards a principled and trust-based partnership', ed. Peter Hustinx and Michael Kennedy, CEPS & QMUL (Bruxelles: Centre for European Policy Studies, August 2018): 6.

[26] See, e.g., more explanation on regional integration in the EU with the ECJ, *Costa* v. *Enel,* C-6/64, judgment, ECLI:EU:C:1964:66, 15 July 1964. Also, Joseph H. H. Weiler and Ulrich R. Haltern, 'The autonomy of the Community Legal Order: Through the Looking Glass', *Harvard International Law Journal,* vol. 37, no. 2 (1996).

regional organisations. This perspective remains debated in the EU, while ASEAN Member States do not view it the same way (yet).[27]

Going through the main components of national sovereignty, namely autonomy, control and legitimacy, may explain the challenges States face when engaging in a regional integration project.[28] Autonomy refers to the independence of a State vis-à-vis external authority, namely other States and organisations. Control refers to the ability of States to produce the effect they desire in their territory and, in some cases, beyond it (extraterritorial jurisdiction); it also refers to their actual capacities to engage in legal relations with other legal actors. Finally, legitimacy—seen as a corollary of sovereignty[29]—refers to the right of the State to formulate rules in a way that is widely accepted and recognised internally and externally.[30] These elements shall be seen as components of States engaging in a regional integration process and potentially as components of the regional organisation established itself.

The EU has gone much further in the process of regional integration, while ASEAN Member States are still at the premises of developing more interconnected intra-regional relations. As it has been extensively written about, the EU experience is only discussed to highlight the similarities or differences with ASEAN's development.

Concerning the component of autonomy, ASEAN does not have any autonomous competence and power, whereas its Member States remain completely autonomous in defining their national legislation and policies. In the EU, the regional institutions can legislate in the matters for which the EU is competent and impose obligations to Member States.[31] Concerning the component of control, States involved in a process of regional integration do not have complete control over the competences conferred upon the regional organisation by the Treaty. In the EU, the Member States have given some control to the regional organisation through the Treaties, whereas ASEAN Member States remain in full control, especially due to the need for unanimous agreement on any regional decision. Concerning the component of legitimacy, a regional organisation may seem legitimate to intervene, as an impetus, when an issue involves a cross-border element. Generally speaking, regional organisation's legitimacy requires more effort than that of States. Yet, States' sovereignty does not necessary imply that its government is legitimate. Therefore, and maybe

---

[27] Amitav Acharya and Alastair Iain Johnston, 'Conclusion: institutional features, cooperation effects, and the agenda for further research on comparative regionalism' in *Crafting Cooperation: Regional International Institutions in Comparative Perspective*, eds., Amitav Acharya and Alastair Iain Johnston (Cambridge: Cambridge University Press, 2007): 253.

[28] ASEAN Senior Officials Meeting on Transnational Crime Working Group on Counter Terrorism (WG on CT)—Terms of Reference, 2nd SOMTC Working Group on Counter-Terrorism, ASEAN Secretariat Paper Agenda Item 4, Kuala Lumpur, 16 June 2008. Walter Mattli, 'Sovereignty Bargains in Regional integration', *Review of international Studies,* vol. 2, no. 2 (2000); Bhanu Mehta (2011): 36.

[29] Best and Christiansen (2008): 443.

[30] Bhanu Mehta (2011): 36.

[31] See, e.g., Art. 82 and ff., TFEU.

more specifically in ASEAN, States' ability to create such regional organisations is compromised by the collective uncertainty on their domestic legitimacy.

Consequently, States may be autonomous, but ineffective alone in bringing about the desired results. States are more willing to cooperate with one another and to even potentially enter an integration process when confronted with a large-scale threat—or issue—that they realise they cannot deal with alone. Therefore, States may accept sacrificing part of their autonomy. It does not necessarily mean they give away their sovereignty. Their commitment to cooperate together in order to reach common the goals drawn up in regional norms does not necessarily diminish their role but rather, it may help them recover a part of the control they would have lost anyway.[32]

Today, ASEAN Member States are caught between rigid commitments vis-à-vis national sovereignty[33] and the international acknowledgement that transnational crime needs a common response.[34]

Based on these considerations, an integration process is a complex and long-term project. A certain level of maturity is necessary for all Member States to secure their own position, their legal system and their identity on an international level.[35] Each Member State develops its own cultural, institutional and legal identity. National identity refers to the capacity of the State to endow people with an overriding sense of who they are as a collective group.[36] Regional integration is unlikely to exist in the absence of adequate mutual identification between the States involved.[37] A regional identity and 'actorhood' can only be consolidated on the basis of its members' identities.[38] When the elements of identity diverge too much, cooperation and a form of approximation of legislations may be more complicated to develop.

---

[32] Weyembergh, 'L'Espace Pénal Européen' (2004).

[33] See, e.g., ASEAN, *Treaty of Amity and Cooperation in Southeast Asia*, Bali, 24 February 1976; *ASEAN Plan of Action to Combat Transnational Crime* (1999); *Joint Declarations for Cooperation to Combat International Cooperation*; Arts. III and IV, ACCT; Art. 2.2(a), *ASEAN Charter.*

[34] Edward Best and Thomas Christiansen, 'Regionalism in international affairs' in *The Globalisation of World Politics: An Introduction to International Politics* eds., John Baylis, Steve Smith, and Patricia Owens (Oxford: Oxford University Press, 2008): 443.

[35] Bhanu Mehta (2011): 34–35.

[36] Ibid.: 47.

[37] Christopher B. Roberts, *ASEAN Regionalism. Cooperation, values and institutionalization*, Routledge Security in Asia Pacific (London: Routledge, 2012): 11.

[38] Best and Christiansen, 'Regionalism in international affairs' (2008): 437; Anna Cornelia Beyer, *Counter Terrorism and International Power Relations: The EU, ASEAN and Hegemonic Global Governance* (London: I.B.Tauris & Co Ltd., 2010); Wunderlich, 'The EU an Actor Sui Generis?' (2012); Wunderlich, 'Comparing regional organisations in global multilateral institutions: ASEAN, the EU and the UN' (2012); Frank Mattheis and Uwe Wunderlich, 'Regional actorness and interregional relations: ASEAN, the EU and Mercosur', *Journal of European Integration,* vol. 39, no. 6 (2017); Thomas Gehring, Sebastian Oberthür, and Marc Mühleck, 'European Union Actorness in International Institutions: Why the EU is Recognized as an Actor in Some International Institutions, but Not in Others', *Journal of Common Market Studies,* vol. 51, no. 5 (2013); Chun Hung Lin, 'ASEAN Charter: Deeper Regional Integration under International Law?', *Chinese Journal of International Law,* vol. 9, no. 4 (2010): para. 18.

Although the EU identity is relatively clear, it has recently been confronted with serious challenges;[39] while ASEAN actorhood is unlikely to emerge soon.

Although heavily challenged in recent years by strong nationalist movements, the EU has been built upon the willingness and ability of its members to transfer certain competences to the regional institutions with the idea that 'united we stand taller'.[40] Trust has always been a means towards European cohesion within the region and beyond. Yet, it is clear that the EU Member States do not intend to dispossess themselves from their national sovereignty, but instead aim to exercise it at more on a supranational level.[41]

As previously shown, the EU has many features that distinguish it from traditional international organisations. Among its characteristics, there are no internal borders and the free flow of goods, persons, services and capital is guaranteed by the founding treaties. The EU citizenship also gives EU citizens rights, including the right to move freely and reside on the territory of any Member State. However, as aforementioned, probably the most important development is the emergence of a separate and autonomous legal order, i.e. the 'EU law'. The applicable ordinary legislative procedure, namely the qualified majority vote, creates a situation where some Member States who have voted against some laws have to apply them nonetheless. Although of different origin and type, the EU could be considered as sovereign in its 'realm' due to it creating legal norms in the fields in which it is competent, which are superior to norms of individual Member States. No longer do the Member States enjoy legal supremacy in areas entrusted to the EU. This is now the case for criminal matters too. The EU Member States started with the establishment of intergovernmental cooperation mechanisms, then they gradually set up regional norms and institutional means to increase effective compliance with EU duties. Such evolution or processes resulted in the communautarisation of cooperation in criminal matters in 2009 via the establishment of the *Treaty of Lisbon*. With this treaty, EU Member States accepted a pooling of sovereignty, delegation of powers and an institutionalisation to the benefit of the EU institutions. This process constitutes a major 'sovereignty trade-off'.[42] Member States have decided to exercise particular component(s) of their sovereignty through the EU as they recognised the advantages from this 'externalisation'.

---

[39] See, e.g., Mario Telò, *L'Europe en crise et le monde* (Bruxelles: Editions de l'Université de Bruxelles, 2016); Mario Telò and Anne Weyembergh, 'Supranationality and sovereignty in an era of increasing complexity and fragmentation' in *Supranational Governance at Stake. The EU's External External Competences caught between Complexity and Fragmentation*, eds., Mario Teló and Anne Weyembergh (Oxon: Routledge, 2020).

[40] Jean-Claude Juncker, State of the Union 2018 Address, 'The Hour of European Sovereignty', European Commission, 12 September 2018, 6.

[41] See, e.g., Jean-Claude Juncker, 'The Hour of European Sovereignty' (2018): 'European sovereignty is born of Member States' national sovereignty and does not replace it. Sharing sovereignty—when and where needed—makes each of our nation states stronger'.

[42] Bhanu Mehta (2011): 35.

Except for Thailand, all ASEAN Member States were colonised. In this circumstance whereby external forces imposed themselves, governments still need to strengthen their own position in internal and external affairs moving forward. Mainly because of this European domination over Southeast Asian colonies and ASEAN Member States' finding it difficult sometimes to control their territory, to control people and resources within national boundaries, these members have adopted the traditional approach vis-à-vis national sovereignty.[43] Concepts such as national sovereignty and territorial integrity were particularly important during the decolonisation process.[44] Such principles acted as a protection mechanism of the recently constituted independent States against external and internal threats and divisions. Looking at the method adopted by ASEAN Member States for their regional development, the list of constitutive elements of the 'ASEAN Way' includes as the first guiding norms protected principles, namely the principles of national sovereignty and of non-interference in internal affairs of other Member States. These principles are reiterated in the *Treaty of Amity and Cooperation in Southeast Asia*, in which the notions of 'mutual respect for [...] sovereignty' and 'non-interference in internal affairs of one another' are core principles.[45] These principles are held protectively by States in this region.[46] Nonetheless, a particularly group of States managed to get together and, to a certain extent, unite together politically under a unified 'ecosystem of peace'.[47,48] Therefore, a common ASEAN identity seems to slowly emerge, yet it still needs to be more precisely formed. Moreover, due to these strong divergences, the level of trust between Member States remains low.

Regional integration may be a means for States to operationalise their sovereignty and, together with other States, take a more important place on the international scene. This aside, a shared sovereignty at the regional level based on the EU model is not on ASEAN's agenda.[49]

Transferring competences to a regional organisation and deepening cooperation between competent national authorities can only happen when their relevant stakeholders trust each other. Mutual trust constitutes the yardstick of regional

---

[43] Ibid.: 48.

[44] Tokár, *Extraordinary Times, IWM Junior Visiting Fellows Conferences* (2001): 2.

[45] Art. 2, *Treaty of Amity and Cooperation in Southeast Asia* (1976). See Alex J. Bellamy, *Security Communities and Their Neighbours: Regional Fortresses or Global Integrators?* (Basingstoke: Palgrave MacMillan, 2004), 95.

[46] Bhanu Mehta (2011): 48.

[47] Kishore Mahbubani, 'The Modern Miracle that is ASEAN' *The Straits Times*, 9 May 2015.

[48] Centre for European Policy Studies (CEPS), 'Lessons from the EU integration process for ASEAN regional integration", Project on Capacity Enhancement for Intensive International Integration of Vietnam towards 2020, CEPS Report (24 July 2015).

[49] ASEAN, Terms of Reference, 2nd SOMTC Working Group on Counter-Terrorism, 16 June 2008. Particularly developed in EU law: Stephen Weatherill, *Cases and Materials on EU Law*, 8th ed. (Oxford: Oxford University Press, 2007): 676; Paul Craig and Gráinne de Búrca, *EU Law: Text, Cases, and Materials*, 5th ed. (Oxford: Oxford University Press, 2011): 184 and ff.

integration; starting as a preliminary step, then operating as a tool of governance, and finally ending up as the result of enhancement of interstate relations. It prompts States to exercise part of their sovereignty through a regional organisation. The different level and form of mutual trust between the members of each region and the members' appreciation of the advantages and disadvantages of regional integration certainly explain the diverging approaches in the EU and ASEAN.

II. **Forging a regional identity: the basis for a more in-depth regional integration?**

While developing their own regional architecture and own identity, ASEAN and EU Member States are making sure to include values, norms and organising principles (Table 4.1).

While it is argued that the EU needs to pay attention to its internal diversity, the latter may be considered more limited compared to the ASEAN intra-regional diversity.[50] After more than 50 years of regional dialogue, diversity is the concept that best captures the Association. Politically, there is a plethora of governance models in the region, stretching from an absolute monarchy to democracies, constitutional monarchies and authoritarian States. Economically, highly developed States and the world's top-ranking economies stand side by side with some of the World's poorest countries. Moreover, the plurality of religions, languages, ethnicities and ways of living add to the internal challenges. Against the backdrop of such divergence, the emergence of a stable and deeply rooted organisation based on non-binding instruments and the principle of equality *inter pares* is a remarkable achievement.

In Southeast Asia, the 'ASEAN Way' provides an institutional framework for policy- and decision-making between leaders, through various informal channels of communication amongst governments, through the intensive and discrete discussions occurring during different international fora, or through the weak role and understaffed nature of the ASEAN Secretariat.[51] This method of governance emphasises the unique socialising nature of the ASEAN decision-making process, and defines interstate relations as a process of identity building.[52]

ASEAN has a lot of work ahead in order to improve its role in the region and beyond. Reaching a regional identity is certainly a difficult objective to aim at in Southeast Asia, where the colonialist-imposed borders do not represent the distribution of the unique populations and their distinct lived-experiences. Individuals do not always feel that they identify as belonging to a particular State, but rather to a specific ethnic group, ones which can transcend borders. The 'weak socio-political

[50] See, e.g., Amitav Acharya, 'Comparative Regionalism: A Field Whose Time has Come?', *The International Spectator*, vol. 47, no. 1 (2012).

[51] Shaun Narine, *Explaining ASEAN: Regionalism in Southeast Asia* (Boulder: Lynne Rienner Publishers, 2002).

[52] Jean-Claude Piris and Walter Woon, *Towards a Rules-Based Community: An ASEAN Legal Service*, Integration Through Law: The Role of Law and the Rule of Law in ASEAN Integration (Cambridge: Cambridge University Press, 2015): 112.

Table 4.1 Comparison between the ASEAN's and EU's basic principles

ASEAN	EU
Art. 2, *ASEAN Charter* 'Principles' (slightly summarised) ASEAN and its Member States shall act in accordance with the following Principles: – respect for independence, sovereignty, equality, territorial integrity and national identity; – shared commitment and collective responsibility in enhancing regional peace, security and prosperity; – renunciation of aggression and of the threat or use of force [. . .]; – reliance on peaceful settlement of disputes; – non-interference in the internal affairs of ASEAN Member State; – respect for the right of every State to lead its national existence free from external interference, subversion and coercion; – enhanced consultations on matters seriously affecting the common interest; – adherence to the rule of law, good governance, the principles of democracy and constitutional government; – respect for fundamental freedoms, the promotion and protection of human rights, and the promotion of social justice; – [. . .] – respect for the different cultures, languages and religions of the peoples of ASEAN while emphasising their common values in the spirit of unity in diversity; – the centrality of ASEAN in external political, economic, social and cultural relations while remaining actively engaged, outward-looking, inclusive and non-discriminatory; and – adherence to multilateral trade rules and ASEAN's rules-based regimes for effective implementation of economic commitments and progressive reduction towards the elimination of barriers to regional economic integration, in a market-driven economy.	Art. 2, *Treaty on the EU* on the values: The Union is founded on the values of respect for human dignity, freedom, democracy, equality, the rule of law and respect for human rights, including the rights of persons belonging to minorities. These values are common to the Member States in a society in which pluralism, non-discrimination, tolerance, justice, solidarity and equality between women and men prevail. Art. 3 on the interests and objectives (slightly summarised) – The Union's aim is to promote peace, its values and the well-being of its peoples. – The Union offers its citizens an area of freedom, security and justice without internal frontiers (free movement of persons with respect to external border controls, asylum, immigration and the prevention and combating of crime). – The Union shall establish an internal market [. . .] It shall combat social exclusion and discrimination, and shall promote social justice and protection, equality between women and men, solidarity between generations and protection of the rights of the child. It shall promote economic, social and territorial cohesion, and solidarity among Member States. It shall respect its cultural and linguistic diversity, and ensure that Europe's cultural heritage is safeguarded and enhanced. – The Union shall establish an economic and monetary union whose currency is the euro. – With the wider world, the Union shall uphold and promote its values and interests and contribute to the protection of its citizens. It shall contribute to peace, security, the sustainable development of the Earth, solidarity and mutual respect among peoples, free and fair trade, eradication of poverty and the protection of human rights as well as to the strict observance and the development of international law [. . .]. Art. 4(2), e.g., slightly limits the regionalisation process: 'The Union shall respect the equality of Member States before the Treaties as well as their national identities, inherent in their fundamental structures,

(continued)

Table 4.1 (continued)

ASEAN	EU
	political and constitutional, inclusive of regional and local self-government. It shall respect their essential State functions, including ensuring the territorial integrity of the State, maintaining law and order and safeguarding national security. In particular, national security remains the sole responsibility of each Member State'.

cohesion of the region's new nation-States, the legitimacy problems of several of the region's postcolonial governments, interstate territorial disputes, intra-regional ideological polarisation and intervention by external powers' as well as other historical, political and legal differences significantly influence the geopolitical landscape of the region.[53] All these elements have had a clear impact on the extent of cooperation between Member States and on ASEAN's institutionalisation. The principle of consensus-based decision-making in the political-security realm is an essential element of cooperation in this region.[54]

While ASEAN's identity is not unified and is a work in progress, the EU has 'institutionalised' its identity. The *Treaty on the EU* (TEU) sets out this purpose in Article 2, which lists the set of values and principles on which the Union is based as well as those powers which has been conferred to them in order to achieve those values. Article 2 defines the Union's self-perception and thus its identity, namely that it is based on a number of foundational values such as respect for human dignity, freedom, democracy, equality, the rule of law and the like. Article 3 TEU enumerates its interests and objectives such as promoting peace as well as its values and the well-being of its peoples and/or offering its citizens an Area of Freedom, Security and Sustice (AFSJ). Despite the proclamation of an EU identity, the *Treaty on the EU* tempers this unity by guaranteeing the protection of national identities.[55]

ASEAN identity is slowly emerging on the basis of shared values which the Member States have identified and accept to defend. Sanctioning this process, the 2007 *ASEAN Charter* provides several elements of shared purposes[56] and principles,[57] but they need to be associated with precise implementation tools.

It is clear that the founding principles diverge from one region to the other. ASEAN's principles are more traditional as they focus on interstate relations. It

[53] Tanja A. Börzel and Thomas Risse, 'From Europeanisation to Diffusion: Introduction', *West European Politics,* vol. 35, no. 1 (2012): 3.

[54] Patrick Low, 'Bad Days for Interntional Trade' *ASEAN Economic Integration Brief* (Jakarta: ASEAN Secretariat, June 2018): 7.

[55] Art. 4(2), TEU.

[56] Art. 1, *ASEAN Charter.*

[57] Art. 2, *ASEAN Charter.*

was with the 2007 *ASEAN Charter* that values and human rights as well as an external dimension to ASEAN's action were added to the list. It is only 6 years later that ASEAN Member States agreed upon a regional *Human Rights Declaration,*[58] supported by the Intergovernmental Commission on Human Rights (AICHR) established in 2009.[59] However, there is no enforcement procedure to ensure an effective implementation of these human rights within the region and no regional court or other similar systems. Guaranteeing human rights is still considered a national prerogative and a sole national concern. In accordance with the 'ASEAN Way', decision-making of the AICHR is based on consultation and consensus. Since its establishment, the AICHR has adopted several key documents, including the Guidelines on the Operations of AICHR and the Guidelines on the AICHR's Relations with Civil Society Organisations (CSOs). Its mode of action is based on Five-Year Work Plan, the last of which covers the period between 2020 and 2025.[60] The objectives of this intergovernmental Commission are mostly to develop strategies for the promotion and protection of human rights and fundamental freedoms in collaboration with the relevant stakeholders, including governments and CSOs.

By contrast, the EU's principles go beyond traditional interstate requirements and elaborate on the values governing their actions within and beyond the region. Currently, human rights are promoted and guaranteed in a harmonised way within the EU, with the contribution of the Court of Justice of the European Union (CJEU). The current state in the region is the result of a progressive integration in the constitutional package of the EU.[61] Upon the establishment of the EU, the Treaty of Rome[62] did not include any consideration to fundamental rights. Over time, the Treaties were amended to ensure a regional protection of fundamental rights by EU institutions and its Member States when they acted within the scope of EU law.[63] For instance, the Treaty of Maastricht included reference to the ECHR and the common constitutional traditions of Member States as general principles of EU law, while the Treaty of Amsterdam affirmed the European 'principles' upon which the EU is founded (then qualified as 'values' in Article 2 TEU of the Lisbon Treaty). It created

---

[58] *ASEAN Human Rights Declaration*, 21st ASEAN Summit, Phnom Penh, 18 November 2012.

[59] *Declaration on the Intergovernmental Commission on Human Rights* and *ASEAN Intergovernmental Commission on Human rights (Terms of reference)*, 15th ASEAN Summit, Cha-Am Hua Hin, 23–25 October 2009.

[60] See Five-Year Work Plan of the AICHR (2021–2025), approved at the 53rd ASEAN Foreign Ministers' Meeting, 9 September 2020; and the previous AICHR Work Plan (2016–2020), adopted on 15 June 2015 and endorsed at the 48th ASEAN Foreign Ministers' Meeting on 3 August 2015.

[61] Emmanuelle Bribosia, 'La future constitution: point culminant de la constituionalisation des droits fondamentaux dans l'Union europêenne' in *La Grande Europe*, ed., Paul Magnette (Bruxelles: Editions de l'Université de Bruxelles, 2004); *Droit de l'Union européenne*, 5th ed. (Bruxelles: Editions de l'Université de Bruxelles, 2014): 54 and ff.

[62] *Treaty establishing the European Economic Community* and related instruments (EEC Treaty) and *Treaty establishing the European Atomic Energy Community* (Euratom), Roma, 25 March 1957.

[63] See, e.g., Art. 51, EU Charter integrated into the EU Constitutional package.

a procedure to suspend the rights foreseen by the Treaties in cases of serious and persistent violations of fundamental rights by a Member State. This evolution has continued with the treaties and secondary legislations, as discussed later in this chapter.

The adoption of human rights standards within regions may facilitate interstate relations. Those standards are promoted and guaranteed through different means in the EU and ASEAN, specifically a more legal approach (in brief, norms and judicial control) in the EU and a more social and political approach (in brief, discussions and soft power) in ASEAN. The protection of human rights constitutes one of the legal components of mutual trust in the EU and, consequently, provides a common basis for intra-regional cooperation in criminal matters. It does not seem to form a core component of Southeast Asia relations, which would explain the traditional meaning given to mutual trust in the region, i.e. based on interpersonal relations.

Therefore, States face serious challenges when deciding to engage in a regional integration project. The regional integration process of States can only go as far as their agreement on shared values and principles as well as their position vis-à-vis national sovereignty. Eventually, the identity and the form of each regional organisation depend on the common ground its members successfully negotiate.

Section 2: All Roads Do Not Necessarily Lead to the Same Regional Institutional and Legal Architecture

Despite a clear prejudice drawn from the assumption that progress in regional integration is defined in terms of EU-style institutionalisation,[64] States tailor their own regional framework to fit their needs and conditions. The historical and geopolitical context plays a significant role in developing mutual trust between States and, subsequently, affects the form the regional organisation eventually takes.

This section compares the regional designs of the EU and ASEAN (II). To achieve this, it is essential to understand the developments that led to their current regional architecture. As the evolution of the EU institutional and legal framework has already been thoroughly covered by experts,[65] this section focuses on the ASEAN developments (I).

---

[64] See, e.g., Shaun Breslin, Richard Higgott and Ben Rosamond, 'Regions in Comparative Perspective', in Shaun Breslin, Christopher W. Hughes, Nicola Philips and Ben Rosamond (eds.), *New Regionalisms in the Global Political Economy* (London: Routledge, 2002), 11.

[65] See, e.g., Ernst Haas, 'International Integration: The European and the Universal Process', *International Organisation,* vol. 15, no. 3 (1961); Pierre Pescatore, *The Law of Integration. Emergence of a New Phenomenon in International Relations, based on the Experience of the European Communities* (Leiden: A.W. Sijthoff, 1974); Cappelletti, Seccombe, and Weiler, eds., *Integration Through Law: Europe and the American Federal Experience* (1986); Jean-Victor Louis, *L'ordre juridque communautaire*, 4th ed. (Luxembourg: Office des publications officielles des Communautés européennes, 1988); Antje Wiener and Thomas Diez, eds., *European Integration Theory* (Oxford: Oxford University Press, 2004); Axel Berkofsky, 'Comparing EU and Asian Integration Processes. The EU a role model for Asia?', European Policy Centre (EPC, 18 January 2005); Sanoussi Bilal, 'Is the EU a Model of Regional Integration? Risks and Challenges' *Briefing for ACP-EU Joint Parliamentary Assembly's Committee on Political Affairs*, European Centre for

This section identifies the place and role of mutual trust in developing the regional architecture. In this respect, the question is whether regional integration may help fostering mutual trust or whether building up trust fosters the establishment of a more integrated system. It is analogous to the question whether it was the chicken or the egg that came first. It is uncertain whether an answer to the question about mutual trust is easier to discover than the one about the chicken and the egg. Nonetheless, it seems that there is a basic minimum of trust needed to establish a regional organisation—whatever form it takes. Additionally, through the enhancement of regional integration, mutual trust is strengthened. This seemingly forms a virtuous circle.

I. The rising of the ASEAN institutional framework: proof that different regional integration approaches are possible?

States respective history obviously marks their capabilities and willingness to engage with one another. The situation in Southeast Asia since the mid-twentieth century has evolved for the countries and thus for the regional organisation. After some initial failed attempts, ASEAN finally emerged (A) and its structure evolved over time allowing legal elements to slowly and sporadically appear (B).

A. The slow emergence of a will to develop a Southeast Asian regional architecture

The Association of Southeast Asia (ASA) was inaugurated on 31 July 1961. Both the Philippines and the Federation of Malaya had initially favoured a deeply institutionalised structure, modelled on the European Economic Community, but Thailand was against anything more than a loosely articulated and non-binding form of intergovernmentalism.[66] The latter solution was accepted because, firstly, it was necessary to maintain Thailand's participation and, secondly, because the two

---

Development Policy Management (Bruxelles, 13 September 2007); Guy Milton and Jacques Keller-Noëllet, 'The Immediate Origins of the European Constitution: From Nice to Laeken' in *Genèse et destinée de la Constitution européenne: Commentaire du Traité établissant une Constitution pour l'Europe à la lumière des travaux préparatoires et perspectives d'avenir*, eds., Giuliano Amato, Hervé Bribosia, and Bruno De Witte (Bruxelles: Bruylant, 2007); Weatherill (2007); Craig and de Búrca (2011); Wunderlich, 'The EU an Actor Sui Generis?' (2012); Wunderlich, 'Comparing regional organisations in global multilateral institutions: ASEAN, the EU and the UN' (2012); Damian Chalmers, Gareth Davies, and Giorgio Monti, *European Union Law*, 3rd ed. (Cambridge: Cambridge University Press, 2014); Marianne Dony, *Droit de l'Union européenne*, 7e ed. (Bruxelles: Editions de l'Université de Bruxelles, 2018); Mario Telò and Anne Weyembergh, eds., *Supranational Governance at Stake. The EU's External Competences caught between Complexity and Fragmentation*, Globalisation, Europe and Multilateralism (Abingdon: Routledge, 2020).

[66] Roberts (2012): 39.

countries hoped that this loosely structure would attract other Southeast Asian States.[67] However, ASA was unsuccessful in attracting States.

Relations lasted for nearly 3 years, from 1963 to 1966. The only modest achievements of the Association were the establishment of channels of communication and a tentative organisational structure. Meetings and conferences were to rotate through the member countries. No permanent secretariat was established in the short life of the organisation, but its slight accomplishments were a starting point for the subsequent organisation, ASEAN.

As was the case for ASA, ASEAN has developed through practice by building up good relations between its members.

At the end of the 1950s and in the 1960s, the Southeast Asia region was composed of very young countries in terms of their national development or nation building. Brunei Darussalam was not an independent country yet, and Singapore was still part of the Federation of Malaya at that time.[68] It is in fact surprising that so early after their national independence a regional project emerged. The founding of ASEAN in 1967 particularly supported by Indonesia, was officially motivated by a strong desire and political commitment to 'promote a sense of regional identity as the basis of a prosperous and peaceful community of Southeast Asia nations'.[69] With a more pragmatic perspective, the intergovernmental organisation was initially and mainly established for economic and commercial purposes[70] to bolster the influence of its Member States on the international scene. ASEAN Member States realised that they would gain far greater influence together in trade and political issues than what they would achieve individually. Establishing economic linkages is also supposed to reduce the likeliness of interstate conflict within the region. Thanks to ASEAN's role, the Member States did not suffer a war against each other since the adoption of its constitutive act, namely the 1967 *ASEAN Declaration*. As stated in this Declaration, the first purpose of the Association is to 'accelerate economical growth social progress and cultural development in the region through joint endeavours in the spirit of equality and partnership in order to strengthen the foundation for a prosperous and peaceful community of Southeast Asian Nations'.[71] Six other purposes followed, including regional peace, collaboration and mutual assistance on matters of common interest in the economic, social, cultural, technical, scientific and

[67] Narine (2002): 11.

[68] Dates of independence of the nine Southeast Asian countries in chronological order: Philippines, 12 June 1898 (from Spain); Indonesia, 17 August 1945 (from the Netherlands); Vietnam, 2 September 1945 (from France); Myanmar, 4 January 1948 (from the British Empire); Lao PDR, 22 October 1953 (from France); Cambodia, 9 November 1953 (from France); Malaysia, 31 August 1957 (from the British Empire); Singapore, 9 August 1965 (from the Federation of Malaya); Brunei Darussalam, 1 January 1984 (from the British Empire). NB: Brunei National Day is actually commemorated when the British control effectively ended, i.e. on 23 February 1984.

[69] ASEAN, *Ten Years of ASEAN* (Jakarta: ASEAN Secretariat, April 1978).

[70] See, e.g., Houchang Flassan-Yari, 'L'ASEAN ou le réveil partiel du Tiers Monde?', *Etudes internationales* vol. 33, no. 2 (2002).

[71] Pt. 1, *ASEAN Declaration* (Bangkok Declaration), Bangkok, 8 August 1967.

administrative fields, etc. More specifically, there was no mention of traditional or non-traditional security issues, except for the promotion of regional peace and stability through abiding respect for justice and the rule of law in the relationship among countries of the region and adherence to the principles of the UN Charter.[72]

Notably, more than 10 years earlier, the European integration project that led to the establishment of the European Communities in the 1950s was also meant to prevent further international armed conflict after the Second World War by developing economic ties.[73]

The primary objectives of ASEAN were similar to those of the European Communities, including economic activities, continuous and balanced growth, increased stability, a more rapid improvement in the standard of living and closer relations. Thus, members of the two regional organisations adopted a similar approach: creating economic ties to reinforce their position worldwide and with the objective of reducing the risk of conflict.

Nonetheless, the form of the approach of the two regions diverges. Member States of the European Communities quickly introduced supranational elements in their regional project within the European Communities, including the European Economic Community, the European Coal and Steel Community and the European Atomic Energy Community. Conversely, ASEAN Member States did not aim for the regional organisation to get power over Member States.[74] The aim was to slowly develop knowledge and begin to trust each other. However, the financial crisis in the 1990s convinced the decision-makers of the necessity to develop the regional institutionalisation and to deepen regional cooperation in ASEAN.[75]

B. An ASEAN architecture sparingly adopting a rules-based approach?

Because of its particular history, ASEAN structure has followed a combination of mainly informal steps characteristic of the 'ASEAN Way' (1) and few formal ones slowly appearing over time (2). In this evolution, it must be discussed whether the

[72] Pt. 2, *ASEAN Declaration.*

[73] Foundation Robert Schuman, 'Declaration of the 9th May 1950 delivered by Robert Schuman' *European Issue* No. 204 (10 May 2011). On 18 April 1951, the *Treaty establishing the European Coal and Steel Community* (ECSC) was adopted. That Treaty, which entered into force on 23 July 1952 for a period limited to 50 years, integrated the economic sectors of the coal and steel industry. Then, the *Treaty establishing the EEC* and the *Euratom Treaty* were signed in Rome on 25 March 1957. Those Treaties, which entered into force on 1 January 1958 for an unlimited period, provided for the further integration of economic sectors by creating a common market as part of the EEC and by pooling nuclear industries under Euratom. As an organisation designed for the common management of the entire economy of the Member States, the EEC soon emerged as the most important Community. It became the main tool for—indirectly—achieving political unification.

[74] See ASEAN, Terms of Reference, 2nd SOMTC Working Group on Counter-Terrorism, 16 June 2008. At the time of ASEAN's formation there was only a very low level of complex integration between the states and the communities of Southeast Asia'. in Acharya (2012): 6; Piris and Woon (2015): 15.

[75] Telò (2016): 11–13.

adoption of the *ASEAN Charter* in 2007 was successful in conferring a legal personality unto the regional organisation (3).

1. The establishment of the 'ASEAN Way': a historically-based tool of regional governance

Recognising the benefit of dealing with some issues collectively, ASEAN Member States have decided to meet more and more regularly over the years. The first Summit between Member States was held in Bali in 1976. The third meeting took place in Manila in 1987 when it was decided that the leaders would meet every 5 years. Consequently, the fourth meeting was held in Singapore in 1992 where the leaders agreed to meet more frequently, deciding to hold the summit every 3 years. In 2001, it has been decided to meet annually to address urgent issues affecting the region. By December 2008, the *ASEAN Charter* came into force and with it, the decision that ASEAN Summit would be held twice in a year. In so doing, the ASEAN Summit has formalised the members' interactions.

The Summit takes place for three days. The usual itinerary is as follows: (1) The leaders of Member States would hold an internal organisation meeting; (2) These leaders would hold a conference together with foreign ministers of the ASEAN Regional Forum; (3) A meeting, known as ASEAN Plus Three, is set for leaders of three Dialogue Partners (People's Republic of China, Japan and South Korea); (4) A separate meeting, known as ASEAN-CER, is set for another set of leaders of two Dialogue Partners (Australia and New Zealand). Ancillary meetings also take place with other external partners.

These meetings are representative of the intra-regional dynamics. Regional cooperation and integration in Southeast Asia have been built upon the consultation, consensual decision-making and flexibility which is characteristic of the 'ASEAN Way'.[76] The 'ASEAN Way' is based on the Indonesian concepts of *musyawarah* (discussion and consultation) and *mufakat* (consensus-seeking). This 'Way' encompasses these six core norms guiding Member States' behaviour and decision-making: (1) sovereign equality, (2) non-recourse to the use of force and the peaceful settlement of conflict; (3) non-interference and non-intervention in internal affairs; (4) non-involvement of ASEAN to address unresolved bilateral conflict between members; (5) quiet diplomacy and (6) mutual respect and tolerance.[77] It provides an umbrella for informal channels of communication between governments that may also occur during the 'ASEAN leaders retreat' which follows each ASEAN Summit.

The 'ASEAN Way' has played a major role in ensuring stability in a region where diversity remains significant and in developing its Member States' potential

[76] Amitav Acharya, *Constructing a Security Community in Southeast Asia. ASEAN and the problem of regional order*, Politics in Asia series (New York: Routledge, 2001). In his book, Amitav Acharya defines the ASEAN Way as 'a process of regional interactions and cooperation based on discreteness, informality, consensus building and non-confrontational bargaining styles'.

[77] Kusuma Snitwongse, 'Thirty Years of ASEAN: Achievements through Political Cooperation', *The Pacific Review*, vol. 11, no. 2 (1998); Jürgen Haacke, *ASEAN's Diplomatic and Security Culture: Origins, Development and Prospects*, 1st ed. (Oxon: Routledge, 2003).

throughout those communities. This method of governance presents some similarities with the EU Open Method of Coordination (OMC). The OMC is a form of intergovernmental policy-making that does not result in adopting regional mandatory legislative measures and does not require Member States to introduce or amend their laws. The OMC is mainly based on jointly identifying and defining objectives (adopted by the Council in the EU; unanimously by ASEAN Member States); on jointly established measuring instruments through statistics, indicators, guidelines (not particularly developed in ASEAN); on benchmarking, i.e. comparing the performance of different countries and exchanging best practices (monitored with periodic evaluations by the European Commission and by Member States through peer reviews; monitored by Member States only in ASEAN). In a certain way, the ASEAN Secretariat may monitor Member States' actions but cannot take unilateral action or report a failed State without the States' agreement.

This method was initially necessary because there was no alternative basis for collaboration given that, at the time of the Association's formation, the differences between the Southeast Asian countries far outweighed their similarities.[78] Due to these historical, political and legal differences and tensions, it is logical for the Association to have adopted a loose regional structure. It took almost 10 years of interactions before the Member States decided to accept a basic element of central coordination through the establishment of the ASEAN Secretariat. Its creation in February 1976 was motivated by the 'need for a central administrative organ to provide for greater efficiency in the coordination of ASEAN organs and for more effective implementation of ASEAN projects and activities'.[79]

As expressed in Article 2 of the 1976 *Treaty of Amity and Cooperation*[80] and further developed in Article 2 of the 2007 *ASEAN Charter*, there is a desire to handle things in a fraternal manner through the dominant method of quiet diplomacy and a resistance against ceding sovereignty to a supranational body. ASEAN diplomacy makes use of informal relationships and discussions to work out consensual positions behind the scenes, rather than holding 'lengthy' intergovernmental confer-

[78] Angela Pennisi di Floristella, 'Are non-traditional security challenges leading regional organizations towards greater convergence? The EU and ASEAN security systems in comparative perspective', *Asia Europe Journal,* vol. 11, no. 3 (2013). See also Rodolfo C. Severino, *Southeast Asia in Search of an ASEAN Community: Insights from the former ASEAN Secretary-General* (Singapore: ISEAS publishing, 2006); Lin (2010).

[79] Preamble, *Agreement on the Establishment of the ASEAN Secretariat*, Bali, 24 February 1976. It was even recently repeated by the Secretary-General of ASEAN for 2018–2022, Wunderlich, 'The EU an Actor Sui Generis?' (2012): 654.

[80] Art. 2, ASEAN, *Treaty of Amity and Cooperation in Southeast Asia* (1976). The ASEAN principles are the following: mutual respect for the independence, sovereignty, equality, territorial integrity and national identity; the right of every State to lead its national existence free from external interference, subversion or coercion; non-interference in the internal affairs of one another; settlement of differences or disputes by peaceful means; renunciation of the threat or use of force; and, effective cooperation among themselves.

ences. This has helped establish networks of officials who negotiate 'on the golf course'.[81]

Although there is still much work to be done in the EU, relations between ASEAN Member States are not as orderly as those between EU Member States. Building mutual trust between Member States is a difficult task, especially between ASEAN Member States. This justifies the nature of dialogue which is to build up an interpersonal/social or, tentatively, political form of mutual trust while focusing less on the development of an autonomous ASEAN legal order. Eventually, trust constitutes a vector or, at least, a step towards the development of a regional architecture. In the EU, trust has developed alongside the adoption of norms. For example, the European arrest warrant would not be effective without mutual trust. Other norms facilitating cross-border cooperation have progressively built mutual trust and in kind they have benefited from it. The emergence of a duty of mutual trust has been imposed in many areas of EU law, including in criminal matters, as a tool for integration; despite trust intuitively refers to a subjective phenomenon that cannot be dictated.[82]

Knowing what has come first—regional law/regional integration or mutual trust—is indeed difficult to identify in both regions.

2. Towards a legal intrusion into the 'ASEAN Way': the establishment of the ASEAN Community

Moving forward, ASEAN Member States unanimously agreed at the ninth ASEAN Summit in 2003 (also called Bali Concord II) on the establishment of an ASEAN Community.[83] It was only at the 12th ASEAN Summit held in January 2007 that the leaders made a strong commitment, in the *Cebu Declaration on the Acceleration of the Establishment of an ASEAN Community*, to facilitate the establishment of an ASEAN Community by the end of 2015. Since the 2003 *Declaration of ASEAN Concord II*, the ASEAN's action has been divided into three pillars, namely the Political-Security Community, Economic Community and Socio-Cultural Community.[84] This ASEAN Community which is based on those three pillars was set for 2020.[85] However, an earlier date was set by the 21st ASEAN Summit, held in Phnom Penh between 17 and 20 November 2012.[86] Through the

[81] Alex J. Bellamy, 'The pursuit of security in Southeast Asia: Beyond realism' in *Contemporary Southeast Asia: regional dynamics, national differences*, ed., Mark Beeson (Basingstoke: Palgrave MacMillan, 2004): 170.

[82] Amitav Acharya, *Constructing a Security Community in Southeast Asia. ASEAN and the problem of regional order*, 3rd ed. (London: Routledge, 2014): 43 and ff.

[83] *Declaration of ASEAN Concord II*, Heads of State/Government, 9th ASEAN Summit, Bali, 7 October 2003.

[84] Pt. 1, *Declaration of ASEAN Concord II* (2003).

[85] *Roadmap for an ASEAN Community 2009–2015*, ASEAN Secretariat, Jakarta, 2009; and, *Cha-Am Hua Hin Declaration on the Roadmap for the ASEAN Community (2009–2015)*, Cha-Am, 1 March 2009.

[86] 20th ASEAN Summit, Phnom Penh, 3–4 April 2012.

implementation of programmes and plans of actions within the three pillars, ASEAN leaders established the ASEAN Community in 2015. In so doing, they entered into the next phase of its consolidation, further integration and stronger cohesiveness. The strengthening of ASEAN integration through the accelerated establishment of an ASEAN Community was explicitly intended to 'reinforce ASEAN's centrality and role as the driving force in charting the evolving regional architecture'.[87]

In so doing, ASEAN has recorded achievements in the realms of the three aforementioned pillars,[88] which serve as a firm foundation to build 'a dynamic, cohesive, resilient, and integrated ASEAN Community'.[89] These pillars are closely interdependent and mutually reinforcing for the purpose of ensuring durable peace, stability and shared prosperity in the region. Through the successive intersectional and more sectorial Roadmaps and Plans of Action,[90] the Association has made tremendous efforts to establish the ASEAN Community.[91] The establishment of the ASEAN Community is considered a major milestone in the regional integration process. Although the ASEAN Community is meant to reinforce ASEAN's centrality and its role as the driving force in charting the development of regional architecture, it is not the ultimate goal. In practice, it only constituted a new phase towards a deeper integration process.

This process has become more institutionalised and slightly rules-based,[92] particularly in the economic community. The 'economic integration' is clearly stated as an objective, while the word 'integration' is not mentioned in the other two pillars.[93] The ASEAN Economic Community has been the most successful pillar thus far.[94] The economic integration has been, until mid-2000s, mainly outward-oriented,

---

[87] ASEAN, *Declaration on the Acceleration of the Establishment of an ASEAN Community by 2015*, Cebu, January 2007.

[88] See, e.g., *ASEAN Political-Security Community Blueprint*, Jakarta, 1 March 2009.

[89] *Declaration of ASEAN Concord II* (2003).

[90] See some cross-cutting documents, like the *Roadmap for an ASEAN Community 2009–2015*; *ASEAN 2025: Forging Ahead Together* (2015); and sectorial documents, as the *ASEAN Work Plan on Combating Illicit Drug Production, Trafficking and Use (2009–2015),* Siem Reap, 17 November 2009; ASEAN Plan of Action Against Trafficking in Persons, Especially Women and Children, 27th ASEAN Summit, Kuala Lumpur, 22 November 2015.

[91] *Roadmap for an ASEAN Community 2009–2015*; *ASEAN Political-Security Community Blueprint* (2009); *ASEAN 2025: Forging Ahead Together* (2015). Also, ASEAN, Terms of Reference, 2nd SOMTC Working Group on Counter-Terrorism (2008).

[92] See, e.g., Acharya, *Constructing a Security Community in Southeast Asia* (2001): 64; Locknie Hsu, 'Towards an ASEAN Charter: Some Thoughts from the Legal Perspective' in *Framing the ASEAN Charter*, ed., Rodolfo C. Severino (Singapore: ISEAS Publishing, 2005): 45–51; Best and Christiansen, 'Regionalism in international affairs' (2008): 442; Lin (2010).

[93] See, e.g., Bali Concord III (2011). Also, Yeo Lay Hwee, 'The EU as a Security Actor in Southeast Asia' in *Security Politics in Asia and Europe*, ed., Wilhem Hofmeister, Panorama: Insights into Asian and European Affairs (Singapore: Konrad-Adenauer-Stiftung, 2009).

[94] According to official statistics, the implementation of the Economic Community has reached 458 out of 506 measures (90.5%): Report of the ASEAN Economic Community Council to the 26th ASEAN Summit, Kuala Lumpur, 27 April 2015.

seeking preferential tariffs and trade deals with the competitive neighbours of East Asia. Currently, the integration of the Economic Community aims to enhance the economy of ASEAN Member States through a single regional market and to strengthen their capacities on the global market. Notably, until recently legally binding agreements signed between ASEAN Member States have been predominantly economic in nature.[95] At this stage, it is worth noticing that, as in the EU, the economic development of the ASEAN Member States varies significantly from one to the other. Within this context, the Initiative for ASEAN Integration (IAI) Task Force provides policy guidance and direction to the development and implementation of the IAI Work Plan.[96] It is designed to assist Cambodia, Lao PDR, Myanmar and Vietnam (also called the 'CMLV countries') to meet the ASEAN-wide targets aimed at narrowing the development gap among the Member States, and between ASEAN and the rest of the world.[97] Although this initiative does not concern criminal matters, the regional programmes developed in the criminal justice area also take into consideration the gap between the Member States. Uncertainty remains about the spill-over effects that ASEAN Single Market has on the increasingly interdependent constellation of economies, i.e. the Asian 'noodle-bowl' that resulted from ASEAN's open regional architecture.[98]

Seventeen years after the Bali Concord II, the fight against transnational crime has not mirrored—or at least has not followed the same evolution as—the regional economical developments. ASEAN countries are undeniably benefiting from economic integration, but they have to consider the evolution of related challenges that are transnational crime, including smuggling of people, goods and capital and trafficking in persons between countries. It is patently evident that transnational organised crime groups have been able to capitalise on regional connectivity and trade flows, while many justice agencies and authorities do not effectively cooperate across borders. Against the backdrop of regional economic development, security and crime challenges have been changing and States now have to work together more frequently and in ways which have not been done in the past. In 2015, while celebrating the achievement of the ASEAN Community, ASEAN Foreign Ministers recognised the need to strengthen ASEAN legal integration to address and combat transnational crime.[99] It is particularly interesting and beneficial to observe whether

[95] Jean-Claude Piris and Walter Woon, *Towards a Rules-Based Community: An ASEAN Legal Service* (Cambridge: Cambridge University Press, 2015): 53.

[96] See the last *Initiative for ASEAN Integration (IAI) Work Plan IV (2021–2025)* (Jakarta: ASEAN Secretariat, November 2020).

[97] ASEAN, *Committee of Permanent Representatives to ASEAN (CPR) Handbook* (Jakarta: ASEAN Secretariat, August 2017), 12: The IAI Work Plan focuses on five strategic areas: food and agriculture; trade facilitations; micro, small and medium enterprises; education; and health and well-being.

[98] Art. 1(15), *ASEAN Charter*.

[99] Pt 39, Joint Communiqué, 48th ASEAN Foreign Ministers Meeting, Kuala Lumpur, 4 August 2015.

or not, and how, ASEAN is complying—or is attempting to comply—with this objective from a short-, medium- and long-term perspective.

Cooperation and integration are regularly associated in the *ASEAN Charter* as well as in the ASEAN Political-Security Community (APSC) Blueprint.[100] Cooperation mechanisms are increasingly incorporated through the various integration perspectives.[101]

3. The adoption of the *ASEAN Charter*: a decisive step towards a rules-based approach?

ASEAN Member States have decided to take a step forward by developing a regional institutional framework, through the adoption of an *ASEAN Charter* on 20 November 2007. This constitutes a significant development by way of inserting legal elements in ASEAN. The Charter highlights the commitment of the Member States to enhancing regional cooperation and integration, especially in developing the ASEAN Political and Security Community (APSC).[102] Whether this instrument revolutionises the development of the regional organisation, or whether it deepens regional integration through law, is still a pending question.

The Eminent Persons' Group (EPG), which was tasked to make recommendations with respect to drafting the *ASEAN Charter*, identified the absence of institutions and procedures to monitor, implement and enforce ASEAN norms as the ASEAN's primary concern. The EPG maintained that ASEAN 'must have a culture of commitment to honour and implement decisions, agreements and timelines'.[103] Thus, it was recommended that a Dispute Settlement Mechanism 'be established in all fields of ASEAN cooperation which should include compliance monitoring, advisory, consultation as well as enforcement mechanisms'.[104] The ASEAN Secretariat would have been entrusted with 'monitoring compliance with ASEAN agreements and actions plans, with the Secretary-General of ASEAN reporting its findings to the ASEAN Council and the Community Councils on regular basis'.[105] ASEAN Council should have had 'the power to take measures to redress cases of serious breaches of ASEAN's objectives, major principles and commitments to important agreements',[106] such as suspending rights and privileges of membership, and possibly, expulsion.

[100] See, e.g., C1 'Strengthening ASEAN Centrality in regional Cooperation and Community Building', in *ASEAN Political-Security Community Blueprint* (2009).

[101] Pt. 7 of the Preamble, B.4.1. and C.1., *ASEAN Political-Security Community Blueprint* (2009).

[102] Preamble, *ASEAN Charter*; ASEAN, 20th ASEAN Summit (2012). See ASEAN, 'Evolving Towards ASEAN 2015' *Annual Report 2011–2012*, ASEAN Secretariat, Jakarta, June 2012. See Victor V. Ramraj et al., eds., *Global Anti-Terrorism Law and Policy*, 2nd ed. (Cambridge: Cambridge University Press, 2012): 112.

[103] Para. 6, *Report of the Eminent Persons' Group on the ASEAN Charter*, December 2006.

[104] Ibid.

[105] Ibid.

[106] Ibid.

While these recommendations were not wholly endorsed, the *ASEAN Charter* did incorporate many of them. The Charter took a major step in the community-building process with a slight rules-based approach,[107] which is a move from regional collaboration towards integration. It expressly confers legal personality upon ASEAN and provides that the rights and duties contained in the Charter shall prevail over other ASEAN instruments in the event that there are conflicting laws or principles.[108] Member States are required under Article 5 of the *ASEAN Charter* to 'take all necessary measures including the enactment of appropriate domestic legislation' to implement the Charter provisions and to comply with membership obligations.

Notably, the *ASEAN Charter* can either be seen as a confirmation of existing practice—institutionalising it—or a developmental modification pursuant to deeper regional integration, particularly economic integration.[109] In the field of security, ASEAN is best characterised by representing a limited security regime as its Member States have only been bound by a medium-low level of complex integration in this domain thus far.

Subsequently, ASEAN affirmed the strong commitment of the Member States to intensify cooperation 'towards an integrated, people-centred and rules-based organisation' at its 20th ASEAN Summit in 2012.[110] Today still, regional integration remains a work in progress.

II. Intergovernmental design v. supranational design: a distinction only seemingly clear

The construct of the two regional organisations has led to two distinctly qualified regional organisations (A). It still remains to be seen whether the two regional organisations' designs increasingly align, especially since they both gained legal personalities. Their respective regional legal frameworks can be examined via three main lines of inquiry (B), from which some conclusions on the main differences and similarities may be drawn. These might explain their diverging approaches thus far (C).

A. Finding common ground in different forms of international organisations: a basis for the development of regional organisations

[107] Art. 1(15), *ASEAN Charter*. Also, Clara Portela, 'The Association of Southeast Asian Nations (ASEAN): Integration, Internal Dynamics and External Relations', Study for the European Parliament, Policy Department Directorate-General for External Policies, EXPO/B/AFET/FWC/2009–01/Lot2/13, PE 433.713 (Bruxelles: European Union, September 2013).

[108] Art. 52(2), *ASEAN Charter*.

[109] Lin (2010); Lee Leviter, 'The ASEAN Charter: ASEAN's Failure or Member Failure?', *New York Journal of International Law and Politics*, vol. 43, no. 4 (2010).

[110] ASEAN, 'Evolving Towards ASEAN 2015' *Annual Report 2011–2012*, ASEAN Secretariat, Jakarta, June 2012; also, *ASEAN 2025: Forging Ahead Together* (Jakarta: ASEAN Secretariat, November 2015), 4.

One measure of the success of a regional legal system is whether it is accepted by those who are subject to it. Reliant upon their consent, they define the legal architecture of the regional organisation according to their ability and willingness to engage in projects of this nature. Each member may give the regional organisation different purposes and/or may have different views on the institutional, legal and factual challenges which they encounter. Over time, the role and place of the EU institutions have become clearer and the Member States have externalised their sovereignty through the regional organisation, whereas ASEAN Member States remain in full control of the organisation's actions.

While disagreements and discrepancies between EU Member States' policies and laws exist, disagreements and discrepancies have greater impact on the functioning and decisions of ASEAN, due to the nature of the 'ASEAN Way'. For instance, Singapore's perspective on the regional security architecture is shaped by realist-bound balance of power considerations—giving States the central role and using the regional framework to reach its own agenda.[111] In contrast, Indonesia is very much in favour of the development of ASEAN as a regional actor distinct from its Member States, and giving it the power to engage in closer cooperation.[112] Due to these tensions, ASEAN's development is limited. That being said, according to former ASEAN Secretary General Ong Keng Yong, the Charter aims to confirm ASEAN as an organisation by conferring legal personality, enhancing institutional accountability and compliance, and reinforces the perception of ASEAN as a real regional actor.[113]

Against this backdrop, it is crucial to state that regional integration does not necessarily entail the creation of a supranational authority. Integration should not be limited to the centralisation of a law-making authority.[114] It can encompass a vast spectrum of activities and processes, ranging from the mere coordination of law-making policy to the merging of distinct systems into a single unified system. In whichever form it takes, regional integration links States much closely together and formalises their interactions.

Regional organisations are often 'divided' between those of a traditional nature or predominant intergovernmental systems and those which are predominantly of a

[111] Chin Kin Wah, 'Singapore's Perspective on the Asia-Pacific Security Architecture' in *Asia-Pacific Security Cooperation: National Interests and Regional Order*, eds., See Seng Tan and Amitav Acharya (New York: M. E. Sharpe Inc., 2004): 188.

[112] Wunderlich, 'Comparing regional organisations in global multilateral institutions: ASEAN, the EU and the UN' (2012): 129.

[113] ASEAN, 'ASEAN leaders sign *ASEAN Charter*' *media release* (2007): available at http://www.aseansec.org/21085.htm (accessed on 10 February 2021).

[114] Jürgen Habermas, *Die Einbeziehung des anderen. Studien zur politischen Theorie* (Frankfurt am Main: Suhrkamp, 1996); Ursula Nelles, 'Definitions of harmonisation' in *Harmonisation and harmonising measures in criminal law*, eds., André Klip and Harmen van der Wilt (Amsterdam: Koninklijke Nederlandse Akad. van Wetenschappen, 2002); Weyembergh, 'Introduction' (2006); Telò and Weyembergh, 'Supranationality and sovereignty' (2020).

supranational nature, usually marked by and leading to a more integrated system or higher degree of regional integration.

The term 'international' is composed of two parts: 'inter' and 'national'. The first part means 'between', while the second means 'of or regarding nations'. Therefore, the term 'international' includes anything involving, regarding or pertaining to two or more nations or States. Several definitions of 'international organisations' have been discussed by the International Law Commission.[115] According to Article 2 (a) of the *Draft articles on the responsibility of international organisations* adopted by the International Law Commission, 'international organisation' means 'an organisation established by a treaty or other instrument governed by international law and possessing its own international legal personality'.

Traditional international institutions are meant to provide a common working environment for members in which they can organise dialogues, enhance mutual understanding, facilitate cooperation, seek to further their interests and promote the common good.[116] It involves formal and informal sets of rules that different actors, including States and potentially other entities,[117] should respect in order to achieve certain outcomes in specific areas.[118] Institutions can contribute to creating norms and promoting compliance with these norms via monitoring mechanisms.[119]

The term 'supranational' is quite different as it is composed of two parts: 'supra', i.e. 'beyond or above', and 'national'. Supranational thus means beyond or above the control or oversight of one nation. Supranational organisations have greater binding powers over Member States than a traditional international organisation does; and thus, the extent of those powers depends on the respective foundational treaty. The evolution towards a supranational organisation is reflected in the ambition to create a

[115] See, e.g., A/CN.4/SER.A/2002/Add.1 (Part 2), *Yearbook of the International Law Commission 2002*, Vol. II (Part II), 'Report of the International Law Commission on the work of its fifty-fourth session', 29 April–7 June and 22 July–16 August 2002, Doc. A/57/10 (New York – Geneva: UN Publications, 2009): 94.

[116] *Final Communiqué of the Bandung Conference* (1955), 19.

[117] Draft articles on the responsibility of international organisations, A/CN.4/SER.A/2011/Add.1 (Part 2), *Yearbook of the International Law Commission 2011*, Vol. II (Part Two), 'Report of the International Law Commission on the work of its sixty-third session', 26 April–3 June and 4 July–12 August 2011, Doc. A/66/10 (New York and Geneva: UN Publications, 2018).

[118] Robert O. Keohane, 'International Institutions: Two Approaches', *International Studies Quarterly,* vol. 32, no. 4 (1988): 383. See also Anne Mette Kjær, *Governance*, Key Concepts in the social sciences (Cambridge: Polity Press, 2004): 8; Barbara Czarniawska, 'Emerging Institutions: Pyramids or Anthills?', University of Gothenburg, GRI (Gothenburg, 2006); Franck Bessis, 'L'institution comme réalisation du collectif', *Tracés: Revue de Sciences Humaines,* vol. 17, no. 2 (2009); Simon Chesterman, 'Does ASEAN exist? The Association of South East Asian Nations as an International Legal Person', *Singapore Year Book of International Law,* vol. 12 (2008); Stephen D. Krasner, 'Structural Causes and Regime Consequences: Regimes as Intervening Variables', *International Organization,* vol. 36, no. 2 (1982): 191.

[119] Michael N. Barnett, 'The United Nations and Global Security: The Norm is Mightier than the Sword', *Ethics and International Affairs,* vol. 9 (1995): 38.

legal system which has supremacy over the national legislations of the Member States.[120]

Both traditional international organisations and supranational organisations share many characteristics. For instance, their legal personality differs from that of the Member States and they are endowed with internal independent organs for which they have their own human and financial resources. However, some elements differentiate them strongly, particularly in terms of the depth of integration reached between Member States. The differences between these organisations make one far better than the other. International organisations can be characterised by three weaker features: (1) Unlike supranational organisations, international (intergovernmental) organisations arguably do not 'limit' the sovereignty of their Member States as they only restrict their external freedom of action, by compelling or preventing States from taking those actions, which are within an organisation's competence.[121] (2) International organisations cannot enforce those binding decisions which are directly applicable to Member States and individuals. (3) International organisations share competence with their Member States. Moreover, these competences are explicitly enumerated in the constitutive treaties and are limited to restricted substantive areas.[122] These elements explain the differences of the EU and ASEAN's respective qualifications.

In normative terms, supranational law is a form of international law that differs from public international law. In the case of supranational law, States expressly submit their right to make decisions on transnational issues to a set of common institutions. It is especially the case in the EU where sovereign States have pooled their authority through a system of institutions and court competent in designated matters. By contrast, the normative effect of ASEAN can rather qualified as general international law, as there is no delegation of competence.

To this extent, analysing each regional organisation's current institutional and legal developments, with an emphasis on the emergence of their legal personality, reveals the divergences between the way in which EU and ASEAN operationalise their unique attributes.

---

[120] Elements of definition are provided by scholars in EU law, such as Weatherill (2007): 676; Craig and de Búrca (2011): 184 and ff. For an interdisciplinary approach on the definition of 'supranationality', Telò and Weyembergh, 'Supranationality and sovereignty' (2020).

[121] Notably, the Security Council of the UN, composed of 15 States, has the power under Chap. VII to determine the existence of a threat to, or breach of, international peace and security, and to make binding resolutions. However, the Security Council does not have any autonomous means to impose its resolutions. Only States and/or the international community can actually implement, control and sanction the failing State(s). The UN organs such as the Human Rights Council may 'only' discuss, report, make recommendations on situations that require States' attention. The decision-making is still in the hands of the States; not of the Organisation as such. In the framework of a supranational organisation, it may be argued that States do not 'limit' but 'exercise' their sovereignty through the regional organisation.

[122] Magdalena M. Martin Martinez, *National Sovereignty and International Organizations* (The Hague: Kluwer Law International, 1996), 71–72.

B. The emergence of a legal personality: has it made changes to the regional organisation and its members?

The legal personality confers some rights to States and international organisations and, consequently, to their representatives.[123] Thus, there is an interest for the EU and ASEAN to be granted a legal personality. This allows them to represent the shared interest of their Member States with a clear and more powerful position on the international scene, allocating them specific rights that are enforceable on the international scene.[124]

Interestingly, the EU acquired a legal personality shortly after ASEAN did. The 2007 Lisbon Treaty, which came into force on 1 December 2009, along with the *Treaty on EU* and the *Treaty on the Functioning of the EU*, disregards the previous three-pillar structure in favour of a single legal personality.[125] Up until the Lisbon Treaty, the European Community was endowed with legal personality, while the EU had not been. Due to its previous structure, the EU was not prevented from representing its Member States in specific matters on an international level. It is interesting to question whether a legal personality adds value to a regional organisation.

An organisation enjoys the specific legal personality that its members have given it, meaning that it possesses the following three attributes: (1) a permanent association of States, with lawful objects, equipped with state organs; (2) a distinction, in terms of legal powers and purposes, between the organisation and its Member States; and (3) the existence of legal powers exercisable at an international level and not solely at the level of the national systems of one or more States.[126]

1. <u>The establishment of a permanent organisation, with lawful objects and equipped with administrative and/or policy-making organs</u>

[123] See, e.g., *Convention on the Privileges and Immunities of the United Nations*, New York, 13 February 1946, UNTS vol. 1, No. 4; *Convention on the Privileges and Immunities of the Specialized Agencies*, New York, 21 November 1947, UNTS vol. 33, No. 521; *Vienna Convention on the Diplomatic Relations*, Vienna, 18 April 1961, UNTS vol. 500, No. 7310; and, Resolution 2625(XXV), *Declaration on Principles of International Law concerning Friendly Relations and Co-operation among States in accordance with the Charter of the United Nations* (1964); see also e.g. Hsu (2005); Acharya, 'Comparative Regionalism' (2012): 6.

[124] *Report of the Eminent Persons' Group on the ASEAN Charter*, December 2006, para. 43. See also ICJ, *Reparation for injuries suffered in the service of the United Nations*, Advisory Opinion, 11 April 1949, I.C.J. Reports 1949. Also, Mattheis and Wunderlich (2017): 727.

[125] Art. 47, TEU.

[126] Ian Brownlie, *Principles of public international law*, 5th ed. (Oxford: Oxford University Press, 1998): 679–80. See also pt. 2, *Final Communiqué of the Bandung Conference* (Afro-Asian Conference), Bandung, 18–24 April 1955. For more discussions about the legal personality of an international organisation, Daillier, Forteau, and Pellet (2009): 449 and ff.

Before the enactment of the 2007 Charter, ASEAN was considered an 'institution without legalisation'.[127] ASEAN was said to lack the 'juridical personality or legal standing under international law'[128] necessary to qualify as a regional legal representative of its Member States and to grant it autonomous capacities. It was nonetheless already a permanent association of States, with lawful objects, equipped from the outset with rudimentary organs, which grew into a Secretariat with time.[129] With the resultant Secretariat that has progressively developed, it could have had a greater role in improving the role of the regional organisation in the different areas, including in assuming responsibility to promote cooperation in criminal matters and protect human rights. However, even since the adoption of the Charter, the Secretariat's role is still limited to its original functions. The main role of the ASEAN Secretariat is to formally support the coordination of Member States' actions.[130] The *ASEAN Charter* codifies the norms, principles, rules and values that must be upheld in the pursuit of common goals, and it provides an institutional framework.[131] However, it does not create vertical obligations and rather, promotes horizontal interstate relations. In any event, the role of the Member States has not changed since the adoption of its regional norms.

The *ASEAN Charter* does not make significant changes to the practice of the institution. It does however formalise the role of ASEAN as an international institution.

The type of legal personality given to the organisation by the *ASEAN Charter* is not a personality in a more meaningful sense.[132] The adoption of the *ASEAN Charter* did not fill in the substantive gaps. The Charter is comparable to primary legislation, while enactments such as regulations and rules of procedure act as secondary legislation.[133] As part of the regional legal architecture, the *ASEAN Charter* refers

[127] Miles Kahler, 'Legalization as Strategy: The Asia-Pacific Case', *International Organization*, vol. 54, no. 3 (2000).

[128] Rodolfo C. Severino, 'Introduction' in *Framing the ASEAN Charter*, ed., Rodolfo C. Severino (Singapore: ISEAS Publishing, 2005): 6. In the same book, Hsu adopted the more nuanced position that ASEAN's legal personality needed 'clarification': Hsu (2005): 45. Also, Seiji Naya et al., eds., *ASEAN Economic Cooperation for the 1990s: A Report Prepared for the ASEAN Standing Committee* (Manila: The Philippines Institute for Development Studies, 1992) 112 (concluding that ASEAN has a 'nascent international legal personality'); Jiang Yu Wang, 'International Legal Personality of ASEAN and the Legal Nature of the China-ASEAN Free Trade Agreement' in *China-ASEAN Relations: Economic and Legal Dimensions*, eds., John Wong, Zou Keyuan, and Zeng Huaqun (Singapore: World Scientific, 2006): 126 (ASEAN would have a 'selective personality').

[129] Severino, 'Introduction' (2005); Chesterman (2008); Piris and Woon (2015).

[130] On the need to build the necessary institutions, Piris and Woon (2015): 68–69.

[131] ASEAN, *Committee of Permanent Representatives to ASEAN (CPR) Handbook* (2017), 4.

[132] Chesterman (2008): 200 and ff.

[133] Ingo Venke and Li-Ann Thio, *The internal Effects of ASEAN External Relations*, Integration Through Law (Cambridge: Cambridge University Press, 2016): 11.

to the *Terms of Reference of the Human Rights Body,*[134] which subsequently established the ASEAN Intergovernmental Commission on Human Rights (Article 14, Charter); the *Agreement on the Privileges and Immunities*[135] (Articles 17, 18 and 19, Charter); and, the *Protocol to the ASEAN Charter on Dispute Settlement Mechanisms*[136] (Article 22, Charter). Concerning the mechanism of dispute settlement, the 2010 Protocol provides a stricter mechanism compared to the one in Chap. VIII of the *ASEAN Charter*. It dictates that consultations need to be held within a fixed time frame and it further paves the way for dispute settlement by an arbitral tribunal. These last two instruments were ratified in 2017.[137] These instruments, which have no enforceability power, are nonetheless working towards a more harmonised situation in the region. This structural legal package is in fact less binding than the TEU and TFEU assembled, which provide more precise rules about the region's horizontal (i.e. between States, between citizens up to a certain point) and vertical relations (i.e. between the EU and its Member States, between the EU and EU citizens and between the States and their nationals). Because this ASEAN dispute settlement body lacks enforceability, it does not provide an effective system of protection of human rights.

By contrast, EU Member States have established durable institutions—which strengthened over time—and decision-making processes. This is especially the case since the adoption of the Lisbon Treaty, where the European Parliament gained decisive powers for the decision-making of EU criminal laws by becoming a co-legislator with the Council of the EU. Similarly, the European Commission and the CJEU play a significant role as they ensure that the EU Member States respect EU criminal law and the respective human rights involved. Therefore, the EU has a well-defined institutional structure for criminal matters.

Consequently, the two regional organisations developed various bodies with distinct purposes and capacities. The EU and its Member States have differential roles in certain regional bodies and matters. Meanwhile, ASEAN Member States are the components of every organ of the organisation.

2. The distribution of competences and exercise of legal powers within each region

One of the most important factors defining features of a regional organisation is whether they independently create legal obligations. In this respect, strong divergences exist between the EU and ASEAN internal legal framework as well as the role of the regional organisation within the region.

---

[134] *Declaration on the Intergovernmental Commission on Human Rights* and *ASEAN Intergovernmental Commission on Human rights (Terms of reference)*, 15th ASEAN Summit, Cha-Am Hua Hin, 23–25 October 2009.

[135] *Agreement on the Privileges and Immunities of the Association of Southeast Asian Nations*, Cha-Am Hua Hi, 25 October 2009.

[136] *Protocol to the ASEAN Charter on Dispute Settlement Mechanisms*, Hanoi, 8 April 2010.

[137] The *Agreement on the Privileges and Immunities* entered into force on 20 April 2017 and the *Protocol to the ASEAN Charter on Dispute Settlement Mechanisms* entered into force on 28 July 2017.

(a) *A diverging distribution of competences in the EU and ASEAN*

The organisation and contents of its particular relationship with the central system (regional institutions) and the system of the constituent units (the Member States) vary profoundly.

The *ASEAN Charter* provides a legal status and institutional framework for codifying regional norms, rules and values; setting targets for the regional organisation; and presenting accountability and compliance mechanisms. However, ASEAN has no power to impose any obligation on its Member States. While ASEAN is meant to become 'the primary driving force in regional arrangements that it initiates and [to] maintain its centrality in regional cooperation and community building',[138] it has acted in a limited capacity as a mediator.[139] The role of its Member States remains the central to the adoption of regional instruments.[140] The ASEAN Summit, gathering the Heads of States and governments, is in fact the 'supreme policy-making body of ASEAN'.[141] This is followed by the three ASEAN Coordinating Councils, each of whom is composed of representatives from the ten Member States, and they are placed in charge of ensuring the implementation of the relevant decisions made at the ASEAN Summit.[142] There is therefore no differentiation between the regional organisation and the Member States.

The situation in the EU differs significantly. The competences which are not conferred upon the Union in the Treaties remain with the Member States.[143] However, in several domains, it has exclusive competences. In these areas, it can impose norms and represent its Member States: the customs union, the internal market, the protection of the euro, fisheries policy and trade policy.[144] In other domains, it shares its competence with its Member States such as the AFSJ which relates to police and judicial cooperation in criminal matters.[145] In judicial cooperation, the Member States remain in control where the EU has not exercised its competence or has explicitly ceased to do so. The EU and the Member States have a duty of sincere cooperation vis-à-vis each other. They are bound by a mutual legal obligation 'to assist each other in carrying out the tasks which flow from the

[138] Art. 41(3), *ASEAN Charter*. ASEAN Member States reaffirm their 'continuous support for ASEAN Centrality in the evolving regional architecture': pt. 2, ASEAN, Chairman's Statement, 5th ASEAN-U.S. Summit to Commemorate the 40th Anniversary of ASEAN-U.S. Dialogue Relations, Manila, 13 November 2017.

[139] See, e.g., Kwei-Bo Huang, 'The transformation of ASEAN as a third-party mediator in intra-regional disputes of Southeast Asia' in *Conflict Management, Security and Intervention in East Asia: Third Party Mediation in Regional Conflict*, eds., Jacob Bercovitch, Kwei-Bo Huang, and Chung-Chian Teng (Oxford: Routledge, 2008).

[140] See, e.g., ASEAN, 'Evolving Towards ASEAN 2015' *Annual Report 2011–2012*, ASEAN Secretariat, Jakarta, June 2012, 4.

[141] Art. 7, *ASEAN Charter*.

[142] Art. 9(4) (a), *ASEAN Charter*.

[143] Arts. 4 and 5, TEU.

[144] Art. 3, TFEU.

[145] Art. 4, TFEU.

Treaties'.[146] In this situation, EU Member States are accountable to the EU. Evidently, its integrated regional structure allows the EU to adopt more precise norms which promotes that the Member States approximate their legislation and cooperate on the respective subject.

Another significant difference between ASEAN and the EU is that the EU legal instruments bind their citizens, not only the Member States. The EU legal order directly affects the citizens' daily lives to an ever-increasing extent. It accords them certain rights. For example, due to the protection of freedom of movement within the EU, any EU citizen is free to travel anywhere within the EU territory. The EU has become a driving force and the guardian of EU law as well as regional cohesion. By contrast, ASEAN norms have no impact on the Member States' citizens. Citizens remain governed exclusively by their national legislation.

(b) *Different regional organisational structures*

ASEAN and the EU are differentiated by two main elements: their voting system and their institutional structure, including the relations between the relevant regional institutions and the Member States.

Firstly, the voting system in ASEAN and in the EU differs significantly. These differences vary to a greater or lesser degree depending on the phase of their own regional development.

It has long been argued that there was no prospect for ASEAN to become 'a supranational entity acting independently of its members'.[147] Member States considered such an entity a potential danger to their autonomy and individuality as well as their own influence at an international level.[148] Following its own 'way', ASEAN Member States have adopted norms that are politically—rather than legally—binding.[149] This stems from the successive Summits where a unanimous voting system is in place.[150] Decisions made by unanimity are arduous and time-consuming, but by nature they are intended to be easier to implement. Consensus aims to strike a balance between the probability of reaching a decision and the likelihood of compliance.[151] As any other traditional international convention or treaty, the ASEAN

[146] Art. 4(3), TEU.

[147] Rodolfo C. Severino, 'Asia Policy Lecture: What ASEAN Is and What It Stands For' The Research Institute for Asia and the Pacific, University of Sydney (22 October 1998).

[148] Shaun Breslin 'Theorising East Asian Regionalism(s): New Regionalism and Asia's Future(s)' in *Advancing East Asian Regionalism,* ed. Melissa G. Curley and Nicholas Thomas (Oxon: Routledge, 2007), 2.

[149] Art. 7(2)(a), *ASEAN Charter*: The ASEAN Summit shall 'be the supreme *policy-making* body of ASEAN' (italics by the author).

[150] Incidentally, the consensus principle is applied pretty much in all regional organisations outside the EU: Constance Chevallier-Govers, *De la coopération à l'intégration policière dans l'Union Européenne* (Bruxelles: Bruylant, 1999).

[151] Notably, the difficulties in arriving at a consensual position were evident in ASEAN's response to Vietnam's invasion of Cambodia in 1979—an episode that was crucial to the evolution of ASEAN as a regional collective actor. Reactions to Vietnam's invasion differed between ASEAN

ones need to be signed, ratified and then the instruments of ratification are registered by the competent authority, namely the ASEAN Secretariat or any other competent authority such as the Government of Malaysia being the Depository State of the *ASEAN Treaty on Mutual Legal Assistance in Criminal Matters.*[152] It is only after a defined number of ratifications, or all ratifications, are deposited that the regional or international convention or treaty enters into force. Due to the unanimity requirement, the provisions of the ASEAN texts are broad and unclear to the extent that their implementation may vary across countries.

The EU decision-making process has evolved considerably: there has been a move from the unanimous voting requirement of the Member States in the EU Council to the qualified majority vote. This change was a lengthy process. First introduced by the *Single European Act*, qualified majority is today the standard EU voting rule for the adoption of regulations and directives, including in criminal matters. Indeed, the qualified majority vote was extended by the Lisbon Treaty in Title V of Part III of the TFEU to cooperation in criminal matters too. The Lisbon Treaty abolished the Third Pillar, which was marked by intergovernmental decision-making, thus generalising the ordinary legislative procedure set out in Article 294 TFEU. The Council acts by qualified majority, and the European Parliament has become co-legislator. Adopted under this procedure, regulations are binding in their entirety and directly applicable in all Member States territories, while directives bind the Member States according to the final result(s). The directives have to be transposed into the national legal frameworks and thus, allow for manoeuvrability to shape the form and means of implementation.

Secondly, the regional organisational structures are also quite different. Consequently, the role and functions of the organs/bodies of these respective regional institutions also differ.

The ASEAN Secretariat is not the only body of the regional organisation in the large sense of what the institution encompasses. Although a slight form of hierarchy might be created, ASEAN abounds in bodies, with similar and even overlapping functions, which are meant to discuss shared issues. This structure seems to link these bodies by reporting their discussions and subsequent results as well as information and intelligence sharing, rather than a relationship based on control or effective oversight (Table 4.2).

As its name indicates, the ASEAN Secretariat plays the sole role of secretariat in the decision-making procedure. It takes notes of the decisions of the different bodies (e.g. political cooperation divisions, security cooperation divisions or human rights divisions), at different levels, and it transmits the reports to other respective bodies

---

members. Thailand was extremely concerned about Vietnam's dominant position in Indochina whereas Indonesia was more worried about China. Consensus was forced by troubles on the Thai–Vietnamese border in 1980, resulting in a unitary ASEAN approach. ASEAN rallied and combined a variety of instruments in order to assert its voice on the international stage. It took its defence of sovereignty and non-intervention to the UN, and UN Resolution 34/22 called for an immediate withdrawal of all Vietnamese forces from Cambodia.

[152] *ASEAN Treaty on Mutual Legal Assistance in Criminal Matters* (2004).

Table 4.2 ASEAN Secretariat organisational structure

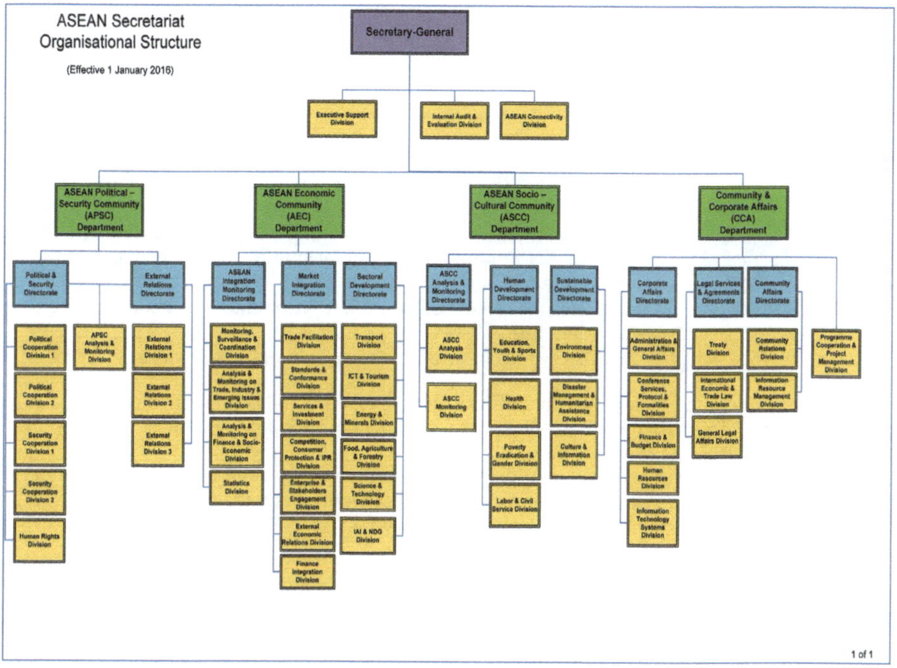

Source: ASEAN Secretariat (as organised in 2023, cf. ASEAN website)

and Member States. Therefore, it would be more accurate to add the Secretariat as part or next to each body.

Below is a schematic of the functions of the main bodies represented in the above chart. The distinctions between the different bodies are not rigid, but rather remain flexible according to the needs and opportunities in each context (Table 4.3).

After providing the necessary explanation on the role of each main body, the decision-making process may be further illustrated as follows (Table 4.4):

Notably, the ASEAN Secretariat has not been highlighted in this schema as it has its place within each body where it takes notes and ensures the coherence of the entire ASEAN policy.

Among these numerous bodies are those involved in the decision-making within the APSC (cf. Table 4.2), that are considered competent to address transnational crime.

ASEAN sectoral bodies (part of the ASEAN Secretariat) monitor and review the implementation by the Member States of their decisions adopted during Summits.[153] In the case of transnational crime, the ASEAN Ministerial Meeting on Transnational

[153] Art XVI, ACCT; Terms of Reference, 2nd SOMTC Working Group on Counter-Terrorism (2008).

Table 4.3 Role of the main ASEAN bodies

ASEAN Summit	• Comprises the Heads of State or Government of the ASEAN Member States and is the **supreme policy-making body**.
ASEAN Coordinating Council	• Comprises the ASEAN Foreign Ministers and supported by the relevant Senior Officials. • Convenes at least twice a year to, among other functions, prepare for the ASEAN Summit and related meetings, coordinate the implementation of the Summit's decisions and agreements. • Coordinates the reports of the ASEAN Community Councils to the ASEAN Summit.
ASEAN Community Council	• Comprises the Political-Security Community Council, the Economic Community Council and the Socio-Cultural Community Council. • Each Community Council coordinates the work of the different sectors under its purview and coordinates on issues that cut across those of other Community Councils.
ASEAN Sectoral Ministerial Bodies	• Comprise Ministers from all ASEAN Member States for a particular sector, such as Defence, Law, Transnational Crime, Drug Matters, Education, to name a few. • Have under their purview the relevant senior officials and subsidiary bodies to undertake their respective functions.
ASEAN National Secretariats	• Serve as the national focal points which, among other roles, coordinate the implementation of decisions at the national level.
Committee of Permanent Representatives	• Comprises the ten Permanent Representatives of Member States to ASEAN at the rank of Ambassadors. The Chairmanship of the Committee is held by the Permanent Representative to ASEAN of the Member State which serves as Chair of ASEAN at the time. • Underpins all of the bodies above.

(AMMTC)—supported by the Senior Officials Meeting on Transnational Crime (SOMTC) and the Directors-General of Immigration Departments and Heads of Consular Affairs Divisions of Ministries of Foreign Affairs Meeting (DGICM)—helps States respect their engagement(s).[154] As for the remaining bodies, these are

[154] For the list of sectoral bodies, Annex 1 to *ASEAN Charter*: available at https://bit.ly/2Z5qpRQ (accessed on 10 March 2019).

Table 4.4 ASEAN' structure in the decision-making procedure

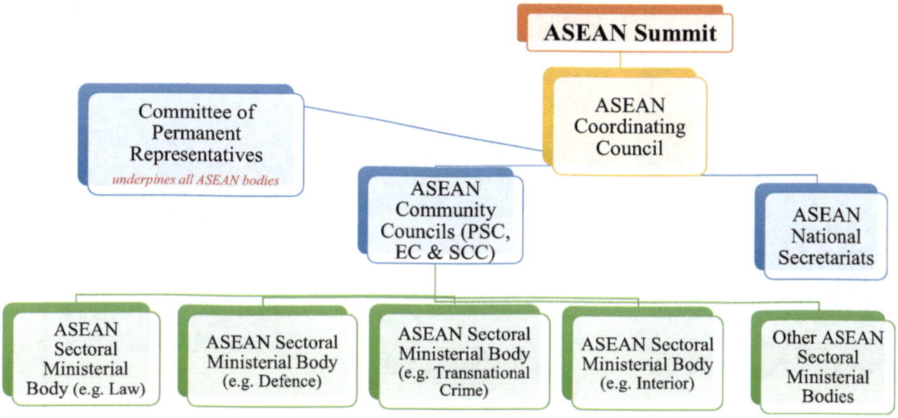

composed of representatives of every Member State. Therefore, together, Member States ensure the implementation of what has been unanimously decided, via support programmes or, but unlikely, through exerting pressure. Nonetheless, it is worth noticing that the obligations they agree upon are substantially broad, which leaves the Member States with significant manoeuvrability. Resultantly, it is unlikely that any violations of a regional Convention or any other Summit decision may occur. Even if such violations do occur, there is no sanction mechanism comparable to the EU infringement procedure.

The full inclusion of the Member States in each body, and at different stages of the decision-making, demonstrates that ASEAN is a good example of a traditional intergovernmental organisation.

By contrast, the EU constitutes a well-known example of a supranational structure. As it has already been well-documented,[155] the EU institutional structure and decision-making shall not be further detailed. For the sake of the comparison, the EU structure and decision-making process can be generally schematised as follows (Table 4.5):

This illustration is an overview of the interactions between the main EU institutions as established by the treaties. There are a number of other bodies that take specialised roles such as the European Central Bank, the European External Action Service, the European Investment Bank, the European Ombudsman, the European

[155] See, e.g., Pescatore (1974); Louis (1988); Wiener and Diez, eds. (2004); Weatherill (2007); Milton and Keller-Noëllet (2007); Craig and de Búrca (2011); Chalmers, Davies, and Monti (2014); Dony (2018).

Table 4.5 EU institutional structure and legislative procedure

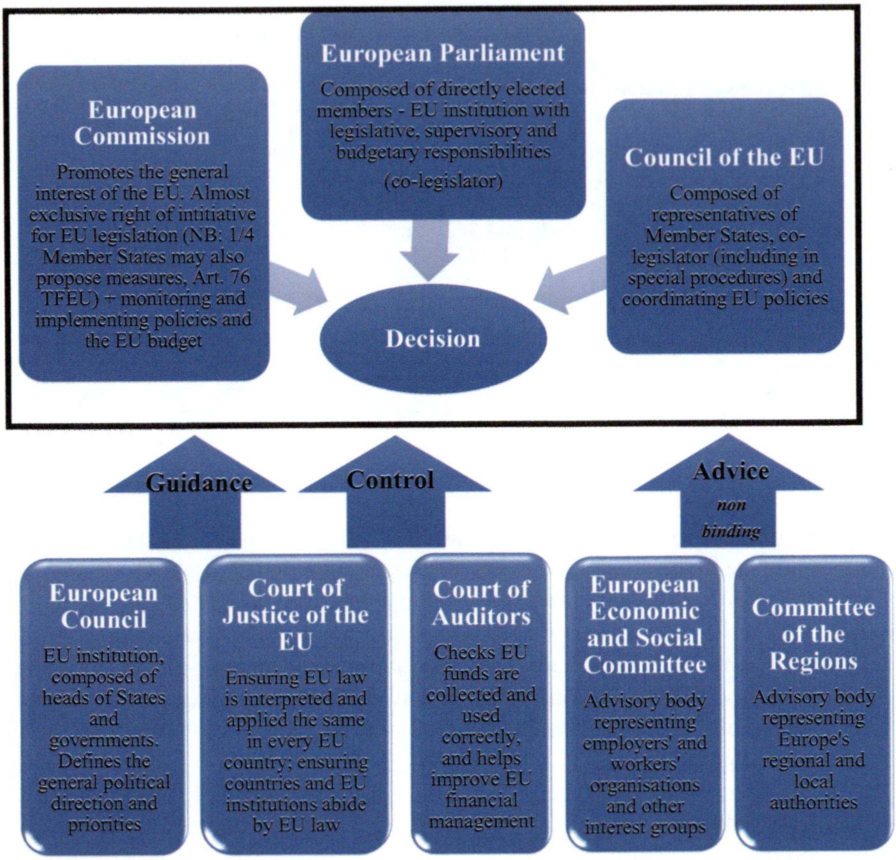

Data Protection Supervisor and other specialised agencies and decentralised bodies.[156]

Compared to ASEAN, the ties between EU bodies and institutions may imply reporting, and information and intelligence sharing, but they may also involve control and/or strict oversight. The latter makes the EU unique amongst the other regional organisations.

[156] Art. 13 TEU. For more on the bodies and their interactions, see the EU website: https://bit.ly/2Z4e3K1 (accessed on 29 April 2019).

(a) *The existence of control over the regional institutions' and its Member States' actions*

No regional court or other regional body exists to control the implementation of ASEAN norms. By contrast, the implementation of EU norms is controlled through the infringement procedure that can eventually reach the CJEU. The European Commission may initiate an infringement procedure when a Member State fails to respect its EU duties and if it does not comply with the opinion delivered by the Commission. The Commission may bring the matter before the CJEU, which can punish the infringing State by imposing financial sanctions.[157] The EU institutions can sanction a Member State for failing to meet a commitment without a preliminary complaint from another Member State; when failing from implementing a regulation or a directive, for example. Thus, Member States shall refrain from deliberately endangering the European project by respecting the principle of loyal or sincere cooperation.[158] Countermeasures decreasingly make sense when the EU intervenes as a legislator and a controller. Conversely, any control in ASEAN comes from the Member States and is of a political nature. An ASEAN Member States may sue another ASEAN Member State before the International Court of Justice (ICJ) though.

In human rights-related matters, the flexible ASEAN institutional architecture leaves significant space in which its Member States can manoeuvre thus, limiting the effectiveness of any common action.[159] This can lead to different forms of implementation of the regional standards, with different procedures of implementation and with a potential margin of appreciation on the scope and purpose of each standard. Unlike in ASEAN, the EU Member States are answerable to its citizens for any harm caused through violations of Union law. The EU citizen can be an active participant in ensuring the coherence of EU law by indirectly challenging Member States' implementation of EU norms where their fundamental rights are infringed. In other words, a citizen may bring an action against its government to its national court, which may require the CJEU interpretation (preliminary proceedings). Moreover, a citizen may also take action directly before the Court, if a decision by an EU institution has affected her/him directly and personally.[160]

(b) *The privileges and immunities of the regional organisations within their own 'territory'*

[157] Art. 258, TFEU.

[158] See Art. 4(3), TEU.

[159] Acharya, *Constructing a Security Community in Southeast Asia* (2001): 63.

[160] See, e.g., on the right to privacy and data protection: CJEU, *Digital Rights Ireland Ltd et Seitlinger e.a.*, Joined Cases C-293/12 and C-594/12, judgment (Grand Chamber), ECLI:EU:C:2014:238, 8 April 2014; *Tele2 Sverige*, Joined Cases C-203/15 and C-698/15, judgement (Grand Chamber), ECLI:EU:C:2016:970, 21 December 2016. There is even an online complaints procedure (https://ec.europa.eu/info/about-european-commission/contact/problems-and-complaints_en)

The place of the two regional organisations has evolved over time within their respective region. Since the creation of ASEAN, the Secretariat has gained a specific status and capacities. Before 2009, the only norm offering a specific regime to ASEAN was the *Agreement Between the Government of Indonesia and ASEAN Relating to the Privileges and Immunities of the ASEAN Secretariat* signed by the Secretary-General of ASEAN in 1979. It only related to its status within the territory of Indonesia.[161] Outside of Indonesia, ASEAN officials travelled as nationals of their respective Member States. This situation changed with the signing of the *Agreement on the Privileges and Immunities of the Association of South East Asian Nations* in 2009;[162] after the adoption of the *ASEAN Charter*. With this Agreement, ASEAN representatives, namely the Secretary-General of ASEAN and its staff, have immunity while they are acting in the performance of and for the independent exercise of their respective duties, functions and responsibilities.[163] Thus, this Agreement provides details on the deriving capacities of the regional organisation and its Secretariat.[164] However, its capacity remains very limited and only deals with diplomatic and administrative issues in the name of Member States. The Agreement specifically provides that due to its legal personality ASEAN has 'the following capacities under domestic laws: to enter into contracts; to acquire and dispose of movable and immovable property; and to institute and defend itself in legal proceedings'.[165] This Agreement clarifies what this legal personality implies for ASEAN, i.e. it makes no practical changes. Moreover, the 2010 *Protocol to the ASEAN Charter on Dispute Settlement Mechanisms* does not provide details, nor does it mention the existence of an ASEAN legal personality.

Similar to ASEAN, the EU institutions and bodies started enjoying privileges and immunities a few years after their establishment. In fact, the 1965 *Protocol (No 36) on the privileges and immunities of the European Communities*[166] provided the European Communities, including their premises, their official documents and their staffs, the customary immunities. These immunities were then transferred to the current EU and remained for the European Atomic Energy Community (EAEC) by the *Protocol (No 7) on the privileges and immunities of the European Union.*[167]

---

[161] *Agreement Between the Government of Indonesia and ASEAN Relating to the Privileges and Immunities of the ASEAN Secretariat*, Secretary-General and Foreign Minister of Indonesia, Jakarta, 20 January 1979.

[162] *Agreement on the Privileges and Immunities of the Association of South East Asian Nations*, Cha-Am, 25 October 2009.

[163] Art. 4, Ibid.

[164] Art. 2, *ASEAN Charter*.

[165] Art. 2, *Agreement on the Privileges and Immunities of the ASEAN* (2009).

[166] *Protocol (No 36) annexed to the Treaties establishing the European Community and the European Atomic Energy Community by the Treaty establishing a single Council and a single Commission of the European Communities of 8 April 1965*, O.J.E.C. L152/13, 13 July 1967.

[167] *Protocol (No 7) on the privileges and immunities of the European Union*, O.J.E.U. C 326/1, 26 October 2012

3. The existence of legal powers exercisable by the two regional organisations on the international scene

Generally speaking, actions matter more than words. The legal personality of a regional organisation seen from an international perspective is more of a capacity than a sign of status.[168] In this respect, there has been an evolution of legal powers exercisable by the two regional organisations at an international level.[169]

The ASEAN legal personality appears to be limited in nature. When the Charter was released, it was underlined that '[d]etails of what ASEAN can or cannot do with its legal personality will be discussed and stated in a supplementary protocol after the signing of the Charter'.[170] Since 2011, ASEAN has had the competence to sign international treaties on its own behalf.[171] However, ASEAN representatives must make sure that Member States unanimously agree on a common position before starting any negotiation with third parties.[172] The *Rules of Procedure for the Conclusion of International Agreements by ASEAN* specifies that the rules do not apply to the international agreements already concluded by Member States collectively.[173] Moreover, it only applies to international agreements creating rights and obligations for ASEAN as a distinct entity from its Member States.[174] Despite this possibility, no international agreement has been signed since 2011 following these rules. Notably, the Joint Declarations, adopted before 2011, between ASEAN and any other third party, namely States or the EU, were signed between the concerned third party and all the ASEAN Member States. Currently, Member States sign and ratify international treaties in their individual capacity.[175] Nonetheless, they are asked to conduct their external relations on the premise of unity and solidarity.[176]

Paradoxically, while the Eminent Persons Group report on the *ASEAN Charter* noted that 'ASEAN's problem is not one of lack of vision, ideas, or action plans, [but] ensuring [their] compliance and effective implementation',[177] some scholars

[168] Daillier, Forteau, and Pellet (2009): 657 and ff.

[169] The external capacities of the two regional organisations are further developed in Chap. 7.

[170] ASEAN Secretariat, 'ASEAN Leaders Sign *ASEAN Charter'* (2007).

[171] ASEAN Coordinating Council, *Rules of Procedure for the Conclusion of International Agreements by ASEAN*, Bali, 17 November 2011.

[172] Rule 4, *Rules of Procedure for the Conclusion of International Agreements by ASEAN* (2011). See also, Chesterman (2008): 204–05; Piris and Woon (2015): 68–69.

[173] Art. 1(2), *Rules of Procedure for the Conclusion of International Agreements by ASEAN* (2011).

[174] Art. 2, Ibid.

[175] See, e.g., *Framework Agreement on Comprehensive Economic Co-Operation Between ASEAN and the People's Republic of China*, Phnom Penh, 5 November 2002.

[176] Art. 41(4), *ASEAN Charter.*

[177] ASEAN, *Report of the Eminent Persons Group on the ASEAN Charter* (2006), 4. See also Hao Duy Phan, *A Selective Approach to Establishing a Human Rights Mechanism in Southeast Asia. The Case for a Southeast Asian Court of Human Rights*, Procedural Aspects of International Law Monograph Series (Leiden-Boston: Martinus Nijhoff Publishers, 2012).

have contradicted this view.[178] Notably, when declaring that the Member States have vision and plans, the report does not specifically mention that Member States have the *same* vision for the region as a whole.

In the case of the EU's AFSJ, several options are possible: the EU may become the sole competent authority to conclude international agreements; an international agreement may be concluded both by the EU and the Member States (mixed agreement); the Member States may conclude international agreements on their own; or the bilateral agreements signed by the Member States may be completed by an agreement concluded by the EU.[179] It is only the communautarisation of cooperation in criminal matters via the Lisbon Treaty that amended the involvement of the EU in these matters, including in the external dimension of the AFSJ. Before the Lisbon Treaty, there was no option for the EU to act in the name of its Member States as the EU itself had no legal personality. In practice however, it did not change much as very few agreements have been concluded by the EU alone in the field since.

C. What may be drawn from this comparison?

The choice between one form of regional integration or another is representative of the intra-regional dynamics. It is strongly linked, among other elements, to their position vis-à-vis the principles of national sovereignty and territorial integrity. The weight and place of these principles are defined by the countries' history and, subsequently, have an impact on their individual position vis-à-vis regional integration. Additionally, the status of their interstate relations, including the level of trust between them, plays a role in the regional dynamics as a whole. In turn, this dynamic increases the level of mutual trust (cf. the chicken and the egg dilemma).

According to this framework, the 'ASEAN Way' seems to last. However, it tends to be supplemented or modified by a new legal culture where greater reliance is placed on rules, institutions and procedures to regulate conduct in order to achieve more efficient and predictable action.[180] For now, ASEAN remains more of a practice-based organisation than a rules-based one—where Member States maintain a central role instead of the regional organisation.

---

[178] See, e.g., Chesterman (2008): 205.

[179] On the possibility for the EU to acquire exclusive competence on the external relations of the domain of the AFSJ, Art. 3(2) TFEU specifies that the EU may have an exclusive competence to conclude an international agreement 'in so far as its conclusion may affect common rules or alter their scope' and is interpreted in CJEU, Opinion 1/13, paras 72–73.

[180] *Declaration on the Establishment of the ASEAN Charter*, Kuala Lumpur, 12 December 2005. See Tommy Koh, Walter Woon and Chan Sze-Wei, 'Charter Makes ASEAN Stronger, More United and Effective' *Straits Times*, 8 August 2007; Venke and Thio (2016): 11. The *Declaration on the Establishment of the ASEAN Charter* (2005) provides that 'the ASEAN Charter will codify all ASEAN norms, rules and values reaffirm that ASEAN agreements signed and other instruments adopted before the establishment of the ASEAN Charter shall continue to apply and be legally binding were appropriate'. Also, Roberts (2012): 174.

As it is still State-centric, ASEAN qualifies as a traditional international organisation or intergovernmental organisation. ASEAN Member States do not want their sovereignty to be impeded by a supranational organisation.[181] Although ASEAN gained a legal personality, it does not possess any autonomous competence. It has no independent power to impose obligations on its members. There is a desire for it to take a more central position though.[182]

The ASEAN legal order 'certainly cannot be likened to a whole-hearted embrace of European supranationalism, but it may be argued that it is more than an arena for the conduct of diplomacy or managed politics'.[183] ASEAN has adopted few elements of institutionalisation over time and has gone towards a more rules-based approach.[184] This approach is becoming slightly more rigid among the Economic Community,[185] while ASEAN Member States have not yet decided if and how to start an integration process in the Political Security Community.

Conversely, the EU's legal order is traditionally perceived as largely autonomous, not only internally (vis-à-vis the Union's own Member States), but also externally (in relation to third States and other international organisations). The source of this perception is to be found in the autonomy of its legal order. Stressing its autonomy was believed to be necessary to establish an independent identity and could perhaps be seen as a disguised claim to sovereignty. Whilst developed by the Court in its jurisprudence, the principle is part of the very foundation of the EU legal order, with unity and the uniform application of rules being an intrinsic part of that order. It is a widely accepted argument that the functionality of the EU ultimately depends on the protection of the principle of supremacy of EU law over national laws when the EU is competent in the specific matter.

Although there are significant differences in the current EU and ASEAN architectures, it must be acknowledged that there are clear similarities in the primary motives for the development of the two regional organisations. They evolve at different points and rates. Even though they differ now, the two regional frameworks may begin to resemble one another with time.

The enactment of the *ASEAN Charter* did not significantly alter the regional organisation's role and place within, and beyond, the region. Similarly, the main change that the Lisbon Treaty provided is not the enactment of a legal personality for the EU, but the communautarisation of the AFSJ and the submission of this field to the supranational decision-making method. Yet, the establishment of a legal person-

[181]Benny Teh Cheng Guan, 'ASEAN's Regional Integration Challenge: The ASEAN Process', *The Copenhagen Journal of Asian Studies,* vol. 20 (2004).

[182]The early 1990s was a turning point as ASEAN sought to affirm its identity and centrality. See also, Pt. 3 of the preamble, *ASEAN Political-Security Community Blueprint*, Jakarta, 2009.

[183]Wunderlich, 'The EU an Actor Sui Generis?' (2012): 659–60.

[184]Roberts (2012): 178.

[185]Bali Concord III (2011). Also, Hwee (2009): 11.

ality for the EU and ASEAN shows commitment from Member States to adopt a regional development based on a certain level of trust.[186]

Throughout their own process, Member States seem increasingly dedicated to ensuring the coherence of their actions and to trust each other to respect their obligations.[187] However, it is clear that the form and level of mutual trust with its three domains (social, political and legal) diverge in the two regions. On the one hand, the approach adopted in Southeast Asia is said to recognise common concerns while accommodating diversity and respecting the institutional integrity and political autonomy of its Member States in all matters where uniformity and centralisation are not necessary or not possible.[188] On the other, a supranational structure was chosen in Europe which facilitates the harmonisation of laws creating legal expectations aimed at fostering trust between competent national authorities.

Section 3: 'Chicken and the Egg' Dilemma—The Symbiotic Relationship Between Regional Integration and Mutual Trust

The members of these two regional organisations have adopted different approaches vis-à-vis regional integration and the role of mutual trust, leading them to two different regional institutional designs thus far (Table 4.6).

In their current state, the main difference between the two regional approaches may be summarised as follows. With regard to the component of autonomy, ASEAN Member States certainly remain relatively autonomous when creating their national legislation and policies, whereas the EU institutions can legislate and impose certain obligations on Member States. The distribution of competences diverges significantly (exclusive and shared competences v. no transfer of competences). With regard to the component of control, the unanimous agreement of all ASEAN Member States is needed for every regional action, whereas EU Member States

---

[186] Argument nourished by the interview with a senior researcher at the Centre for International Law of the NUS and participant in the ASEAN Integration Through Law (ASEAN ITL) Project, Singapore 1 June 2016.

[187] See for ASEAN, e.g. pt. 4, Chairman's Statement, 5th ASEAN-U.S. Summit (2017); Piris and Woon (2015); Min-hyung Kim, 'Theorizing ASEAN Integration', *Asian Perspective,* vol. 35 (2011). See for the EU, for example, Hempel, Leon, Michael Carius and Carla Ilten, 'Echange d'Informations et de Données entre Services Répressifs au sein de l'Union Européenne' (under the supervision of CEPS), Study for the European Parliament (Brussels: European Parliament, April 2009); Saskia Hufnagel and Carole McCartney, eds., *Trust in International Police and Justice Cooperation*, Oñati International Series in Law and Society (Oxford: Hart Publishing, 2017); Cecilia Rizcallah, 'The challenges to trust-based governance in the European Union: Assessing the use of mutual trust as a driver of EU integration', *European Law Journal,* vol. 25, no. 1 (2019); Auke Willems, 'Mutual trust as a term of art in EU criminal law: revealing its hybrid character', *European Journal of Legal Studies,* vol. 9, no. 1 (2016).

[188] Börzel and Risse (2012): 3.

Table 4.6 Brief comparative table of regional integration designs

	Regional structure	Characteristics	Type of regional integration
ASEAN	Regional intergovernmental community	Decision-making and every body of the regional organisation in the hands of the Member States; No autonomous power; Weak recognition as a collective actor.	'Integration through practice' Informal political integration; premise of economic integration through law.
EU	Regional supranational community	Decision-making autonomous from the Member States; Clearer place and recognition on the international scene, with an independent identity.	'Integration through law' Mainly formal institutionalisation; and clear integration process in the various fields, and more recently in the AFSJ.

cannot have complete control over delegated issues (see. qualified majority vote). With regard to the component of legitimacy, the regional organisation may have the legitimacy to be a driving force in cross-border matters according to the limits of what its members are willing to 'cede'. Legal and political diversity keeps governing the Southeast Asian region, unlike in the EU where integration inter se of the various laws and systems of the constituent units allow the Union to function uninterruptedly. It is clear that some sort of externalisation and pooling of sovereignty, at the regional level in Southeast Asia, along the lines of what the EU has, is not on the agenda (and should not necessarily be).[189] ASEAN is marked by its continuous practice of consensus-based decision-making. Although ASEAN appears to be moving towards a more institutionalised structure, it by no means endorses a formal, legal and supranational model similar to that of the EU. ASEAN continues to be an intergovernmental organisation with a minimal level of both regional integration and institutionalisation.

Despite these differences, similarities do tend to appear. For instance, the members have given their regional organisations a legal personality and have allowed their regional organisation to operate at an international level. Moreover, there are similarities between the primary motives for creating the two regional organisations.

Therefore, their discrepancies may be explained either by the different stages of development they have reached thus far or by the different paths they took. Only time will tell which of these two hypotheses ends up being correct. Even though regional structures are not frozen in time.

Their diverging regional architectures impact the nature and functioning of the regional actions. As their names suggest, one is a union while the other is an association. States involved in a union work together jointly under a constitutive act, being the Lisbon Treaty, giving the EU institutions and agencies some competences over States' actions. In contrast, States involved in an association develop

[189] Roberts (2012): 178.

their relations on a subject of common interest. Associated States decided to preserve more strenuously their sovereignty. Thus, the constitutional regional frameworks play their part in the way intra-regional interactions are governed and cooperation is developed.

In analysing the two regional approaches, this chapter addressed mostly the *capability-building component*. The EU and ASEAN have adopted their own tailored-made regional legal architecture. As the ASEAN regional framework was established after the EC/EU's, ASEAN officials may have learned lessons from the EU and applied appropriate ones when developing their own regional framework. Notably, the most relevant example of an EU-inspired norm is the *ASEAN Charter*. However, dominating the ASEAN method of governance, the 'ASEAN Way' has ensured a constant dialogue between members, leading to numerous opportunities for mutual learning (cf. cluster on *information and experience sharing*) about each other respective legal framework(s) in order to improve the national and, potentially, regional criminal justice systems. One of the methods used for sharing experience in the EU is the evaluation procedure, as used by the European Commission,[190] while such a procedure does not exist in ASEAN. Those evaluations aim for competent authorities to learn and implement the appropriate legislations, best practices and methods in their specific field.

In its regional integration process, the EU has gone beyond its Member States differences[191] due to the form mutual trust that competent national authorities, and then its institutions, have developed vis-à-vis each other. By way of fostering trust, the establishment of common norms has helped ensuring good relations between Member States in various matters, including criminal matters (from 'integration through practice' to 'integration though law').[192] In this respect, the EU is considered the most advanced model of regional integration through law.[193] Conversely, ASEAN Member States have fostered channels of communication to develop better understandings and knowledge of each other's policies and legislations ('integration through practice'). In contrast, they have not engaged in any form of approximation of national legislations, but rather only employ slow and minimal regional (weak—or almost non-existing—'integration through law').

[190]See, e.g., European Commission, COM(2014) 554 final, Report from the Commission to the European Parliament and the Council on the implementation of Council Framework Decision 2008/919/JHA.

[191]Klaus-Dieter Borchardt, *The ABC of EU law* (Luxembourg: EU Publications Office, 2017): 89.

[192]On the discussions about the nature of regional organisations and their integration process, see, e.g., Pescatore (1974); Cappelletti, Seccombe, and Weiler, eds., *Integration Through Law: Europe and the American Federal Experience* (1986); Piris and Woon (2015); Telò and Weyembergh, eds., *Supranational Governance at Stake* (2020).

[193]Wunderlich, 'The EU an Actor Sui Generis?' (2012); Wunderlich, 'Comparing regional organisations in global multilateral institutions: ASEAN, the EU and the UN' (2012); Wiener and Diez, eds. (2004); Telò and Weyembergh, eds., *Supranational Governance at Stake* (2020); Bilal (2007); Berkofsky (2005).

Mutual trust certainly constitutes an important tool of governance for removing borders between people and between domestic legal systems and its absence may prevent Member States from reaching their shared objective(s). Giving the two regional organisations a legal personality has not harmonised the two regional institutional architectures. In this context, mutual trust follows the actual social, political and legal regional developments. In the EU where interactions have been strongly legalised, mutual trust tends to have been legalised as well. In ASEAN where interactions are not legalised but instead, mostly social, or political at best, mutual trust tends to be based on social, or potentially political, arrangements.

Yet, it is unclear whether regional integration or mutual trust came first, as it is difficult to identify whether it is the chicken or the egg which came first. Instead, a virtuous circle operates between these two elements, bolstering one another over time.

Finally, the development of a regional legal framework might constitute a determinant push, but is certainly the necessary structure, for comprehensive actions, including the fight against terrorism, through the approximation of the relevant national legislations (Chap. 5) and the streamlining of cooperation between competent national authorities within each region (Chap. 6).

Chapter 5
The Symbiotic Relations Between Mutual Trust & Regional Counterterrorism Arsenals: The Different Outcomes of Three-Tier Vertical Normative Dialogues

A new layer of governance between the broad international framework and the more specific national legislations was added to strengthen collective counterterrorism actions: a regional layer. This new layer constitutes a very interesting ground upon which to develop mutual trust between competent national authorities, as it is caught between a too-broad international framework, that does not allow for more than social trust, and more precise national laws and regulations where the need for trust is more limited.

The regional level facilitates the establishment of institutions and the adoption of norms setting common standards (*capability building* cluster of the matrix) between the Member States of the respective regional organisations as well as the mutual learning between foreign authorities (*information and experience sharing* cluster) stimulating cooperation. A parallel appears between, on the one hand, the evolution of regional institutional and normative architecture(s) in counterterrorism and cross-border relations between the competent national authorities getting more formal and, on the other hand, the development of mutual trust—from a social towards a more legal form.

This chapter and the subsequent one verify whether the regional organisations, identified as the most appropriate level to provide an efficient response against serious transnational crime, have sufficiently developed to accept this responsibility.

While Chap. 6 investigates whether the EU and ASEAN add value when establishing mechanisms of cooperation, this particular chapter investigates whether the EU and ASEAN provide the same added value when reaching a harmonised criminalisation of terrorist offences within their respective regions. To achieve this, this chapter analyses the vertical interactions of norms, i.e. between international, regional and national norms, in order to understand each region's normative capacity regarding counterterrorism efforts. In other words, this chapter examines the normativity of the two regional legal orders; as initiators, influencers, vectors or recipients of anti-terrorism and human rights norms, according to the vertical international and national normative levels. It discusses the approximation of the

C. C. Cocq, *Mutual Trust in Regional and Interregional Cooperation on Counterterrorism*, United Nations University Series on Regionalism 26,
https://doi.org/10.1007/978-3-031-36612-3_5

Member States' legislations as well as the adoption of the main legal frameworks employed to achieve cooperation, as potential means towards enhancing mutual trust or creating preliminary trust development (cf. the chicken and the egg dilemma).

As mentioned before, mutual trust is often invoked as an alternative to harmonisation which maintains diversity. However, trust is easier to build and foster when the respective stakeholders share common values and agree on shared objectives.[1]

In terrorism-related matters, mutual trust is particularly difficult to establish and operationalise. Trust in one another... maybe... it depends on the subject... but, in any case, no blind trust. It is argued, especially by most of EU's authorities, that the approximation of the relevant legislations may support the various counterterrorism efforts. This is the approach adopted by the EU.[2] Approximating criminal laws was initially (i.e. under the Third Pillar of the Maastricht Treaty) meant to replace internal borders checks. Preventive, proactive and reactive measures were essentially meant to ensure that people did not use this freedom of movement for criminal purposes. By contrast, ASEAN Member States have not (yet) turned their attention to this process, most probably due to the sensitive nature of terrorism, the significant differences between countries and the current lack of means to do so.

In the EU, the approximation of substantive and procedural criminal legislations supports a common response against terrorism for three distinct reasons. Firstly, it facilitates the fight against crime: approximating substantive and procedural criminal laws might be necessary to effectively deal with serious crime, otherwise criminals might take advantage of the differences between criminal justice systems by using some countries as safe havens (cf. 'forum shopping'). It ensures the uniform criminalisation of the same behaviours and the application of the same procedural rules which lead to equivalent outcomes. Unlike ASEAN, this has been a focus of the EU. Secondly, it facilitates cooperation between competent national authorities through various mechanisms based on mutual trust. This is especially the case in the EU with, for example, mutual recognition. Approximating substantive and procedural national provisions avoids the risk of a perilous situation where cooperation, including data sharing, occurs in a case where there are no common rules (usual in ASEAN). Thirdly, and especially in the EU, the approximation of procedural criminal law and fundamental rights standards fulfils the crucial so-called shield function (as opposed to the 'sword function') of criminal law, which corresponds with the commitment of the Member States to respect and protect individual rights when implementing criminal justice.[3] The approximation of fundamental rights constitutes an added value. It ensures comparable minimum standards of human

---

[1] See, e.g., Anne Weyembergh, *L'harmonisation des législations: condition de l'espace pénal européen et révélateur de ses tensions* (Bruxelles: Editions de l'Université de Bruxelles, 2004).

[2] Art. 83(2), TFEU.

[3] Weyembergh, *L'harmonisation des législations* (2004); Anne Weyembergh, 'The Functions of Approximation of Penal Legislation within the EU' *Maastricht Journal of European and Comparative Law*, vol. 12, no. 2 (2005).

rights, including data protection (a key fundamental right in the context of increased data sharing). This aspect has not yet been identified as an objective, or a means to enhance cooperation in ASEAN. Based on the current state of the national laws, the opportunity for their approximation will be explored.

This chapter examines the vertical normative forces (top-down and bottom-up influences) which define the position and role of regional organisations concerning the prevention and combating of terrorism. Notably, none of the three legal orders manifests from unidirectional influences. International norms influence regional and national legal orders, but might also be influenced by regional and national norms. These interactions might also apply at the regional and national levels. Each legal order influences the others, co-constructing one another.

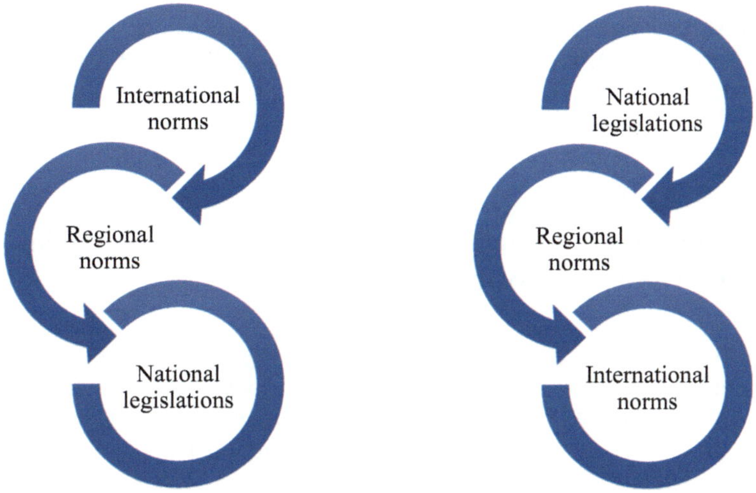

The origin and the ways in which one influences the other are not always easy to determine. The objective of this analysis is not to identify each influence on every legal order, but rather to identify the position and role of the two regional organisations in the counterterrorism panorama. This includes the potential benefits from the respective regional legal order to the development of mutual trust within their own realm.

For these reasons, the first section of this chapter examines the various top-down and bottom-up dynamics which influence international and regional norms (Section 1). Subsequently, the second section provides the same analysis of the vertical influences between the national legislations and the respective regional legal frameworks (Section 2). From this analysis, the position and role of the EU and ASEAN are determined, if any, in facilitating a similar (or, at least, equivalent) criminalisation of terrorist offences within their respective region. Furthermore, it determines how the regionalisation of the criminalisation might constitute an end or support mutual trust in pursuit of enhanced cross-border cooperation. Accordingly, due attention is given to human rights guarantees (i.e. in the human rights-related instruments and in the counterterrorism instruments) when counterterrorism measures are implemented.

The evaluation of the respective influences of the international, regional and national counterterrorism norms, and their impact on the effectiveness of the criminalisation of terrorist offences, shall provide the relevant competent national authorities with a better understanding of the role of the regional organisations.

For the sake of clarity, the order of the regional organisation analysed first changes between the first and second section; i.e. the first section starts with the analysis of ASEAN while the second starts with the EU. As Section 1 adopts a 'funnelling approach', ASEAN shall be the first regional organisation examined due to its stronger similarities with the international legal framework. In Section 2, the EU is examined first as it provides a more precise framework (i.e. legal and institutional structure, concepts and definitions) which helps the understanding of, and the comparison with, ASEAN (where it is still in the early stages of development).

Section 1: Regional Legal Orders in Counterterrorism—What Normative Value Do They Bring to the International Normative Panorama?

This section questions the ways in which the emergence of regional legal orders might benefit the global international framework on counterterrorism. It contrasts the manner in which the EU and ASEAN receive international counterterrorism and human rights-related norms and how these norms might potentially influence global norms in return ('mutually influential' or just 'influencer-and-influenced' relationship).

From a top-down perspective, certain international norms serve as models for developing regional instruments. However, in their respective way, the EU and ASEAN's legal frameworks do not always strictly follow the (same) path of international norms. Pr. Acharya describes this phenomenon as the 'localisation of norms', which refers to an 'active construction (through discourse, framing, grafting, and cultural selection) of foreign ideas by local actors, which results in the latter developing significant congruence with local beliefs and practices'.[4] This localisation of norms aims to integrate external or hierarchically superior norms into specific local contexts. Through this process, international norms might be magnified by infusing these norms within States, or regional organisations, and by teaching the authorities and citizens to accept the values embedded in international law.[5] In brief, the objective is for actors to internalise norms and change their behaviour accordingly.

[4] Acharya, 'How Ideas Spread: Whose Norms Matter?' (2004).

[5] Phan, *A Selective Approach to Establishing a Human Rights Mechanism in Southeast Asia* (2012).

The EU and ASEAN have adopted their own norms with respect for the abilities of their Member States and their willingness to work towards an agreed upon objective. Yet, EU and ASEAN Member States still need to respect international norms by providing common minimum standards.[6] Their different approaches are representative of the divergent understandings of and purposes for mutual trust.

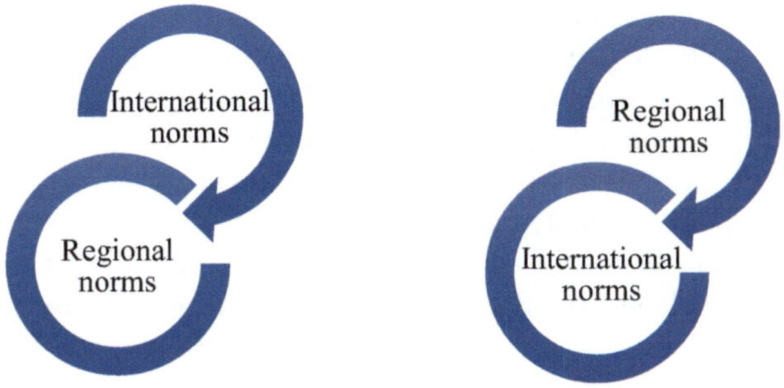

Despite significant differences between the regional legal orders, it is worth noticing that counterterrorism norms tend to have flourished in their number and complexity (I) in comparison to human rights norms (II).

I. Agreeing on a shared objective and ways to reach it: the foundation of mutual trust?

Although the international community adopted counterterrorism norms long before the 9/11 attacks, the counterterrorism priority moved up respective national security agendas and further internationalised after the attacks. The attacks on the World Trade Centre and the Pentagon have triggered a wide variety of reactions, such as the international community moving from military intervention to counter-radicalisation measures which include pro-active and re-active criminal justice actions.

The European and Southeast Asian regions have particularly been the targets of national and transnational terrorist threats. For example, the Philippine government has long struggled with terrorist groups, including the Da'esh group wishing to create a second Caliphate for Southeast Asia in the country. Moreover, the 2002 and 2009 bombings in Bali reinforced the notion of the Southeast Asian's regional vulnerability to transnational terrorism. Similarly, European countries have long faced national and transnational terrorist threats. The 2004 train bombings in Madrid, the 2005 attacks on London's public transport system, the 2015 attacks on *Charlie Hebdo* and on the Bataclan concert hall in Paris, and the 2016 Brussels bombings tragically reminded the danger of the terrorist threat facing Europe. The long-standing terrorist experience in the two regions has led States to adopt national

[6] Art. 38, *Statute of the International Court of Justice* (1945); Arts. 30–33, *Convention on the Law of Treaties* (1969). It is worth noticing that Brunei Darussalam, Indonesia, Singapore and Thailand are not parties to the latter Convention.

and regional counterterrorism norms and enhance them over time. In fact, the two regional legal orders close some of the gaps in the international framework.

As criminal matters are a central feature of national sovereignty, States tend to be reluctant to delegate any power to a supranational body. They first necessitated an intergovernmental response. ASEAN and EU—or, previously, EC—Member States only adopted cohesive positions, namely declarations or plans of action in ASEAN or decisions or framework decisions in the EU. It is only in the 1990s in the EU and in the 2000s in ASEAN that regional binding instruments emerged. However, the strong discrepancies between the EU and ASEAN rules-based approach have had an impact on the type and depth of the regional counterterrorism requirements.

In this endeavour, the diversity between countries plays a significant role. The more diverse the political and legal context is, the more difficult it is to integrate and adapt external norms to a specific context, or even to adopt regional norms independently.[7] This explains how Southeast Asian's diversity, and the strong concern vis-à-vis their national sovereignty, prevent ASEAN from adopting more precise and binding norms than international ones. Conversely, the EU norms provide a more specific and narrower legal framework for its Member States.

Therefore, the UN has had a superior top-down influence on ASEAN legal arsenal against terrorism than on the EU's (A). This fact can be broadened to other forms of transnational crime (B).

A. Criminalising terrorist offences: a more superior top-down influence in ASEAN than in the EU

The primary EU and ASEAN laws, respectively, the TEU and TFEU, and the *ASEAN Charter*, state that their Member States shall uphold the *UN Charter* and other international instruments.[8] The UN Organisation, especially the Security Council, has in fact assumed a crucial role in the fight against terrorism by calling upon States to criminalise terrorism and cooperative actions (1). This influence is more visible in ASEAN (2) than in the EU (3). By contrast, an influence of the EU and ASEAN's norms on the international ones is not easily identifiable.

1. The complicated inception of international anti-terrorism norms

Proposals to substantially develop the United Nations' role in counterterrorism were initially viewed with scepticism. Many States and experts within the UN Secretariat doubted that this level could add significant value. Contrary to the initial estimation, States are now convinced that the UN Conventions constitute a necessary global framework for international cooperation.

---

[7] Acharya, 'How Ideas Spread: Whose Norms Matter?' (2004).

[8] Art. 2, *ASEAN Charter;* and, Art. 3(5), TEU. In case of disputes, the EU has developed its own infringement procedures, whereas Art. 28 *ASEAN Charter* only refers to Art. 33(1) of the UN Charter or any other international legal instruments to which ASEAN Member States are parties to resolve any dispute peacefully.

States started engaging with terrorism in the 1970s, after the Munich massacre in 1972, with a focus on hostage situations. Interestingly, the United Nations intervened 7 years after the facts with the *International Convention against the Taking of Hostages.* The UN's fight against terrorism has been conservative and limited to specific forms of terrorist threats, including attacks against diplomats and the use of explosives for terrorism purposes.[9] Each of these conventions defines terrorist offences in accordance with the object of the convention. Yet, the 1999 *International Convention for the Suppression of the Financing of Terrorism,* ratified or accessioned by all ASEAN and EU Member States, defines the offences related to the Convention in Article 2 as:

> any action 'directly or indirectly, unlawfully and wilfully, provides or collects funds with the intention that they should be used or in the knowledge that they are to be used, in full or in part, in order to carry out: (a) an act which constitutes an offence within the scope of and as defined in one of the treaties listed in the annex; or (b) any other act intended to cause death or serious bodily injury to a civilian, or to any other person not taking an active part in the hostilities in a situation of armed conflict, when the purpose of such act, by its nature or context, is to intimidate a population, or to compel a government or an international organisation to do or to abstain from doing any act'.

Due to paragraph (b) of the article, the Convention provides a more transversal definition of terrorist offences. Notably, certain elements of this second section have been introduced into the 2005 *Draft Comprehensive Convention against International Terrorism* (although this draft has not been adopted).[10]

Due to the 9/11 terrorist attacks, there was an urge to prevent and combat international terrorism by the entire international community. However, the lack of consensus for the path forward has prevented the General Assembly and the States combined to adopt effective measures against terrorism. Therefore, the UN Security Council intervened and designated itself as the main international 'legislator' on this issue.[11] It is worth noting that the Security Council was already encouraging States to adhere to all relevant instruments and emphasised the need for enhanced cooperation among States, international and regional organisations, before the 9/11 attacks.[12] However, the UNSCR 1373(2001) shifted from encouraging to imposing, under Chap. VII of the *UN Charter*, obligation on States to prevent and suppress terrorist offences. Subsequently, the Security Council continuously adopted resolutions in response to these evolving security threats with, among the most recent issues, the foreign terrorist fighters (S/RES/2178(2014)) and the strong connections between organised crime and terrorism (S/RES/2482(2019)). The UN Security

---

[9] *Convention on the Prevention and Punishment of Crimes against Internationally Protected Persons* (1973); *International Convention for the Suppression of Terrorist Bombings* (1997).

[10] Art. 2, *Draft Comprehensive Convention against International Terrorism*: A/59/894, Letter dated 3 August 2005 from the Chairman of the 6th Committee addressed to the President of the General Assembly, Appendix II '*Draft Comprehensive Convention against International Terrorism.* Consolidated text prepared by the Coordinator for discussion', 59th session, 12 August 2005.

[11] See, e.g., Daillier, Forteau, and Pellet, *Droit international public* (2009): 782–83.

[12] S/RES/1269(1999), *The responsibility of the Security Council in the maintenance of international peace and security*, 4053rd meeting, 19 October 1999.

Council and, more particularly, the Counter Terrorism Committee (CTC) is considered to be the leading body within the current global anti-terrorism architecture.[13] The UN CTC was established by the UNSCR 1373(2001) on *Threats to international peace and security caused by terrorist acts*. The CTC is designed to monitor the implementation of this resolution's requirements by States.[14]

Comprehensively developed in 2006 in the UN Global Counter-Terrorism Strategy,[15] those resolutions of the UN's Security Council (UNSC) and General Assembly (UNGA) require the criminalisation of terrorist offences as well as international, regional or sub-regional cooperation in the area of criminal justice. Despite these efforts, the absence of a precise definition of 'terrorist offences' within any of the international instruments, including the 1999 Convention, is insufficient to ensure that the same behaviours are uniformly defined in each country.[16] For this reason, the Security Council resolutions impose on States to adopt and implement measures, including the criminalisation of terrorist offences, and the development of interstate cooperation, amongst others.

Without a common vision and method to counter terrorism, even social trust is difficult to build between national officials. It is difficult to see how the competent authorities from different countries could trust one another enough to cooperate when they do not share an understanding on what such cooperation would entail. An obstacle for cooperation arises when there is no clear agreement between States on which individuals or organisations qualify as terrorists (e.g. the continued debate between the same individuals either being labelled as 'terrorists' or 'freedom fighters'). Moreover, in the current state of international law and international relations, trust is difficult to build, which might hinder cooperation. Cooperation may in fact be hindered by the number of States engaged at such level and by the turnover of States' representatives (cf. social dimension of mutual trust).

In the context of counterterrorism, regional approaches are meant to be more specific than the broad international requirements. Yet, they vary from one regional organisation to another.

2. <u>A Southeast Asian counterterrorism legal architecture following the UN impulses</u>

As it is the case globally, terrorism is not a new phenomenon in ASEAN (cf. separatist groups, Jemaah Islamiyah, etc.). As is the case for the EU,

[13] S/PV.4734 (provisional), *Threats to international peace and security caused by terrorist acts*, 'Chairman of the Counter-Terrorism Committee established pursuant to resolution 1373(2001) concerning counter-terrorism, Sir Jeremy Greenstock', 4734th meeting, 4 April 2003, 3; and, S/PV.4752 (provisional), Sergei Lavrov, Russia's Ambassador to the UN, 4752nd meeting, 6 May 2003, 9.

[14] See on the website of the CTC: https://www.un.org/sc/ctc/about-us/.

[15] A/RES/60/288(2006), *UN Global Counter-Terrorism Strategy*.

[16] See, e.g., Llobet Angli, "What does 'terrorism' mean?" (2013): 19.

counterterrorism in Southeast Asia has long been considered 'a *national security* problem'.[17]

Counterterrorism first appeared in the texts of the ASEAN instruments in the 1990s.[18] Since then, ASEAN counterterrorism instruments have progressed thanks to the international impulse, especially with the 1997 *International Convention for the Suppression of Terrorist Bombings* and the 1999 *International Convention for the Suppression of the Financing of Terrorism*, which were integrated, among others, into the *ASEAN Convention on Counter-Terrorism* in 2007.

In joint statements and declarations, terrorism was typically grouped under the broader umbrella of transnational crime, along with drug trafficking, money laundering, arms smuggling and trafficking in persons.[19] Pr. Chow noted that there was mention of terrorism in the Chairman's Statements at the ASEAN Regional Forum (ARF) which was prior to July 2001, as well as in the 'ASEAN Vision 2020' which was issued in 1997, and the subsequent *Hanoi Plan of Action* which outlined the steps to achieve the ASEAN Vision 2020.[20]

Two months after 9/11, the leaders at the seventh ASEAN Summit issued a *Declaration on Joint Action to Counter Terrorism*, which condemned the 9/11 attacks and stated that terrorism was a 'direct challenge to the attainment of peace, progress and prosperity of ASEAN'.[21] This Declaration also contained a vague commitment to 'counter, prevent and suppress all forms of terrorist acts in accordance with the Charter of the United Nations and other international law, especially taking into account the importance of all United Nations Resolutions'[22] as well as the commitment to reinforce their national and cross-border measures. The 9/11 attacks, 2002 Bali bombings and the acknowledgement of the other transnational forms of terrorist threats have thus fostered the adoption of a regional and multilateral counterterrorism strategy.[23] The eighth ASEAN Summit in 2002 condemned the Bali bombings in the *Declaration on Terrorism* and reaffirmed the leaders' commitment to 'practical cooperative measures'.

Terrorism has been identified as a threat to all sectors of society—economic, political and socio-cultural—at both the national and regional level.[24] Amid the

---

[17] Alistair Millar and Eric Rosand, 'Implementing the UN General Assembly's Global Counter-Terrorism Strategy in the Asia-Pacific' *Asian Security*, vol. 3, no. 3 (2007): 184.

[18] This is a reasonable timing as ASEAN emerged in 1967. Developing its 'ASEAN Way', the Association slowly focused first on economic and traditional security issues and then on non-traditional security issues.

[19] See, e.g., *ASEAN Declaration on Transnational Crime* (1997); Joint Communiqué of the Second AMMTC (1999); *ASEAN Plan of Action to Combat Transnational Crime* (1999).

[20] Jonathan T. Chow, 'ASEAN counterterrorism cooperation since 9/11' *Asian Survey*, vol. 45, no. 2 (2005).

[21] *ASEAN Declaration on Joint Action to Counter Terrorism* (2001).

[22] Preamble, Ibid.

[23] Chow, 'ASEAN counterterrorism cooperation since 9/11' (2005).

[24] *ASEAN Political-Security Community Blueprint* (2009).

integration of counterterrorism into the regional security agenda, the principles of sovereignty, non-interference, quiet diplomacy and consensus have been reflected in the various regional instruments. The pledges for enhanced actions against terrorism were not associated with the adoption and implementation of effective measures. Moreover, there remains a persistent conceptual haze over the regional perceptions of terrorism. For this reason, ASEAN has refrained from defining terrorism due to the risk that a proposed definition might be perceived as anti-Islamic by the region's Muslim communities.[25]

As a consequence, the 2007 *ASEAN Convention on Counter Terrorism* (ACCT), adopted 6 years after the 9/11 attacks, remains particularly lenient with its requirements. The Convention entered into force on 3 June 2011 after the ratification of the 4th of May by Brunei Darussalam (the sixth ratification). Malaysia was last to ratify the Convention on 11 January 2013. This is surprising given that Malaysia has suffered from terrorism and was particularly keen to cooperate with other regional countries concerning this issue.[26]

Going into further detail, the ACCT is based on the different international instruments enacted with the purpose of combating terrorism.[27] The Convention refers to 14 international instruments dealing with terrorism but does not provide its own regional definition of terrorist offences. It specifies nonetheless that the terrorist acts included in these international instruments are those which are intended 'to intimidate a population, or to compel a government or an international organisation to do or to abstain from doing any act, are under no circumstances justifiable by considerations of a political, philosophical, ideological, racial, ethnic, religious or other similar nature'.[28] This specific intention (*dol specialis*) is inspired by the 1999 *Convention for the Suppression of the Financing of Terrorism.* Interestingly, the addition that '[terrorist acts] are under no circumstances justifiable by considerations of a political, philosophical, ideological, racial, ethnic, religious or other similar nature'. Moreover, the preamble adds that 'terrorism cannot and should not be associated with any religion, nationality, civilisation or ethnic group'.[29] Particularly characteristic of the ASEAN approach (i.e. consensual decision-making and respect of each other's sensitivity), these provisions aim to prevent any discrimination from arising during the fight against terrorism. Then, the *dol specialis* is not provided under Article II 'Criminal acts of terrorism' related to the definition of terrorist offences, but rather it appears under 'General provisions' referring to Article

---

[25] Rommel C. Banlaoi, *Counter Terrorism Measures in Southeast Asia: How Effective Are They?* (Manila: De La Salle University, Yuchengco Center, 2009).

[26] See the table of ratifications of the ACCT: available at http://agreement.asean.org/agreement/detail/49.html (accessed on 14 January 2016).

[27] These instruments are listed in Art. II, ACCT. Notably, Arts. V on the non-application of the Convention and VII on the State jurisdiction are almost identical to Arts. 3 and 6 of the *Convention for the Suppression of Terrorist Bombings* (1997).

[28] Art. IX(1), ACCT.

[29] Preamble, ACCT.

II. Despite the absence of a regional definition, States are required to cooperate, which includes the sharing of relevant information.[30]

With regard to its scope, the ACCT amalgamates provisions from several instruments such as the 1997 *International Convention for the Suppression of Terrorist Bombings* and the aforementioned 1999 Convention. For example, Articles V on the non-application of the ACCT and VII on the State jurisdiction are, respectively, almost identical to those in Articles 3 and 6 of the 1997 Convention. The provisions of the *ASEAN Convention on Counter Terrorism* are therefore just as vague as those on at an international level.

As the requirements and implementation of the ACCT depend on international instruments, it is necessary to know the state of the ASEAN Member States' ratifications in order to understand the impact of the Convention on their respective legislation. Among the treaties listed in article II of the ASEAN Convention, all Member States ratified, or later acceded to, the 1970 *Convention for the Suppression of Unlawful Seizure of Aircraft*, the 1971 *Convention for the Suppression of Unlawful Acts against the Safety of Civil Aviation*, the 1988 *Protocol for the suppression of Unlawful Acts of Violence at Airports Serving International Civil Aviation, supplementary to the Convention for the Suppression of Unlawful Acts against the Safety of Civil Aviation* (except Indonesia who recently signed it in 1988), the 1997 *International Convention for the Suppression of Terrorist Bombings* and the 1999 *International Convention for the Suppression of the Financing of Terrorism*. Certain international treaties were only ratified or accessioned by some Member States, such as the 1973 *Convention on the Prevention and Punishment of Crimes against Internationally Protected Persons*, the 1979 *International Convention against the Taking of Hostages* and the 1979 *Convention on the Physical Protection of Nuclear Material*.[31] Due to the discrepancies between members in the ratification of these instruments, the implementation of the ASEAN convention may differ across Member States. Yet, the variations of implementation in ASEAN are unlikely to be an issue given the broad and rather vague nature of the requirements enshrined in both the international and regional conventions. Other elements are more likely to create discrepancies between national approaches in the implementation of the ACCT. For instance, the Convention states that all actions should be subject to domestic laws and requires States to perform their duties 'in a manner consistent with the principles of sovereign equality and territorial integrity of States and that of non-interference in the internal affairs of other Parties'.[32]

Bearing this in mind, the regional convention does nothing to foster the approximation of national legislations and only proposes ASEAN Member States to cooperate in this vague framework.

The consensual decision-making of the 'ASEAN Way' is intended to build links, through the identification of common objectives and the emergence of mutual

---

[30] Art. VI, ACCT.

[31] See Appendix 1 related to the ratifications of the most relevant instruments.

[32] Art. III, ACCT.

understanding between counterparts. By acknowledging the terrorist threat, States have identified a common objective and have thus developed a certain level of trust (in its social dimension) manifesting in transnational interactions. The Association is meant to support States' compliance to the norms adopted and slowly build the political dimension of mutual trust and to facilitate cross-border cooperation in the long term. There is no specific legal benefit in the ASEAN's anti-terrorism arsenal though.

3. A more autonomous and in-depth EU counterterrorism legal framework

As in ASEAN, there was discussion about introducing a counterterrorism policy years before September 2001. Yet, no instrument was adopted which was specifically devoted to terrorism.[33] A proposal for a Framework Decision on combating terrorism was finally presented by the Commission on 19 September 2001;[34] one week after the 9/11 attacks. This Framework Decision was inspired by the 1997 *Convention for the suppression of terrorist bombing* and even more so by the 1999 *Convention for the suppression of financing of terrorism.*[35] The proposal was negotiated during a favourable time period, which led to the adoption of the 2002 *Framework Decision on combating terrorism.*[36]

The 2002 Council Framework Decision (CFD) was quite 'ambitious',[37] as it could not be based on a pre-existing definition of terrorism, at either the international or European level. This Framework Decision, and especially Articles 1–4, was meant to put into practice ex-Article 31e) TUE (currently Article 83 TFEU), which explicitly refers to terrorism as one of the priorities for the approximation of Member States' substantive criminal laws. This form of approximation was repeatedly required in the Conclusions of the 1999 Tampere European Council and of the 2000 Santa Maria da Feira European Council,[38] yet it had not happened prior to 2002.

The 2002 CFD defines terrorist offences in Article 1 as:

> offences under national law, which, given their nature or context, may seriously damage a country or an international organisation where committed with the aim of (1) seriously intimidating a population, or (2) unduly compelling a Government or international organisation to perform or abstain from performing any act, or (3) seriously destabilising or

---

[33] Francesca Galli and Anne Weyembergh, 'Introduction' in *EU counter-terrorism offences. What impact on national legislation and case-law?*, eds., Francesca Galli and Anne Weyembergh (Bruxelles: Editions de l'Université de Bruxelles, 2012): 13 and ff.

[34] European Commission, Proposal for a Council Framework Decision on combating terrorism, COM(2001) 521 final, 19 September 2001.

[35] Galli and Weyembergh, 'Introduction' (2012): 16.

[36] *Council Framework Decision 2002/475/JHA on combating terrorism.*

[37] Eugenia Dumitriu, 'The EU's Definition of Terrorism: The Council Framework Decision on Combating Terrorism' *German Law Journal*, vol. 5, no. 5 (2004).

[38] Tampere European Council, Conclusions of the Presidency (1999); Santa Maria da Feira European Council, Conclusions of the Presidency, 19–20 June 2000.

> destroying the fundamental political, constitutional, economic or social structures of a country or an international organisation.

Moreover, Article 2 defines a terrorist group as 'a structured group of more than two persons, established over a period of time and acting in concert to commit terrorist offences' and a structured group as 'a group that is not randomly formed for the immediate commission of an offence and that does not need to have formally defined roles for its members, continuity of its membership or a developed structure'.[39]

During the negotiations, the EU Member States made significant efforts to define the offences more narrowly and to find a suitable balance between the effectiveness of counterterrorism actions and the protection of fundamental rights, including the rights to the defence.[40] However, in spite of these efforts, the EU definition was criticised by some commentators for being too imprecise and general, and thus not in compliance with the principle of legality in its substantive dimension.[41]

This CFD is advantageous, when compared to the international legal framework and other regional frameworks, as it defines the three elements of an offence: the material acts as defined in ordinary criminal law provisions; the gravity of the acts (i.e. the acts, given their nature or context, need to be capable of seriously damaging a country or an international organisation) and the intention, including the general criminal intent (*dol generalis*) and the special intent, also called *dol specialis* (i.e. the acts must be guided by a 'terrorist intent'[42]).

The criminalisation of terrorist offences at the EU level mainly aimed to improve police and judicial cooperation in terrorism-related cases and to apply some exceptional measures (harsher penalties[43] and exceptional procedural rules[44]).[45]

The 2002 CFD was followed by the 2008 *Council Framework Decision amending the 2002 Council Framework Decision on combating terrorism.* The latter approximated three new offences, namely public provocation, recruitment and training for terrorist activities. This framework decision was adopted based on

---

[39] Art. 2(1), *Council Framework Decision 2002/475/JHA on combating terrorism*; repeated in Art. 2(3) *Directive 2017/541 on combating terrorism.*

[40] See, e.g., Weyembergh, 'Consequences of Brexit for European Union Criminal Law' (2017).

[41] On the influence of the UN definition on the EU instrument, see the position of the Netherlands supported by Denmark, Portugal and the United Kingdom (Council of the European Union, doc 12647//01 rev. 10). See also Council of the European Union, 'Proposal for a Council Framework Decision on combating terrorism', doc. 12647/2/01 rev. 2, Brussels, 8 November 2001. On the value of the UN instruments on the EU instruments, see also Erling Johannes Husabø and Asbjørn Strandbakken, eds., *Harmonization of Criminal Law in Europe* (Antwerpen – Oxford: Intersentia, 2005).

[42] Art. 1, *Council Framework Decision 2002/475/JHA.*

[43] Art. 5(2), *Council Framework Decision 2002/475/JHA.*

[44] See, e.g., Maria Luisa Cesoni, ed., *Nouvelles méthodes de lutte contre la criminalité: la normalisation de l'exception. Etude de droit comparé (Belgique, Etats-Unis, Italie, Pays-Bas, Allemagne, France)* (Bruxelles: Bruylant, 2007).

[45] See Galli and Weyembergh, 'Introduction' (2012): 19.

the requirements of the 2005 Council of Europe (CoE) *Convention on the Prevention of Terrorism.*[46] This EU norm was particularly criticised for criminalising behaviours increasingly over and above actual terrorist attacks.

After the adoption of the Lisbon Treaty and the attacks in Paris, the European Commission proposed a new Directive to replace the former CFDs and added the obligation to criminalise travelling abroad for terrorist purposes and to ensure the protection of the rights of victims.[47] By presenting its proposal in December 2015, the Commission aimed to update the EU legal framework on counterterrorism and bring EU legislation in line with international developments, such as the UNSCR 2178(2014) and the 2015 *Additional Protocol to the Council of Europe Convention on the Prevention of Terrorism.*[48] Interestingly, the 2005 CoE Convention did not criminalise the act of receiving training for terrorism, which was also lacking in the 2008 CFD. This lacuna was remedied by the 2015 Additional Protocol and introduced in the 2017 Directive.

The EU anti-terrorism norms have also been influenced by the international requirements but go much further beyond in terms of their substantive requirements and their binding nature, and more specifically their enforceability (cf. infringement procedure and CJEU).

Compared to ASEAN, the EU has adopted a more legalistic approach, which has enhanced the development and implementation of mutual trust, by adding a legal dimension to it, and may even have replaced the need for mutual trust. Some experts argue that by parties having to respect norms, it leaves no room, no need even, for trust.

The international instruments have had an impact on the two regions (top-down), but there is no clear evidence that the regional developments have influenced international norms.

Similarities between ASEAN and the EU's developments can be highlighted. They both began with the premise that terrorism is a national security concern. However, it became, at least partly, regionalised primarily to ensure that the economy sector was protected. Eventually, counterterrorism became a separate objective. However, the EU has detached itself from the sole international requirements by approximating national criminal laws according to its own method and ensuring that Member States' comply with EU law. By contrast, the ASEAN legal framework on counterterrorism merely mimics international norms.

These instruments form part of the basis for building trust in the social dimension on an international level in both ASEAN (prominently) and the EU; for building

[46] Council of Europe, *Convention on the Prevention of Terrorism* (2005). The latter establishes the obligations of States parties thereto to criminalise public provocation to commit a terrorist offence and recruitment and training for terrorism, when committed unlawfully and intentionally.

[47] *Directive 2017/541 on combating terrorism.*

[48] European Parliament, 'Combating terrorism' *Briefing*, EU Legislation in Progress, PE 599.269, September 2017: available at https://bit.ly/3pdF3kE (accessed on 11 September 2019).

mutual trust in the political dimension in both ASEAN (work in progress) and the EU; and for building trust in the legal dimension within the EU.

B. Criminalising transnational crime: between strong top-down influence in ASEAN and cross-fertilisation in the EU

Apart from the instruments focusing on terrorism, other regional instruments that are relevant in the fight against terrorism relate to 'ordinary' criminal offences, mainly those dealing with instruments on serious transnational crime on a broader sense. In particular, the 2000 *United Nations Convention against Transnational Organized Crime* (UNTOC), which broadly defines serious crime as the 'conduct constituting an offence punishable by a maximum deprivation of liberty of at least 4 years or a more serious penalty',[49] has become the legal basis for approximating, at a minimum, legislations on transnational organised crime and in fostering interstate cooperation.

The UNTOC inspired the relevant regional norms. Particularly, the 2015 *ASEAN Convention against Trafficking in Persons, Especially Women and Children* is the transposition of a combination of the UNTOC and one of its protocols, namely the 2000 *UN Protocol to Prevent, Suppress and Punish Trafficking in Persons, Especially Women and Children.* Some provisions of these two instruments were literally copied, including the definition of 'serious crime' and 'organised criminal group' as provided in the UNTOC. As in the UNTOC, transnational organised crime was defined by a combination of three factors: the seriousness of the criminal activity (determined in accordance with the penalty), the involvement of criminal organisations and the presence of a transnational character.[50]

The international and regional provisions regarding their objective (Article 2 of the UN Protocol and Article 1 of the ASEAN Convention) are quite similar, except for the part 'and to ensure just and effective punishment of traffickers' added to the ASEAN Convention. The scope of these two instruments is identical. In addition to criminalising trafficking in persons (respectively, Article 5 of the UN Protocol and Article 5(1) and (2) of the ASEAN Convention) and preventing such trafficking (respectively, Articles 9 and 11), the ASEAN Convention also criminalises the participation in an organised criminal group (Article 6), the laundering of proceeds of crime (Article 7), and corruption (Article 8) as it is provided in Article 5–9 of the UNTOC.

At this point, it is noteworthy that all ASEAN Member States ratified or accessed the UNTOC and protocols, with Brunei Darussalam being the last State ratifying the Protocol on trafficking in persons on 30 March 2020. Locally, the *ASEAN Convention against Trafficking in Persons* entered into force on 8 March 2017, after the

[49] Art. 2(b), UNTOC (2000). See Chap. 2 for more details.

[50] Para. 12, UN Economic and Social Council, E/CN.15/1998/5, *International Cooperation in Combating Transnational Crime*, 'Implementation of the Naples Political Declaration and global action plan against organized transnational crime: Question of the elaboration of an international Convention against organized transnational crime, and other possible instruments', Commission on Crime Prevention and Criminal Justice, 7th session, 21–30 April 1998.

sixth ratification by the Philippines. This Convention is now ratified by all Member States.

Due to the broad international and regional definitions of offences and the vagueness of the criminalisation, ASEAN Member States enjoy room for discretion when implementing these provisions, which only provide minimum requirements (appearing to form a type of 'best-effort' requirement). The strong similarities between the international and ASEAN norms, and the absence of additional provisions brought by ASEAN norms, ease the implementation of these regional norms.[51]

There is a clear top-down influence from the international to the regional level, with a clear absence of benefits provided by the ASEAN Convention to the regional legal order.

Contrary to the developments in ASEAN, the EU has made serious progress in the criminalisation of serious crime over the past 30 years. The EU intervened before the adoption of the UNTOC by adopting a *Joint Action on 21 December 1998 on the criminalisation of participation in a criminal organisation.*[52] The Joint Action defines a criminal organisation as being 'a structured association, established over a period of time, of more than two persons, acting in concert with a view to committing offences which are punishable by deprivation of liberty or a detention order of a maximum of at least 4 years or a more serious penalty, whether such offences are an end in themselves or a means of obtaining material benefits and, where appropriate, of improperly influencing the operation of public authorities'.[53] This definition served as a basis for the international negotiations, which reveals the reason for the UN and EU definitions being so similar.[54]

Repealing this Joint Action, the *Council Framework Decision of 24 October 2008 on the fight against organised crime*[55] aimed to approximate national criminal laws for the purpose of facilitating judicial and police cooperation, including mutual recognition.[56] This Council Framework Decision transformed the last part of the definition 'whether such offences are an end in themselves or a means of obtaining material benefits and, where appropriate, of improperly influencing the operation of public authorities' into 'to obtain, directly or indirectly, a financial or other material

[51] All ASEAN Member States ratified the Convention.

[52] *Joint Action of 21 December 1998 adopted by the Council on the basis of Article K.3 of the Treaty on European Union on making it a criminal offence to participate in a criminal organisation in the Member States of the European Union*, O.J.E.C. L351/1, 29 December 1998. See also the Amsterdam European Council, Presidency Conclusions, D/97/2, Brussels, 16–17 June 1997, 11–12.

[53] Art. 1, *Joint Action of 21 December 1998 on making it a criminal offence to participate in a criminal organisation in the Member States of the European Union.*

[54] Weyembergh, *L'harmonisation des législations* (2004); Weyembergh, 'The Functions of Approximation of Penal Legislation within the EU' (2005).

[55] Art. 9, *Council Framework Decision 2008/841/JHA on the fight against organised crime.*

[56] Para. 3 of the preamble, Ibid.

benefit'.[57] This EU definition has changed according to the UNTOC's. Since then, there has been no amendment to this framework decision.

As with counterterrorism, the fight against organised crime has clearly benefited from many cross-cutting (e.g. Europol Regulation and Eurojust Regulation) and sectorial instruments (e.g. Directives on combating money laundering and on combating fraud and counterfeiting of non-cash means of payment).

This example illustrates the way in which the EU sometimes inspires and is inspired by international legal frameworks (cross-fertilisation). In contrast, ASEAN has clearly followed international guidance (top-down influence).

II. The adoption of regional human rights standards: influenced by or influencing international norms?

The sensitive balance between firmly countering terrorism and developing, or upholding, effective means of protecting human rights is particularly difficult to achieve and preserve.[58] States have historically prioritised the development of security measures over human rights-based guarantees. However, ensuring an equivalent protection of human rights might be an additional guarantee to build mutual trust and, eventually, to facilitate cooperation between competent national authorities. This is the approach adopted by the EU, while it is not the case in ASEAN (A).

By developing mechanisms of data sharing—identified as essential to the prevention and combating of terrorism—particular rights become endangered, especially the right to privacy which encompasses the right of protecting personal data (B). Providing an equivalent protection might aid the flow of data and prevent risks of human rights violations.

A. Variable protection of human rights in the process of building up mutual trust in criminal matters

Few—and/or vague—norms on human rights have emerged in parallel with the adoption of strong binding security-related instruments. Due to the high priority given to security, international standards of human rights can be threated whenever counterterrorism measures are adopted.[59] Notably, terrorism has led to the adoption of specific norms and measures, whereas human rights norms have not developed to the same extent (1). This is predominantly the case in ASEAN (2) whereas the EU

---

[57] Art. 1, Ibid.

[58] Kalliopi K. Koufa, 'The UN, Human Rights and Counter-terrorism' in *International Cooperation in Counter-terrorism. The United Nations and Regional Organizations in the Fight Against Terrorism*, ed., Giuseppe Nesi, Law, Politics & International Relations (London: Routledge, 2006): 67–68.

[59] See the Report by the International Bar Association's Task Force on International Terrorism, *International Terrorism: Legal Challenges and Responses* (Ardsley-New York: Transnational Publishers, 2003): 57, note 21.

does aim at improving the balance between security and the protection of human rights (3).

1. A large international umbrella for the protection of human rights

The United Nations, other international, or regional organisations and bodies, recognised rights and freedoms by way of conventions,[60] declarations,[61] resolutions, codes of conduct,[62] minimum rules,[63] principles and guidelines[64] and other non-binding instruments.[65]

Historically, the *Universal Declaration of Human Rights* (UDHR) is an international cornerstone in the proclamation of human rights. Although not a binding treaty, the rights enshrined in the UDHR are an expression of the fundamental values shared by the international community. It has profoundly influenced the development of international human rights law. States have increasingly and consistently invoked thee values for seven decades. The Declaration has become part of customary international law.[66] The Universal Declaration has given rise to international binding instruments, such as the *International Covenant on Civil and Political Rights* (ICCPR) and the *International Covenant on Economic, Social and Cultural Rights* (ICESCR).[67] In particular, the rights proclaimed in the UDHR and then repeated in the ICCPR are to be considered 'a common standard of achievement for all peoples and all nations'.[68]

---

[60] See, e.g., *International Covenant on Civil and Political Rights*, New York, 16 December 1966, UNTS, vol. 999, No. 14668; *Convention against Torture and Cruel, Inhuman or Degrading Treatment or Punishment*, New York, 10 December 1984, UNTS, vol. 1465, No. 24841.

[61] See, e.g., A/RES/40/34, *Declaration of Basic Principles of Justice for Victims of Crime and Abuse of Power*, 96th plenary meeting, 29 November 1985.

[62] See, e.g., A/RES/34/169, *Code of Conduct for Law Enforcement Officials*, 106th plenary meeting, 17 December 1979.

[63] See, e.g., A/RES/40/33, *United Nations Standard Minimum Rules for the Administration of Juvenile Justice* ('Beijing Rules'), 96th plenary meeting, 29 November 1985; Council of Europe, *Recommendation No. R(87)3 of the Committee of Ministers to Member States on the European Prison Rules*, 404th meeting, 12 February 1987.

[64] See, e.g., A/RES/43/173, *Body of Principles for the Protection of All Persons under Any Form of Detention or Imprisonment*, 76th plenary meeting, 9 December 1988; A/CONF.144/28/Rev.1, Eighth United Nations Congress on the Prevention of Crime and the Treatment of Offenders, *Guidelines on the Role of the Prosecutors*, Havana, 27 August–7 September 1990; Council of Europe, *Guidelines on Human Rights and the Fight Against Terrorism*, Committee of Ministers, 804th meeting, 11 July 2002.

[65] Further examples in the Report by the International Bar Association's Task Force on International Terrorism, *International Terrorism* (2003): 57, note 21.

[66] See, e.g., Hurst Hannum, 'The Status of the Universal Declaration of Human Rights in National and International Law' *Georgia Journal of International and Comparative Law*, vol. 25, no. 1 (1996): 289; Daillier, Forteau, and Pellet, *Droit international public* (2009): 419–20.

[67] *International Covenant on Economic, Social and Cultural Rights*, New York, 16 December 1966, UNTS vol. 993, No. 14531.

[68] Preamble, *Universal Declaration of Human Rights* (hereafter referred to as 'UDHR'), 10 December 1948, A/RES/217A(III), 183rd plenary meeting, UN Doc A/810.

Terrorism violates essential rights and freedoms of people, such as the right to life (Article 6 ICCPR), the right not to be held in slavery (Article 8 ICCPR) and the right to liberty and security of person (Article 9 ICCPR). Of concern is that violations of human rights are not the exclusive prerogative of criminals. It is incumbent upon States that the instruments related to human rights be respected when adopting measures to counter terrorism. The response to terrorist offences by overreacting government authorities can lead to serious breaches of human rights and freedoms. Beside the abovementioned rights, some other rights and freedoms, such as the right to privacy (Article 12 UDHR; Article 17 ICCPR), the right to freedom of thought, conscience and religion (Article 18 ICCPR), the right to freedom of expression (Article 19 ICCPR), the right of peaceful assembly (Article 21 ICCPR), the right to freedom of association (Article 22 ICCPR) and the right not to be discriminated against (Article 24 ICCPR), tend to be endangered by public authorities while adopting counterterrorism measures.[69] Unfortunately, the rights and freedoms are often broadly defined and not associated with any practical means of implementation, which does not support its implementation and enforceability.

Under this weak international human rights framework, the UN organisation's norms, especially the Security Council resolutions directly, and seriously, affect human rights obligations of States and might potentially neutralise the capacity of national human rights norms and institutions to operate effectively.[70]

For instance, in March 2019, the UNSCR 2462(2019)[71] focusing on terrorism financing has had exceptionally problematic implications for humanitarian and civil society actors in fragile and/or high conflict environments. This resolution expands the definition of material support to terrorism. However, it provides no meaningful protections for human rights. The implementation of these provisions has already targeted civil society actors, dissidents and human rights defenders in multiple States.[72]

The UNSCR 2482(2019) linking terrorism to organised crime has raised further concern for human right violations.[73] It is feared that organised crime 'will be named as a threat to global peace and security to justify the invocation of the Charter'.[74] Although it might already be the case in certain jurisdictions, this would have the effect of extending an exception system related to terrorism into the ordinary-law system. In the exception system, terrorism provisions give wider latitude for actions to competent authorities (e.g. longer duration of police custody, lower level of evidence to arrest a suspected terrorist) than those ordinary crimes.

---

[69] Koufa, 'The UN, Human Rights and Counter-terrorism' (2006): 53–54.

[70] See, e.g., Ní Aoláin, 'The Massive Perils of the Latest U.N. Resolution on Terrorism' (2019).

[71] S/RES/2462(2019), *Threats to international peace and security caused by terrorist acts: Preventing and combating the financing of terrorism*, 8496th meeting, 28 March 2019.

[72] Ní Aoláin, 'The Massive Perils of the Latest U.N. Resolution on Terrorism' (2019).

[73] S/RES/2482(2019), *Threats to international peace and security caused by terrorist acts*, 8582nd meeting, 19 July 2019.

[74] Ní Aoláin, 'The Massive Perils of the Latest U.N. Resolution on Terrorism' (2019).

This represents the global trend of prioritising security above guaranteeing human rights and freedoms.

Among the international mechanisms and bodies in charge of human rights protection, the UN Human Rights Committee (HRC) needs to be highlighted. It is a body of independent experts in charge of monitoring the implementation of the ICCPR by the States parties. States parties are required to submit regular reports to the Committee on the implementation of the rights enacted in the Covenant. The Committee examines the reports, addresses its concerns and provides recommendations in the form of 'concluding observations'. The HRC is an advisory body that cannot engage infringement procedures against States parties that do not respect the provisions of ICCPR.

As one of the UN political bodies, the UN Human Rights Council, formerly the UN Commission on Human Rights, is an intergovernmental body responsible for strengthening the promotion and protection of human rights around the globe, for addressing situations of human rights violations, and making recommendations regarding any violation. It has the capacity to discuss all thematic human rights issues and situations which require their attention throughout the year. Interestingly, the Commission nominated, for the first time in April 2005, a Special Rapporteur on the promotion and protection of human rights and fundamental freedoms while countering terrorism. This Special Rapporteur is missioned to enhance the link between security measures and human rights guarantees, but can only provide recommendations.[75]

Even though it lacks a binding control system, the United Nations has encouraged regional human rights systems to establish this control since the late 1960s.[76] For instance, and among the most well-known regional systems, the Council of Europe

[75] See, e.g., A/HRC/40/63, *Promotion and protection of all human rights, civil, political, economic, social and cultural rights, including the right to development*, 'Right to privacy. Report of the Special Rapporteur on the right to privacy' 14th session, Agenda item 3: Promotion and protection of all human rights, civil, political, economic, social and cultural rights, including the right to development, 27 February 2019; A/74/335, *Promotion and protection of human rights and fundamental freedoms while countering terrorism*, 'Report of the Special Rapporteur on the promotion and protection of human rights and fundamental freedoms while countering terrorism', 74th session, 29 August 2019; UN Human Rights Special Procedures, 'Views of the United Nations Special Rapporteur on the promotion of and protection of human rights and fundamental freedoms while countering terrorism to the Secretariat-General's ending report pursuant to UNSCR 2482(2019) addressing the issue of linkage between terrorism and organized criminal groups (OCG)': available at https://bit.ly/3tSatk7 (accessed on 8 December 2020); UN Human Rights Special Procedures, 'ODIHR Expert consultation meetings on human rights challenges related to information gathering and sharing and new technologies in border management in the counter-terrorism and freedom of movement context. Intervention of the Special Rapporteur on the promotion and protection of human rights and fundamental freedoms while countering terrorism', 15 June 2020: available at https://bit.ly/3tRWYkm (accessed on 8 December 2020).

[76] A/RES/32/127, *Regional arrangements for the promotion and protection of human rights*, 105th plenary meeting, 16 December 1977.

already provided a serious system of human rights protection with the *European Convention on Human Rights* (ECHR),[77] binding all EU Member States and more, which implementation has been guaranteed by the European Court of Human Rights (ECtHR).[78] The EU also has its own binding regional human rights framework in the form of the *EU Charter of human rights* which is guaranteed by the Court of Justice of the EU (CJEU). Meanwhile, ASEAN has adopted the *ASEAN Declaration on Human Rights* devoid of any regional court to ensure compliance by its Member States.

The international legal framework leaves a wide space in which States and regional organisations can manoeuvre. This loose framework has been transposed in Southeast Asia. In contrast, the EU, predominantly influenced by the Council of Europe, has a much more binding regional system of human rights protection.

2. A powerless regional human rights legal architecture in Southeast Asia...

As previously demonstrated, ASEAN Member States are not particularly willing to have a binding regional legal order concerning counterterrorism. They are even less dedicated to establishing regional human rights norms. The lack of interest in being bound to international human rights is demonstrated by Brunei Darussalam, Malaysia, Myanmar and Singapore having neither ratified nor accessioned the ICCPR yet.[79] In any event, it is argued that '[a] mere ratification of human rights treaties by Member States must not be considered sufficient evidence to suggest that a conclusive presumption exists'.[80] However, an '*actual* observance of the treaties signed must be ensured'[81] in order to confirm the presumption that Member States will comply with the relevant regional and international human rights laws. The lack of national implementation by some Member States of the ICCPR, a key convention, may hinder the development of an effective regional human rights-based system. Standards might diverge and protection might differ among countries, which can become problematic when Member States work together in areas concerning human rights, such as terrorism.

Despite these discrepancies, Member States reached a unanimous agreement on the *ASEAN Human Rights Declaration* (AHRD) at the 21st ASEAN Summit on 18 November 2012.[82] This declaration is the fruit of a long procedure representative

---

[77] CoE, *European Convention for the Protection of Human Rights and Fundamental Freedoms*, ETS No. 5, Rome, 4 November 1950.

[78] CoE, *European Convention for the Protection of Human Rights and Fundamental Freedoms*, Rome, 4 November 1950, entered into force on 3 September 1953. The first members of the ECtHR were elected on 21 January 1959 by the Consultative Assembly of the CoE and had their first session on 22–28 February.

[79] See the table of ratifications of the relevant international and regional instruments in Appendix 1.

[80] *N.S. and others*, Joined Cases C-411/10 and C-493/10, judgment, ECLI:EU:C:2011:865, 21 December 2011. See also Xanthopoulou, *Fundamental Rights and Mutual Trust in the Area of Freedom, Security and Justice* (2020): 167.

[81] Ibid.

[82] *ASEAN Human Rights Declaration*, 21st ASEAN Summit, Phnom Penh, 18 November 2012.

of the ASEAN Way. Primarily, the ASEAN Intergovernmental Commission on Human Rights (AICHR) was created in 2009 to promote and protect human rights and fundamental freedoms of the peoples of ASEAN and as such to regionalise human rights standards.[83] The Commission then drafted the Declaration. In the process, Member States aimed to overcome the strong discrepancies between national legislations and policies in this field.

Notably, before the adoption of the AHRD, the previous ASEAN Secretary-General Surin Pitsuwan recognised that:

> The experience of the European Convention of Human Rights... tends to show that the regional protection of human rights can achieve full success only if it constitutes an element in a policy of integration on the part of the States of a given region. Only at this price is it possible to permit the blow struck by regionalism in the matter of human rights against the necessary universalism which springs from the intrinsically identical nature of all human beings.[84]

One of the main distinctions between the ASEAN and EU instruments on human rights rests on the difference in the terminology used: 'Declaration' and 'Charter'. These two instruments do not have the same normative force. The term 'declaration' is often deliberately chosen to indicate that the parties do not intend to create binding obligations, but merely intend to declare certain aspirations. Ascertaining the intention of the parties may be a difficult task. Some instruments entitled 'declarations' were not originally intended to have binding force, but their provisions may have reflected customary international law or may have subsequently gained binding nature as customary law. This is the case for the *Universal Declaration of Human Rights*.[85] Similarly, the ASEAN Declaration is not legally binding, but can acquire force and influence in regional human rights law over time, especially as it was adopted unanimously. By contrast, the term 'charter' is used for formal and solemn instruments, such as the treaty founding an international organisation like the United Nations ('The Charter of the United Nations').[86] This term grants rights or privileges to any national, regional or international organisation.[87]

Clearly stated in the Phnom Penh Statement on the adoption of the AHRD, the Member States are committed to 'the full implementation of the AHRD to advance

[83] *ASEAN Intergovernmental Commission on Human Rights (Terms of reference)*, 15th ASEAN Summit, Cha-Am Hua Hin, 23–25 October 2009.

[84] Karel Vasak, 'Introduction' in *The International Dimensions of Human Rights*, eds., Karel Vasak and Philip Alston (Westport: Greenwood Press, 1982): 455.

[85] UN Treaty Collection, 'Declaration' in *Glossary*: available at https://treaties.un.org/pages/overview.aspx?path=overview/glossary/page1_en.xml#declarations (accessed on 8 June 2017). See René Cassin, 'La Déclaration universelle et la mise en oeuvre des droits de l'homme' *Recueil des Cours de l'Académie de Droit International*, vol. 79 (1951).

[86] UNICEF, 'Definition of key terms' *Introduction to the Convention on the Rights of the Child*: available at https://www.unicef.org/french/crc/files/Definitions.pdf (accessed on 8 June 2017).

[87] *Dictionary of Law* (Oxford: Oxford University Press, 5th ed., 2003).

the promotion and protection of human rights in the region'.[88] The Declaration is meant to be a framework for increased protection of human rights in the region and to contribute to the ASEAN Community's building and regional integration process.[89]

The Declaration encompasses civil and political rights as well as socio-economic and cultural rights. Similar rights exist in the ICCPR and ICESCR and in the AHRD, such as the right to liberty and security of person (Article 12), the right to privacy (Article 21), the right to freedom of thought, conscience and religion (Article 22), the right to freedom of opinion and expression (Article 23), the freedom of peaceful assembly (Article 24) and the right not to be discriminated against (Articles 3 and 22). The implementation of the AHRD is required by the UN,[90] which might be considered as easy task as most of these rights are also enshrined in the ICCPR. However, this argument is limited since not all ASEAN Member States are party to the ICCPR.

The Declaration frequently conditions the implementation of human rights to national law in accordance with the willingness and ability of the Member States.[91] This formulation can be used by governments as a justification to drop below international standards. This concern has been raised by various experts.[92]

The state-centric approach stated in the Declaration has prevailed over entrusting such role on the regional community as a whole, or empowering individual citizens and non-governmental organisations. ASEAN Member States might interpret and promote human rights differently. National debates about how to translate these human rights into their laws still remain. Member States deal with their own legacy; knowing that certain Members might have experienced a very recent authoritarian

---

[88] *Phnom Penh Statement on the Adoption of the ASEAN Human Rights Declaration*, 21st ASEAN Summit, Phnom Penh, 18 November 2012; and, preamble, *ASEAN Human Rights Declaration* (hereafter referred to as 'AHRD') (2012).

[89] See, e.g., *ASEAN 2025: Forging Ahead Together* (2015).

[90] See the recommendations from the UN Committee on the Rights of the Child to Vietnam, Thailand, Laos, Singapore, Myanmar: Concluding observations regarding Vietnam, 22 August 2012, CERD/C/VNM/CO/3-4, para. 81; Concluding observations regarding Thailand, 17 February 2012, CRC/C/THA/CO/3-4, para. 87; Concluding observations regarding the Lao People's Democratic Republic, 8 April 2011, CRC/C/LAO/CO/2, para 77; Concluding observations regarding Singapore, 4 May 2011, CRC/SGP/CO/2-3, para. 73; Concluding observations regarding Myanmar, 14 March 2012, CRC/C/MMR/CO/3-4, para. 100.

[91] See, e.g., right to life (pt. 11); right of asylum (pt. 16); *ne bis in idem* principle (pt. 20(3)); right to vote (pt. 25); right of assembly and of association (pt. 27(1)) in AHRD (2013).

[92] UN Office of the High Commissioner for Human Rights (OHCHR), 'ASEAN Human Rights Declaration should maintain international standards. An Open Letter from the coordination Committee of the Special Procedures of the Human Rights Council on the Draft ASEAN Human Rights Declaration', 18 November 2012: http://www.ohchr.org/EN/NewsEvents/Pages/DisplayNews.aspx?NewsID=14864&LangID=E (accessed on 9 June 2017); "UN experts raise concerns over 'landmark' Southeast Asian human rights declaration" *UN News Centre*, 16 November 2012: available at http://www.un.org/apps/news/story.asp?NewsID=43520#.WTpiAz_IxE4 (accessed on 9 June 2017).

regime or still do. The tremendous changes that might be required to ensure an effective protection of human rights in some countries may prevent a harmonised protection at the regional level in the short or medium term.

The rights and freedoms proclaimed in the Declaration are at risk when counterterrorism measures are implemented. Even more so due to the fact that the protection of human rights is not closely tied to the other norms related to criminal matters. The *ASEAN Convention on Counter Terrorism* only states in its preamble that 'reaffirming our commitment to protect human rights, fair treatment, the rule of law, and due process'. Security and human rights seemingly belong to separate areas. Conversely, security manifests in the protection of human rights as the Declaration elevates security as a right to be enjoyed by everyone.[93] The Declaration ensures that '[e]very person and the peoples of ASEAN have the right to peace within an ASEAN framework of security and stability, neutrality and freedom, such that the rights set forth in the Declaration can be fully realised'.[94] Accordingly, Member States must ensure security of people in the region (top-down relation) and security between the Member States themselves (more traditional horizontal inter-state relations).

ASEAN has not created any regional mechanism comparable to the EU infringement procedure, where control is exercised by the CJEU or the ECtHR. Nonetheless, ASEAN citizens have the right to an effective and enforceable remedy, which is determined by the national court or any other national competent authority. This right applies to 'acts violating the rights granted to that person by the constitution or by law', not by the ASEAN Declaration directly, which is the case in the EU. Clearly, the Declaration has no direct effect on the national law of ASEAN countries. This may limit the construction of a unified understanding by ASEAN on human rights. It might also negatively affect intra-regional cooperation.

The AICHR aims to foster the effective implementation of the AHRD through soft collaborations and dialogues. AICHR's mandate concerns matters related to human rights cooperation with other ASEAN bodies, external partners and stakeholders. It organises workshops as platforms for exchanging and sharing experiences, best practices and lessons on the implementation of human rights.[95] These workshops can include external experts from other regional human rights systems, such as Europe, Inter-America and Africa as well as representatives from government agencies, national human rights institutions and civil society organisations.[96] However, while the 'minimum standards' established in this Declaration have been

---

[93] Pt. 12, AHRD.

[94] Pt. 38, AHRD.

[95] ASEAN Intergovernmental Commission on Human Rights (AICHR), 'Sharing national experience on human rights implementation in ASEAN', 23 December 2014: available at https://bit.ly/3rMUS3M (accessed on 9 December 2015).

[96] AICHR, 'AICHR Workshop on Regional Mechanisms: Best practices on implementation of human rights' (with partial support from UN Women and Regional EU-ASEAN Dialogue Instrument), 21 November 2014.

criticised for reducing the level of protection of human rights,[97] the AICHR has been described as being 'toothless'.[98,99]

Apart from the UN Office of the High Commissioner on Human Rights (OHCHR) which continues to ensure that ASEAN Member States respect their engagement vis-à-vis international human rights standards,[100] the AICHR and ASEAN Secretariat do not have investigative powers, lack the power to impose any specific objective and cannot sanction a State that violates the Declaration. There is no ASEAN court competent to pursue the States if they do not respect the Declaration or any other regional obligation(s) they might have. The ADHR and AICHR's purpose are to 'promote' rather than 'protect' human rights.[101]

Therefore, the ASEAN regional human rights protection system remains legally weak and is developing slowly.[102] This explains why mutual trust between ASEAN competent national authorities is not based on common human rights standards, but instead on interpersonal relations. The Declaration may nonetheless constitute a common ground for further discussions in this field and, potentially in the future, for enhancing cross-border cooperation.

As has been shown, the human rights international legal framework has been directly transplanted into the regional level (top-down). The *ASEAN Declaration on Human Rights* appears to be more akin to a political statement than to a legally binding instrument. Nonetheless, the Declaration and the work of the AICHR constitute a step towards a minimal approximation of human rights standards within the region. With this in mind, counterterrorism measures still pose a threat given the overwhelming prioritisation of security.

The absence of common human rights standards within ASEAN does not constitute an obstacle to cooperation. Agreeing on shared high priority concern seems enough to foster such cross-border cooperation.

---

[97] Note from Michel Forst, Committee's Chair, taken from "UN Experts raise concerns over 'landmark' Southeast Asian human rights declaration" *UN News Centre*, 16 November 2012: available at http://www.un.org/apps/news/printnewsAr.asp?nid=43520 (accessed on 14 February 2018).

[98] "ASEAN's 'Human Rights' Council: Not Off to a Great Start", *The Wall Street Journal* (25 October 2009); Roberts, *ASEAN Regionalism* (2012): 154.

[99] Before the adoption of the Declaration, concerns from the Office of the High Commissioner for Human Rights, 'ASEAN Human Rights Declaration should maintain international standards. An Open Letter from the Coordination Committee of the Special Procedures of the Human Rights Council on the draft ASEAN Human Rights Declaration', November 2012: available at https://bit.ly/372438b (accessed on 31 May 2017).

[100] See the table of ratification in the Appendix 1. See also, 'UN official welcomes ASEAN commitment to human rights, but concerned over declaration wording' *UN News Centre*, 19 November 2012: available at https://bit.ly/2Z9Q7EU (accessed on 18 June 2017).

[101] Roberts, *ASEAN Regionalism* (2012): 154.

[102] Gerard Clarke, 'The Evolving ASEAN Human Rights System: The ASEAN Human Rights Declaration of 2012' *Northwestern Journal of International Human Rights*, vol. 11, no. 1 (2012).

3. ... in contrast with a binding human rights protection system essential in building up mutual trust and enhancing cooperation within the EU

Establishing a sound balance between counterterrorism and protection of human rights is also a challenge in the EU. Despite having an effective regional human rights framework, many experts recognise that the balance between security measures and the protection of human rights remains difficult to guarantee in the region.[103]

When the European Communities (EC) were founded, human rights were not at the forefront of integration efforts.[104] Yet, the EC Member States were already bound by the ECHR and the ICCPR. In time, the EU created its own human rights instrument: the *Charter of Fundamental Rights of the European Union*, which is applicable to the EU institutions and bodies, with respect to the principle of subsidiarity, and to national authorities when they are implementing EU law.[105]

Aiming at guaranteeing the protection of human rights and fundamental freedoms in the criminal justice process, the EU has, on the one hand, integrated a—yet vague—reminder in counterterrorism instruments of the need to protect human rights, and, on the other hand, adopted more specific means to ensure the protection of procedural rights during the criminal proceedings.

Some concerns have been highlighted during the preparatory work and in the final texts of the EU counterterrorism instruments. Numerous safeguards have been discussed during the negotiations of the 2002 CFD. These discussions led to the introduction of a provision specifying that the respect of the CFD shall not have the effect of altering the obligation to respect fundamental rights and fundamental legal principles as enshrined in Article 6 of the TEU.[106] This late addition may be reassuring, but it might also be symptomatic of the negotiators' uneasiness when faced with the risks that such instruments present to EU citizens' fundamental rights.[107] The following 2008 CFD suffers from the same critical reservations. The addition of three new offences has raised concerns regarding its impact on the principle of legality, the freedom of expression and freedom of association and assembly, for instance. In 2017, the *Directive on combating terrorism* improved the democratic deficit from which the two previous framework decisions suffered.[108] The different approach between the two CFD and the directive might be explained

[103] See, e.g., Galli and Weyembergh, 'Introduction' (2012): 13 and ff.

[104] CEPS, 'Lessons from the EU integration process for ASEAN regional integration', Project on Capacity Enhancement for Intensive International Integration of Vietnam towards 2020, CEPS Report (24 July 2015).

[105] *Charter of Fundamental Rights of the European Union* (2000). See more on the place of the Charter in Chaps. 3 and 4.

[106] Art. 1(2), *Council Framework Decision 2002/475/JHA on combating terrorism.*

[107] See Galli and Weyembergh, 'Introduction' (2012): 16.

[108] *Directive (EU) 2017/541 of the European Parliament and of the Council of 15 March 2017 on combating terrorism and replacing Council Framework Decision 2002/475/JHA and amending Council Decision 2005/671/JHA*, O.J. L88/6, 31 March 2017.

by the fact that the two council framework decisions had been adopted under the Third Pillar of the TEU, without the involvement of the European Parliament, whereas the Directive was adopted following the co-decision legislative procedure, with the European Parliament as a co-legislator.

In the three successive instruments, human rights and fundamental freedoms are the primary reference in the preamble and their protection in counterterrorism action constitutes a warning in the core of the three texts.[109] It constitutes a negative obligation to not endanger human rights while preventing and combating terrorism. The references to human rights protection are not precise enough to imply specific actions, except the rights of victims of terrorism provided for in the 2017 Directive.[110]

As the Charter is not specific enough and because human rights are not only at risk during terrorism-related proceedings but also in any criminal proceeding, the EU passed several specific instruments as part of the so-called procedural rights package. This package was mainly endorsed in the 2009 *Roadmap for strengthening procedural rights of suspected or accused persons in criminal proceedings*.[111] Adopting and strengthening common procedural rights within the EU is meant to realise the area of justice, based on mutual trust and mutual recognition, and to ensure the balance between facilitating investigation and prosecution of cross-border crimes and measures protecting the rights of suspects and the accused. This resulted in the adoption of important regional norms: the *Directive 2010/64/EU on the right to interpretation and translation in criminal proceedings*; the *Directive 2012/13/EU on the right to information in criminal proceedings*; the *Directive 2013/48/EU on the right of access to a lawyer in criminal proceedings and in European arrest warrant proceedings, and on the right to have a third party informed upon deprivation of liberty and to communicate with third persons and with consular authorities while deprived of liberty*; the *Directive 2016/343 on the strengthening of certain aspects of the presumption of innocence and of the right to be present at the trial in criminal proceedings*; the *Directive 2016/800 on procedural safeguards for children who are suspects or accused persons in criminal proceedings*; and, the *Directive 2016/1919 on legal aid for suspects and accused persons in criminal proceedings and for*

---

[109] Art. 1, *Council Framework Decision 2002/475/JHA on combating terrorism*; Art. 2, *Council Framework Decision 2008/919/JHA on combating terrorism*; and, Art. 23 as well as Title V related to the protection of, support to, and rights of victims of terrorism, *Directive 2017/541 on combating terrorism.*

[110] Title V (on protection of, support to, and rights of victims), *Directive 2017/541 on combating terrorism.*

[111] *Resolution of the Council of 20 November 2009 on a Roadmap for strengthening procedural rights of suspected or accused persons in criminal proceedings*, O.J. C295/01. This package encompasses a directive on the right to interpretation and translation, a directive on the right to information about rights in criminal proceedings, a directive on the right to access to a lawyer, the right for a detained person to communicate with family members, employers and consular authorities and recommendations on the right to protection for vulnerable suspects. Notably, during the negotiations of the Roadmap, some Member States presented suggestions for other rights to be included, as the right to remain silent and the presumption of innocence.

requested persons in European arrest warrant proceedings.[112] Apart from this procedural rights package linked to suspects' and accused persons' rights, the *Directive 2012/29/EU establishing minimum standards on the rights, support and protection of victims of crime* should be mentioned as well.[113]

Unlike ASEAN, the EU has moved away from the international system. Not only did it further develop the normative regional architecture on human rights and create an enforcement procedure guaranteeing them, but it also integrated human rights considerations into instruments related to criminal matters. There is an existing top-down influence from international norms to the EU, but such influence tends to find its origin in the Council of Europe's norms rather than in the UN's. The main unique feature of the EU is its development of much more detailed and integrated sets of human rights rules guaranteed by the CJEU, which can interpret the Directives' provisions and can also sanction the recalcitrant Member States. The EU has attempted to improve the effectiveness of the protection of human rights, especially since this constitutes an essential component of mutual trust basis of cross-border cooperation.

A top-down influence from the international framework to these two regional legal orders seems to exist. The question remains as to whether it is a real top-down influence or whether it is simply a matter of chronological order (i.e. the later establishment of regional organisations, and regional human rights norms, compared to the international ones). The international (and CoE) human rights norms were adopted before the EU and ASEAN human rights norms or human rights-related provisions in anti-terrorism norms.

---

[112] *Directive 2010/64/EU of the European Parliament and of the Council of 20 October 2010 on the right to interpretation and translation in criminal proceedings*, O.J. L280/1, 26 October 2010; *Directive 2012/13/EU of the European Parliament and of the Council of 22 May 2012 on the right to information in criminal proceedings*, O.J. L142/1, 1 June 2012; *Directive 2013/48/EU of the European Parliament and of the Council of 22 October 2013 on the right of access to a lawyer in criminal proceedings and in European arrest warrant proceedings, and on the right to have a third party informed upon deprivation of liberty and to communicate with third persons and with consular authorities while deprived of liberty*, O.J. L294/1, 6 November 2013; *Directive (EU) 2016/343 of the European Parliament and of the Council of 9 March 2016 on the strengthening of certain aspects of the presumption of innocence and of the right to be present at the trial in criminal proceedings*, O.J. L65/1, 11 March 2016; *Directive (EU) 2016/800 of the European Parliament and of the Council of 11 May 2016 on procedural safeguards for children who are suspects or accused persons in criminal proceedings*, O.J. L132/1, 21 May 2016; *Directive (EU) 2016/1919 of the European Parliament and of the Council of 26 October 2016 on legal aid for suspects and accused persons in criminal proceedings and for requested persons in European arrest warrant proceedings*, O.J. L297/1, 4 November 2016. On the victim side, procedural rights have also been adopted, such as *Directive 2012/29/EU of the European Parliament and of the Council of 25 October 2012 establishing minimum standards on the rights, support and protection of victims of crime, and replacing Council Framework Decision 2001/220/JHA*, O.J.E.U. L315/57, 14 November 2012.

[113] *Directive 2012/29/EU establishing minimum standards on the rights, support and protection of victims of crime.*

Despite this development, the EU has gone further than the international norms through the adoption of legal instruments associated with a regional enforcement procedure. By contrast, as a simple vessel of international law, ASEAN does not add value to the protection of human rights. This has been reflected in the respective regional approach vis-à-vis mutual trust. ASEAN bases its mutual trust on the political agreement to reach identifiable objectives. The EU has added the guarantee of human rights to the identification of a shared objective to enhance mutual trust, and thus facilitates direct cooperation.

B. Serious challenges for the right to privacy in a world where having data is everything

The right to privacy, including the right to the protection of personal data, is either highly debated in multilateral fora such as the United Nations,[114] regional organisations, including in the EU[115] or, on the contrary, may be put aside in some other fora such as ASEAN.[116] These rights, and the associated ones, were codified in international and regional human rights instruments, interpreted by treaty bodies and regional courts, evaluated by special procedures of the Human Rights Council (HRC), and underwent periodic review.

---

[114] A/RES/68/167, *The right to privacy in the digital age*, 68th plenary meeting, 21 January 2014; para. 34, A/CONF.222/L.6, *Doha Declaration on integrating crime prevention and criminal justice into the wider United Nations agenda to address social and economic challenges and to promote the rule of law at the national and international levels, and public participation* (2015).

[115] See all the negotiations preceding the adoption of the *Directive 2016/681 on the use of Passenger Name Record (PNR) data for the prevention, detection, investigation and prosecution of terrorist offences and serious crime*, O.J. L119/132; *Directive 2016/680 on the protection of natural persons with regard to the processing of personal data by competent authorities for the purposes of the prevention, investigation, detection or prosecution of criminal offences or the execution of criminal penalties, and on the free movement of such data*, O.J. L119/89; *General Data Protection Regulation 2016/679*; *Europol Regulation; and Regulation (EU) 2022/991 of the European Parliament and of the Council of 8 June 2022 amending Regulation (EU) 2016/794, as regards Europol's cooperation with private parties, the processing of personal data by Europol in support of criminal investigations, and Europol's role in research and innovation*, O.J.E.U. L169/1, 27 June 2022. Also, European Parliament, Committee on Civil Liberties (LIBE Committee), Justice and Home Affairs, Draft Report on the US NSA surveillance programme, surveillance bodies in various Member States and their impact on EU citizens' fundamental rights and on transatlantic cooperation in Justice and Home Affairs, 2013/2188 (INI), 8 January 2014. See, e.g., Paul de Hert and Vagelis Papakonstantinou, *The data protection regime applying to the inter-agency cooperation and future architecture of the EU criminal justice and law enforcement area*, Study for the LIBE Committee, PE 510.001 (Bruxelles: European Parliament, 2014); Anne Weyembergh, Inès Armada and Chloé Brière, 'The Inter-Agency Cooperation and Future Architecture of the EU Criminal Justice and Law Enforcement Area', Study for the LIBE Committee, PE 510.000 (Bruxelles: European Parliament, 2014).

[116] Nothing has emerged at the ASEAN level. A multilateral forum in Asia Pacific, Asia-Pacific Economic Cooperation (APEC), has worked on this issue for longer than ASEAN and as ASEAN link the data protection to economic considerations. APEC is composed of 21 States with only seven ASEAN Member States: Brunei, Indonesia, Malaysia, Philippines, Singapore, Thailand and Vietnam.

1. A vague international guidance for privacy issues

The ICCPR requires States to act positively in protecting individuals from unjustified interferences into the right to privacy, and the rights to freedom of opinion and expression. In particular, Article 17 ICCPR states that (1) '[n]o one shall be subjected to arbitrary or unlawful interference with his privacy, family, home or correspondence, nor to unlawful attacks on his honour and reputation' and that (2) '[e]veryone has the right to the protection of the law against such interference or attacks'.

No right to the protection of personal data is directly guaranteed by an international instrument. However, as developed especially in the UNGA Resolution of December 2013, the right to privacy constitutes the umbrella under which the right to protection of personal data is promoted. Subsequently, the General Assembly adopted the Resolution entitled 'The right to privacy in the digital age'.[117] Despite being lengthier, this resolution does not add more precision to the definition of the right to privacy and to the means which should be implemented to ensure its effectiveness. The resolution only calls on States to take measures to put an end to rights violations, review practices and policies of communications surveillance and establish oversight mechanisms. The value added by this resolution rests in its call for an effective remedy for individuals whose right to privacy has been violated as well as its request for the Human Rights Committee to establish a special procedure. At this stage, no global binding norm has thus emerged on data protection more specifically.

These rights are not absolute. Restrictions to the right to privacy must meet the well-known three-part test: (1) any limitation on expression must be provided for by law;[118] (2) may only be imposed for legitimate grounds;[119] and, (3) must conform to the strict tests of necessity and proportionality.[120] A regime of permissible limitations to human rights appears to be the prevailing paradigm for justifying methods of cooperation. The permissible limitations on the right to privacy should

[117] A/RES/68/167, *The right to privacy in the digital age*, 68th plenary meeting, 21 January 2014.

[118] The law must be precise, public and transparent, and avoid providing State authorities with unbounded discretion to apply the limitation: UN Human Rights Committee, CCPR/C/GC/34, *General Comment No. 34* 'Article 19: Freedoms of opinion and expression. General remarks', 102nd session, 12 September 2011.

[119] Art. 19(3), ICCPR.

[120] HRC, 'Human Rights Council discusses freedom of opinion and expression and freedoms of peaceful assembly and of association', 17 June 2015: available at https://bit.ly/3jEQGQF (accessed on 18 September 2016). Para. 29 and ff, A/HRC/29/32, *Promotion and protection of all human rights, civil, political, economic, social and cultural rights, including the right to development*, 'Report of the Special Rapporteur on the promotion and protection of the right to freedom of opinion and expression, David Kaye', 29th session, 22 May 2015.

be read strictly, particularly in an age of pervasive surveillance—whether passive or active, mass or targeted—and exponential transnational data transfer.[121]

In this context, the EU has been the theatre of many debates and developments concerning the right to privacy and protection of personal data.[122] As it provides definition and more in-depth legal details, it is discussed first due to its tendency to influence debates in ASEAN, where no specific debate on the right to privacy has taken place.

2. Reinforcing mutual trust through the establishment of equivalent data protection standards within the EU

The EU has been strongly inspired by two main international organisations that are particularly grounded in the region, namely the Organisation for Economic Cooperation and Development (OECD) and the Council of Europe (CoE). In particular, two important instruments dealing with data protection adopted in the early 1980s made an impact on European countries, namely the OECD *Guidelines Governing the Protection of Privacy and Transborder Flows of Personal Data*[123] and the CoE *Convention for the Protection of Individuals with regard to Automatic Processing of Personal Data.*[124] These instruments set out definitions and minimum standards and the debates before the ECtHR have made a clear impact on international discussions and on the elaboration of global standards.[125]

The EU is eager to facilitate the flow of data among competent authorities to ensure the prevention, detection, investigation and prosecution of serious crimes. It even appears as the first point of the 2005 Hague Programme on 'Strengthening security' prior to the section on preventing and combating terrorism. It has become the driving force of any European measure aiming to prevent and combat terrorism.[126] In this context, the right to privacy, including data protection, is at great risk during this age of Big Data and digital expansion.

---

[121] Para. 29, A/HRC/29/32.

[122] See, e.g., CJEU, *Digital Rights Ireland Ltd*, Joined Cases C-293/12 and C-594/12, 8 April 2014.

[123] OECD, *Guidelines on the Protection of Privacy and Transborder Flows of Personal Data,* 23 September 1980.

[124] CoE, *Convention for the Protection of Individuals with regard to Automatic Processing of Personal Data*, ETS No. 108, Strasbourg, 28 January 1981.

[125] See, e.g., paras. 30–31, A/HRC/40/63, *Promotion and protection of all human rights, civil, political, economic, social and cultural rights, including the right to development*, 'Right to privacy. Report of the Special Rapporteur on the right to privacy' 40th session, Agenda item 3: Promotion and protection of all human rights, civil, political, economic, social and cultural rights, including the right to development, 27 February 2019.

[126] See, e.g., *Council Framework Decision 2006/960/JHA on simplifying the exchange of information and intelligence between law enforcement authorities of the Member States of the European Union*; *Regulation 1986/2006 regarding the access to SIS II by the services in the Member States responsible for issuing vehicle registration certificates*; *Regulation 1987/2006 on the establishment, operation and use of the SIS II*; *Council Decision 2009/934/JHA adopting the implementing rules governing Europol's relations with partners, including the exchange of personal data and classified information*; *The Stockholm Programme* (2010); *Directive 2016/681 on the use of PNR data for*

Article 7 of the *EU Charter of Fundamental Rights* guarantees the protection of the right to privacy.[127] The right to protection of personal data has even emerged as an independent fundamental right; confirmed by its inclusion in Article 8 of the Charter.[128] Then, absent so far in the EU 'constitutional' Treaties, the Lisbon Treaty introduced Article 16 of the *Treaty on the Functioning of the European Union* that ensures the right to the protection of personal data.

Besides these provisions in the Charter and the Lisbon Treaty, several specific instruments were adopted. The first instrument was the 1995 *Directive on the protection of individuals with regard to the processing of personal data and on the free movement of such data*[129] that provided the first regional legal norm on the sole protection of data. It took more than two decades for a specific instrument to emerge which deals with the processing and sharing of data within the EU in criminal matters.[130] With the adoption of the Lisbon Treaty and the integration of the Third Pillar related to police and judicial cooperation into the 'ordinary' EU competence, new EU instruments saw the light in 2016. The *Regulation on the protection of natural persons with regard to the processing of personal data and on the free movement of such data (General Data Protection Regulation)*[131] replaced

the prevention, detection, investigation and prosecution of terrorist offences and serious crime; Europol Regulation; Regulation 2022/991 as regards Europol's cooperation with private parties, the processing of personal data by Europol in support of criminal investigations, and Europol's role in research and innovation.

[127] *Charter of fundamental rights of the European Union*, O.J.E.C. 2000/C 364/01, 18 December 2000.

[128] Art. 52(1) EU Charter: 'Any limitation on the exercise of the rights and freedoms recognised by this Charter must be provided for by law and respect the essence of those rights and freedoms. Subject to the principle of proportionality, limitations may be made only if they are necessary and genuinely meet objectives of general interest recognised by the Union or the need to protect the rights and freedoms of others'. As the place of the right to privacy in criminal matters has been well developed in the European doctrine, it will not be elaborated further in this book: see e.g. Gloria González Fuster, Paul De Hert, and Serge Gutwirth, "Privacy and Data Protection in the EU Security Continuum" *INEX Policy Brief*, no. 12 (2011); Franziska Boehm, *Information Sharing and Data Protection in the Area of Freedom, Security and Justice. Towards Harmonised Data Protection Principles for Information Exchange at EU-Level* (Verlag Berlin Heidelberg: Springer, 2012); Gloria González Fuster, *The Emergence of Personal Data Protection as a Fundamental Right of the EU*, vol. 16 (Cham: Springer, 2014); Maria Tzanou, *The Fundamental Right to Data Protection. Normative Value in the Context of Counter-Terrorism Surveillance* (Oxford: Hart Publishing, 2017); EU Agency for Fundamental Rights and Council of Europe, *Handbook on European Data Protection Law* (Luxembourg: Publications Office of the European Union, 2018).

[129] *Directive 95/46/EC on the protection of individuals with regard to the processing of personal data and on the free movement of such data.*

[130] *Council Framework Decision 2008/977/JHA of 27 November 2008 on the protection of personal data processed in the framework of police and judicial cooperation in criminal matters*, O.J. L350/60, 30 December 2008; then, *Council Decision 2009/371/JHA of 6 April 2009 establishing the European Police Office (Europol)*, O.J.E.U. L121/37, 15 May 2009 and their following amendments and associated texts.

[131] Regulation (EU) 2016/679 of the European Parliament and the Council of 27 April 2016 on the protection of natural persons with regard to the processing of personal data and on the free

the previous 1995 Directive and the *Directive on the protection of natural persons with regard to the processing of personal data by competent authorities for the purposes of the prevention, investigation, detection or prosecution of criminal offences or the execution of criminal penalties, and on the free movement of such data*[132] replaced the 2008 *Council Framework Decision on the protection of personal data processed in the framework of police and judicial cooperation in criminal matters.*[133] The new texts improved upon the previous ones by considering the evolution of means of communications and of the actors involved in the gathering, processing, and sharing of data.[134] In particular, the 2016 Directive requires Member States to 'protect the fundamental rights and freedoms of natural persons and in particular their right to the protection of personal data; and ensure that the exchange of personal data by competent authorities within the Union, where such exchange is required by Union or Member State law, is neither restricted nor prohibited for reasons connected with the protection of natural persons with regard to the processing of personal data'.[135] These instruments are meant to ensure the legitimacy and lawfulness of data processing.[136] The EU has thus progressed the most in developing data protection requirements which must be applied by competent national and regional authorities.

Identical to the international level, the ECtHR and CJEU apply the same three-part test: (1) the restriction to the right to privacy must be prescribed by the law, i.e. having a proper legal basis; (2) it must serve a legitimate aim; and (3) it must be necessary and proportional[137] in a democratic society.[138] This test has been

movement of such data, and repealing Directive 95/46/EC (General Data Protection Regulation), O. J. L119/1, 4 May 2016.

[132] *Directive (EU) 2016/680 of the European Parliament and the Council of 27 April 2016 on the protection of natural persons with regard to the processing of personal data by competent authorities for the purposes of the prevention, investigation, detection or prosecution of criminal offences or the execution of criminal penalties, and on the free movement of such data, and repealing Council Framework Decision 2008/977/JHA*, O.J. L119/89, 4 May 2016.

[133] *Council Framework Decision 2008/977/JHA on the protection of personal data processed in the framework of police and judicial cooperation in criminal matters.*

[134] See, e.g., Céline C. Cocq, 'EU Data Protection Rules Applying to Law Enforcement Activities: Towards an Harmonised Legal Framework?' *N.J.E.C.L.*, vol. 7, no. 3 (2016).

[135] Art. 1(2), *Directive 2016/680 on the protection of natural persons with regard to the processing of personal data by competent authorities for the purposes of the prevention, investigation, detection or prosecution of criminal offences or the execution of criminal penalties, and on the free movement of such data.*

[136] Art. 4, *Directive 2016/680.*

[137] See, e.g., para. 59, *The Sunday Times* v. *the United Kingdom*, App. No. 6538/74, judgment (plenary), 2 EHRR 245, 26 April 1979. The Court concluded that the word 'necessary' in the ECHR means that the restriction must be something more than useful, reasonable or desirable. On the criterion of proportionality, see, e.g., para. 50, *Klass* v. *Germany*, App. No. 5029/71, judgment (merits), 2 E.H.R.R. 214, 6 September 1978.

[138] See, e.g., *Digital Rights Ireland*, Joined Cases C-293/12 and C-594/12, 8 April 2014; *Maximillian Schrems* v. *Data Protection Commissioner*, C-362/14, judgment (Grand Chamber), ECLI:EU:C:2015:650, 6 October 2015; and, *Data Protection Commissioner*

employed numerous times, especially in cases related to methods of data collection and sharing. Like the ECtHR, the CJEU case-law has also imposed criteria on the EU and its members for when they interact with external actors and when entering into agreements.[139]

Accordingly, the CoE and EU norms on this subject, as well as their related case-law, certainly have become key references globally, including in ASEAN.

In the EU, mutual trust is built on the premise that all Member States have adopted equivalent human rights standards, including the right to privacy. Approximating these rights ensures that the data shared is used in respect to the same standards. It is meant to strengthen mutual trust and to facilitate cross-border cooperation.

3. Intra-regional cooperation without guaranteeing the rights at risk: an issue for mutual trust in ASEAN?

Global data protection concerns have pushed some ASEAN Member States to adopt norms regarding data protection. In turn, certain ASEAN Member States, namely Indonesia, the Philippines and Singapore, co-supported specific UN Resolutions on the right to privacy in the digital age. Regardless, as an organisation, ASEAN does not have any influence in the international domain.

The regional level does not provide for any further details on the protection of the right to privacy and on data protection more specifically compared to the international level. The *ASEAN Human Rights Declaration* (AHRD) explicitly encompasses the right to the protection of personal data within the right to privacy.[140] The meaning may be similar to that of the ICCPR, but it is phrased differently. In ASEAN, the right to privacy is seen as a positive right to be protected, while it constitutes a negative obligation towards the States and other public authorities according to the ICCPR. Nonetheless, it is unlikely that these provisions lead to discrepancies in practice.

Moreover, and as seen previously, the regional organisation does not provide for any enforcement mechanism or any direct access for citizens from ASEAN countries to the AICHR to ensure compliance by governments regarding this right.

Despite the absence of approximation in this field, competent authorities share data sporadically based on interpersonal relations. Law enforcement authorities consider that the risk of misuse of data is nearly non-existent as they are the only

---

v. *Facebook Ireland Limited and Maximillian Schrems* (Shrems II), C-311/18, judgment (Grand Chamber), ECLI:EU:C:2020:559, 16 July 2020.

[139] See CJEU, *Digital Rights Ireland* (2014); *Tele2,* C-203/15, 4 May 2015; *Schrems* (2015) and (2020).

[140] Art. 21, *AHRD*: 'Each person has the right to be free from arbitrary interference with his or her privacy, family, home or correspondence including personal data, or to attacks upon that person's honour and reputation. Every person has the right to the protection of the law against such interference or attack'.

ones who process it and it is used solely for justice purposes.[141] Prosecutors integrate the data received into the case file the same way they would have for any data collected at the national level. There is no differentiation of treatment between data gathered by the national authorities of the jurisdiction where the prosecution is taking place and data gathered by foreign national authorities and then shared with their counterpart where the prosecution is taking place.[142]

Therefore, the low level of human rights protection, including data protection, is one of the factors which explain why trust among Southeast Asian competent national authorities remains based on interpersonal relations.[143]

In conclusion, it seems that the top-down influence of international norms over regional ones prevails. However, the localisation of international norms into the regional realm[144] did not happen the same way in the EU and as it has in ASEAN. The EU was mainly inspired by the Council of Europe rather than by global norms. In return, the EU norms have also inspired the international norms (bottom-up), especially human rights norms (cross-fertilisation). In contrast, ASEAN tends to pick and choose the type of top-down influence it is willing to accept.

With these vertical interactions, mutual trust is being built through the categories of capability building (e.g. development of the relevant regional norms in counterterrorism and human rights) and information and experience sharing (e.g. sharing norms' content and experience between the different levels of decision-making).

After analysing the top-down and bottom-up dynamics between the international and regional legal orders on terrorism and human rights, the place and role of the EU and ASEAN concerning their respective Member States shall be put into light. The influence between the regional organisations and their respective Member States reveal another significant factor which explains the difference(s) between the EU and ASEAN counterterrorism approaches.

[141] Interviews with, notably: an official from the Anti-Terrorism Council-Programme Management Center, General Santos City, 20 April 2016; an official from the Technical Support Coordinating Unit, Directorate for Intelligence, National Headquarters, Philippine National Police, and official from the City Prosecutor Office, Department of Justice of the Philippines, General Santos City, 20 April 2016; and a group interview with officials from the Directorate General of ASEAN Cooperation from the Ministry of Foreign Affairs of the Republic of Indonesia, Office specialised in Multilateral and Bilateral Treaties on Transnational Crime, Legal Department, Jakarta, 15 June 2016.

[142] Interviews with, notably: an official from the State Prosecutor Office from the Philippines (2016), op. cit.; an official from the Directorate General of International Affairs, Department of the Office of the Attorney General in Thailand, Bangkok, 24 June 2016.

[143] Argument nourished by an interview with a senior researcher at the ISIS Malaysia, Foreign Policy and Security Studies, Kuala Lumpur, 8 June 2016.

[144] As a reminder, the localisation of norms refers to the 'active construction (through discourse, framing, grafting, and cultural selection) of foreign ideas by local actors, which results in the latter developing significant congruence with local beliefs and practices'. Acharya, 'How Ideas Spread: Whose Norms Matter?' (2004).

Section 2: Regional Legal Orders in Counterterrorism—Tailored by and for Their Respective Member States

There is a considerable difference between the relative equivalence among the European countries and the more fragmented Southeast Asian region. In particular, the various countries' experiences in the recent years have framed differently their respective political and legal national frameworks, especially in terrorism-related issues. States use various sets of legal (e.g. anti-terrorism laws) and administrative (e.g. blacklisting, freezing of assets) measures, giving more importance to one measure than another. Moreover, in both regions, Member States may be categorised according to those who have pre-existing specific counterterrorism policies and legislations (e.g. France, Spain, Germany; Indonesia, Malaysia, Singapore) and those who did not have any specific definition and regime against terrorism prior to the adoption of counterterrorism regional legislations (and potentially still do not have any) (e.g. Belgium; Brunei Darussalam, Cambodia, Lao PDR, Myanmar, the Philippines, Thailand, Vietnam).

This section highlights the other end of the spectrum by assessing to the extent to which the respective regional counterterrorism legal frameworks are a product of two opposing influences (top-down and bottom-up) between the national legislations and regional norms concerning counterterrorism and human rights.

By complementing the first section, the function of the regional organisations as intermediaries between international fora and States will be uncovered. It must not be forgotten though that, in criminal matters such as terrorism-related cases, States remain the primary drivers.

This section does not extend to the analysis of each country's national policies and legislation. Pinpointing the most relevant similarities and differences sufficiently reveals the impact of the two-directional influences on the respective regional legal orders.

Due to the vertical angle adopted in this chapter as well as the significant differences between the two regions, the relations between the EU and its members and between ASEAN and its members are analysed separately. In line with the chronological order of development of the regional organisations, the examination begins with the most furnished and legalised framework, namely the EU (I), and then be followed by ASEAN (II).

Their vertical dialogue should serve to build up their own form of mutual trust; and, should consequently have a different impact on the relations between competent authorities on both the horizontal (between national authorities) and vertical (between national authorities and regional organisation) levels.

I. Reaching a comprehensive regional counterterrorism framework: a fruitful vertical dialogue between the EU and its Member States

This section investigates the mutual influence between the EU and its Member States on the development of counterterrorism norms (A) and on human rights-related norms (B). The EU's impetus for approximation is the avoidance of the problem of incompatibility between national laws, particularly for the purpose of improving cooperation.[145] Looking for common minimum denominators, the EU Member States have already elevated their legislation to quite a high level of harmonisation. With the objective of finding its regional position, the top-down law-making is based on, supported, completed or replaced by a bottom-up law--making process.

A. Reaching a harmonised regional counterterrorism legal framework through a fruitful vertical dialogue between national and EU norms

In past decades, the EU has been an epicentre for terrorist attacks, from nationalist groups, such as the Euskadi ta Askatasuna (ETA) or Irish Republican Army (IRA), to transnational ones, such as the Rote Armee Fraktion, the Brigate Rosse and Action Directe. Consequently, the concept of 'euro-terrorism' appeared and became popular in the 1980s to designate the activities of the transnational left, ultra-left groups or far-right groups.[146] Facing this transnational threat, Member States adopted different approaches, but have increasingly worked together in order to prevent and combat this threat.

Tense regional debates related to terrorism and to the threat that government's reaction may pose to human rights have occurred. These regional debates have nourished national debates and, reciprocally, have been nourished by them. These top-down and bottom-up influences are meant to ensure a comprehensive regional anti-terrorism approach representative of the different constitutional traditions.

---

[145] See Weyembergh, *L'harmonisation des législations* (2004); Anne Weyembergh, *Le rapprochement des législations, condition de l'espace pénal européen et révélateur de ses tensions* (Bruxelles: Éditions de l'Université de Bruxelles, 2004); Weyembergh, 'The Functions of Approximation of Penal Legislation within the EU' (2005).

[146] See, e.g., Cesoni, *Nouvelles méthodes de lutte contre la criminalité: la normalisation de l'exception. Etude de droit comparé (Belgique, Etats-Unis, Italie, Pays-Bas, Allemagne, France)* (2007).

1. Primary EU legislation going deeper into the requirement of approximation in criminal matters

The approximation of substantive criminal law began under the Third Pillar of the Maastricht Treaty. It was then pursued under the Amsterdam and Nice Treaties. Based on Article 31e) of the previous TEU, there was a growing number of initiatives towards the approximation of substantive criminal law, especially in the fields of organised crime, terrorism and illicit drug trafficking.

Before the adoption of the Lisbon Treaty, the assessment of progress in criminal matters was positive from a quantitative point of view. However, the results were criticised from a qualitative point of view for different reasons, such as the low level of ambition of most instruments, which were limited to a lowest common denominator approach,[147] and their limited approximating impact.[148,149] Although limited, approximation of legislations by the EC legislation (under the First Pillar) had already been authorised by the European Court of Justice in two main decisions of 2005 and 2007 *Commission* v. *Council*.[150]

Before the Treaty of Amsterdam, criminal law initiatives of the EU aimed at compensating the abolition of checks at the internal borders. As such, a new objective was enshrined, namely the establishment and maintenance of an Area of Freedom Security and Justice (AFSJ). Over time, the fight against crime became an end in itself.[151] The EU and its Member States now aim to ensure the safety and security of all EU citizens and other people on its territory.[152]

With the Lisbon Treaty, the whole field of police and judicial cooperation was transferred to the TFEU and was consequently communautarised with everything that it implies, including the qualified majority voting process.

Both in substantive and procedural criminal law, the EU legislator is only entitled to establish minimum rules (lowest common denominator). The approximation of national legislations is provided for in Article 82(2) TFEU regarding procedural laws, and in Article 83 TFEU regarding substantive laws. The approximation process in the procedural field is meant to ensure an effective protection of human

[147] See, e.g., Galli and Weyembergh, 'Introduction' (2012): 19. Also, Caeiro and Lemos, 'Content and impact of approximation' (2013).

[148] Flore, *Droit pénal européen. Les enjeux d'une justice pénale européenne* (2009): 133–34.

[149] Vervaele, 'Mutual Trust in Gathering of Evidence at the EU Level' (2014).

[150] ECJ, *Commission* v. *Council*, C-176/03, judgment (Grand Chamber), ECLI:EU:C:2005:542, 13 September 2005; *Commission* v. *Council*, C-440/05, judgment (Grand Chamber), ECLI:EU: C:2007:625, 23 October 2007.

[151] See, e.g., Vervaele, 'Mutual Trust in Gathering of Evidence at the EU Level' (2014): 217.

[152] See, e.g., Council of the EU, 'The European Union Counter-Terrorism Strategy', No. 14469/5/05, Brussels, 30 November 2005; European Commission, Communication from the Commission to the European Parliament and the Council, 'Final implementation report of the EU Internal Security Strategy 2010–2014', COM(2014) 365 final, Brussels, 20 June 2014; Council of the EU, Presidency, Draft Council Conclusions on the Renewed European Union Internal Security Strategy 2015–2020, No. 9798/15, Brussels 10 June 2015.

rights in criminal proceedings[153] as well as to facilitate police and judicial cooperation.

The legal basis for the approximation of substantive criminal laws grew from one littera (former Article 31e) TEU) to an entire article (Article 83 TFEU). Article 31e) focused on a list of offences, namely organised crime, terrorism and illicit drug trafficking, whereas the current article with the minimum rules 'concerning the definition of criminal offences and sanctions in the areas of particularly serious crime with a cross-border dimension'.[154] This article was criticised for being too broad. Each of these expressions is rather vague and creates uncertainty.[155] For example, what do 'minimum rules' entail? Does it only focus on a minimum level of penalty? What constitutes a 'serious crime'? Must the offences necessarily be cross-border in nature to involve an action from the EU? These questions have not been addressed by any EU text.[156] For instance, terrorism is a serious crime, yet by nature it is not necessarily a transnational crime. A terrorist attack might occur and be limited to a single country. Does it then follow that a purely national terrorist offence without any cross-border element is out of the realm of action of the EU? This would be the case if there were no special need to combat terrorist offences on a common basis,[157] which is not the case. Terrorism was clearly identified as a common threat that needs to be handled in concert, even when all the elements of the offence remain within the jurisdiction of one country.[158]

Despite imprecisions in some terms (intentional or not), norms have been adopted in the AFSJ. Its integration into the EU competence has led to an increasing number of binding instruments (i.e. directives and regulations) in criminal matters. The legal tool to be used and the respective decision-making procedure are clarified.

The nature and increasing number of challenges require a regional, or at least a transnational, response. However, values and principles encompassed in national constitutions need to be considered and respected when drafting new EU norms. In so doing, the objective is to avoid any negative impact of the EU law on the national constitutions. These considerations include, among others, the will to make the EU decision-making more transparent, explaining why the European Commission launches *ex ante* evaluations, analysing the opportunity and feasibility of adopting new regional norms that would harmonise national legislations in criminal matters. The Commission considers the role of these *ex ante* evaluations as well as the *ex post*

---

[153] Art. 82(2)(b),TFEU.

[154] Art. 83(1), TFEU. The Council can always identify other areas of crime that may need approximation (on the provision that they are unanimously decided).

[155] For further developments, see, e.g., Vervaele, 'Mutual Trust in Gathering of Evidence at the EU Level' (2014): 219.

[156] See further development on this aspect in Chap. 2.

[157] Art. 83(1), TFEU.

[158] See, e.g., Ní Aoláin, 'The Massive Perils of the Latest U.N. Resolution on Terrorism' (2019). Also, European Commission, Communication from the Commission to the European Parliament, the Council, the European Economic and Social Committee and the Committee of the Regions, 'The European Agenda on Security', COM(2015) 185 final, Strasbourg, 28 April 2015, 2.

evaluations essential to ensure EU policies remain cohesive.[159] The *ex ante* and *ex post* evaluations are part of the collaborative work between EU Member States and the EU.[160] *Ex ante* and *ex post* evaluations are intended to design and evaluate EU policies and laws to ensure that they achieve their objectives in the most efficient and effective way possible. They also facilitate the sharing of knowledge, experiences and best practices between the Member States. Before undertaking any legislative procedure, the *ex ante* evaluations aim to ensure the acceptance of Member States in new EU policies and norms.

Whereas the importance of *ex ante* evaluation has been increasingly recognised in line with the reflections on European governance and a better regulation process,[161] one could consider that it would have been of even greater importance when the AFSJ was of an intergovernmental nature. Due to the unanimity required by the EU Council for the adoption of framework decisions, such evaluation reduces the risks of legal blockage due to an incompatibility of the proposed norm with a specific country's constitutional principle. This occurred when the 2002 and 2008 Council Framework Decisions on combating terrorism were created. Currently, the significance of such evaluation remains, despite the qualified-majority voting, as constitutional obstacles take precedent where there is a conflict of law.

The benefits provided by the ordinary decision-making procedure introduced by the Lisbon Treaty in the field, also makes it possible for Member States to intervene via their representatives at the European Parliament, as one example. With the involvement of the European Parliament, the decision-making process is intended to be more democratic when compared to the previous intergovernmental decision-making procedures. States might always invoke a fundamental incompatibility with their criminal justice system to oppose the approximation.[162] This possibility has never been invoked though; due probably to the *ex ante* evaluations.[163]

---

[159] European Commission, 'The Programming Period 2015–2020. Monitoring and Evaluation of European Cohesion Policy. Guidance document on ex-ante evaluation', European Regional Development Fund, European Social Fund and Cohesion Fund, January 2014: available at https://bit.ly/3eSgSoZ (accessed on 29 September 2019).

[160] See Chap. 3.

[161] Commission of the European Communities, 'European Governance—A white paper', COM (2001) 428 final, O.J.E.C. C287/1, 12 October 2001; Commission of the European Communities, Communication from the Commission, 'European Governance: Better lawmaking', COM(2002) 275 final, Brussels, 5 June 2002. See also the adoption of a Scrutiny Board provides quality control and support for Commission impact assessments and evaluations at early stages of the legislative process: European Commission, Regulatory Scrutiny Board, 'Rules of Procedure of the Regulatory Scrutiny Board' replacing the Rules of Procedure of the Regulatory Scrutiny Board of 5 October 2016, Ares(2016)5764766), Ares(2020)2060246, Brussels, 15 April 2020.

[162] Arts. 82(3) and 83(3), TFEU.

[163] See, e.g., the 'Study on minimum sanctions in EU Member States', JUST/2013/JPEN/PR/0047/A4, Study for the European Commission, Contractor: ECORYS NL with ECLAN (sub-contractor).

2. The gradual regionalisation of the criminalisation of terrorist offences

The impact from continuous terrorist attacks on the adoption and/or in speeding up the adoption of regional counterterrorism norms cannot be overlooked. Each text has followed a significant attack, namely the 9/11 attacks, the attacks in Madrid (2004) and London (2005) and the attacks in Paris (2015) and Brussels (2016).

Although the adoption of a specific instrument dealing with terrorism had already been debated,[164] the first framework decision was proposed eight days after the 9/11 attacks.[165] A political agreement defining terrorist offences was swiftly agreed upon in December 2001[166] and the proposal was finally adopted, under the Third Pillar, on 13 June 2002.[167] This Council Framework Decision was amended in 2008[168] and a final Directive[169] replaced these two framework decisions. These instruments are the manifestation of intense dialogues between the regional and national authorities, bringing their unique national identity to the legal debates.

(a) *Council Framework Decision 2002/475/JHA: the cornerstone of the fight against terrorism*

At the time of the 9/11 attacks, the national laws of the six countries which already criminalised terrorist offences were a particular point of reference for the framework decision. These countries were the United Kingdom[170] (one of the

---

After demonstrating the constitutional issues that the adoption of an EU legislation on this subject would encounter, the European Commission refrained from proposing anything.

[164] See among other documents, Plan of Action of the Council and the Commission on how best to implement the provisions of the Treaty of Amsterdam on an area of freedom, security and justice, text adopted by the Justice and Home Affairs Council of 3 December 1998, O.J.E.C. C19, 23 January 1999; the scoreboard of the Commission before the 9/11 attacks, Commission of the European Communities, Communication from the Commission to the Council and the European Parliament. Biannual update of the scoreboard to review progress on the creation of an Area of 'Freedom, Security and Justice' in the EU (second half of 2000), COM(2000) 782 final, Brussels, 30 November 2000; Commission of the European Communities, Communication from the Commission to the Council and the European Parliament. Biannual update of the scoreboard to review progress on the creation of an Area of 'Freedom, Security and Justice' in the EU (first half of 2001), COM(2001) 278 final, Brussels, 23 May 2001, 33–34.

[165] European Commission, Proposal for a Council Framework Decision on combating terrorism, COM(2001) 521 final, 19 September 2001.

[166] Council of the EU, Proposal for a Council Framework Decision on combating terrorism, doc 14845/1/01 DROIPEN 103, CATS 49, REV 1, Brussels, 6–7 December 2001.

[167] *Council Framework Decision 2002/584/JHA on the European arrest warrant.*

[168] *Council Framework Decision 2008/919/JHA on combating terrorism.*

[169] *Directive 2017/541 on combating terrorism.*

[170] Section 1, *Terrorism Act 2000*: "(1) 'terrorism' means the use or threat of action where (a) the action falls within subsection (2), (b) the use or threat is designed to influence the government or to intimidate the public or a section of the public, and (c) the use or threat is made for the purpose of advancing a political, religious or ideological cause. (2) Action falls within this subsection if it (a) involves serious violence against a person, (b) involves serious damage to property, (c) endangers a person's life, other than that of the person committing the action, (d) creates a serious risk to the health or safety of the public or a section of the public, or (e) is designed seriously

countries with the most advanced legislation in this matter and still a EU member at the time), France,[171] Germany,[172] Italy,[173] Portugal[174] and Spain.[175] These anti-terrorism legislations diverged though. Certain countries such as Germany did not criminalise terrorist acts committed by an independent individual, i.e. someone not belonging to a terrorist group (also called 'lone wolves'). Some countries qualified the elements of terrorist acts via common law offences with the aggravating circumstances of terrorism. In all pre-existing anti-terrorism laws, the intent was specific: the use or threat of violence designed to influence a public authority (i.e. government, international organisation) or to intimidate the public or a section of the public. These national definitions and characteristics have been of great influence in the negotiations of the first framework decision (bottom-up influence).[176]

Some examples highlight the different national dynamics. For instance, the French legislation followed the evolution of the threat. Even before 9/11, France had been particularly prolific in the adoption of counterterrorism policies and laws. France adopted a definition of terrorist offences in 1986, which evolved over time.[177] With its long experience in terrorism, Spain also had anti-terrorism laws before the

---

to interfere with or seriously to disrupt an electronic system. (3) The use or threat of action falling within subsection (2) which involves the use of firearms or explosives is terrorism whether or not subsection (1)(b) is satisfied'.

[171] *Loi No. 86-1020 du 9 septembre 1986 relative à la lute contre le terrorisme et aux atteintes à la sûreté de l'Etat*, J.O.R.F. 0210, 10 September 1986 and Art. 421-1 French Criminal Code (CC): 'Constituent des actes de terrorisme, lorsqu'elles sont intentionnellement en relation avec une entreprise individuelle ou collective ayant pour but de troubler gravement l'ordre public par l'intimidation ou la terreur, les infractions suivantes [...]'.

[172] Art. 129a), *Strafgesetzbuch* (StGB) on terrorist organisations.

[173] Arts. 270bis, 280, 289bis, Italian CC.

[174] Art. 300, Portuguese CC.

[175] Art. 571, Spanish CC criminalises terrorist offences committed in an armed group or in collaboration with and armed groups; and Art. 577 when terrorist offences are not committed in the framework of an armed group.

[176] Anne Weyembergh, 'L'impact du 11 septembre sur l'équilibre sécurité/liberté dans l'espace pénal européen' in *Lutte contre le terrorism et droits fondamentaux* eds., Emmanuelle Bribosia and Anne Weyembergh (Bruxelles: Bruylant, 2002); Emmanuelle Bribosia and Anne Weyembergh, eds., *Lutte contre le terrorisme et droits fondamentaux* (Bruxelles: Bruylant, 2002); Oehmichen, *Terrorism and Anti-Terror Legislation. The Terrorised Legislator?* (2009); O'Neill, *The Evolving EU Counter-Terrosim Legal Framework* (2012); Roach, 'Secret evidence and its alternatives' (2012); Galli and Weyembergh, *Approximation of substantive criminal law in the EU* (2013); Llobet Angli, "What does 'terrorism' mean?" (2013); Caeiro and Lemos, 'Content and impact of approximation' (2013); Murphy, *EU Counter-Terrorism Law* (2012); Bribosia and Weyembergh, 'Confiance mutuelle et droits fondamentaux' (2016); Hufnagel and McCartney, *Trust in International Police and Justice Cooperation* (2017).

[177] See all the laws between *Loi No. 86-1020 relative à la lutte contre le terrorisme*; and, *Loi No. 2019-222 du 23 mars 2019 de programmation 2018-2022 et de réforme pour la justice*, J.O.R.F. 0071, 24 March 2019; with, for instance, *Loi No. 2004-204 du 9 mars 2004 portant adaptation de la justice aux évolutions de la criminalité*, J.O.R.F. 59, 10 March 2004; *Loi No. 2014-1353 du 13 novembre 2014 renforçant les dispositions relatives à la lutte contre le terrorisme*,

adoption of the first EU norm. Terrorist offences are referred to as those committed with the objective or aim of subverting the constitutional order or seriously disturbing public peace and perpetrated by people belonging to, acting in the service of or collaborating with armed bands, organisations or groups with this purpose or aim in mind.[178] Only terrorist organisations were criminalised. By contrast, due to its authoritarian history (Nazi regime), Germany has long been recalcitrant to enact specific provisions on terrorism. Prosecutors tend to have built up cases against suspected terrorists based on general provisions related to serious violent offences (*schweren Gewalttat*) associated with aggravating circumstances of endangering the State.[179] However, 'participating in a terrorist organisation' has been criminalised long before the 2002 CFD, as is the case for France and Spain. The Act of 18 August 1976[180] for the first time created offence in Section 129a *Strafgesetzbuch* (StGB—Criminal Code). This Section, criticised for its wide scope and potential to undermine human rights, dealt with any support to a terrorist organisation, and even the unsuccessful advertising for such support or attempted instigation or assistance to garner it.[181] Enacted in the aftermath of 9/11, Section 129b StGB encompasses the creation of foreign organisations and allows the government to punish certain demonstrations which provide support for such organisations.[182] Subsequently, the criminalisation of recruitment for terrorist purposes was introduced prior to the 2008 CFD, and even before the 2002 CFD, in Section 129(1) relating to the formation of criminal organisations, more generally, and Section 129a(5) regarding the formation of terrorist organisations.

The EU definition has been influenced by the existing national provisions and, in return, has reflected these elements on the Member States' legislations, especially those who did not have anti-terrorism legislation prior to 2002.

J.O.R.F. 0263, 14 November 2014; *Loi No. 2015-912 du 24 juillet 2015 relative au renseignement*, J.O.R.F. 0171, 26 July 2015.

[178] Art. 571 Spanish CC, inserted by Organic Law 5/2010 of 22 June 2010 reforming the Penal Code.

[179] See Sections 89a (regarding the preparation of a serious violent offence endangering the State), 89b (criminalising the fact of establishing contacts for the purpose of committing of serious violent offence endangering the State) and 91 (related to the encouragement of the commission of a serious violent offence endangering the State) StGB.

[180] *Gesetz zur Änderung des Strafgesetzbuches, der Strafprozessordnung, des Gerichtsverfassungsgesetzes, der Bundesrechtanwaltsordnung und des Strafvollzugsgesetzes vom 18 August 1976*, BGBl I: 2181 (also called Anti-Terror-Gesetz).

[181] Gloria González Fuster, Paul De Hert, and Serge Gutwirth, 'Privacy and Data Protection in the EU Security Continuum' *INEX Policy Brief*, no. 12 (2011); Boehm, *Information Sharing and Data Protection in the Area of Freedom, Security and Justice* (2012); Gloria González Fuster, *The Emergence of Personal Data Protection as a Fundamental Right of the EU*, vol. 16 (Cham: Springer, 2014); Maria Tzanou, *The Fundamental Right to Data Protection. Normative Value in the Context of Counter-Terrorism Surveillance* (Oxford: Hart Publishing, 2017); European Union Agency for Fundamental Rights and Council of Europe, *Handbook on European data protection law* (Luxembourg: Publications Office of the European Union, 2018).

[182] *Strafrechtsänderungsgesetz*, BGBl I Nr. 61, 29 August 2002: 3390.

Among the countries without a definition of individual terrorist offences prior to 2002, two different groups of States can be distinguished: those that did not have provisions on terrorist offences, such as Belgium; and those with provisions on some terrorist offences, such as Germany. These two countries highlight differing reception of the framework decision. While Belgium literally transposed the definition provided in the framework decision, Germany did not. On the one hand, the Belgian Law of 19 December 2003,[183] implementing the 2002 CFD and the 1999 *Convention for the repression of terrorism financing,* inserted a new Title *Iter* in Book II of the Criminal Code (CC) entitled *terrorist offences* and introduced 'terrorist offences' (Articles 137 and 138); 'offences relating to a terrorist group' (Articles 139 and 140); and 'contribution to the commission of a terrorist offence committed independently from a terrorist group' (Article 141). This law also revised specific provisions of the Belgian Code of Criminal Procedure (Articles 6 and 10*ter*; Article 90*ter*). On the other hand, Germany is among the Member States which refrained for a certain period from transposing the EU definition of 'terrorist offences' into their legislation. Thus, the reception of the subsequent EU instruments has diverged.

Therefore, there was a bottom-up influence from some Member States on the 2002 CFD, while there was also a top-down influence of the regional norm on other Member States.

(b) *Council Framework Decision 2008/919/JHA: criminalising inchoate terrorist offences*

The 2002 framework decision was amended in 2008 to further criminalise behaviours at an earlier stage. It added public provocation, recruitment and training for terrorism to the list of terrorist offences.[184] As discussed in the previous section, the second framework decision was mostly inspired by the CoE *Convention on the Prevention of Terrorism.*[185]

Although the influence of the CoE over the 2008 CFD is evident, certain Member States had criminalised specific relevant behaviours prior to this Convention. For example, Germany criminalised some of the 2008 CFD's behaviours even before the adoption of the 2002 CFD. Provocation to commit a terrorist offence has been encompassed in the provisions related to the incitation to hatred (Section 130 StGB); attempt to cause the commission of offences by means of publication (Section 130a StGB); and, dissemination of depictions of violence (Section 131 StGB). Moreover, Germany criminalised training for committing serious violent offences (Section 130a(2)2 StGB) prior to the adoption of the 2008 CFD. France also provided specific provisions on terrorism that criminalise training as part of the participation in a terrorist group (Article 421-1 CC) since it enacted the Law of 30 December 1996.[186]

[183] *Loi C-2003/09963 du 19 décembre 2003 relative aux infractions terroristes,* M.B. 29 December 2003.

[184] Art. 1(1), *Council Framework Decision 2008/919/JHA on combating terrorism.*

[185] CoE, *Convention on the Prevention of Terrorism* (2005).

Member States have predominantly been receivers (top-down) rather than influencers (bottom-up) of the 2008 CFD. Certain States who have been proactive prior to 2002 have further adapted their legislations after the 2008 CFD. For instance, France criminalised recruitment with the Law of 21 December 2012 introducing provisions in Article 421-2-4 CC. Interestingly, unlike for the 2002 CFD, the French laws evolved after the 2008 CFD to respect the EU requirements regarding the apology for terrorism or incitation of terrorism. Law 2014-1353[187] inserted a specific incrimination for public provocation to commit terrorist offences in the new Article 421-2-5 CC based on the more general offence of apology for crimes incriminated in the 1881 *Loi sur la liberté de la presse* (Law on the Freedom of the Press).

Among the national laws which were unfamiliar with terrorist offences prior to the 2002 CFD, the Belgian Law of 18 February 2013 modified Book II, Title I*ter* of the Criminal Code,[188] and in so doing followed the EU norm once again. It inserted new offences (Art. 140*bis* on incitement, 140*ter* on recruitment, 140*quater* on training) and amended Articles 137 and 138 CC concerning terrorist attempts. It went beyond the EU requirements by also criminalising passive training (Art. 140*quinquies*). Other laws followed which aimed to improve States' actions against terrorism.[189]

(c) *Directive 2017/541: consolidating the intergovernmental framework decisions and responding to new challenges*

Adopted under the new co-decision procedure, this instrument amended and repealed the two framework decisions, but almost entirely mimicked the CFDs' definitions.[190]

An impact assessment of the 2008 CFD led to the publication of the *Report on the implementation of Council Framework Decision 2008/919/JHA on combating ter-*

[186] *Loi No. 96-1235 du 30 décembre 1996 relative à la détention provisoire et aux perquisitions de nuit en matière de terrorisme*, J.O.R.F. 1, 1 January 1997.

[187] Art. 5, *Loi No. 2014-1353 renforçant les dispositions relatives à la lutte contre le terrorisme*. This law inserted Art. 421-2-5 CC.

[188] *Loi C-2013/09097 du 18 février 2013 modifiant le livre II, titre I^er^ter du Code pénal*, M.B. 4 March 2013.

[189] *Loi C-2015/09385 du 20 juillet 2015 visant à renforcer la lutte contre le terrorisme*, M.B. 5 August 2015; *Loi C-2016/09200 du 27 avril 2016 relative à des mesures complémentaires en matière de lutte contre le terrorisme*, M.B. 9 May 2016; *Loi C-2016/30017 du 25 décembre 2016 portant des modifications diverses au Code d'instruction criminelle et au Code pénal, en vue d'améliorer les méthodes particulières de recherche et certaines mesures d'enquête concernant Internet, les communications électroniques et les télécommunications et créant une banque de données des empreintes vocales*, M.B. 17 January 2017; *Loi C-2017/11752 du 30 mars 2017 modifiant la loi du 30 novembre 1998 organique des services de renseignement et de sécurité et l'article 259bis du Code Pénal*, M.B. 28 April 2017.

[190] Arts. 2–3, *Directive (EU) 2017/541 of the European Parliament and of the Council of 15 March 2017 on combating terrorism and replacing Council Framework Decision 2002/475/JHA and amending Council Decision 2005/671/JHA*, O.J. L88/6, 31 March 2017.

rorism[191] in 2014. This *ex post* evaluation was used as a tool to draft the *Directive on combating terrorism.* The Directive was proposed by the Commission on 2 December 2015, 19 days after the attacks in Paris and following the UNSCR 2178(2014)'s requirements,[192] after the adoption of the Additional Protocol to the CoE *Convention on the Prevention of Terrorism*[193] on the phenomenon of foreign terrorist fighters and of the standards of the Financial Action task Force (FATF) regarding the financing of terrorism.[194,195] With (suspected) terrorists fleeing to other countries, further harmonising the EU position on the threat of foreign terrorist fighters was considered a necessity. Adapting to the new challenges, the Directive integrated new provisions requiring the criminalisation of travelling—and facilitating of travelling—abroad for terrorist purposes.[196]

The quick response to the UN resolution and the CoE protocol is explained by the large number of foreign terrorist fighters originating from EU countries (mostly from Belgium, France, Germany and the UK), estimated to be approximately 4.000 individuals.[197]

Similarly, certain Member States had legislations prior to the adoption of the UNSCR 2178(2014), such as the UK.[198] Other Member States followed the UNSCR and adopted norms before the Directive, such as Belgium, Bulgaria, Germany, Italy, Luxembourg, Portugal and Spain.[199] Notably, France adopted a law in November

---

[191] European Commission, 'Report from the Commission on the implementation of Council Framework Decision 2008/919/JHA of 28 November 2008 amending Framework Decision 2002/475/JHA on combating terrorism", COM(2014) 554.

[192] S/RES/2178(2014), *Resolution Condemning Violent Extremism, Underscoring Need to Prevent Travel, Support for Foreign Terrorist Fighters.*

[193] CoE, *Additional Protocol to the Council of Europe Convention on the Prevention of Terrorism*, ETS No. 217, Riga, 22 October 2015.

[194] Financial Action Task Force, *International Standards on Combating Money Laundering and the Financing of Terrorism and Proliferation.* FATF Recommendations, Paris, February 2012 and updated in June 2019.

[195] See Monika Hohlmeier's speech at the European Parliament, Rapporteur of the European Parliament's Committee on Civil Liberties, Justice and Home Affairs on the proposal of Directive on combating terrorism, Brussels, 15 February 2017: available at http://www.europarl.europa.eu/doceo/document/CRE-8-2017-02-15_EN.html#creitem36 (accessed on 27 September 2019).

[196] Arts. 9–10, *Directive 2017/541 on combating terrorism.*

[197] Amandine Scherrer ed., 'The return of foreign fighters to EU soil. Ex-post evaluation', Study of the European Parliamentary Research Service, PE 621.811 (Brussels: European Parliament, May 2018); Europol, EU Terrorism Situation and Trend Report, *TE-SAT 2017* (The Hague: European Police Office, 15 June 2017).

[198] Sections 6 and 8, *Terrorism Act 2006*, Chap. 11, 30 March 2006.

[199] See, e.g., *Loi C-2013/09097 modifiant le livre II, titre I^{er}ter du Code pénal* inserting Arts. 140*quinquies* and 140*sexies* in the Belgian CC and *Loi C-2015/09385 visant à renforcer la lutte contre le terrorisme*; *Gesetz zur Änderung der Verfolgung der Vorbereitung von schweren staatsgefährenden Gewalttaten* (GVVG-Änderungsgesetz – GVVG-ÄndG), BGBl Teil I Nr. 23, 12 June 2015: Seite 926, modifying Arts. 89a and b StGB; *Ley Orgánica 2/2015, de 30 de marzo, por la que se modifica la Ley Orgánica 10/1995, de 23 noviembre, del Código Penal, en material de delitos de terrorismo* inserting Art. 575 in the Spanish CC.

2014,[200] immediately after the adoption of the UNSCR, which criminalised travelling for the purpose of terrorism.

The influence of Member States over the Directive can be evaluated in two ways. Firstly, as members of these international fora, States are the source of the relevant international provisions. Secondly, having enacted laws after the adoption of the international norms and standards, Member States have 'indirectly' influenced the Directive. For instance, Austria stated that national criminal laws must be more coherent, comprehensive and uniform throughout the EU to effectively prevent and prosecute offences committed by foreign terrorist fighters.[201] Thus, the most visible influence on this Directive comes from international fora (top-down) rather than from Member States (bottom-up). The Directive did provide an EU position and ensured the harmonisation of the national provisions.

It is noteworthy that the three successive EU instruments have been the objects of different dynamics. In fact, there has clearly been cross-fertilisation between regional and national levels, which varies according to the respective instruments.

Along with the development of regional counterterrorism norms, Member States must ensure that fundamental rights and freedoms are effectively guaranteed when counterterrorism measures are adopted and implemented.

B. Regional human rights standards in criminal matters: a long-awaited step towards building up more effective mutual trust

States have been known to prioritise the security threat without fairly balancing these measures with human rights protections. Nonetheless, human rights considerations have been integrated into different levels: into the EU primary law (1), into counterterrorism norms (2) and into specific secondary legislation on criminal justice proceedings (3).

1. The insertion of human rights protection into the EU 'constitutional' architecture: a strong influence of Member States

Beside the 'constitutional' Treaties, namely the *Treaty on the European Union* and *Treaty on the Functioning of the European Union*, the *EU Charter of*

[200] *Loi No. 2014-1353 du 13 novembre 2014 renforçant les dispositions relatives à la lutte contre le terrorisme*, J.O.R.F. 0263, 14 November 2014inserting Arts. 421-2-6 and 224-1 in the French CC.

[201] The President of the Bundesrat of the Republik Österreich, 'Mitteilung an die Europäische Kommission, den Rat und das Europäische Parlament gemäss Art. 23f Abs. 4 B-VG des EU-Ausschusses des Bundesrates vom 8 März 2016. COM(2015)625 final Vorschlag für eine Richtlinie des Europäischen Parlaments und des Rates zur Terrorismusbekämpfung und zur Ersetzung des Rahmenbeschlusses 2002/475/JI zur Terrorismusbekämpfung', 9 March 2019, 2. Also, at the beginning of the negotiations, Ard van der Steur, the Minister for Justice of The Netherlands and President of the Council, at that time, said in March 2016: 'I am pleased that especially today, on the EU Annual Commemoration Day for the Victims of Terrorism, we can deliver on our common endeavour to deal with new forms of terrorism and the threat posed by foreign terrorist fighters. We need to show now we stand united'. Council of the EU, 'Directive on combating terrorism: Council ready to start negotiations with Parliament', *press release*, 11 March 2016.

fundamental rights, most particularly, has reached the same legal value as the treaties, and the CJEU's decisions are binding. Adding legal weight to the Charter was intended to guarantee its legitimacy.[202] In particular, Article 8 of the Charter, with Article 16 TFEU, on the protection of personal data has increasingly gained weight in the debates regarding the elaboration of technologies and technical means in the fight against serious crime.

The role of the Member States was significant both prior to and after the adoption of the Charter. The Cologne European Council of June 1999 believed that 'this Charter should contain the fundamental rights and freedoms as well as basic procedural rights guaranteed by the European Convention for the Protection of Human Rights and Fundamental Freedoms and derived from the constitutional traditions common to the Member States, as general principles of Community law'.[203] The influence by national constitutions and legislations on the drafting of the Charter was visible from the start. It was also decided that the Charter should be elaborated upon by a body composed of representatives of the Heads of State and Government and of the President of the Commission as well as by members of the European Parliament and national parliaments.[204] Representatives of the European Court of Justice participated as observers. Representatives of the Economic and Social Committee, the Committee of the Regions and social groups as well as experts had a more consultative role.[205]

Tense debates took place during national parliaments' sessions and at the IGC (Inter-Governmental Conference). For example, certain French parliamentarians considered that the adoption of the Charter was not in the best interests of French citizens as it lowered national standards.[206] These concerns also appeared in other countries, including Germany. In response, Article 53 of the Charter states that:

---

[202] Carly Nyst, 'Privacy, Protection of Personal Information and Reputation Rights' *Discussion Paper Series: Children's Rights and Business in Digital World*, ed. Patrick Geary and Amaya Gorostiaga, UNICEF, UNICEF Child Rights & Business Unit.

[203] Conclusions of the Cologne European Council: extract concerning the Charter of fundamental Rights, Presidency Conclusions, 'Annex IV: European Council Decision on the drawing up of a Charter of fundamental rights of the European Union', 3–4 June 1999.

[204] The body in charge of such elaboration was composed of 16 members of the European Parliament and 2 representatives of each national parliament of the 15 Member States, being the number of Member States at that time. Tampere European Council: annex on the body to draft a Charter of Fundamental Rights (15 and 16 October 1999), Annex: Composition method of work and practical arrangements for the body to elaborate a draft EU Charter of fundamental rights, as set out in the Cologne Conclusions.

[205] Conclusions of the Cologne European Council, 'Annex IV: European Council Decision on the drawing up of a Charter of fundamental rights of the European Union', 3 and 4 June 1999. Decision welcomed by the European Parliament: European Parliament, Resolution on the establishment of the Charter of Fundamental Rights (16 September 1999), O.J.C.E. C54, 25 February 2000.

[206] Assemblée nationale (France), Débats parlementaires—Session ordinaire de 2000-2001 (195ème séance): compte-rendu intégral de la 3ème séance du mardi 5 juin 2001, J.O.R.F. Année 2001, No. 39 [2] A.N. (C.R.), 6 June 2001, 3863–3906.

> Nothing in this Charter shall be interpreted as restricting or adversely affecting human rights and fundamental freedoms as recognised, in their respective fields of application, by Union law and international law and by international agreements to which the Union or all the Member States are party, including the European Convention for the Protection of Human Rights and Fundamental Freedoms, and by the Member States' constitutions.

As with any text negotiated between parties, this article is a compromise for different interests. Indeed, strong debates occurred, especially regarding the level of protection of fundamental rights between the respective legal orders. Yet, in the end, Article 53 does not clearly regulate relations between EU law and national norms.

A small group of Member States led by the UK[207] opposed any legal status of the Charter, claiming that it would present issues for its incorporation into the EU and national legal frameworks.[208] It would have hindered the involvement of some Member States in regional activities. In response, the final report expressed the compromise reached by those who wished to develop its regional integration and those who wished to consider the Charter as merely an enactment of the current legal situation within the EU.[209]

Due to the early reluctances of certain Member States, the Charter formed part of the primary law much later on, through the adoption of the Lisbon Treaty. The Treaty gave it a direct effect via Article 6(1) TEU.

While the EU Member States have had an impact on the adoption of the Charter, they have also maintained control over human rights standards.

Firstly, conflicts arose between national constitutional principles and regional norms regarding the level of human rights protection for many years.[210] Legal

[207] with Denmark, Ireland, Latvia, the Netherlands (government only) and Sweden.

[208] Daniel Flore, 'Une justice pénale européenne après Amsterdam' *Journal de Tribunaux - Droit Européen,* (1999); Daniel Flore, 'Droit pénal matériel et Union européenne' in *Quelles réformes pour l'espace pénal européen?*, eds., Gilles De Kerchove and Anne Weyembergh (Bruxelles: Editions de l'Université de Bruxelles, 2003).

[209] Clemens Ladenburger, 'Fundamental Rights and Citizenship of the Union' in *Genèse et destinée de la Constitution européenne: Commentaire du Traité établissant une Constitution pour l'Europe à la lumiére des travaux préparatoires et perspectives d'avenir*, eds., Giuliano Amato, Hervé Bribosia, and Bruno De Witte (Bruxelles: Bruylant, 2007): 314–16.

[210] See the most significant case: the dialogue between German judicial authorities and the ECJ. In ECJ *Internationale Handelsgesellschaft mbH* v. *Einfuhr- und Vorratsstelle für Getreide und Futtermittel,* C-11/70, ECLI:EU:C:1970:114, 17 December 1970, the Bundesverfassungsgericht (German Constitutional Court) stated that, in the present state of evolution of the Community, it would not renounce its right to uphold German fundamental rights in the face of a conflict with Community law. The Constitutional Court did not accept that Community law must take priority even over German fundamental rights. However, in this case, the German Court accepted that the Community legislation did not violate German fundamental rights. The reservations noted by the Constitutional Court included the fact that the European Parliament was not at the time directly elected and that the Community law did not include a precise catalogue of fundamental rights. The dissenting opinion emphasised that the Constitutional Court was bound by EC law. Later, *Solange II - Wünsche Handelsgesellschaft* decision of 22 October 1986, BVerfGE 73, 339, 2 BvR 197/83, Europäische Grundrechte-Zeitschrift, 1987, 1, [1987] 3 CMLR 225. In this case, the German Constitutional Court abandoned its reservations about the standard of European fundamental rights protection subsequent to its decision in the *Internationale Handelsgesellschaft*. In *Wünsche*

conflicts may have slightly decreased due to the progressive clarifications of the relations between the regional and national legal orders by the CJEU; but, some remain, as is evidenced by the relations between the CJEU and the Constitutional Court of Germany in cases.[211] The emergence of other regional human rights-related norms, which may be more precise, and the subsequent approximation of national norms in this regard have also helped reduce any arising conflicts.

Secondly, the Charter states that '[t]he provisions of th[e] Charter are addressed to the institutions and bodies of the Union with due regard for the principle of subsidiarity and to the Member States only when they are implementing Union law'.[212] Thus, minimal human rights standards shall be similar in every country as long as their action falls within the EU's competence. For the rest, States remain the guardians of the respect of human rights in their own territory; under the control of the Strasbourg Court though.

Thirdly, the Charter expressly offers the possibility for Member States to uniquely frame specific rights or liberties. However, leaving room for discretion does not necessarily result in increased protection.[213]

Regarding ambiguities in Article 53, the CJEU has created necessary clarification. It differentiates several scenarii that depend on the nature of the EU norm which establishes the type of relation between the EU and national laws: (1) a Member State may adopt a norm limiting EU primary law as long as it can justify that such a limitation, motivated by its constitutional order, complies with the requirements of the Treaty;[214] (2) when implementing secondary law that exhaustively governs a specific matter (without leaving any margin of appreciation to Member States), Member States are not allowed to adopt any norm protecting fundamental

Handelsgesellschaft, the German court decided that it would no longer examine the compatibility of Community legislation with German fundamental rights as long as the European Court continues to protect fundamental rights adequately. In other words, the German Constitutional Court is willing to trust the ECJ to strike down Community legislation that is contrary to fundamental rights. Then, e.g., pts. 12 and 13, ECJ, Case C-309/96, *Daniele Annibaldi* v. *Sindaco del Comune di Guidonia et Presidente Regione Lazio,* judgment, ECLI:EU:C:1997:631, ECR [1997] I-07493, 18 December 1997.

[211] CJEU, *M.A.S. and M.B.*, C-42/17, judgment, EU:C:2017:936, 5 December 2017; pts. 79–81, *Pelham e.a.*, C-476/17, judgment, EU:C:2019:624, 29 July 2019; and, *Spiegel Online*, C-516/17, judgment, EU:C:2019:625, judgment, 29 July 2019. Koen Lenaerts, 'La Charte dans l'ordre juridique de l'Union européenne', paper presented at the Opening, *La Charte a 20 ans: Regards croisés pour un anniversaire*, Bruxelles, 9 October 2020 (2020).

[212] Art. 51(1), *EU Charter of fundamental rights.*

[213] The EU Charter conditions the implementation of rights to national legislations: 'in accordance with the national laws governing the exercise of...' or 'according to the procedures laid down by law'. See, e.g., Arts. 3, 9, 10, 14, 16, 28, 30 and others.

[214] Nik de Boer, 'Addressing rights divergences under the Charter: Melloni. Case C-399/11, Stefano Melloni v. Ministerio Fiscal, Judgment of the Court (Grand Chamber) of 26 February 2013' *Common market law review*, vol. 50, no. 4 (2013).

rights, or any other norm, that would undermine the primacy, effectiveness and unity of EU law;[215] (3) when implementing secondary law that does not exhaustively govern a specific matter, Member States may establish different levels of protection of fundamental rights insofar as it does not jeopardise the primacy, effectiveness and unity of EU law.[216,217]

When any of these scenarii occur, the Charter is not to be interpreted as limiting or infringing those fundamental rights guaranteed in national constitutions and, conversely, national constitutions are not to be used to decrease the level of protection enshrined in the Charter. Therefore, the Charter constitutes the common minimum denominator in the protection of fundamental rights within the EU and, in some cases, greater levels of protection provided in national constitutions may prevail.

The elaboration of the Charter has clearly been nurtured by certain Member States' influence (bottom-up). In return however, Member States have been influenced by the Charter and needed to ensure their legislation complies with the EU obligations (top-down).

Historically, human rights considerations seem to be dissociated from security measures. However, anti-terrorism measures have slightly and slowly taken human rights into consideration.

2. The place of human rights in the anti-terrorism texts

Within the EU's counterterrorism legal arsenal, there is little provision for fundamental rights and freedoms.

The 2002 CFD refers to human rights in the preamble and briefly in Article 1(2), stating that the framework decision 'shall not have the effect of altering the obligation to respect fundamental rights and fundamental legal principles as enshrined in Article 6 of the Treaty on European Union'. The 2008 CFD does not change anything in this regard. The intergovernmental framework decisions did not impose any particular obligation on the chief of the Member States with regard to protecting human rights while combating terrorism. They only refer to the Charter, which was not binding at that time, and other human rights texts.

Regarding the 2017 Directive, no article in the proposal required Member States to guarantee fundamental rights and freedoms. It was only referred to once in the proposed preamble.[218] As it was not considered sufficient, certain governments did

215 CJEU, *Melloni*, C-399/11, 26 February 2013, paras. 60–63.

216 CJEU, *Akerberg Fransson*, C-617/10, ECLI:EU:C:2013:105, 26 February 2013, para. 29; *M.A. S. and M.B.*, C-42/17 (2017).

217 Lenaerts, 'La Charte dans l'ordre juridique de l'Union européenne' presented at the *La Charte a 20 ans: Regards croisés pour un anniversaire* (9 October 2020); Nicolas Cariat, 'Article 53. Niveau de protection' in *Charte des droits fondamentaux de l'Union européenne*, eds., Fabrice Picod, Cecilia Rizcallah, and Sébastien Van Drooghenbroeck, Droit de l'Union européenne (Bruxelles: Bruylant, 2020): 1329 and ff.

218 Recital 19, European Commission, Proposal for a Directive of the European Parliament and of the Council on combating terrorism and replacing Council Framework Decision 2002/475/JHA on combating terrorism, COM(2015) 625 final, Brussels, 2 December 2015.

not fully endorse the new Directive; although they all recognised the necessity to adopt a new instrument for addressing the threat posed by foreign terrorist fighters. For instance, the Cyprus Parliamentary Committee on Legal Affairs expressed 'doubts whether the proposed Directive [...] constitutes the best possible option to address the threat of terrorism', especially as this Directive is 'exceptionally' presented without any impact assessment.[219] Cyprus was concerned about the potential impact that the Directive might have on human rights. The balance between ensuring the security of EU citizens and their fundamental rights and freedoms was also a concern for other countries (e.g. Austria, Romania[220]). The Parliament amended the proposal by adding an Article 23 on 'fundamental rights and freedoms'[221] to respond to representatives of Member States' and national parliaments' concerns. Furthermore, the Directive enshrines protection and support for the rights of victims of terrorism. This is significant progress in terms of human rights.[222] It gives the Directive a more holistic nature when tackling terrorism.

Eventually, despite concerns from Member States, the Directive was adopted by the European Parliament with 498 votes for, 114 votes against, and 29 abstentions.[223]

Yet, it may be wondered whether an instrument that provides for a special regime in terrorism-related matters should not be associated with an equivalent special regime for human rights.

3. <u>What better protection than a *lex specialis* for human rights to be applied during criminal proceedings?</u>

Getting into the specifics of the rights of importance in criminal law matters, the package of procedural rights of suspected and accused persons in criminal

---

[219] Republic of Cyprus, 'Opinion submitted by the Standing committee on Legal Affairs of the House of Representatives of the Republic of Cyprus with regard to the Commission's proposal for a Directive of the European Parliament and of the Council on combating terrorism and replacing Council Framework Decision 2002/475/JHA on combating terrorism, COM(2015) 625,—executive summary in English', 1: available at https://bit.ly/3jPnB51 (accessed on 29 September 2019).

[220] Romanian Parliament, Senate, 'Opinion of the Romanian Senate regarding the Proposal for a Directive of the European Parliament and of the Council on combating terrorism and replacing Council Framework Decision 2002/475/JHA on combating terrorism COM(2015) 625 final', Bucharest, 17 February 2016.

[221] Art. 23, *Directive on combating terrorism*: '1. This Directive shall not have the effect of modifying the obligations to respect fundamental rights and fundamental legal principles, as enshrined in Article 6 TEU. 2. Member States may establish conditions required by, and in accordance with, fundamental principles relating to freedom of the press and other media, governing the rights and responsibilities of, and the procedural guarantees for, the press or other media where such conditions relate to the determination or limitation of liability'. For the details of the amendments at the Parliament: https://bit.ly/3acvi1P (accessed on 29 September 2019).

[222] Arts. 24–26, 2017 *Directive on combating terrorism.*

[223] European Parliament, Results of vote in Parliament, 2015/0281(COD), final vote 16 February 2017: available at https://oeil.secure.europarl.europa.eu/oeil/popups/sda.do?id=27513&l=en (accessed on 29 September 2019).

proceedings has been of great influence in fostering cross-border cooperation. This package constitutes the *lex specialis* of human rights in criminal matters.

As previously discussed, the EU establishes rules on the right to information, the right to interpretation and translation, the right to have legal representation, the right to be presumed innocent and to be present at trial, the right to legal aid, and provides special safeguards for children suspected and accused in criminal proceedings. Adopting the package of six directives on procedural rights for suspected and accused persons in criminal proceedings[224] was a response to this concern. However, in light of their strong historical resistance to the package, certain Member States have delayed in their implementation of the various directives or have refrained to do so thus far.[225]

Besides the compliance issue, Member States might also adopt diverging understandings of the key terminology and implement the six directives differently.[226] Due to the vague wording of the provisions, the scope of the rights might vary from one country to another and discrepancies between the EU and national laws may appear. Interestingly, when national standards are higher than EU ones, it might cause a differentiation between national cases and transnational ones, with potentially a better protection for the concerned individual in national cases than those which contain an extraterritorial element.[227] This would contradict the very principle of freedom of movement upon which the EU was founded.[228]

---

[224] *Resolution of the Council of 20 November 2009 on a Roadmap for strengthening procedural rights of suspected or accused persons in criminal proceedings* leading to *Directive 2010/64/EU on the right to interpretation and translation in criminal proceedings*; *Directive 2012/13/EU on the right to information in criminal proceedings*; *Directive 2013/48/EU on the right of access to a lawyer in criminal proceedings and in European arrest warrant proceedings, and on the right to have a third party informed upon deprivation of liberty and to communicate with third persons and with consular authorities while deprived of liberty*; *Directive 2016/343 on the strengthening of certain aspects of the presumption of innocence and of the right to be present at the trial in criminal proceedings*; *Directive 2016/800 on procedural safeguards for children who are suspects or accused persons in criminal proceedings.*

[225] See, e.g., European Parliament, Report on the implementation of Directive 2012/29/EU establishing minimum standards on the rights, support and protection of victims of crime, Plenary sitting, 2016/2328(INI), 14 May 2018; European Commission, Report from the Commission to the European Parliament and the Council, COM(2018) 857 final, Brussels 18 December 2018.

[226] Wouter Van Ballegooij, 'The Cost of Non-Europe in the area of Procedural Rights and Detention Conditions', Study for the European Parliament, European Parliament Research Service (Bruxelles: European Union, December 2017): 25: available at https://www.europarl.europa.eu/RegData/etudes/STUD/2017/611008/EPRS_STU(2017)611008_EN.pdf (accessed on 6 May 2021).

[227] See, e.g., CJEU, *Melloni*, C-399/11, 107; Wouter Van Ballegooij and Petra Bárd, "Mutual Recognition and Individual Rights: Did the Court Get It Wouter Van Ballegooij and Petra Bárd, "Mutual Recognition and Individual Rights: Did the Court Get It Right?" *New Journal of European Criminal Law*, vol. 7, no. 4 (2016).

[228] CJEU, *Procura della Repubblica* v. *M.*, C-398/12, Opinion of Advocate General Sharpston, ECLI:EU:C:2014:65, 6 February 2014, para. 45: 'A person should not lose the protection that he enjoys under national criminal law through exercising his free movement rights (...)'.

Moreover, data is increasingly made available to competent national authorities within the EU and databases are increasingly interoperable.[229] For this reason, EU institutions and the Member States have been developing a comprehensive approach when introducing data protection mechanisms and rules. Even before Snowden's revelations in 2013, the post-Lisbon Treaty strategy encompassed fundamental rights strategy documents, including those comprised in the 2010 Comprehensive Approach on Personal Data Protection in the EU. Evidently, data protection has become an even more topical issue since 2013. The most recent updates of the regional legal framework in this field have added real value to the EU panorama with the 2016 *General Data Protection Regulation* (GDPR) and, more specific to criminal matters, with the *Directive (EU) 2016/680 on the protection of natural persons with regard to the processing of personal data by competent authorities for the purposes of the prevention, investigation, detection or prosecution of criminal offences or the execution of criminal penalties, and on the free movement of such data*.[230,231] These instruments have been impactful during and after their adoption on EU Member States' legislations and on the EU bodies and national organisations. For instance, in an organisational perspective, in order to ensure the effective protection of this right in national and transnational cases, Member States needed to establish the necessary national authorities.

Interestingly, terrorist attacks have accelerated the adoption of EU legislations, whereas data protection instruments were only adopted 3 years after heated debates between Member States, and other relevant stakeholders.

To create a stronger link between security measures and human rights protection, the European Commission acted as the initiator and driving force. The Member States have then influenced the content of the various texts of the package. With this package, the EU aims to achieve harmonised and effective implementation of relevant rights during the criminal proceedings. Ultimately, the Commission controls the correct implementation of the norms. There is therefore a clear dialogue (cross-fertilisation) between the EU and its Member States. Such harmonisation has clearly fostered trust between competent national authorities by re-adjusting the balance between crime control measures and human rights protection.

---

[229] *Regulation 2019/818 on establishing a framework for interoperability between EU information systems in the field of police and judicial cooperation, asylum and migration.*

[230] *Directive 2016/680 on the protection of natural persons with regard to the processing of personal data by competent authorities for the purposes of the prevention, investigation, detection or prosecution of criminal offences or the execution of criminal penalties, and on the free movement of such data.*

[231] See, e.g., the EU Data Protection Reform, the Proposal for an EU Passenger Name Record (PNR) both under negotiations, as well as the Data Protection Umbrella Agreement between the EU and the US, the PNR Agreements between the EU and the United States (2012), Canada (2006) and Australia (2008). See also, Stefan M. Aubrey, *The New Dimension of International Terrorism* (Zürich: vdf Hochschulverlag AG an der ETH, 2004); Gérard Chalian and Arnaud Blin, eds., *The History of Terrorism from Antiquity to ISIS* (Oakland: University of California Press, 2016).

C. The EU: an effective legislator and controller of the implementation of the regional instruments

Approximation of legislations establishing common minimum denominators in both counterterrorism and human rights has helped operationalising cooperation mechanisms, such as the European arrest warrant,[232] or mechanisms of data sharing. The minimum approximation of certain aspects of criminal law has permitted mutual recognition-based instruments to function. This is a somewhat ironic twist in the EU's legal history since the initial reason for the adoption of mutual trust-based instruments was to serve as an alternative to harmonisation.

The EU is competent to control the implementation of human rights as provided in EU law. As aforementioned, after those implementation deadlines set in the regulations and directives have lapsed, the Commission is competent to check that EU Member States fully and correctly implemented the regulations, or incorporated the provisions of the directives into their national laws. If Member States do not implement the EU directives on terrorism or on procedural rights, the European Commission can then initiate an infringement procedure and, if the recalcitrant States do not comply with the Commission's opinion, the matter may be brought before the CJEU, which can punish them by imposing financial sanctions.[233] Apart from the infringement proceedings, one should not forget the CJEU preliminary ruling competence allowing a national court to seek the opinion of the CJEU about secondary law provisions in order to provide a uniform interpretation. Notably, there has been no case directly linked to an instrument approximating substantive criminal laws,[234] but there have been cases of instruments approximating procedural criminal laws.[235]

Due to the approximation of the definition of 'terrorist offences' and the subsequent criminalisation thereof, EU norms have contributed to a relatively harmonised response within the region. Moreover, providing minimum rules regarding procedural rights of suspects or accused persons has added the necessary element to enhance mutual trust and to ensure effective cross-border cooperation. It grants

---

[232] *Council Framework Decision 2002/584/JHA on the European arrest warrant.*

[233] Art. 258, TFEU.

[234] Some attempts have been made to refer preliminary rulings to the CJEU, such as the attempt by the NGO *la Ligue des droits de l'Homme* and the Belgian *Conseil des Ministres* suggesting the Belgian Constitutional Court refer to the CJEU in the context of the annulment request introduced by the first one against the relevant implementing internal law. Belgian Constitutional Court, Ruling No. 125/2005, 13 July 2005, paras. A.8.2. and A.9., refused.

[235] See, e.g., CJEU, *Kovalkovas*, C-477/16 PPU (2016) on the European arrest warrant. CJEU, *Gambino*, C-38/18, judgment, ECLI:EU:C:2019:628, 29 July 2019 on minimum standards on the rights, support and protection of victims of crime. CJEU, *DK and Spetsializirana prokuratura*, C-653/19 PPU, judgment, ECLI:EU:C:2019:1024, 28 November 2019 on the presumption of innocence. CJEU, *Kolev and others*, C-612/15, judgement (Grand Chamber), ECLI:EU:C:2018:392, 5 June 2018, and *VW*, C-659/18, judgment, ECLI:EU:C:2020:201, 12 March 2020 on the right of access to a lawyer.

guarantees to competent national authorities that their counterparts would address the situation identically.

The EU norms, which have been analysed, are not solely the result of regional decision-making (top-down), but are also strongly influenced by national inputs (bottom-up). The regional legal framework, including the control by the EU institutions over the Member States' actions, is the product of a cross-fertilisation process between the EU norms and the Member States' legislations.

ASEAN Member States have not investigated the opportunity of approximating norms related to terrorism and human rights. This opportunity is nonetheless analysed in this next part by highlighting some similarities between national laws and considering the elements that may prevent this approximation.

II. Making an ASEAN comprehensive counterterrorism legal order rise out of diversity? Looking for a common ground

As previously discussed, ASEAN's decision-making is not autonomous from its members. This section investigates the relations between the two levels of decision-making, namely the national and regional levels in the fields of counterterrorism and human rights. This section first analyses whether the few regional norms have had an impact on national laws (A). Then, it elaborates upon the potential for approximation of the ASEAN Member States' legislations (B).

The difficulties that States must overcome—difficulties that could be stronger compared to those in the EU—are highlighted as well as the potential similarities that could facilitate the approximation of the relevant legislations. Although it might have been considered, there has been no real attempt to approximate relevant legislations thus far. It has not been considered that approximating national legislations would foster mutual trust between competent national authorities and facilitate transnational cooperation.

In this regional context, governments have an influence on the development of ASEAN norms as members (bottom-up) and deciders (top-down) of the Association. Thus, the term 'cross-fertilisation' between the regional and national levels can hardly describe the situation.

A. ASEAN: A forum without top-down influence and added value

ASEAN is a simple representation of its members. There is no top-down influence from ASEAN over Member States.[236] The Member States form the ASEAN's decision-making structure. Looking for a common ground, some national cases highlight the differences preventing a potential approximation and/or the similarities that constitute a fertile ground for such approximation.

[236] Jean-Claude Piris and Walter Woon, *Towards a Rules-Based Community: An ASEAN Legal Service*, Integration through Law: The Role of Law and the Rule of Law in ASEAN Integration (Cambridge: Cambridge University Press, 2015), 115–16.

The regional counterterrorism legal framework has nonetheless been designed to enhance the action of its Member States and to attempt a slight approximation of their approaches when combating terrorism (1) and protecting human rights (2).

1. Regional approximation of anti-terrorism norms: a shy statement of political willingness from ASEAN Member States

The first mention of harmonisation in criminal matters arose in the 1997 *Declaration on Transnational Crime* and the 1999 *Plan of Action to Combat Transnational Crime*. Nonetheless, they were not followed by meaningful legal approximation.

The *ASEAN Declaration on Transnational Crime* led to the establishment of ASEAN Centre on Transnational Crime which aims to coordinate regional efforts against transnational crime and to engage in the exchange of critical information, harmonisation of policies (not laws) and the coordination of operations.[237] In 1998, the Member States expressed in the *Manila Declaration on the Prevention and Control of Transnational Crime* their 'determination and political will'[238] to take concrete actions by, among other things, 'improving the functioning of the institutions, in particular the criminal justice systems, reviewing, modernizing and harmonizing, as appropriate, existing laws and regulations to ensure the continued relevance, efficiency and adaptability to modern manifestations of organized crime' and by 'enacting new laws and regulations, responding to the complexity and sophistication of various forms of transnational crime, so as to bridge the gaps in legal systems which can be exploited by organized criminal groups'.[239] Yet, the vague wording remains leaves a large margin of manoeuvrability for Member States to implement the Declaration. There is no definition of crime or no specific rule required, for example. These declarations remained political statements. Similarly, the 1999 *Plan of Action* stated that Member States must engage with one another to ensure the harmonisation of their relevant national policies under the 'legal matters' section, yet it does not specifically foresee any harmonisation of national legislations.

These documents mostly focus on cooperation, including information sharing and coordination of policies rather than on an effective approximation of norms. The

---

[237] Pt. 4, *ASEAN Declaration on Transnational Crime* (1997); pt. A(b)2, *Plan of Action to Combat Transnational Crime* (1999) and pt. C7 states the engagement of the Member States to ensure the harmonisation of relevant national policies among Member States. These Centres have never seen the light (Piris and Woon, *Towards a Rules-Based Community* (2015): 115–16.) but instead the Jakarta Centre for Law Enforcement Cooperation (JCLEC) was established in July 2004, a couple of months before the adoption of the *ASEAN Treaty on Mutual Legal Assistance in Criminal Matters* (2004). But, the JCLEC's purpose does not include any harmonisation of policies or legislations. True to its name, it is only a centre of trainings for law enforcement, where exchange of best practices as well as information and intelligence may take place informally.

[238] Pt. 2, *ASEAN Declaration on the Prevention and Control of Transnational Crime* (1998).

[239] Pt. 2(c) and (d), *ASEAN Declaration on the Prevention and Control of Transnational Crime* (1998).

slight approximation of national policies ensures that Member States are heading in the same direction. The wording used in the different ASEAN texts demonstrates that the Member States are not willing to engage in the process of legal approximation.

An alternative way to approach the approximation of relevant parts of legislations is based on the idea of strengthening national, sub-regional and regional capabilities and capacities to counter terrorism.[240] In this sense, several fora exist: the ASEAN meetings taking place between the respective competent authorities, the different centres dedicated to build up cooperation between competent national authorities such as the Jakarta Centre for Law Enforcement Cooperation (JCLEC), Southeast Asian Regional Centre for Counter-Terrorism (SEARCCT) or International Law Enforcement Academy (ILEA). However, these fora are usually a way to adopt common positions on security threats which are so broad that they do not lead to any precise and meaningful approximation of laws. By sharing experiences in implementing counterterrorism means (i.e. practices, technological tools, policies, regulations, laws), a certain form—minimal though—of approximation might take place.

The 2002 *Work Programme to Implement the ASEAN Plan of Action to Combat Transnational Crime* has similar requirements to previous instruments on transnational crime. However, on the issue of harmonisation, discrepancies can be found. The Work Programme states that Member States shall '[w]ork towards the harmonisation of relevant national policies, where applicable, among ASEAN Member Countries by exchange of information'[241] in the areas of trafficking in persons, and arms smuggling; neglecting illicit drug trafficking, sea-piracy, money laundering, *terrorism*, international economic crime and cybercrime. ASEAN documents discuss policies rather than laws. These policies imply actions from States, including the adoption of appropriate legislations. For each crime targeted, the Work Programme requires States to 'establish a compilation of national laws and regulations of ASEAN Member Countries, including international treaties and agreements, pertaining to terrorism leading towards establishing a regional repository of such laws'[242] within a certain timeframe. Relating to terrorism, Member States are requested to '[w]ork towards the criminalisation of terrorism in ASEAN Member Countries'.[243] However, there is no mention of harmonisation of anti-terrorism legislation. Focusing on capability and capacity building, States convened specialised workshops, seminars and training courses on new forms of terrorism such as bio-terrorism and cyber-terrorism for law enforcement officials. During these

[240] Pt. B(b)5, *ASEAN Plan of Action to Combat Transnational Crime* (1999); Pts. I.2.1. and II.3.1., *ASEAN Comprehensive Plan of Action on Counter Terrorism* (2009). See also, Beyer, 'ASEAN Counterterrorism: Participation and Causes' (2010): 104.

[241] Pt. 2.2.b), Work Programme to Implement the ASEAN Plan of Action to Combat Transnational Crime, Kuala Lumpur, 17 May 2002: available at https://bit.ly/2Zc3xjW (accessed on 6 June 2017).

[242] Pt. 6.6., Ibid.

[243] Pt. 6.2.a), Ibid.

meetings, discussions include the review of existing laws and legislation in these areas.[244]

At a later stage and specific to counterterrorism, Indonesia hosted the Second ASEAN Government Legal Officers Programme on Anti-Terrorism in August 2003 which discussed the possibility of criminalising terrorist activities and approximating laws thereof in the region and the establishment of an ASEAN Regional Operational Convention to Combat Terrorism.[245] Eventually, the first—and only (thus far)—binding regional instrument was adopted. The 2007 *ASEAN Convention on Counter Terrorism* specifies its objective to establish a 'framework for regional cooperation to counter, prevent and suppress terrorism in all its forms and manifestations and to deepen cooperation among law enforcement agencies and relevant authorities of the Parties in countering terrorism'.[246] This Convention aims to provide the legal framework for competent national authorities to cooperate in the fight against terrorism. However, it provides no definition of 'terrorist offences' and it has not been used to the extent of imposing specific and precise legal obligations, such as demanding the Members States to modify their national legislations or adopt new ones in this matter. The Convention and the associated *ASEAN Comprehensive Plan of Action on Counter Terrorism*[247] are only meant to foster cooperation mechanisms (Article VI).

ASEAN counterterrorism norms bring no added value to the approximation of the national legislations compared to international norms. In other words, ASEAN Member States respecting international requirements also respect ASEAN norms. Consequently, there is no specific top-down influence from the regional level to the national level.

Looking at the types of instruments, ASEAN represents an interesting case to debate the normativity of the various texts. Although this aspect will not be developed exhaustively in this monograph, specific elements are of interest when analysing the role of the different norms in the counterterrorism regional architecture. It provides clues about the logic behind the adoption of one instrument compared to another and, eventually, how this choice impacts the development of mutual trust between competent authorities.

The ASEAN instruments are predominantly plans of action or declarations, and with only a few conventions. In the field of counterterrorism, ASEAN Member States adopted only one convention which is more binding according to international law.[248] Does it mean that the requirements of the ACCT have more impact on the national legislations compared to the plans of action or the declarations? A convention can be more binding on paper, but it may have less impact on national legislations due to the substance of the provisions themselves. By contrast, plans

[244] Pt. 6.5.d), Ibid.

[245] Sundram Pushpanathan, 'ASEAN efforts to Combat terrorism', Phuket, 20 August 2003.

[246] Art. I, ACCT.

[247] *ASEAN Comprehensive Plan of Action on Counter Terrorism* (2009).

[248] Art. 38, ICJ Statute; and *Convention on the Law of Treaties* (1969).

of actions tend to be more detailed and more demanding towards Member States. The precision of their provisions might have more influence on States than its formal nature. These plans of action are the most important basis for capacity building actions, such as trainings for competent national authorities which enhances the operational capacities of these authorities.

There might be two main reasons which explain this particular approach: the weight of national sovereignty and the desired objective.

Firstly, as previously demonstrated, Member States are ready to adopt a binding regional instrument in only two cases. The first case would arise if they have already adopted the necessary national norms. The regional norm would thus be a demonstration of the Member States' agreement on a specific subject. The second case, which is not incompatible with the first, would be the Member States agreeing on broad requirements, which would not have any specific binding impact on each party. The regional norm would constitute a political statement acknowledging that this matter needs to be tackled by the Association's members. Thus far, the regional decisions of all Member States have political value vis-à-vis each other and vis-à-vis third States and international organisations.

Secondly, the objective identified in the various instruments fosters and facilitates cooperation within ASEAN.[249] This is highlighted by the preamble of the ACCT, in its Article I, and further detailed in Article VI 'Areas of cooperation'. The Convention requires Member States to cooperate, but the *Comprehensive Plan of Action on Counter Terrorism* delves into the specifics of the actions expressed in the convention.[250] In other words, the ACCT only constitutes a large umbrella for the development of plans of actions that, despite their weak legal value, provide for 'more specific' requirements.

Interestingly, the approach has not changed with the adoption of the 2015 *ASEAN Convention on trafficking in persons.*

The fact that all Member States agree on counterterrorism requirements, as broad as they might be, and transpose the international provisions constitutes a demonstration of political willingness to combat terrorism. Currently, the UNODC and other stakeholders can meet each government and advocate for the application of the ACCT and the associated plan of action.[251]

2. A clear absence of legal and political willingness to regionalise human rights standards

[249] *ASEAN Declaration on Joint Action to Counter Terrorism* (2001); the various Joint Declarations between ASEAN and third States and the EU; *ASEAN Convention on Counter-Terrorism* (2007).

[250] *ASEAN Comprehensive Plan of Action on Counter Terrorism* (2009).

[251] See Jérémy Douglas, "Preface" in Hernán Longo et al., "Promoting Effective Responses to the Foreign Terrorist Fighters: Situation in Southeast Asia" (Bangkok: United Nations Office on Drugs and Crime), iii.

As aforementioned, there is no regional instrument concerning human rights binding upon all Member States. The *ASEAN Declaration on Human Rights* is an instrument of soft power.[252] This lacuna has been pointed out by Dr. Phan who, after the adoption of the Declaration, argued that '[t]he region needs a human rights mechanism with more legal force'.[253] This Declaration can be interpreted as either a weak sign of the Member States' goodwill to respect their international requirements in this domain or a way for Member States to start considering effective measures to protect these rights. Notably, the OHCHR has shown its concern regarding the standards proposed by the Declaration and their implementation.[254]

The implementation of the Declaration is limited to 'in accordance with national law', which can be used by governments to lower down the standards. Therefore, the Declaration leaves a too wide margin for interpretation. Such limitation can shield States from scrutiny by international human rights mechanisms concerning the excessive use of force by law enforcement officers, especially in terrorism-related cases.[255] One example among others of human rights issues in the region relates to Indonesia: the Asian Human Rights Commission (AHRC)—a regional, non-governmental, human rights organisation in Asia, external to the ASEAN system—stated that '[learning] of the current situation on the war against terrorism in Indonesia. [It] deplore[s] the action of the Police of the Republic of Indonesia, in particular Special Detachment Anti-Terror Unit (Densus 88). They have not seriously learned from their previous experience. The agenda on war against terrorism has caused human rights violations. Similar cases recur without law-enforcement or accountability'.[256]

As seen previously, there is no ASEAN text specifically related to data protection. The *ASEAN Human Rights Declaration* requires, broadly though, that Member States protect 'the right [of every person] to be free from arbitrary interference with his or her privacy, family, home or correspondence including personal data

[252]For more on the legal value of the Declaration, see Chap. 4.

[253]Phan, A Selective Approach to Establishing a Human Rights Mechanism in Southeast Asia (2012), 29.

[254]See the table of ratification in Appendix 1. See also, 'UN official welcomes ASEAN commitment to human rights, but concerned over declaration wording' *UN News Centre*, 19 November 2012: http://www.un.org/apps/news/story.asp?NewsID=43536#.WTphCz_IxE4 (accessed on (8 June 20017).

[255]HRC, 'ASEAN Human Rights Declaration should maintain international standards. An Open Letter from the Coordination Committee of the Special Procedures of the Human Rights Council on the draft ASEAN Human Rights Declaration' (2012).

[256]Statement, 'INDONESIA: War against terrorism should respect human rights and the Rule of Law' *Asian Human Rights Commission*, AHRC-STM-015-2018, 6 March 2018: available at http://www.humanrights.asia/news/ahrc-news/AHRC-STM-015-2018 (accessed on 12 March 2018).

[...]. Every person has the right to the protection of the law against such interference or attacks'.[257]

As also aforementioned, ASEAN diverges from the EU in its absence of infringement procedures against a Member State as well as the absence of a regional court of justice. Neither the ASEAN Secretariat nor the AICHR are able to sanction a State who is in violation of the Declaration. The AICHR does not have the authority to issue binding decisions to redress human rights violations and to effectively change State behaviour.

At this stage, ASEAN Member States are not willing to adopt binding regional standards as they may not meet them. The current context is not conducive to the development of protection of those fundamental rights at risk during criminal proceedings.

Regarding the role of the regional organisation, it must be concluded that there is a weak—or even no—top-down influence in counterterrorism and human rights matters. It might even be argued that there is no autonomous influence of the regional organisation as it represents the gathering of Member States' political willingness when working together towards a specific objective. As such, it can be concluded that there is rather a form of horizontal influence among Member States.

B. **Diversity prevailing among ASEAN Member States' legislations: making approximation utopic?**

ASEAN Member States still maintain independent legislations and legal systems.[258] The members do not see the added value in approximating their legislations to fulfil their common objective, which is to establish and enhance cooperation against terrorism. This section investigates nonetheless the possibility of there being fertile ground for approximation (within the limits of this research's objective and access to relevant data). Importantly, the author acknowledges that certain documents are either only accessible in unknown languages for her or not accessible to the public and thus are unable to be included in the analysis. This limitation does not extend to the primary and required documents. Nor does the limitation prevent conclusions from being drawn with regard to the object of this book.

1. Overcoming discrepancies between national anti-terrorism norms: a feasible task?

[257] Art. 21, *ASEAN Human Rights Declaration*.

[258] Tan Hsien-Li and Simon Tay, 'Southeast Asian cooperation on anti-terrorism: the dynamics and limits of regional responses' in *Global Anti-Terrorism Law and Policy*, eds., Victor V. Ramraj et al. (Cambridge: Cambridge University Press, 2005): 400.

Certain Member States have been more active than others, especially due to the different levels of threat and experiences of terrorism. Particularly affected by Islamist terrorism, Indonesia has been especially active in enacting anti-terrorism laws. As in some EU countries, Indonesian anti-terrorism laws evolved in response to the different terrorist attacks.[259]

Importantly, the Member States have not necessarily ratified the same international conventions thus far, which might create differences in the criminalisation of terrorist offences.[260] In fact, many discrepancies exist between the different national sets of anti-terrorism legislation, and especially regarding the issue of foreign terrorist fighters (FTFs). Regarding this terrorist evolution, the UNODC reported in 2015 that Southeast Asian national legislations needed to be updated in order to provide criminal justice officials 'with adequate and effective tools to address certain offences, such as the recruitment of FTFs, the travelling of would-be FTFs and incitement to terrorism'.[261]

The UNODC report carried out a brief analysis of the implementation of the international requirements by the Southeast Asian countries taking a list of 15 terrorist behaviours as the table of analysis of the Southeast Asian national legislations: (1) planning (of terrorist acts); (2) preparation (of terrorist acts); (3) perpetration (of terrorist acts); (4) organisation; (5) financing of terrorist acts, organisations and individuals; (6) financing of the travel of FTFs; (7) equipping; (8) provision of training; (9) receiving training; (10) transporting; (11) travel of FTFs; (12) recruiting; (13) criminal association; (14) inciting and (15) glorification of terrorism.[262] These elements are compared between ASEAN Member States' legislations.

Certain Member States have enacted more or less comprehensive and specific counterterrorism laws over recent years. Three Member States are said to fully comply with the UNSCR 2178(2014) requirements,[263] namely Brunei Darussalam, Singapore and Vietnam, while others still 'rely on the common offences in the criminal codes, which in some cases might be insufficient to effectively investigate and prosecute terrorism-related cases'.[264] This might be true for specific offences related to the foreign terrorist fighters, such as the act of receiving training; transporting and the travelling of suspected (future) foreign terrorist fighters. How-

[259] Greta Nabbs-Keller, 'Indonesia's anti-terror law: crisis to consensus' *The Interpreter*, 25 October 2018: https://bit.ly/3rSLdIZ (accessed on 31 October 2019).

[260] See the table of ratifications in Appendix 1.

[261] Longo et al., 'Promoting Effective Responses to the Foreign Terrorist Fighters: Situation in Southeast Asia' (2015), 8.

[262] As used in Ibid., 8.

[263] See table related to the compliance of ASEAN Member States' legislations with the different forms of terrorist offences in Appendix 3.

[264] Longo et al., 'Promoting Effective Responses to the Foreign Terrorist Fighters: Situation in Southeast Asia' (2015), viii.

ever, the main offences, namely the preparation, perpetration, organising, financing of terrorist acts, organisations and individuals have been criminalised in each country.

Using the example of Brunei Darussalam, the 2011 *Anti-Terrorism Order* complied—indirectly sometimes—with some of the requirements of the UNSCR 2178(2014) regarding foreign terrorist fighters, even before its adoption.[265] At the time of writing, certain offences have not been criminalised as of yet, such as the incitement and glorification of terrorism, the planning and preparation of terrorist offences. Notably, it does not specifically criminalise passive training, but it could be interpreted as doing so as the law criminalises the solicitation of support including the provision of a skill (Article 9[266]). Similarly, financing the travel of FTFs might indirectly be addressed by Article 5 which criminalises the act of financially supporting 'for the purpose of committing or facilitating the commission of a terrorist act or of the purpose of benefiting any person who is committing or facilitating the commission of a terrorist act [...]'.

Going further into the national provisions on terrorism, this section aims to update and elaborate upon the UNODC report in certain aspects, especially by looking at the various definitions of terrorist offences, and briefly assessing the criminalisation of these offences.[267]

Analysing the ten sets of anti-terrorism legislation has revealed the diversity of the Member States' approaches as well as the ways in which the elements of the definitions provided by the 1997 *International Convention for the Suppression of Terrorist Bombings* and the 1999 *International Convention for the Suppression of the Financing of Terrorism.* The national definitions of 'terrorist' or 'terrorist act' can differ from one country to another according to three aspects: (1) the material elements, (2) the *dol generalis* (i.e. the general criminal intent) and (3) the *dol specialis* (i.e. the specific terrorist intent).

---

[265] *Anti-Terrorism Order 2011*, Brunei Darussalam Government Gazette, No. S45/2011, 1 August 2011.

[266] Art. 9 *Anti-Terrorism Order 2011*: "(1) Any person who knowingly—(a) solicits support for, or gives support to, any terrorist group, or (b) solicits support for, or gives support to, the commission of a terrorist act, is guilty of an offence and liable on conviction to [...]. (2) In this section, 'support' includes but is not limited to (a) an offer to provide, or the provision of, forged or falsified travel documents to a member of a terrorist group; (b) an offer to provide, or the *provision of a skill or an expertise for the benefit of, at the direction of or in association with a terrorist group*; or (c) entering or remaining in any country for the benefit of, or at the direction of or in association with a terrorist group' (italics by the author).

[267] See the table related to the compliance of ASEAN Member States' legislations with the different forms of terrorist offences in Appendix 3. The report notes that 'many jurisdictions need to adjust their definition of terrorism and terrorist acts'. See Longo et al., 'Promoting Effective Responses to the Foreign Terrorist Fighters: Situation in Southeast Asia' (2015): viii.

1. Firstly, ASEAN Member States have diverse material elements. Certain countries have various lists of terrorist acts (i.e. Brunei Darussalam, Lao PDR,[268] Vietnam[269]), while others predominantly refer to (an)other law(s) or international convention(s) or to common law criminal acts (i.e. Cambodia,[270] Indonesia,[271] Thailand[272]). Certain countries employ parts of both, like Myanmar[273] and the Philippines[274] namely, by listing the infractions in the definition as well as also detailing them in other parts of the law or in (an)other law(s). Interestingly, the 2012 *Anti-Terrorism Order* of Brunei[275] almost completely mirrors the definition of 'terrorist act' from the 2001 *United Nations (Anti-terrorism measures) Regulations* of Singapore;[276] the Singaporean definition has evolved slightly over

[268] Art. 7, *Law on Anti-Money Laundering and Counter-Financing of Terrorism*, No. 50/NA, 21 July 2014.

[269] Doing so vaguely, Arts. 115 and 299, *Criminal Code*, No. 100/2015/QH13, National Assembly, 27 November 2015. Art. 3, *Anti-Terrorism Law*, No. 28/2013/QH13, National Assembly, 12 June 2013.

[270] Arts. 76 and 78, *Law on Counter Terrorism of 20 July 2007*, Nation Religion King, Royal Gazette, Year 7, No. 55, week 4, 27 July 2007. The definitions do not provide for any constitutive element except for: 'act intended to cause death or serious bodily injury to a person other than a person taking an active part in armed hostilities in a situation of armed conflict'. The definition rather refers to offences under 'this Law, or under the law of a foreign State, that is within the scope of any of the treaties listed in the annex to the International Convention for the Suppression of the Financing of Terrorism done at New York'.

[271] Indonesia criminalises terrorist offences based on the criminal intent and on the fact that any offence 'create mass casualties, by forcibly taking the freedom, life or property of others or causes damage or destruction to vital strategic installations or the environment or public facilities or international facilities'. See, e.g., *Government Regulation in Lieu of Legislation (GRL) of the Republic of Indonesia No. 1/2002 combating criminal acts of terrorism*, President of the Republic of Indonesia, State Gazette, 18 October 2002; *Undang-undang (UU) tentang Perubahan atas Undang-Undang Nomor 15 Tahun 2003 tentang Penetapan Peraturan Pemerintah Pengganti Undang Undang Nomor 1 Tahun 2002 tentang Pemberantasan Tindak Pidana Terorisme Menjadi Undang-Undang*, No. 5, Pemerintah Pusat, LN.2018/NO.92, TLN NO.6216, LL SETKAB: 30 HLM, 21 June 2018.

[272] Section 135/1, *Criminal Code*, B.E. 2499, 1956; amended for the Criminal Code (No. 17), B.E. 2547, 2003; Section 3, *Anti-Terrorist Financing Act 2013*, B.E. 2556, 1 February 2013.

[273] Section 3(b), *Counter-Terrorism Law 2014*, No. 23/2014, 7th Waxing of Nayone, 1376 ME, 4 June 2014.

[274] Section 3, *The Terrorism Financing Prevention and Suppression Act of 2012*, Republic Act No. 10168, Republic of the Philippines, 20 June 2012 and the most recent *Act to prevent, prohibit and penalize terrorism, thereby repealing Republic Act No. 9372, otherwise known as the 'Human Security Act of 2007' (also called The Anti-Terrorism Act of 2020)*, Republic Act No. 11579, 22 July 2020.

[275] *Anti-Terrorism (Amendment) Order 2012*, No. 48/2012, Constitution of Brunei Darussalam (Order made under Article 83(3)), Brunei Darussalam Government Gazette, 2 July 2012.

[276] *United Nations (Anti-terrorism measures) Regulations* (Chap. 339, Section 2(1)), Regulation 1, G.N. No. S 561/2001, The Statutes of the Republic of Singapore, 13 November 2001.

time. The Malaysian definition of 'terrorist act' greatly resembles those of Brunei and Singapore, with a few discrepancies.[277] Based on previous relations, certain States might influence one another. These three countries, i.e. Brunei Darussalam, Singapore and Malaysia, most represent this trend.

2. Secondly, the *dol generalis*, i.e. the intent to commit a criminal offence, is not formulated uniformly across the different legislations. Although it is always a necessary requirement for the criminalisation of offences, certain definitions of terrorist offences do not clearly state the need for intent.[278] As the main source of inspiration for the anti-terrorism laws, the 1999 *International Convention for the Suppression of the Financing of Terrorism* states that States will criminalise terrorist acts committed 'by any means, directly or indirectly, unlawfully and wilfully'.[279] Some Member States such as Lao PDR,[280] Thailand,[281] Vietnam[282] and the Philippines (prior to 2012)[283] do not require criminal intent to punish certain terrorist offences. It was only in 2012 that the Philippines modified its legislation to transpose the 1999 Convention's provision,[284] and when Brunei

[277] *Penal Code,* Act 574, Laws of Malaysia, first enacted in 1963 (F.M.S. Cap. 45) latest amendment made by Act A1487 which came into operation on 31 December 2014). The Malaysian Penal Code defines differently a 'terrorist act' as involving serious bodily injury to a person, endangering a person's life and causing a person's death while, in the same category, the two other countries criminalise 'serious violence against any person'. The Malaysian Code adds nuclear material as a dangerous element to release, distribute or expose the public to. Finally, this Code enlarges the possible actions in points G and H of the Brunei provision with 'designed *or intended to* disrupt <u>or</u> <u>*seriously interfere with'*</u> (italics and underlining by the author: the italics differentiate the Malaysian and the two other definitions, and the underlining is similar between the Malaysian and Singapore definitions, but not to the Brunei definition).

[278] By referring to other offences, some anti-terrorism provisions do not specify the intent. See, e.g., Section 3, *Anti-Terrorist Financing Act 2013*, B.E. 2556, Government of Thailand, 1 February 2013. Interestingly, the Section 3(b) of the Burmese *Counter-Terrorism Law 2014* (No. 23/2014, 4 June 2014) states the intent for some specific offences (italics by the author). See, e.g., *Intentional* offence committed unlawfully against civil aviation and airport as prescribed in Chap. 4; *Intentional* offence committed unlawfully in order to harm maritime travel as prescribed in Chap. 8; *Intentional* offence committed unlawfully in order to harm underwater resource exploration unit at offshore shelf as prescribed in Chap. 9. The other offences listed (15) do not require intent as such. It may be required in the Chapters referred to.

[279] Art. 2(1), *International Convention for the Suppression of the Financing of Terrorism* (1999).

[280] Art. 7, Lao *Law on Anti-Money Laundering and Counter-Financing of Terrorism*, 21 July 2014.

[281] Section 135/1, Thai *Criminal Code* (2003).

[282] Art. 3, Vietnamese *The Anti-Terrorism Law* (2013); Arts. 113 and 299, *Criminal Code* (2015).

[283] Section 3, *Human Security Act of 2007*, Republic Act No. 9372, Republic of the Philippines, 6 March 2007.

[284] Section 3, *The Terrorism Financing Prevention and Suppression Act of 2012*, Republic Act No. 10168, Republic of the Philippines, 20 June 2012; and even more clearly in the recent law: Section 4, *Act to prevent, prohibit and penalize terrorism, thereby repealing Republic Act No. 9372, otherwise known as the 'Human Security Act of 2007' (The Anti-Terrorism Act of 2020)*, Republic Act No. 11579, 22 July 2020.

Darussalam's legislation adopted the same definition.[285] Interestingly, Brunei Darussalam transposed the 1999 Convention's provision in two stages. The *Anti-Terrorism (Amendment) Order 2012*[286] clarifies intent in the definition of 'terrorist' provided in *Anti-Terrorism Order 2011* by adding 'directly or indirectly, unlawfully and wilfully'.[287] This 2012 Order also added a definition and criminalisation of 'terrorist group'. This evolution was elucidated further by *The Anti-Terrorism Act of 2020*, which considered the challenges presented by foreign terrorist fighters, although slightly too late.[288] Marginally distancing themselves from the UN definition in the wording, Cambodia, Indonesia and Myanmar still require the general intent for committing a crime.[289] Finally, Malaysia does not clearly refer to any general criminal intent in the terrorism-related provisions, but mentions the specific intent that can be found in other criminal provisions.[290]

3. Thirdly, the specific intent necessary to qualify as a 'terrorist' offence is referred to in the 1999 Convention, which states that 'the purpose of such act, by its nature or context, is to intimidate a population, or to compel a government or an international organization to do or to abstain from doing any act'.[291] Certain Member States entirely transposed this provision, namely Brunei Darussalam,[292] Malaysia[293] and Singapore.[294] Certain countries complied with this provision, but elaborated upon it further and/or differently, such as Cambodia,[295] Indone-

[285] Brunei *Anti-Terrorism Order 2011* as modified by *Anti-Terrorism (Amendment) Order 2012*, No. 48/2012, Darussalam Government Gazette, 2 July 2012.

[286] Section 1 amending Section 2 of *Anti-Terrorism (Amendment) Order 2012*.

[287] Section 2(2), *Anti-Terrorism Order 2011*: 'terrorist acts' under (b)(ii) 'where the use or threat is intended or reasonably regarded as intending to—(A) influence of compel the Government, any other government or any international organisation to do or abstain from doing any act; or (B) intimidate the public or a section of the public'.

[288] Philippine *Anti-Terrorism Act of 2020*.

[289] In Cambodia, Arts. 76 and 78, *Law on Counter Terrorism* of 20 July 2007, Royal Gazette, Year 7, no. 55, week 4, 27 July 2007. In Indonesia, Section 6, *GRL No. 1/2002 combating criminal acts of terrorism*, 18 October 2002, The President of the Republic of Indonesia; and, *Law No. 15 of 2002* of the Republic of Indonesia *on the Eradication of the Crime of Terrorism as a Law*, 4 April 2003, Laws of the Republic of Indonesia. In Myanmar, Section 3(b), *Counter-Terrorism Law 2014*, No. 23/2014, 4 June 2014.

[290] There is no mention of knowledge, wilfulness, or any other way of qualifying the intent of an individual to commit a crime. *Penal Code*, Act 574, F.M.S. Cap. 45, 1963; latest amendment made by Act A1487 which came into operation on 31 December 2014.

[291] Art. 2(1)b, *International Convention for the Suppression of the Financing of Terrorism* (1999).

[292] Brunei *Anti-Terrorism Order 2011* as modified by *Anti-Terrorism (Amendment) Order 2012*.

[293] Defining 'terrorist act', see *Penal Code*.

[294] Defining 'terrorist act', *Terrorism (Suppression of Financing) Act 2002* (Chap. 325), No. 16 of 2002, Revised in 2003, The Statutes of the Republic of Singapore, 29 January 2003.

[295] Art. 76(1)(b), Cambodian *Law on Counter Terrorism* of 20 July 2007.

sia,[296] Myanmar,[297] the Philippines,[298] Thailand[299] and Vietnam.[300] The provisions enshrined in Lao's legislation are slightly more confusing.[301]

Establishing a common definition might improve cross-border cooperation. However, other elements need to also be considered when examining the discrepancies between criminal procedures. Specifically concerning terrorism-related cases, certain Member States have enacted special procedures which may lead to the introduction of extraordinary powers conferred to investigators, public prosecutors and judges; the elaboration of investigating methods;[302] a liberalisation of the use of

---

[296] Sections 4(c) and (d), and 6, *Indonesia GRL 1/2002 combating criminal acts of terrorism*; and, *Law No. 15 of 2002 on* the GRL of the Republic of Indonesia *on the Eradication of the Crime of Terrorism as a Law,* 4 April 2003, Laws of the Republic of Indonesia. Section 6 provides for 'to create a widespread atmosphere of terror or fear in the general population [or to create mass casualties, by forcibly taking the freedom, life or property of others or causes damage or destruction to vital strategic installations or the environment or public facilities or international facilities]'. And, Section 4 mentions the fact of compelling the government or any international organisation to take or not take an action.

[297] Section 3(b)(13), Burmese *Counter-Terrorism Law 2014*. This provision is not associated with the different offences but is listed apart, which makes the section and requirements for criminalising terrorist offences confusing.

[298] Section 3, Philippine *Human Security Act of 2007*.

[299] Section 125/1, Thai *Criminal Code* stating that an offence shall be qualified as terrorist if 'such act is made by the aim to treated or enforce Thai Government, Foreign Government of International Organization make or not to make any act to cause seriously injury or for making a disorder by causing the people to be terrified [...]'.

[300] Art. 299(1), Vietnamese *Criminal Code* (2015) and Art. 3, *The Anti-Terrorism Law* (2013). The Criminal Code qualify offences as terrorist ones if the act brings terror in the public; the Anti-Terrorism Law adds the fact of 'compel[ling] the people's authorities, foreign organizations and international organizations, cause difficulties to the international relations of the Socialist Republic of Vietnam or cause panic situation in the public'.

[301] Art. 7, Lao *Law on Anti-Money Laundering and Counter-Financing of Terrorism* (2014) criminalises acts of terrorism are an event in which natural persons, groups of people, organisations or terrorist organisation within or outside of the territory of the Lao PDR receive finances to conduct an act of terrorism, with the details as:

1. *Acts that effect the national security, socio-economic foundation, foreign and international organisations, cause difficulties to international relations of the Lao PDR or chaos to people in the society;* (This part should be understood as the *dol specialis*, but it is listed as an independent criminal act.)
2. Acts that affect lives, health, freedom, or deemed as a physical and psychological coercion and threat
3. Seizure, damaging properties, invasion, attack, obstruction, causing damages and chaos to computer communication and Internet systems or digital instruments of state organisations, legal persons and natural persons; [...]

See the complete list in Appendix 2 on the national definitions of terrorist offences in ASEAN.

[302] See, e.g., Art. 30, Indonesia *Anti-Terrorism Law*; Section 16, Philippine *Anti-Terrorism Act of 2020*. The extraordinary powers given to investigative authorities must be sanctioned by the court. A judicial warrant is needed prior to surveillance and interception of communications. These provisions in the HSA were considered unconstitutional by H. Harry L. Roque Jr. because it

evidence,[303] including oral communications, and intelligence reports. Taking these discrepancies into account, competent national authorities must share their knowledge, information and intelligence, skills, and practices of their respective systems in order to, eventually, be able to develop cooperation mechanisms.[304]

Specific conclusions can be drawn by this brief analysis of the definitions of 'terrorist offences'.

1. The national anti-terrorism legislations differ from one another. Further clarity and coherence would benefit Member States in transnational cases to prevent and combat terrorism. National anti-terrorism provisions have diverged depending on which respective international instrument is used as reference point. For example, the Cambodian anti-terrorism provisions refer directly to different international norms. Yet, even the 1999 UN Convention, the main reference point, has been transposed differently from one country to another.
   The main difference between national legislations in ASEAN today, as well as the main difference in the EU prior to the adoption of the 2002 CFD, is that all ASEAN Member States have provisions on terrorism, while this was not the case in the EU. The approximation took place among a smaller number of Member States that already had anti-terrorism legislations in the EU in addition to countries that did not have any, which might have facilitated the task. By contrast, the pre-existing anti-terrorism provisions in every ASEAN country might constitute an obstacle for the approximation process in Southeast Asia. Member States might not appreciate the need to approximate their legislations and in turn amending their legislations.
2. The anti-terrorism provisions tend to exist in various national laws and have not been compiled in the national criminal code, whenever such codes do exist. For example, Singapore criminalises all the previously listed 15 behaviours in five different laws.[305] The amendment to the legislation in 2002 has updated the means and procedural guarantees previously provided for. Indeed, three months after the 9/11 attacks, 13 individuals suspected of association with the Jemaah Islamiyah (JI), later designated by the UN as being associated with Al-Qaida, were detained without trial under the Internal Security Act (ISA)—a piece of

violates, among other rights and liberties, the right to privacy. See H. Harry L. Roque, Jr., 'The Human Security Act and the IHL Law of the Philippines: of security and insecurity' in Longo et al., 'Promoting Effective Responses to the Foreign Terrorist Fighters: Situation in Southeast Asia' (2015).

[303] See, e.g., Art. 26(1), Indonesia *Anti-Terrorism Law*.

[304] Ramraj et al., *Global Anti-Terrorism Law and Policy* (2012): 323 and ff.

[305] Singapore *Terrorism (Suppression of Financing) Act 2002* revised in 2003; *Public Order Act* (Chap. 257A), No. 15 of 2009, Revised in 2012, 9 October 2009; *Criminal Procedure Code* (Chap. 68), No. 15 of 2010, Revised in 2012, 2 January 2011; *Organised Crime Act 2015*, No. 26 of 2015, Government Gazette No. 27, 21 august 2015; *Public Order and Safety (Special Powers) Act 2018*, No. 26 of 2018, Government Gazette No. 20, 20 April 2018; *Serious Crimes and Counter-Terrorism (Miscellaneous Amendments) Act 2018*, No. 51 of 2018, Government Gazette No. 31 December 2018.

legislation dating back to the conclusions of World War II.[306] The first laws specifically targeting terrorism were adopted after the 9/11 attacks, except in Malaysia which adopted its first anti-terrorism legislation two months prior to the attacks.[307]

Interestingly, the same conclusion can be drawn from the analysis of the EU Member States' legislations prior to the 21st century. Certain Member States have also had terrorism-related provisions scattered among their various legislations.

3. Due to the absence of coherence and comprehensiveness in the respective anti-terrorism legislations, the definition of 'terrorist' or 'terrorist act'—and the offences associated with these definitions—vary as well as the methods of their criminalisation. Specific offences, especially those related to foreign terrorist fighters, have not been criminalised by all ASEAN Member States under specific anti-terrorism laws, instead doing so through the use of 'common law' provisions. As in the EU, certain countries such as Brunei Darussalam, Malaysia, the Philippines, Singapore, Thailand and Vietnam have, for the most part, historically relied on the requirements on 'common law' provisions.
4. ASEAN national legislations have detached terrorist offences from any political characteristic; putting a stop to the limitation of extradition of persons suspected or accused of terrorism. For instance, Indonesian law enacted subsequent to the Bali bombings rejected a previous draft that had defined terrorism as a crime with a political motive, and emphasised that terrorism should not be considered a political crime and that it should not be applied in a manner which discriminates against any particular religion.[308]
5. The penalty also diverges among Member States. Half of the Member States still have the death penalty, namely Indonesia,[309] Malaysia,[310] Singapore,[311]

---

[306] Michael Hor, 'Singapore's anti-terrorism laws: reality and rhetoric' in *Global Anti-Terrorism Law and Policy*, eds., Victor V. Ramraj et al. (Cambridge: Cambridge University Press, 2012).

[307] *Anti-Money Laundering, Anti-Terrorism Financing and Proceeds of Unlawful Activities Act 2001,* Act 613, Laws of Malaysia, Gazette, 4 July 2001.

[308] Indonesian *GRL 1/2002 combating criminal acts of terrorism*; *Law No. 15 of 2002 on* the GRL of Indonesia *on the Eradication of the Crime of Terrorism as a Law*.

[309] World Coalition against the Death Penalty, 'Indonesia': available at http://www.worldcoalition.org/Indonesia (accessed on 14 November 2019). According to this report, the last person was executed in 2016. There were at least 308 individuals on death row at the end of 2018, including at least seven women. Amnesty International, 'Death Sentences and Executions in 2018', ACT/50/9870/2019, 10 April 2019, 19; and, Institute for Criminal Justice Reform, 'Perpetuating Lies. 2018 Indonesian Death Penalty Report', 27: available at https://bit.ly/3ag7KcK (accessed on 14 November 2019).

[310] World Coalition against the Death Penalty, 'Malaysia': available at http://www.worldcoalition.org/Malaysia (accessed on 14 November 2019). According to this report, the last person was executed in 2017. There were around 1275 individuals on death row at the end of 2018.

[311] World Coalition against the Death Penalty, 'Singapore': available at https://bit.ly/3qeNsWl (accessed on 14 November 2019). The last execution took place in 2015.There were at least 40 people on death row at the end of 2018. Amnesty International, 'Death Sentences and Executions in 2018' ACT 50/9870/2019, 10 April 2019, 19.

Thailand[312] and Vietnam.[313] Notably, Brunei Darussalam, Lao PDR and Myanmar are de facto abolitionists.[314] Cambodia and the Philippines are the only two States to have officially abolished the death penalty. In general, the death penalty can be imposed upon any individual who has committed a terrorist offence whenever such a sentence is permissible.

Lastly, none of the Member States' legislations refer to the *ASEAN Convention on Counter Terrorism* or any other ASEAN norm, but rather refer to the relevant international norms. This is additional proof that the regional norms do not constitute any additional value to the Southeast Asian legal landscape. Evidently, there is no top-down influence from the regional level to the national level, but rather from the international level directly to the national level.

If ASEAN Member States were to engage in discussions with the purpose of adopting a common regional definition of terrorist offences, a systematic approach must be taken to ensure that terrorist offences are uniformly criminalised. This task is difficult due to the absence of comprehensive approach on behalf of each Member State (e.g. different anti-terrorism legislations or different provisions dispersed among several legislations, or no clear legal terminology and associated criminalisation). Nonetheless, a minimum common denominator is outside the realm of possibility. A common definition including the *dol generalis* and *dol specialis* could be grounded in the 1999 Convention.

[312] World Coalition against the Death Penalty, 'Thailand': available at https://bit.ly/3peDwuI (accessed on 14 November 2019). Thailand's death row had a total of 551 people at the end of 2018. Interestingly, Thailand carried out executions for the first time during 2018 since 2009. Amnesty International, 'Death Sentences and Executions in 2018' Ibid., 19.

[313] World Coalition against the Death Penalty, 'Vietnam': available at https://bit.ly/3tPxnIV (accessed on 14 November 2019). At least 600 people were on death row in Vietnam at the end of 2018. During this year, there were 85 executions and 122 new death sentences. Amnesty International, 'Death Sentences and Executions in 2018' Ibid., 19.

[314] World Coalition against the Death Penalty, 'Lao PDR': available at https://bit.ly/3rNPn4A (accessed on 14 November 2019). Lao PDR is abolitionist de facto. Human Rights Council, A/HRC/29/7, *Universal Periodic Review* 'Report of the Working Group on the Universal Periodic Review, Lao People's Democratic Republic', 29th session, 23 March 2015, and Human Right Committee, 'List of issues in relation to the initial report of Lao People's Democratic Republic. Addendum. Replies of Lao People's Democratic Republic to the list of issues' CCPR/C/LAO/Q/1/Add.1, 8 June 2018, para. 29; Ramraj et al., *Global Anti-Terrorism Law and Policy* (2012): 271. Also, Amnesty International reported that at the end of 2018, there were 315 people on death row, including 311 inmates who were convicted for drug-related crimes. Because of restrictive State practices concerning the release of information related to the death penalty, it is difficult to verify the number of people on death row. See See Amnesty International, 'Death Sentences and Executions in 2018' ACT 50/9870/2019, 10 April 2019, 6 and 23. World Coalition against the Death Penalty, 'Brunei Darussalam': available at https://bit.ly/3qf62hl (accessed on 14 November 2019). Brunei Darussalam has not executed anyone since 1957; World Coalition against the Death Penalty, 'Myanmar': available at http://www.worldcoalition.org/Myanmar (accessed on 14 November 2019). According to this report, the last person was executed in 1988.

ASEAN Member States recognise that once one individual leaves their country, that person is difficult to pursue and prosecute.[315] Therefore, an approximation of the relevant legislations would help Member States to cooperate when combating terrorism.

2. Fundamental discrepancies between ASEAN Member States' approach to human rights making unlikely an approximation of legislations in a near future

ASEAN national governments' actions prioritise security above human rights protection. Yet, the national delegates that contributed to the 2015 UNODC report on the Southeast Asian response to foreign terrorist fighters (FTFs) underlined the importance of striking a fair balance between preventing and combating terrorism and protecting human rights.[316]

In this respect, it must be remembered that four Member States, namely Brunei Darussalam, Malaysia, Myanmar and Singapore, are not parties to the ICCPR as of yet. Out of 17 human rights instruments that impact the matter at the heart of this research, the only conventions that received unanimous approval by the ASEAN Member States are the 1979 *Convention on the elimination of all forms of discrimination against women,*[317] the 1989 *Convention in the rights of the child* and its 2000 *Optional Protocol on the involvement of children in armed conflict* and the 2006 *Convention on the rights of persons with disabilities*.[318] Conversely, the key conventions dealing with rights and freedoms which might be more heavily impacted by terrorism or, more importantly, by States' response to such terrorism, have not been addressed by States with much enthusiasm. For instance, only the Philippines ratified the 1989 *Second Optional Protocol to the International Covenant on Civil and Political Rights* aiming at the abolition of the death penalty.[319] Another example is the topic of torture and other cruel, inhuman or degrading treatment or punishment: Malaysia, Myanmar and Singapore have not signed the 1984 *Convention against torture and other cruel, inhuman or degrading treatment or punishment*, and Brunei Darussalam only recently signed it in 2015;[320] and, the 2002 *Optional Protocol to the Convention against Torture and Other Cruel, Inhuman or Degrading Treatment or Punishment* has only been ratified and acceded by

[315] Longo et al., 'Promoting Effective Responses to the Foreign Terrorist Fighters: Situation in Southeast Asia' (2015), 18.

[316] Ibid.: 23–24.

[317] Interestingly, this Convention is specifically referred to in the preamble of the AHRD.

[318] *Convention on the Elimination of All Forms of Discrimination against Women*, New York, 18 December 1979, UNTS vol. 1249, No. 20378; *International Convention on the Rights of the Child*, New York, 20 November 1989, UNTS vol. 1577, No. 27531; *Optional Protocol to the Convention on the Rights of the Child on the involvement of children in armed conflict*, New York, 25 May 2000, UNTS vol. 2173, No. 27531; and, *Convention on the Rights of Persons with Disabilities*, New York, 13 December 2006, UNTS vol. 2515, No. 44910.

[319] *Second Optional Protocol to the International Covenant on Civil and Political Rights, aiming at the abolition of the death penalty*, New York, 15 December 1989, UNTS vol. 1642, No. 14668.

[320] The Sultan of Brunei Darussalam stated on the 5th of May 2019 its intention to ratify the Convention. But, it has not happened yet.

Cambodia and the Philippines.[321] The Member States' lack of ratification of the 17 instruments is representative of the low importance that ASEAN countries give to human rights issues.[322]

In this context, some relevant trends must be highlighted.

Firstly, certain States adopted norms which endanger the human rights of individuals caught in criminal justice proceedings. For example, Brunei Darussalam had to appear before the UN Human Rights Council on 10 May 2019 after the government enacted the 2013 Sharia penal code, which contains punishments such as death by stoning, amputation and whipping.[323] Certain punishments made permissible by this code constitute torture and acts of cruel, inhuman or degrading treatment. These are prohibited by the 1984 *Convention against Torture and Other Cruel, Inhuman or Degrading Treatment or Punishment* which was signed by Brunei Darussalam though. This too contravenes the AHRD. These punishments might also breach Brunei's obligations as a party to the 1989 *Convention of the Rights of the Child* and the 1999 *Convention on the Elimination of All Forms of Discrimination against Women.*[324] Surprisingly, Brunei Darussalam was nevertheless praised in the UN Human Rights Review for its efforts to improve human rights in its country, despite its 'stoning of gays'.[325]

---

[321] *Convention against Torture and Cruel, Inhuman or Degrading Treatment or Punishment*, New York, 10 December 1984, UNTS vol. 1465, No. 24841; and, *Optional Protocol to the Convention against Torture and Other Cruel, Inhuman or Degrading Treatment or Punishment*, New York, 18 December 2002, UNTS vol. 2375, No. 24841.

[322] For a detailed list of ratification, see Appendix 1.

[323] Neela Ghoshal, 'Don't go easy on Brunei at UN Rights Review. Death penalty, whipping, and amputation remain on Statute Books' *Human Rights Watch*, 9 May 2019.

[324] See, e.g., Advocates for Justice and Human Rights, 'Brunei Darussalam: implementation of Syariah Penal Code is anathema for Human Rights' International Commission of Jurists, 2 April 2019; Maja Kocijancic, 'Statement of the Spokesperson on the implementation of the Penal Code Order in Brunei-Darussalam', EEAS, Brussels, 3 April 2019; European Parliament, 'Motion for a Resolution with request for inclusion in the agenda for a debate on cases of breaches of human rights, democracy and the rule of law pursuant to Rule 135 of the Rules of Procedure on Brunei' 2019/2692(RSP), 16 April 2019; 'Brunei's Pernicious New Penal Code' *Human Rights Watch*, 22 May 2019.

[325] UN Watch, 'Brunei Praised in Human Rights Review Despite New Stoning of Gays Penal Code' Geneva, 10 May 2019. 'According to a count by UN Watch, 61 out of 91 countries that spoke praised the government for its human rights record. An additional 21 countries expressed some praise for Brunei's alleged progress, in addition to applying genuine scrutiny. If one includes these statements, then 82 out of 91 countries, or 90%, expressed praise for the country'. Must be listed the countries that particularly supported the review: Egypt, Equatorial Guinea, Cambodia, China, Cuba, the Philippines, Saudi Arabia, Bangladesh, Bahrain, Algeria, UAE, Sudan, Palestine, Sri Lanka, Russia and Qatar. Those countries are not particularly known for their action in the defence of human rights. However, a minority of countries—including Canada, France, Norway, Sweden and Switzerland—rightly called out Brunei's use of a Sharia law penal code, limitations on gays and women's rights and restrictions on the media.

Also, Singaporean authorities, as in many countries around the world, have increased the use of administrative detention, without criminal charge or trial.[326] Adopting administrative measures in this way avoids judicial scrutiny. The primary explanation given by public authorities when adopting these measures is that they are a means of preventing terrorist offences. This type of exception regime has developed to prevent and counter terrorism. However, this form of regime tends to be prolonged and subsequently integrated into the ordinary regime.

As the most active in counterterrorism, Indonesian and Malaysian's measures need to be mentioned.

Indonesia, a democracy party to the ICCPR, has been the theatre of many tense debates and demonstrations concerning the development of anti-terrorism laws.[327] Among the most relevant human rights issues which deserve mention are the arbitrary or unlawful killings by government security forces; torture by police; arbitrary detention by the government; harsh and life-threatening conditions in prisons and detention centres; political prisoners; censorship, including laws addressing treason, blasphemy, defamation and decency, site blocking; corruption and attempts by the government to undermine efforts to prosecute corrupt officials.[328] Many anti-terrorism laws, such as the Law No. 15 of 2003, were strongly criticised. This law is in violation of the independence of the judiciary due to the involvement of the Military and the State Intelligence Agency (BIN) in eradicating terrorist acts. There is no clear division of competence between the Police, Military and the BIN. This has resulted in human rights violations such as deprivation of liberty, illegal arrest and detention in particular.[329] The investigators can use data collected by intelligence services directly to develop facts and indict without informing the accused as to how they obtained such data. Moreover, the method used to gather data (e.g. use of torture or other illegal means) is not governed by this Law.[330] Another related problem is the Government's delay in developing a proper

[326] ECOSOC, E/CN.4/2002/157, Letter dated 19 March 2002 from the Permanent Representative of Singapore to the United Nations Office at Geneva addressed to the Chairperson of the Commission on Human Rights, 'Question of the violation of human rights and fundamental freedoms in any part of the world. Civil and political rights. Effective functioning of human rights mechanisms', 58th session, 25 March 2002.

[327] See, e.g., the recent proposal of modification of the Criminal Code that could threaten a wide range of civil liberties: Kate Lamb, 'Indonesia's criminal code: what is it, why does it matter, and will it be passed?' *The Guardian*, 26 September 2019.

[328] U.S. Department of State 'Indonesia 2018 Human Rights Report', Country Reports on Human Rights Practices for 2018, Bureau of Democracy, Human Rights and Labor: available at https://www.state.gov/wp-content/uploads/2019/03/INDONESIA-2018.pdf (accessed on 18 November 2019).

[329] Statement, 'INDONESIA: War against terrorism should respect human rights and the Rule of Law' *Asian Human Rights Commission*, AHRC-STM-015-2018, 6 March 2018: available at http://www.humanrights.asia/news/ahrc-news/AHRC-STM-015-2018 (accessed on 12 March 2018).

[330] Notably, Indonesia ratified the *Convention against Torture and Cruel, Inhuman or Degrading Treatment or Punishment* (1984) but is not party to the *Optional Protocol to the Convention against Torture and Other Cruel, Inhuman or Degrading Treatment or Punishment* (2002).

and accountable complaint mechanism to address human rights violations. Victims and families of victims can only use ordinary mechanisms such as General Crimes to seek compensation. In practice, it is incredibly difficult to implement.

Malaysia is intensely active against terrorism and it too has been criticised for the threat that its anti-terrorism legislations pose to human rights. Of particular interest are the *Malaysian Security Offences (Special Measures) Act 2012* (SOSMA), the *Prevention of Terrorism Act*, *Prevention of Crime Act* and the *Sedition Act.*[331] The main issue with SOSMA is that certain provisions deny an accused a fair trial, something which they would normally be entitled to, if they are being investigated and tried under the normal Criminal Procedure Code and Evidence Act.[332]

Secondly, the incongruity between the applicable text of the laws and their effective implementation tends to be significant. For instance, Lao PDR has developed provisions ensuring the protection of the rights of the suspects or the person charged with terrorist offences or related offences, particularly in the *Law on Criminal Procedure*, but the effective control of the implementation of these rights remains extremely weak.[333] Similarly, Cambodia's Constitution of 1993 encompasses a Chapter on 'the Rights and Obligations of Khmer Citizens' (Articles 31–50) consisting of 20 articles, including 17 on rights. Additionally, according to the 1991 Paris Agreement that led to the adoption of the Cambodian Constitution,[334] judicial courts were established and empowered to enforce the rights provided under the Constitution. For over a decade, efforts have been made to establish an independent judicial system, yet they have not achieved the intended results. In practice, the judiciary remains corrupt, inefficient and controlled mostly by the ruling party (the Cambodian People's Party). Flagrant violations of human rights by State agents have been identified, but successful prosecutions have been rare.[335] Unfortunately, these examples can be found almost entirely throughout the region.

---

[331] Amer Hamzad Arshad, 'The case against oppressive laws' *The Star*, 17 August 2018.

[332] *Evidence Act*, Act 56, Laws of Malaysia, first enacted in 1950 (Ordinance No. 11 of 1950), latest amendment made by Act A1527 which came into operation on 1 November 2017; *Criminal Procedure Code*, Act 593, Laws of Malaysia, first enacted in 1935 (F.M.S. Cap. 6), latest amendment made by Act A1431 which came into operation on 31 July 2012.

[333] Para. 23, HRC CCPR/C/LAO/Q/1/Add.1, *Consideration of reports submitted by States parties under Article 40 of the Covenant*, 'List of issues in relation to the initial report of Lao People's Democratic Republic. Addendum. Replies of Lao People's Democratic Republic to the list of issues', 123rd session, 20 June 2018.

[334] A/46/608 and S/23177, Letter from the Permanent Representatives of France and Indonesia to the United Nations addressed to the Secretariat-General concerning the situation in Cambodia, 46th session, 30 October 1991; *The Constitution of the Kingdom of Cambodia*, Constitutional Assembly, 2nd Plenary Session, Phnom Penh, 21 September 1993, translation supervised by the Constitutional Council, March 2009.

[335] A/HRC/42/60, *Annual report of the UN High Commissioner for Human Rights and reports of the Office of the High Commissioner and the Secretary-General. Technical assistance and capacity-building*, 'Situation of human rights in Cambodia. Report of the Special Rapporteur on the situation of human rights in Cambodia', 42nd session, 27 August 2019.

Highlighting human rights issues is necessary to understand the potential impact on an approximation of legislations and on interstate cooperation. Human rights norms are even less likely to be approximated in comparison to counterterrorism norms. The use of terrorism as a trump card to justify the development of exceptional security legislations prevails over human rights concerns.

Therefore, there is no bottom-up influence from the Member States to the regional legal framework concerning the protection of human rights. An approximation of human rights norms is unlikely to occur in the near future.

Despite these problematic elements, the United Nations considered that human rights improvements are being made in certain ASEAN Member States, such as Thailand. However, progress is far slower in other Member States. The situation in Myanmar needs to be acknowledged, given the grave abuses and injustices which continue to be committed against the Rohingya people. The ratification status of major international human rights treaties, especially those regarding complaint procedures provided in these treaties (e.g. the Individual Complaint Procedure under the ICCPR[336]) and the implementation and reporting process suggests that certain countries are actively engaging in the international human rights protection system. By contrast, others are not supportive of, if not opposed to, any international mechanisms or bodies which include strict procedures to monitor the implementation of human rights obligations.

Therefore, human rights have been promulgated at the regional level through the *ASEAN Human Rights Declaration*. Nonetheless, this merely reflects the weak and broad political willingness by the Member States to introduce this concern for future deliberation and inclusion into ASEAN policies. It adds no legal value and does not effectively and directly impact Member States' legislations. Moreover, the Declaration states that the Member States reaffirm their commitment 'to the Universal Declaration of Human rights, the Charter of the United Nations, the Vienna Declaration and Programme of Action, and other international human rights instruments *to which ASEAN Member States are parties* (own added emphasis)'.[337] The last section is representative of the absence of top-down influence of regional norms on national legislations. The Declaration is not intended to impose any obligations on its members.

Referring back to one of the aforementioned examples, the ASEAN Member States, through the AHRD, affirmed that '[n]o person shall be subject to torture or to cruel, inhuman or degrading treatment or punishment'.[338] Since the adoption of this provision, Brunei signed the *Convention against Torture and Cruel, Inhuman or Degrading Treatment or Punishment* and Vietnam ratified it. Hopefully, the Declaration might be—or become—an incentive for Member States to further develop

[336] *Optional Protocol to the International Covenant on Civil and Political Rights*, New York, 16 December 1966, UNTS, vol. 999, No. 14668.

[337] Preamble para. 3, *ASEAN Human Rights Declaration* (2012) (italics by the author).

[338] Pt 14, AHRD.

their legislations in ways which comply with these rights and freedoms; but it is doubtful.

One may consider that the text already limits greatly its purpose, the AHRD expressly states that '[t]he enjoyment of human rights and fundamental freedoms must be balanced with the performance of corresponding duties as every person has responsibilities to all other individuals, the community and the society where one lives. It is ultimately the primary responsibility of ASEAN Member States to promote and protect all human rights and fundamental freedoms'.[339] The Declaration limits the implementation of these rights to duties to protect society, including ensuring its security, according to the willingness and abilities of the Member States.

In a non-legally binding perspective, there have been recent ASEAN developments in the field of human rights though. Dialogues and fora discussing these matters continue to multiply. For instance, a forum was provided for the launch and presentation of the key findings of the ASEAN Intergovernmental Commission on Human Rights (AICHR) on Access to Justice. During the forum, there was a clear reinforcement of the idea that multi-sectorial and cross-border collaboration is essential to ensure access to justice for all concerned. Moreover, the AICHR and Representative of Singapore, Ambassador Barry Desker, stated that the rule of law and human rights underpins citizen's confidence and ensures stability among ASEAN societies. He also added that access to justice needs to be realised through inclusive and collaborative approaches, which form the core of ASEAN values.[340] It is particularly interesting that Singapore defended this view as it has ratified or accessed very few international human rights-related norms.[341]

Due to the nature of consent of these operating rules at the fora, the decisions taken are either a form of political recognition regarding the need to tackle an identified issue or a way to politically signify that Member States have adopted the necessary legislations protecting these rights. Regardless, these regional efforts do not guarantee the effective protection of human rights by the Member States as they retain sole responsibility and there continues to be a lack of a regional enforcement mechanism. In this respect, the AICHR has demonstrated its limited role to promote human rights and act as a convenor in spearheading regional and national strategies.

Focusing on the rights and freedoms linked to counterterrorism, there have been few discussions and progress towards a regional legal approach. No specific procedural guarantee has been established by ASEAN norm(s) concerning the rights of an

---

[339] Pt. 6, AHRD.

[340] 'ASEAN human rights body holds forum on access to justice' *ASEAN Secretariat News*, 18 December 2018: https://asean.org/asean-human-rights-body-holds-forum-access-justice/ (accessed on 7 May 2019).

[341] Singapore ratified or accessed four international human rights instruments, namely the *Convention on the Elimination of All Forms of Discrimination against Women* (1979); *International Convention on the Rights of the Child* (1989); its *Optional Protocol to the Convention on the Rights of the Child on the involvement of children in armed conflict* (2000); and, *Convention on the Rights of Persons with Disabilities* (2006), out of 17 instruments identified in this research. See Appendix 1 regarding ASEAN Member States' ratifications.

accused in criminal cases. National stakeholders are still at the stage of organising dialogues and sharing best practices. For instance, chief justices, senior judges and members of the Council of ASEAN Chief Judges (CACJ); representatives of the AICHR and the ASEAN Senior Law Officials Meeting (ASLOM); and regional human rights experts attended the dialogue organised on 11 December 2018. It must also be mentioned that the AICHR held the Judicial Colloquium on the Sharing of Good Practices Regarding International Human Rights Law in Kuala Lumpur on 13–15 March 2017. During this process, the AICHR recognised that certain fair trial rights have been expressly stated in the AHRD, and that dialogue is important to learn about how the judicial authorities fulfilled their role to interpret and apply laws on the subject of fair trial rights. As such, judges from ASEAN Member States shared their experiences and good practices on the manners in which the judiciaries implement the legal protection afforded to an accused. The challenges facing each legal system were also discussed. Furthermore, possible gaps between national legal standards and international human rights standards were identified. The outcome of this dialogue was the adoption of recommendations focusing on key points of interest, namely on the right to counsel, the right to be informed of the grounds of his/her arrest, the right to access documents, the right to a speedy trial, the right to bail, the right to a presumption of innocence, the right to cross-examine witnesses, the right to legal aid, the prohibition of double jeopardy, and the right to non-retroactive punishment. Against this backdrop, the ASLOM is supposed to develop a Model Law, as done by the UN, which outlines the common standards to be implemented within the region when processing accused persons in criminal matters. It is also intended to further organise training and capacity building workshops to enhance cooperation and dialogue between competent national authorities on matters of human rights.[342]

To conclude the matter of human rights, there is either minimal or no regionalisation in ASEAN and a low probability of any occurring in the near future; converse to the situation in the EU.

In ASEAN, tackling terrorism is a top priority on the agenda to the extent that protection of human rights seems to be much lower in the items of their agenda, which could arguably be considered similar up to a certain extent in the EU. Member States do not consider human rights standards to be a basis for mutual trust and collective cooperation. It is mostly, and even solely, based on the identified common objective of preventing and countering terrorism.

[342] 'AICHR and CACJ hold ASEAN human rights dialogue on the rights of accused persons in criminal cases' *ASEAN Secretariat News*, 11 December 2018: available at https://asean.org/aichr-cacj-hold-asean-human-rights-dialogue-rights-accused-persons-criminal-cases/ (accessed on 7 May 2019).

Elevating common human rights standards might aid to improve mutual trust. Indeed, it would create legal expectations and, subsequently, smoothen cooperation. The creation of an environment where people can exercise their rights fosters horizontal mutual trust.[343]

Thus, the lowest common denominator approach dictates the pace of regionalisation of counterterrorism and human rights norms in the two regions. The distinguishing feature is that the lowest common denominator between Member States is higher in the EU.

Section 3: The Results of Vertical Influences over the Construct of Regional Legal Frameworks—A Fostering of Mutual Trust Facilitating Cooperation?

The EU and ASEAN legal frameworks in counterterrorism and related human rights matters are being developed in accordance with the varied combinations of top-down and bottom-up influences in each region. The outcome of each region's unique combination has variably impacted the dimension(s) that mutual trust take(s).

Firstly, this chapter demonstrates the manner in which the three-level cross-fertilisation of norms has led to different outcomes in the EU and ASEAN. The cross-directional vertical interactions between international, regional and national norms have resulted in differing legal outcomes in the EU and ASEAN.

Regarding the first set of dynamics (between international and regional norms), there has been little localisation of norms in ASEAN, while the EU has integrated international norms and taken further legal steps.

On the East side of the Ural mountain divide, ASEAN has been a simple vector of international law without any distortion in counterterrorism, while it is argued that the *ASEAN Declaration on Human Rights* has lowered international standards. ASEAN has no power over its Member States in the same way a supranational organisation could have. The only potential influence is political.

On the West side of the Ural, the EU is a vector of international law, but functions mostly as an independent regional actor. The EU has not necessarily distorted international norms, but instead has provided quite precise instructions to its Member States. Interestingly, the EU is not only a receiver, but it is also an influencer of international norms. Most significantly, the cross-fertilisation between the norms adopted by the Council of Europe and the EU's is more visible.

Regarding the second set of dynamics (between regional and national norms), there is a significant difference between ASEAN and the EU.

In ASEAN, the lack of coordination and institutional linkages between the national and regional levels—along with the lack of consistent political will of national governments—have, as part of the main reasons, prevented the

[343] HRC, 'ASEAN Human Rights Declaration should maintain international standards' (2012).

development of a top-down influence. The ASEAN Conventions' provisions are too vague to constitute a real added value when approximating national laws. Moreover, Member States remain the sole actors responsible for the functioning of the regional organisation, which might explain the reason that there are no clear two-level relations between ASEAN and its members. However, it is unlikely that common regional definitions and standards will emerge in the near future (no bottom-up influence). Horizontal mutual influences between States cannot be denied though (e.g. the relations between anti-terrorism norms of Brunei, Singapore and Malaysia).

In the EU, there has been a cross-fertilisation between the regional and national norms. Over time, the Member States have given the regional organisation the tools to ensure the harmonisation of EU policies and norms resulting in a top-down influence from the EU over its members. However, Member States have kept the power to push for, and influence, the elaboration of regional norms (bottom-up influence). This dialogue between the regional and national actors aims to ensure the effective and harmonised implementation of regional norms.

Secondly, through these three-level interactions, this chapter shows one angle in the process of building mutual trust, namely the normative angle. In so doing, it focused on the adoption of regional norms, the potential approximation of national legislations in counterterrorism and human rights protection (*capability building)*, and on the *knowledge and experience sharing* occurring between competent authorities (i.e. horizontally and vertically). These efforts are intended to facilitate the development of mutual trust between the relevant competent authorities, and subsequently, foster cross-border cooperation.

The question remains as to whether the approximation of legislations aids in building mutual trust or whether mutual trust constitutes a preliminary step to any effort for approximation. In other words, back to the dilemma: which came first, chicken or the egg?

Present at all three levels of analysis, interpersonal trust (i.e. social dimension of mutual trust) is insufficient to ensure sustainable cooperative relations. Developing the political dimension of mutual trust is a progressive step but retains an element of uncertainty. The various ASEAN and EU declarations, which state the willingness of the Member States when employing counterterrorism actions, do not bind the parties to any precise means and results. Some States progress further by adding a legal dimension to the other two dimensions. This progression constitutes a stabilisation of relations in the long term. A national policy is easier to modify or repeal than a law. Such sustainability might have hindered cooperation between ASEAN Member States who do not want to be legally bound, whereas the more legalistic approach adopted by the EU has most certainly facilitated cross-border cooperation.

Within their respective legal architecture in counterterrorism and human rights, the two regional organisations with the support of their Member States have developed their respective understanding of 'mutual trust'. Member States' choices over their own regional norms in counterterrorism and human rights as well as the consequences on the different dimensions of mutual trust have then impacted the development of cross-border cooperation within each region, as will be demonstrated in the next chapter.

Chapter 6
Sharing Data with Peers from the Same Region: A Matter of Mutual Trust

The EU and ASEAN have proclaimed their ambition to ensure the cohesion of their responses against terrorism. With this purpose in mind, ASEAN has almost solely focused on cooperation and coordination compared to the EU, which took the position that harmonising its Member States' legislations would foster and enhance the cooperation and coordination.

Within their respective regional legal frameworks, intra-regional cooperation mechanisms between the competent national authorities[1] are essential for an effective fight against serious transnational crime. Notably, judicial cooperation is not part of this study. However, because the latter, and particularly mutual legal assistance, also covers exchange of information, it is sporadically mentioned to explain the progressive development of direct and horizontal cooperation mechanisms within the two regions.

Among the main cooperative activities to be pursued to counter serious transnational crime, information and intelligence sharing maintain top priority. Gathering and processing relevant data is necessary for the investigation, detection and prosecution of terrorist offences. It is even more so for the prevention of terrorist attacks. With the huge impact on human lives (physical and psychological consequences) and on government foundation, preventing terrorist offences has indeed become essential. The timely access to accurate and up-to-date information and intelligence is considered a crucial element for law enforcement authorities to successfully detect, prevent and investigate crime or criminal activity. Sharing information and intelligence provides opportunities to develop crime-fighting strategies and determine the resources needed to conduct multi-layered operations that often require the establishment of teams of interested foreign competent national authorities

[1] As defined in Chap. 2, competent national authorities refers, in this book, to all police authorities, and other law enforcement services, intelligence services and other public authorities existing in the Member States, which are responsible under national law for preventing and combating criminal offences.

C. C. Cocq, *Mutual Trust in Regional and Interregional Cooperation on Counterterrorism*, United Nations University Series on Regionalism 26,
https://doi.org/10.1007/978-3-031-36612-3_6

(*knowledge and experience sharing* cluster). When information collected is made available to foreign authorities, it enables these authorities to identify the criminal activities, to develop knowledge about actual or potential criminal activity that occurs beyond their jurisdiction and cooperate with each other. Horizontal cooperation between competent national authorities is thus very important against transnational crime.

In a virtuous circle, sharing data and best practices, as well as establishing channels of communications is essential to build up trust. In return, mutual trust allows streamlining and strengthens data sharing.[2] Along the way, information and intelligence sharing establishes—and is facilitated by—networks between competent national authorities.[3]

The development of cooperation has only been possible because authorities have started to trust in the 'terms and conditions' of their engagements vis-à-vis each other and in reaching their shared objective(s). ASEAN and EU Member States agreed to enhance information and intelligence sharing, in particular that relating to terrorists and terrorist organisations, their movement and funding and any other information needed to protect lives, properly and the security of all modes of travel. Indeed, States need to take appropriate actions, consistent with national law and applicable international law, including human rights law, to ensure that their competent national authorities have access to relevant information, as appropriate, about suspected terrorists, including foreign terrorist fighters.[4]

Despite recognising the added value of data sharing, the effectiveness of cross-border cooperation remains hampered by mistrust and the desire of States to keep key information and/or intelligence to themselves to protect their national sovereignty and territory from any external security threat. In particular, vertical and horizontal trust issues[5] have prevented the effectiveness of cooperation mechanisms.

On the one hand, vertical trust between citizens and their governments was damaged, especially in Western countries, following different scandals that proliferated since 2013, most importantly with Snowden's revelations. Sharing data along with data gathering and processing constitutes a legitimate means in the fight against terrorism. National security agencies around the world are collecting and sharing

---

[2]Malcolm Anderson, 'Trust and Police Co-operation' in *Police and Justice Cooperation and the New European Borders*, eds., Malcolm Anderson and Joanna Apap, European Monographs (The Hague: Kluwer Law International, 2002).

[3]Didier Bigo, *Polices en Réseaux: L'Expérience Européenne* (Paris: Presse de Science Po, 1996).

[4]Pt. 7, S/RES/2396(2017).

[5]See table in the introduction of Chap. 3.

intelligence more than ever before,[6] sometimes with tragic consequences.[7] There are indeed sufficient examples in world history of misuse of data for data gathering, sharing and use to be a valid and reasonable concern. By their actions, governments and their representatives might endanger people's rights and freedoms, especially the right to privacy and data protection. In this context, there have been numerous polemic discussions on the way to address the risks posed by the increasing means of gathering, processing and sharing at the disposal of competent authorities; but, very worrying, also at the disposal of the private sector.[8] Re-establishing and enhancing this bottom-up vertical trust has forced the decision-makers to re-evaluate and to update the international and EU norms on the right to privacy.[9]

On the other hand, horizontal forms of trust between competent national authorities of different countries of a same region or of different regions and potentially between regional organisations have become a significant objective to ensure a quick response against terrorism. However, horizontal trust might be hindered by different historical and political considerations, as well as by the sensitivity of certain data. For example, no State is going to pass on highly sensitive information which might reveal the existence of a highly placed informant in the centre of an organised crime group to another State where the level of corruption is high.[10] Tackling corruption is thus an additional necessity to facilitate cooperation.

Besides, whilst politics and the law help to set the framework within which cooperation can take place, the prevailing culture between field actors to a large extent determines how cooperation occurs in practice.[11] Competent authorities also encounter practical obstacles while aiming to achieve their objectives. All the political will, legal framework and enthusiasm in the world amount to nothing if the physical ability or actual capacity to implement the desired cooperation is lacking. The facilities and opportunities that international organisations like Interpol or regional ones like Europol and—though very limited at the moment—Aseanapol offer would be less effective if officers tasked with international requests lack the

---

[6]Chesterman, *One Nation Under Surveillance* (2011).

[7]Commission of Inquiry into the Actions of Canadian Officials in Relation to Maher Arar, *Report of the Events relating to Maher Arar* (Ottawa: Government of Canada, 2006).

[8]See, e.g., CJEU, *Digital Rights* (2014); *Tele2* (2016).

[9]At the international level, A/RES/68/167, *The right to privacy in the digital age*, 68th plenary meeting, 21 January 2014; and, A/RES/69/166, *The right to privacy in the digital age*, 69th session, Agenda item 68(b), 18 December 2014. At the EU level, *Directive 2016/680 on the protection of natural persons with regard to the processing of personal data by competent authorities for the purposes of the prevention, investigation, detection or prosecution of criminal offences*; *General Data Protection Regulation 2016/679*; *Regulation 2016/794 on the European Union Agency for Law Enforcement Cooperation (Europol)*.

[10]Roger Gaspard, 'Tackling international crime. Forward into the era' in *Combating international crime. The longer arm of the law*, ed., Steven David Brown (London: Routledge, 2008): 25.

[11]Steven David Brown, 'Ready, willing and enable' in *Combating international crime. The longer arm of the law*, ed., Steven David Brown (London: Routledge, 2008): 35.

technical means to receive the details, to conduct the necessary enquiries or, having done so, to transmit the result.[12]

These are reasons why developing mechanisms of data sharing is a real challenge. When reflecting on this challenge, it is interesting to observe that 'low level' peer-to-peer cooperation works often better than higher-level cooperation between officials. It might be considered as paradoxical given that cooperation between field competent national authorities usually involves operational cooperation, with a potential sharing of personal data and specific data on ongoing investigations. By contrast, cooperation is of a more strategic nature between government officials or other high-level officials. At that level, information and intelligence shared usually remain more general (e.g. sharing experiences of terrorist trends or on their counterterrorism policies and laws), but might of course also be sensitive, especially from a political point of view.

This study focuses on horizontal forms of trust between competent national authorities, as well as vertical forms of trust between the latter and regional bodies of the same region. Forms of horizontal trust between regional bodies from the same region may also be tackled, but more incidentally.

This chapter does not quantitatively assess the concrete effectiveness of cooperation in each region (e.g. number of data exchanges; number of cross-border cases leading to a prosecution; number of suspected terrorists arrested on the basis of specific cases of transnational cooperation). Rather, it analyses and compares the development of intra-regional methods of cross-border cooperation. It examines how each of the regional organisations, and their respective Member States, have developed cross-border cooperation, with a particular focus on data sharing, in order to prevent and combat terrorism, and whether trust plays a role in developing such mechanisms of cooperation. In line with the previous chapter, the objective is also to examine the link with the worldwide framework (e.g. the UN and Interpol) and its impact on each regional approach to cross-border cooperation.

With that purpose in mind, this chapter presents and discusses two types of complementary intra-regional actions. On the one hand, horizontal cooperation mechanisms have diversified and become more numerous; among them, direct sharing of data between competent national authorities has been particularly enhanced (Section 1). On the other hand, various actors and other multilateral platforms have emerged over time and have been increasingly invested in fostering and smoothening cooperation and in particular data sharing (Section 2). Cooperation mechanisms and actors differ strongly from one region to the other, reflecting the geographical, political and economic make-up of each region.[13] The causal link between, on the one hand, the development of cooperation mechanisms and the establishment of actors and platforms facilitating the flow of data, and, on the other hand, the role of mutual trust is highlighted throughout this chapter.

---

[12]Ibid.: 37.

[13]Nicholas Rees, 'EU and ASEAN: Issues of regional security' *International Politics*, vol. 47, no. 3/4 (2010): 408.

Section 1: A Correlation Between the Different Dimensions of Mutual Trust and the Different Forms of Horizontal Cross-Border Cooperation

Mutual trust, by the operationalisation of one or several of its dimensions, plays a key role in the development of an environment conducive of cross-border data sharing. A correlation exists between the development of mutual trust, and its various components, and the form horizontal cross-border cooperation takes.

Bearing this in mind, the global scene is not particularly conducive of streamlined and steady cooperation between competent national authorities. Indeed, the global legal panorama is not precise enough to impose specific obligations on States regarding horizontal cooperation mechanisms in the field of counterterrorism (I). In this context, the EU and ASEAN have marked their engagement to further develop cooperation, especially when facilitating the exchange of data. In so doing, they have adopted different approaches that are resultantly more or less effective than the other (II).

I. Formal strategic relations and informal operational horizontal cross-border cooperation reflecting the social dimension of mutual trust

Since international terrorism disregards national borders, competent authorities should also benefit from some sort of 'relaxation' of the concept of national jurisdiction to be able to counter this criminal behaviour. Law enforcement operations should be able to 'mirror' this disregard. A closer cooperation between competent national authorities in sharing data is thus strongly encouraged.

That being said, it must not be ignored that collaboration between law enforcement agencies is plagued by competing agendas of law enforcement authorities themselves or of their governments, by limited resources, or by nationalist or national sovereignty reflexes when it comes to sharing information. Inevitably, cultural and social norms, along with individual experiences, impact cross-border relations. Cooperation rests on the willingness and ability of States to create an international environment ripe for information sharing through the negotiation of bilateral and regional agreements. This might explain the form and degree of mutual trust at the different jurisdictions, including the international (A) and regional ones (B), and the subsequent impact that might have on the emergent horizontal cross-border cooperation.

A. An overly broad worldwide legal umbrella for cross-border cooperation

At the UN level, a difference is to be made between sectorial instruments adopted in the field of terrorism and transversal ones, i.e. not specific to counterterrorism.

International terrorism-related conventions require States to cooperate together in order to reach the objective(s) set in the Convention(s) in which such requirement is attached to.[14] However, these instruments do not detail the form such cooperation should take.

On a sectorial basis, the Council of Security, whose resolutions are binding on the States, has not been more effective in fostering operational cooperation between competent national authorities. Certain resolutions might require competent authorities to 'intensify and accelerate the timely exchange of relevant operational information and financial intelligence regarding actions, movements and patterns of movement of terrorist or terrorist networks, including foreign terrorist fighters'.[15] However, it does not specify the method, the extent and degree of such cooperation.

The absence of progress in providing more precise global responses is demonstrated in the similarities of requirements over the years. For instance, the report 'Implementation of Security Council resolution 2178(2014) by States affected by foreign terrorist fighters' published in 2016 insists on the urgent need for effective flows of information at the national and international levels.[16] The report identifies priorities for law enforcement, including the centralised and coordinated exchange of information at the national level and the urgent need for an operational 24/7 alert system that enables users to share information immediately with frontline officers. Frontline officers are not only law enforcement officers but also immigration officers or customs authorities. This report even considers that there might be 'a causal relationship between inadequate information exchange and the risk of terrorist attack'.[17]

Taking a look at other sectorial instruments shows that the loose nature of cooperation requirements at UN level is not specific to the field of counterterrorism. Article 28(2) of the *UN Convention against Transnational Organized Crime* (UNTOC) does not provide much detail either. Notably, instruments require States to cooperate 'by exchanging accurate and verified information'.[18] In this respect, States are asked to take effective measures, on the one hand, to 'enhance and, where necessary, to establish channels of communication between their competent authorities, agencies and services in order to facilitate the secure and rapid exchange of

[14] See, e.g., Art. 15(b), *International Convention for the Suppression of Terrorist Bombings* (1997) that states that States Parties shall cooperate in the prevention of the offences set forth in article 2, particularly '(b) By exchanging accurate and verified information in accordance with their national law, and coordinating administrative and other measures taken as appropriate to prevent the commission of offences as set forth in article 2'. This follows the requirement of adoption of domestic legislation to prevent and counter terrorist offences (a). Similarly, Art. 18(3), *International Convention for the Suppression of the Financing of Terrorism* (1999); Art. 7(1)(b), *International Convention for the Suppression of Acts of Nuclear Terrorism* (2005). Also, UNODC, *Handbook on criminal justice responses to terrorism*, Criminal justice handbook series (New York: UN publication, 2009), 61.

[15] See, e.g., pt. 19, S/RES/2462(2019); pt. 2, S/RES/2482(2019).

[16] United Nations Security Council, 'Implementation of Security Council 2178(2014) by States affected by foreign terrorist fighters: A compilation of three reports (S/2015/338; S/2015/683; S/2015/975)', United Nations, Counter-Terrorism Committee Executive Directorate (New York: United Nations, 31 August 2016).

[17] Ibid.: 24.

[18] See e.g. Art. 15(b), *International Convention for the Suppression of Terrorist Bombings* (1997).

information concerning all aspects of the offences covered by [the] Convention' and, on the other, to facilitate effective coordination between the competent national authorities and to promote the exchange of personnel and experts, including the posting of liaison officers.[19]

On a global level, there is no binding transversal instrument that requires States to adopt or respect a specific method of cross-border cooperation between competent national authorities, even less so when direct and horizontal data sharing is at stake. The UN has nonetheless been looking for common minimum denominators and attempted to foster an effective implementation of the objectives identified by the States through soft power. For this purpose, it developed certain manuals or model laws.[20] This is especially the case in the field of judicial cooperation, as shown by the *UN Model Treaty on Mutual Legal Assistance in Criminal Matters*. Other sectorial soft law instruments have been adopted too, such as the *Manual on International Cooperation in Criminal Matters related to Terrorism*. Models and manuals present the advantage of being more detailed regarding the form(s) cooperation might or should take to be more effective. For example, the principle of *aut dedere aut judicare* (obligation to extradite or prosecute) has increasingly gained importance over the years and has gradually been incorporated into numerous bilateral and multilateral treaties in criminal matters.[21] Yet, the details regarding the legal basis, purpose and content of the obligation tend not to be particularly detailed and might require the adoption of more precise bilateral agreements and national provisions. These details are provided in the *Manual on International Cooperation in Criminal Matters* that provides with examples of applications of the principle.[22] However, they are deprived of any binding nature.

Therefore, the international legal framework for cooperation remains vague and limited. A global response is difficult to implement because of the historical, cultural, political and legal differences between States. The combination of those differences with the importance of national sovereignty and the principle of non-interference in internal affairs results in States' resistances to take part in international cooperation mechanisms that might be considered as endangering their sovereignty and potentially their national security. Without a binding instrument, the UN has instead fostered interstate dialogues and cooperation on a more

[19] Art. 27(1), UNTOC (2000). All EU and ASEAN Member States are parties to the convention.

[20] UNODC, Terrorism Prevention Branch, *Model legislative provisions against terrorism* (Vienna: UNODC Publications, February 2009); *Manual on International Cooperation in Criminal Matters related to Terrorism* (Vienna: UNODC publications, July 2009); *UN Model Treaty on Mutual Legal Assistance in criminal Matters*, A/RES/45/117 (68th plenary meeting, 14 December 1990) as amended by A/RES/53/112 (53rd session, 20 January 2000).

[21] See, e.g., Art. 146, *Geneva Convention relative to the Protection of Civilian Persons in Time of War*, Geneva, 12 August 1949, UNTS vol. 75; Art. 4, *Convention for the Suppression of Unlawful Seizure of Aircraft*, The Hague, 16 December 1970, UNTS vol. 860, No. 12325; and, amongst the recent instruments, Art. 11, *Convention for the Suppression of Acts of Nuclear Terrorism* (2005).

[22] UNODC, *Manual on International Cooperation in Criminal Matters related to Terrorism*, Module 3 (2009), 143–162.

strategic level on the basis of non-binding instruments and through soft power. The UN brings its added value especially in the building of States' capabilities by creating a broad political and legal umbrella as well as ties and bridges for cooperation. The UN leaves States with the task of finding ways to cooperate on a more operational level.

The looseness of provisions encompassed in international norms and the state of government-to-government relations seem to nourish each other. This explains why the higher in the hierarchy cooperation takes place, the more strategic and formal cooperation is. Following the same dynamic, the precision of provisions encompassed in binding and more 'local' norms, for example, domestic laws or EU law, and the state of direct horizontal cross-border between law enforcement authorities, through formal or informal channels of cooperation, seemingly nourish each other too.

B. Interpol: the main worldwide platform for operational cooperation

Although increasingly providing strategic assessments of criminal threats, Interpol is well known for its significant operational role. Interpol is the only structure that gathers law enforcement agencies of 194 States from across the world and enables them to collaborate bilaterally and multilaterally using a common platform. In essence, Interpol aims 'to ensure and promote the widest possible mutual assistance between all criminal police authorities within the limits of the laws existing in the different countries and in the spirit of the 'Universal Declaration of Human Rights'; to establish and develop all institutions likely to contribute effectively to the prevention and suppression of ordinary law crimes'.[23] More specifically, Interpol is meant to facilitate the transnational flow of data concerning any offences.

According to Article 3 of Interpol's Constitution, Interpol is strictly forbidden 'to undertake any intervention or activities of a political, military, religious or racial character'. This provision finds its origin in one specific event and a general concern. Firstly, it was recognised that Interpol was used as an arm of the Nazi regime. Although Hitler promised to maintain the strictly non-political character of Interpol's mission, called 'International Criminal Police Commission' at that time, it was effectively absorbed by the Nazi regime. Besides, its list of presidents during that era includes prominent Nazi figures such as Otto Steinhäusl, Arthur Nebe and Reinhard Heydrich. In order to prevent another misuse of this international organisation's resources, the General Assembly adopted Article 3 and elaborated on its interpretation. Since 1951, Interpol is not bound by the qualification of the elements of the offences made by States but an offence's nature (i.e. political, military, religious or racial) is defined on a case-by-case basis by taking into account a number

[23] INTERPOL, *Constitution of the International Criminal Police Organisation – INTERPOL*, I/CONS/GA/1956 (2017), General Assembly, 25th session, Vienna, 1956.

of elements developed in Article 34(3) of Interpol's Rules on the Processing of Data.[24,25] In this context, terrorism was long excluded, *de facto,* from an offence's subjects of cooperation through Interpol. Then, with the evolution of international law, the practice of Interpol has evolved in relation to the application of Article 3. The adoption by the General Assembly of Resolutions AGN/53/RES/6 and AGN/53/RES/7 in 1984 changed the interpretation of Article 3 in crucial respects. Resolution AGN/53/RES/6 on Violent Crime commonly referred to as Terrorism used the term 'terrorism' for the first time. Resolution AGN/53/RES/7 lists offences that to be considered 'political' in nature while also stating that it was not possible to give a precise definition of 'political, military, religious or racial matters' and that each case should be examined separately.[26] It thus follows the international motion towards a depoliticisation of terrorist offences for the purpose of facilitating cross-border cooperation.[27] Secondly, the countries' legislations and policies still differ very much from each other and tensions between States remain. This international context is not conducive to trust and to a same precise understanding of criminal offences, including terrorist ones.

Interpol provides its Member States and designated partner organisations five core functions or services:

1. Secure global police communications services: Interpol designed and implemented a state-of-the-art global communications system for the law enforcement community, called 'I-24/7'. Connecting States via the Interpol National Central Bureaus (NCBs), this communication tool allows for the transmission of data about suspected individuals, criminals and crimes between competent national authorities requiring assistance with ongoing transnational investigations in a secure, real-time manner. This network links police agencies, the Secretariat General offices, NCBs and other bureaus or sub-bureaus. It also enables authorised users to share sensitive and urgent information with their counterparts around the globe.
2. Global databases and data services: Once police have the capability to communicate internationally, they need access to information which can assist investigations or help prevent crime. Interpol has therefore developed and maintains 18 global databases and data services, covering key information, including personal data, such as names, fingerprints, photographs, DNA profiles of

[24] Art. 34(3), 'INTERPOL's Rules on the Processing of Data' III/IRPD/GA/2011(2019), Resolution AG/2019/RES/02 adopting amendments to INTERPOL's Rules on the Processing of Data, 88th General Assembly session.

[25] Interpol, General Assembly Resolution AGN/20/RES/11 (1951).

[26] Interpol, AGN/53/RES/6 (1984), 'Violent Crime commonly referred to as Terrorism'; AGN/53/RES/7 (1984), 'Application of Article 3 of the Constitution'. See, James Sheptycki, 'Brand Interpol' in *Trust in International Police and Justice Cooperation*, eds., Saskia Hufnagel and Carole McCartney, Oñati International Series in Law and Society (Oxford: Hart Publishing, 2017): 109.

[27] See, specifically mentioning Interpol's role, S/RES/2395(2017).

individuals under investigation or wanted for arrest as well as data concerning Stolen and Lost identification and Travel Documents (SLTD), stolen vehicles, stolen works of art and illicit weapons related to criminal cases. Competent national authorities voluntarily populate these databases and search them in real time as part of their investigations. In particular, international requests for cooperation or alerts, also called 'Interpol Notices', allow police officers to share information related to specific crimes.[28]

3. Operational police support services: Interpol provides operational police support services in the diverse priority crime areas, such as drugs and organised crime, financial and high-tech crime, fugitives, public safety and terrorism, trafficking in human beings (including crimes against children) and corruption. Interpol convenes theme-oriented specialised working groups which bring together experts from around the world to share expertise and develop and promote best practice concerning investigation techniques.
4. Operational and strategic analysis: Interpol conducts thematic criminal analysis in order to, *inter alia*, detect new crime trends, trace criminal networks, determine *modus operandi* and identify perpetrators. In addition to specific crime area support, Interpol operates a Command and Co-ordination Centre ('CCC') 24/7, linking the General Secretariat, regional offices and all NCBs for urgent police-related matter or emergency. The CCC coordinates the exchange of information between Member States requesting assistance with international investigations. It also assumes a crisis-management role during serious incidents and serves as the first point of contact for any Member State which might require assistance with a crisis situation. In addition, upon request of a State, Interpol can deploy Incidence Response Teams (IRT) which have the capacity to provide a range of investigative and analytical support to the local law enforcement authorities at the scene of an incident.
5. Training and Development: Interpol enhances the capacity of Member States to effectively combat serious transnational crime and terrorism, through the provision of (a) focused police training initiatives and of (b) on-demand advice, guidance and support in building dedicated crime-fighting components with national police forces. The latter includes the sharing of knowledge, skills and best practices about policing through Interpol channels and the establishment of global standards on how to combat specific forms of crimes.

Besides the different Interpol offices, the Interpol Global Complex for Innovation (IGCI), established in Singapore in 2014, must be discussed. Adapting its support to evolving threats, the IGCI is designed to equip the world's law enforcement agencies with the tools and knowledge to better tackle the criminal threats of the twenty-first century, particularly cybercrime, by providing a sophisticated research and development facility for the identification of crimes and criminals, innovative training, operational support and partnerships. The IGCI is not merely another regular

[28] On the different types of Notices, see the following link: https://www.interpol.int/How-we-work/Notices/About-Notices (accessed on 28 February 2020).

regional office, but rather aims to be a more specialised office complementing the headquarters in France. By having Interpol in the region, there is an element of proximity that helps to disseminate knowledge and allows for direct contact, especially as the IGCI provides the authorities with trainings.

The perpetual challenge for Interpol as a hub of information and intelligence is the need for accurate sources as well as timely and relevant information. Despite the range of data systems available and the progress made by certain States in connecting them, Interpol remains far from being a streamlined global data sharing facility. Irrespective of any technical and technological issues of compatibility, many States do not have national or local databases of key and critical information, and/or do not have the legislations fostering the exchange of data with external partners. The opportunity for effective data sharing is significantly increased where it can be shown to be useful and where the recipient(s) might be relied upon to respect the level of confidentiality attached to it.[29]

On a global level, discrepancies and tensions between countries are far from being uncommon. Building up and maintaining mutual trust is accordingly not an easy task. In particular, as there is no legal obligation for law enforcement officers to cooperate together, mutual trust is not acting in its legal dimension, but is rather defined by its political and social dimensions. Competent national authorities develop these dimensions of mutual trust to facilitate cooperation and streamline the flow of data.

C. A combination of cooperation activities to build up mutual trust

Although such cooperation is generally required by international organisations, as the United Nations, and facilitated by Interpol, States are unlikely to cooperate when they do not trust each other and/or when their objectives differ. The UN has recognised that the lack of mutual trust impedes the good development and functioning of cooperation mechanisms.[30] The UN pinpoints trust as a necessary support and complement to the legal rules and willingness of competent authorities. Legal and political requirements cannot replace or avoid the need for the social dimension of mutual trust between competent authorities. However, despite international calls to cooperate by sharing data, best practices and experiences, achieving this on a global scale is hardly effective in practice, especially due to the climate of mistrust amongst States. This mistrust results from significant differences between political regimes and legislations in criminal matters (both substantive and procedural), from differences in terms of degree of human rights protection, including data protection, and from overly bureaucratic procedures when confronted with transnational cases.

---

[29] Stuart Cameron-Waller, 'Interpol. A global service provider' in *Combating international crime. The longer arm of the law*, ed., Steven David Brown (London: Routledge, 2008): 56.

[30] See, e.g., pts. 33, 40, 77 and 141, S/2015/683, Letter dated 2 September 2015 from the Chair of the Security Council Committee established pursuant to resolution 1373(2001) concerning counter-terrorism addressed to the President of the Security Council, Annex 'Implementation of Security Council Resolution 2178(2014) by States affected by foreign fighters', Second report, 2 September 2015.

In this global legal framework, the competent national authorities combine formal and informal interactions across borders. There are rules on cooperation but there is also a grey zone allowing field officers to cooperate outside any legal framework. In both cases, mutual trust is essential. On the one side, trust is unavoidable for formal mechanisms of cooperation to be operationalised and, on the other, informal cooperation would not even exist without mutual trust between the relevant authorities. International summits constitute an important opportunity for such relations. In addition to official dialogues and interactions, many subjects are actually discussed unofficially as asides.

These two forms of interactions are inductive and conducive of the building of trust. In both cases, but certainly most significantly in informal interactions, social skills catalyse cooperation among people, i.e. foreign counterparts.[31] This is the reason for the UN Office on Drugs and Crime (UNODC) organising training, workshops and other events for competent national authorities to meet, familiarise with each other and discuss current and future cooperation (*information and experience sharing* cluster). This occurs in both regions; but it must be noted that the UNODC is much more active in ASEAN in this aspect. It is quite clear that informal cooperation works better between peer-to-peer officers who actually know one another and who share the same *esprit de corps*. However, the quite quick turnover of officers, particularly noticeable in ASEAN, is the main issue which arises when there is only a social dimension associated with mutual trust.

Thus, as an international 'legislator', the UN provides a very broad legal umbrella (light *capability building*) and, as a support via its agencies, it helps States develop tools and means to combat terrorism, including fostering cross-border cooperation (*capacity building*; rather strategic *knowledge and experience sharing*). In contrast, it can be argued that the work done through Interpol is much more operational than that which is fostered by the United Nations. Interpol is bared from having any direct influence on national legal frameworks (no *capability building*). It focuses solely on *information and experience sharing*. However, a smooth flow of data can only occur when law enforcement authorities have the political, legal and technological means to cooperate. For this reason, Interpol has also assisted countries through its expertise and technical support (*capacity building*).

The UN, through the General Assembly[32] and the Security Council,[33] has promoted regional organisations' work against threats to peace and security, including terrorism. Following the UN requirements, States are required to make use of relevant regional frameworks, as intermediary platforms, to build up mutual trust,

---

[31] Neil Fligstein, 'Social Skill and the Theory of Fields' *Sociological Theory*, vol. 19, no. 2 (2001).

[32] See, e.g., A/70/328, *Cooperation between United Nations and regional and subregional organizations on mediation.* Report of the Secretary-General, 87th session, 19 August 2015.

[33] Among the recent resolutions, almost all of them include a reference to the necessary role of the regional organisations: e.g. S/RES/2178(2014); S/RES/2195(2014); S/RES/2199(2015); S/RES/2368(2017); S/RES/2395(2017); S/RES/2396(2017); S/RES/2482(2019).

and to share information and intelligence for the prevention and combating of terrorism.

II. Regional cooperation mechanisms fostered by and/or vectors of mutual trust: two different methods and level of engagements

Regional organisations take into account their local specificities and they are, therefore, intended to be more effective in developing cooperation mechanisms. However, the Member States' willingness to engage in integrated and binding forms of cooperation is much higher in the EU (A) than in ASEAN, where it is almost non-existing (B). The two regions are analysed in chronological order of development.

A. Looking for more efficiency in intra-EU cooperation: the operationalisation of the three-dimensional mutual trust

Cooperation in criminal matters within the EU started under the umbrella of conventions adopted in the framework of the Council of Europe, e.g., the 1957 Council of Europe (CoE) *European Convention on Extradition* and its four protocols[34] and the 1959 *European Convention on Mutual Assistance in Criminal Matters,*[35] and complemented by the 1978 Additional Protocol[36] and 2001 second Additional Protocol.[37] The 1959 CoE Convention laid down the multilateral will of States parties to develop mutual legal assistance in criminal matters and developed an interesting model for cooperation complementing the mechanism of cooperation on extradition.[38] However, these conventions remained quite traditional, with much respect given to national sovereignty. Yet, whereas the CoE has played a significant normative role in developing judicial cooperation in criminal matters, its normative role in fostering cooperation between law enforcement authorities has remained extremely limited. Focusing on the terrorism-related instruments, only the most recent norms require States to cooperate in that field.[39] Although 'law enforcement authorities and other bodies' are, in general, identified as key actors in the prevention

---

[34] Council of Europe, *European Convention on Extradition*, ETS No. 24, Paris, 13 December 1957, ratified by all EU Member States. Also, *Additional Protocol to the European Convention on Extradition*, ETS No. 86, Strasbourg, 15 October 1975; *Second Additional Protocol to the European Convention on Extradition,* ETS No. 98, Strasbourg, 17 March 1978; *Third Additional Protocol to the European Convention on Extradition,* ETS No. 209, Strasbourg, 10 November 2010; *Fourth Additional Protocol to the European Convention on Extradition,* ETS No. 212, Vienna, 20 September 2012.

[35] CoE, *European Convention on Mutual Assistance in Criminal Matters*, ETS No. 30, Strasbourg, 20 April 1959, ratified by all EU Member States.

[36] CoE, *Additional Protocol to the European Convention on Mutual Assistance in Criminal Matters*, ETS No. 99, Strasbourg, 17 March 1978, ratified by all EU Member States.

[37] CoE, *Second Additional Protocol to the European Convention on Mutual Assistance in Criminal Matters*, ETS No. 182, Strasbourg, 1 February 2001, ratified by all EU Member States, except for Greece and Luxembourg which only signed this Protocol.

[38] Vervaele, 'Mutual Trust in Gathering of Evidence at the EU Level' (2014).

[39] Art. 2, CoE, *Convention on the Prevention of Terrorism* (2005).

of terrorism,[40] and the importance of exchange of information is underlined,[41] Article 4 of the *Convention on the Prevention of Terrorism* dealing with international cooperation does not name any specific competent national authorities in charge of this task. In contrast, cooperation between law enforcement authorities has been institutionalised and regulated in the EU.

The EU legal framework related to police and judicial cooperation is extremely developed and much has been written about it.[42] For this reason, the description of the EU legal framework on cooperation does not pretend to be exhaustive and thus does not need to be described in great detail below. However, the main trends need to be highlighted to demonstrate how the EU has been working on the development of a regional legal framework that has fostered direct peer-to-peer cooperation, going far beyond international norms. Whereas it is only after 9/11 that the EU legislator approximated national substantive criminal legislations to support cooperation in the field of counterterrorism (cf. Chap. 5), cooperation on terrorism-related issues started long before that. But, most of the relevant instruments developing cooperation, including those fostering information exchange, are of a transversal nature, not specific to counterterrorism. There is hardly any requirement for cooperation in any of the 2002 and 2008 Council Framework Decisions as well as the 2017 Directive.[43] Notably, information sharing was the subject of intense discussions during the debates on the proposal for the *Directive on combating terrorism* at the LIBE Committee.[44] However, without successful agreement, no provision requiring cooperation appeared clearly in the final version of the 2017 Directive. The necessity of sharing information and good practices appears briefly in the Directive and lacks any precision on the form and manner in which such cooperation should take

[40] Art. 3(1), Ibid.

[41] Art. 3(2), Ibid.

[42] For an extensive, but non-exhaustive, list, see the bibliography. Among others, see, e.g., Didier Bigo, *Polices en Réseaux: L'Expérience Européenne* (Paris: Presse de Science Po, 1996); Chevallier-Govers, *De la coopération à l'intégration policière dans l'Union Européenne* (1999); Daniel Flore, 'Le mandat d'arrêt européen: première mise en oeuvre d'un nouveau paradigme de la justice pénale européenne' *Journal des Tribunaux*, vol. 121, no. 6050 (2002); Anne Weyembergh, 'La Coopération Pénale Européenne Face au Terrorisme: Rupture ou Continuité?' in *Le Droit International Face au Terrorisme*, eds., Karine Bannelier et al. (Paris: Pedone, 2002); Weyembergh, 'L'Espace Pénal Européen' (2004); Hufnagel and McCartney, *Trust in International Police and Justice Cooperation* (2017); Carrera et al., 'Criminal Justice and Police Cooperation between the EU and the UK after Brexit' (2018); Anne Weyembergh, 'Enhanced cooperation in criminal matters: past, present and future' in *Vielfalt des Strafrechts im internationalen Kontext*, eds., Robert Kert and Andrea Lehner (Wien: Neuer Wissenschaftlicher Verlag, 2018).

[43] Art. 9(2), *Council Framework Decision 2002/475/JHA on combating terrorism*; Art. 19(3), *Directive 2017/541 on combating terrorism*.

[44] See Monika Hohlmeier's speech at the European Parliament, Rapporteur of the European Parliament's Committee on Civil Liberties, Justice and Home Affairs on the proposal of Directive on combating terrorism, Brussels, 15 February 2017: available at http://www.europarl.europa.eu/doceo/document/CRE-8-2017-02-15_EN.html#creitem36 (accessed on 27 September 2019).

place.[45] These instruments have nonetheless aided competent national authorities to ensure that similar substantive provisions apply, i.e. that terrorist offences are defined in a similar way in the different EU countries, and thus that they have the necessary substantive basis to support streamlined cooperation amongst competent national authorities.

Apart from these EU counterterrorism norms, transversal ones have been adopted to facilitate cross-border cooperation. Enhanced methods of information and intelligence sharing have indeed been at the centre of cross-border cooperation undertakings against transnational crime, including terrorism.[46] These methods have evolved considerably from pure intergovernmental and traditional nature (1) towards a more integrated EU response vis-à-vis transnational criminal challenges (2).

1. Pure intergovernmental cooperation: the first steps towards the development of mutual trust and data sharing

In the absence of an EU autonomous regional legal framework, the sharing of information and intelligence was primarily based on formal bilateral or multilateral (such as those of the Council of Europe or the Benelux ones) agreements in the field of judicial cooperation and on informal cooperation between law enforcement authorities. It slowly shifted towards EU specific methods of cooperation along with the regional integration process, without preventing Member States from creating enhanced cooperation either outside the EU institutional framework or, later on, within such Union framework (cf. the next part).

When the European Communities (EC) were established, cooperation in criminal matters was not among their competences. It was, at that time, hampered by fears of losing national prerogatives. The first efforts to strengthen police and judicial cooperation between the EC members date back to the 1970s. Outside the Communities framework, within the 'European Political Cooperation', these efforts were motivated by the need to respond to transnational security threats, particularly terrorism.[47] It is in this context that in 1976, the TREVI[48] Group (*Terrorisme, Radicalisme, Extrémisme et Violence Internationale*) was established. This group operates at three levels: the Ministerial level (meetings of Interior Ministers), the TREVI Senior Officials group and the working parties (meetings of Interior/Home Ministry officials, senior police officers, immigration and customs officials and internal security service representatives). TREVI aimed at providing a common operational response, through the harmonisation of methods and most importantly

[45] In several paragraphs of the preamble, *Directive 2017/541*.

[46] On the definitions of 'information' and 'intelligence', see Cocq, "'Information' and 'intelligence'" (2017); also see Chap. 2.

[47] Weyembergh, 'L'impact du 11 septembre sur l'équilibre sécurité/liberté dans l'espace pénal européen' (2002).

[48] TREVI was the forum of the operational cooperation between ministries of justice and internal affairs of the Member States. It was formalised on 29 June 1972 in Luxembourg at a meeting between the European Community Interior Ministers and it functioned till the entering into force of the TEU.

by sharing experiences, best practices, information and intelligence on current trends against terrorist groups such as the IRA, the Red Brigade and the Baader–Meinhof group including sharing (*information and experience sharing*). The TREVI Group swiftly grew to encompass the combating of other forms of transnational crime.[49] TREVI Group I was in charge of information sharing related to terrorist activities and was assigned to police cooperation in this area. TREVI Group II dealt with exchange of information related to breaches of the peace and worked on training, equipment and technical problems such as ballistic examinations. TREVI Group III was created in 1985 to combat organised crime. TREVI Group IV, created in 1988, dealt with the circulation of people. The TREVI cooperation ended on 1 November 1993 when the Treaty on the EU entered into force, which encompasses a Third Pillar concerning cooperation in the field of 'justice and home affairs'. This pillar included the EU asylum policy, rules governing the crossing of the Union's external borders, immigration policy and policy regarding third-country nationals, combating drug addiction and fraud on an international scale, judicial cooperation in civil and criminal matters, and customs and police cooperation.

Apart from the TREVI Group, the French President Giscard d'Estaing presented its project leading towards the creation of a European area for judicial cooperation in criminal matters during the European Councils of 1976, 1977 and 1978.[50] The objective of these initiatives was to tighten interstate relations in the field of criminal justice. However, as the texts adopted were not ratified by all the Member States, they never entered into force.

With the 1986 *Single European Act*, the objective was to establish a single market and to facilitate the free movement of persons within the region. However, due to disagreements among Member States with regard to its implementation, the initial deadline to lift controls at internal borders could not be met. Realising this limit during the negotiations, five Member States, namely France, Germany, Belgium, Luxembourg and the Netherlands, signed the *Schengen Agreement* on 14 June 1985.[51] The 1985 *Agreement between the Governments of the States of the Benelux Economic Union, the Federal Republic of Germany and the French Republic on the gradual abolition of checks at their common borders*, also known as Schengen I, intended to establish an area where checks at common borders would be abolished, but would be transferred to external borders and reinforced.[52] In order to safeguard a high level of security, parties were meant to open discussions on several subjects, including drawing up arrangements for police cooperation, examining difficulties that might arise in applying agreements on international judicial assistance and

[49] TREVI Group, Programme of Action relating to the reinforcement of police cooperation and of the endeavours to combat terrorism or other forms of organized crime, June 1990, para. 3.

[50] Weyembergh, 'L'Espace Pénal Européen' (2004): 249.

[51] *Schengen Agreement of 14 June 1985 between the Governments of the States of the Benelux Economic Union, the Federal Republic of Germany and the French Republic on the gradual abolition of checks at their common borders*, Schengen, 14 June 1985.

[52] Art. 17, *Schengen Agreement.*

extradition and seeking means to combat crime jointly. The 1985 Agreement was then complemented by the 1990 *Convention implementing the Schengen Agreement* (CISA),[53] through which the parties agreed specifically to assist each other for the purpose of preventing and detecting criminal offences via identified central bodies.[54] This was a new step towards a more integrated police and judicial cooperation.

The CISA contains concrete and innovative provisions regarding police cooperation. Certain provisions deal with cross-border surveillance (Article 40), or cross-border 'hot pursuit' over land borders (Article 41). These provisions are particularly representative of the States Parties' will to go beyond the existence of borders and to establish a real Schengen area. In addition to police cooperation, the Convention provides for obligations in the field of judicial cooperation. In this respect, two types of provisions are to be mentioned as they are representative of a clear increase of ambitions in line with the idea of 'area'. On the one hand, those provisions on mutual legal assistance provide for the possibility of a direct transmission of rogatory letters between judicial authorities, thus avoiding the use of diplomatic channels (Article 53). On the other hand, the enactment of the *ne bis in idem* principle, which receives a transnational scope, also demonstrates this trend (Article 54). Other interesting provisions concern extradition (Articles 59–66) and the transfer of prisoners (Articles 67 and ff.).

On a more practical note, the Schengen Information System (SIS) was established, which emerged as an operational, computer-aided recording and query system to search for persons and objects, operated among the Schengen Contracting States, while respecting data protection standards. The SIS is often considered the keystone of the Schengen Agreement. Its purpose is 'to maintain public policy and public security, including national security, in the territories of the Contracting Parties and to apply the provisions of this Convention relating to the movement of persons in those territories, using information communicated via this system'.[55] It encompasses two parts: a central technical support, namely C-SIS, and a national part, namely the N-SIS. The national systems do not support online cross-border information sharing; only the C-SIS does.[56] Each State maintains its own national system.[57] The national part of the SIS is made up of two sub-parts: the computer system as such and the national Bureau responsible for its operational management called SIRENE (Supplementary Information Request at the National Entry). This last instance establishes a single point of contact in every country, available on a permanent basis. It is the Schengen equivalent of the Interpol National Central

[53] *Convention implementing the Schengen Agreement of 14 June 1985 between the Governments of the Benelux Economic Union, the Federal Republic of Germany and the French Republic*, Schengen, 19 June 1990 (hereafter referred to as 'CISA').

[54] Arts. 39–47, CISA.

[55] Art. 93, CISA.

[56] Vendelin Hreblay, *La libre circulation des personnes. Les accords de Schengen*, Politique d'aujourd'hui (Paris: Presses Universitaires de France, 1994): 164 and ff.

[57] Art. 92(3), CISA.

Bureaus (NCBs). These SIRENEs are connected by protected telecommunications systems and constitute the human interface of the SIS. The success of this system is to have combined the conjunction of officials from different origins (police, border officers, magistrates) and a permanent material structure. SIRENE's main tasks are data sharing and providing advice and information on the procedures implemented.

The SIS is accompanied by strict requirements on data quality and data protection. The access to data by competent national authorities, namely those competent to carry out controls at the borders, is governed by Article 101 dealing with the access to data entered in the SIS and the right to search such data directly. These authorities have access to information only for the purpose of their mission (purpose limitation). Personal data integrated in the SIS for search purposes are retained until the end of their purpose, for maximum 3 years.[58] Personal data integrated in the system on the basis of indications cannot be retained for longer than 1 year. Additionally, non-personal data cannot be retained for longer than 10 years.[59]

Yet, the *Schengen Convention* provides that, as regards the automatic processing of personal data, the Contracting Parties have to ensure the protection of personal data 'at least equal to that resulting from the Council of Europe *Convention for the Protection of Individuals with regard to Automatic Processing of Personal Data* of 28 January 1981'.[60] The Convention might provide the rules, while the Member States are in charge of ensuring a minimum of protection. Discrepancies might therefore exist between Member States' legislations, which might impact cross-border cooperation. Besides, only States, owners of their data, are competent to modify, complete, rectify and erase their data.[61] Already with the CISA, individuals have the right to access data entered in the SIS according to national legislation. This access might be refused if this is indispensable for the performance of a lawful task in connection with the alert or for the protection of the rights and freedoms of third parties.[62] The individuals concerned can also request that their personal data be deleted.[63]

Since its establishment, the SIS has evolved considerably, both geographically (SISOne4ALL) and content-wise (introduction of new alerts categories, types of data and rules governing the access to data in SIS II). The SIS has become the most widely used and efficient IT/Alerts systems of the EU in criminal matters.

The added value of this system is undeniable. Detections (known as 'hits') processed by the SIRENE Bureaus, which are used to measure the usage and relevance of the system, have more than doubled in number between 2014 and 2019, reaching on average 777 hits per day in 2019. In operational terms, this means that SIS II supports competent national authorities' actions. The numbers

[58] Art. 112, CISA.

[59] Art. 113, CISA.

[60] Art. 126(1), CISA.

[61] Art. 106(1), CISA.

[62] Art. 119, CISA.

[63] Art. 110, CISA.

demonstrate the usefulness of the system. For instance, in 2017, SIS II was accessed more than 5.1 billion times by Member States, triggering more than 240.000 hits on foreign alerts (alerts issued by another country).[64] In 2019, SIS II was accessed more than 6.6 times than it was in 2014. The number of alerts also increased, growing from more than 76 million at the end of 2018 to more than 91 million at the end of 2019.[65]

Since Summer 2022, the Regulation on the establishment, operation and use of the SIS in the field of police cooperation and judicial cooperation in criminal matters grants Europol the right to access and search data in SIS as well as additional rights to process and exchange data provided by EU Member States, within its mandate, after an alert in SIS is revealed by a search of Europol in the system. It also allows Europol to propose that information alerts be entered into SIS under specific conditions.[66]

2. The progressive move towards a more integrated EU response vis-à-vis transnational criminal challenges

After the initial steps achieved outside the EC/EU institutional framework, cross-border cooperation in criminal matters was integrated into the intergovernmental Third Pillar of the 1992 Treaty of Maastricht. At that time, Schengen cooperation continued to develop outside the EU structure. The 1997 Treaty of Amsterdam maintained the predominant intergovernmental nature of the Third Pillar but brought it closer to the Community model. With the Protocol on Schengen annexed to the Treaty of Amsterdam, the 'Schengen *Acquis*' was incorporated in the EU's 'Acquis'.[67]

[64] Council of the EU, 'SIS II – 2017 Statistics' eu-LISA to Delegations, No. 8279/18, Brussels, 24 April 2018.

[65] For the numbers of 2019, Report of the EU Agency for the Operational Management of Large-Scale IT Systems in the Area of Freedom, Security and Justice (eu-LISA), 'SIS II – 2019 Annual Statistics' (March 2020). The number of searches obviously fell 44% in 2020 due to the covid-19 pandemic: 'SIS II – 2020 Annual Statistics' (March 2021).

[66] European Commission, *Regulation (EU) 2018/1862 on the establishment, operation and use of the Schengen Information System (SIS) in the field of police cooperation and judicial cooperation in criminal matters, amending and repealing Council Decision 2007/533/JHA, and repealing Regulation (EC) No 1986/2006 of the European Parliament and of the Council and Commission Decision 2010/261/EU*, O.J.E.U. L312/56, 7 July 2018; as amended by *Regulation (EU) 2022/1190 of the European Parliament and of the Council of 6 July 2022 amending Regulation (EU) 2108/1862 as regards the entry of information alerts into the Schengen Information System (SIS) on third-country nationals in the interest of the Union*, O.J.E.U. L185/1, 12 July 2022.

[67] See the Protocol to the Amsterdam Treaty integrating the Schengen *Acquis* in the framework of the EU and its annex identifying what is the Schengen *Acquis*, available at: https://europa.eu/european-union/sites/europaeu/files/docs/body/treaty_of_amsterdam_en.pdf (accessed on 11 July 2017). Also, the last instrument demonstrating its integration into the EU legal framework, *Regulation 2018/1862 on the establishment, operation and use of SIS in the field of police cooperation and judicial cooperation in criminal matters*.

(a) *The development of judicial cooperation*

Since the introduction of criminal matters into the EU competence, the EU's activities in the field have progressively intensified. The deepening of the European integration and the increasing mobility of persons, goods, services and capital in the regional internal market made it become clear that there was a growing need for a stronger legal regime of judicial cooperation in criminal matters among EU Member States.[68] Among the representative efforts made under the Third Pillar of the Maastricht Treaty, one should mention the EU Convention of 1995 on simplified extradition procedure,[69] the EU Convention of 1996 on extradition[70] as well as the 2000 *Convention on Mutual Assistance in Criminal Matters between the Member States of the European Union*[71] (EU MLA Convention) and its Protocol of 2001.

The EU MLA Convention did not intend to replace the Council of Europe's arsenal in the field, but to instead complement it. Two main objectives were pursued. It intended, firstly, to modernise MLA and, secondly, to make MLA more effective between EU Member States and specific to the EU legal framework. The 2000 Convention includes a series of provisions that adapt mutual assistance to new technologies. Compared to the 1959 *European Convention on Mutual Assistance*, the 2000 Convention diversifies the number of investigative acts, including hearings by videoconference (Article 10), hearings of witnesses and experts by teleconference (Article 11) and interceptions of telecommunications (Articles 17–22). Among the changes aimed at improving MLA, one can mention the four following ideas: an extension of competent authorities, the generalisation of direct contacts, the relaxation of the classic *locus regit actum* rule and the establishment of Joint Investigation Teams (JITs).

The MLA Convention widens the understanding of competent authorities beyond the classic 'judicial authorities' (public prosecutors, investigating magistrates),[72] opening the possibility to include administrative law enforcement agencies under certain conditions.[73] These administrative authorities are competent only if they have punitive sanctioning powers and if most of the evidence gathering occurs at a pre-stage of criminal investigation and prosecution.

The Convention clearly favours direct contact. Direct contact does not mean that a request from a requesting authority in State A automatically has legal value in State

[68] Vervaele, 'Mutual Trust in Gathering of Evidence at the EU Level' (2014).

[69] *Council Act of 10 March 1995 adopted on the basis of Article K.3 of the Treaty on European Union, drawing up the Convention on simplified extradition procedure between the Member States of the European Union*, O.J.E.C. C78/1, 30 March 1995.

[70] *Council Act of 27 September 1996 adopted on the basis of Article K.3 of the Treaty on European Union, drawing up the Convention relating to extradition between the Member States of the European Union*, O.J.E.C. C313/11, 23 June 1996.

[71] *Council Act of 29 May 2000 establishing in accordance with Article 34 of the Treaty on European Union the Convention on Mutual Assistance in Criminal Matters between the Member States of the European Union*, O.J.E.C. C197/1, 12 July 2000.

[72] Art. 3, CoE, *European Convention on Mutual Assistance in Criminal Matters* (1959).

[73] Art. 3(1), *Convention on Mutual Assistance in Criminal Matters between the Member States of the European Union* (2000).

B of the requested authority. These warrants must be converted into a national decision in the requested State through *exequatur* proceedings. It means that under the terms of Article 6(1) requests are transmitted directly between judicial authorities without going through the ministries of justice. The possibility of going through the central authorities is maintained, but only in special cases which should remain exceptional (Article 6(2)).

When executing a request for mutual assistance, the Requested States apply their own procedure, but they accept in principle to respect any procedure that the Requesting State has expressly requested them to follow, provided however that it is not contrary to the fundamental principles of their own law (Article 4). In doing so, the 2000 Convention softens the classic *locus regit actum* adage, by enabling the *forum regit actum* adage. The main interest in this change is, of course, to strengthen, in the requesting Member State, which is also the judgment State, the usefulness of the information and evidence collected in the Requested State. Accordingly, and to ensure as far as possible the admissibility of evidence, the requesting authority should, in the request, ensure that it clearly expresses the formalities and procedures which must be applied in the Requested State.[74] The MLA Convention also contains the legal basis for the establishment of JITs, composed of judicial, police and/or customs officials of the Member States, and even of Europol. This method was later developed in the *Council Framework Decision 2002/465/JHA on Joint Investigation Teams.*[75] This mechanism has proved effective in terms of transmission of information and evidence collected. For a limited period and for a well-defined purpose, a JIT brings together investigators from several countries. It is therefore an *ad hoc* 'pluri-national' team set up to carry out criminal investigations in one or more Member States which create the team. Its creation requires a written agreement between the authorities concerned. This agreement details its operating procedures and its composition. The team may be composed of persons from the police, customs or other competent law enforcement services and of judicial authorities from at least two Member States. Once created, the JIT offers clear advantages over the mutual legal assistance regime normally applicable: operational powers for agents even outside their home territory, free exchange of information within the team, access to investigative measures in all the States concerned without going through a letter rogatory. Although they were not specifically used for counterterrorism, JITs have become a crucial tool in this field. It has been particularly useful in the aftermath of the Paris and Brussels attacks in 2015 and 2016.

The 2000 MLA Convention was enriched in 2001 with an Additional Protocol,[76] aiming to improve MLA in the banking sector. The 2001 Protocol mainly aims to manage mutual assistance relating to three types of mutual assistance requests in this

[74] Vervaele, 'Mutual Trust in Gathering of Evidence at the EU Level' (2014): 217.

[75] *Council Framework Decision 2002/465/JHA on Joint Investigation Teams.*

[76] *Protocol established by the Council in accordance with Article 34 of the Treaty on European Union to the Convention on Mutual Assistance in Criminal Matters between the Member States of the European Union*, O.J.E.C. 326/2, 21 November 2001.

sector: requests for information on bank accounts (Article 1), on banking transactions (Article 2) and requests for monitoring banking transactions (Article 3). These requests were already covered by the general instruments of mutual legal assistance. But the protocol details the binding regime for mutual aid in this sector and thus makes it possible to overcome the specific obstacles faced by mutual aid. It also includes various provisions relating to certain classic grounds for refusing assistance. The protocol removes or mitigates other grounds for refusing mutual assistance. It especially removes the ground for refusal based on banking secrecy,[77] which was not explicitly referred to, but could be considered as covered by Article 2(2) of the 1959 Convention and was often invoked by certain Member States.

These EU norms were inspired by the CoE's instruments (not by the UN MLA Model Treaty) and intended to develop and strengthen direct cooperation between Member States. The EU norms have in turn greatly influenced the CoE's work as is evidenced by the second Protocol to the CoE Convention on MLA[78] completely mimicking the 2000 EU MLA Convention.

Since the adoption of the 1999 Tampere Programme, under the Third Pillar of the Amsterdam and Nice Treaties, judicial cooperation in criminal matters was founded on the principle of mutual recognition. With this mutual recognition process, judicial cooperation in the EU has a much more ambitious and integrated process than in the wider CoE framework.

As previously shown, the principle of mutual recognition was implemented through the adoption of several EU legislative instruments, among which the 2002 *Council Framework Decision on the European Arrest Warrant* (EAW) *and surrender procedures between Member States.*[79] This mechanism has simplified and accelerated extradition proceedings, as shown by the successive evaluation reports by the European Commission, especially by its most recent report of 2020.[80] It has been presented by many as the success story of the EU area for criminal justice. It has been especially helpful when prosecuting terrorist offenders. For instance, Salah Abdeslam (French national with Moroccan origin and Belgian resident) who was among the perpetrators of the attacks on 13 November 2005 at the Bataclan (France) was arrested in Molenbeek-Saint-Jean (Belgium) and judged by French authorities. French and Belgian investigative authorities exchanged information and evidence through bilateral channels (including JITs) and Europol's channel. He was arrested in Brussels on 18 March 2016 and surrendered to France on 27 April 2016 in execution of the European arrest warrant issued by the French authorities on

---

[77] Art. 7, *Protocol to the Convention on Mutual Assistance in Criminal Matters* (2001).

[78] *Second Additional Protocol to the European Convention on Mutual Assistance in Criminal Matters* (2001).

[79] *Council Framework Decision 2002/584/JHA on the European arrest warrant.*

[80] European Commission, 'Report from the Commission to the European Parliament and the Council on the implementation of Council Framework Decision of 13 June 2002 on the European arrest warrant and the surrender procedures between Member States', COM(2020) 270 final, Brussels, 2 July 2020. Also, Vervaele, 'Mutual Trust in Gathering of Evidence at the EU Level' (2014); Xanthopoulou, *Fundamental Rights and Mutual Trust in the Area of Freedom, Security and Justice* (2020).

19 March 2016. This instrument is another piece against criminals trying to use national borders as protection.[81]

Besides, among EU legislative acts implementing the mutual recognition principle, must be highlighted the *Council Framework Decision 2003/577/JHA of 22 July 2003 on the execution in the European Union of orders freezing property or evidence*[82] and the *Council Framework Decision 2008/978/JHA of 18 December 2008 on the European evidence warrant for the purpose of obtaining objects, documents and data for use in proceedings in criminal matters.*[83] However, due to difficulties occurring in the negotiations, the latter was a complete failure. It was subsequently replaced by the 2014 *Directive on the European investigation order*[84] which was adopted after the Lisbon Treaty entered into force.

The *Directive on the European Investigation Order* (EIO) illustrates the increasing level of integration of judicial cooperation within the EU, but also and more particularly, reaching a better balance between the efficacy priority and the protection of human rights. It aims at speeding up the assistance provided by one country to another in criminal investigations.

The EIO is a judicial decision issued, or validated by a judicial authority, in an issuing Member State to have one or several specific investigative measures carried out in another Member State. The EIO is deliberately wide ranging to take into account the differing roles of the police and prosecutors in the different countries. Article 3 within the Directive states that the EIO shall cover 'any investigative measure' with the exception of measures exempted and listed in the Directive. The executing Member State must recognise the EIO unless one of the grounds for non-recognition or grounds for postponement exist. It constitutes a move away from a request for assistance in obtaining evidence, to an order for specified measures to be undertaken and for evidence already in the possession of a State to be transferred without delay.[85]

An EIO can be issued in four cases: (1) with respect to criminal proceedings that are brought by, or that might be brought before, a judicial authority in respect of a criminal offence under the national law of the issuing State; (2) in proceedings brought by administrative authorities in respect of acts which are punishable under

---

[81] On the development of the transposition and implementation of the *Council Framework Decision 2002/584/JHA on the European arrest warrant and the surrender procedures between Member States* and the remaining issues in respecting the time frames, see European Commission, 'Report on the implementation of Council Framework Decision of 13 June 2002 on the European arrest warrant and the surrender procedures between Member States' (2020). Despite these issues, this terrorist case shows that cooperation can be smoother because of the identification of a similar goal and of its high-level importance for public security.

[82] *Council Framework Decision 2003/577/JHA on the execution of orders freezing property or evidence.*

[83] *Council Framework Decision 2008/978/JHA of 18 December 2008 on the European evidence warrant for the purpose of obtaining objects, documents and data for use in proceedings in criminal matters*, O.J.E.U. L350/72, 30 December 2008.

[84] *Directive 2014/41/EU of the European Parliament and of the Council of 3 April 2014 regarding the European Investigation Order in criminal matters*, O.J. L130/1, 1 May 2014.

[85] Art. 3, Ibid.

the national law of the issuing State by virtue of being infringements of the rules of law and where the decision might give rise to proceedings before a court having jurisdiction, in particular, in criminal matters; (3) in proceedings brought by judicial authorities in respect of acts which are punishable under the national law of the issuing State by virtue of being infringements of the rule of law, and where the decision might give rise to proceedings before a court having jurisdiction, in particular, in criminal matters; and, (4) in connection with proceedings referred to in the three previous types of procedure which relate to offences of infringements for which a legal person can be held liable or punished in the issuing State.[86]

The EIO must be recognised without any formality by the executing authority. This authority must ensure its execution in the same way and under the same modalities as if the investigative measure concerned were ordered by an authority of the executing State, unless that authority decides to invoke one of the grounds for non-recognition or non-execution or one of the grounds for postponement provided for in the Directive.[87] The EIO aimed to achieve a better balance between efficacy, on the one hand, and protection of human rights, on the other, than in the Framework Decision on the European arrest warrant.[88]

Parallel to the development of mutual recognition, the establishment of ECRIS (European Criminal Records Information System) should also be mentioned. The 2009 *Council Framework Decision on the organisation and content of the exchange of information extracted from the criminal record between Member States*[89] complements, for EU Member States, Article 13 of the 1959 *European Convention on Mutual Assistance* and its protocols and replaces Article 22 of this very Convention. In addition to the obligation for the central criminal record of the sentencing State to immediately notify each conviction to the central criminal record of the State of nationality, the framework decision obliges the central criminal record of the State of nationality, on the one hand, to keep the data in question and, on the other hand, to transmit them to the central criminal record of another Member State which requests this information.[90] As ECRIS only concerns EU citizens, it was then complemented by ECRIS-TCN (for third-country nationals). Whereas ECRIS is not a centralised

[86] Art. 4, Ibid.

[87] Art. 9(1), Ibid.

[88] Notably, the grounds for non-execution of the EIO (Art. 11) are more limited than for the European Arrest Warrant (Arts. 3 and 4). Compared to the latter instrument, there is no ground for mandatory non-execution in the EIO Directive. Moreover, the grounds for non-execution must not infringe fundamental rights as enshrined in Article 6 TEU. While the principles of proportionality and necessity are mentioned in the preamble of the *Council Framework Decision 2002/584/JHA on the European Arrest Warrant*, it is stated in Article 6(1) of the EIO Directive. See, e.g., Inès Armada, 'The European Investigation Order and the Lack of European Standards for Gathering Evidence: Is a Fundamental Rights-Based Refusal the Solution?' *N.J.E.C.L.*, vol. 6, no. 1 (2015).

[89] *Council Framework Decision 2009/315/JHA of 26 February 2009 on the organisation and content of the exchange of information extracted from the criminal record between Member States*, O.J. L93/23, 7 April 2009.

[90] This framework decision of February 2009 was the subject of an implementation measure through the decision of 6 April 2009 on the creation of ECRIS (*Council Framework Decision 2009/316/*

information system but rather a connection of national criminal records, ECRIS-TCN is centralised and operated by the EU Agency for large-scale IT systems (eu-LISA).[91]

These successive steps demonstrate the increasing integration of judicial cooperation within the EU. The EU has distanced itself from the traditional relations between sovereign States which involves the deliberation of whether a specific individual should be handed over or whether mutual legal assistance should be provided.

(b) *The development of police cooperation*

After the Tampere Conclusions of 1999, which have proven to be crucial in the field of judicial cooperation, the European Council agreed in 2004 on a new 5-year plan known as The Hague Programme.[92] Operating until 2009, this multiannual programme of work covered all aspects of the AFSJ. Heavily influenced by the 9/11 terrorist attacks, it encompassed an important number of measures to enhance information and intelligence sharing, and to improve cross-border cooperation between law enforcement authorities. The Hague Programme consecrated the principle of availability pursuant to which, within the Union, a law enforcement officer of one Member State who needs information to perform his duties may obtain the information from the corresponding authorities of another Member State holding the information—taking into account the requirements of on-going investigations in the requested State.[93] This is a principle that is linked to police cooperation just as the principle of mutual recognition is linked to judicial cooperation in criminal matters. While mutual recognition aims to guarantee the free movement of criminal decisions, the principle of availability aims to guarantee the free movement of information. The Hague Programme also insisted that Member States should make full use of new technology to facilitate the exchange of information through reciprocal access to or interoperability of national databases, or direct (online) access to existing central EU databases, such as the SIS.[94]

JHA on the establishment of the European Criminal Records Information System (ECRIS) in application of Article 11 of Framework Decision 2009/315/JHA, O.J. L93/33, 7 April 2009).

[91] *Regulation (EU) 2018/1726 of the European Parliament and of the Council of 14 November 2018 on the European Union Agency for the Operational Management of Large-Scale IT Systems in the Area of Freedom, Security and Justice (eu-LISA), and amending Regulation (EC) No 1987/2006 and Council Decision 2007/533/JHA and repealing Regulation (EU) No 1077/2011*, O.J. L295/99, 21 November 2018; *Regulation (EU) 2019/816 of the European Parliament and of the Council of 17 April 2019 establishing a centralised system for the identification of Member States holding conviction information on third-country nationals and stateless persons (ECRIS-TCN) to supplement the European Criminal Records Information System and amending Regulation (EU) 2018/1726*, O.J. L135/1, 22 May 2019.

[92] *The Hague Programme* (2005).

[93] Para 2.1., *The Hague Programme*.

[94] Ibid.

A first step on the way to implement the availability principle was the adoption of the *Prüm Convention* on 27 May 2005 by Belgium, Germany, Spain, France, Luxembourg, the Netherlands and Austria. Its accession was opened to all EU Member States.[95] Similar to the rationale of the Schengen agreements launched also outside the EU institutional framework by a reduced number of Member States, the *raison d'être* of the Convention was stated in its preamble: 'in an area with free movement of persons it is important for Member States of the European Union to step up their cooperation, in order to combat terrorism, cross-border crime and illegal migration more effectively'. The Convention intended to create a system to intensify cross-border cooperation in order to face the abovementioned threats through the automated exchange of information. Among the most powerful provisions are the automated searching and comparison of DNA profiles and the automated searching of dactyloscopic data, fingerprints and vehicle registration data. The Convention did not fully implement the availability principle as it did not ensure the free movement of information, nor allowed for direct access to it by foreign counterparts. However, it is in the field of vehicle registration data where the Convention was most ambitious and saw greatest automation. For DNA and fingerprints, it was obviously more difficult as it is much more sensitive from a human rights perspective. The *Prüm Convention* was subsequently integrated into EU law and extended to all Member States through the *Council Decision 2008/615/JHA on the stepping up of cross-border cooperation, particularly in combating terrorism and cross-border crime* and the *Council Decision 2008/616/JHA on the implementation of Decision 2008/615/JHA*.[96]

On 8 December 2021, the European Commission presented a proposal for a Regulation on automated data exchange for police cooperation ('Prüm II') that aims to find a solution for efficient automated exchange of data between EU law enforcement agencies; ensure that all EU law enforcement authorities have access to relevant data; ensure that the relevant data in the Europol's database is available to EU law enforcement authorities; and, provide access to the actual data regarding a 'hit'.[97]

[95] Art. 51, *Convention between the Kingdom of Belgium, the Federal Republic of Germany, the Kingdom of Spain, the French Republic, the Grand Duchy of Luxembourg, the Kingdom of the Netherlands and the Republic of Austria on the stepping up of cross-border cooperation, particularly in combating terrorism, cross-border crime and illegal migration* (*Prüm Convention*), Prüm, 27 May 2005.

[96] *Council Decision 2008/615/JHA of 23 June 2008 on the stepping up of cross-border cooperation, particularly in combating terrorism and cross-border crime*, O.J. L210/1, 6 August 2008; *Council Decision 2008/616/JHA of 23 June 2008 on the implementation of Decision 2008/615/JHA of 23 June 2008 on the stepping up of cross-border cooperation, particularly in combating terrorism and cross-border crime*, O.J. L210/12, 6 August 2008.

[97] European Commission, Proposal for a Regulation of the European Parliament and of the Council on automated data exchange for police cooperation ('Prüm II') amending Council Decisions 2008/615/JHA and 2008/616/JHA and Regulations (EU) 2018/1726, 2019/817 and 2019/818 of the European Parliament and of the Council, COM(2021)784 final, Brussels, 8 December 2021.

Aside from the *Prüm Convention* (whose integration into the EU framework and the Europol Regulation are examined later), an array of other norms concerning police cooperation or indirectly linked to police cooperation have been adopted. These include the 2005 *Council Decision on the exchange of information and cooperation concerning terrorist offences*[98] and the 2006 'Swedish Framework Decision',[99] both of which were adopted prior to the Lisbon Treaty. Although the Schengen Information System already required Member States to exchange information on criminal issues linked to immigration, the importance of these two instruments is not to be neglected in the field of exchange of information in criminal matters. Specific to terrorist offences, the 2005 Council Decision provides for the information that can be shared with Europol and Eurojust. Member States are required to designate a specialised service within its law enforcement authorities to be equally responsible for streamlining the sharing of information with Europol and facilitating judicial cooperation between Member States and Eurojust.[100] Later, the 'Swedish Framework Decision' expanded the requirement of data sharing by establishing the rules under which Member States' law enforcement authorities can exchange information and intelligence effectively and expeditiously for the purpose of conducting criminal investigations or criminal intelligence operations. The Framework Decision is meant to ensure that procedures for cross-border data exchanges are not stricter than those applying to exchanges at national level. It regulates the conditions for exchanging information and intelligence, including time limits and admissible justifications for refusing to share data.

(c) *Developments pertaining both to judicial and police cooperation*

Other instruments belonging both to judicial cooperation in criminal matters and police cooperation were adopted after the Lisbon Treaty, such as the 2016 *Directive on the use of passenger name record (PNR) data,*[101] and the Regulations on the interoperability between EU information systems in both the field of borders and visa (2019/817), and the field of police and judicial cooperation, asylum and migration (2019/818).[102] Among them, some key mechanisms of cooperation

---

[98] *Council Decision 2005/671/JHA of 20 September 2005 on the exchange of information and cooperation concerning terrorist offences*, O.J. 253/22, 29 September 2005.

[99] *Council Framework Decision 2006/960/JHA on simplifying the exchange of information and intelligence between law enforcement authorities of the Member States of the European Union.* See also *Directive (EU) 2023/977 of the European Parliament and of the Council of 10 May 2023 on the exchange of information between the law enforcement authorities of Member States and repealing Council Framework Decision 2006/960/JHA*, O.J.E.U. L134/1, 22 May 2023.

[100] Art. 2, *Council Decision 2005/671/JHA on the exchange of information and cooperation concerning terrorist offences.*

[101] *Directive2016/681 on the use of PNR data for the prevention, detection, investigation and prosecution of terrorist offences and serious crime.*

[102] *Regulation (EU) 2019/817 of the European Parliament and of the Council of 20 May 2019 on establishing a framework for interoperability between EU information systems in the field of borders and visa and amending Regulations (EC) No 767/2008, (EU) 2016/399, (EU) 2017/ 2226, (EU) 2018/1240, (EU) 2018/1726 and (EU) 2018/1861 of the European Parliament and of*

facilitating and fostering the flow of data in criminal matters within the EU may be highlighted.

For the purpose of improving data sharing, the EU has more recently focused its attention on the development of interoperable information systems.[103] Interoperable systems are designed to exchange raw materials for investigative purposes, which at a later stage could become actual evidence at trial. Such systems challenge existing cooperation dynamics and redefine the role of the actors involved.

It is questionable whether, and to what extent, interoperable information systems[104] could become the next step towards an even more integrated mode of cooperation within the AFSJ.[105] In this attempt of reforming the whole EU data sharing system, the *Regulation 2019/818 on the interoperability between EU information systems in the field of police and judicial cooperation* has an ambitious purpose.[106]

This Regulation, together with Regulation 2019/817,[107] establishes a framework to ensure interoperability between the following EU information systems: the Entry/Exit System (EES), the Visa Information System (VIS), the European Travel Information and Authorisation System (ETIAS), Eurodac, the Schengen Information System (SIS) and the European Criminal Records Information System for third-country nationals (ECRIS-TCN). The objectives of these two Regulations are, *inter alia*, to improve the effectiveness and efficiency of border checks at the EU's external borders and to combat illegal immigration by connecting all centralised databases in the AFSJ. In addition, the Regulations seek to streamline law enforcement access to stored information in order to contribute to the prevention, detection and investigation of terrorist offences and of other serious crime, and to facilitate the identification of unknown persons. For these databases to be useful, the stored information need not only be complete, accurate and reliable, but also instantly available.[108] Interestingly, the Regulations also adapt the procedures and conditions

---

the Council and Council Decisions 2004/512/EC and 2008/633/JHA, O.J. L135/27, 22 May 2019; *Regulation (EU) 2019/818 of the European Parliament and of the Council of 20 May 2019 on establishing a framework for interoperability between EU information systems in the field of police and judicial cooperation, asylum and migration and amending Regulations (EU) 2018/1726, (EU) 2018/1862 and (EU) 2019/816*, O.J.E.U. L135/85, 22 May 2019.

[103] Boehm, *Information Sharing and Data Protection in the Area of Freedom, Security and Justice* (2012).

[104] Information systems or databases are information management arrangements or tools which result in either specific software, IT systems or organisational infrastructures supporting different kinds of inter-jurisdictional information-sharing activities.

[105] Francesca Galli, 'Interoperable Law Enforcement. Cooperation Challenges in the EU Area of Freedom, Security and Justice' *EUI Working Paper,* Working Paper, no. 15 (2019).

[106] Art. 2, *Regulation 2019/818 on establishing a framework for interoperability between EU information systems in the field of police and judicial cooperation, asylum and migration.*

[107] *Regulation 2019/817 on establishing a framework for interoperability between EU information systems in the field of borders and visa.*

[108] Art. 1(1) and (4), *Regulation 2019/818 on establishing a framework for interoperability.*

for the designated authorities and for Europol to access the EES, VIS, ETIAS and Eurodac for the same purpose of prevention, detection or investigation of terrorist offences or of other serious criminal offences.

Such interoperability is facilitated by the EU Agency for the Operational Management of Large-Scale IT Systems in the AFSJ (eu-LISA). This Agency, established in 2011 and given a larger mandate in 2018, provides a long-term solution for the operational management of these EU databases.[109] Currently, the Agency manages Eurodac, SIS II and VIS and is developing the EES, ETIAS and ECRIS-TCN. Through eu-LISA, these systems are being built and/or adapted to ensure their interoperability and to improve the access to information stored in these various EU databases and the management at an EU level. Systems interoperability is meant to ensure information availability, improve the effectiveness of service delivery while reducing costs, and ensure improved identity management across eu-LISA IT systems.

Nonetheless, Member States are confronted with many serious legal, ethical, technical and technological difficulties when trying to implement such interoperability. Technical but important, not all Member States have the financial and technical means to implement the necessary system that would ensure the effectiveness of this mechanism of cooperation. From a legal perspective, interoperability may be considered an alternative to the approximation of national legislations (as once was considered the principle of mutual trust).[110] Certainly, the interoperability of databases respects the differences between national legislations, but an approximation facilitates cooperation as States would be more willing to include specific data in these databases which would be handled the same way in a foreign country; and guarantee the respect of fundamental rights. In fact, the EU aimed to ensure that national substantive and procedural criminal laws are sufficiently approximated and that the EU human rights standards are effectively applied. Critics have indeed continuously highlighted the data protection risks created by this interoperability. Apart from the concerns related to the necessity and proportionality of such cooperation mechanism, the interoperability is a challenge for data protection, data security and the allocation of data responsibilities. This becomes more complicated as competent national authorities are confronted with a plurality of legal bases, channels, procedures and technical tools for different categories of data. Notably, as these databases are meant to serve different purposes and to be accessed by different authorities, their interconnections might challenge the principle of purpose limitation.[111] Effective data protection and data security safeguards are

[109] *Regulation 1077/2011 establishing a European Agency for the operational management of large-scale IT systems in the area of freedom, security and justice*; *Regulation 2018/1726 on the eu-LISA*.

[110] Galli, 'Interoperable Law Enforcement. Cooperation Challenges in the EU Area of Freedom, Security and Justice' (2019): especially 8 and ff.

[111] Art. 5(1)(b), *General Data Protection Regulation 2016/679*; Art. 4, *Regulation 2019/818 on establishing a framework for interoperability between EU information systems in the field of police and judicial cooperation, asylum and migration*.

therefore necessary to prevent any improper access or misuse of data—this is exactly that which the EU has aimed to develop.[112]

Therefore, by aiming for interconnectivity between the different national and regional systems, the EU has much to work towards. Nonetheless, the EU has clearly demonstrated the significant progresses it made in further integrating cooperation between competent national authorities. The EU legal framework is thus moving away from the traditional relations between sovereign States.[113]

3. The emergence and nourishment of a three-dimensional mutual trust

Through the aforementioned successive steps, the EU Member States have progressively entered the virtuous circle of mutual trust which nourishes cooperation, and vice versa. This circle is meant to streamline the flow of data, increase the amount of data shared and enhance the quality of cross-border cooperation.

The informal exchange of data outside any regulated channel of communication and without the proper safeguards has limited results and still depends on the good relations between the respective field officers. Understanding the risks of informal cooperation (i.e. unlawfulness of the method of data gathering; privacy and data protection violations), Member States under the Third Pillar and then the EU, under the ordinary co-decision procedure, have adopted norms which foster direct peer-to-peer cooperation. Informal cooperation has not disappeared though.

By agreeing on a common objective (i.e. preventing and combating terrorism), States have set the ground for developing the political dimension of mutual trust between EU national officials; in addition to the social dimension of trust. At this stage, such trust fosters both the formal and informal interactions between competent national authorities from law enforcement officers to decision-makers. However, such trust relies on a political variable which is quite unstable and changeable.

A legal dimension was included in the concept of mutual trust when adopting a common definition of terrorist offences, criminalising these offences and requiring the respect of EU standards related to human rights and fundamental freedoms. The

[112] See, e.g., *Directive 2016/680 on the protection of natural persons with regard to the processing of personal data by competent authorities for the purposes of the prevention, investigation, detection or prosecution of criminal offences or the execution of criminal penalties, and on the free movement of such data*; *Regulation 2019/818 on establishing a framework for interoperability between EU information systems in the field of police and judicial cooperation, asylum and migration*. Also, the EU Data Protection Reform, the Proposal for an EU Passenger Name Record (PNR) both under negotiations, as well as the Data Protection Umbrella Agreement between the EU and the US, the PNR Agreements between the EU and the United States (2012), Canada (2006) and Australia (2008). See also, González Fuster, De Hert, and Gutwirth, 'Privacy and Data Protection in the EU Security Continuum' (2011); Cocq, 'EU Data Protection Rules Applying to Law Enforcement Activities' (2016); Cocq and Galli, 'Data retention regime within the EU' (2016); Bräutigam and Miettinen, *Data Protection, Privacy and European Regulation in the Digital Age* (2016).

[113] Notably, the Lisbon Treaty did not eliminate extra-EU form of cooperation. Member States may still establish enhanced cooperation between themselves within the framework of the Union. This method of cooperation is aimed at overcoming the issue posed by certain insurmountable differences between Member States. Art. 87(3) TFEU, in the limits provided in Arts. 322–334 TFEU.

legal dimension may also be found in the array of norms requiring EU competent national authorities to cooperate together in sharing data, for example.

As a consequence, the concept of mutual trust, with its three dimensions, was developed and operationalised to ensure a smoother and more effective cooperation between competent national authorities. The EU mechanisms of cooperation are meant to be implemented in accordance with the principle of mutual trust (e.g. the 'Swedish Initiative' or the EIO).

B. A long way to go before a 'legally effective' intra-ASEAN cooperation: mutual trust in the making?

Aside from the near-total absence of approximation of the relevant national legislations, other elements have been identified as actual barriers to cooperation within ASEAN. These include, amongst others, the differences of governments' structure and policy; the language barrier; budget deficits; the turnover time of competent authorities in the different countries; corruption and/or the absence of data sharing systems.[114]

The peculiarity of Southeast Asian security culture and values is centred on a kind of 'bottom-up approach' (from the national to the regional level). However, certain UN instruments have a top-down influence. The UN Model Treaties on International Cooperation in Criminal Matters (on MLA for instance) serve as models when the Member States conclude bilateral, sub-regional or regional agreements.[115] In practice, ASEAN efforts to address the terrorist threat have mostly been conducted on an *ad hoc* basis, through bilateral or sub-regional initiatives or alternatively between Member States and third partners.[116] Regional cooperation is slowly increasing though.[117]

---

[114] Argument nourished by interviews with, notably: a Europol Liaison Officer to Interpol Global Complex for Innovation, Singapore, 31 May 2016; a professor at the NUS, Singapore, 3 June 2016; official from the Regional Programme on Human Trafficking/Smuggling of Migrants at the UNODC-ROSEAP, Bangkok, 19 May 2016; official from the Information, Legal Affairs and Transnational Crime in the ASEAN Framework in charge of International Relations at the Ministry of Interior, Royal Government, Phnom Penh, 4 June 2016; official from the Regional Programme on Border Management at the UNODC-ROSEAP, Bangkok, 17 June 2016; official from the Terrorism Prevention Programme at the UNODC-ROSEAP, Bangkok, 11 July 2016.

[115] See the UNODC website on Model Laws and Treaties: https://www.unodc.org/unodc/fr/legal-tools/model-treaties-and-laws.html (accessed on 31 December 2019). On their impact, see, e.g., *Manila Declaration on the Prevention and Control of Transnational Crime* (1998).

[116] Argument nourished by interview with a senior research fellow at the ISEAS, retired from the ASEAN Secretariat (political and security field of ASEAN cooperation), Singapore, 3 June 2016.

[117] See, e.g., *ASEAN Declaration on Transnational Crime*, Manila, 20 December 1997; *ASEAN Declaration on Joint Action to Counter Terrorism*, Bandar Seri Begawan, 5 November 2001; *ASEAN Treaty on Mutual Legal Assistance in Criminal Matters*, Ministers of Justice/Law Attorneys-General, Kuala Lumpur, 29 November 2004; ASEAN Plan of Action Against Trafficking in Persons, Especially Women and Children, 27th ASEAN Summit, Kuala Lumpur, 22 November 2015; *Declaration in Combating Transnational Crime*, Tenth ASEAN Ministerial Meeting on Transnational Crime, Kuala Lumpur, 30 September 2015; *ASEAN Comprehensive Plan of Action on Counter Terrorism*, Nay Pyi Taw, 30 June 2009; ASEAN, *Joint Statement of the*

1. A slow but progressive recognition of the added value of a regional cooperative response against terrorism in a context of tensions and significant differences

The main difference between the two regions is that ASEAN Member States must still overcome strong obstacles to develop effective means of cooperation. Amongst many others, these obstacles include their cultural, historical, political and legal diversity; the historic animosities towards and suspicions of one another; and their strong attachment to national sovereignty.[118] This is especially true in the field of counterterrorism as States 'differ very much in their susceptibility to and experience of terrorism and hence it is extremely difficult to obtain an effective ASEAN-wide response to it'.[119]

Among the 'difficult' relations, some relevant examples may be highlighted. For a long time, Philippine competent national authorities had difficulty working with Malaysia due to Malaysia's long history of supporting the Moro National Liberation Front (MNLF) and the Moro Islamic Liberation Front (MILF) from the late 1960s to 1980s as well as the Sabah territorial dispute.[120] Indonesia's intransigence towards Malaysia and Singapore's methods applied to the arrest of suspected terrorists as well as towards past security issues when Singapore established a huge spy ring in Indonesia in the mid-1990s and when Malaysia turned a blind eye to Free Aceh Movement's (GAM) activities within the Malaysian border. Moreover, the weakest countries, namely the 'CLMV countries' (Cambodia, Lao PDR, Myanmar and Vietnam), are suspicious about intelligence sharing and tend to have a strong position regarding non-interference in internal affairs. However, as it is considered a necessity, data sharing and cooperation have increasingly improved over the course of the war on terror, with a specific focus on transnational Islamist terrorism.

In this context, certain Southeast Asian States have been more active in cooperating in the field of counterterrorism, even before the creation of ASEAN. In fact, it took some time for all Member States to actually engage in the ASEAN Political and Security Community (APSC) and adopt norms fostering cooperation in criminal matters, and even more so regarding terrorism-related matters. Prior to and during the development of ASEAN, cooperation has been more effective between law enforcement authorities on a bilateral or sub-regional level.[121] In fact, the development of ASEAN norms and platforms of dialogues is usually completed by sub-regional, potentially more operational, agreements.

ASEAN Directors-General of Immigration Departments and Heads of Consular Affairs Divisions of the Ministries of Foreign Affairs (DGIM) on the Prevention of the Movement of Foreign Terrorist Fighters, 20th meeting of the DGIM, Bali, 23 September 2016; *Revised ASEAN Comprehensive Plan of Action on Counter Terrorism*, 11th AMMTC, Manila, 20 September 2017.

[118] Roberts, *ASEAN Regionalism* (2012): 178.

[119] Robert O'Neill, Chairman of the International Institute for Strategic Studies, Shangri-La Dialogue, 30 May–1 June 2003.

[120] Zachary Abuza, *Militant Islam in Southeast Asia: Crucible of Terror* (Boulder: Lynne Rienner Publishers, 2003): 25.

[121] Sapphaisal, *Fighting Terrorism in Southeast Asia* (2004): 25.

Notably, bilateral cooperation occurs on a case-by-case basis and in accordance with their respective national laws, such as the 1979 *Law of the Republic of Indonesia concerning Extradition.*[122] Extradition remains governed by traditional international law and does not imply direct horizontal cooperation. ASEAN, due to the *Model ASEAN Extradition Treaty,*[123] aids in harmonising national laws on extradition, which can facilitate cooperation. Despite being of interest, bilateral relations do not particularly represent the dynamics created by multilateral dialogues amongst ASEAN Member States.

(a) *Recognising the need for cross-border cooperation against transnational crime leading to strategic regional channels of discussions and sub-regional operational arrangements*

While ASEAN was in its early stages in the 1970s, cooperation in criminal matters became topical in the EU (even before any effort of harmonisation of national substantive and procedural criminal laws). In ASEAN, it was only towards the end of the 1990s that cooperation was identified as a means of combating transnational crime. Transnational cooperation is particularly needed in this region as borders are porous and immigration controls and systems of visa administrations are weak. Administration requirements might also be circumvented through corruption.[124] For these reasons, Southeast Asian countries have been qualified as 'countries of convenience'[125] for international terrorist individuals and groups.

In a context of tensions and diversity, the first mention of cooperation in criminal matters in an ASEAN text appears at the same time as ASEAN Member States identified security threats that needed to be handled in concert, namely in the 1997 *ASEAN Declaration on Transnational Crime*. Cooperation is essential in combating terrorism as well as illicit drug trafficking, arms smuggling, money laundering, traffic in persons and piracy. The first attempts to enter into the specifics of cooperation occurred in the 1998 *Declaration on a Drug Free ASEAN*. Nothing other than regional declarations were adopted and they only resulted in fostering strategic discussions.

Moreover, the 1997 Declaration specifically identified information exchange as a necessary means to combat these crimes. Since then, ASEAN Senior Ministers have been meeting regularly, through the ASEAN Ministerial Meetings on Transnational Crime (AMMTC), and the ASEAN Senior Officials Meetings on Transnational Crime (SOMTC). These meetings usually lead to declarations or plans of actions, such as the 2004 *ASEAN Declaration Against Trafficking in Persons particularly*

[122] *Law of the Republic of Indonesia concerning Extradition*, No. 1/1979.

[123] *Model ASEAN Extradition Treaty*, 10th ASEAN Law Ministers Meeting (ALAWMM) taking place on 11–12 October 2018, Vientiane, 12 October 2018.

[124] Sapphaisal, *Fighting Terrorism in Southeast Asia* (2004): 13.

[125] Mark Manyin et al., *Terrorism in Southeast Asia*, CRS, Report for Congress (updated on 18 November 2003), 3–4.

Women and Children[126] or the 2009 *ASEAN Comprehensive Plan of Action (PoA) on Counter Terrorism*[127] and its updated version.[128]

Therefore, during the early stages of ASEAN development, regional cooperation, whatever its form, was not an obvious task. This might explain why the first forms of regional interactions in criminal matters remain strategic, as were their outcomes.

As strategic responses are not sufficient, effective operational responses to transnational security issues are required. Take, for instance, the threat that piracy in the Strait of Malacca poses for Indonesia, Malaysia and Singapore. Tensions between these countries have led these three States to pursue individual strategies. However, facing their incapacity to deal with the threat alone, they decided to work together in order to address this problem.[129] Realising the added value of interstate cooperation, more operational sub-regional arrangements have emerged to complement the broad and strategic regional interactions.

As another example, on 7 May 2002, before the Bali attacks, a tripartite cooperation was initiated by Indonesia, Malaysia and the Philippines, which signed an *Agreement on Information Exchange and Establishment of Communication Procedures* in order to facilitate the exchange of information in matters of transnational crime, especially terrorism.[130] This trilateral pact covers ten areas of cooperation such as intelligence sharing, extradition, transparency of banking systems and certain transnational issues like piracy, smuggling, illegal arms shipment and narcotics.[131] This group was subsequently joined by Cambodia and Thailand. A noteworthy fact is that Singapore is excluded from this pact.

Operational cooperation against transnational crime involves various competent authorities. Other examples show the diversity of actors involved in sub-regional cooperation arrangements. For example, the Indonesian and Singapore armed forces conducted a joint counterterrorism exercise in July 2012. In June 2017, the Philippines, Indonesia and Malaysia signed an *Agreement on Patrolling Shared Maritime Border* whereby naval military personnel from these countries coordinate efforts in order to give chase to Islamic militants who navigate the seas of these nations. The Trilateral Maritime Patrol Arrangement, while mostly a maritime-based operation, may also involve air and land military assets in order to secure the Sulu Sea, located to the northeast of Borneo and southwest of the Philippines. This agreement does not

---

[126] *ASEAN Declaration against Trafficking in Persons particularly Women and Children*, Vientiane, 29 November 2004.

[127] *ASEAN Comprehensive Plan of Action on Counter Terrorism* (2009).

[128] *Revised ASEAN Comprehensive Plan of Action on Counter Terrorism* (2017).

[129] Ralph Emmers, Comprehensive security and resilience in Southeast Asia: ASEAN's approach to terrorism and Piracy, 2007, 132, Working Paper, S. Rajaratnam School of International Studies, Singapore.

[130] Art. III(i), *Agreement on Information Exchange and Establishment of Communication Procedures*, between the Republic of the Philippines, the Republic of Indonesia and Malaysia, Putrajaya, 7 May 2002.

[131] See also, Senia Febrica, *Maritime Security and Indonesia: Cooperation, Interests, and Strategies* (Abingdon: Routledge, 2017): 141.

exist within the criminal justice realm. It is however representative of the difference between the ASEAN agreements and sub-regional ones. The ASEAN norms may be incentives and an umbrella for Member States to develop more operational agreements in compliance with the specific objective identified at the ASEAN level.

Interestingly, most of the agreements involve Indonesia, Malaysia, the Philippines and Singapore. In addition to the sub-regional agreements, there are bilateral agreements between Malaysia and Singapore, Singapore and the Philippines, Indonesia and Malaysia, and Indonesia and the Philippines. Most of these agreements involve operational cooperation, which includes police to police cooperation (also called 'P2P' cooperation), intelligence services cooperation, intelligence and information sharing, training and the like. This shows a certain level of mutual trust between these countries. It might be based on common history (in the case of Malaysia and Singapore's agreement), mutual understanding and similar interests.

Interestingly, the premises of operational cooperation within the EU were more important for terrorism, while this is not the case in ASEAN, where cooperation has been discussed for different forms of transnational crime and where operational sub-regional arrangements have focused on various topical issues.

Compared to the EU, a limited form of freedom of movements across borders appeared in the ASEAN legal framework with the adoption of the 2012 *Agreement on the Movement of Natural Persons*. This agreement aims to facilitate the movement of natural persons, but only those engaged in the conduct of trade in goods, trade in services and investment.[132] Interestingly, this regional freedom of movement emerged after the development of regional instruments in criminal matters; after the adoption of the 2004 *ASEAN Treaty on Mutual Legal Assistance in Criminal Matters* and 2007 *ASEAN Convention on Counter-Terrorism* for instance. The development at this stage of such a limited freedom of movement is representative of both the ASEAN level of regional integration and its approach towards fundamental rights and freedoms.

Beside the unwillingness to pool resources and work together, another potential issue is the (un)ability of each country to address transnational crime, which is linked to the capacity of the State to implement appropriate measures via national laws. In general, the more effective States have been Singapore, Indonesia and Thailand—with Laos, Cambodia, Myanmar and Vietnam being the laggards.[133]

(b) *Initial steps towards ASEAN-wide cooperation in preventing and countering terrorism: strategic or operational responses?*

The absence of common regional definitions of the crimes, including 'terrorist offences', has not prevented Member States from adopting a growing number of regional legal instruments promoting cooperation, with a particular focus on

[132] Art. 1(b), *ASEAN Agreement on the Movement of Natural Persons*, Phnom Penh, 19 November 2012. This Agreement entered into force on 14 June 2016.

[133] Aurel Croissant and Daniel Barlow, 'Folowing the Money Trail: Terrorist Financing and Government Responses in Southeast Asia' *Studies in Conflict & Terrorism*, vol. 30, no. 2 (2007).

information and intelligence sharing. It is in fact what is first mentioned in the regional instruments dealing with criminal matters.[134]

In the process of 'regionalising' their actions against terrorism, Member States have engaged in discussions during the AMMTC since the mid-1990s. However, the ASEAN commitment to the fight against terrorism was particularly catalysed by the September 11 attacks. The fear that the Al Qaeda terrorist network was setting up local cells, particularly in Kuala Lumpur and Bangkok to exploit the regional loose border and financial controls, and cooperate with indigenous regional terrorist groups such as Jemaah Islamiyah (JI), MILF and Abu Sayyaf Group (ASG) led the Bush Presidency to qualify Southeast Asia as the 'second front' in the fight against terrorism. As a consequence, ASEAN issued a *Declaration on Joint Action to Counter Terrorism* in 2001 whose measures have been incorporated in the Terrorist Component of the Work Programme to implement the 2002 ASEAN Plan of Action to combat Transnational Crime.

A new phase was inaugurated after the Bali bombings of 2002, which brutally killed approximately 200 people and injured some 200 more, as well as the series of attacks in 2005. Indonesia had to come to terms with the existence of radical elements pursuing a pan-Islamic project within its borders and became more willing to undertake forms of multilateral initiatives. The negative effects of the bombings, which were reflected on a 38% fall of tourism arrivals in Indonesia, a rise to 3.5 million by 2008 in the number of displaced persons (victims of counterterrorism measures) and an average reduction of GDP by 3%, exacerbated the need to overcome unilateral policies in favour of more coordinated approaches. Unsurprisingly, ASEAN leaders not only reiterated their commitment to the fight against terrorism but also their willingness to establish a regional cooperation centre in Kuala Lumpur in order to raise the level of cooperation, coordination and information sharing. They did so, most visibly, in the 2007 *ASEAN Convention on Counter-Terrorism* (ACCT) and the 2009 *ASEAN Comprehensive PoA on Counter Terrorism* and its revised version.[135]

As the ASEAN regional legal framework remains deficient, sub-regional and bilateral agreements are still prominent if practical measures, such as information exchange and joint activities, are to be implemented. Apart from sub-regional and bilateral mechanisms of cooperation, ASEAN Member States agreed on common training programmes and projects leading to the creation of various documents relating to the fight against transnational crime or to specific crimes. Those amongst them worth highlighting are the Vientiane Action Programme 2004–2010 which announced the adoption of the 2004 *ASEAN Treaty on Mutual Legal Assistance in*

[134] See, e.g., Preamble, *ASEAN Declaration on Transnational Crime* (1997); *Plan of Action to Combat Transnational Crime* (1999); Pt. 5, *Declaration on Joint Action to Counter Terrorism* (2001); Art. VI, ACCT.

[135] 2007 ACCT; *ASEAN Comprehensive Plan of Action on Counter Terrorism* (2009); *Revised Comprehensive Plan of Action on Counter Terrorism* (2017).

Criminal Matters (ASEAN Treaty on MLACM), the 2007 ACCT, and, later on, the Model ASEAN Extradition Treaty in 2018.[136]

Interestingly, both UN and ASEAN instruments proclaim their intention to cooperate together, especially for sharing information and intelligence (e.g. UNODC Model Law on Mutual Legal Assistance in Criminal Matters[137]/ ASEAN Treaty on MLACM), and propose models for their members (e.g. UN Model Treaty on Extradition/Model ASEAN Extradition Treaty).

This brief discussion concerning the ASEAN cooperative approach towards terrorism during its infancy stages, and the sub-regional dynamics, illustrates the high sensitivity of criminal matters. Defining their objective and the core of their cooperation tends to remain vague and undefined, which hinders their engagement with one another.

2. The weak added value of regional norms in fostering horizontal data sharing

Peer-to-peer cooperation is the most effective (e.g. 'P2P' cooperation) form of cooperation.[138] This method of cooperation remains bilateral, unofficial and non-institutionalised within ASEAN. Its Member States prefer bilateral cooperation over regional cooperation. Apart from law enforcement cooperation, intra-regional relations between judicial authorities are also officially framed by the ASEAN Treaty on MLACM. However, judicial cooperation seems almost non-existent in practice.[139] The ASEAN Treaty on MLACM is not used often enough and is too slow to keep the required pace to effectively prevent and combat terrorist offences. For this reason, informal peer-to-peer cooperation is preferred. Thus, prosecutors tend to prefer requesting that the police of their own country cooperate with their counterparts of another country. Police cooperation is regarded to be significantly more effective than judicial cooperation. Besides, the information shared by a police officer from one country A with a police officer of another country B usually falls under the same regime as any other information gathered in this latter country.

Accordingly, judicial cooperation is briefly touched upon, through the requirements related to mutual legal assistance in particular, due to its impact on the development of mutual trust within the region and on the dynamics leading to peer-to-peer data sharing.

(a) *The ASEAN Treaty on Mutual Legal Assistance in Criminal Matters: the first legal stepping-stone for horizontal cooperation?*

[136] *Model ASEAN Extradition Treaty*, 10th ALAWMM (2018). At that time, the ASEAN Ministers reviewed their respective extradition laws.

[137] UNODC, *Model Law on Mutual Legal Assistance in Criminal Matters* (Vienna: UNODC Publications, 2007).

[138] Interestingly, the same goes for immigration to immigration 'I2I' cooperation.

[139] Argument nourished by interviews with notably: an official from the State Prosecutor Office from the Philippines (2016), op. cit.; official from the Directorate General of International Affairs (2016), op. cit.

The ASEAN Treaty on MLACM is based on the UN Model Treaty on Mutual Legal Assistance in Criminal Matters, which was last amended in 2000.[140] This transversal treaty aims to facilitate, among other things, the exchange of evidence and other kinds of information related to investigations, prosecutions and trial proceedings. This treaty constitutes a step towards the facilitation of judicial cooperation in criminal matters within the region.

This Treaty expresses the Member States' desire 'to improve the effectiveness of the law enforcement authorities of the Parties in the prevention, investigation and prosecution of offences through cooperation and mutual legal assistance in criminal matters'.[141] Despite prevention being mentioned in the preamble, it is not discussed in the core of the treaty. In fact, the treaty only deals with the investigations, prosecution and resulting proceedings. As it is the first ASEAN binding instrument related to serious transnational crime,[142] this treaty constitutes the first framework for sharing information and evidence between its Member States.

Content wise, as with the UN Model Treaty, the ASEAN Treaty requires Member States to provide the widest possible mutual assistance to one another (Articles 1(1) of both texts). In terms of scope, it is slightly broader than the UN Model Treaty, while the list of types of acts covered is indeed longer (see Article 1(2) ASEAN Treaty and Article 1(2) UN Model Treaty). It is particularly representative of the sensitivity of national sovereignty to notice that Article 2(2) of the ASEAN Treaty provides that '[n]othing in this Treaty entitles a Party to undertake in the territory of another Party the exercise of jurisdiction and performance of functions that are reserved exclusively for the authorities of that other Party by its domestic laws', a provision which does not exist in the UN Model Treaty. The UN Model only provides that assistance may be refused if '[t]he requested State is of the opinion that the request, if granted, would prejudice its sovereignty, security, public order (*ordre public*) or other essential public interest'.[143] Similarly, the grounds for refusal or cases of limitations are much more numerous in the ASEAN Treaty (Article 3) compared to the ones in the UN Model Treaty (Article 4). In this respect, whereas the UN Model Treaty only lists six optional grounds for refusal, the ASEAN Treaty lists 11 mandatory grounds for refusal, and three optional. As in the UN Model Treaty, the ASEAN Treaty provides that MLA cannot be refused solely on the ground of bank secrecy (Article 3(5)).

Format wise, this treaty provides, as the UN Model Treaty does, for rules regarding the format and the content of the requests from one State to another (Articles 5 and 6 UN Model Treaty; Articles 5–7 ASEAN Treaty). These requests

[140] *UN Model Treaty on Mutual Legal Assistance in Criminal Matters*, A/RES/45/117 (68th plenary meeting, 14 December 1990) as amended by General Assembly resolution A/RES/53/112 (53rd session, 20 January 2000). With the latest version: 2007, *Model Law on Mutual Legal Assistance in Criminal Matters*.

[141] Preamble, *ASEAN Treaty on Mutual Legal Assistance in Criminal Matters* (2004).

[142] Millar and Rosand, 'Implementing the UN General Assembly's Global Counter-Terrorism Strategy in the Asia-Pacific' (2007).

[143] Art. 4(1)(a), *UN Model Treaty on Mutual Legal Assistance in Criminal Matters*.

are made and received by designated central authorities (respectively, Articles 4 and 3), without specifying their nature. Nonetheless, judicial authorities tend to be the actual national authorities in charge.[144] However, requests can be transmitted via Interpol or Aseanapol in urgent cases and if permitted by national laws (Article 5).

This transfer of information and evidence requires the consent of the requested State on the use or disclose or transfer of information or evidence provided by the requesting State for purposes other than those stated in the request.[145] Notably, Member States are unlikely to share information which they consider to be sensitive for their national security, and historically this has included terrorism-related cases and it might continue to be in specific cases.

As has been demonstrated by the comparison between the ASEAN Treaty and the UN Model Treaty, the only way in which ASEAN goes beyond the UN is through the definition of the scope of the instrument and its nature, namely a binding legal instrument for ASEAN Member States. By contrast, the UN Model Treaty is, as its name specifies it, only a model for States. The UN Model Treaty is included in a General Assembly resolution, which was passed without the need for a vote and does not need to be ratified.

All ASEAN Member States have ratified the ASEAN Treaty (Thailand being the last to do so on 31 January 2013). Interestingly, this agreement is not part of the legal ASEAN bloc, which means that it was not negotiated under the ASEAN umbrella and not deposited in the ASEAN legal database. It was only as a result of Malaysia's proposal that the negotiations took place and that the Treaty was signed and deposited in Malaysia.

Questions remain regarding the practical implementation of the MLA Treaty. Key judicial actors insisted that the procedure provided for by the instrument is too heavy and time-consuming.[146] It is thus hardly used. Although binding, this instrument remains too broad in its requirements, which reduces its actual impact on cross-border cooperation. Yet, 5 years after its entry into force, the senior officials recognised the value of the Treaty on judicial cooperation but also pointed out the difficulties for effective implementation. Particular focus has been placed on the ways in which the role of central authorities can be enhanced.[147]

In essence, this Treaty, although important, does not represent a turning point for building trust and facilitating cooperation.[148] It mostly emphasises the level of willingness of the Member States to cooperate with one another.

---

[144] Argument nourished by interview with, notably, official from the Department of the Office of the Attorney General in Thailand (2016), op.cit.

[145] Art. 8, *ASEAN Treaty on Mutual Legal Assistance in Criminal Matters* (2004).

[146] Interview with, notably, official from the Department of the Office of the Attorney General in Thailand (2016), op.cit.

[147] 'ASEAN: ASEAN countries seek to foster mutual legal assistance in criminal matters', *Asia News Monitor*, Bangkok, 1 May 2018.

[148] Interview with, notably, official from the Department of the Office of the Attorney General in Thailand (2016), op.cit.

Interestingly, there is no other binding treaty which has been adopted by ASEAN Member States that regulates cross-border cooperation. As extradition requires a higher level of mutual trust, it might explain why no binding ASEAN extradition treaty has been adopted yet. However, progress has been made in this field given that the ASEAN Law Ministers agreed on a Model Treaty in October 2018.[149] The discussions on extradition leading to the adoption of a binding text would represent a step forward in building mutual trust.

(b) *The ASEAN Convention on Counter Terrorism: a sectorial instrument without any precise added value for cooperation*

The *ASEAN Convention on Counter Terrorism*[150] committed the members to 'a framework of regional cooperation to counter, prevent and suppress terrorism in all its forms and manifestations and to deepen cooperation among law enforcement agencies and relevant authorities of the Parties in countering terrorism'.[151] Compared to the 2015 *ASEAN Convention against Trafficking in Persons, Especially Women and Children* that went further by requiring Member States to harmonise their relevant legislation in order to increase cooperation while bearing in mind the necessary protection of human rights, the ACCT did not. On the one hand, the ACCT does not clearly approximate Member States' legislations and, on the other hand, it does not refer to human rights in the core of its text but only briefly in the preamble. The preamble states that the Member States recall:

> the Charter of the United Nations and relevant principles of international law, the relevant international conventions and protocols relating to counter terrorism and relevant resolutions of the United Nations on measures aimed at countering international terrorism, and reaffirming [their] commitment to protect human rights, fair treatment, the rule of law, and due process as well as the principles enshrined in the Treaty of Amity and Cooperation in Southeast Asia done at Bali on 24 February 1976.

Although the ACCT remains weak in these two aspects, this instrument did pave the way for the realisation of a consistent regional policy. The main added values of this convention are its nature (a binding instrument) and its scope (requiring competent national authorities to cooperate together). As Article I states, the ACCT aims to deepen cooperation among law enforcement agencies and other relevant authorities in countering terrorism. Article VI contains a rather long list of appropriate measures that *may* be included in the areas of cooperation, in conformity with the domestic laws of the respective Parties. Certain measures worth mentioning are the enhancing of cross-border cooperation, intelligence exchange and sharing of information as well as enhancing existing cooperation towards developing regional databases under the purview of the relevant ASEAN bodies. They agreed to enhance and facilitate the flow of information and intelligence about terrorists and terrorist organisations, their movement and funding, and any other information needed to

[149] *Model ASEAN Extradition Treaty* (2018).

[150] The ACCT came into force in May 2011.

[151] Rees, 'EU and ASEAN: Issues of regional security' (2010): 411.

protect lives, property and the security of all modes of travel.[152] This Article VI remains rather vague in the sense that it uses the verb 'may' and does not specify any particular method of cooperation, such as method of data sharing, special investigative techniques or joint investigation teams.[153] Article VI is somehow complemented by Article IX, according to which the '[...] Parties *shall, where possible* (emphasis added), establish channels of communication between their competent agencies to facilitate the exchange of information to prevent the commission of offences covered in Article II of the Convention'. One might notice the subtle pairing of the word 'shall' with the words 'where possible'.

The associated 2009 *ASEAN Comprehensive PoA on Counter Terrorism* aimed to go a bit further in planning the 'establishment of institutionalised mechanisms for the exchange of information and intelligence on the surveillance and tracking of suspected terrorist organisations including their associated organisations and their activities with a view to preventing their acts of terror'.[154] Regarding the exchange of information and intelligence, the Plan of Action refers to Interpol's database and Interpol National Central Bureaus as contact points, as well as other tools and resources to be used as channels of cooperation. Interestingly, while already existing at the time of the adoption of the ACCT, Aseanapol is not considered a more useful—or even useful—way of processing, analysing and exchanging data.

It is worth noting that the PoA is not a binding instrument,[155] which implies that Member States are not accountable if they do not respect its requirements. This explains why the Member States often adopt one general binding instrument and another slightly more precise but non-binding agreement associated with it.

Notably, neither the ACCT nor the PoA have been a better turning point than the ASEAN MLA Treaty at enhancing effective cooperation against terrorism within the region.

Activities from the three clusters elaborated in Chap. 3 (*capability building, capacity building* and *information and experience sharing*) have been stated in the ACCT and elaborated in the associated PoA. With these norms, Member States nurture the relationship between data sharing and mutual trust building at the regional, sub-regional or bilateral levels; even if involuntarily. However, their engagement is weak due to the lack of capability and capacity of some Member States and the lack of political and legal understanding between national authorities.

---

[152] ASEAN, 'ASEAN Efforts to Counter Terrorism' Paper prepared for the UN Counter-Terrorism Committee, 4 July 2012: available at https://bit.ly/3d6tVnj (accessed on 5 November 2020).

[153] Art. I, ACCT.

[154] Pt. 10, *ASEAN Comprehensive Plan of Action on Counter Terrorism* (2009).

[155] Plans of action (PoA) have no binding force in the positivist appreciation of international law. The normative force of norms can be appreciated due to three significant factors: the normative value, the legal scope and the normative guarantee. On the analysis of the normative force, see, e.g., Thibierge and alii, *La force normative* (2009). The ASEAN Member States unanimously agreed with the terms of the different PoA giving it a certain normative value. On the other sides of the triangle developed by Thibierge, the PoAs clearly lack normative guarantee but can have a legal scope/a legal impact on the participants' actions.

The regional anti-terrorism documents provide for a broad umbrella under which the objectives of the Member States are set. The ACCT and its PoA provide strategic guidelines and objectives without any legally binding obligation. This umbrella has led to strategic cooperation between high-ranking officers or government officials. Moreover, this has fostered the establishment of trainings, networks and channels of communications, among other initiatives, which are used by field officers.

Certain improvements are worth noticing, but transnational cooperation remains a sensitive issue, especially dealing with national security.[156] This explains the additional involvement of bilateral or sub-regional operational agreements and activities supporting or implementing the more general engagement of ASEAN Member States to cooperate together, including information and intelligence sharing.

Nine years after the adoption of the PoA, ASEAN Member States have initiated discussions about an 'Our Eyes' Initiative (OEI), namely a new intelligence-sharing initiative. In October 2018, Indonesia's Defense Minister even invited EU Member States to join. The OEI, which derives its name from the 'Five Eyes' intelligence network, was officially proposed by Indonesian Defense Minister Ryamizard Ryacudu in 2017 as an information-sharing platform for Member States designed to facilitate the exchange of intelligence on terrorism, radicalism and violent extremism. The OEI was initially conceptualised to be an initiative between Indonesia, Malaysia and the Philippines. Discussions between Member States and the representative of the ASEAN Secretariat focus on the development of mechanisms of cooperation for the exchange of strategic information. Significant challenges remain for this transnational endeavour to become reality though. Many of these are tied to deep-seated issues, from interstate distrust to differences in organisational culture and to bureaucratic rivalries within the agencies of individual countries. As these issues make it difficult to operationalise OEI between the initial three countries, they are growing with its expansion across all Member States (becoming the ASEAN OEI, or AOEI), and possibly beyond those to include dialogue partners as well.[157]

In conclusion, the EU and ASEAN political and legal architectures have had an impact on the components of their own 'mutual trust' and its dimension as well as on the type of cooperation mechanisms used (formal and informal interactions). Among these mechanisms, information and intelligence sharing constitutes a basis for, and a

[156] It is also the case in Europe, see, e.g., Rozemarijn van der Hilst, 'Ranking in terms of their human rights risks, the detection technologies and uses surveyed in WP09', DETECTER, 30 November 2011, 17; Oldrich Bures, *EU Counterterrorism Policy. A Paper Tiger?* (Surrey: Ashgate, 2011); Benjamin J. Goold 'Mind the (Information) Gap: Making Sense of the European Union's Strategic Approach to Transnational Organised Crime' *in* Felia Allum and Stan Gilmour (eds.), *Routledge Handbook of Transnational Organized Crime* (London: Routledge, 2011).

[157] Prashanth Parameswaran, "Where is the New ASEAN 'Our Eyes' Intelligence Initiative Headed?" *The Diplomat* (5 February 2019); Prashanth Parameswaran, 'ASEAN Our Eyes Meeting Spotlights Counterterrorism Cooperation' *The Diplomat* (10 March 2020); Vierstraete-Verlinde, 'EU ACTIONPLAN on CT and P/CVE, South-East Asia PRIORITIES' (2019): 10.

result of, the development of mutual trust and mutual understandings in both regions (cf. virtuous circle).

Adding to the social dimension of mutual trust, the political and legal dimensions brought cooperation between EU competent national authorities a step further towards efficiency. Over time, the EU and its Member States have adopted an increasing number of norms fostering cooperation, establishing the rules governing such cooperation and developing the mechanisms and channels of communication. Cooperation mechanisms applying to competent national authorities went into far greater detail in comparison to that which was required by international norms. Although increasingly formalised, cross-border cooperation between competent national authorities maintain a sense of informality, especially between law enforcement authorities.

By contrast, mutual trust, and cooperation in criminal matters, is not associated with precise legal obligations in ASEAN. Mutual trust remains mostly a social construct, especially between frontline officers. Yet, it tends to be associated with a political component at a higher level of the hierarchy. The regional norms do not approximate the relevant national legislations. In addition, the requirements are too vague to be effective. Cross-border horizontal cooperation remains mostly informal and occurs on a case-by-case basis.

Consequently, the increasing data flow has made the fight against terrorism more effective within the EU. Meanwhile, it can be argued that the situation in ASEAN does not meet the criteria to qualify as 'legally effective', due to it being fostered, for the most part, by social interactions and supported by a broad political engagement and vague legal framework. In the current state, it remains unclear whether ASEAN is in the early phase of the process towards a three-dimensional mutual trust (similar to the EU's) or whether it is setting a separate course.

In their respective legal frameworks, regional key actors and platforms of discussions were established to support cooperation and facilitate peer-to-peer data sharing. The structure, objective, scope and competence of these actors differ according to the regional context and the purpose they chose.

Section 2: The Introduction of Multilateral Platforms for Cooperation and Regional Actors—Nourishing the Virtuous Circle 'Mutual Trust/Data Sharing'

The urge for an appropriate response against terrorism and for cross-border cooperation has prompted authorities to adapt pre-existing platforms of discussions and actors as well as to create new ones. These platforms and regional actors were established to provide traditional actors with further support in facilitating cross-border cooperation, including data sharing. The different international actors and platforms (I) as well as the regional and sub-regional ones (II) have facilitated the development of transnational cooperation and the flow of data among competent national authorities.

Although the impact of the different dimensions of mutual trust on the effectiveness of cooperation mechanisms is not always clearly visible, it is even less so on the development of these platforms. Mutual trust plays two main roles in the establishment of actors and platforms of discussions and in fostering cross-border cooperation. Firstly, mutual trust is necessary for States to agree on a delegation of competence or, at least, to accept the support of regional actors and to use regional platforms. Secondly, mutual trust might even be considered more important to ensure the good functioning of these actors and platforms, and to streamline competent national authorities' tasks.

I. International actors and their strategic and operational actions: what foundations for mutual trust?

Although many international influencers exist, the UN and Interpol are the most representative of the complementarity of approaches in the fight against terrorism. The actions of these international actors fulfil the three axes of the matrix: capability building, capacity building and information and experience sharing. The UN has been active in these three axes, with a greater focus on strategic cooperation (data sharing between decision-makers) while Interpol focuses rather on operational cooperation (data sharing, including personal data, between field officers) than on strategic cooperation. One should explain how their action has had an impact on the development of mutual trust between competent national authorities.

A. Informal and/or strategic cooperation fostered by the UN bodies' activities

The United Nations Organisation is a traditional international organisation that has no autonomous binding power over the Member States, except for the resolutions of the Security Council adopted under Chap. VII of the Charter. By contrast, the resolutions adopted during sessions of the General Assembly are not legally binding. The UN has asked States to take all necessary measures to prevent and combat terrorism mainly via the General Assembly (UNGA) or Security Council (UNSC) resolutions or via multilateral conventions. As many States have adopted legislation and measures in response, it can be said that the UN has influenced the adoption of regional and national norms facilitating the fight against terrorism with, depending on the countries, a human rights-based approach (*capability building*).

It is through its agencies, and most specifically the UN Office on Drugs and Crime (UNODC) and, progressively, the new UN Office of Counter-Terrorism (UNOCT), that the UN has played a role in capability building, capacity building and information and experience sharing.

The UNOCT[158] was established in 2017 to, amongst other tasks, support Member States in implementing the *UN Global Counter-Terrorism Strategy*. This Strategy is composed of four pillars, including actions encompassed in the three axes of the matrix for the development of mutual trust (*capability and capacity building* actions, and *information and experience sharing* measures).[159] The UNOCT coordinates the actions of many other UN bodies by ensuring the implementation of the Strategy, which primarily involves the UNODC.

Amongst other bodies, the Terrorism Prevention Office at the UNODC is indeed in charge of supporting States implement this Strategy. It assists them to enhance their legislation in order to meet the UN standards and requirements through regional, sub-regional and national workshops.[160] These involve the relevant competent national authorities and tailor-made technical assistance (based on the highlighted strength and weaknesses of each country) to improve their capacity to implement anti-terrorism legislation in accordance with international standards and obligations (*capability* and *capacity building*). Such events offer criminal justice officials the opportunity to exchange views, develop a useful network, discuss best practices and share experience, ultimately aiming to equip them with the specialised skills and knowledge required to effectively prevent, investigate, detect and prosecute terrorism cases (*information and experience sharing*). The UNODC also provides and disseminates a set of tools and publications, such as the publication entitled 'Preventing terrorist acts: a criminal justice strategy integrating rule of law standards in implementation of United Nations anti-terrorism instruments'.[161]

As a soft power working in different parts of the world, the UNODC's task is two-fold. Firstly, and as its main purpose, the UNODC works with the national authorities concerning the enhancement of their legislations on counterterrorism and human rights in compliance with international norms. At the different conferences, workshops and training every stakeholder shares its experience and knowledge, which might help others to adapt their own response against terrorism. Secondly, the UNODC works on developing cooperation by arranging for the relevant national authorities to meet, creating networks of peers and informal channels of

---

[158] A/RES/71/291, *Strengthening the capability of the United Nations system to assist Member States in implementing the United Nations Global Counter-Terrorism Strategy*, 87th plenary meeting, 15 June 2017.

[159] A/RES/60/288(2006), *United Nations Global Counter-Terrorism Strategy*.

[160] See, e.g., in ASEAN, the Training for Collaborative Intelligence Investigation and Prosecution of Terrorism-Related Cases. Roll-Out Training, General Santos City, 18–22 April 2016; the Inter-Regional conference on Wildlife and Timber Trafficking between ASEAN, Asian and African Countries, Bangkok, 20–22 June 2016; the Second Regional Conference on Enhancing Cooperation on Border Management in ASEAN: Towards a More Interconnected and Safer ASEAN Community, Bangkok, 25–26 April 2016.

[161] See, e.g., UNODC, Assistance Tools and Publications: available at https://bit.ly/3rOFzaB; including the Counter-terrorism Legislation Database: available at https://bit.ly/3d4Fcog; and Counter-terrorism Learning Platform: available at https://bit.ly/378jThS; UNODC, Terrorism Prevention Branch, Menu of Services, Legislative and Capacity-Building Assistance to Prevent and Combat Terrorism, e-book: available at https://bit.ly/3qfKCk3 (accessed on 12 February 2021).

communications (*information and experience sharing*). Events, potentially organised by the UN, focus rather on strategic cooperation, highlighting the shared threats, common difficulties and strength, than on any operational channels or mechanisms of cooperation. Operational cooperation still remains mostly informal and occurs alongside the official meetings. Eventually, the UNODC promotes common legal norms and standards which are meant to ensure a better mutual understanding and knowledge (*capability building*).

As such, the UNODC facilitates experience sharing between national authorities at different levels of competence (e.g. ministers, chiefs of police, frontline officers, etc.) and developing the capabilities and capacities of States in need by providing them with the necessary legal and technical means to prevent and combat terrorism.

Although the UNGA and UNSC norms remain too global to harmonise States' response and to facilitate effective cooperation, the UN has tried to create a broad common background—both legal and political—for mutual trust (slight *capacity building* impact) to emerge. In this framework, the UN's activities have participated somewhat in the birth, enhancement and/or formalisation of mutual trust between competent national authorities.

That being said, there are significant discrepancies between the extent and depth of the UN action in the EU and ASEAN. ASEAN is the region where the UN has been more active.

Among the main reasons for this, it must be highlighted that the EU Member States are all considered 'developed countries', while Southeast Asian countries are mostly decolonised countries and/or 'developing countries'. ASEAN Member States take technical assistance from Dialogue Partners, such as third countries, and relevant specialised agencies as the UNODC in Bangkok and other international organisations, particularly with regard to training and acquisition of equipment. While ASEAN recognises the role played by other international organisations in Southeast Asia, such as the United Nations Asia and Far East Institute for the Prevention of Crime and the Treatment of Offenders (UNAFEI) and the Asia Crime Prevention Foundation (ACPF), in assisting Member States in their development,[162] there has been no precise assessment of the manner in which the UN bodies have actually affected the prevention and combating of crime and the cooperation between Member States.[163] More specifically, the UN Commission on Crime Prevention and Criminal Justice was seen of particular interest before the adoption of the *ASEAN Treaty on Mutual Legal Assistance in Criminal Matters*.[164] It helped Member States cooperate on the basis of common international rules. The UNODC

[162] Pt. 14, *Manila Declaration on the Prevention and Control of Transnational Crime* (1998).

[163] Interpol, 'ASEANAPOL partnership with INTERPOL boosts regional security, INTERPOL Chief tells Laos meeting' *media release*, 31 May 2011.

[164] Pt. 9(d), *Declaration on the Prevention and Control of Transnational Crime*.

was also of particular importance in the drafting and adoption of the *ASEAN Convention on Counter Terrorism.*[165]

Due to the presence of UN offices in Southeast Asia and the direct contacts between UN officers and national and regional authorities through networking, trainings or conferences, ASEAN Member States are claimed to have gained technical and technological means as well as a better understanding and knowledge of each other's terrorist threats, means and methods in order to cooperate together with more effectiveness. By contrast, the presence of the UNODC headquarters and of the special representative office in Europe does not imply a similar influence vis-à-vis EU Member States. It is patently evident that the UNODC has a stronger presence and impact in ASEAN than in the EU.

Based on the three identified clusters, mutual trust has been fostered and supported mostly by the UNODC in ASEAN, while this international actor has been much less of an influencer in the EU. In fact, on the West side of the Ural mountain divide, mutual trust has rather been forged by the Council of Europe and the EU itself.

The UN has mostly supported the social and political dimensions of mutual trust. Through this process, it has mainly focused on capability and capacity building. The third axis has mainly been a subsidiary effect of working on the prior ones. Through its activities, it has fostered strategic, more than operational, interactions between competent national authorities (from high-level decision-makers to field agents). Nonetheless, the format of cooperation fostered remains on an informal level, but might be serve as the basis for more formal bilateral agreements in the future.

B. Formal and informal and/or operational cooperation through Interpol

Complementarily to the UN and its bodies, Interpol has coordinated operational cooperation in sharing operational data, including personal data. Firstly, it is a significant operational channel of communication and hub of information (*information sharing*). Secondly, it provides expertise and support to national law enforcement authorities through trainings or specific investigative support such as forensics, analysis and assistance in locating fugitives (*capacity building*).

Regional agencies and task forces, police committees and secretariats have also been created to promote and deliver more intense local cooperation. Interpol has supported local and regional activities when appropriate and where they can boost effectiveness.[166] It thus attempts to ensure its presence in different regions of the world. Beside their headquarters being in France and the IGCI being in Singapore, Interpol has established a regional bureau in Bangkok with the Thailand liaison office as well as the special representative office to the EU in Brussels.

In ASEAN, Interpol plays an 'institutionalised' role in operational cooperation, in addition to the informal cooperation between competent national authorities.

[165]Interview with an official from the Embassy of the Republic of Indonesia in Singapore, Singapore, 6 June 2016.

[166]Cameron-Waller, 'Interpol. A global service provider' (2008): 58.

Member States prefer to go through its system rather than through their own regional system, namely Aseanapol's system. Ronald K. Noble, Interpol Secretary General at that time, told chiefs of police of ASEAN that their collaboration with global law enforcement initiatives is fundamental to strengthen regional security.[167]

Besides, the Interpol regional office in Bangkok engages in collaboration with other actors present in the region, namely the UNODC and the local law enforcement agencies, to fight serious crime. For instance, in 2013, an Annual Southeast Asia Working Party on Crimes against Children was established between Interpol Liaison Office for Asia and South Pacific, the UNODC and the Royal Thai Police.[168] Interpol has participated in various events, including in the Inter-Regional Conference on Wildlife and Timber Trafficking between ASEAN, Asian and African Countries organised by the UNODC-ROSEAP in Bangkok in June 2016[169] and terrorism-related ones. The objective is to tighten relations with the different entities, namely international and regional organisations, that share the mission of preventing and combating terrorism.

The choice of ASEAN Member States to act globally through international organisations rather than to deepen intra-regional cooperation is quite representative of their position vis-à-vis the purpose of the regional organisation.

In the EU, although remaining a key actor in international cooperation, the interest in Interpol as a hub of information has diminished over time in internal EU matters due to the added value brought by Europol in terms of data exchange, specifically in terms of data processing, analysis and storage. Its chief role and importance have shifted towards that of a bridge—a channel of communication—between the EU Member States and external countries.

Interpol has supported the social dimension of mutual trust. In this process, it has mainly focused on capacity building and information and experience sharing. In so doing, it has fostered operational exchange of data between competent national authorities. Going through the Interpol system, the format of cooperation fostered is rather formal, but it does not exclude certain informal cooperation which might tangentially take place between authorities, who do not want the data to appear elsewhere.

The divergences and potential tensions between countries hinder mutual trust between competent national authorities and might constitute a break in interstate cooperation. This is even more applicable to international relations where there is no legal obligation to cooperate and, thus, where social trust dominates.

---

[167] 'ASEANAPOL partnership with INTERPOL boosts regional security' *media release*, 31 May 2011.

[168] UNODC, 'INTERPOL-UNODC meeting agrees to form annual Southeast Asia Working Party on crimes against Children' *press release*, Bangkok, 27 March 2013: available at https://bit.ly/3rNmS7k (accessed on 26 January 2023).

[169] 'Inter-Regional Conference on Wildlife and Timber Trafficking between ASEAN, Asian and African Countries', organised by the UNODC-ROSEAP with the support of the ASEAN Secretariat and the Royal Thai Police, Bangkok, 20–22 June 2016.

In this context, the international actors and platforms have been entrusted to carry out certain activities meant to facilitate cooperation against transnational crime, including terrorism. In this respect, the UN and Interpol have different competences and tasks.

Using these platforms does not institutionalise or legalise cooperation at the international level. They mainly bring competent authorities together through building bridges for strategic and/or operational cooperation. With the exception of the EU where a certain formalisation of cooperation has occurred, transnational cooperation remains predominantly informal, even with these actors' support (e.g. UN and Interpol).

II. The emergence of regional platforms and actors: a step, a support and/or a result of the building up of mutual trust?

As in Chaps. 4 and 5, the 'chicken and the egg' dilemma also applies to the relation between the development of platforms for cooperation or actors and the building up of mutual trust. In essence, the question that needs to be addressed is whether the development of these platforms or actors helps building up trust or, conversely, whether mutual trust constitutes a preliminary step to the creation and strengthening of these platforms and/or actors.

In a context where global operational cooperation suffers from distrust between States, the EU has developed its institutional capacities and those of its regional bodies and agencies (A) beyond what ASEAN Member States have been willing to develop at the regional or sub-regional levels (B). Due to interesting chronological similarities between the two regional organisations, the section focuses first on the different EU bodies and then ASEAN ones.

A. The integration of key European regional actors and channels of communication into the virtuous circle of 'mutual trust/cooperation'

Before addressing the EU framework, the ways in which the Council of Europe (CoE) has indirectly fostered cooperation must be mentioned again. The CoE supports the capabilities and capacities of its members regarding the effective implementation of its standards in criminal justice.

As aforementioned in this chapter, the CoE provides a more specific legal background in terms of judicial cooperation in criminal matters for States parties compared to the international one. Two of the most relevant CoE structures or bodies are the PC-OC (Problèmes Criminels—Operation of Conventions) and the Criminal Law Co-operation Unit.

The PC-OC is a committee of experts in the field of international cooperation in criminal matters working under the authority of the European Committee on Crime Problems (CDPC) and composed of representatives of the central authorities of the 47 CoE Member States and observers. It monitors the application of the CoE conventions related to international cooperation in criminal matters (including mutual legal assistance) and may propose new instruments in this field. It also produces helpful tools, such as country information, model forms, practical guidelines, etc., for practitioners who deal with these instruments.

The Criminal Law Co-operation Unit is also worth mentioning. Through cooperation activities and projects, this unit assists the beneficiary countries to integrate the CoE standards in their criminal justice systems. It aims to help States improve their legislation and practice related to the work of the law enforcement authorities as well the execution of penal sanctions and measures. Obviously, may it be said, the overall work of the Council of Europe focuses mainly on improving human rights, democracy and the rule of law. Eventually, the CoE publishes the results of its analyses in guidelines.[170] In this respect, the CoE also has an impact on the capacities of the different States concerned (*capacity building*). It does not aim to facilitate information sharing, but experience may be shared during the trainings, conferences and other activities organised by the Criminal Law Co-operation Unit.

In so doing, the Council of Europe contributes to the development of the social, political and legal dimension of mutual trust between competent national authorities, including those of the EU Member States.

1. From platforms of discussions conducive to cooperation…

Platforms of discussions have slowly emerged and evolved alongside, and in support of, norms facilitating horizontal cooperation between competent national authorities.

Initially, Member States established platforms for cooperation gathering representatives of the ministries, to share information and experience. These platforms have disappeared or, more often, evolved along with the integration process to become EU bodies or agencies.

Taking, for instance, the TREVI Group and the other attempts to enhance cross-border cooperation, which evolved into working groups within the EU institutional framework as well as springboards for launching new platforms such as the establishment of a European Police Chiefs Operational Task Force under the impulse of the 1999 Tampere European Council. The latter was then replaced, with the Lisbon Treaty, by the Standing Committee on Internal Security (COSI), losing the representativeness of police force along the way. TREVI also resulted in the establishment of Europol.

Over time and for the purpose of responding to the new challenges, EU platforms have multiplied and have fostered, mostly informal, cross-border cooperation. They have provided competent national authorities with regional support for their objective to prevent and combat serious transnational crime, including terrorism.

Due to the absence of competence of the EU in the field of national security, there is no EU body or agency for intelligence services. Nonetheless, regional platforms have appeared for intelligence authorities to share experience, best practices and information. Some are worth mentioning briefly.

One of the most important cooperation platforms is the Club de Berne which gathers intelligence authorities from EU Member States as well as Norway and

[170] See the CoE guidelines of criminal law cooperation: available at https://www.coe.int/en/web/criminal-law-coop (accessed on 28 January 2023).

Switzerland. This Club was founded in 1969, before the TREVI Group or any other judicial or law enforcement gathering. Here, the directors of domestic intelligence services meet annually.

In 2001, the Club de Berne founded a Counter Terrorism Group (CTG), in which members regularly exchange information on incidents and discuss follow-up measures. Since 1 July 2016, this Club and its CTG run an operational platform in The Hague. The domestic intelligence services there maintain a common database and a real-time information system. Details are secret, so parliamentary control of its activities is barely possible. The CTG is intended to network more closely with police structures of the EU or individual Member States. As such, this Club is more operational than others such as the Intelligence Analysis and Situation Centre (IntCen),[171] which is a civilian intelligence grouping affiliated to the European External Action Service (EEAS). This Centre evaluates reports on terrorist threats that domestic intelligence services from the EU provide and briefs the EU Council Working Group on Terrorism and Member States ministries.

Other platforms established to foster cooperation between competent national authorities against terrorism must also be mentioned. In the EU framework, the Group 13+[172] meetings which gather national senior officials in justice and home affairs, experts, but also the European Commission and the EU Counter-Terrorism Coordinator, are among the platforms worth mentioning. Notably, Group 13+ has specifically discussed ways to enhance the informational exchange on foreign terrorist fighters.[173] Moreover, the different competent authorities are represented in numerous groups such as the Paris Group[174] and the SIGINT Seniors Europe

---

[171] The EU IntCen was known as the EU Situation Centre (EU SitCen). The EU SitCen was established as a directorate of the Council General Secretariat, directly attached to the office of the High Representative. The same year, staff from Member States' intelligence services was seconded to SitCen. After several intermediary steps, and the entry into force of the Lisbon Treaty, EU SitCen came under the authority of the new High Representative Catherine Ashton. EU SitCen was transferred to the EEAS on 1 January 2011. Following restructuring, the EU SitCen was renamed the EU Intelligence Analysis Centre (EU IntCen) in March 2012.

[172] Since 2013, Interior Ministers of Belgium, Denmark, Germany, France, Great Britain, Ireland, the Netherlands, Sweden and Spain have been meeting as the 'EU 9 Group' to discuss the topic of 'foreign fighters'. The extension to Austria, Poland and Italy, as well as the EU Member State holding the Presidency, has enlarged the group to 'Group 13+'. Meetings take place in the run-up to or alongside the meetings of the Council for Justice and Home Affairs of the EU. The meetings, which do not take formal decisions, ensure 'an open, informal exchange on the current threat situation' and aim 'on measures to improve the collective capacity to combat international terrorism at European level'.

[173] Council of the European Union, the Presidency to the Standing Committee on Operational Cooperation on Internal Security, Permanent Representatives Committee and the Council, 'Foreign Fighters – Enhancing the information exchange', No. 13777/16, Brussels, 4 November 2016.

[174] Since 2016, the secret service coordinators of several European countries have gathered in the 'Paris Group'. This group was set up 'in response to the terrorist attacks on European territory' and serves as 'an open and trusting exchange on various security issues of intelligence relevance' says the German Federal Government. Fifteen European governments now gather in the Paris Group, including Austria, Belgium, Denmark, France, Germany, Italy, Ireland, the Netherlands, Poland,

meetings[175] gathering secret services, the EUMS INT Directorate[176] gathering military authorities and the Police Working Group on Terrorism (PWGT)[177] gathering senior police officers specialised in the fight against terrorism.

Overall, their concern, objectives and tasks may overlap, which might question their relevance and effectiveness in the fight against terrorism. Besides, the lack of transparency of these platforms prevents the democratic analysis of their actions.

These different platforms, affiliated or not to the EU institutions, have facilitated some of the activities spanning the three clusters composing mutual trust. Through them, officials or field agents of the Member States have shared experiences, best practices, information and intelligence. In the capability building process, these platforms might constitute fora where stakeholders learn about each other's respective legal frameworks, especially each other's criminal justice systems. In the capacity building process, trainings and other meetings for competent national authorities help them elaborate the most appropriate methods and techniques to prevent and counter terrorism. Moreover, these platforms' core tasks are to facilitate the flow of data, potentially through channels of communications, and develop networks of peers. Therefore, the main driving force of cooperation through these

---

Spain, Great Britain, Norway and Sweden. The group has no chairman and no secretary, no formal decisions are taken. Other representatives of European institutions and other multilateral fora can also be invited to meetings.

[175] The SIGINT Seniors encompasses members of the international secret services responsible for digital surveillance (Signals Intelligence). The group is led by the US secret service NSA and consists of the SIGINT Seniors Europe (SSEUR) and SIGINT Seniors Pacific departments. SIGINT Seniors Europe was reportedly established in 1982 to exchange information about the Soviet military. After 9/11, the focus was changed to terrorism and the group increased from nine to 14 members (USA, Canada, Great Britain, Australia and New Zealand as well as Belgium, Denmark, France, Germany, Italy, the Netherlands, Norway, Spain and Sweden). SIGINT Seniors Europe meets annually, allegedly focusing on cooperation on new surveillance techniques. Members communicate via their self-installed system SIGDASYS.

[176] The EUMS INT Directorate operating a military structure processes classified information provided by Member States or transmitted from EU operational areas. It exchanges information with the EU IntCen. Both centres form the Single Intelligence Analysis Capacity (SIAC), under the authority of the High Representative for Foreign Affairs and Security Policy. They are considered to be the main users of intelligence data from the EU Satellite Centre SitCen. The situation reports, analyses and briefings are distributed to, among others, the Ministries of Defence, the Foreign Offices, the Ministries of the Interior, the Domestic and Foreign Secret Services, the Military Secret Service and the Army.

[177] The PWGT was founded in 1979 by the German Federal Criminal Police with the Special Branch of the Metropolitan Police of London, the Bijzondere Zaken Centrale of the Dutch Centrale Recherche Informatiedienst and the Belgian Gendarmerie for the 'exchange of information in terrorist attacks'. Today, the group includes the police headquarters of all EU Member States as well as Norway, Iceland and Switzerland. Although the name suggests a focus on terrorism, its participants also exchange information on extremism or other crime. Since 2000, the PWGT has also helped to prevent political violent activities. The cooperation is also aimed at facilitating operational measures. Notably, the establishment of Europol makes a form of cooperation such as the PWGT superfluous.

various platforms is the social, and political at best, dimension of the mutual trust they built together.

These platforms are specifically promoted by the various EU security programmes, particularly since the integration and institutionalisation of cooperation in criminal matters (see. the 2005 The Hague Programme, 2010 Stockholm Programme or 2014 Strategic guidelines of the European Council[178]).

2. ... to regional actors entrusted and trust-conductor facilitating the flow of data

Competent national authorities have increasingly worked together to build mutual trust. This endeavour has led to several institutional outcomes.

Specific to the fight against terrorism, the Counter-Terrorism Coordinator (CTC) should be quickly mentioned. This position was created following the *Declaration on combating terrorism* adopted after the terrorist attacks in Madrid on 11 March 2004.[179] This declaration identified the relations between the different bodies and agencies in the field of internal security and their interplay as a crucial determinant for any future action of the EU.[180]

Although this function was created after certain EU bodies were established, it has been a crucial support to EU institutions and bodies in the fight against terrorism. The CTC's task is to ensure the dialogue and coordination between the different EU institutions, bodies and agencies competent to prevent and combat terrorism. The CTC coordinates the work of the Council in this matter, presents policy recommendations and proposes priority areas for action to the Council, monitors the implementation of the EU counterterrorism strategy, maintains an overview of all EU instruments, reports to the Council and follows up Council decisions, coordinates with the relevant preparatory bodies of the Council, the Commission and the EEAS, and improves communication between the EU and third countries.

Key EU bodies and agencies have been established to ensure the sustainability of intra-regional cooperation in the field of serious transnational crime, by offering secure channels for information and intelligence sharing and providing authorities with regional strategic and operational analysis. The EU bodies and agencies facilitating police (a) and judicial (b) cooperation, such as Europol[181] and Eurojust,[182] tend to be the result of an evolution of specific preliminary established interstate platforms. Additionally, new transversal European agencies facilitating bilateral and multilateral sharing of data have been established, such as eu-LISA.[183]

---

[178] European Council, General Secretariat of the Council to Delegations, Conclusions, Brussels, 26–27 June 2014.

[179] European Council, *Declaration on combating terrorism*, 2574th Council meeting, Brussels, 30 March 2004.

[180] Anne Weyembergh, Inès Armada, and Chloé Brière, 'The Inter-agency cooperation and future architecture of the EU criminal justice and law enforcement area', Study for the European Parliament (Bruxelles: European Union, 2014).

[181] Art. 88, TFEU.

[182] Art. 85, TFEU.

[183] *Regulation 2018/1726 on the eu-LISA.*

In fact, as consistency and complementarity are crucial to avoid overlap or gaps in the EU criminal area, the EU has increasingly worked to ensure a good articulation between the different EU agencies and bodies (c).

The multiplication of regional agencies and bodies over the past is representative of the evolution of the regional virtuous circle linking mutual trust and data sharing or, in this case, linking mutual trust and the development of regional actors.

(a) *Agencies and bodies competent in law enforcement cooperation: the clear demonstration of the virtuous circle's outcome*

Since TREVI, Member States have taken successive steps that led to the establishment of the EU law enforcement agencies, such as Europol, followed by the European Police College.

Police cooperation between law enforcement authorities took a crucial turn when Europol was conceived and established by the adoption of the 1995 *Convention on the establishment of a European Police Office (Europol Convention).*[184] Some authors even 'suggested that the EU wanted a Europol because Interpol was not providing what it needed'.[185] Europol, however, was initially given specific terms of reference that essentially required it to focus on the top level of transnational crimes, whereas Interpol had a much broader mandate. Besides, their roles particularly differ concerning the development and handling of criminal intelligence. Moreover, Europol has a more restrictive jurisdictional limitation, compared to Interpol. Despite Europol's advantages in the processing, analysis, storage and sharing of data, the agency remains competent within the EU and its external partners only. Regardless, Interpol is, and will remain, a significant and key service provider for States all over the world.

Europol has become a major player within the EU for supporting and strengthening cooperation between Member States in the fight against terrorism. Historically, its duties have been hindered by the lack of trust among Member States (low social trust between competent national authorities, lack of political trust between Member States and let's not even mention legal trust). It also suffered from a lack of vertical trust from national authorities who resisted, at first, having to provide it with necessary information, including information relating to terrorism (see. the many calls addressed by the CTC to Member States and their competent national

---

[184] *Council Act of 26 July 1995 drawing up the Convention based on Article K.3 of the Treaty on European Union on the establishment of a European Police Office (Europol Convention)*, O.J.E.C. C316/1, 27 November 1995. For the history and development of Europol, Weyembergh, Armada, and Brière, 'The Inter-agency cooperation and future architecture of the EU criminal justice and law enforcement area' (2014): 11 and ff; Bunyan, 'Trevi, Europol and the European State' (1993); Sabine Gless, 'Europol' in *Research Handbook on EU Criminal Law*, eds., Valsamis Mitsilegas, Maria Bergström and Theodore Konstadinides (Cheltenham: Edward Elgar, 2016); Céline C. Cocq and Francesca Galli, 'The evolving role of Europol in the fight against terrorism at the EU level: Deficient flows of information and future prospects' in *Trust in international police and justice cooperation*, eds., Saskia Hufnagel and Carole McCartney, Oñati International Series in Law and Society (Oxford: Hart Publishing, 2017).

[185] Cameron-Waller, 'Interpol. A global service provider' (2008): 58.

authorities to increase transmission of information). This resistance has of course been a source of concern as it has hampered Europol's activities and efficiency. The difficulty to establish and develop trust is precisely the reason behind the gathering of all law enforcement agencies in the same building: improving mutual interpersonal knowledge and direct peer-to-peer cooperation.

In response to the attacks in Paris in November 2015, a new European Counter Terrorism Centre (ECTC) was established in January 2016. In fact, attempts were made prior to the attacks. But, once again, the events fostered the creation of the Centre by adding necessity to the missing level of trust. This Centre is meant to become a central information hub in the fight against terrorism in the EU 'providing analysis for on-going investigations and contributing to a coordinated reaction in the event of major terrorist attacks'.[186] Through Europol, competent national authorities cooperate and coordinate their actions in such a way as to ensure an effective and efficient response to terrorism. This is a clear example of institutionalisation of mutual trust being applied to the facilitation of cooperation in criminal matters.

Nourished by the trust that Member States and their national authorities have built, Europol's legitimacy has grown. Reciprocally, Europol has fostered mutual trust in facilitating the dialogue between competent national authorities to perform effectively.[187] This development has been very dependent upon Member States' ability and willingness to engage with Europol and with each other via Europol. In this process, meetings have been—and still are—crucial to raise awareness of the agency's competence and to develop personal contacts to streamline cooperation in order to share best practices and information (*information and experience sharing*) more effectively. There is in fact a clear causal relationship between legitimacy and effectiveness. The more Europol becomes legitimate and trusted by the competent authorities, the more it builds further mutual trust and gains effectiveness.[188] Integrating elements of protection of human rights while further developing Europol's tasks and functions (e.g. the data protection rules applying to the processing and exchange of information, the sharing of best practices and experience, the data analysis and processing and the trainings) as well as its own channel of communication, the Secure Information Exchange Network Application (SIENA), is meant to improve mutual trust between competent national authorities in the agency (*capacity building*) and, as consequence, the fight against terrorism. Europol has found its place in the EU security landscape, becoming a credible actor in the eyes of national authorities. As such, cross-border cooperation through Europol has become both formal and informal.

---

[186] Europol, 'Europol's European Counter Terrorism Centre Strengthens the EU's Response to Terror' *media release*, 25 January 2016; see also Europol, 'Annex 4: Europol Counter-Terrorism Activities', *TE-SAT 2016* (The Hague: European Police Office, 2016): 49 and ff.

[187] Cocq and Galli, 'The evolving role of Europol in the fight against terrorism at the EU level' (2017).

[188] Michael Barnett, 'Social Constructivism' in *The Globalisation of World Politics: An Introduction to International Politics*, eds., John Baylis, Steve Smith, and Patricia Owens (Oxford: Oxford University Press, 2008): 165.

Complementary to Europol, the European Police College (CEPOL) was established under the impulse of the 1999 Tampere European Council. It was initially meant to be a network of existing national training institutes, without precluding the establishment of a permanent institution at a later stage.[189] The *Council Decision 2005/681/JHA,*[190] later amended by *Regulation 2015/2219,*[191] made CEPOL an entity of the Union with the aim of training senior police officers of the Member States and facilitating cooperation between national police forces by organising and coordinating training activities with a European policing dimension and supporting information sharing. CEPOL works closely with other agencies, including Europol.

Supported by CEPOL's action, Europol is an essential actor in the pre-trial phase as it gathers, processes and shares information and intelligence. With the rules governing police cooperation through Europol, mutual trust has become three-dimensional. The prominence that Europol has earned over the years is the direct result of the aforementioned virtuous circle which involves building mutual trust between competent national authorities as well as the progressive institutional and legal developments nourishing each other, culminating in a streamlined data flow.

The EU Agency for the Operational Management of Large-Scale IT Systems in the AFSJ (eu-LISA)[192] constitutes a platform for competent national authorities to access the various databases it manages, including Eurodac, SIS and VIS, and develops, including the EES, ETIAS and ECRIS-TCN. By centralising the databases, the EU has ensured their interoperability and access to information, and has thus smoothened the sharing of data within the EU. Such interoperability has been made possible due to the numerous safeguards the EU has developed over the years, including human rights and data security standards, as well as the subsequent mutual trust developed between competent national authorities. Mutual trust within the EU is based on shared human rights safeguards, on common legislations regarding the gathering, processing, sharing and use of data in criminal proceedings and on interpersonal relations facilitated by regional bodies and platforms.

Cooperation between law enforcement authorities has gone from intergovernmental to a more integrated system involving regional actors such as Europol, institutionalised and technically implemented channels of communication.[193]

---

[189] *Council Decision 2000/820/JHA of 22 December 2000 establishing a European Police College (CEPOL)*, O.J. L336/1, 30 December 2000.

[190] *Council Decision 2005/681/JHA establishing the European Police College (CEPOL) and repealing Decision 2000/820/JHA*, O.J. L256/63, 1 October 2005.

[191] *Regulation (EU) 2015/2219 of the European Parliament and of the Council of 25 November 2015 on the European Union Agency for Law Enforcement Training (CEPOL) and replacing and repealing Council Decision 2005/681/JHA*, O.J. L319/1, 4 December 2015.

[192] *Regulation 1077/2011 establishing a European Agency for the operational management of large-scale IT systems in the area of freedom, security and justice*; *Regulation 2018/1726 on the eu-LISA*.

[193] Integrating and institutionalising police cooperation at the EU level, the Stockholm Programme—as well as the General Conclusions of the 2014 Council of the EU—particularly

These agencies, and their evolution most importantly, are representative of the development of mutual trust between competent national authorities as well as the necessity for working together closely in the fight against terrorism. Their evolution is also representative of the growing trust between national competent authorities towards EU actors; or the growing need for national authorities to trust each other to prevent and combat serious transnational crime.

(b) *Agencies and bodies competent in judicial cooperation: two different outcomes of the virtuous circle*

In a complementary manner, while Europol serves to improve cooperation between competent national law enforcement authorities, Eurojust[194] does similar between judicial authorities. Eurojust's main action is to support and strengthen coordination and cooperation between national judicial authorities in relation to serious crime affecting two or more Member States. Eurojust is thus also charged with facilitating MLA and the exchange of information between judicial authorities. This aspect was already present in the initial 2002 Decision.[195] The sharing of information was further elaborated upon in the 2009 Council Decision, amending the 2002 Council Decision by including Articles 13 and 13a regarding the exchange of information with the Member States and between national members as well as regarding the information Eurojust provides to competent national authorities. But, the task of analysing information does not seem to appear in the Council Decision[196] nor in the 2018 Regulation.[197] The analysis of data can be carried out by the national member for the purpose of determining whether such data are relevant to Eurojust's tasks and can be included in the case management system. It is only in 2022 that Eurojust was attributed a task of 'analysis' but only with regard to genocide, crimes against humanity, war crimes and related criminal offences.[198]

With the purpose of improving data sharing, Eurojust has gone a step further in the centralisation of judicial cooperation in terrorism matters. Proposed in 2018 by a

---

underlines the role of the European agencies and institutions. *The Stockholm Programme* (2010); European Council, Conclusions of the European Council (26–27 June 2014), General Secretariat of the Council to Delegations, EUCO 79/14, Brussels, 27 June 2014.

[194] *Eurojust Regulation.*

[195] The direct exchange of information between national members through Eurojust was specified in Article 6(a)(v); the processing of data is provided for in the Decision insofar as it is done for the purpose of the exchange (Art. 14), as well as the storage of information (Arts. 16 and 21): *Council Decision 2002/187/JHA setting up Eurojust.*

[196] In the 2002 Eurojust Decision, there was no mention of analysis. Interestingly, the only mention of 'analysis' is the one carried out by Europol (Art. 7(d) and (f)).

[197] *Regulation (EU) 2018/1727 on the European Union Agency for Criminal Justice Cooperation (Eurojust) and replacing and repealing Council Decision 2002/187/JHA*, O.J. L295/138, 21 November 2018.

[198] *Regulation (EU) 2022/838 of the European Parliament and of the Council of 30 May 2022 amending Regulation (EU) 2018/1727 as regards the preservation, analysis and storage at Eurojust of evidence relating to genocide, crimes against humanity, war crimes and related criminal offences*, O.J.E.U. L 148/1, 31 May 2022.

group of countries amongst the most affected by terrorism, namely Belgium, France, Germany and Spain,[199] a European judicial Counter-Terrorism Register (CTR) was launched at Eurojust. This Register aims to reinforce Member States' judicial response to terrorist threats. The CTR, which entered into force on 1 September 2019, centralises key judicial information to establish links in proceedings against suspects of terrorist offences. The CTR is managed by Eurojust in The Hague on a 24-h basis and provides proactive support to national judicial authorities. This centralised information is dedicated to help prosecutors coordinate more actively and identify the suspects or networks that are being investigated in specific cases with potential cross-border implications.[200] Eurojust's system is beginning to resemble Europol's more closely. This provides hints about the intentions of the EU decision-makers in facilitating the inter-agency cooperation and the flow of data.

Interestingly, trust has been mentioned several times by Mr. Frédéric Baab—former French National Member at Eurojust and initiator of the CTR—at the press conference which launched the CTR at Eurojust.[201] In his experience, lacking trust has hindered cooperation and prevented competent national authorities from sharing data about terrorism-related cases. Yet, one wonders if the recent steps were taken because of an enhancement of mutual trust or merely out of necessity. Either way, these improvements have fostered mutual trust between competent national authorities via the respective agencies.

Besides Eurojust, a 'new generation' judicial body has been established, namely the European Public Prosecutor Office (EPPO), but this time via enhanced cooperation.[202] The Treaty on the EU kept in Title IV the possibility for Member States to establish enhanced cooperation between themselves within the framework of the Union's non-exclusive competences. Trying to solve the issue posed by potential insurmountable differences between Member States, this possibility was created in order for a certain number of Member States to establish a form of cooperation that is designed to enhance the process of integration without undermining the Union's cohesion. The possibility to launch enhanced cooperation was also specifically mentioned in Art. 86 TFEU, focusing on the EPPO.[203]

---

[199] "Déclaration commune de la France, de l'Allemagne, de l'Espagne et de la Belgique en faveur de la creation d'un 'registre judiciaire européen antiterroriste' auprès d'Eurojust", 20 June 2018: available at https://bit.ly/3aeVuJl (accessed on 4 December 2020).

[200] Eurojust, 'Launch Eurojust of Judicial Counter-Terrorism Register at Eurojust. Speeding up and Strengthening the Judicial Response to terrorism' *news release*, 5 September 2019: available at https://bit.ly/3pjMGGm (accessed on 12 February 2021).

[201] Frédéric Baab, until recently French National Member at Eurojust and initiator of the Counter-Terrorism Register, 'Press conference on Launch of Judicial Counter-Terrorism Register at Eurojust', Main press room, Justus Lipsius building of the Consilium of the EU, 5 September 2019.

[202] *Council Regulation 2017/1939 on the EPPO.*

[203] Art. 86(1), TFEU.

Now operational, the EPPO has become the most supranational EU body in criminal matters, amongst the 22 participating Member States.[204] Agencies such as Europol and Eurojust remain intergovernmental in their functioning as they do not replace the national authorities and are deprived of binding powers vis-à-vis national authorities. By contrast, the EPPO is a fully independent and a decentralised prosecution office of the EU. It may even constitute a step further in regional integration as it is equipped with binding powers towards the national authorities.[205] For this reason, it is said that the EPPO concretises the passage from horizontal towards vertical cooperation. It is built on two levels: the central and the national decentralised level. The central level consists of the European Chief Prosecutor, its two Deputies and twenty-two European Prosecutors (one per country). The decentralised level consists of European Delegated Prosecutors located in the participating countries. The central level supervises the investigations and prosecutions carried out at the national level. As a rule, the European Delegated Prosecutors carry out the investigation and prosecution in their own country. However, the EPPO's material scope of competence has, thus far, been limited to frauds against the budget of the EU. This being said, Article 86 TFEU provides for the possibility of extending its scope of action to other forms of serious transnational crime, including terrorism. Proposals have been made to this end, but extensions of this nature are subject to European Council unanimity and, for the time being, the Member States are unenthusiastic about granting the extension.[206]

Regional actors and institutionalised channels of communication have clearly integrated the virtuous circle: mutual trust—data sharing (through the development of regional actors and channels of communication). Their establishment is representative of the progressive development and enhancement of mutual trust—and its three dimensions—in the EU. Indeed, along with a legalisation of the principle of mutual trust, horizontal cross-border cooperation between competent national authorities has become more institutionalised, resulting in the emergence of legitimate regional actors.

(c) *Inter-agency collaboration against terrorism: a crucial demonstration of deepening of mutual trust within the EU*

Regional bodies and agencies have been key actors in the building of trust based on the development of the competent national authorities' capacities (*capacity building*) and on *information and experience sharing* in a common regional legal framework (*capability building*). They facilitate direct peer-to-peer cooperation among judicial authorities and among law enforcement authorities, taking steps

[204] See the list of participating members at https://www.eppo.europa.eu/en/members (accessed on 25 February 2023).

[205] Telò and Weyembergh, 'Supranationality and sovereignty in an era of increasing complexity and fragmentation' (2020).

[206] See, e.g., Chloé Brière, 'Le Parquet européen: analyse critique d'une réussite tempérée par d'importants défis à relever' *Cahiers de droit europeen*, vol. 55, no. 1 (2019).

towards formalisation, institutionalisation and legalisation. Achieving a sound articulation and complementarity of the actions of these increasingly numerous bodies and agencies is inherently required. Fostering intra-regional collaboration between regional bodies and agencies demonstrates an important level of trust within the EU. Although not going into detail about their collaboration,[207] specific developments reveal the challenges of such endeavours as well as the added value for cross-border cooperation. Accordingly, it demonstrates how inter-agency collaboration is a progressive step towards the goal of strengthening mutual trust within the region.

Ensuring the coherence of the EU's action against terrorism, collaboration between agencies or bodies is increasingly required in various political and legal documents, including the legal instruments constituting the legal basis for each of them. However, organising this coherence and inter-agency collaboration in practice is challenging in light of the differences (including structural) which exist between these different actors.

Firstly, looking at the traditional bilateral inter-agency collaboration between Europol and Eurojust, it is interesting to note that a form of connection between their tasks was already mentioned in 2002, when Eurojust was established.[208] Their bilateral collaboration improved over time becoming streamlined and more operational. Over time, the EU has increasingly brought their governing organisational structures into alignment and created synergy between them, particularly between Eurojust's CTR and Europol's ECTC. This synergy was made, from the start, in the proposal for the establishment of the CTR in 2018. Inter-agency cooperation seems to take an important operational turn. This inter-agency sharing of data is quite interesting as it seems independent from Member States.[209] This might indicate a higher level of trust in the EU institutions. Yet, Member States are not excluded from this interaction as they remain the owner of the data throughout the entire process. As such, they decide whether to share the data and control how and for what purpose the data is used (cf. purpose limitation). Therefore, Member States agree on the Europol-Eurojust exchange of information. Such inter-agency cooperation aims to make police and judicial cooperation within the region more interconnected and coordinated.

In addition to this traditional form of bilateral inter-agency collaboration, new actors have increasingly been involved in the prevention and combating of serious

[207] For a deeper analysis of this inter-agency collaboration, see, e.g., Weyembergh, Armada and Brière, 'The Inter-agency cooperation and future architecture of the EU criminal justice and law enforcement area' (2014); Chloé Brière, 'Cooperation of Europol and Eurojust with external partners in the fight against crime: a legal appraisal' in *The External Dimension of EU Agencies and Bodies. Law and Policy*, eds., Herwig C. H. Hofmann, Ellen Vos and Merijn Chamon, Law (Cheltenham: Edward Elgar Publishing, 2019).

[208] Arts. 7(d) and (f), 26(1) and 27(1)(a), *Council Decision 2002/187/JHA setting up Eurojust*.

[209] Weyembergh, Armada, and Brière, 'The Inter-agency cooperation and future architecture of the EU criminal justice and law enforcement area' (2014): 14–19.

transnational crime, such as Frontex.[210] This agency is meant to 'cooperate with Europol and Eurojust and provide support to Member States in circumstances requiring increased technical and operational assistance at the external borders in the fight against cross-border crime and terrorism'.[211] The relations between Frontex and Europol have particularly grown in recent years and have become essential not only to ensure the security at the external borders, but also to support investigations. The Agency is not meant to launch or coordinate counterterrorism operations or investigations, but it contributes to the fight against terrorism through its operational assistance to the Member States focusing on the external borders, and in cooperation with other EU internal security partners. In fact, border management agencies can support their internal security counterparts by providing valuable information and intelligence, including personal data, and even collect evidence to support counterterrorism operations and/or investigations. Responding to the new security challenges (cf. migration crisis), the 2016 Regulation expanded the sources from which personal data can be gathered and the type of information that can be processed. This Regulation has also allowed Frontex to use its own staff to collect personal data. This possibility of data collection was motivated by the fact that there have been cases of terrorists or radicalised individuals ready to commit terrorist acts using the flow of migrants to enter the EU territory (see for instance, the threat posed by Islamist foreign terrorist fighters coming back from Syria and Iraq or the far-right foreign terrorist fighters coming back from the Russia-Ukraine conflict[212]).

These regional actors have been helpful in building and nourishing trust amongst competent national authorities. Reciprocally, mutual trust has strengthened their legitimacy and emphasised the importance of their role to facilitate cooperation as well as enabled them to achieve their objective(s). They have evolved into more ambitious structures and objectives. They have also developed greater complementarity. Better inter-agency collaboration has allowed them to gain more legitimacy over the years.

B. A socialisation of competent national authorities within ASEAN through regional platforms for cooperation and regional actors

As highlighted previously, ASEAN must address certain equivalent security threats as identified in Europe, including terrorism, illegal drugs, human trafficking,

[210] *Council Regulation (EC) 2007/2004 of 26 October 2004 establishing a European Agency for the Management of Operational Cooperation at the External Borders of the Member States of the European Union*, O.J. L349/1, 25 November 2004; and, *Regulation (EU) 2016/1624 of the European Parliament and of the Council of 14 September 2016 on the European Border and Coast Guard and amending Regulation (EU) 2016/399 of the European Parliament and of the Council and repealing Regulation (EC) No 863/2007 of the European Parliament and of the Council, Council Regulation (EC) No 2007/2004 and Council Decision 2005/267/EC*, O.J. L251/1, 16 September 2016.

[211] Art. 8(1)(m), *Regulation 2016/1624 on the European Border and Coast Guard.*

[212] See, e.g., Anne Weyembergh and Céline Cocq (eds.), 'Foreign terrorist fighters: Enhancing the synergies between the EU's internal and external strategies', special issue, *N.J.E.C.L.*, Vol. 14, No. 2, 2023.

smuggling, money laundering and piracy. Nonetheless, Member States have addressed them in very distinct manners, reflecting the heterogeneous nature of ASEAN,[213] and the underlying norms and practices accepted by its members.[214] Competent national authorities are proposed, and even incited, to cooperate on the basis of regional norms such as the ASEAN Treaty on MLA, or even the ACCT. Despite this, they have no precise legal obligation to do so. ASEAN Member States remain the main or even sole actors in the development and enhancement of cross-border cooperation in the fight against terrorism.

In light of the diversity among its members, ASEAN's approach to security matters rests on quiet diplomacy, dialogue and discussion between the relevant competent national authorities, ranging from top decision-makers to field agents. Decisions and measures, respectively, range from the most strategic to the most operational.

Though Southeast Asian States have been dealing with transnational crime for decades, regional cooperation flourished in the late 1990s. The development of regional cooperation has in fact been a slow and difficult process. When Singaporean Defence Minister NG Eng Hen mentioned that problem transcends borders and nationality, he added that '[w]hen we work together, it strengthens capabilities and interoperability, and demonstrates our shared commitment to counter terrorism in the region'.[215] Transnational security issues have persuaded Southeast Asian States to work together, at the sub-regional and regional levels and beyond.[216] Peer-to-peer cooperation is nonetheless hindered by a lack of trust between certain governments.

1. The development of regional and transregional platforms for strategic rather than operational cooperation

As a traditional intergovernmental organisation, ASEAN works in quite a similar mode to the UN system, although without the Security Council's power to impose actions on Member States. Competent national authorities have been meeting under

---

[213] Telò, *L'Europe en crise et le monde* (2016): 110.

[214] See one of the most prolific authors on the subject, Acharya, *Constructing a Security Community in Southeast Asia* (2001); Acharya and Johnston, 'Comparing Regional Institutions: an Introduction' (2007); Acharya and Johnston, 'Conclusion: institutional features, cooperation effects, and the agenda for further research on comparative regionalism' (2007); Acharya, *Constructing a Security Community in Southeast Asia* (2014).

[215] Defence Minister NG Eng Hen in 'ASEAN and other countries should do more to combine resources in terrorism fight: Ng Eng Hen' *Channel NewsAsia*, 11 December 2016: available at https://www.gov.sg/news/content/channel-newsasia%2D%2D-asean-and-other-countries-should-do-more-to-combine-resources (accessed on 28 December 2019).

[216] Ralph Emmers, *Non-Traditional Security in the Asia-Pacific: The Dynamics of Securitization* (Singapore: Marshall Cavendish, 2004): 45. For example, Singapore has adopted a rhetoric of security towards sea piracy and maritime terrorism and translated it into an effective response and deterrence policy. Singapore remains, however, at risk as ships need to cross the Straits of Malacca before or after reaching its port facilities. Singapore is acutely aware that its maritime security is dependent on close cooperation with its neighbours, both at a bilateral and multilateral level. The same situation occurs for terrorism.

the umbrella of ASEAN (a) and other regional or transregional centres (b) to discuss subjects of concern and reach strategic to operational decisions.

(a) *ASEAN: an umbrella for collaboration between its Member States*

ASEAN is constituted by a multiplication of platforms for competent national authorities to discuss shared issues, collaborate and cooperate. These platforms are worth being mentioned as they represent opportunities for information and experience sharing. They are characterised by multiple intertwined actions.

Firstly, these meetings are channels of communication between the relevant officials and other stakeholders thus creating informal networks. Although they are not institutionalised, the interactions of the relevant national authorities at these meetings can involve sharing information but, most importantly, experience. The interactions generated by these meetings are more likely to be strategic rather than operational, even during side dialogues. Operational interactions usually occur afterwards on the basis of interpersonal relations created at these meetings. The closer to the field authorities are, the more likely operational interactions might get.

Secondly, they constitute important platforms of mutual learning about each other's respective legal frameworks. Such sharing might inspire States to identify the most appropriate response against terrorism within their own constitutional framework. In the long run, it might even facilitate a certain level of approximation of the relevant legislations.

Going into the specifics of cooperation in non-traditional security issues, ASEAN Ministers of Interior and Home Affairs on transnational crime signed the 1997 *ASEAN Declaration on Transnational Crime*, and formed the ASEAN Ministerial Meeting on Transnational Crime (AMMTC), initially to be held every 2 years. The AMMTC is part of the numerous platforms for Member States to discuss, at different levels of competence, the transnational security issues they encounter and aim to deal with collectively.[217] The role of AMMTC has been to serve as the highest policy-making and coordinating body on ASEAN cooperation on transnational crime amidst other meetings, institutions and plans that deal with the subject, including the Senior Officials Meeting on Transnational Crime (SOMTC); the Directors-General of Immigration Departments and Heads of Consular Affairs Divisions of the Ministries of Foreign Affairs (DGICM); the ASEAN Chiefs of National Police (Aseanapol). The AMMTC has evolved since, including through its expansion to ASEAN Plus Three meetings with Japan, South Korea and China which were first held in 2004.

During their various meetings, Member States have constantly reaffirmed the need to enhance information sharing, strengthen legal measures, as well as boost training and capacity building efforts to combat terrorism.[218] These meetings do not

[217] *Terms of Reference of the ASEAN Ministerial Meeting on Transnational Crime*, 11th AMMTC, Manila, 20 September 2017.

[218] See, e.g., Work Programme to Implement the ASEAN Plan of Action to Combat Transnational Crime, Kuala Lumpur, 17 May 2002.

lead to specific mechanisms of cooperation. They are part of the slow formalisation of the Member States' intent to share best practices, experience and strategic or, potentially, operational information.

The past few years have seen specific efforts made by ASEAN Member States to strengthen cooperation concerning transnational crime. During Malaysia's ASEAN chairmanship, Member States signed the new Kuala Lumpur *Declaration in Combating Transnational Crime*[219] in 2015 and agreed to various measures, including holding the AMMTC annually instead of biannually starting in 2016, and adding three new areas—illicit trafficking in wildlife, illicit trafficking in timber and people smuggling—in addition to the pre-existing eight other areas (drug trafficking, terrorism, economic crimes, human trafficking, money laundering, piracy, weapon smuggling and cybercrime).[220] These events and the declaration of unchanged objectives and means are representative of the absence of progress in developing cooperation mechanisms.

The SOMTC, one of the sub-AMMTC regional platforms, gathers the senior officials involved in the subjects of the various working groups, especially the Working Group on terrorism (SOMTC WG on CT).[221] It is in charge of adopting the relevant policy and guidelines in transnational crime, including terrorism. These meetings require Member States to collaborate and cooperate, but they have no power to force any specific action. Cooperation at this level remains of a policy nature. In practice, States use these meetings to adopt common but wide objectives. States are free to act together or separately to achieve these objectives and to adopt measures suiting their own legal and institutional frameworks. Typical of a collaborative approach, the emphasis is on the objectives rather than on the methods used to achieve them. These SOMTC working groups have influenced the 11 distinct areas of cooperation which have been discussed above. More specifically, the SOMTC WG on CT was formalised during the seventh SOMTC held in Vientiane in June 2007. The Working Group has been held annually and was deemed necessary to facilitate discussions about the development of terrorism cases in the region as well as ways to enhance cross-border cooperation.

Notably, while the AMMTC adopted the *ASEAN Convention on Counter Terrorism*, this SOMTC WG on CT serves as a permanent mechanism for monitoring and reviewing the implementation of the Convention and *ASEAN Comprehensive PoA on Counter Terrorism*. This review process does not imply specific requirements or any infringement procedure, but it is merely a dialogue between parties to facilitate coherent regional implementation. Concurrently, law enforcement authorities have the general authorisation and soft requirement to cooperate with one another. However, such cooperation would fall outside of the purview of any specific regional legal framework (on an informal basis only).

---

[219] *Declaration in Combating Transnational Crime*, 10th AMMTC, Kuala Lumpur, 30 September 2015.

[220] Prashanth Parameswaran, 'What did ASEAN's latest Transnational Crime Meeting achieve?' *The Diplomat*, 23 September 2017.

[221] ASEAN, Terms of Reference, Agenda Item 4, 2nd SOMTC Working Group on Counter Terrorism (2008).

(b) *Building competent national authorities' capacities* via *trans-ASEAN platforms*

As the ASEAN channels of cooperation remain diplomatic, or strategic at best, Member States separately or with other parties, including third countries or international organisations, have established platforms to improve their collaboration and cooperation efforts in criminal matters.

ASEAN Member States have quite successfully created stable centres which have specific purposes, despite their early attempts being unsuccessful. The idea of an ASEAN Centre on Transnational Crime proposed in the 1997 *Declaration on Transnational Crime* was abandoned. Filling this void, certain Member States, notably Indonesia, Malaysia and Thailand, have established centres dedicated to the prevention and combat of transnational crime, including terrorism. These included the Jakarta Centre for Law Enforcement Cooperation (JCLEC) in Indonesia, the Southeast Asia Regional Centre for Counter-Terrorism (SEARCCT) in Malaysia and the International Law Enforcement Academy (ILEA) in Thailand. These three centres were created under the impulse or in collaboration with third partners, namely the UN, the USA and Australia, and due to their external funding. These platforms were established and are governed by the respective ASEAN Member States, not ASEAN as a regional grouping.[222] They are meant to continuously develop new strategies, including regional ones, techniques and tactics for law enforcement authorities to counter terrorism.

The three centres were established to support competent national authorities, especially field agents, in their action against transnational crime. For this purpose, these three centres provide trainings and workshops for competent national authorities to develop effective cooperation within the region. They are also an opportunity to share best practices, experiences and knowledge. With respect to these tasks, these centres bare strong resemblance to CEPOL in Europe. However, CEPOL differs from these centres insofar as it is an EU agency while these centres are not part of the ASEAN bodies. Besides, CEPOL provides training and support to all EU Member States while each centre's training might not include all ASEAN Member States or might include external partners.

Notably, conducting activities in areas specifically related to counterterrorism, SEARCCT also provides a research-based approach to its projects and training programmes. Interestingly, SEARCCT has focused heavily on the prevention of terrorism through programmes of countering violent extremism involving the local communities, reaching beyond the criminal law approach.

These centres and other platforms of dialogue, training and experience and information sharing are meant to enhance cooperation and build trust in the process. They gather authorities working on two of the three clusters, which serve to build trust among themselves: capacity building, and information and experience sharing.

---

[222] Pt. A.1.p.v., Bali Concord III (2013–2017); Beyer, 'ASEAN Counterterrorism: Participation and Causes' (2010): 104–05.

2. The emergence of an ASEAN regional 'actor': does Aseanapol provide added value?

Unlike in the EU, ASEAN Member States have not adopted regional legal obligations for competent national authorities to cooperate through regional actors with autonomous competences. Yet, ASEAN Member States have developed Aseanapol, which is a platform to facilitate cross-border cooperation between competent national authorities (a). A regional actor, associated with legal obligations, is unlikely to be adopted as long as the members remain reluctant to adopt any form of regional institutionalisation, with an autonomous organisation and regional norms imposing precise obligations on the Member States. In this respect, Aseanapol can be compared to Europol, yet it is far from being as institutionalised and operational as Europol is today (b).[223]

(a) *The birth of an ASEAN body with a broad and unclear competence but short arms*

At the first conference in 1981, Aseanapol was just a forum of discussion between Chiefs of ASEAN Police. Over time, Aseanapol has become a notable body in the Southeast Asian panorama concerning criminal matters that might hopefully—or not—become a regional body to be reckoned with. Member States are committed to cooperate to prevent and counter transnational crime, including terrorism. For this purpose, they are dedicated to enhance information and intelligence sharing between competent national authorities and with Aseanapol, amongst other ASEAN bodies and partners.[224]

While Aseanapol could have been established to facilitate police cooperation, it must be noted that the 2004 *ASEAN Treaty on MLA* mentions Aseanapol as a possible channel of communication—alongside Interpol—in urgent cases and where permissible according to the law of the Requested State.[225] This reference could even question the scope of the *ASEAN Treaty on MLA*. It could also question the entire process of cross-border cooperation in criminal matters, including those very services which actually ensure cross-border cooperation between law enforcement officers and between judicial authorities. However, as it has been demonstrated throughout this dissertation, the reference to Aseanapol as a channel of communication and partner of cooperation does not imply any specific legal obligation for Member States and their competent authorities.

Moving slightly towards institutionalisation, ASEAN Member States decided, at the 25th Aseanapol Conference in Bali in 2005, to establish a Permanent Secretariat.

[223] Céline C. Cocq, 'Development of regional legal framework for intelligence and information sharing in the EU and ASEAN' *Tilburg Law Review – Journal of International and European Law, special issue: Privacy and National Security in the Digital Age*, vol. 20, no. 1 (2015).

[224] See, e.g., *ASEAN Declaration on Transnational Crime* (1997); *Plan of Action to Combat Transnational Crime* (1999); *Comprehensive Plan of Action on Counter Terrorism* (2009).

[225] Art. 5(2), *ASEAN Treaty on Mutual Legal Assistance in Criminal Matters* (2004). This possibility remains what it is, i.e. a possibility ('*may* be transmitted through [. . .] ASEANAPOL').

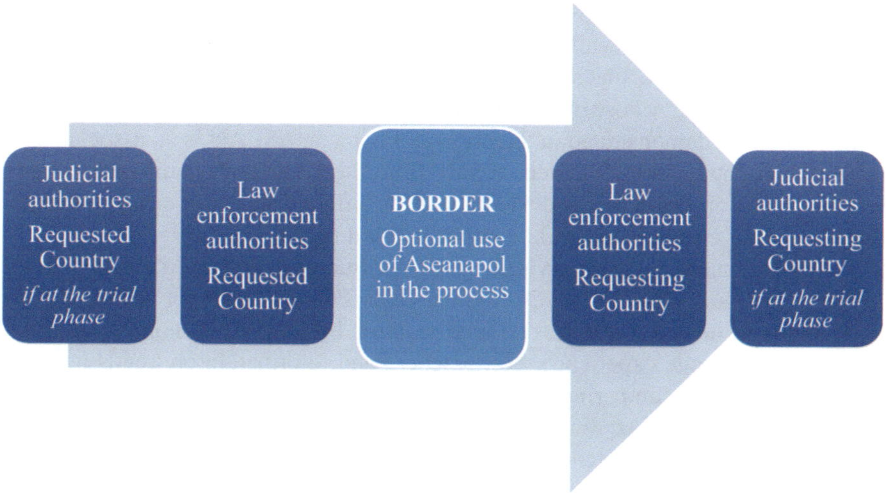

Diagram 6.1 The schematic de facto transnational flow of data (requested or looked for) between ASEAN Member States

This Secretariat has been fully operational since 1 January 2010.[226] This Permanent Secretariat aims to '(1) ensure the effective implementation of all resolutions adopted at the Aseanapol Conferences; (2) serve as a coordination and communication mechanism to allow members to establish and to maintain all channels of interaction amongst members; (3) foster mutual assistance and cooperation amongst members; and (4) endeavour to increase regional cooperation efforts against transnational crime'.[227] The objective of this body is so broad that it might not take place between judicial authorities, but through police officers who actually execute the terms of the cooperation. As aforementioned, cross-border cooperation tends to be operationalised by law enforcement officers. Data, being either pre-trial information and/or evidence, flows through police authorities to cross borders (Diagram 6.1).

(b) *Aseanapol: towards a Southeast Asian Europol?*

When considering the future of Europol, it has often questioned whether Europol was developing in such as was to as to become the European equivalent of the FBI and whether such an outcome would be feasible and/or desirable.[228] However, the

[226]Pt. 10, Aseanapol, 25th ASEAN Chiefs of Police Conference, Bali, 16–20 May 2005.

[227]Aseanapol's website: http://www.aseanapol.org/about-aseanapol/objectives-and-functions (accessed on 14 November 2020).

[228]Europol 'Is Europol a European FBI?' *FAQ*: available at https://www.europol.europa.eu/faq/europol-european-fbi (accessed on 13 November 2020); Joe Barnes, 'EU's FBI force! Plan to hire 100.000 border agents made by candidate to replace Juncker" Express: available at https://bit.ly/2NgGC49 (accessed on 13 November 2020); Matthias Monroy, "Europol Regulation: towards a 'European FBI?'": available at https://digit.site36.net/2020/08/04/europol-regulation-towards-a-european-fbi/ (accessed on 13 November 2020).

constitutional architecture governing these two agencies is completely different: the USA is a federal country while the EU is a union of sovereign countries that reserve the use of coercion to the realm of the State. Similarly, it could be questioned whether Aseanapol, whose name suggests a localised form of Europol's, would mimic them. As demonstrated in the previous chapters, ASEAN is an association of sovereign countries, which differs greatly from the Union. Their differences have had an impact on the different development (or different stages of development) of the Aseanapol's legal framework, competence and tasks.

Europol is an agency supervised by EU institutions, unlike Aseanapol or the former European Police Chiefs Operational Task Force. Aseanapol is indeed more comparable to the European Task Force required by the 1999 Tampere European Council to exchange experience, best practices and information on trends in cross-border crime. Yet, comparing Aseanapol and Europol, as they both stand today, some conclusions may be drawn as follows.

Firstly, the European agency's status and objective are regulated by a regionally binding norm, namely the 2016 *Europol Regulation*. Aseanapol's role and actions are governed by its *Terms of Reference*, which are not publicly available and do not impose any legally binding obligations.

Looking at the relevant authorities, cooperation is generally required between the 'duly authorised representatives'[229] or 'relevant authorities'.[230] Information and intelligence may be shared between competent national authorities (in the general meaning of this designation) on the basis of certain ASEAN norms, but when it relates to sharing data through Aseanapol and its database, only police officers are authorised to do so.

Through an examination of Aseanapol and Europol's respective objectives,[231] certain similarities and differences can be highlighted. On the one hand, both Aseanapol and Europol aim to foster cooperation in cross-border cases; though the presentation of Aseanapol's objective is less precise than the one of Europol. On the other hand, Aseanapol seems to have, in reality, a rather strategic role in facilitating interactions amongst members, while Europol is much more operational. In fact, Europol is associated with other norms requiring competent national authorities to cooperate together (see. previous section), which is not the case for Aseanapol (see. the non-binding documents requiring ASEAN Member States to cooperate).

Looking at the human rights standards governing Europol and Aseanapol's activities, Europol is bound by the human rights standards fixed by the EU primary norms and its own internal standards. As there is only the *ASEAN Declaration on Human Rights* that is not binding upon competent national authorities and even less upon Aseanapol. Discussions about human rights are scarce—if not inexistent—within

---

229 Art. II(2) (v), *Agreement on Information Exchange and Establishment of Communication Procedures* (2002).

230 Art. I, 2007 ACCT.

231 Aseanapol's website: http://www.aseanapol.org/about-aseanapol/objectives-and-functions (accessed on 14 November 2020); Art. 3, *Europol Regulation*.

Aseanapol. Moreover, for the purpose of ensuring a better protection of human rights, the European Parliament and an independent body composed of data protection experts from each EU Member State's independent data protection authority, namely the Joint Supervisory Body, control the application of data protection standards by the agency. This sort of control mechanism does not exist within Aseanapol.

Europol is thus governed by binding norms, including human rights safeguards, and is much more institutionalised than Aseanapol.

Secondly, Aseanapol and Europol's missions look roughly similar, up until a certain point. The means available to the ASEAN Chiefs of Police and the Secretariat of Aseanapol diverge drastically from their Europol counterparts though.

Regarding cooperation through data sharing, Aseanapol is meant to enhance the exchange of best practices and experiences, the exchange of information on a case-by-case basis about current investigations and to provide support on transnational actions. Unlike Europol, this forum does not physically gather competent national authorities in its headquarters to help with these tasks. Due to the *ASEAN Convention on Counter Terrorism*'s requirements, Aseanapol can be an interesting forum of discussion on the implementation of the Convention provisions. Interestingly, the ACCT does not mention Aseanapol, although Aseanapol already existed at the time of the Convention's adoption. Aseanapol is referred to in the associated PoA, amongst the axes of actions. Member States are supposed to work in close cooperation with Aseanapol on the improvement of information sharing concerning lost and stolen passports, lost and stolen vehicles, fingerprints, wanted persons, etc.[232] A similar requirement already exists and is operational in the EU (see especially the SIS).

Interpol, with its databases, constitutes the main operational international partner of the ASEAN Member States. In terrorism-related matters, the PoA associated with the ACCT requires from Member States to exchange data via the INTERPOL-UNSC Special Notices, Orange Notices, fingerprints, DNA and other terrorism-related data. The PoA specifies that Member States need to enhance their capacity and the flow of terrorism-related information, including through Aseanapol and Interpol.

Aseanapol fosters the transfer of data between competent national authorities on the model of the Interpol 24/7 interface, rather than the Europol's SIENA.[233]

The Aseanapol Database System (e-ADS) is considered a useful tool for easier exchange of information, particularly regarding stolen and lost travel documents, stolen motor vehicles, wanted and missing persons, and membership to syndicates and other organised crime groups.[234] Through this database, Aseanapol aims to build a

[232] See, e.g., Art. 5(1), *ASEAN Treaty on Mutual Legal Assistance in Criminal Matters* (2004); Pt. 8, ASEAN Comprehensive Plan of Action on Counter Terrorism (2009).

[233] Interview with an official from the Special Branch's Counter-Terrorism Division of the Royal Malaysian Police (2016), op. cit.; group interview at the Aseanapol Headquarters hosted in the Royal Malaysian Police with officials from the Indonesian National Police, from the Philippine National Police, and from the Indonesian National Police, Kuala Lumpur, 8 June 2016.

[234] 31st Aseanapol Database System Technical Committee Meeting, Taguig, 17–21 March 2014. Interestingly, this database located in Singapore is not hosted at Aseanapol headquarters in Kuala Lumpur.

more effective and regionally institutionalised mechanism of information exchange. Interestingly, no official legal instrument provides for the establishment and functioning of the e-ADS; or this information has not been made public. Nowhere is it written that Member States shall nourish the Aseanapol database and should share data through this forum. This system includes a web portal where the geographically dispersed ASEAN Police Force users can upload and access information or use this portal as a forum to post and reply to messages.[235] Notably, a crucial part of the e-ADS is its interface to the Interpol system. This interface eliminates the need to manually update information to the Interpol information system, thus saving time and resources.[236] Only the Aseanapol Database System Technical Committee ensures the proper implementation and enhancement of this e-ADS.

Regarding data analysis, this is where the divergence becomes even more prominent. Aseanapol is not tasked with the analysis of data, which is the added value of Europol over Interpol. Far from currently being at the same level as Europol's databases with the Europol Information System (EIS) and the Analysis Work Files (AWFs), the e-ADS[237] is dedicated to store criminal and crime-related information, also facilitates data cross-checking and provides a system for rapid, reliable and secure 24/7 exchange of criminal information. No mention is made about the analysis of the data which populates this database.

Analysing the added value of this regional body, no report on the activities of Aseanapol and, more particularly, on the scope of the e-ADS has been published yet. Only very short briefs on the holding of the meetings are published without precise information on the object of the discussions and on the effectiveness of cooperation through Aseanapol, or the work undertaken to improve its effectiveness. Therefore, Aseanapol's action, including the impact of its database on cooperation, is difficult to assess. The only reference point is what the respective practitioners are willing to mention about this regional body.

Aseanapol is labelled as a 'gentlemen's club' by certain officials.[238] Aseanapol is nonetheless a useful forum to build mutual knowledge, trust and even to exchange operational information on specific criminal threats, mostly on a case-by-case basis. Yet, this regional forum is poorly promoted and supported by ASEAN Member States. In fact, the capacity building role of Aseanapol is not considered as effective as the UNODC's. ASEAN instruments make clear reference to UN entities such as the UNODC. Conversely, almost no reference is made to Aseanapol. Similarly, the Member States still prefer going through Interpol for information sharing rather than through Aseanapol. Member States do not see the added value of the Aseanapol

---

[235] Singapore Technologies Electronics Limited, 'ASEAN Police Forces. Develop e-Community with STEE-InfoSoft solution' *STENGG,* vol. 19, no. 2, 14: available at https://bit.ly/3rQqs0y (accessed on 24 April 2015).

[236] Ibid.

[237] This database located in Singapore is not hosted at Aseanapol headquarters located in Kuala Lumpur.

[238] An expression used by several people interviewed by the author. These interviewees prefer to remain anonymous in their contribution to this subject.

database and the channel of communication, when compared to the services offered by Interpol.[239]

The place and role of Aseanapol and the other platforms of cooperation are representative of the ASEAN institutional and legal developments. They build mutual trust between competent national authorities through capacity building activities and through channels of information and experience sharing. These activities are meant to facilitate direct peer-to-peer cooperation among competent national authorities. Notably, mutual trust remains mostly social in nature. ASEAN norms in criminal matters might mention Aseanapol as a body to be used for cooperation purposes, but no norm is actually precise and binding enough (see. the constitutive acts of each body) to make the ASEAN body more operational. Moreover, the development of ASEAN platforms and bodies facilitating law enforcement cooperation has been the only focus of officials. This is not conducive to human rights guarantees—at least when one balances the development of cross-border cooperation in criminal matters.

The virtuous circle previously designed (see also Diagram 6.2) has not reached the same dynamics as in the EU. Mutual trust has been developed in its social dimension mainly; in its political dimension by agreeing on shared objectives (typical of the collaborative approach); but with a limited legal dimension (with no specific means adopted and, most importantly, no legal obligation for Member States). Consequently, regional cross-border cooperation, through various regional discussion platforms, is almost entirely based on social mutual trust, and the absence of regional actors facilitating data sharing is due to the unwillingness—or low willingness—to engage in a regionalisation process. Bilateral agreements which serve as the actual legal basis for more operational cooperation seem to have prevailed in the region for now.

Throughout this section, it has been demonstrated that a three-dimensional mutual trust has facilitated the sustainability of the EU and its Member States' actions against terrorism and the creation of regional bodies fostering cooperation between competent national authorities. By contrast, the loose ASEAN approach constitutes a minimal demonstration of political willingness to engage with each other for the purpose of combating terrorism. Its broad regional legal framework might explain the absence of effective regional actors facilitating cross-border cooperation. Cooperation continues to depend on the respective people in authority, i.e. from the decision-makers to the frontline officers, which might hinder the sustainability of cross-border cooperation. Europol and other regional actors are representative of the development in the EU of mutual trust in its three dimensions, whereas Aseanapol shows that mutual trust can be politically motivated, but it is actually its social dimension which is being operationalised.

[239] Interview with an official from the Special Branch's Counter-Terrorism Division of the Royal Malaysian Police (2016), op. cit.; group interview at Aseanapol (2016), op. cit.

Diagram 6.2 The virtuous circle applied to the development of regional bodies facilitating the sharing of data

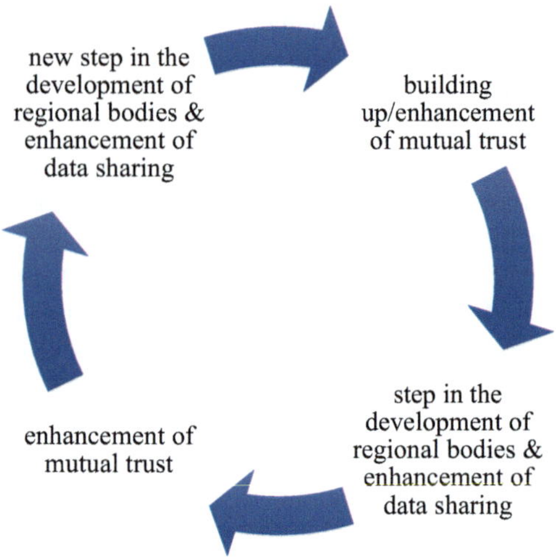

Importantly, this virtuous circle seems to rotate at different speeds depending on the region; slower in ASEAN than in the EU. To this point, shall be added that ASEAN Member States have entered this circle later than the EU. In the future, it will be interesting to observe whether ASEAN's virtuous circle mimics the stage the EU is at today.

Section 3: Mutual Trust and Data Sharing Nourishing and Building upon Each Other—An Endless Virtuous Circle

International norms require States to make use of, among other platforms, the regional frameworks to build up mutual trust and share information and intelligence for the prevention and combating of terrorism. However, the divergences and potential tensions between countries hinder mutual trust amongst competent national authorities and might hinder interstate cooperation.

In this context, the UN and Interpol can have a similar objective. However, they have different competences and tasks, and adopt different strategies. They mainly bring competent authorities together through building networks for strategic and/or operational cooperation. In any case, informal international cooperation remains predominant, even with these actors' support. The international institutions once again provide a wide umbrella for States to cooperate with one another under, including regional frameworks.

In this respect, the EU Member States have established ambitious cooperation mechanisms as well as regional bodies and entities aiding the transnational flow of data, which is not the reality in ASEAN. The top-down influence from the international norms is clearer towards ASEAN's than towards the EU's. ASEAN has more similarities with the UN structures compared to the EU, where norms have gone into much further detail regarding the cooperation requirements and further, and where the regional actors have played a more significant role in fostering cooperation. This can be explained in part by chronological differences, whereby the premises of intra-regional cooperation in criminal matters emerged much earlier in the EU (1970s) than in ASEAN (late 1990s). However, it remains unclear whether ASEAN is at an early phase of a three-dimensional mutual trust process, similar to the one existing in the EU, or whether it is travelling along a different path.

The role of the two regional organisations varies depending on which side of the Ural it is based. The EU has been a strong supporter and has become a strong leader in fostering cross-border cooperation while ASEAN has acted as a platform on which its Member States may, if they wish to do so, cooperate.

Evaluating the effectiveness of the EU and ASEAN approaches is not a simple task, especially when focusing on the prevention and combating of terrorism. It is not always easy to quantify or qualify interstate relations. For instance, the amount of data shared regionally between Member States cannot be numbered with precision. This is even more patent with regard to cooperation in criminal matters amongst competent national authorities given that it is mostly informal, even in the EU. During the prevention phase, it is more complicated—or even impossible—to identify which crime has failed or was foiled by the action of competent national authorities, thanks to a potential cross-border cooperation. Nonetheless, the analysis of the regional and national norms, of the mechanisms established to facilitate the fight against terrorism and of the authorities' actions clarifies the nature of cooperation in both regions. In this perspective, the EU increasingly privileges the formal approach to the enhancement of informal cooperation, although the latter remains key to peer-to-peer cooperation. The adoption of regional mechanisms of cooperation helps the fight against international terrorism, as does the existence of shared databases as well as regional actors and platforms for cooperation.

Due to the regional legal and institutional evolution and the development of a three-dimensional mutual trust, the EU and its members have been able to entrust regional bodies and agencies, such as Europol, Eurojust or Frontex, with facilitating cooperation among competent national authorities. In return, these bodies and agencies constitute a step further in building mutual trust and, subsequently, in enhancing cross-border cooperation. ASEAN Member States have agreed on specific platforms of dialogue, but they remain the only ones in the driving seats with full control over any of their actions. These platforms are meant to facilitate the social and political dimensions of mutual trust. Thus, the formal interactions between competent national authorities are particularly strategic in ASEAN, while the interactions may be both strategic and operational in the EU. Informal interactions have not disappeared from the EU legalistic panorama and are usually of an operational nature, while cooperation is more strategic and unofficially (i.e. not going through any official channel of communication) operational in ASEAN.

Notably, unlike in the EU, human rights guarantees are not part of the elements needed to build mutual trust and, subsequently, they are officially a non-existent consideration when facilitating cooperation within ASEAN. The mere identification of a common objective, i.e. preventing and combating terrorism, and the agreement on the means, i.e. cross-border cooperation, is considered sufficient in ASEAN. Yet, the absence of a shared consideration for human rights within the Southeast Asian region tends to limit the scope of cooperation as certain States and stakeholders do not trust each one of their counterparts.

Chapter 7
Finding a Path Through Multiheaded Interregional Relations in Counterterrorism: What Place Is There for Mutual Trust in the EU-ASEAN Dialogue?

The emergence and development of regional organisations has changed the traditional dynamics of international relations. Regional organisations get added to the increasing number of actors involved in one way or another in the international panorama (i.e. States, regional organisations, private companies, international associations, international NGOs, etc.). The diversity and number of actors have increasingly made international interactions more complex.[1]

As regional organisations have different attributes and competences, they cannot all be considered similar entities. The differences between the EU and ASEAN are representative of this complexity. The core EU characteristics are at a high level of legal integration and are supranational by nature. The competences that are not conferred upon the Union in the Treaties remain with the Member States.[2] However, in several domains, it has exclusive competences. In these areas, it represents its Member States including the customs union, the internal market, the protection of the euro, fisheries policy and trade policy.[3] In other sectors, it shares its competence with its Member States. This is especially true in the Area of Freedom, Security and Justice, especially covering cooperation in criminal matters (AFSJ—Title V, TFEU).[4] By contrast, ASEAN is clearly intergovernmental in nature. ASEAN's voice represents the unanimous agreement of all the Member States.

Despite having different institutional and legal architectures, both regional organisations were established for similar reasons, namely maintaining peace among States in their region through strengthened trade relations. From those reasons, it has

[1] See Telò and Weyembergh, 'Supranationality and sovereignty in an era of increasing complexity and fragmentation' (2020).

[2] Arts. 4 and 5, TEU.

[3] Art. 3, TFEU.

[4] Art. 4, TFEU.

C. C. Cocq, *Mutual Trust in Regional and Interregional Cooperation on Counterterrorism*, United Nations University Series on Regionalism 26,
https://doi.org/10.1007/978-3-031-36612-3_7

been deduced that they share the 'same DNA'.[5] This DNA seems to have driven these two regional organisations towards similar objectives, namely establishing a regional environment conducive to trade and investment and guaranteeing the internal security and stability.

The EU and ASEAN share similar traditional as well as non-traditional security threats. These include similar terrorist threats.[6] The two regions have been victims of terrorist attacks, especially nationalist and Islamist terrorism, and have had to address the issue of returning foreign terrorist fighters. Worryingly, the EU and ASEAN are the main regions of origin of the foreign terrorist fighters who went to Iraq and Syria.[7] As a consequence, the EU and ASEAN have declared terrorism to be a significant threat to each respective region's peace and stability and have then recognised the importance of cooperation in this matter.[8] The identification of this shared threat as well as some interregional connections between terrorism cases have fostered ASEAN-EU cooperation.[9]

Criminal threats might be more appropriately addressed within regions, but interregional dialogue might be useful given that the criminals could cross the external borders of one region; despite potentially stricter controls at the external borders compared to the internal ones. When two regions are confronted with similar issues, developing interregional relations might be beneficial. Relations of this sort can facilitate the sharing of best practices, experiences and knowledge. Eventually, the objective of interregional dialogue is to reinforce actions within and between the regions. However, reaching a common understanding between regions is even more complicated than at the 'internal' regional level. Indeed, the respective position of each regional organisation and their Member States as well as the discrepancies between both regions, including their regional institutional structures and national systems, play a role in interregional discussions and negotiations.

On the basis of their own regional developments in transnational matters, including in non-traditional security matters (criminal matters), the EU and ASEAN are increasingly engaging in dialogue. Following the Bali bombing, the EU and ASEAN made the fight against terrorism a key priority in their cooperation in

---

[5]EU Delegation to Indonesia and Brunei Darussalam, 'EU-ASEAN: Natural Partners' *news release*, January 2013: 1.

[6]Wilhelm Hofmeister and Patrick Rueppel, eds., *Maritime Security and Piracy. Common Challenges and Responses from Europe and Asia*, EU-Asia Dialogue. Shaping a Common Future for Europe and Asia—Sharing Policy Innovation and Best Practices in Addressing Common Challenges (Singapore: Konrad-Adenauer Stiftung Ltd.—European Policy Centre, 2014); Ewers-Peters, 'The EU as an Interorganizational Influencer?' (2018): 376.

[7]Interview on the phone with an official from the EU Counter-Terrorism Coordinator Office, Brussels, 8 April 2020.

[8]See, e.g., Declaration of the Council of the European Union, Special Council meeting, General Affairs, 11,795/01, Brussels, 12 September 2001; *ASEAN Declaration on Joint Action to Counter Terrorism* (2001).

[9]Vierstraete-Verlinde, 'EU ACTIONPLAN on CT and P/CVE, South-East Asia PRIORITIES' (2019).

security matters. In their 2003 *Joint Declaration on Cooperation to Combat Terrorism,*[10] they adopted a multifaceted joint strategy comprising different dimensions to address the root causes of terrorism. However, even if some analysts consider ASEAN–EU cooperation concerning counterterrorism to be improving,[11] such cooperation remains relatively superficial and restricted to mutual trust-building initiatives.

Different channels of interactions between these two regions exist, which can be categorised into five ideal-types: relations between EU and ASEAN Member States (interstate bilateralism); relations between the regional organisations themselves (bilateral, inter-organisational interregionalism[12]); relations between a regional organisation and one or several Member States of another region (hybrid interregionalism); institutionalised relations between States from different regions but in the absence of any specific regional organisation (transregionalism); and, cooperation born from the formal or informal membership of the regional organisations and/or their Member States in common transnational or global governance mechanisms, such as the UN (multilateralism).

Diverging positions and purposes do not facilitate interregional interactions, but they might explain this web of interactions. Actors tend to establish new channels when the pre-existing ones are unable to meet the set requirements (e.g. when the parties do not manage to reach an agreement). This chapter highlights the challenges posed by the increasingly high number of existing channels of dialogue.

In this web of interactions, some authors argue that inter-organisational interactions occur 'if one institution (the source institution) affects the development or performance of another institution (the target institution)'.[13] In this case, the relations between the EU and ASEAN include the extent to which the EU, in particular, is able to exert influence on the policies and norms of ASEAN. The EU does support and collaborate with ASEAN and its Member States in order to create an effective interregional partnership. Originally, opportunities for the EU to become more involved in criminal matters in Southeast Asia presented themselves in the aftermath of the Asian financial crisis and particularly during the post-9/11 era. While the EU demonstrated its desire to have ASEAN as a politically coherent international partner

[10] *Joint Declaration on cooperation to combat terrorism,* 14th EU-ASEAN Ministerial Meeting, 5811/03, Brussels, 27–28 January 2003.

[11] Rees, 'EU and ASEAN: Issues of regional security' (2010).

[12] Inter-organisational interactions may be defined as 'links, relationships and modes of interaction between two or more international organizations'. Joachim A. Koops, 'Inter-organisation approaches' in *Routledge Handbook on the European Union and International Institutions*, eds., Knud Erik Jørgensen and Katie Verlin Laatikainen (Oxon: Routledge, 2013): 72; Ewers-Peters, 'The EU as an Interorganizational Influencer?' (2018): 368.

[13] Thomas Gehring and Sebastian Oberthür, 'The causal mechanisms of interaction between international institutions' *European Journal of International Relations*, vol. 15, no. 1 (2009): 127.

within a multilateral world,[14] the fact that nine out of ten ASEAN countries were colonised has given rise to an underlying sensitivity towards any sign of pressure or preaching from external actors. ASEAN Member States have in fact demonstrated a strong will to develop and preserve their 'Way' as an alternative to the EU regional integration model. However, although it chose not to completely mimic EU standards, it was not able to fully insulate itself from an EU influence.

Why the EU is interested in developing more in-depth collaboration with ASEAN and its Member States remains unsettled. The heritage of colonisation is certainly one motive for EU Member States wanting to keep ties with their former colonies, either through a sense of responsibility or for economic reasons. Apart from these two considerations, the reasons motivating the EU to further engage with ASEAN in criminal matters are not entirely clear. The terrorist threat is certainly a shared interest, but it does not inherently require strong interregional collaboration. One questions whether the EU sees ASEAN countries as a source of security threats, including terrorist threats, and whether the EU prefers to prevent these threats (such as the rising of a Southeast Asian Caliphate[15]) by working with ASEAN and its Member States. Yet, the number of terrorists travelling between Europe and Southeast Asia continues to be low and seemingly does not require an interregional endeavour of this nature. Such a collaboration exists though and may concern terrorism-related issues. One most probable case would be that the EU might consider this collaboration to be a means towards an end, namely ensuring the European investments, developing tighter economic ties and facilitating the flow of persons and goods between the two regions.

In this context, it is salient to question whether mutual trust has a role to play in ASEAN-EU relations, and if so, in which ways. In order to answer this question, one has to first address the following ones: At which level do these interregional relations occur (i.e. diplomatic/strategic/operational relations)? Which dimension(s) do (es) mutual trust adopt in the relations between the two regions, including the regional organisations and their respective Member States? The overarching issue central to the investigation is whether such interregional relations constitute an added value in the fight against terrorism in either region as well as at an international level.

[14] Naila Maier-Knapp, 'How the EU Promotes Regional Security in Southeast Asia' *Southeast Asian Studies*, ed. Occasional Paper Series, University of Freiburg (Freiburg: University of Freiburg, March 2018): 6..

[15] Navhat Nuraniyah and Sulastri Osman, 'Southeast Asian fighters in the new "caliphate": Implications for Indonesia's militant Islamist movement' *RSIS Commentaries,* Commentary, no. 133 (2014). In the news, Agence France-Press 'Islamic militants plan Southeast Asian caliphate' *The Inquirer*, 20 August 2014: available at https://bit.ly/2LLBLrn (accessed on 23 March 2020); Rohan Gunaratna, 'The Caliphate's Influence in Southeast Asia' *The Asian Dialogue*, 14 February 2017: available at https://bit.ly/3jKgRoT (accessed on 23 March 2020).

In order to clarify the interregional situation, this chapter first investigates those EU and ASEAN internal rules which govern the externalisation of their policies in order to establish their roles in the international domain (Section 1). Then, it describes the complexity of the multiheaded and multifaceted relations between the EU and ASEAN relating to counterterrorism (Section 2).

Section 1: Shaping the 'Public Face' of the Regional Organisations According to Their 'Internal' Features

While consolidating their internal policies, the members of regional organisations have also agreed upon their external policies. They tend to reflect and potentially extend their internal policy onto the international scene. In so doing, the EU and ASEAN have developed their own 'public face' to project to the world (I). In accordance with their respective legal and political fundamental principles, the EU and ASEAN adopted tailor-made 'terms and conditions' to ensure that their interregional relations would be fruitful (II).

I. The EU and ASEAN's 'Public Faces' Determining Their Respective External Counterterrorism Actions

The EU and ASEAN's capacities to play a role in the international scene (their 'actorness'[16]) are based on their respective internal rules. After elaborating upon this concept, which is rooted in political sciences, and integrating it into this legal study (A), the specific internal rules in each region are examined to determine the actual actorness of each regional organisation (B).

A. Interregional Relations Determined by the 'Actorness' of the Main Actors

The actorness of an entity refers to its capacity to behave actively and deliberately in relation to other actors in the international system.[17] In other words, it is the ability

[16] On the use of this term, see, e.g., Beyer, *Counter Terrorism and International Power Relations* (2010); Wunderlich, 'The EU an Actor Sui Generis?' (2012); Wunderlich, 'Comparing regional organisations in global multilateral institutions: ASEAN, the EU and the UN' (2012); Gehring, Oberthür, and Mühleck, 'European Union Actorness in International Institutions' (2013); Mattheis and Wunderlich, 'Regional actorness and interregional relations: ASEAN, the EU and Mercosur' (2017).

[17] David Allen and Michael Smith, 'Western Europe's presence in the contemporary international arena' *Review of International Studies*, vol. 16, no. 1 (1990); Charlotte Bretherton and John Vogler, *The European Union as a Global Actor*, Politics & International Relations, 2nd ed. (London: Routledge, 2005): 20. It was also defined as the capacity to 'develop presence, to become identifiable, aggregate interests, formulate goals and policies, make and implement decisions' by Jürgen Rüland, 'Inter- and Transregionalism: Remarks on the State of the Art of a New Research Agenda' National Europe Centre Paper No. 35 (Canberra, Australian National University: Workshop on Asia-Pacific Studies in Australia and Europe: A Research Agenda for the Future, 5–6 July 2002), 6.

of an entity to exert influence on the external world. A regional organisation's actorness is built upon their capacity, legitimacy and recognition. They need to have the legitimacy and capacity to act and to mobilise resources in order to fulfil their objective(s). They also need to be perceived as competent and legitimate actors by the other subjects of international law. Notably, it is possible for a regional organisation to be unsuccessful with its external policies while still being recognised as an international actor. Some authors who analysed this question identify four criteria determining the actorness of an organisation: 'shared values and principles, the ability to formulate coherent policies, policy instruments and the legitimacy of decision-making processes'.[18] In this sense, the concept of actorness holds that entities, such as regional organisations, can be more than just the sum of their parts, namely their respective Member States.[19]

These four criteria are generated by the international legal and political context in which they exist and evolve, and by the socio-historical 'internal' ground from which they grow.

Firstly, the global legal and political architecture constitutes a structural factor shaping the relevance of the regional organisations within the international scene.

An entity can only be considered a member of the international community if the international norms adopted are directly intended for them. According to the classical doctrine, only States should be recognised as members of the international community. However, other actors have been integrated on the basis of the ICJ Advisory Opinion in 1949. The Court stated that '[t]he subjects of law in any legal system are not necessarily identical in their nature or in the extent of their rights, and their nature depends upon the needs of the community'.[20] Compared to States which inherently derive legal personality from their existence and are characterised by their national sovereignty, other actors, such as regional organisations, are limited to that legal personality which is granted to them by Member States, in accordance with international law.[21] Regional organisations have been identified as relevant actors in several international norms and policies, including UN resolutions.[22] However, formal and informal rules and procedures of global governance institutions frame the significance of EU and ASEAN participation as actors, which has led the EU and ASEAN to different places in the international domain as of yet.

---

[18] Wunderlich, 'The EU an Actor Sui Generis?' (2012): 656.

[19] Mattheis and Wunderlich, 'Regional actorness and interregional relations: ASEAN, the EU and Mercosur' (2017): 724.

[20] ICJ, *Reparation for injuries suffered in the service of the United Nations*, Advisory Opinion (1949).

[21] See, e.g., Daillier, Forteau, and Pellet, *Droit international public* (2009): 445.

[22] See, e.g., A/RES/49/57, *Declaration on the Enhancement of Cooperation between the United Nations and Regional Arrangements or Agencies in the Maintenance of International Peace and Security*, 84th plenary meeting, 9 December 1994; S/RES/1631(2005) *on cooperation between the United Nations and regional organisations in maintaining international peace and security*. Also, S/RES/2462(2019); S/RES/2482(2019).

Secondly, the actorness of a regional organisation depends on the socio-historical background of the Member States which encompass the organisation as well as of the specific process of regional integration which they have selected. In essence, the norms and principles which determine the character of a regional actor are linked to their historical origin. The process of regional integration determines the normative core around which the structure and self-understanding of an actor is constructed. It shapes their institutionalisation and decision-making structures. Thus, to emerge as an international actor, regional projects need to be institutionalised, at a minimum, with formal and/or informal rules.[23] Formalised institutions and decision-making structures enhance cohesion between the members.

In this respect, the EU approach, dominated by a preference for formal and legal settings, tends to enhance its actorness. By contrast, the lower level of ASEAN institutionalisation characterised by a preference for dialogue, consensus-based decision-making and non-binding agreements limits its actorness. Yet, ASEAN seems to emulate lessons learned from the EU's experience, which could improve its actorness in time and allow them to overcome its capability-expectations gap. ASEAN architecture is more prone to volatility, which potentially undermines the ability of the organisation to have a unified voice.[24] Therefore, ASEAN's present place in the international system remains uncertain.

Either way, the fact that the EU and ASEAN can be collective actors and have their own role in international affairs does not prevent their members from exercising their own roles.[25] This ability stems from the fact that they remain sovereign actors.

After qualifying and explaining the operationalisation of an actor's capacities in the international scene, the next part goes into further detail by analysing the internal rules governing the external relations of the EU and ASEAN.

B. The Internal Rules Determining the 'Public Face' of the EU and ASEAN Concerning Counterterrorism

The EU has long been criticised for its lack of a common voice and uniformity regarding foreign policy and external relations. As the former U.S. Secretary of State Henry Kissinger supposedly said, 'Who do I call if I want to speak to Europe?' With the successive revisions of EU treaties, even if still complex, the EU position has improved.[26] Interestingly, the EU faces the same problem when it wants to communicate with other regions. The question is especially salient when they want to interact with ASEAN, which is a regional organisation that does not seem to exist as an autonomous entity.

---

[23] Wunderlich, 'The EU an Actor Sui Generis?' (2012): 661.

[24] Mattheis and Wunderlich, 'Regional actorness and interregional relations: ASEAN, the EU and Mercosur' (2017): 725.

[25] Wunderlich, 'The EU an Actor Sui Generis?' (2012): 657.

[26] Marise Cremona, Joerg Monar, and Sara Poli, eds., *The External Dimension of the European Union's Area of Freedom, Security and Justice* (New York: Peter Lang, 2011).

For the purpose of clarifying this complexity, the internal rules dealing with the external action of each regional organisation in counterterrorism need to be examined following the chronological order of their establishment (i.e. the EU and then ASEAN).

1. The external dimension of the EU's counterterrorism policy: a legalistic approach

The EU wishes to increase its influence in international affairs by promoting values such as peace and security, democracy and human rights, while also collaborating with external parties. For this purpose, the EU aims to become an international player which would further promote its own regional integration project as well as influence other regions and organisations worldwide.[27] In counterterrorism, the EU's complex competence regarding internal affairs is reflected in its external policy (a), which eventually has an impact on the externalisation of its understanding of mutual trust (b).

(a) *The EU's complex internal features reflected in its external arrangements*

With the 1957 Rome Treaty founding the European Economic Community (EEC), this international organisation was explicitly given competence to conduct international trade relations through its 'Common Commercial Policy' and to conclude international agreements through which it could associate itself with third countries. As European integration progressed, the EEC, later European Community (EC) and now EU, acquired powers in various areas such as foreign and security policy, justice and home affairs, environmental policy, energy policy and so on.

Alongside the principles of subsidiarity and proportionality sits the principle of conferral of competences.[28] This principle dictates that the EU can only act within the limits of the competences that have been conferred upon it by the EU treaties.[29] There are four types of competences:

- exclusive (Article 3 TFEU): only the EU can act in these areas;
- shared between the EU and its Member States (Article 4 TFEU): Member States can act only if the EU has chosen not to, e.g. area of freedom, security and justice (AFSJ);
- the EU may set up arrangements within which its members must coordinate policies (Article 5 TFEU); and,
- the EU may support, coordinate or supplement Member States' actions (Article 6 TFEU).

This principle also applies in the EU's external activities, as the EU can only act externally in fields in which it has been conferred competences. The nature of its

[27] Sandra Lavenex and Frank Schimmelfennig, 'EU rules beyond EU borders: Theorizing external governance in European politics' *Journal of European Public Policy*, vol. 16, no. 6 (2009); Ewers-Peters, 'The EU as an Interorganizational Influencer?' (2018): 365.

[28] Art. 5 TEU.

[29] Arts. 2–6 TFEU.

competences impacts whether it has the capacity to act on its own, or in collaboration with Member States. Such complexity is mirrored in the conclusion and ratification of international agreements, which can be signed by the EU alone (e.g. free trade agreements), or by the EU and its Member States (e.g. investment agreements). Besides, external relations between the EU and external partners are based on either express provisions of the EU Treaties, or implied external dimensions of substantive policy fields.[30] It is indeed possible for the EU to obtain exclusive competence in the case of external action through the application of Article 3(2) TFEU, including in the case of the AFSJ.

In the fight against terrorism, the EU has adopted a multifaceted approach. This approach might involve different actors and various levels and distribution of competence. Such multiplicity can lead to conflicts about legal bases.[31] The most notable domains of competence which must be highlighted are the EU foreign security policy (e.g. military action, humanitarian aid), of which the Common Foreign and Security Policy (CFSP) is a part, as well as the external dimension of its internal policies in criminal matters, as part of the AFSJ (e.g. the cooperation mechanisms, including data sharing, or the protection of human rights, including data protection standards).

The CFSP is governed by a distinct legal regime, which is marked by stronger inter-governmentalism. It has specific institutional features, such as the limited participation of the European Commission and the European Parliament in the decision-making procedure and the exclusion of any legislative activity.[32] The CFSP is defined and implemented by the European Council, i.e. the Heads of States and Governments of EU Member States, as well as the Council of the EU, i.e. the representatives of each competent national ministry. The President of the European Council and the High Representative of the Union for Foreign and Security Policy represent the EU in matters of the CFSP.

Demonstrating the interconnections between these two domains of competence, it must be noted that AFSJ-related actions and measures may be undertaken under CFSP powers if it serves its objectives.[33] However, although the EU is bound by

---

[30] See, e.g., Valsamis Mitsilegas, 'Internal and external dimensions of trust in Europe's area of criminal justice' in *Europe in Crisis. Crime, Criminal Justice and the Way Forward. Essays in Honour of Nestor Kourakis*, eds., Calliope D. Spinellis et al. (Athens: Sakkoulas, 2017); Dony, *Droit de l'Union européenne* (2018): 629 and ff.

[31] CJEU, *European Parliament* v. *Council (Mauritius Agreement)*, C-658/11, judgement (Grand Chamber), ECLI:EU:C:2014:2025, 24 June 2014. The case concerns the conclusion of an Agreement for the transfer and prosecution of suspected pirates arrested in the framework of Operation Atalanta between the EU and Mauritius.

[32] Art. 47 TEU and Arts. 2(4) and 218(3), TFEU.

[33] CJEU, *European Parliament* v. *Council of the European Union (Mauritius Agreement)*, C-658/11, Opinion of Advocate General Bot, ECLI:EU:C:2014:41, 30 January 2014, paras. 117–118. See also, Marise Cremona, 'External Unity, Institutional Complexity and Structural Fragmentation' in *Supranational Governance at Stake. The EU's External Competences caught between Complexity and Fragmentation*, eds., Mario Teló and Anne Weyembergh, Globalisation, Europe, and Multilateralism (Oxon: Routledge, 2020): 75.

fundamental rights when acting within the CFSP, the vindication of individual rights through courts is more difficult in this domain.[34]

Unfortunately, the Member States' foreign security policies can diverge from the EU's, which might cause, among other things, representation issues between the EU and its Member States in international organisations.[35] During the 2003 Iraq crisis, for instance, the EU failed to put forward a common foreign policy position due to the diverging opinions and interests of its Member States.

Focusing on terrorism as a criminal matter, this chapter examines the AFSJ's external dimension. Both Title V in Part Three of the TFEU related to the AFSJ and Part Five on the Union's External Action do not mention any police or judicial cooperation with third parties. Yet, the EU can still externalise its internal policy and values in order to create common ground for collaboration with external partners.[36]

Although the EU and its Member States exercise powers in tandem both internally and externally,[37] the harmonisation of national laws and the implementation of coordinating mechanisms are meant to reach and consolidate a common position. Due to the overlap of competences, negotiations might be more complicated and agreements more difficult to reach. The EU and the Member States conclude the agreement under the provisions falling in the scope of their respective competences (cf. mixed agreements). As explained in the ECJ's Opinion 2/91, an 'agreement may be concluded in an area where competence is shared between the Community and the Member States. In such a case, negotiation and implementation of the agreement require joint action by the Community and the Member States'.[38] Although the Member States remain sovereign actors, the EU can sign international agreements with external partners on its own, on the provision that it is necessary to fulfil the EU's internal action and it is agreed upon by the Council.[39]

The EU AFSJ external dimension in counterterrorism has seen a lot of development following the 9/11 attacks. After this event, the EU concluded several agreements with key external partners.[40] For instance, after the 2004 terrorist attacks in

[34] The European Parliament has no decision-making power and the principles of subsidiarity and proportionality are hard to enforce. The institutional specificities of the AFSJ, namely the involvement of the European Parliament in the decision-making process, may be lost. See ibid.

[35] Marianne Dony, 'The EU's external relations and their evolving legal framework' in *The European Union and Global Governance*, ed., Mario Teló (Abingdon: Routledge, 2009).

[36] Art. 205, TFEU and Arts. 216–221 TFEU on the conclusion of external agreements by the EU, especially Art. 216 showing the implicit external powers of the EU in the AFSJ.

[37] Art. 4(2)(j), TFEU. Also, Arts. 82–89 TFEU on judicial and police cooperation. Also, see Chap. 6.

[38] ECJ, Opinion delivered pursuant to the second subparagraph of Article 228 (1) of the EEC Treaty—Convention N° 170 of the International Labour Organization concerning safety in the use of chemicals at work, Opinion 2/91, ECLI:EU:C:1993:106, 19 March 1993, pt. 12. See also, Marianne Dony, 'Retour sur les compétences externes implicites de l'Union' *Cahiers de droit européen*, vol. 54, no. 1 (2018): 123.

[39] Art. 218, TFEU.

[40] See, e.g., the agreements of Europol with external partners, such as the *Agreement between the United States of America and the European Police Office* signed in Brussels on 6 December 2001,

Madrid, the *European Council Declaration* of 25 March 2004 set out several objectives, including the deepening of the international consensus and enhancing international efforts to prevent and combat terrorism as well as targeting actions which prioritise third-party States or regional partners where counterterrorist capacity or commitment to combating terrorism requires enhancement.[41]

Although the Treaty of Lisbon constitutes a turning point in the externalisation of the AFSJ, three challenges remain, including (1) the discrepancies between national foreign policies, (2) the relations between the EU and its members in international affairs and (3) the distribution of competences between EU institutions and bodies.

1. Prior to the Lisbon Treaty, the multitude of, and potentially divergent, policies of the Member States with external partners have hampered the process of achieving a common position given that consensus was required.[42] Although the Treaty has extended the use of qualified majority voting in the Council to new areas, including in the AFSJ, divergences still exist and may hinder the decision-making outcomes. The EU Member States are not prevented from pursuing their own foreign policy goals regarding police and judicial cooperation, and from developing bilateral relations with external partners, as long as the EU has not already concluded an international agreement which governs said cooperation and relations, as to avoid conflict of law (albeit in respect of the principle of sincere cooperation enshrined in EU law, cf. *Open Skies* judgement[43]). In fact, the Treaty contains a set of common principles and objectives which must be respected by the EU and its members in order to realise EU policies within the region and beyond.[44]
2. The recognition of the EU legal personality in Article 47 TEU reinforced the EU's legitimacy on the international scene and strengthened its autonomous position, next to the one of its members. With this recognition, the Lisbon Treaty has simplified and harmonised the procedures for concluding international treaties and agreements, as well as the EU representation in international organisations and negotiations, in the sense that EU representatives, regardless of their institutional affiliation, in principle now sit behind one single nameplate: 'European Union'. However, it has not simplified the internal distribution of

European Council 14,581/01, Justice, Home Affairs and Civil Protection, 2396th Council meeting, Brussels, 6–7 December 2001; *Supplemental Agreement between the Europol Police Office and the United States of America on the exchange of personal data and related information*, 20 December 2002. In the same line, Eurojust has concluded agreements with 12 third countries, including the USA. See, e.g., Brière, 'Cooperation of Europol and Eurojust with external partners in the fight against crime: a legal appraisal' (2019). See also the *Joint Declaration on cooperation to combat terrorism,* 14th EU-ASEAN Ministerial Meeting, 5811/03, Brussels, 27–28 January 2003.

[41] European Council, *Declaration on combating terrorism* (2004).

[42] Commission of the European Communities, 'Towards a New Asia Strategy', Communication from the Commission to the Council, COM(94) 314 final, Brussels, 13 July 1994: 10.

[43] ECJ, *Commission of the European Communities* v. *Belgium*, C-471/98, judgement, ECLI:EU:C:2002:628, 5 November 2002.

[44] Art. 21 TEU and Art. 7 TFEU; the latter addressing the consistency of the EU's actions.

competences and tasks between the different EU institutions and bodies, nor with its Member States. The practice shows that the EU's international representation remains unclear and uncertain.

3. Despite having a nameplate, it is not always evident who will sit behind it, leading to (legal) arguments between the European Commission and the European External Action Service (EEAS), and at times the Member States. Counterterrorism falls within the purview of several EU actors, such as the High Representative of the Union for Foreign and Security Policy (CFSP), the European Commission's Directorate General for European Civil Protection and Humanitarian Aid Operations (DG ECHO) and Directorate General for International Cooperation and Development (DG DEVCO), as well as the EEAS in collaboration with EU Counter-Terrorism Coordinator (CTC). The EEAS does not centralise the competence in external affairs. Rather, it coordinates all of the EU programmes vis-à-vis external partners and provides expertise on the various relevant subjects. The EEAS engages in various projects funded by the EU Commission, including the DG DEVCO. It should also be mentioned that the relevant EU agencies, such as Europol and Eurojust, are gaining more and more powers to cooperate with external partners in police and judicial matters.

The actions of these various actors have been partially coordinated by the EU CTC since its nomination. The European Council Conclusions of June 2014 states that 'an effective EU counter terrorism policy is needed, whereby all relevant actors work closely together, integrating the internal and external aspects of the fight against terrorism'.[45] As such, the EU CTC's role has been reaffirmed. In addition to its internal tasks, the CTC coordinates with the relevant preparatory bodies of the Council, the Commission and the EEAS to harmonise the external dimension of the EU's counterterrorism policy. The CTC ensures that the EU plays an active role in this field and works on improving the communication between the EU and third countries. In this respect, the CTC regularly meets with government officials and stakeholders outside of the EU to share views on counterterrorism cooperation. The CTC has also engaged in discussions with the Executive Director of the UN Counter-Terrorism Committee Executive Directorate (CTED). As an aside, it can be said that there has been no meeting between the CTC, or any of their advisers, and ASEAN Member States authorities as of yet. The first meeting was scheduled to take place in Summer 2020 between Gilles de Kerchove, the Counter-Terrorism Coordinator at the time, and national authorities in Jakarta, Kuala Lumpur and Singapore, but these meetings were indefinitely postponed due to the global health threat posed by COVID-19.[46]

Although the variety of actors, the distribution of competences and the different approaches between the EU and its members still constitute complex features of the EU counterterrorism external activities, the Lisbon Treaty has improved the effectiveness of the EU as an actor by addressing the problems of consistency, coherence

[45] Pt. 10, Conclusions of the European Council, EUCO 79/14 (2014).

[46] An official from the EU Counter-Terrorism Coordinator Office in discussion with the author, interview carried out on the phone (2020).

and representation.[47] These elements are the core components of the autonomous actorness of the EU.

(b) *The externalisation of the EU's understanding of mutual trust: between theory and practice*

The Union pursues its internal policies and actions abroad, insofar as it safeguards its values, fundamental interests and security.[48] The EU's external activities are guided by the principles which inspired its creation, development and enlargement, namely 'democracy, the rule of law, the universality and indivisibility of human rights and fundamental freedoms, respect for human dignity, the principles of equality and solidarity, and respect for the principles of the United Nations Charter and international law'.[49]

As previously illustrated, the protection of human rights is a key component of mutual trust in the EU. This pursuit of balance between security and human rights' protection has always been at the core of the EU's actions, within the EU as well as abroad. However, the actual power of the EU to export its level of human rights protection can hardly be analysed. In political sciences, 'power' may refer to a phenomenon that is exercised when one actor gets another actor to do something that the latter would not otherwise have done.

In theory, the EU aims to ensure an equivalent level of protection of human rights in its external action. The EU and its Member States are required to not lower the EU's human rights standards, nor circumvent them. Just as human rights standards are a component of mutual trust in the EU, so too are they a component in their external policies.

In practice, the EU does not *de facto* possess the power to export its human rights standards. With other powerful actors, it is difficult for the EU to export its standards. Depending on its interlocutor(s), preventing and countering terrorism seems to be that important as it results in the EU lowering its human rights standards. By working with these external partners, the EU might have progressively influenced them though. For instance, the EU has been working with the United States of America (USA) despite concerns related to the level of protection of human rights in their relations. Yet, some improvements in this aspect must be noted.[50]

---

[47] See, e.g., Cremona, 'External Unity, Institutional Complexity and Structural Fragmentation' (2020).

[48] Art. 21(2), TEU.

[49] Art. 21, TEU; and Art. 205, TFEU; also, Art. 2, TEU.

[50] See, e.g., European Data Protection Supervisor (EDPS), Opinion of 9 December 2011 on the Proposal for a Council Decision on the conclusion of the Agreement between the United States of America and the European Union on the use and transfer of Passenger Name Records to the United States Department of Homeland Security, O.J.E.U. C35/03, 9 February 2012; *Agreement between the United States of America and the European Union on the protection of personal information relating to the prevention, investigation, detection, and prosecution of criminal offences*, O.J.E.U. L336/3, 10 December 2016.

Although human rights and fundamental freedoms are values that the EU needs to ensure within its region and beyond, it cannot be said that the principle of mutual trust is exportable directly and automatically via the EU's external policies.[51] The European Commission has in fact indicated that '[t]here is no presumption of mutual trust [in its legal dimension] outside of the EU institutional framework underpinned by common principles'.[52]

Preventing and combating terrorism while also respecting equivalent human rights standards has driven the EU external action.[53] In particular, the EU's activities regarding the gathering, analysing and sharing data have also been externalised.[54] To this end, the EU and its Member States should seek to create a balance which incorporates sufficient protection.

Data flow is more streamlined between Member States than in relations with external partners. Yet, a significant exception is the United-Kingdom which—even when it was still a EU member—was also taking part (and continues to do so) in the Five Eyes Alliance between Australia, Canada, New Zealand and the USA.[55] This intelligence-gathering and intelligence-sharing programme constitutes an integrated global surveillance arrangement that covers the majority of the world's communications. Interestingly, Singapore revealed itself to be one of the other unofficial members of this alliance. This alliance has been particularly criticised for its disregard of peoples' right to privacy.[56] Similarly, some EU Member States might still have close ties with third countries, especially their former colonies. This is sometimes reflected in the conclusion of bilateral cooperation agreements enabling the exchange of information.

---

[51] See, e.g., Anne Weyembergh and Sarah Khabirpour, 'Quelle confiance mutuelle ailleurs?' in *La confiance mutuelle dans l'espace pénal européen – Mutual trust in the European Criminal Area*, eds., Gilles De Kerchove and Anne Weyembergh, European Studies (Bruxelles: Editions de l'Université de Bruxelles, 2005).

[52] European Commission, Task Force for the Preparation and Conduct of the Negotiations with the United Kingdom under Article 50 TEU, 'Police and judicial cooperation in criminal matters' presentation at the Council Working Party (Art. 50) on 15 June, TF50 (2018) 51—Commission to EU 27, 18 June 2018.

[53] See, among other recent declarations, pt. 3, Council of the European Union, 'Council Conclusions on EU External Action on Preventing and Countering Terrorism and Violent Extremism' General Secretariat of the Council to Delegations, No. 8868/20, Brussels, 16 June 2020.

[54] Council of the EU, *EU Plan of Action on Combating Terrorism*, 10,586/04, Brussels, 15 June 2004.

[55] The Five Eyes Alliance, comprised of the United States National Security Agency (NSA), the UK's Government Communications Headquarters (GCHQ), Canada's Communications Security Establishment Canada (CSEC), the Australian Signals Directorate (ASD) and New Zealand's Government Communications Security Bureau (GCSB), is the continuation of an intelligence partnership formed in the aftermath of the Second World War.

[56] See, e.g., Nyst and Crowe, 'Unmasking the Five Eyes' global surveillance practices' (2014); Céline C. Cocq, 'Snowden's Impact on ASEAN Relations' *Perspectives Internationales*, vol. Tribune 'Asie' (Paris: Science Po Paris, 26 May 2014): available at http://perspectivesinternationales.com/?p=1092 (accessed on 1 June 2014).

Other than the general protection of human rights, specific rules apply when EU Member States or EU agencies share data with third countries or other agencies. Before the adoption of the *EU Charter of Fundamental Rights*, Article 25 of Directive 95/46[57] already provided that the level of data protection afforded by a third country should meet the requirements of adequacy in order to allow data to be transferred to this country in a commercial context. Subsequently, the 2016 *General Data Protection Regulation* (GDPR),[58] which replaced the Directive 95/46, implemented the express obligation laid down in Article 8(1) of the EU Charter to protect personal data. It also expressly requires 'an adequate level of protection' where personal data is transferred to a third country. The Court, in the *Schrems* case,[59] affirms a continuum of data protection when EU law authorises the transfer of personal data to third countries. The Court recognises that the word 'adequate' does not require a third country to ensure a level of protection identical to that which is guaranteed in the EU legal order. However, the adequate level of protection must be understood as requiring the third country to ensure, by reason of its domestic law or its international commitments, a level of protection of fundamental rights and freedoms that is essentially equivalent to that which is guaranteed within the EU. The Court explained that if there was no such requirement, the objective of ensuring a high level of data protection would be disregarded, and this high level of data protection could easily be circumvented by transfers of personal data from the EU to third countries for the purpose of being processed in those countries.[60] The Court has thus introduced a threshold of protection of fundamental rights for third countries, when sharing data (in and out) with the EU. The rules providing for the assessment of the adequacy of the level of data protection are elaborated in further detail in Article 45(2) of the GDPR, which was adopted on the basis of the 2015 Court's decision in its *Schrems* case.

The data transfer to third countries for law enforcement purposes falls outside the GDPR. This gap was already filled in by the *Council Framework Decision 2008/977/JHA on the protection of personal data processed in the framework of police and judicial cooperation in criminal matters,*[61] which was then replaced by *Directive 2016/680 on the protection of natural persons with regard to the processing of personal data by competent authorities for the purposes of the prevention, investigation, detection or prosecution of criminal offences or the execution of criminal*

[57] *Directive 95/46/EC on the protection of individuals with regard to the processing of personal data and on the free movement of such data.*

[58] *General Data Protection Regulation 2016/679.*

[59] CJEU, *Maximillian Schrems* v. *Data Protection Commissioner*, C-362/14, judgement (Grand Chamber), 6 October 2015; reaffirmed in *Data Protection Commissioner* v. *Facebook Ireland Limited and Maximillian Schrems* (Shrems II), C-311/18, judgement (Grand Chamber), 16 July 2020.

[60] Para. 73, *Schrems* (2015).

[61] *Council Framework Decision 2008/977/JHA of 27 November 2008 on the protection of personal data processed in the framework of police and judicial cooperation in criminal matters,* O.J.E.U. L350/60, 30 December 2008.

penalties, and on the free movement of such data.[62] This Directive, like the GDPR, contains provisions for transfers of data to third countries on the basis of an assessment of an adequate level of protection in the third country.[63]

EU external agreements are subject to the same fundamental rights requirements as internal legislation,[64] and therefore cooperation with external parties should not affect the protection guaranteed by EU law. Yet, the power of influence of a third country introduces an additional dynamic.[65] In some cases, the EU has thus adopted contradictory, and at times openly controversial, positions. It was criticised that the EU could have been more lenient, regarding its standards, with some third countries due to their significant power and centrality in the matters at stake. For example, the operational agreements between Europol and other countries such as the USA could have been adopted more out of opportunity rather than on the basis of the due diligence.[66] Similarly, the PNR agreements between the EU and USA or Canada are useful examples of the EU being criticised for endangering the EU's human rights standards of its people. While the former was adopted and drafted due to intense political pressures, the latter has been rejected by the Court of Justice of the EU (CJEU) because, as it stood, it might have indeed endangered the fundamental rights guaranteed by the EU Charter.[67]

---

[62] *Directive (EU) 2016/680 of the European Parliament and the Council of 27 April 2016 on the protection of natural persons with regard to the processing of personal data by competent authorities for the purposes of the prevention, investigation, detection or prosecution of criminal offences or the execution of criminal penalties, and on the free movement of such data, and repealing Council Framework Decision 2008/977/JHA*, O.J.E.U. L119/89, 4 May 2016.

[63] Arts. 35–40, *Directive (EU) 2016/680.*

[64] CJEU, *Opinion 1/15 of the Court (Grand Chamber)*, opinion, ECLI:EU:C:2017:592, 26 July 2017, paras. 67, 93 and 214.

[65] Cremona, 'External Unity, Institutional Complexity and Structural Fragmentation' (2020): 77.

[66] See, e.g., *Agreement between the United States of America and the European Police Office*, European Council, Justice, Home Affairs and Civil Protection, 14,581/01, 2396th meeting, Brussels, 6 December 2001; *Supplemental Agreement between the Europol Police Office and the United States of America on the exchange of personal data and related information*, Copenhagen, 20 December 2002.

[67] See, e.g., *Agreement between the United States of America and the European Union on the use and transfer of passenger name records to the United States Department of Homeland Security*, O.J.E.U. L215/5, 11 August 2012; EDPS, *Opinion of 9 December 2011 on the Proposal for a Council Decision on the conclusion of the Agreement between the United States of America and the European Union on the use and transfer of Passenger Name Records to the United States Department of Homeland Security* (2012); European Commission, 'Security Union: Commission reports on the implementation of the EU-US TFTP and PNR Agreements' *press release*, Brussels, 19 January 2017. Also, Council of the European Union, *Agreement between Canada and the European Union on the transfer and processing of Passenger Name Record*, No. 12657/5/13, Brussels, 23 June 2014; CJEU, *Opinion 1/15 of the Court (Grand Chamber)*, opinion, ECLI:EU:C:2017:592, 26 July 2017; *Opinion of Advocate General Mengozzi,* Opinion 1/15, Request on an opinion submitted by the European Parliament, ECLI:EU:C:2016:656, 8 September 2016; Arianna Vedaschi, 'Privacy and data protection versus national security in transnational flights: the EU–Canada PNR agreement' *International Data Privacy Law*, vol. 8, no. 2 (2018).

The EU has increased its legitimacy as an independent international actor, alongside its Member States. The greater the legitimacy, the more likely it will be to convince others to cooperate on shared interests and exchange information and experience. The EU's capacities to externalise its internal policy in criminal matters through the development of mutual trust is dependent upon its level of legitimacy. In this context, cooperation between the EU and its external partners is slowly developing and the EU tries to disseminate its values in order to facilitate such a cooperation with its partners. As the level of protection of human right in the EU is not met everywhere in the world, cooperation tends to be limited.

2. The ASEAN's counterterrorism policy: A localisation rather than an externalisation

Southeast Asia's newly independent States provided a stable structure for themselves in order to deal with intra-regional relations, contain intra-regional conflicts, resist external influences and position themselves on the international scene.[68] The development of ASEAN is about regional reassurance and enhancing regional mutual trust.[69]

Following the same internal dynamics as presented previously, ASEAN diplomacy makes use of informal and non-official relations and discussions to work out consensual positions behind the scenes.[70] Consensual decision-making is meant to ensure that 'each and every action taken in the name of ASEAN must either contribute to or be neutral, but not detract from the perceived national interests of individual ASEAN Member States'.[71] *A fortiori*, the ASEAN fundamental principles of sovereignty and non-interference also govern the foreign policy behaviours of the regional organisation.[72]

(a) *A complex internal structure reflected in the ASEAN actorness: All members' acting in synergy*

The internal rules defining the competence of ASEAN in the conduct of its external relations are quite scarce. The *ASEAN Charter* has provided few elements of coordination between the regional organisation and its Member States.

Firstly, the Charter provides that ASEAN Member States, in the conduct of their external relations, shall 'coordinate and endeavour to develop common positions and

---

[68] Mely Caballero-Anthony, 'Regionalisation of Peace in Asia: Experiences and Prospects of ASEAN, ARF and UN Partnership' *Institute of Defence and Strategic Studies,* Working paper, no. 42 (2003).

[69] Jeannie Henderson, *Reassessing ASEAN*, The International Institute for Strategic Studies (London: Routledge, 1999).

[70] Wunderlich, 'The EU an Actor Sui Generis?' (2012): 662. Informal interactions are also privileged in international relations in Africa and between the EU and the African Union: Ewers-Peters, 'The EU as an Interorganizational Influencer?' (2018): 373.

[71] Bilson Kurus, 'The ASEAN Triad: National Interest, Consensus-Seeking, and Economic Cooperation' *Contemporary Southeast Asia*, vol. 16, no. 4 (1995): 405.

[72] ASEAN, *Treaty of Amity and Cooperation in Southeast Asia* (1976).

pursue joint actions' on the basis of unity and solidarity.[73] ASEAN Member States shall work in harmony to secure decisions with external partners favourable to the region. The central role of the Member States, within a firmly intergovernmental structure, and the consensual decision-making method have impacted ASEAN's external policies. Member States need to agree on these external policies during ASEAN Summits and to ensure they are implemented consistently and coherently.[74] Therefore, any form of collaboration with external partners is complicated to develop and guarantee, which might explain the broad provisions of the various external agreements.

Secondly, the legal personality was attributed by the Charter to 'ASEAN, as an inter-governmental organisation',[75] and not as a regional organisation with autonomous powers. ASEAN represents its Member States through an intergovernmental approach; not as an independent actor. Yet, the *ASEAN Charter* was designed to signal a shift from the 'ASEAN Way' in international affairs; as it was supposed to do in internal affairs. Equipped with a legal personality, ASEAN has sought an appropriate status within the UN system and within other sub-regional, regional, international organisations and institutions to ensure a common voice for the Southeast Asian nations.[76] ASEAN's efforts to do so have been unsuccessful as they have hardly secured a harmonised position for themselves on the international scene thus far. ASEAN's legal personality has not particularly enhanced its own standing and ability to participate in international affairs. It nonetheless constitutes a good step in the development of the ASEAN's legitimacy to represent its Member States as a whole. In totality, outside of its region, the organisation seems to represent even less than the sum of its parts.[77]

As in the EU, ASEAN is composed of various bodies whose action(s) can have an external dimension. In addition to their actions within the region, these bodies[78] formed by the relevant authorities of all Member States could coordinate their external action to provide a harmonised voice for ASEAN.

Leading the movement, the Chairmanship of ASEAN held by a Member State, changing every year, coordinates the action of the main ASEAN bodies. Besides its internal actions, the Member State assuming the Chairmanship 'represent[s] ASEAN in strengthening and promoting closer relations with external partners'.[79] Notably, Cambodia held the Chairmanship in 2022 and Indonesia has taken over in 2023.

---

[73] Art. 41(4), *ASEAN Charter.*

[74] Art. 41(5) and (6), *ASEAN Charter.*

[75] Art. 3, *ASEAN Charter.*

[76] Art. 45, *ASEAN Charter.*

[77] Chesterman, 'Does ASEAN exist?' (2008).

[78] See the ASEAN Structure in Tables 4.2. and, most precisely, 4.3. in Chap. 4. For instance, ASEAN sectoral ministerial bodies comprise Ministers from all Member States for a particular sector, such as Defence, Law, Transnational Crime, Drug Matters, Education, to name a few.

[79] Art. 32(d), *ASEAN Charter.*

The ASEAN Coordinating Council,[80] in consultation with the Community Councils, determines the procedures for ASEAN to conclude international agreements[81] and it decides on the participation of ASEAN in sub-regional, regional, international organisations and institutions, besides the UN.[82] While the Chairmanship ensures the general representation of ASEAN Member States abroad, Member States could also be represented by specific Country Coordinators. Each Country Coordinator rotates taking overall responsibility for coordinating and promoting the interests of ASEAN in its relations with each external partner (dialogue partners, sectoral dialogue partners and development partners).[83] The Country Coordinators differ from one external partner to another and also change every 3 years. Notably, ASEAN Country Coordinator for the EU was Singapore until July 2021 and was replaced by the Philippines for the subsequent 3 years.[84] It is thus possible that a State holds the Chairmanship and others act as Coordinators.

ASEAN's external action has been supported by the 2011 *Rules of Procedure for the Conclusion of International Agreements by ASEAN*.[85] Since then, ASEAN has been able to sign international treaties on its own behalf on the basis of the Member States' common position.[86] These *Rules of Procedure* only apply to international agreements creating rights and obligations for ASEAN as a distinct entity.[87] Notably, the Joint Declarations adopted before 2011 between ASEAN and third parties, namely third States or the EU, were signed between the concerned third party and all the ASEAN Member States. Since 2011, no internationally binding agreement has been signed by ASEAN, but Member States continue to sign and ratify international treaties in their individual capacities in unity and solidarity.[88]

Eventually, the Member States' progress in implementing the potential—but currently non-existent—ASEAN agreements and other decisions would be facilitated and monitored by the Secretary General.[89]

---

[80]The ASEAN Coordinating Council gathers the Ministers of Foreign Affairs. Art. 8, *ASEAN Charter*.

[81]Art. 41(7), *ASEAN Charter*.

[82]Art. 45, *ASEAN Charter*.

[83]Art. 42(1), *ASEAN Charter*.

[84]ASEAN 'ASEAN Dialogue Coordinatorship July 2015–July 2024': available at https://bit.ly/2OBMbel and https://bit.ly/3d9qAUO (accessed on 13 April 2020).

[85]ASEAN Coordinating Council, *Rules of Procedure for the Conclusion of International Agreements by ASEAN*, 19th ASEAN Summit, Bali, 17 November 2011.

[86]Ibid. Also, Chesterman, 'Does ASEAN exist?' (2008): 204–05; Piris and Woon, *Towards a Rules-Based Community* (2015): 68–69.

[87]Art. 2, *Rules of Procedure for the Conclusion of International Agreements by ASEAN* (2011). Also, Art. 1(2), *Rules of Procedure for the Conclusion of International Agreements by ASEAN* (2011).

[88]See, e.g., *Framework Agreement on Comprehensive Economic Cooperation Between ASEAN and the People's Republic of China*, Phnom Penh, 5 November 2002.

[89]Art. 11(2) b, *ASEAN Charter*.

While coordinating its action on counterterrorism, ASEAN does not have an equivalent of the EU CTC responsible for organising its relations within the region and with its external partners. The ASEAN Chairmanship and the Coordinating Council are the main external interlocutors. However, external partners could also be involved in more specific meetings of ASEAN bodies, especially the ASEAN Ministerial Meeting on Transnational Crime (AMMTC) and the Senior Officials Meeting on Transnational Crime (SOMTC), as the Working Groups of the AMMTC and SOMTC on counterterrorism. While some forms of collaboration are institutionalised such as the 'Plus Three' (China, Japan, South Korea),[90] many are not. Notably, these 'Plus Three' countries are also the main partners in the AMMTC. The EU and other key partners such as Australia, the USA or the UNODC could be invited to participate as experts, supporters and/or observers at any respective meeting.[91] The EU is also an actor involved in the SOMTC, but the EU and ASEAN officials convene only on the side of their annual meetings. In this respect, ASEAN distinguishes between 'Dialogue and Sectoral Partners' and 'external parties'.[92] While the first category seems to target the partners clearly identified by ASEAN and with which it already has 'formal' relations, the second category seems to encompass third countries and other parties with whom ASEAN has a light form of cooperation (e.g. on a case-by-case basis), or with whom ASEAN aims to develop a form of collaboration. The EU is the only organisation among the dialogue partners.[93] Despite certain 'formalised' interactions, with Dialogue Partners in particular, ASEAN external engagements in counterterrorism do not imply precise and binding actions.

Aseanapol, as the body meant to facilitate cooperation between law enforcement authorities, does not have any competence to engage with third countries or other organisations.

Therefore, the complexity of the ASEAN institutional organisation is reflected in its external relations, where such external relations are provided for. Institutionally, ASEAN remains deprived of any independent actorness. From an external perspective, the ASEAN external relations might look like an 'hydra organisation' with the

[90] See, e.g., 10th ASEAN Plus Three Ministerial Meeting on Transnational Crime (10th AMMTC +3) Consultation, Joint Statement, Bangkok, 28 November 2019.

[91] For instance, pt. 1.3. (b), European Union External Action (EUEA)—ASEAN Secretariat, *ASEAN-EU Plan of Action (2018–2022)*, Manila, 6 August 2017. Taking another example, Australia participates in the SOMTC Plus Australia Consultation. So far, 14 SOMTC + Australia Consultations have been held. Moreover, ASEAN-Australia Special Summit with the theme 'Enhancing Regional Security and Prosperity', including the side event, namely the ASEAN-Australia Counter-Terrorism Conference, Sydney, 17–18 March 2018.

[92] See, e.g., pt. 25 *'Extra-Regional Cooperation'*, ASEAN Plan of Action to Combat Transnational Crime (1999); pts. 2.4 and 20, ASEAN Comprehensive Plan of Action on Counter Terrorism (2009).

[93] The others are States: China, Japan, Republic of Korea, India, Australia, New Zealand, the USA, Russia and Canada.

Member States all sitting in the driver's seat. The Member States, or their relevant ministries, altogether represent the Association more so than the ASEAN Secretariat.

(b) *ASEAN's external interface: An importer, not exporter*

ASEAN Member States tend to be recipients of external partners' foreign policy in counterterrorism. In particular, the EU-ASEAN actions encompass the mutual learning of each other's respective legal frameworks, the organisation of trainings with external partners, other capacity building exercises, as well as the sharing of information and best practices. The various joint declarations signed between ASEAN and other partners[94] are relatively similar in scope and content, except for minor variations which depend on the agenda as well as the capabilities and resources of each partner.

Military-wise, the ADMM-Plus[95] concept note, drafted in 2007, states that the engagement of the Member States with external partners 'is for the benefit of ASEAN'.[96] It specifies that the purpose of the ADMM-Plus is to 'bring expertise, perspectives and resources from extra-regional countries to bear on shared security challenges' and to 'benefit ASEAN member countries in building capacity to address shared security challenges'.[97] The ADMM-Plus has established six Experts' Working Groups (EWGs) to deal with non-traditional security challenges, including one on terrorism.

While gladly accepting the support of external partners, ASEAN nonetheless aims to conduct their external affairs without larger powers imposing their preferences on ASEAN's domestic affairs. In fact, ASEAN's external policy allows Member States to redefine 'foreign norms' to suit the Association's 'cognitive priors and identities'.[98] When engaging with ASEAN, a given external norm is localised instead of being indiscriminately accepted.[99] For instance, specific developments to ASEAN's architecture over the years, such as the slight addition of a rules-based approach to its 'ASEAN Way', might be due to the influence of the EU on the Southeast Asian region. Yet, ASEAN Member States have adapted such external influence to align with their own objectives and to respect any regional impediments. Regardless, this evolution certainly has facilitated ASEAN relations with the EU.

---

[94] See, e.g., *Joint Declaration on co-operation to combat terrorism*, 14th EU-ASEAN Ministerial Meeting, 5811/03, Brussels, 27–28 January 2003; *Joint Declarations for Cooperation to Combat International Terrorism* between ASEAN and: United States of America, Bandar Seri Begawan, 1 August 2002; India, Bali, 8 October 2003; Australia, Jakarta, 1 July 2004; New Zealand, Vientiane, 29 July 2005; Canada, Kuala Lumpur, 28 July 2006.

[95] The ADMM-Plus is a biennial meeting of the defence ministers of the ASEAN Member States and their Dialogue Partners (Australia, China, India, Japan, New Zealand, South Korea, Russia and the United States).

[96] Pt. 3, ASEAN Defence Ministers' Meeting-Plus (ADMM-Plus), *Concept paper*, 2nd ADMM, Singapore, 13–15 November 2007.

[97] Ibid.

[98] Acharya, 'How Ideas Spread: Whose Norms Matter?' (2004): 239.

[99] Ibid.

ASEAN's external relations in non-traditional security matters are mainly framed by joint declarations.[100] For instance, the 2003 *ASEAN-EU Joint Declaration* stresses the commitment of the EU and ASEAN to the relevant international instruments (*capability building*). It also announces their determination to exchange information on their measures implemented to fight against terrorism (*information and experience sharing*), 'including on the development of more effective policies and legal, regulatory and administrative frameworks'[101] (*capability building*). The joint declaration also states that the EU will assist ASEAN Member States to build capacity (*capacity building*). These relations are more strategic than operational. Even when promoting cooperation between Europol and Aseanapol, relations remain mostly strategic and focus on mutual learning.

Promoting knowledge against terrorist threats and sharing of experience, the EU could provide funding through projects, such as the 'EU-UNODC Joint Initiative for Supporting Southeast Asian Countries to Counter Terrorism'. This initiative has fostered training and research on counterterrorism. As a result of this initiative, Thomas K. Samuel published research in 2016 for the Southeast Asia Regional Centre for Counter-Terrorism (SEARCCT), entitled *Radicalisation in Southeast Asia: A Selected Case Study of Daesh in Indonesia, Malaysia and the Philippines.*[102] This publication served as the basis for SEARCCT to work with other national and ASEAN key actors on counter-radicalisation through training and other capacity building activities.

In general, the external relation foreseen by the ASEAN texts is, at best, diplomatic or strategic. In fact, the provisions related to ASEAN's external action are not particularly developed. Concerning information and intelligence sharing, such a mechanism of cooperation is not legally shaped; but, broadly mentioned and generally associated with the sharing of best practices. Moreover, the wording clearly demonstrates the absence of an operational angle in the ASEAN's external relations. As information and intelligence sharing between competent national authorities within the region—on a strategic level and, even more so, on an operational level—is an objective which ASEAN Member States have barely approached, data sharing, especially for operational purposes, with external partners is close to unthinkable currently. Nonetheless, some ASEAN Member States are more cooperative with certain external partners than with other ASEAN members. For instance, although focusing on intelligence sharing, Singapore has been much more active in sharing data, for operational purposes, with the partners of the Five Eyes Alliance than with other ASEAN members. Interestingly, the *ASEAN Convention on Counter Terrorism* does not mention any external collaboration. By contrast, the PoA

[100] See the list in the table of legislations.

[101] Pt.6, *EU-ASEAN Joint Declaration on co-operation to combat terrorism* (2003).

[102] Thomas K. Samuel, *Radicalisation in Southeast Asia: A selected case study of Daesh in Indonesia, Malaysia and the Philippines* ((Kuala Lumpur: Southeast Asia Regional Centre for Counter-Terrorism, 2016): available at https://www.unodc.org/documents/southeastasiaandpacific/Publications/2016/Radicalisation_SEA_2016.pdf (accessed on 7 January 2021).

associated with the Convention promotes the engagement of the Member States with their dialogue partners and external parties. The form of cooperation foreseen focuses on the implementation of the joint declarations with their dialogue partners, on the sharing of best practices and lessons learnt in countering terrorism and on capacity building and technical cooperation in the areas identified by the PoA. The wording shows that such cooperation remains at a strategic level.[103]

Similarly, the wording which qualifies the relations between Europol and Aseanapol—two bodies meant to facilitate cooperation, including operational cooperation—indicates that their relations will remain strategic, at least for now. They signed a *letter of intent* on 8 November 2016 to strengthen cooperation, which demonstrates that they intend to collaborate for the purposes of establishing cooperative links between the two bodies. Brigadier General Yohanes Agus Mulyono, Executive Director of the Aseanapol Secretariat, commented that 'The Letter of Intent aims to improve mutual cooperation and ensure greater complementary in promoting the *strategic partnership* of EUROPOL and ASEANAPOL as two regional bodies bound by shared basic values. This initiative will reinforce the ties of both agencies and synergies their efforts towards a common goal of effectively addressing transnational crimes and ensuring internal security in their respective region'.[104] They aim to reach a shared objective through strategic means.

As it was previously demonstrated, ASEAN's understanding of mutual trust does not encompass the protection of human rights. On this aspect as well, ASEAN remains an importer of external policies. ASEAN Member States participate in international and transregional fora related to human rights issues, including in security-related fora where human rights are discussed. Yet, localisation of these external norms and policies by each ASEAN Member State still plays a significant role in the regional external policy.

With regard to the sharing of information and intelligence, there is no regional data protection rule or any other rule governing the sharing of data with external partners or parties. This might seem logical given that there is no regional norm governing the exchange of data across borders. The rules on human rights, including data protection, could be part of bilateral agreements; unlikely though because of the absence of national norms in this respect. As ASEAN Member States have different legislations including different data protection standards, engagement with external justice authorities is thus often inconsistent—and in some cases minimal or non-existent—preventing ASEAN from having a common voice on the international

[103] See also ASEAN-EU Enhanced Partnership Action Plan (2013–2017), Bandar Seri Begawan Plan of Action to strengthen the ASEAN-EU Enhanced Partnership (2013–2017), ASEAN-EU Ministerial Meeting in Bandar Seri Begawan, 27 April 2012; ASEAN-EU Plan of Action (2018–2022) (2017).

[104] Europol, 'Europol and Aseanapol agree upon enhanced cooperation' *press release*, 8 November 2016 (italics by the author).

scene.[105] Therefore, ASEAN's actorness is almost mute as an entity or very limited to the sum of its members.

The ways in which the EU and ASEAN conduct their foreign relations concerning counterterrorism reveal clear discrepancies. Those discrepancies are representative of their internal organisation and distribution of competence. As a consequence, ASEAN's actorness is much more limited than the EU's. Their roles on the international scene even tend to be complementary: ASEAN being more passive than the EU and behaving like a beneficiary of external influence, including by the EU's.

In this context, developing an interregional dialogue could present challenges. Building mutual trust between the two regions to develop cooperation in various domains, including terrorism, cannot begin on the basis of the specificities that the EU has attributed to it (i.e. the legal dimension of mutual trust and strong role of human rights). On the contrary, agreeing on a common minimum denominator is a necessary step towards the development and strengthening of relations between parties.

II. The EU and ASEAN Actorness on the International Scene: Determining Factors Governing Interregional Relations

The actorness of the EU and ASEAN depends on the international context (structural factors enabling their participation and recognition in multilateral organisations) and regional institutionalisation (form of representation, cohesion and capabilities).[106] Their legal personality, negotiation capacities, resources and instruments are political and legal elements which establish a regional organisation's actorness.

Influenced by their members and by external partners, regional institutions forge certain types of behaviour and instil particular values and principles that define the regional organisations with their own form of presence and identity[107] while establishing their place on the international scene (A) and building relations between regional organisations (B).

Based on these elements, specific questions arise: who would represent better the EU or ASEAN interests in the global domain? Are the regional organisations or their respective Member States better suited? Are the regional organisations' and their respective Member States' actions coherent, mutually supportive, or perhaps contradictory? The answers to these crucial questions depend on the region involved, the context at a specific moment (e.g. stage of their regional integration, political context, etc.) or the areas of concern. However, certain elements may provide the

[105] UNODC Southeast Asia, 'ASEAN officials and diplomatic partners gather in Bangkok to discuss criminal justice cooperation', Bangkok, 22 March 2017: available at https://bit.ly/37bdmmr (accessed on 30 April 2017).

[106] Wunderlich, 'Comparing regional organisations in global multilateral institutions: ASEAN, the EU and the UN' (2012): 127–28.

[107] Ibid.: 129.

main lines of appreciation in terms of each regional organisation's capacities and presence on the international scene.

A. The Progressive Recognition of Regional Organisations on the International Scene

The challenges of globalisation and post-Cold War restructuring have created opportunities for regional organisations to participate in global governance within the UN alongside States.

In 1992, the UN General Secretary's report 'An Agenda for Peace' called for greater cooperation between the UN and regional arrangements and organisations.[108] Throughout the last two decades, the UN worked to gradually deepen its contacts with regional organisations. Several regional organisations now have the status of permanent observers at the General Assembly. Beginning in 1993, the UN General Assembly convened several high-level meetings with regional organisations to discuss global challenges.[109] Following the first high-level meeting between the UN and regional organisations, the General Assembly adopted the 'Declaration of Enhancement of Cooperation between the UN and Regional Organisations in the Maintenance of International Peace and Security' in 1994. This Declaration recognised 'the importance of the role of regional arrangements or agencies in dealing with such matters relating to the maintenance of international peace and security as are appropriate for regional action [...]'.[110] Moreover, interregional relations was already predicted at that time. The Declaration provided that cooperation between regional arrangements or agencies could take the form of 'exchange of information'.[111]

The formalisation of relations between the UN and regional organisations reached an entirely new level following several commitments at the 2005 World Summit, the sixth highest-level meeting between the UN and regional organisations.[112] There is explicit support for a stronger relationship between the UN and regional organisations via formalised agreements and, where appropriate, the involvement of regional organisations in the Security Council. Since then, several steps took place to enhance

[108] A/47/277-S/24111, Report of the Secretary-General pursuant to the statement adopted by Summit Meeting of the Security Council on 31 January 1992, 'An Agenda for Peace, Preventive diplomacy, peacemaking and peace-keeping', 17 June 1992.

[109] See, e.g., GA/11639, 'Strengthened Cooperation between United Nations, Regional Organizations Vital to International Peace, Security' (2015); A/70/328, *Cooperation between United Nations and regional and subregional organizations on mediation* (2015). See also Luk Van Langenhove and Ramesh Thakur, 'Enhancing Global Governance through Regional Integration' *Global Governance*, vol. 12, no. 3 (2006): 236.

[110] A/RES/49/57, *Declaration on the Enhancement of Cooperation between the United Nations and Regional Arrangements or Agencies in the Maintenance of International Peace and Security*, 84th plenary meeting, 9 December 1994, pt. 3(a).

[111] Ibid., para. 4.

[112] A/RES/60/1, *2005 World Summit Outcome*, 8th plenary meeting, 16 September 2005; S/RES/1631.

cooperation between the UN and the regional organisations. With the porous distinction between traditional security issues and non-traditional ones, regional organisations are progressively recognised as key actors and encouraged by the UN to act in non-traditional security matters, such as terrorism.[113]

Despite this general recognition, regional organisations differ and thus the nature of their respective actorness varies. Therefore, one could query whether regional organisations, such as the EU (1) and ASEAN (2), have the necessary capacities to effectively operate on the international scene.

1. The EU: A *sui generis* international actor?

The EU is an international actor, with a distinct legal and political existence outside of its Member States. It has emerged as a significant partner for the UN across a broad range of areas such as development, climate change, peace building, humanitarian assistance, health concerns and the promotion of good governance.

Like the UN, the EU is 'championing multilateralism'.[114] It has long supported the work done at the UN, including in the prevention of radicalisation leading to violent extremism and terrorism. The EU is committed to strengthening the UN's efforts to address the global threat of terrorism in full compliance with international law, including international human rights law, international humanitarian law and international refugee law, in line with the UN Global Counter-Terrorism Strategy.[115] The gathering of all EU Member States is also amongst the biggest contributors to the UN budget.

However, there are also serious questions regarding the EU's external representation, internal cohesion and consistency. The place of the EU within the UN is a complicated matter. The EU has retained its permanent observer status in the General Assembly since 1974.[116] In addition, the General Assembly upgraded the status of the EU in May 2011 by adopting a resolution granting the EU the right to reply and the ability to make oral amendments.[117] This allows the EU to present common positions, make interventions, present proposals and participate in the UN's general debates. The EU now has its own voice within the UN General Assembly and can

[113] See, e.g., S/RES/2482(2019), *Threats to international peace and security caused by terrorist acts*, 8582nd meeting, 19 July 2019, highlighting the concern of the UNSC over terrorism benefiting from transnational organised crime.

[114] See, e.g., Council of the European Union, Council Conclusions on EU Priorities in UN Human Rights Fora in 2020, General Secretariat of the Council to Delegations, No. 5802/20, Brussels, 17 February 2020.

[115] Pt. 12 of the Annex, Ibid.

[116] A/RES/3208(XXIX), *Status of the European Economic Community in the General Assembly*, 2266th plenary meeting, 11 October 1974.

[117] A/RES/65/276, *Participation of the European Union in the work of the United Nations*, 65th session, 3 May 2011.

thus be active as a separate entity. The EU is represented by a multiplicity of actors: the President of the European Council, the High Representative of the Union for Foreign Affairs and Security Policy, the European Commission and the EU delegations, as well as by its 27 Member States, of which one (France) is a permanent veto-holding member of the Security Council.[118] Importantly, the EU Member States are obligated to coordinate their actions at all international fora.

Given its size, potential and normative priorities, the EU might be expected to be a driving force within the UN, on human rights issues for instance. However, this is far from being the case.[119] The EU is more often reactive than proactive. The EU often lacks internal cohesion, with its Member States but also with different EU institutions being more inclined to follow their own agendas. The EU might appear to constitute a single actor. In reality however, it masks a diversity of different actors with individual interests and opinions. Different EU Member States often support different positions. For example, the dispute between the EU and China in 2005 over textile imports revealed significant differences within the EU; with the UK, Germany and the Nordic countries supporting freer trade and Spain, France and Italy seeking to limit imports. Also, the UK has often been criticised for adopting a more transatlantic position, as opposed to defending the EU's interests. Hence, the EU is forced to assign a great amount of time and energy to internal coordination in order to arrive at a common position.

Despite some internal disagreements, the EU has been able to have productive interactions with the UN and other regional and international organisations. For instance, the EU has worked together with the UN to improve their common operational cooperation in crisis management, including through the sharing of data and analysis (leading to joint analyses) and the planning of peace and security operations (facilitating operational aspects).[120]

Interestingly, the EU has also enhanced its own actorness in developing the one of other regional organisations. The EU's action 'can take the form of supporting regional organisations elsewhere via capacity-building or of the export and projection of its own institutional and normative preferences',[121] which is actually what it does for ASEAN. As such, interregional relations allow for the EU to be recognised as an actor in its own right on the international scene, especially as a supporter or

[118]Before Brexit, the EU had two representatives with the United Kingdom.

[119]Paul Taylor, 'The EU in Geneva: Coordinating Policy in the Economic and Social Arrangements of the United Nations System' in *The European Union at the United Nations. Intersecting Multilateralisms*, eds., Katie Verlin Laatikainen and Karen E. Smith, Palgrave Studies in European Union Politics (Basingstoke: Palgrave Macmillan UK, 2006).

[120]European Parliament, 'Motion for the European Parliament Resolution on the role of the EU within the UN. How better achieve EU foreign policy goals' 2015/2104(INI), Committee on Foreign affairs, Rapporteur: Paavo Väyrynen, 21 October 2015, para. 24 in 'The EU within the UN system'.

[121]Börzel and Risse, 'From Europeanisation to Diffusion: Introduction' (2012); Mattheis and Wunderlich, 'Regional actorness and interregional relations: ASEAN, the EU and Mercosur' (2017): 725.

provider. The EU could help the Southeast Asian regional organisation develop its international actorness and benefit from it in the process.

Methodologically, the power exerted by the Union in its external relations, whatever the interlocutors, has been qualified as a civilian power,[122] soft power,[123] normative power,[124] etc.[125] In fact, the EU regards itself as a norm promoter in global governance, a success story for regional integration, and an alternative world order model to the US's existing hegemony.[126] All these concepts usually indicate that there is something unique about the EU's action on the international scene namely, an 'EU Way' of conducting international relations. Its action is connected to the way post-World War II European integration itself has progressed: avoiding interstate conflicts through integration founded on multilateral, legally binding instruments operated by supranational institutions. Whatever the position of officials or scholars on this matter, the EU might nonetheless quite simply be described as an entity which belongs in a category of its own (a *sui generis* international actor).

2. ASEAN: A simple showcase of its members' common position?

Although ASEAN was not initially meant to be an international actor, but rather a forum where its Member States can interact and collaborate, small steps have slowly been made towards gaining its recognition.

As of yet, the ASEAN Secretariat has no executive and legislative powers. It exclusively aims to ensure the 'greater efficiency in the coordination of ASEAN organs and for more effective implementation of ASEAN projects and activities'.[127] ASEAN's ability to achieve collective action is constrained by its Member States' sovereignty. This left the association unable to respond to the transnational challenges of the 1990s, such as the Asian financial crisis or the East Timor crisis. ASEAN was heavily criticised and its credibility was tarnished.[128] The fact that one notices and analyses ASEAN's capability deficiency is indicative of its presence in global affairs, but this does not reflect its actual regional cohesion.

However, certain changes have occurred since the creation of ASEAN regarding its capacity to represent its Member States and to act independently outside of the

[122] Hedley Bull, 'Civilian Power Europe: A Contradiction in Terms?' *Journal of Common Market Studies*, vol. 21, no. 2 (1982).

[123] Joseph S. Jr. Nye, *Soft Power: The Means To Success In World Politics* (New York: PublicAffairs, 2005).

[124] Ian Manners, 'Normative Power Europe: A Contradiction in Terms?' *Journal of Common Market Studies*, vol. 40, no. 2 (2002).

[125] See also, European Parliament, 'Motion for the European Parliament Resolution on the role of the EU within the UN' 2015/2104(INI), Paavo Väyrynen (2015).

[126] Björn Hettne, 'Interregionalism and World Order: The Diverging EU and US models' in *European Union and New Regionalism*, ed., Mario Telò (Aldershot: Ashgate, 2007).

[127] Presentation of the ASEAN Secretariat: available at https://asean.org/asean/asean-secretariat/ (accessed on 20 November 2020).

[128] Henderson, *Reassessing ASEAN* (1999).

region. Although the *ASEAN Charter* asserts a legal personality for the regional organisation, it appears to have a limited form of international legal personality.

Due to the *ASEAN Charter*, ASEAN as an intergovernmental organisation has started gaining institutional means (cf. Chap. XII 'External Relations' of the *ASEAN Charter*) and recognition (see. 2007 *Memorandum of Understanding on the future of UN–ASEAN cooperation*[129]). As set forth in the Charter, ASEAN obtained the competence to sign international treaties on its own behalf in 2011.[130] However, it clearly stated that before entering in any negotiation procedure, ASEAN representatives must ensure that Member States unanimously agreed upon a common position.[131] The 2011 *Rules of Procedure for the Conclusion of International Agreements by ASEAN* specifies that the rules do not apply to those existing international agreements which have been collectively concluded by ASEAN Member States.[132] Moreover, it only applies to international agreements which create rights and obligations for ASEAN as a separate entity from its Member States.[133] Notably, the Joint Declarations adopted before 2011 between ASEAN and any other third party, namely other States or the EU, were signed by all ASEAN members. Since 2011, Member States have continued to sign and ratify the different international treaties in their individual capacity. For now, there has been no treaty signed between ASEAN, as an independent entity, and third parties. ASEAN Member States are nonetheless asked to conduct their external relations in alignment with ASEAN's unity and solidarity.[134]

There are three types of external agreements that ASEAN and its Member States may conclude. Firstly, there are the agreements which ASEAN could conclude with international organisations. These agreements do not bind Member States, nor do they have internal effects on national legal orders. However, they might strengthen the monitoring and facilitating of the Secretariat in relation to Member States' treaty obligations and thus have internal effects within the ASEAN legal order. Secondly, agreements with external partners usually take the form of international treaties between States parties. Thirdly, there are joint ASEAN agreements which might help to interpret or ensure the implementation of international treaties between ASEAN Member States and external partners. These agreements are signed by the Member States in one column and by the other party (or parties) in another. In any case, most of the external agreements have modalities of entering into force or modalities of termination suggesting that the Member States need to act jointly.

[129] *Memorandum of understanding between the Association of Southeast Asian Nations (ASEAN) and the United Nations (UN) on ASEAN–UN cooperation*, New York, 27 September 2007.

[130] ASEAN Coordinating Council, *Rules of Procedure for the Conclusion of International Agreements by ASEAN*, Bali, 17 November 2011.

[131] Rule 4, 2011 *Rules of Procedure for the Conclusion of International Agreements by ASEAN*. See also, Chesterman, 'Does ASEAN exist?' (2008): 204–05; Piris and Woon, *Towards a Rules-Based Community* (2015): 68–69.

[132] Art. 1(2), *Rules of Procedure for the Conclusion of International Agreements by ASEAN*.

[133] Art. 2, Ibid.

[134] Art. 41(4), *ASEAN Charter*.

Notably, as in the EU, the response to non-traditional security threats in ASEAN is still State-centric in approach; even more so vis-à-vis external partners.

Through different means, including with aid from of these various types of agreements, ASEAN has built up its actorness through its interaction with other key international actors, such as the UN and the EU.

Cooperation between the UN and ASEAN has evolved. It traditionally focused on development issues and emerged in 1972 with the first agreements on cooperation between ASEAN and UN agencies, funds and programs. In 1977, the United Nations Development Programme (UNDP) became a significant ASEAN Dialogue Partner. In the post-Cold War world, ASEAN began to move away from a focus on regional peace and stability to explore 'broader regional coordination in a substantial number of economic issues, as well as so-called functional areas that addressed particular microeconomic and social issues'.[135] Since then, ASEAN Member States realised the advantages of operating as a group and were determined to enhance ASEAN towards being a functioning regional organisation.[136] Despite its considerations for regional security, ASEAN's primary purpose remains the support of Southeast Asia's state-building projects in the face of challenges posed by globalisation and structural change.

Supporting different facets of the ASEAN's development, a relatively dense network of institutional cooperation between the UN, its several associated agencies (such as UNDP, Food and Agriculture Organization, ESCAP, UNODC-ROSEAP), and ASEAN has emerged since the end of the Cold War.[137] It is noteworthy that as early as January 1949, the establishment of the UN Economic and Social Commission for Asia and Pacific (ESCAP) in Bangkok began improving the relations between the UN and Southeast Asian countries. Since then, contacts have increased and cooperation has been strengthened, particularly since 4 December 2006. At that time, ASEAN obtained the Observer status at the UN.[138] Then, on 25 September 2007, the Secretary-General of ASEAN and the Secretary-General of the UN signed a *Memorandum of Understanding* (MoU) *on the Association of Southeast Asian Nations (ASEAN) and the United Nations (UN) on ASEAN-UN cooperation*. Among other things, this MoU stated the need 'to make appropriate administrative arrangements to ensure effective cooperation and liaison between the [two] Secretariats'.[139] The most recent UN–ASEAN Summit took place in November 2022. In this

[135] César de Prado, 'Regions in the world: The EU and East Asia as foreign policy actors' *International Politics*, vol. 47, no. 3/4 (2010): 362.

[136] Donald E. Weatherbee, *International Relations in Southeast Asia: The Struggle for Autonomy*, ed., Samuel S. Kim, Asia in World Politics, 2nd ed. (Lanham: Rowman & Littlefield Publishers, 2009).

[137] The UN has also organised two peacekeeping operations in the region: one in Cambodia and, more recently, in East Timor. Indonesia and Malaysia that have regularly contributed to UN peacekeeping missions around the world supported these operations.

[138] A/RES/61/44, *Observer Status for the Association of Southeast Asian Nations in the General Assembly*, 64th plenary meeting, 4 December 2006.

[139] Art. 2(5), *Memorandum of understanding on ASEAN–UN cooperation* (2007).

Summit, as in previous ones, the Chairperson reiterated the importance of addressing the threats and challenges posed by terrorism and violent extremism.[140]

Interestingly, this MoU was signed prior to the adoption of the *ASEAN Charter* in November 2007 and even prior to the adoption of the 2011 *Rules of Procedure for the Conclusion of International Agreements by ASEAN*. Therefore, ASEAN obtained its legal personality after the UN signed the agreement with ASEAN, which has not prevented the Secretary General for ASEAN to sign this MoU. It cannot be deduced from this signature that the ASEAN Secretariat nor the Chairperson had the requisite power to represent the regional organisation yet. It was only later that ASEAN's credibility as a player in the international arena has been strengthened.

Today, ASEAN faces challenges when attempting to promote itself as an international actor.

The representation problem of ASEAN has long been perpetuated by its weak organisational capability.[141] As with the EU, ASEAN's representation is two-fold: it is represented by its Member States who found ways to cooperate within the UN and, by acting collectively, have enhanced the visibility of the grouping. An early example was the response to Vietnam's invasion of Cambodia in 1979, an episode which was crucial for the evolution of ASEAN as a regional collective actor within the UN.[142] ASEAN's coordinated efforts within the UN made it impossible for Vietnam to gain access to international capital and aid from many key donors and international agencies. ASEAN Member States supported a coherent position for more than a decade and its international weight increased significantly together with its profile and influence.[143]

Another element which might hinder ASEAN's position is financial. ASEAN Member States' contribution to the ASEAN Secretariat is extremely modest due to their lack of financial means. Their contribution to the UN budget is even less. The weight of the ASEAN Member States on the international scene is quite light, which served as the motivation for their own project of regional integration. ASEAN is overly reliant on external resources in almost every aspect of its operations. Relations with external partners are thus extremely important.[144]

---

[140] Pt. 14–15, Chairman's Statement of the 12th ASEAN-United Nations Summit, 'ASEAN Addressing Challenges Together', Phnom Penh, 11 November 2022; see also, pt. 9, Chairman's Statement of the 10th ASEAN-UN Summit, 'Advancing Partnership for Sustainability' Bangkok/Nonthaburi, 3 November 2019.

[141] Haacke, *ASEAN's Diplomatic and Security Culture* (2003): 165–90.

[142] Jürgen Rüland, 'Southeast Asian Regionalism and Global Governance: "Multilateral Utility" or "Hedging Utility"?' *Contemporary Southeast Asia*, vol. 33, no. 1 (2011): 102.

[143] Acharya, *Constructing a Security Community in Southeast Asia* (2001); Wunderlich, 'Comparing regional organisations in global multilateral institutions: ASEAN, the EU and the UN' (2012): 135.

[144] Lukas Maximilian Müller, 'Governing Regional Connectivity in Southeast Asia. The Role of the ASEAN Secretariat and ASEAN's External Partners' *Southeast Asian Studies at the University of Freiburg*, Occasional Paper Series, no. 42 (2018): 6.

Despite its internal weaknesses and the obstacles it encounters, ASEAN is still developing its own form of regional governance.

Based on their internal rules and external action, the EU and ASEAN have demonstrated different forms of actorness. Although they fall into the same broad category of 'regional organisation', their respective features and characteristics differ considerably. The autonomous nature of the EU in international relations, as a representative of is Member States, seems to be more asserted than the ASEAN's, which has almost no autonomous power and a very weak stronghold on the international scene.

B. Adopting the 'Terms and Conditions' of the EU-ASEAN Dialogue: A First Step Towards the Operationalisation of Their Respective Actorness

Interregionalism has two potential advantages for enhancing the actorness of regional organisations, especially of the EU. Firstly, the emergence of other regional actors makes the EU less exceptional by overcoming the $n = 1$ problem. It normalises the EU and generates greater levels of acceptance in global governance fora by creating comparable 'others'. Secondly, it generates a platform for mutual recognition and interaction between regional organisations.[145]

1. Interregionalism: A form of operationalisation of the EU and ASEAN international actorness?

The EU has a long-standing partnership with ASEAN. This 'group-to-group dialogue' began informally in 1972 and was formalised in 1977 with regular senior official and ministerial meetings.[146] The two organisations emphasised the importance of the shared values and common interests that bind them in a long-standing and unique relationship as 'partners in integration'.[147]

Unfortunately, despite repeating their shared intent to accelerate efforts towards strengthening all areas of dialogue and cooperation, little progress has been made in the fight against serious transnational crime in the past 40 years. Currently, one of the applicable planning documents, namely the Plan of Action to Implement the ASEAN-EU Strategic Partnership (2023–2027) (as the one before), primarily identifies the need for enhanced dialogue and deeper political and security cooperation between the two regions. This Plan of Action refers among other instruments to the renewed ASEAN-EU Work Plan to Combat Terrorism and Transnational Crime (2022–2024). It supports the implementation of the various ASEAN-EU agreements as well as the ASEAN counter-terrorism objectives, referred to in the different

---

[145] Mattheis and Wunderlich, 'Regional actorness and interregional relations: ASEAN, the EU and Mercosur' (2017): 724.

[146] Lay Hwee (2009) 9.

[147] *Nuremberg Declaration on an EU-ASEAN Enhanced Partnership*, Nuremberg, 15 March 2007; Council of the EU, 'Press statement of the ASEAN-EU commemorative summit on the occasion of the 40th anniversary of the establishment of ASEAN-EU dialogue relations', Press office—General Secretariat of the Council, Déclarations et Observations 654/17, 14 November 2017.

ASEAN instruments, and proposes to continue working together by exchanging best practices and knowledge.[148]

Specifically relating to terrorism, the EU and ASEAN have declared that they are working together to counter this threat. However, none of the interregional documents develops operational ways to achieve this goal.

In this aspect, as in many others, the devil is in the details. The terminology is important and needs to be defined. When words are associated with specific meaning and consequences, they create legitimate expectations on each partners' side. Conversely, a lack of common terminology might prevent reliable communication and collective understanding. In this specific situation, the terms and conditions of the EU-ASEAN relations remain vague and overly broad in their agreement about methods and commitments. However, it has not prevented the two regions from engaging in specific programmes aimed at fostering EU-ASEAN relations.

2. Defining the contours of the EU-ASEAN interregional relations

Defining the object and purpose of their relations is the necessary basis to start any form of relations. The determination of the object, purpose and means of each party is essential to define the common ground upon which to facilitate their interactions.

The international and regional debates surrounding the definition of 'terrorism' or 'terrorist offences' have been discussed in Chap. 2. Moreover, working in international and regional contexts, the relevant national and regional actors and the channels of interactions have been more specifically defined and discussed in Chaps. 2 and 6. However, the relevant authorities in interregional relations might be more limited in number and diversity when compared with intra-regional relations. In fact, the decision-makers and other relevant strategic actors define the lines of actions in their external relations. Analysing the relations between the EU and ASEAN's competent authorities implies a preliminary understanding of the framework governing the interregional relations. For this reason, this chapter examines their respective regional policies in counterterrorism in relation to one another and the development of channels of interregional interactions.

The approach towards this security threat differs between countries and between regions. Some authors even argue that the EU and ASEAN do not share the same conception of security.[149] In fact, counterterrorism actions might fall into two main categories: 'traditional security issues' in ASEAN or 'security and defence' in the EU, on the one side, and 'non-traditional security issues' in ASEAN or 'criminal matters' in the EU, on the other. From a defence perspective, the EU and ASEAN are platforms of collaboration. Unlike in ASEAN, the EU established a European Defence Agency with the mandate of supporting the Member States and the Council in their effort to improve European Defence capabilities in the field of crisis

[148] Section 1.3, Plan of Action to implement the ASEAN-EU Strategic Partnership (2023–2027), Phnom Penh, 4 August 2022.

[149] Hwee, 'The EU as a Security Actor in Southeast Asia' (2009): 12 and ff.

management and to maintain the European Defence Policy.[150] However, neither the EU nor ASEAN have a regional army at their disposal, nor do they even possess the ability to call on the armies of their Member States for a specific purpose decided by the regional organisation. From a criminal perspective, the EU has adopted a more integrated approach against terrorism, especially since the Lisbon Treaty. By contrast, an improved cooperation between ASEAN competent national authorities in criminal matters is a slow work in progress in a context where States' legislations remain significantly independent from one another.

Determining the two regions' approaches vis-à-vis each other clarifies each partners' obligations and expectations.

Each region brings its own identity and approach to the interregional dialogue. Firstly, not only can the values and interests of the regional organisations and their respective Member States diverge, but the objectives they pursue could too. The consistency of each regional organisation' behaviour and an increase in the convergence is nonetheless essential to ensure long-lasting interregional relations. Secondly, as seen previously, the EU approach is more rules-based. The discourse of the EU as a normative power constructs a particular identity, while also attempting to change other parties through the spread of certain norms and standards.[151] By contrast, the ASEAN approach remains more practice-based. These differences can hinder the production of useful mutual commitments that would constitute a meaningful step forward. Despite diverging approaches, the two regions have decided to work together to reinforce an inclusive and rules-based international order and to support the effective functioning of regional institutions.[152]

The precise intents and actions of the two regions—through their representatives—vis-à-vis each other are unclear. There is a tendency in official documents or doctrine to use broad interaction terms such as 'cooperation', 'collaboration' and 'coordination' without giving these terms a precise definition and specific legal consequences.[153]

Since the 2003 *EU-ASEAN Joint Declaration on cooperation to combat terrorism,* the successive EU-ASEAN joint declarations in criminal matters are elaborated under 'Political and Security Cooperation'.[154] These instruments mostly use 'cooperation' to qualify the interregional relations in all subjects, including transnational

---

[150] *Council Joint Action 2004/551/CFSP of 12 July 2004 on the establishment of the European Defence Agency*, O.J. L245/17, 17 July 2004; updated by the *Council Decision (CFSP) 2015/1835 of 12 October 2015 defining the statute, seat and operational rules of the European Defence Agency*, O.J. L266/55, 13 October 2015.

[151] Thomas Diez and Ian Manners, 'Reflecting on Normative Power Europe' in *Power in World Politics*, eds., Felix Berenskoeter and M. J. Williams (London: Routledge, 2007): 174.

[152] Council of the EU, 'Press statement of the ASEAN-EU commemorative', 14 November 2017.

[153] For the definitions of these terms, see Chap. 2.

[154] *Nuremberg Declaration on an EU-ASEAN Enhanced Partnership* (2007); Plan of Action to strengthen the ASEAN-EU Enhanced Partnership (2013–2017) (2012). Author's italics in the text.

crime and human rights.[155] In particular, the *EU-ASEAN Joint Declaration on cooperation to combat terrorism* only uses 'cooperation' to qualify the interregional interactions. The word 'collaboration' is seldom used in the various documents and it unlikely involves distinct commitments to those for 'cooperation'. 'Coordination' is also rarely included in EU-ASEAN documents but, where it is, it is always defined as an objective to be targeted.[156] Coordination seems to imply a better ordering of tasks to enhance the effectiveness of authorities' action. Thus, the words 'collaboration' and 'cooperation' seem to have been used interchangeably thus far, while the word 'coordination' is rarely used.

Their regional integration model, their actorness and their external policies have revealed that the two regional organisations have distinct means and objectives on the international scene. However, the EU and ASEAN claim to collaborate and cooperate in the fight against terrorism.[157] The analysis of the different EU-ASEAN documents and their practical interactions with one another indicate that the interregional relation between the EU and ASEAN more accurately constitutes a strategic collaboration, as opposed to an operational cooperation. They share common objectives and interact on a strategic basis, but they do not cooperate on specific cases and do not exchange specific information. This type of interaction only exists—if it exists—on a bilateral basis between States of each of the two regions, and not between the regional organisations themselves.

Evidently, the terminology in the official documents is not always accurate. This becomes an issue where the principle of transparency and accountability are concerned. As many interregional interactions are not public, the vocabulary used to qualify their interactions should be more precise in order to explain the level and form of relations that the EU and ASEAN have in this regard. However, this ambiguity and vagueness might be useful in the current state of international relations, especially when dealing with sensitive matters such as terrorism.

---

[155] *Nuremberg Declaration* (2007); Plan of Action to strengthen the ASEAN-EU Enhanced Partnership (2013–2017); EUEA, 'The European Union and the Association of South East Asian Nations: Towards an Ever Stronger Natural Partnership', Fact Sheet, No. 140722/03, Brussels, 22 July 2014; Council of the EU, 'Press statement of the ASEAN-EU commemorative summit' (2017); Plan of Action to implement the ASEAN-EU Strategic Partnership (2023–2027), Phnom Penh, 4 August 2022.

[156] Co-Chair's Statement of the 20th EU-ASEAN Ministerial Meeting, Brussels, 23 July 2014; EUEA, Fact sheet EU-ASEAN relations, Brussels, 7 April 2016.

[157] See *ASEAN-EU Joint Declaration on Cooperation to Combat Terrorism*, (2003); European Council of the EU, 'Council Conclusions on EU-ASEAN relations', press release, 22 June 2015: available at https://bit.ly/3pgNqfe (accessed on 12 February 2021); ASEAN-EU Post-Ministerial Conference, Vientiane, 25 July 2016: available at https://bit.ly/3jO3Yu3 (accessed on 12 February 2021). Also, Céline C. Cocq and Sarah Teo, 'Countering Terrorism: Challenges and Opportunities in ASEAN-EU Cooperation' in *Interregionalism and the European Union. A post-revisionist approach to Europe's place in a changing world*, eds., Louise Fawcett, Frederik Ponjaert, and Mario Telò (Farnham: Ashgate, 2015).

Section 2: A Multiheaded and Multifaceted Interregional Dialogue—Synergistic Relations Between the EU and ASEAN

As was presented in the previous section, the external relations of the EU and ASEAN are a means for them to be recognised as international actors. Three forms of external relations of regional organisations can be discerned: relations with third countries (bilateralism); relations with other regional organisations (interregionalism) and direct or indirect involvement in other transnational or global governance mechanisms (multilateralism). These various forms of interactions are present in the EU-ASEAN relations.

Interregionalism might be regarded as a successful way to facilitate strategic interactions in various subjects. Establishing a common ground based on an understanding of the objective is essential to improve their relations. In fact, the outcome of the EU-ASEAN relations on mutual interests is considered to be positive.[158]

Yet, the analysis of the EU-ASEAN relations also reveals the limits of their interregional relations. Their internal complexities and the distribution of competences between the regional organisations and their respective Member States do not facilitate the interregional interactions. With the view that a 'region-to-region' qualification would be better suited to the situation, the EU, as a more centralised supranational organisation, has aimed to ensure that ASEAN, multi-pronged today between the ASEAN Secretariat (or any ASEAN representative) and the Member States, emerges as an effective regional organisation, within and beyond Southeast Asia (I). The objective for the EU is to enable a balanced and fruitful interregional dialogue in counterterrorism with another regional organisation, namely ASEAN (II).

I. Interregionalism: Creating a New Constructive Path Through International Relations

It must be recognised that the EU is not the only partner of ASEAN and its Member States. The UNODC and some third countries have a strong presence in the region and have influenced—especially through the funding of different programmes—the development of ASEAN Member States in matters of interest for the funding country and the receiving one. However, as with any other regional organisation, the EU could be a valuable partner for ASEAN.

Acknowledging the fact that the EU is interested in engaging with the development of ASEAN, a number of questions arise. The first question is whether, and how, the EU could adapt its policies and standards to the Southeast Asian region. The second is whether ASEAN, as a regional organisation and/or its ten Member

[158] An official from the EU Counter-Terrorism Coordinator Office in discussion with the author, 8 April 2020. See also, Rees, 'EU and ASEAN: Issues of regional security' (2010): 415.

States, would call for, recognises and/or accepts the EU's influence. Lastly, there needs to be an analysis on the ways in which ASEAN and its Member States might potentially have imported and localised these external policies.

After analysing the converging point between the two regional organisations' policies (A), the actual influence of the EU in the development of ASEAN's actorness in counterterrorism needs to be highlighted (B).

A. A Confrontation Between the EU's External Policies and the Reluctances of ASEAN vis-à-vis External Influences: A Difficult Process of Localisation

The EU has recognised the increasing role of Asia in the world economy. For this reason, it started to develop strong economic and political ties with the different Asian actors, including ASEAN.[159] The maintenance of peace and stability in Asia is an important factor not only for the protection of the Union's interests in this region, including economic ones, but also for the respect of international obligations and agreements on which the Union itself depends for its security. It is therefore essential for the Union to develop its capacity in order to play a proper role in the region[160] and adopt the most adequate approach towards its Southeast Asian partners.

The EU is using these relations to project its own model of institutionalised actorness.[161] The EU could be a leader, a reference, a sponsor and/or an implementer in Southeast Asia.[162] Before determining the role of the EU, each method need to be defined.

A leader proposes the accomplishment of certain objective(s), not the adoption of specific norm(s) or policy(-ies) that could help reaching the objective(s). It often applies socialisation mechanisms in order to convince the receiver(s) to adopt the identified goal. The leader could use processes with positive connotations, as persuasion and teaching, and/or with negative connotations, via naming or shaming strategies.[163]

A reference acts as a model for others to adopt norms or policies in a specific field. The influence can take various forms. Firstly, the receiver could fully copy the norm (s) and/or policy(-ies) adopted by the reference. Secondly, the norm(s) or policy(-ies) adopted by the reference is(are) adapted to the local realities. Lastly, the receiver (s) pick(s) and choose(s) parts of the norm(s) or policy(-ies) from a set of actors fulfilling their role as references.[164]

---

[159] Commission of the European Communities, 'Towards a New Asia Strategy', COM(94) 314.

[160] Ibid., 7.

[161] Mattheis and Wunderlich, 'Regional actorness and interregional relations: ASEAN, the EU and Mercosur' (2017): 723.

[162] Categorisation particularly developed by Giulia Tercovich, *The EU inter-regional influence in comparison: the case of the institutionalization of ASEAN disaster management* (Université libre de Bruxelles and University of Warwick, PhD degree, dissertation, 2019): 89–95.

[163] Ibid., 89–90.

[164] Ibid., 90–93.

A sponsor financially sustains the steps which lead to the objective identified by the receiver and agreed to by the sponsor (in both of their interests). The support can be direct, such as directly financing the instruments analysed; or it can sustain the process indirectly by sponsoring the activities supporting the norms and tools discussed (resource dependence).[165]

Finally, the implementer can be placed in charge of the technical implementation of the norm(s) or of the tools that serve to reach the objective(s). The type of influence exercised by the implementer is direct and often results in the full adoption of norms or tools which are already implemented elsewhere, usually by the implementer. In fact, the implementer is often chosen as it already has experience implementing similar norms or policies.[166]

Taking this categorisation into account, the EU tends to prefer being categorised into two main types. In these various roles, the EU could exert influence both actively and passively.

Firstly, the presence of the EU is clear in the region, but its leadership is not strong. The main added value of the EU is therefore not its leadership.

Secondly, the EU sponsorship is characterised by its financial support to regional and national programmes in order to help the development of the region's capacities, in economic, social, political or security matters. Such support might target specific countries (see the development strategies for the 'CLMV' economies) or even ASEAN. In terrorism-related matters, the EU has partnered with the UNODC to fund programmes that UNODC-ROSEAP, due to its strong presence and legitimacy in the region, aims to implement. It also works directly with ASEAN in supporting the implementation of its regional instruments.

Thirdly, and in its primary capacity, the EU serves as a benchmark, a reference, especially because of its experience in developing a comprehensive regional legal framework. The influence of the EU norms and policies on those of ASEAN is quite visible. ASEAN Member States have adapted certain EU norms to local constraints and objectives. The EU tends to serve as a template regional organisation and thus the EU has pro-actively engaged in promoting its model.[167] For instance, it has been said that the *ASEAN Charter* has been inspired by the EU constitutional framework. In this sense, the EU influences the development of the ASEAN institutional framework. Having a similar structure is meant to facilitate successful cooperation between the two regions. The EU's project of regional integration is 'widely perceived as not just an example, but a model for regional economic integration'.[168] This is true even if regional organisations, such as the African Union or ASEAN, seek to create their own institutions and move away from the EU format. They are nevertheless inspired by its institutional structure.[169] In particular, ASEAN Member

[165] Ibid., 93–96.

[166] Ibid., 96–99.

[167] Ewers-Peters, 'The EU as an Interorganizational Influencer?' (2018): 370.

[168] Bilal, 'Is the EU a Model of Regional Integration? Risks and Challenges' (2007)..

[169] Ibid.: 3; Ewers-Peters, 'The EU as an Interorganizational Influencer?' (2018): 372.

States have adopted a 'pick and choose' approach vis-à-vis the EU and other external partners' policies and norms.[170] With this approach, the EU's external action seemingly aims to strengthen its own action by exporting its unique policy and normative preferences to other parties. Conversely, ASEAN's engagement with third partners primarily seeks to control the extraction of normative and material resources to strengthen its own internal action.

Therefore, ASEAN and its Member States have not fully adopted the EU norms, but tend, when it suits the receiving party, to localise them.[171] External norms can be imported for a local and specific usage only.[172] Regional and national decision-makers redefine external norms, which they take as generally useful and desirable, but not fully consistent with their regional or national history, political and legal framework (hence the need for their redefinition). The same regional and national decision-makers might also reject those external norms which they do not view as worthy of selection, borrowing and adoption in any form.[173] The 'localised' norms are more likely to be accepted and integrated by 'local' decision-makers and to be respected by any recipient (e.g. stakeholders and/or citizens). It is the support from local actors that is vital in determining the norm's acceptance and the preservation of their legal autonomy.

In fact, it is not surprising that, after gaining independence, ASEAN Member States and their leaders might question, or potentially reject, the norms of an international or European order established at a time of European dominance and might seek to replace or modify them with ones which are consistent with their interests and identities.[174] Southeast Asian countries may have known the Europeans during the colonial times as disrespectful of local cultures, traditions, human rights and individual liberties. This may explain some reservation by some Asian countries and leaders to accept similar norms and structures that nowadays are broadly respected in the EU. But, it is also true that international norms could paradoxically be invoked and supported by weaker States, including the principles of sovereignty and non-interference, in order to strengthen their place on the international scene.[175]

Finally, it should not be forgotten that their interregional relations, and the influence of the EU in the Southeast Asian region, could be hindered by tensions which might arise between the EU and ASEAN concerning certain situations in Southeast Asia. For instance, the situation in Myanmar has been a problem between the EU and ASEAN.[176] The EU has imposed diplomatic sanctions on Myanmar. On

---

[170]Ewers-Peters, 'The EU as an Interorganizational Influencer?' (2018): 377.

[171]Amitav Acharya, 'Norm Subsidiarity and Regional Orders: Sovereignty, Regionalism, and Rule-Making in the Third World' *International Studies Quarterly*, vol. 55, no. 1 (2011): 97.

[172]Acharya, 'How Ideas Spread: Whose Norms Matter?' (2004): 252.

[173]Acharya, 'Norm Subsidiarity and Regional Orders' (2011): 98.

[174]Ibid.: 99.

[175]Ibid.: 101–02.

[176]Hui Ying Lee 'ASEAN's Limited Role in Solving the Rohingya Crisis' *The Diplomat*, 12 October 2018.

the ASEAN side, its commitment to the 'Asian Way' of diplomacy limits its ability to criticise Myanmar, although it has slowly exerted more pressure on the junta and appears to be adopting a more assertive stance. This has placed a strain on EU–ASEAN relations, making meetings difficult. Yet, on 14 December 2022, the EU Member States and ASEAN Member States, except Myanmar, met to discuss this situation.[177] These types of issues could limit the possibilities for cooperation at some levels between the EU and ASEAN.[178]

B. The Effect of the EU's Action on the Development of the ASEAN Actorness in Counterterrorism

The EU aims to contribute to security, solidarity, mutual respect among peoples and human rights beyond the European region,[179] and, in so doing, be recognised as an important international actor, including by ASEAN (1). In its dialogue with ASEAN, the EU aims to uphold and promote its values, standards and its interests while also combating transnational crime, including terrorism (2).

1. <u>The EU's flexible approach towards ASEAN: Its cautious recognition as a relevant actor and a regional legal model</u>

The EU has slowly understood that the further they stray from EU territory, the less it makes sense to spread their policies, norms, standards and institutions (a process referred to as 'Europeanisation'[180]). In particular, the EU has recognised that its approach in Asia needs to be 'flexible and modular'[181] in order to anticipate changes in the region and must be geared towards the particular circumstances of the different countries and the region. It could also be said that 'the further we move away from Europe, the fewer incentives the EU has to offer to promote its policies and institutions and the more it has to rely on mechanisms of persuasion and of communication to make its case'.[182] The adoption and adaptation of norms, rules and institutional models, equivalent to those of the EU, into domestic and regional structures mostly involves active processes of interpretation, incorporation of new norms and rules into a pre-existing legal and political framework, and also resistance to particular rules and regulations.[183] As previously shown, this localisation process might be more or less complex depending on the norms and policies, on the objectives of the partners and on the relations established between them. The EU might be confronted with strong—or even simply incompatible—differences with

---

[177] John Sifton 'Europe and ASEAN should work together on Myanmar crisis' Human Rights Watch, 13 December 2023: available at https://www.hrw.org/news/2022/12/13/europe-and-asean-should-work-together-myanmar-crisis (accessed on 12 March 2023).

[178] Rees, 'EU and ASEAN: Issues of regional security' (2010): 415.

[179] Art. 3 TEU.

[180] Börzel and Risse, 'From Europeanisation to Diffusion: Introduction' (2012): 2.

[181] Commission of the European Communities, 'Towards a New Asia Strategy', COM(94) 314, 14.

[182] Börzel and Risse, 'From Europeanisation to Diffusion: Introduction' (2012): 8.

[183] Ibid.

their partner's legislation or policy. Therefore, the EU attempts to build a bridge with ASEAN and its members in various domains in order to establish a 'fruitful' dialogue between the two regional organisations.[184]

ASEAN has been 'moving towards the need to build institutions and there are more serious attempts and studies to understand how the EU works'.[185] The outcome was the adoption of the *ASEAN Charter*, which was influenced by the EU-style of institutionalisation. With it, ASEAN has imported parts of the EU method of governance. The 14th ASEAN Summit in 2009 agreed on a roadmap to create a three-pillar structure comprised of an ASEAN Community, based on an ASEAN Political-Security Community, an ASEAN Economic Community and an ASEAN Socio-Cultural Community. This can be interpreted as an indicator of the EU's success as a model for regionalism. After more than 40 years, ASEAN might mostly retain its practice-based approach, but is slowly transforming into a rule-based community endowed with a legal personality. The ASEAN Summit structure and the Chairmanship are similar to the European Council and the Presidency. In essence, the *ASEAN Charter* 'heavily emulates EU concepts and terminology and represents what could have been a lean version of the Constitutional Treaty'.[186] Yet, ASEAN's external competences differ significantly from the EU's and it is still clearly avoiding supranational institutions. ASEAN tends to transpose its internal governance system to its external relations; slowly adding a more rule-based approach into its practice-based external policy. The degree to which the EU has inspired the *ASEAN Charter* has yet to be strongly debated.[187]

The threat of international terrorism provided the EU 'with new opportunities for greater involvement on non-traditional security issues of terrorism, piracy and money laundering'.[188] The European Commission's Communication in 2003 called for the revitalisation of the EU's relations with ASEAN Member States. This Communication identifies six strategic priorities of the EU towards ASEAN: (1) Supporting regional stability and fight against terrorism; (2) Promoting human rights, democratic principles and good governance; (3) Mainstreaming Justice and Home Affairs issues such as migration, organised crime and piracy; (4) Injecting a new dynamism into regional trade and investment relations; (5) Continuing to support the development of less prosperous countries and (6) Intensifying dialogue

---

[184] See, e.g., Paul Mandl (ARISE Team Leader), 'ASEAN Regional Integration Support from the EU (ARISE) Programme holds Closure Event' *press release*, Mission of the European Union to ASEAN, Jakarta, 8 July 2017; project YAKSHA to reinforce EU-ASEAN cooperation in cybersecurity: see https://project-yaksha.eu/

[185] Yeo Lay Hwee, 'EU-ASEAN Relations and Policy Learning' in *Europe-Asia Relations: Building Multilateralisms*, eds., Richard Balme and Brian Bridges, Palgrave Studies in European Union Politics (Basingstoke: Palgrave MacMillan, 2008): 92.

[186] Börzel and Risse, 'From Europeanisation to Diffusion: Introduction' (2012).

[187] See, e.g., Severino, *Southeast Asia in Search of an ASEAN Community* (2006); Kim, 'Theorizing ASEAN Integration' (2011).

[188] Hwee, 'The EU as a Security Actor in Southeast Asia' (2009): 12.

and cooperation in specific policy areas.[189] This new phase of EU-ASEAN relations is no longer purely driven by economic considerations. The EU support for regional integration and political and security dialogue became an important component of the partnership.

With respect to the first priority, the EU has supported the ASEAN Member States efforts to adopt and implement effective measures against terrorism. As the lowest common denominator is pacing the relations with ASEAN and its Member States, the EU has an interest in raising their standards as well as their capabilities and capacities. The successive ASEAN-EU Plans of Action adopted until now do not go beyond the strategic level of cooperation. It nonetheless focuses on the three axes of mutual trust building with, for instance, the implementation of the *ASEAN Convention on Counter Terrorism* and the *ASEAN Comprehensive Plan of Action on Counter Terrorism*[190] and the establishment of regular EU-ASEAN policy dialogues on counterterrorism, capacity building exercises and information and experience sharing.[191] On the basis of these Plans of Action, it seems that the ACCT and its PoA constitute the minimum common denominator and, although it seems bold to argue, this could also imply a mostly one-sided trade of expertise (from the EU to ASEAN Member States). Indeed, 'ASEAN has welcomed EU engagement in helping member states address non-traditional security threats such as countering terrorism, development assistance to alleviate poverty and close the development gap between the more developed and less developed ASEAN Member States, humanitarian assistance, and most recently, peacekeeping in Aceh'.[192]

While the influence of the EU over the ASEAN legal framework seems undeniable, the degree of the EU's influence is still determined by ASEAN.

2. The EU's agenda in supporting ASEAN's regional integration and response against non-traditional security issues

The EU faces competitors while elaborating its agenda in the Southeast Asian region. Among these competitors are the sharp rise of China and India on the Asian continent as well as the United States' growing interest in the region.

The EU has nonetheless managed to have a certain influence in the region; following its own interests and those of ASEAN Member States, and according to the distinctive ASEAN features and needs. The slow development of interregional relations between the EU and ASEAN is in fact determined by two main and contradictory considerations: on the one hand, an equal relationship can be more fruitful and, on the other, Southeast Asian governments are highly sensitive about

[189] Commission of the European Communities, Communication from the Commission, 'A new partnership with South East Asia', COM(2003) 399 final, Brussels, 9 July 2003.

[190] Pt. 1.3. (c), EUEA—ASEAN Secretariat, ASEAN-EU Plan of Action (2018–2022).

[191] Plan of Action to strengthen the ASEAN-EU Enhanced Partnership (2013–2017); ASEAN-EU Plan of Action (2018–2022); Plan of Action to implement the ASEAN-EU Strategic Partnership (2023–2027).

[192] Hwee, 'The EU as a Security Actor in Southeast Asia' (2009): 15.

issues pertaining to their sovereignty. Yet, several criminal matters, such as terrorism, have clearly been identified as shared threats and reasons to engage in such interregional dialogue.

The EU has supported ASEAN's actions through various means, including financial support, expertise and technical assistance. The EU provides ASEAN with financial support, but it could set conditions on how funds are to be used by recipient organisations or countries. Analysing the most recent budget cycle (2014–2020), ASEAN received 170 million euros from the EU to support integration projects, which include projects and programmes on security cooperation in the region.[193] However, in comparison with the EU-African Union (AU) relationship, the EU's financial assistance for ASEAN's projects seems rather small.[194]

With the funding, the Union provides assistance and expertise to ASEAN to improve internal cooperation in the areas of information sharing and capacity building. The transfer of expertise indicates how, and to what extent, the target organisation or country relies on the source of organisation's experience on and knowledge about certain issues.[195,196]

The EU has sought to increase its technical assistance to enhance regional cooperation through capability building, capacity building and information and experience sharing with the goal of addressing the various security threats.[197] The EU has supported different missions for a more connected and integrated ASEAN. However, those missions are difficult to implement as the EU faces multiple interlocutors, namely the ASEAN Secretariat and, mostly, ASEAN Member States (2). Despite the reluctance of ASEAN Member States, the EU aims to foster (bilateral) inter-organisational interregional relations between the EU and ASEAN Secretariat by supporting the ASEAN centrality and regional institutionalisation (1).

1. Primarily, the EU has adopted a regionally centred approach supporting the ASEAN Secretariat to be a driving force for promoting dialogue, moderation and cooperation for peace, security, stability and prosperity in the region.[198] Looking for another regional partner, the EU has aimed to develop the ASEAN actorness.[199] The EU has been ASEAN's most significant partner in this regard.

The two organisations emphasised the importance of the shared values and common interests. UN principles such as independence, sovereignty, equality and

---

193 European Commission, 'EU proposes to scale up its partnership with ASEAN' *press release*, Brussels, 19 May 2015.

194 Ewers-Peters, 'The EU as an Interorganizational Influencer?' (2018): 377.

195 Ewers-Peters, 'The EU as an Interorganizational Influencer?' (2018): 370.

196 Ewers-Peters, 'The EU as an Interorganizational Influencer?' (2018): 377.

197 Rees, 'EU and ASEAN: Issues of regional security' (2010): 414.

198 Nuremberg pt. 4; Pt. 1.2. (a), EUEA—ASEAN Secretariat, ASEAN-EU Plan of Action (2018–2022); Council of the EU, 'Press statement of the ASEAN-EU commemorative summit' (2017).

199 Hwee, 'The EU as a Security Actor in Southeast Asia' (2009): 15.

territorial integrity are central values in their relations, as it was referred to in the 2017 EU-ASEAN Summit or more recently in the 2022.[200] These principles are repeatedly uttered at each ASEAN Summit; something the EU rarely does. Evidently, it is once again the lowest common denominator which dictates the pace of these interregional relations.

The EU has offered to strengthen the institutional capacity of the ASEAN Secretariat through different means. It has worked mainly through ASEAN-EU Programmes for Regional Integration Support (APRIS I and II), which have run from 2003 to 2010, but also through other EU-funded programmes (e.g. the 2013–2016 ARISE programme supporting the implementation of regional integration initiatives, ARISE-Plus and E-READI). These programmes, and the ones that succeed them,[201] nonetheless focus on economic development instead of political and security matters. This might be explained by the fact that ASEAN currently has no intention of engaging in a deep discussion about potential integration into the Political-Security Community. By focusing on the economic development, the EU's relations with ASEAN seem to have contributed to the persistent impression among Southeast Asian countries that the EU is primarily an economic power.

By financially supporting ASEAN programmes, the EU has influenced the direction of the ASEAN policy in the matter(s) of these programmes. While this might lead to positive effects concerning Southeast Asian economic, commercial, legal or institutional development, it could also limit the ASEAN's ownership of the adopted policies as the financial assistance has created a 'donor dependence' (see. sponsorship).[202] The situation has evolved over time though. While the EU was previously able to verbalise its conditions, the situation has changed with the arrival of alternative donors such as the UN or other countries such as New Zealand, Australia and the USA. ASEAN Member States have edged towards self-ownership and autonomy.[203] It is only upon request that external expertise complements any

[200] 'Press statement of the ASEAN-EU commemorative summit' (2017); ASEAN-EU Commemorative Summit 2022, Joint Leader's Statement, 45th anniversary of ASEAN-EU Dialogue Relations, Brussels, 14 December 2022.

[201] See European Commission, Regional Programming For Asia Strategy Document (2007–2013), Brussels, 31 May 2007, only focused, among other Asian countries on eight ASEAN countries, i.e. Cambodia, Indonesia, Laos, Malaysia, Myanmar, Philippines, Thailand and Vietnam: available at https://bit.ly/379bA5m (accessed on 27 July 2017); ASEAN Regional Integration Support (2013–2017); available at http://arise.asean.org/ (accessed on 27 July 2017) concerned the full region but it is clear that the countries the most concerned by this programme are the same eight countries. Brunei Darussalam and Singapore are considered the richest and the most developed countries in the region. See also ASEAN-EU Cooperation Programmes 2014–2020: available at https://bit.ly/3aYIbfb (accessed on 12 February 2021).

[202] On this link of dependency but applied on the EU's action in another region, see, e.g., Annemarie Peen Rodt and Jide Martyns Okeke, 'AU-EU "Strategic Partnership": Strengthening Policy Convergence and Regime Efficacy in the African Peace and Security Complex?' *African Security*, vol. 6, no. 3–4 (2013): 221; Ewers-Peters, 'The EU as an Interorganizational Influencer?' (2018): 374.

[203] Ewers-Peters, 'The EU as an Interorganizational Influencer?' (2018): 374.

financial support.[204] The EU could still attempt to export its standards, principles, norms and practices on the subject at stake, when the expertise of the EU is requested. It could even attempt to add conditions to the funding of certain programmes.

For the purpose of promoting its standards, the EU attempts to adapt them to the specific Southeast Asian context. This has slowly occurred in the case of human rights-related matters. The human rights component was already part of the Union's action in 1994.[205] Its general approach was to encourage Asian States to endorse the relevant international instruments. These programmes, which involve not only national officials but also practitioners, usually aim to increase regional cooperation by developing trust among competent authorities. The main obstacle to cooperation is the defiance which might exist among relevant actors within ASEAN. A way to overcome this lack of trust could be the adoption of a political or legal agreement. This agreement would necessarily be based on a common understanding and knowledge of each other.

Encouraging a more central and legalistic architecture in ASEAN, the EU has also supported complementary axes: a regional freedom of movement with the ASEAN Common Visa[206] associated with a more centralised system of cooperation in criminal matters through Aseanapol. In the latter case, Europol and Aseanapol have started to converse with each other to exchange experiences and best practices.[207] However, for the time being, there is no operational agreement between Europol and any of the ASEAN Member States. There is no exchange of information between the two regional 'bodies'. International exchanges of information are executed either through Interpol or according to bilateral interstate agreements.

2. Secondly, the EU has directed its activities at ASEAN Member States given the lack of a centralisation of their actions at the regional level. Yet, the EU has not directly concluded any bilateral agreements with any of the ASEAN Member States for developing operational relations in criminal matters. This is not surprising as the EU has only concluded a few external agreements related to cooperation in criminal matters with specific third countries, especially and mainly the USA, Iceland, Norway, Switzerland and Japan.[208] The main agreements concluded by the EU with ASEAN Member States are either hybrid interregional relations (between the EU and one or several ASEAN Member State(s)) or inter-organisational interregional relations (between the EU and ASEAN as the grouping of its Member States) which deal mainly with economic, development and democracy related matters. The objective is to build up useful partners for the EU. Interestingly, the 2003 European Security Strategy

---

[204] Ibid.

[205] Commission of the European Communities, 'Towards a New Asia Strategy', COM(94) 314, 12.

[206] *ASEAN Framework Agreement on Visa Exemption*, Kuala Lumpur, 25 July 2006 (not in force).

[207] Letter of Intent between Europol and Aseanapol, 85th Interpol General Assembly, Bali, 8 November 2016.

[208] Cremona (2011).

neglected any mention of ASEAN and the EU's participation in the ASEAN Regional Forum (ARF).[209] This could be explained by the fact that this forum includes more than just ASEAN Member States. Eventually, operational communication is more significant between the Member States of each region. Terrorism-related matters, more so than others, continue to be a sensitive issue at the core of the Member States' integrity and competence. For this reason, bilateral relations between States from the two regions remain more prominent.[210]

Initially, the EU aimed to make its partnership with the Association fruitful on the international scene. The EU has indeed contributed to the ASEAN institutional design. Then, realising that the ASEAN Member States did not share this objective, the EU has exerted influence over both the regional organisation and its Member States through various channels, including EU-ASEAN Summits, or through the designing of trainings, meetings and dialogues with ASEAN Member States. Conversely, ASEAN Member States have not been able to successfully shape their policy towards the EU. In fact, the relationship is still considered asymmetrical.[211]

Despite the significant discrepancies between the two regional organisations, interregional relations are meant to be fruitful for both parties. The recognition of ASEAN provided by the EU, a fellow regional entity, in a growing number of sensitive policy fields such as counterterrorism serves as a legitimising factor for the Southeast Asian leaders, for the regional organisation, and could also balance the EU-ASEAN interregional relations.

Caught between inter-organisational interregionalism (ASEAN-EU relations) and hybrid interregionalism (relations between the EU and one or several ASEAN Member State(s)), the EU has attempted to pursue its interregional strategy through broader fora involving third parties (transregionalism). This makes ASEAN Member States less exposed to the power asymmetries any group-to-group interaction with the EU might imply due to the relatively weak ASEAN.

II. Hope for an Inter-organisational Interregional Relation?

At the ASEAN-EU Commemorative Summit organised on 14 November 2017, the two regional organisations proudly declared to be 'two of the world's most advanced and successful regional organisations' as they succeeded in ensuring 'peace, security, stability, inclusive growth and sustainable development' as well

[209] Hwee, 'The EU as a Security Actor in Southeast Asia' (2009): 16–17.

[210] On the main facts related to the relations between the EU and ASEAN, especially its members, see, e.g., European Parliament, 'Fact sheets on the European Union. Southeast Asia': available at https://www.europarl.europa.eu/factsheets/en/sheet/183/southeast-asia (accessed on 21 November 2020). More specifically, see Delegation of the European Union to Indonesia and Brunei Darussalam, 'The European Union and Indonesia hold their 5th Security Policy Dialogue' *joint press release*, Brussels, 21 October 2020: available at https://bit.ly/3pgT2Xd (accessed on 21 November 2020).

[211] Ewers-Peters, 'The EU as an Interorganizational Influencer?' (2018): 377–78.

as 'in addressing global challenges and reinforcing regionalism and multilateralism'.[212]

Against their respective achievements, the relationship between the European Community (later, the European Union) and ASEAN is considered to be a model of group-to-group interregionalism.[213] In fact, the European Community became the first regional partner of ASEAN. The EU-ASEAN relations have involved two levels of actors (States and organisations) with different forms of relations (i.e. inter-organisational interregionalism, hybrid interregionalism and/or interstate bilateralism). EU-ASEAN cooperation in the last 40 + years has expanded in scope and depth, despite the various ups and downs in the partnership.[214]

As per its definition, 'interregionalism' refers to the 'interaction of one region with another' and is often portrayed a 'double regional project' responding to the need to pool an ever-greater percentage of resources in recognition of other interregional or the global dynamics'.[215] Interregionalism is deeply rooted in the EU's external relations[216] and is evident in EU-ASEAN dialogue. For the EU, interregionalism serves several functions, including promoting regional integration and exporting its own norms and ideas.[217] As aforementioned, the EU aims to enhance its own actorness through the construction of other regional organisations. ASEAN has also become more active in intensifying its relations with other regional groupings. The 'ASEAN Way' provides the foundation for the ARF, the ASEAN Plus Three, the ASEAN-EU relationship and the ASEM process.

Interestingly, ASEAN has not only determined the pace of the progress of its own development and of its external relations, but has also selected the fora where dialogues may occur. With its role as a sponsor and a reference, the EU has taken every opportunity to facilitate the interregional dialogue and to fulfil its objective to disseminate its standards. In these fora, the lowest common denominator principle applies. In this process, some actors tend to dangerously lower their standards, which (might) constitute(s) a serious issue, especially if it lowers the standard of protecting human rights or derogating the duty to others.

---

[212]Council of the EU, 'Press statement of the ASEAN-EU commemorative summit' (2017).

[213]Hettne, 'Regional Actorship: A Comparative Approach to Interregionalism' (2014).

[214]Hwee, 'The EU as a Security Actor in Southeast Asia' (2009): 10.

[215]Julie Gilson, 'New Interregionalism? The EU and East Asia' *Journal of European Integration*, vol. 27, no. 3 (2005); Salvador Santino F. Regilme Jr., 'It Takes Two to Tango: A Constructivist Analysis of EU-ASEAN Interregional Relations' in *Global Power Europe*, eds., Astrid Boening, Jan-Frederik Kremer, and Aukje van Loon (Berlin: Springer, 2013): 240.

[216]Wunderlich, 'The EU an Actor Sui Generis?' (2012); Wunderlich, 'Comparing regional organisations in global multilateral institutions: ASEAN, the EU and the UN' (2012); Gehring, Oberthür, and Mühleck, 'European Union Actorness in International Institutions' (2013); Regilme Jr., 'It Takes Two to Tango: A Constructivist Analysis of EU-ASEAN Interregional Relations' (2013); Louise Fawcett, Frederik Ponjaert, and Mario Telò, eds., *Interregionalism and the European Union. A post-revisionist approach to Europe's place in a changing world* (Farnham: Ashgate, 2015); Maier-Knapp, 'How the EU Promotes Regional Security in Southeast Asia' (2018); Ewers-Peters, 'The EU as an Interorganizational Influencer?' (2018).

[217]Wunderlich, 'The EU an Actor Sui Generis?' (2012): 660.

A. Establishing and Enhancing EU-ASEAN Relations Through a Slow and Partial Development of Mutual Trust at the Governmental Level

Taking into account the date of ASEAN's creation, this regional organisation has a long-standing partnership with the EU. Since 1972, this interregional relation has developed through regular meetings centred on strategic information exchange and cooperation in an increasing number of fields. The development of this relation is based on a low level of institutionalisation, respecting the preferences of the ASEAN side, usually meetings at ministerial, ambassadorial and senior official levels, supplemented by expert working groups. These meetings have led each region to build their respective collective identity and to develop a certain understanding of each other. This interregional relation has become more formalised with regular senior officials and ministerial meetings.[218] Through these meetings, the social dimension of mutual trust may have begun developing. However, the quick turnover of the representatives, especially on the ASEAN's side, could constitute an issue in the long run.

This interregional relation was formalised with the first ASEAN-EC Ministerial Meeting (AEMM) in 1978 and the ASEAN-EC Cooperation Agreement in Kuala Lumpur of 1980,[219] which qualified ASEAN as a 'viable and cohesive grouping'. Although the early years of their relation placed emphasis on economic interests, a common political strategy quickly emerged due to the necessities created by the Cold War.[220] The Maastricht Treaty transformed European integration by creating the EU, enhancing institutional cohesion, adding new policy areas and paving the way for enlargement. Meanwhile, Southeast Asia had emerged as a political and economic region to be reckoned with. There were moves towards closer economic integration as evidenced, for example, by the ASEAN Free Trade Area.[221] Reacting to the new economic realities, the EU called for increased cooperation with ASEAN.[222] In each field, they have engaged in a mutual learning process to boost each one's opinion of the other and create more opportunities for cooperation.[223] Today, the EU is ASEAN's second largest trading partner.[224]

---

[218] Lay Hwee (2009) 9.

[219] *Cooperation Agreement between Member Countries of ASEAN and European Community*, Kuala Lumpur, 7 March 1980.

[220] Maier-Knapp, 'How the EU Promotes Regional Security in Southeast Asia' (2018): 3–4.

[221] See the list of ASEAN Agreements and Declarations in trade, starting from the *Agreement in the Common Effective Preferential Tariff Scheme for the ASEAN Free Trade Area*, Singapore, 28 January 1992: available at https://bit.ly/2MTga0Q (accessed on 30 April 2020); Bali Concord III (2011). See also, Hwee, 'The EU as a Security Actor in Southeast Asia' (2009): 11.

[222] European Commission, 'EU-ASEAN: Creating a new dynamic' *press release*, 3 July 1996: available at http://europa.eu/rapid/press-release_IP-96-580_en.htm (accessed on 2 September 2015).

[223] See, e.g., Commission of the European Communities, 'Towards a New Asia Strategy', COM (94) 314, 19.

[224] CEPS, 'Lessons from the EU integration process for ASEAN regional integration' (2015).

Over time, the subjects of these interregional relations have become more varied and have been deepened in specific aspects such as regional integration and economic development.

On the one hand, they have deepened their collaboration, especially regarding the ASEAN integration process. The two regional organisations resolve to work together to reinforce an inclusive and rules-based international order and to support the effective functioning of regional and multilateral.[225] At the 2017 ASEAN-EU Commemorative Summit, President Donald Tusk reiterated the EU's support to the ASEAN integration process. The objective is to reach the level of a partnership between two 'quite equal' regional organisations. This aspect was meant to constitute a significant step towards the building of the legal dimension of mutual trust.

On the other hand, the EU and ASEAN have diversified their discussions on subjects of mutual interest, including human rights and criminal matters. At the 2017 ASEAN-EU Commemorative Summit, Donald Tusk even highlighted opportunities for strengthened EU-ASEAN cooperation, such as those relating to security and global challenges.[226] This type of joint declaration demonstrates the willingness of the two regional organisations to tackle shared issues. On this basis, it can be said that the EU and ASEAN manage to agree on shared objectives, such as counterterrorism, founding the political dimension of mutual trust between their two regions.

To these ends, further advancing ASEAN-EU cooperation at interstate and regional levels, as well as partnership in multilateral fora on key global issues, including terrorism, was recognised as having enormous potential.

Looking at the interstate bilateralism, inter-organisational interregionalism and hybrid interregionalism, the EU and ASEAN, and their respective Member States, have established and enhanced diplomatic and strategic relations. In ASEAN, they have encouraged the dialogue between the Committee of Permanent Representatives to ASEAN[227] and the EU Mission to ASEAN in Jakarta[228] to elevate the partnership between the two regional organisations at a strategic level.[229] In the EU, ASEAN diplomatic representatives accredited to the EU are part of different working groups with EU officials in Brussels.

[225] Council of the EU, 'Press statement of the ASEAN-EU commemorative summit' (2017).

[226] Ibid.

[227] The CPR is constituted by the Permanent Representatives of ASEAN Member States at the rank of Ambassadors based in Jakarta. The Chairmanship of the Committee is in line with the annual rotation of ASEAN Chairmanship. According to its Terms of Reference and the ASEAN Charter, the CPR covers multiple layers of the ASEAN structure. The CPR's tasks may be categorised as follows: a) Monitoring and implementing Leaders' decisions; b) Coordinating cross-pillar issues; c) Strengthening relations with ASEAN's external partners and d) Providing substantive and administrative direction and support to the ASEAN Secretariat.

[228] The establishment of a dedicated EU Ambassador to ASEAN who took up duties in Jakarta in September 2015 was a form of deepening of their collaboration. This step is representative of the development of the EU-ASEAN relations.

[229] Pt. 1.1. (c), ASEAN-EU Plan of Action (2018–2022).

Besides, the EU and ASEAN Member States also take the general path of diplomacy through different avenues, such as multilateral fora. Looking at the multilateral and transregional fora, must be identified the various bodies within the UN system, the Asia-Europe Meeting (ASEM) and the ARF.[230] The EU and ASEAN have used them to discuss further and with other partners subjects of their interests and/or present the common position—when applicable—to other international actors. The EU and ASEAN have both garnered recognition and visibility through these fora, including ASEM. The ASEM Summit is a biennial meeting between the Heads of State and Governments, the President of the European Council, the President of the European Commission and the Secretary-General of ASEAN. In addition, ASEM Ministers and Senior Officials meet in their respective sectoral dialogue. The EU participates at the ASEM meetings, alongside its Member States, positioning itself as a relevant actor. Like the EU, the participation of the ASEAN Secretariat within ASEM reinforces the notion of ASEAN as an international actor. ASEM has helped to further the notion of the EU and ASEAN actorness through a series of coordinating mechanisms whereby the EU and ASEAN Member States frequently act as groups.[231] Notably, apart from the two regional organisations and their respective Member States, other European or Asian countries have been included, such as Norway, Switzerland, China, Kazakhstan and South Korea. The number of ASEM partners totals 53 today. Moreover, the EU has deepened its engagement with ASEAN in criminal matters through the more focused ARF, as well as through strengthened policy dialogue with ASEAN and its Member States and peer support for ASEAN institutions (where requested). The presence and actions of the EU and ASEAN through such fora, which may encompass third countries, aim to demonstrate their international actorness on various subjects, especially in criminal matters.

B. The Development of EU-ASEAN Interregional Cooperation in Counterterrorism: Two-level Tracks for a Two-fold Approach

Given the differences between the EU and ASEAN's characteristics (e.g. their level of regional integration, their rules-based/practice-based approach, the harmonisation of their relevant norms), it is likely that cooperation will remain mostly diplomatic in nature or, potentially, strategic on sporadic occasions. It is unlikely that operational agreements between the two regional organisations will be enacted in the near future.

1. <u>Diplomatic and strategic interregional relations: Establishing ground for mutual trust</u>

The EU-ASEAN interregional relations have formally been institutionalised through ASEAN-EU ministerial meetings and the EU's own participation at side

[230] Pt. 1.1. (b), Ibid.

[231] Mattheis and Wunderlich, 'Regional actorness and interregional relations: ASEAN, the EU and Mercosur' (2017).

meetings of the ASEAN Ministerial Conferences. Their relations have expanded to include political and security matters through official ministerial meetings between the two regional organisations.

Since 1978, the two regional organisations have repeated their commitment to improve the cooperation between them to promote counterterrorism cooperation. In this respect, the EU strives to convince ASEAN Member States to improve their counterterrorism measures and offers technical support in exchange for meeting its terms. Common declarations were signed by the EU and ASEAN to promote the enhancement of interregional cooperation, in the field of security/criminal matters, but attempted to do so while respecting human rights, rule of law and democracy.[232]

As the lowest common denominator applies to their interregional relations, ASEAN has determined the fora in which discussions happen and has dictated the pace of their collaboration.

As previously shown, the interregional relations can be grouped into two main categories: the direct EU-ASEAN relations on counterterrorism and the institutionalised relations under broader umbrellas.

When examining the impact of the various EU-ASEAN interactions on counterterrorism, there has been a slight formalisation of interregional interactions. Bilateral cooperation between the respective Member States exists. They might have an impact on the interregional relations, especially considering the relations between the former colonising countries and the colonised ones. Interestingly, Indonesia—a former Dutch colony—is known to enjoy close relations with a number of European States relating to counterterrorism.[233] On a more regional level, the EU Counter Terrorism Coordinator (CTC) has not developed direct ties with ASEAN Member States and even fewer with the ASEAN Secretariat. The EU CTC instead supports the EEAS's actions, including the organisation of events related to counterterrorism. A minor progression in the dialogue between the EU and ASEAN, and its Member States in this matter has been the appointment in 2018 of a Counter-Terrorism/

[232] *ASEAN-EU Joint Declaration on Cooperation to Combat Terrorism* (2003); *Nuremberg Declaration on an EU-ASEAN Enhanced Partnership* (2007); *Phnom Penh Agenda for the Implementation of the ASEAN-EU Plan of Action (2009–2010)*, Phnom Penh, 28 May 2009; Plan of Action to strengthen the ASEAN-EU Enhanced Partnership (2013–2017); EUEA, 'Towards an Ever Stronger Natural Partnership' (2014); Co-Chair's Statement of the 20th EU-ASEAN Ministerial Meeting, No. 140723/03, Brussels, 23 July 2014; EUEA, *Fact sheet EU-ASEAN relations*, Brussels, 7 April 2016; ASEAN-EU Plan of Action (2018–2022). See also Beyer, *Counter Terrorism and International Power Relations* (2010): 65; Cocq and Teo, 'Countering Terrorism: Challenges and Opportunities in ASEAN-EU Cooperation' (2015); Cocq, 'The EU and ASEAN approaches in fighting terrorism: collaboration or cooperation?' (2016); Céline C. Cocq, 'Finding a path through a multiheaded interregional relationship: The EU's action vis-à-vis ASEAN region in criminal matters' in *The Supranational at Stake? The EU's External Competence caught between Complexity and Fragmentation*, eds., Mario Teló and Anne Weyembergh, Globalisation, Europe and Multilateralism (Oxon: Routledge, 2020).

[233] Hikmahanto Juwana, 'Anti-terrorism efforts in Indonesia' in *Global Anti-Terrorism Law and Policy*, eds., Victor V. Ramraj et al. (Cambridge: Cambridge University Press, 2012): 297.

Security Expert Counsellor at the EU Delegation to Indonesia and Brunei Darussalam and Mission to ASEAN in Jakarta.

Apart from these few permanent representatives, EU-ASEAN relations are primarily based on regular meetings. Three main interregional mechanisms of collaboration can be highlighted—EU-ASEAN Joint Cooperation Committee, EU-ASEAN Senior Officials Meeting and EU-ASEAN Foreign Ministers Meeting—and the Ministerial Meetings act as the supervisory channel for cooperation. All three channels deal with communication, and information and experience sharing between the EU and ASEAN.[234]

In addition to these 'direct' relations, the other variations in interregional interactions between the EU and ASEAN, and their respective members, can occur under broader umbrellas. The purpose and functioning of some of the fora already mentioned, namely the UN, ASEM and ARF, must be highlighted to discern the ways in which they pertain to the development of mutual trust and cooperation in counterterrorism.

While their presence within the UN has already been mentioned, the latter two need to be further elaborated upon.

Established in 1996, ASEM does not only address security issues. It deals with any political, economic, financial, social, cultural and educational issues of common interest to the parties. Interestingly, '[w]hile the agenda of ASEM was initially dominated by trade issues, the Seoul Summit expanded cooperation to engage with the regional concept of comprehensive security in response to such problems as environmental degradation, human rights, transnational migration and crime, the trafficking of persons and international terrorism'.[235] More precisely, the ASEM leaders have stated their commitment to join forces to fight the plague of terrorism and underline the need to bring to justice those responsible for the attacks in accordance with the Charter of the United Nations and other obligations under international law.[236] However, this forum remains overwhelmingly strategic, if not entirely diplomatic. It generally defers the responsibility to States to actually prevent and combat terrorism and violent extremism.

The ARF is the only multilateral regional forum focusing solely on security issues in the broad meaning of the term. It was inaugurated in Bangkok on 25 July 1994. The EU participates on behalf of its Member States alongside the ASEAN Member States, Australia, Bangladesh, China, India, Japan, Canada, Mongolia, New Zealand, Democratic People's Republic of Korea, Republic of Korea, Pakistan, Papua New Guinea, Russia, Sri Lanka, Timor-Leste and the United States. The EU's active

---

[234] Ewers-Peters, 'The EU as an Interorganizational Influencer?' (2018): 376.

[235] ASEM, 'Partnership for Prosperity and Stability in the New Millennium', Final Chair Statement, 3rd ASEM Summit (ASEM3), Seoul, 20–21 October 2000, pt. 9. See also, Roberts, *ASEAN Regionalism* (2012): 107.

[236] See, e.g., Statement of ASEM Leaders on International Terrorism, Ulaanbaatar, 15 July 2016; ASEM Foreign Ministers' Meeting (Madrid, 15–16 December 2019), Chair's Statement, 16 December 2019, pts. 18–19.

engagement in the ARF is proved by its co-chairmanship of the thematic work stream on transnational and counterterrorism for the period of 2020–2022.[237]

The ARF objective is two-fold. Firstly, the ARF aims to foster constructive dialogue and consultation on political and security issues of common interest and concern and, secondly, it aims to enhance participants' efforts to confidence-building and preventative diplomacy in the Asia-Pacific region.[238] The ARF also sponsors, for example, the Chemical Biological Radiological and Nuclear (CBRN) Centre of Excellence in Southeast Asia which was officially opened in March 2013 and constitutes a platform for exchanging risk management strategies.[239] The discussions remain of a strategic and diplomatic nature. They are far from being operational.

The pace of the interregional relations in counterterrorism between the two regions remains steady regardless of which forum is selected. The declarations and other documents adopted at these meetings demonstrate the objective(s) and progress—or the absence of progress—in the subject(s) of their inter-organisational collaboration. In January 2003, ASEAN and EU foreign ministers pointed out, in the *EU-ASEAN Joint Declaration on Cooperation to Combat Terrorism,* the leading role of the UN in the fight against terrorism and committed themselves to implementing UN resolutions and supporting the Counter-Terrorism Committee. Terrorism cannot be defeated on a military level alone, but also needs to be addressed by through economic, diplomatic and legal measures, and by examining and mitigating the root causes. The successive Joint Declarations contain engagements, including capability and capacity building measures and the exchange of information and experiences. The joint declarations focus on the EU's support of counterterrorism measures implemented by ASEAN Member States. The development of their relations is determined by the 'ASEAN Way' and ASEAN's progression in the different fields.[240] Similarly, in hybrid interregional relations, the pace of their relations' development is determined by the ASEAN Member States with whom the EU interacts.

In either case (i.e. inter-organisational and hybrid interregionalism), the EU also conditions its level of engagement to the respect of some minimum standards. It does so within ASEAN where the EU is arguably well-suited to act both as a sponsor and reference point.

Ultimately, these efforts are fed into the EU's longer-term goal of deepening regional integration in Southeast Asia through reiterated and multilevel interactions, while providing support whenever it is requested by the Southeast Asian competent

[237] Pt. 1, ASEAN-EU Commemorative Summit 2022, Joint Leader's Statement, 45th anniversary of ASEAN-EU Dialogue Relations, Brussels, 14 December 2022.

[238] *Nuremberg Declaration on an EU-ASEAN Enhanced Partnership* (2007).

[239] See, e.g., EUEA, 'Towards and Ever Stronger Natural Partnership' (2014); 'Co-Chairs' Statement of the 20th EU-ASEAN Ministerial Meeting' Brussels, 23 July 2014; 'EU-ASEAN Relations' Fact Sheet, Brussels, 7 April 2016.

[240] Commission of the European Communities, 'Towards a New Asia Strategy', COM(94) 314: 9.

authorities. In that respect, the embedding of cooperation in criminal matters among the region's major players will be of great benefit to both regional organisations and is something that the EU will continue to actively support.

It must not be forgotten that terrorism-related matters should be addressed in a manner which meets the requirements for the protection of human rights. Effectively preventing and combating terrorism cannot be achieved through security measures and criminal justice responses alone. A coherent and comprehensive approach is required.

In this aspect too, the EU has tried to influence the ASEAN legal framework, especially as human rights are a significant part of mutual trust in the EU's view. Cooperation in criminal matters cannot take place without a certain set of safeguards. These safeguards are more significant in the EU than at the international level. Thus, the EU-ASEAN relations in criminal matters would benefit from a closer collaboration between the EU and the ASEAN in order to guarantee the balance between ensuring the security of their respective citizens and protecting their human rights. The EU has adopted a legalistic approach on human rights too. However, confronted to strong obstacles in its endeavour in Southeast Asia (i.e. the localisation process), the EU has had to soften its approach, taking the context and the current regional development into account.

The EU in addition to other ASEAN Dialogue Partners has been involved with the ASEAN Intergovernmental Commission on Human Rights (AICHR) to discuss mutual areas of interest for future cooperation.[241] Regular ASEAN-EU policy dialogues on human rights have been convened since the visit by the AICHR to the EU in 2015; much later than the first discussions in criminal matters. Prior, and subsequent, to these meetings, the AICHR, as the overarching human rights institution of ASEAN, coordinated with other ASEAN human rights bodies. The policy dialogues provide avenues to foster close relations between AICHR and the EU to share experiences, views and best practices on human rights issues of mutual concern, as well as to identify potential areas for future cooperation in the promotion and protection of human rights.

Interestingly, radicalisation leading to terrorism, as a cross-cutting issue, is a subject of concern for both the EU and ASEAN. ASEAN Member States have addressed violent extremism and radicalisation leading to terrorism prior to it being raised as a European issue. It has been discussed with a more preventive and human rights-oriented perspective by the competent authorities. The dynamics of the EU-ASEAN relations on this front might be a bit different as ASEAN Member States—some of them most particularly as Malaysia or Indonesia—have had a longer experience in this field than the EU.

The diversity of fora and channels of communication gathering EU and ASEAN officials who may be replaced between the scheduled meetings does nothing to build the social dimension of mutual trust. The political agendas determined at these

[241] For example, the AICHR conducted study visits to a number of Dialogue Partners, including the European Union in 2015; AICHR, 29th meeting, ASEAN Secretariat, Jakarta, 12–15 May 2019.

meetings are broad enough not to impose any specific obligations on the Member States. Thus, the political dimension of mutual trust is overly vague. The two regions possess similar objectives security-wise but not necessarily human rights-wise; and they have dissimilar means and pacing to achieve their objectives. Evidently, there is no legal dimension to mutual trust in these interregional relations relating to counterterrorism. EU-ASEAN interregional cooperation on criminal matters lack the normative congruence needed for a more multidimensional mutual trust to crystallise at this level.

2. Unforeseeable operational cooperation under the current level of mutual trust between the EU and ASEAN

In addition to the strategic relations it generates, the *EU-ASEAN Joint Declaration on Cooperation to Combat Terrorism* also encourages the parties to further improve mutual assistance and cooperation, particularly through information sharing. EU-ASEAN cooperation in criminal matters can take place at different levels, i.e. at an interstate level (2) or interregional level (1), and under different forms (i.e. strategic or operational).

Firstly, international cooperation between competent national authorities through the regional law enforcement bodies, Europol and Aseanapol, would be a demonstration of a certain level of regional integration and mutual trust within each region and between the two regions.[242] However, operational cooperation between these bodies is unlikely to occur until such time as Aseanapol develops into a fully-fledged support structure for law enforcement agencies in ASEAN. This would constitute a significant step towards strategic and operational cooperation. An enhancement of this nature to Aseanapol's tasks and capacities would certainly aid the inter-organisational interregional relations on criminal matters; and potentially even raise Aseanapol to an operational level. As Aseanapol and Europol stand today, only cooperation between ASEAN law enforcement agencies and Europol are encouraged to provide mutual support and to facilitate the exchange of best practices and expertise in the areas of shared interests.[243]

Information and intelligence[244] sharing is more effective and coherent if States agree on a common definition or coherent listing of terrorist offences. As of yet, the two regional organisations have not brought their definitions or listings into alignment. While the EU defined terrorist offences,[245] ASEAN's sole legal instrument specific to terrorism[246] simply refers to a series of international conventions. The vagueness of the terminology used, the lack of a common understanding regarding

[242] Beyer, 'ASEAN Counterterrorism: Participation and Causes' (2010): 113.

[243] Pt. 1.3. (f), ASEAN-EU Plan of Action (2018–2022); pt.1.3. (h), Plan of Action to implement the ASEAN-EU Strategic Partnership (2023–2027).

[244] There is a clear lack of any mention of intelligence in the cooperation between the EU and ASEAN.

[245] Since the *Council Framework Decision 2002/475/JHA on combating terrorism*.

[246] 2007 *ASEAN Convention on Counter Terrorism*.

terrorist offences, the different choices in strategies considered effective in the fight against terrorism and, probably, the absence of pressing necessity to cooperate at this level have limited any interregional cooperation on counterterrorism.

Besides, and most importantly, Europol and Aseanapol's different functions and organisational structures tend to deter any form of agreement between these two bodies. The organisation and functioning of these two bodies are representative of the different levels of regional integration in the EU and ASEAN. While in theory it might seem to be 'an Asian equivalent of Europol', Aseanapol remains a forum of discussion for ASEAN Chiefs of Police without any legal competence.[247]

For now, collaboration between Europol and Aseanapol focuses on the two first dimensions of mutual trust, i.e. social and eventually political, through exchange of best practices and experience. This could lead to strategic cooperation, rather than operational cooperation. It is interesting to see that, in general, social trust has led to operational cooperation between field agents, while this is not the case between institutions.

As a point of comparison, the Interpol-Europol collaboration can serve as a reference point or benchmark for future Europol-Aseanapol collaboration.

On 5 November 2001, Europol and Interpol agreed to establish and maintain cooperation in combating serious forms of organised international crime within the field of their competence. For this purpose, they are supposed to exchange operational, strategic and technical information, coordinate their activities, including through the development of common standards, actions plans, training and scientific research as well as through the secondment of liaison officers.[248] In this framework, the transmission of data, including personal data, is conditioned by the principles of legality and purpose limitation.[249] Such advanced possibilities of data sharing were justified by the need for efficiency in the fight terrorism.[250] Notably, this agreement was negotiated and approved by the Council of the EU before the 9/11 attacks. Interpol approved it just afterwards, on 26 September.

In 2011, Europol and Interpol established a secure communication line for the transmission and exchange of information.[251] This secure line does not imply an interoperability of the Europol and Interpol databases. The principles governing the transmission remain the same.

---

[247] Leslie Holmes, 'Dealing with Terrorism, Corruption and Organised Crime: The EU and Asia' in *The Palgrave Handbook of EU-Asia Relations*, eds., Thomas Christiansen, Emil Kirchner and Philomena Murray (Basingstoke: Palgrave Macmillan, 2013): 157.

[248] Art. 2, *Cooperation Agreement between Interpol and Europol*, Brussels, 5 November 2001. The text of the agreement was approved by the Council of the European Union on 27 June 2001, and by the Interpol General Assembly at its 70th session, held in Budapest, on 26 September 2001.

[249] Art. 5, *Cooperation Agreement between Interpol and Europol.*

[250] Interpol, 'Interpol and Europol sign cooperation agreement' 5 November 2001: available at https://bit.ly/3aXrwJa (accessed on 23 November 2020).

[251] Art. 1, *Memorandum of Understanding on the establishment of a secure communication line between Europol and Interpol*, Lyon, 11 October 2011.

In this respect, it is worth noticing that Europol is not the owner of the data encompassed in the Europol Information System (EIS). The data inserted in the EIS remains under the full control of the inputting entity, namely the Member State who sent the data to Europol. Thus, Europol could transmit data, including personal data, but under the conditions set by the data owner. These conditions must be clear and restrictive if the data owner does not want the data to be shared with all Interpol's members and for any purpose. Therefore, Europol and Interpol are intermediaries between EU Member States, on the one hand, and third countries, on the other.

Drawing a parallel between the Europol-Interpol relations, if Europol chooses to cooperate with an international agency which encompasses ASEAN Member States, why would it not cooperate with Aseanapol under the same terms and conditions? Although for this to happen, ASEAN Member States need to share data in criminal matters through Aseanapol and ensure that the principles of data protection, data security and other necessary conditions are guaranteed. Additionally, the parties must want to engage in such an endeavour.

Going into the details of Europol's external action, the EU agency could conclude strategic and operational agreements with third parties, i.e. countries or organisations such as Aseanapol. While both types of agreement are aimed at enhancing cooperation between Europol and the third party, there is one major difference: strategic agreements are limited to the exchange of general intelligence as well as strategic and technical information, whereas operational agreements allow for the exchange of information, including personal data. A parallel with the definitions of 'strategic analysis' and 'operational analysis' brings more details to the object of the agreement. The former refers 'to [the] process[ing of] relevant information concerning a particular problem or to develop or improve initiatives by the competent authorities', while the latter refers 'to [the] obtain[ing of] information on one or more of the criminal activities [...] which relates to a case, person or organisation, in order to commence, assist or conclude [...] bilateral or multilateral investigations of an international nature, provided that two or more Member States are among the parties concerned'.[252] By contrast, Aseanapol is not governed by any legal rules regarding its potential external action. Such external action was not foreseen when this body was established.

According to their respective rules, Europol and Aseanapol have recently started to talk to each other[253] to exchange experiences and best practices on transnational criminal matters, including terrorism. For example, Europol, with Aseanapol and

[252] Art. 2(b) and (c), *Europol Regulation*. See also Cocq and Galli, 'The evolving role of Europol in the fight against terrorism at the EU level' (2017).

[253] Letter of Intent between Europol and Aseanapol, 85th Interpol General Assembly, Bali, 8 November 2016. Later, see, e.g., Muhammad Faris, 'Visit of the Head of the Europol Office at the ASEAN Secretariat Office on 18 April 2018', Kuala Lumpur, 31 May 2018: https://bit.ly/3tSQGRJ (accessed on 7 May 2020).

Interpol, initiated a new EURASEAN investigative network on combating cyber fraud in 2017.[254]

Observing the steps adopted at the regional levels, mutual trust between the two regions seems to be built upon the identification of shared objectives, interpersonal relations and political engagements. There is no legal obligation for the two regional organisations and their respective Member States to cooperate against terrorism.

Secondly, and potentially by default, cooperation in criminal matters remains more effective and might become more operational between countries, under bilateral agreements. The EU has not undertaken any form of negotiations with an ASEAN Member State, which could lead to a legally binding agreement on cooperation in criminal matters. The EU has only engaged in such a path in Asia with Japan, regarding mutual legal assistance in criminal matters.[255]

The consecutive Plans of Action have nonetheless encouraged the establishment of linkages between law enforcement agencies in ASEAN and the EU with a view to sharing experiences and best practices in combating transnational crime, including terrorism.[256] There may thus be more precise and legally binding bilateral obligations between some States from one and another region. Mutual trust at this level is easier to reach in security-related matters; maybe more so between certain former colonisers and their historic colonies (e.g. France with Vietnam).

Eventually, reaching the necessary level of mutual trust to develop cooperation is difficult, especially operational cooperation. In this context, the EU and ASEAN have been working to build mutual trust and mutual understanding. However, mutual trust, at this interregional level, does not involve any legal dimension given that the EU and ASEAN's institutional and legal differences are too significant. According to the three axes of mutual trust building, the EU and ASEAN have focused their attention on the social and, sporadically, political dimensions. These steps are essential before their relations can be improved.

Therefore, EU-ASEAN relations in the field of criminal matters lack the necessary level of mutual trust and their networks do not have the requisite stability to further deepen cooperation in counterterrorism. There is no privileged channel for exchange of information between the regions. International exchanges of information are conducted either through Interpol or on the basis of bilateral agreements between States of each region.

[254] Europol, 'New EURASEAN Investigative Network on Combating Cyber Fraud' *News Article*, 26 July 2017: https://bit.ly/3jL16y5 (accessed on 7 May 2020).

[255] *Agreement between the European Union and Japan on mutual legal assistance in criminal matters*, O.J.E.U. L39/20, 12 February 2010.

[256] *Nuremberg Declaration on an EU-ASEAN Enhanced Partnership* (2007); Plan of Action to strengthen the ASEAN-EU Enhanced Partnership (2013–2017); ASEAN-EU Plan of Action (2018–2022).

Section 3: Asymmetric Interregional Relations Based on the EU and ASEAN's Respective Actorness

The divergent EU and ASEAN legal and institutional architectures have impacted their actorness as well as the nature and functioning of their interregional actions.

The asymmetrical nature of EU-ASEAN interregional relations has fostered institutional learning and socialisation. On the one side, the EU desires to trigger and contribute to transformations in ASEAN for the opportunity to export its own policies, practices and institutions as well as its norms and values. Yet, by recognising the reluctances of ASEAN Member States, the EU has tried to boost regional integration in ASEAN, without pushing for the transposition of its own system in Southeast Asia. Although the EU is the most important partner of ASEAN in its regional development, it should not be forgotten that the EU is not the only source of domestic and regional changes.[257] The EU's main influence has been limited to ASEAN's regional integration and normative development.[258] Given their strong attachment to national sovereignty, the localisation of external norms related to criminal matters, including EU norms, by ASEAN Member States remains selective. On the other side, asymmetry strengthened ASEAN's group cohesion. Faced with a more institutionalised partner, ASEAN Member States are incentivised to work more closely together. However, ASEAN seems to only superficially mimic the legal structure of the EU to gain international recognition. ASEAN still has much work to do before being established as a regional organisation capable of having an effective and independent role beyond the region. All of these elements in combination explain the choice for a more diplomatic and strategic-oriented approach of ASEAN Member States whenever they speak for the Association.

The discrepancies between the two regional organisations have limited the development of a three-dimensional mutual trust which facilitates effective interregional cooperation. However, these 'regional organisation to regional organisation' relations have fostered, to a certain degree, both the EU and ASEAN's actorness on the international scene. Group-to-group relations may even be viewed as a means to simplify international relations.

Therefore, although interregional relations exist, they are hardly occurring between the two regional organisations (i.e. strategic inter-organisational interregionalism). By contrast, relations seem to be particularly more effective between the EU, on the one hand, and ASEAN Member States, on the other (i.e. hybrid interregionalism); or between the Member States of each regional grouping, i.e. EU Member States with ASEAN Member States (i.e. interstate bilateralism).

In this context, terrorism as a shared security challenge has catalysed the manifestation of various forms of cooperation between ASEAN and the EU, in both

---

[257] Börzel and Risse, 'From Europeanisation to Diffusion: Introduction' (2012): 15.

[258] Ewers-Peters, 'The EU as an Interorganizational Influencer?' (2018): 379–80.

closed bilateral (e.g. direct contacts between the representatives of the regional organisations or of their Member States) and multilateral fora (e.g. within broader multilateral fora such as UN, ARF and ASEM meetings). Using various platforms, ASEAN and the EU develop group-to-group contacts to strengthen their respective actions and, where appropriate, coordinate their position within wider fora. The EU-ASEAN relations have facilitated the sharing of experience and intelligence regarding the diverse forms of terrorist threat and have also enhanced their respective institutional and legal framework to improve their internal and interregional action against terrorism.

Therefore, the interregional relations between the EU and ASEAN constitute an added value in the fight against terrorism. Unfortunately, such a conclusion might not be reached in human rights-related matters, which remain a secondary concern.

Chapter 8
Conclusion

> *Every kind of peaceful cooperation among men is primarily based on mutual trust and only secondarily on institutions such as courts of justice and police.*
> *Albert Einstein*

Although not every region of the world agrees with the second part of Einstein's assertion, the first part is universally accepted. Reaching a certain level of mutual trust is indeed crucial in building and enhancing cross-border cooperation.

Throughout this monograph, many questions have revolved around the role of mutual trust in facilitating cross-border cooperation. Although there is no straightforward answer to the numerous associated questions, key issues are highlighted and some important conclusions may be drawn (Section 1). In so doing, this book proposes new lines of research inquiry within the field of legal studies (Section 2).

Section 1: Mutual Trust—The Three-Dimensional Principle That Holds All Relationships

This study highlighted the numerous issues hindering cross-border cooperation between competent national authorities in counterterrorism. By addressing them, these authorities may better streamline their relations and increase cooperation.

I. Defining the Terminological and Conceptual Framework: A Premise for In-depth Discussions on Transnational Cooperation

Primarily, this study identified many difficulties when searching for common terminology for cross-border cooperation. This is not only due to a difference in language but also to the different definitions associated with specific consequences. Yet, competent authorities would gain from having a common language and, more importantly, from working together in building up more trustful relations.

C. C. Cocq, *Mutual Trust in Regional and Interregional Cooperation on Counterterrorism*, United Nations University Series on Regionalism 26,
https://doi.org/10.1007/978-3-031-36612-3_8

A. **Un-existing, Unclear and/or Debated Terminology**

While requiring States to cooperate, international and regional organisations do not often provide clear and unanimously accepted definitions of key concepts, including definitions of offences, actors and forms of interactions. This issue is more evident in ASEAN than in the EU. Despite its institutionalised and legal architecture, which strongly facilitates cooperation in criminal matters, there is still a lot of room for informal cooperation between competent authorities within the EU. With its very loose—or, it might even be said, non-existent—legal architecture in criminal matters, ASEAN does not provide precise definitions and more resembles the UN broad framework.

Despite this terminological blur, competent authorities have found ways to cooperate in the fight against terrorism. While uniform definitions would increase the effectiveness of transnational cooperation, the absence of harmonised definitions dangerously provides parties with much room of manoeuvre. In this context, mutual trust is key yardstick in transnational relations.

B. **Mutual Trust: A Three-dimensional Yardstick**

Mutual trust is a flexible concept with social, political and legal dimensions, with each dimension developed in this order. This concept, elevated to the rank of fundamental principle in the EU, knows varying statuses, understandings, degrees, and occurs at different levels within the respective regions. They also have different implications. Regardless of the regional framework (EU or ASEAN), trust (or 'mutual trust') has been a useful tool to foster cooperation between competent national authorities. It is built upon legal and/or non-legal incentives to ensure its purpose, i.e. to make sure that competent national authorities work together against transnational crime.

It remains unclear whether mutual trust constitutes a driving force, a complementary element or a consequence of the development of cross-border cooperation. Either way, this concept has been identified as essential to create the conditions that enhance cross-border cooperation in the two regions while preserving, as far as possible, the specific identities of national criminal justice systems. Although mutual trust was not meant to disturb the legal diversity within the EU AFSJ, it ended up fostering the adoption of minimum standards in the field of EU criminal law as well as enforceable EU human rights standards. By contrast, in ASEAN, mutual trust has not had any specific effect on either the regional norms or national laws. In this respect, mutual trust remains particularly traditional in its understanding within this region.

The various activities used to build mutual trust were categorised under three clusters which were identified after preliminary observations and tested throughout this study: capability building; capacity building and knowledge and experience sharing. These categories shape the matrix used throughout this study.

II. Comparative Regionalism: Putting the Analytical Matrix to the Test

The matrix highlights the interactions between mutual trust and the establishment and enhancement of cooperation in criminal matters through different angles: the respective regional legal architectures, the criminalisation of terrorist offences and cross-border cooperation.

A. First Step: The Respective Regional Legal Architectures

The members of these two regional organisations have adopted different approaches vis-à-vis regional integration and the role of mutual trust, leading them to two different regional institutional designs thus far.

In their current state, the main differences between the two regional approaches can be summarised as follows. Concerning the autonomy, ASEAN Member States certainly remain autonomous when creating their national legislations and policies, whereas the EU institutions can legislate and impose certain obligations on Member States. This is also shown by the distribution of competences which diverges significantly (exclusive and shared competences v. no transfer of competences). Concerning the notion of control, the unanimous agreement of all ASEAN Member States is needed for each regional action, whereas EU Member States cannot have complete control over delegated issues (see qualified majority vote). Concerning the notion of legitimacy, the regional organisation might have the legitimacy to be a driving force in cross-border matters according to the limits of what its members are willing to 'cede'. Internal tensions as well as legal and political diversity are much more prominent in Southeast Asia than in Europe. Therefore, a regional pooling of sovereignty in Southeast Asia, such as in the EU, is not on the agenda. ASEAN is marked by its continuous practice of consensus-based decision-making. Although the Association appears to be moving towards a more institutionalised structure, it by no means endorses a formal, legal and supranational model similar to that of the EU. ASEAN continues to be an intergovernmental organisation with a minimal level of both regional integration and institutionalisation. Yet, these differences are not drastic and few small similarities tend to slowly appear. For instance, the EU and ASEAN members have given their regional organisations a legal personality and have allowed their regional organisation to operate on an international level.

Through their capability-building actions, the EU and ASEAN have adopted their own tailored-made regional legal architectures. As the ASEAN regional framework was established after the EC/EU's, ASEAN officials might have learned lessons from the EU when developing their own regional framework (cf. localisation process). One of the most relevant examples of an EU-inspired norm is the *ASEAN Charter*. However, the 'ASEAN Way' has ensured a constant dialogue between members, leading to numerous opportunities for mutual learning (cf. information and experience sharing) about one another's respective legal framework(s) in order to improve their national and, potentially, regional criminal justice systems.

In its regional integration process, the EU has gone beyond its Member States' differences thanks to the mutual trust that competent national authorities, and then institutions, have developed vis-à-vis each other ('integration through practice' followed by 'integration through law'). By way of fostering this trust, the establishment of common norms has ensured sustainable relations between Member States. ASEAN Member States have fostered channels of communication to develop better understandings and knowledge about one another's policies and legislations ('integration through practice'). In contrast with the EU, they have not engaged in any approximation of national legislations, but rather only employ slow and minimal regional institutionalisation with legal power (weak—or almost non-existing—'-integration through law').

Mutual trust certainly constitutes an important tool of governance for removing borders between domestic legal systems and its absence might prevent Member States from reaching their shared objective(s). Mutual trust follows the social, political and legal developments in each region. In the EU where interactions have been strongly legalised, mutual trust tends to have been legalised as well. In ASEAN where interactions are not legalised, but instead are mostly social, or political at best, mutual trust tends to be based on social or potentially political arrangements.

However, it is unclear whether regional integration or mutual trust arose first, in much the same way as it is difficult to identify whether the chicken or the egg comes first. Undoubtedly, there exists a virtuous circle which operates between these two elements, bolstering one another over time.

B. **Second Step: The Two-fold Action Against Terrorism**

The second step of the comparative analysis was determined by the UN's two-fold action against terrorism, namely the criminalisation of terrorist offences and the development of cooperation in order to eliminate any safe havens for perpetrators.

1. The criminalisation of terrorist offences

Some level of approximation is generally considered necessary to smoothen cooperation between competent national authorities. A framework for mutual trust with assurances, creating legitimate expectation for partners, would help Member States further ensure that they do not serve as safe haven for criminals. The EU has adopted this perspective, while ASEAN Member States have not (yet).

The EU and ASEAN legal architectures in counterterrorism, which encompass anti-terrorism and human rights norms related to the threat and/or to the response to it, are the result of the varied combinations of top-down and bottom-up influences. The various cross-directional vertical interactions between international, regional and national norms have led to the current legal situation in ASEAN and the EU. The outcome of each region's unique combination has variably impacted the dimension (s) which mutual trust takes.

Regarding the set of dynamics between international and regional norms, the two regional organisations might have served as vectors of international norms, but the EU adds more to the international normative panorama than ASEAN.

On the East side of the Ural mountain divide, ASEAN has only been a vector of international requirements regarding the criminalisation of terrorist offences and cross-border cooperation without any distortion. There is an area where ASEAN has strayed from international requirements: the level of protection of human rights. It is indeed argued that the *ASEAN Declaration on Human Rights* has lowered international standards. ASEAN has no power over its Member States. The only potential influence it has is political, and this is often due to external pressures from key dialogue partners.

On the West side of the Ural mountain divide, the EU is a vector of international law but functions mostly as an independent regional actor. The EU has provided more precise instructions to its Member States. Interestingly, the EU is not only a subsidiary of international norms to its Member States, but it is also an influencer of international norms. There has been a more visible cross-fertilisation between the EU norms and those of another important international actor in this field of counterterrorism and police and judicial cooperation, including the Council of Europe.

Regarding the set of dynamics between regional and national norms, there is a significant difference between ASEAN and the EU.

In ASEAN, the lack of coordination and institutional linkages between the national and regional levels—along with the lack of consistent political will—have prevented the development of a top-down influence. The ASEAN Conventions' provisions are too vague to constitute a real added value when approximating national laws. As ASEAN Member States remain the sole actors responsible for the functioning of the regional organisation, there are no dual-level relations between ASEAN and its members. As there is a clear confusion between the national and regional levels, there is no top-down influence from a regional actor over the Member States and there can hardly be a bottom-up influence given that the members form the Association. In fact, the influence would be more accurately qualified as horizontal or interstate. Member States influence each other during ASEAN meetings or any other bilateral or multilateral fora. For instance, the influence between Brunei, Singapore and Malaysia's anti-terrorism norms is patently evident. The combination of these influences produces a consensus, which is then later enshrined as a regional norm.

In the EU, there has been a cross-fertilisation between the regional and national norms. Over time, the Member States have given the regional organisation the tools to ensure the harmonisation of EU policies and norms resulting in a top-down influence from the EU over its members. However, Member States can continually push for, and influence, the emergent regional norms (bottom-up influence). This dialogue between the regional and national actors aims to ensure the effective and harmonised implementation of regional norms. This applies to both terrorism norms and human rights norms, although more significantly so to the adoption of terrorism-related norms.

Therefore, the three-tier vertical normative interactions between international, regional and national 'legislators' highlight the most influential normative actor within each region, while developing the EU and ASEAN legal architecture governing terrorism-related issues. The result of these vertical interactions provides the respective regional legal frameworks within which activities meant to build and maintain mutual trust are conducted. This explains the differences between the two regions' choices of activities and the differences in impact that the various activities have on the development of mutual trust in one region or the other.

The question remains as to whether the approximation of legislations aids in building mutual trust or whether mutual trust constitutes a preliminary step to any effort for approximation. Back to the dilemma: which came first, the chicken or the egg?

As it exists at the international, regional and national levels, interpersonal trust (i.e. social dimension of mutual trust) is insufficient to ensure sustainable cooperative relations. Developing a political dimension of mutual trust is a step forward but retains an element of uncertainty. The various ASEAN declarations and the EU policy declarations do not bind the parties through any precise means and results. The EU Member States have added a legal dimension to the other two dimensions. This progression constitutes a stabilisation of relations in the long term. This last step might be an issue for those ASEAN Member States who do not want to be legally bound, whereas the more legalistic approach adopted by the EU has facilitated cross-border cooperation.

Within their respective legal architecture in counterterrorism and human rights, the two regional organisations have developed their respective understanding of 'mutual trust' in parallel according to their own approach towards cross-border cooperation.

2. The development of cross-border cooperation to eliminate any safe haven to terrorists

Based on the two previous angles of analysis (i.e. level of regional integration/ regional legal architectures and regional criminalisation of terrorist offences), the focus turns towards the actual intra-regional cooperation between competent national authorities through information and intelligence sharing.

Although international norms require States to make use of, among other platforms, the regional frameworks to build mutual trust and share information and intelligence for the prevention and combating of terrorism, the divergences and tensions between countries hinder mutual trust amongst competent national authorities and might also hinder interstate cooperation.

In this context, the UN and Interpol have different competences and tasks and adopt different strategies which strive for a similar objective: the establishment, development and enhancement of cross-border cooperation. Nonetheless, informal international cooperation remains predominant, even with these actors' support. The international institutions once again provide a wide umbrella for States to cooperate, leaving room for regional organisations to intervene.

The EU and ASEAN Member States firmly agree on the idea to cooperate to combat serious transnational crime, including by way of intensifying cooperation through information and intelligence sharing. However, there are strong discrepancies between the EU and ASEAN cooperative dynamics.

The EU Member States have established ambitious cooperation mechanisms as well as regional bodies and entities aiding the transnational flow of data, which is not the reality in ASEAN. The protection of national sovereignty remains more dominant in ASEAN and trustful relationships need to be enhanced. ASEAN is working on these challenges through dialogues organised in different kinds of fora for both increasing cooperation in criminal matters and developing common standards, including on human rights. The cooperative dynamics within ASEAN share more similarities with international ones, which means that there is a broad obligation for States to cooperate, but the requirements are not specific and there is no control or enforcement mechanism.

The main discrepancies can be explained in part by chronological differences, whereby the premises of intra-regional cooperation in criminal matters emerged much earlier in the EU (1970s) than in ASEAN (late 1990s). However, it remains unclear whether ASEAN is at an early phase of a three-dimensional mutual trust process, similar to the one existing in the EU, or whether it is travelling along a different path.

The role of the two regional organisations varies depending on which side of the Ural they are located. The EU has been a strong supporter of, and become a strong leader in, fostering cross-border cooperation, while ASEAN is limited to being a platform upon which its Member States can cooperate.

Evaluating the effectiveness of the EU and ASEAN approaches is a complex task, especially when focusing on the prevention and combating of terrorism. At certain times, it is difficult to precisely quantify or qualify the respective interstate relations. For instance, the amount of data shared regionally between Member States cannot be enumerated accurately. This is even more evident when one examines cooperation in criminal matters among competent national authorities, given that a large part of cross-border cooperation is informal, including data sharing. This applies to a greater extent in ASEAN than it does in the EU. During the prevention phase, it is more complicated—even almost impossible—to identify all crime which either failed or was foiled by the action of competent national authorities. Nonetheless, the analysis of the regional and national norms of the mechanisms established to facilitate the fight against terrorism and of the authorities' actions clarify the nature of cooperation in both regions. According to this perspective, the EU has privileged the formal approach to the enhancement of informal cooperation privileged by ASEAN. The adoption of norms organising regional mechanisms of cooperation helps fight against international terrorism, as does the existence of actors and platforms for cooperation.

The EU and its members have been able to entrust regional bodies and agencies with facilitating cooperation among competent national authorities. In return, these bodies and agencies constitute a further step to build mutual trust and, subsequently, enhancing cross-border cooperation. ASEAN Member States have agreed on specific platforms of dialogue, but they remain the sole drivers, retaining full control over any of their actions. These platforms are meant to facilitate the social and political dimensions of mutual trust.

These elements have facilitated formal interactions between competent national authorities on a strategic level in ASEAN, while the interactions in the EU are both strategic and operational. Informal interactions have not disappeared from the EU panorama and are usually of an operational nature.

Notably, unlike in the EU, human rights guarantees are not part of the elements needed to build mutual trust and, subsequently, they are officially a non-existent consideration when facilitating cooperation within ASEAN. The mere identification of a common objective, i.e. preventing and combating terrorism, and the agreement on the means, i.e. cross-border cooperation, are considered to be sufficient in ASEAN. However, the absence of a shared consideration for human rights within the Southeast Asian region tends to limit the scope of cooperation. The absence of similar human rights standards or the different levels of protection might dissuade countries from working together, especially external partners.

III. Interregionalism: The Challenge of Building Mutual Trust on Top of Two Different Regional Organisations

The asymmetrical nature of EU-ASEAN interregional relations has fostered institutional learning and socialisation. On the one side, the EU wants to catalyse and contribute to transformations in other regional and international organisations and sees it as an opportunity to export its own policies, practices and institutions as well as its norms and values. However, recognising the reluctances of ASEAN Member States, the EU has tried to boost regional integration in ASEAN without pushing for the transposition of its own system into Southeast Asia. Although the EU is the most important partner of ASEAN in its regional development, it should not be forgotten that the EU is not the only source of domestic and regional change(s). The EU's main influence has been limited to ASEAN's regional integration and normative development. Given ASEAN Member States' strong attachment to national sovereignty, the localisation of external norms related to criminal matters, including EU norms, remains selective. On the other side, faced with a more institutionalised and more autonomous regional partner, ASEAN Member States are incentivised to work more closely together. However, ASEAN still has much work to do before establishing itself as a regional organisation capable of having an effective and independent role separate from its members. These elements in combination explain the decision of Member States to adopt a more diplomatic and strategic-oriented approach—whenever they speak for the Association.

The discrepancies between the two regional organisations might have limited the development of a three-dimensional mutual trust (i.e. social, political and legal dimensions) facilitating interregional cooperation.

Although interregional relations exist, they hardly occur between the two regional organisations (i.e. strategic inter-organisational interregionalism). By contrast, relations seem to be particularly more effective between the EU, on the one hand, and ASEAN Member States on the other (i.e. hybrid interregionalism); or between the Member States of each regional grouping, namely one EU Member State with one ASEAN Member State (i.e. interstate bilateralism).

Nonetheless, these 'regional organisation to regional organisation' relations have fostered, up to a certain degree, both the EU and ASEAN's actorness on the international scene. Group-to-group relations could possibly be a means for simplifying international relations.

In this context, terrorism as a shared security challenge has catalysed the manifestation of various forms of cooperation between ASEAN and the EU, in both closed bilateral (e.g. direct contacts between the representatives of their respective regional organisations or of their Member States) and multilateral fora (e.g. within broader multilateral fora such as UN, ARF and ASEM meetings). Using these platforms, ASEAN and the EU develop group-to-group contacts which strengthen their respective actions and, where appropriate, coordinate their positions within wider fora. The EU-ASEAN relations have facilitated the sharing of experience, information and intelligence regarding the diverse forms of terrorist threats and have enhanced their respective institutional and legal framework which should also improve their internal and interregional action against terrorism.

Therefore, though limited, the EU-ASEAN interregional relations might constitute an added value in the fight against terrorism. Unfortunately, the same conclusion might not be made for human rights-related matters, which remain a secondary concern.

Section 2: Opening an Avenue for Further Legal Research in Comparative Regionalism and Interregionalism

A general assessment of the results of this analysis (I) opens space for a large variety of possibilities for legal and interdisciplinary research (II).

I. Final Assessment

This monograph investigated whether the EU, with its highly institutionalised form of cooperation, has ensured greater consistency and sustainability, when addressing non-traditional security matters, than ASEAN.

As such, the correlation between the development of mutual trust in its different dimensions, on the one hand, and the development of cross-border cooperation, on the other, was further elaborated upon. While it is not possible to draw a clear and indisputable conclusion on the 'chicken and the egg dilemma' of the order in which one caused the other to emerge, some conclusions can still be drawn from this study.

The discussions throughout this book highlighted the existence of a virtuous circle which nourishes mutual trust and the regionalisation of the fight against terrorism.

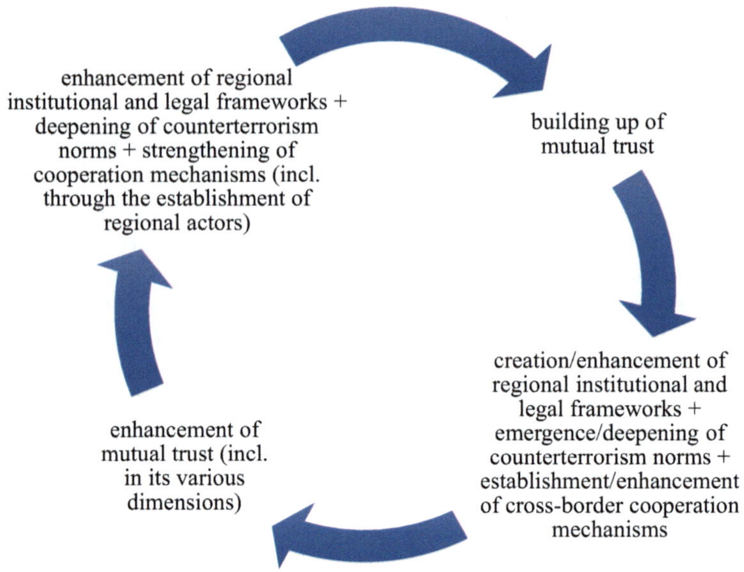

1. Firstly, the stronger mutual trust is between Member States, the greater their willingness is to delegate elements of their sovereignty to the regional organisation. Mutual trust starts being built with social interactions. Then, a political dimension can be added to it. The emergence of the legal dimension of mutual trust is concomitant with a certain level of delegation of sovereignty to a regional organisation. Then, it is unclear whether the strengthening of mutual trust, with its legal dimension, has facilitated a delegation of competences to the regional organisations or whether, by delegating competences, mutual trust has been strengthened. Yet, a certain level of mutual trust is definitely necessary to start such delegation.

Whereas the EU and ASEAN undertook initiatives aimed at recalibrating and adapting their security systems and models of cooperation to face transnational criminal issues, their values, approaches and forms of cooperation diverge. It is undeniable that the institutional and legal regional architectures diverge drastically between the EU and ASEAN.

Regarding the regionalisation projects, the scientific literature shows that there is no single model of regionalism and regional actorness. Evidently, no universal 'law of integration' can be deduced from the European example.[1] As aforementioned and elaborated upon in this study, differences are also represented by the name of the organisations. There is, on one side, a Union and, on another, an Association. If the Association were to become more integrated, it would be interesting to see whether there would seek to amend the name to include the word 'Union'. In the futuristic

[1] Haas, 'International Integration: The European and the Universal Process' (1961): 289.

Japanese animation movies *Psycho-Pass,*[2] an organisation by the name of Southeast Asian Union (SEAUn) exists and constitutes a confederation of the same Southeast Asian countries as the real-life countries. Will this remain a fantasy or will the movies correctly have predicted the future?

2. Secondly, the more the legal dimension of mutual trust is built between Member States, the more they are willing to adopt regional norms in counterterrorism requiring them to criminalise, in a similar way or not, terrorist offences. Conversely, the more anti-terrorism legislations align, the more likely Member States trust each other's legal systems, which would in turn facilitate cross-border cooperation.

Interestingly, mutual trust is not supposed to involve any approximation of legislations. However, such approximation has been determinant in developing the legal dimension of mutual trust. The adoption of regional norms which define and criminalise terrorist offences has fortified the relations between Member States and created legal expectations between competent national authorities.

When there is no regional counterterrorism legal framework, mutual trust might be at best two-dimensional, specifically, social and political. In this case, mutual trust does not foster the approximation of legislations, yet interstate agreements based on mutual understandings and associated with conditions can still be concluded.

3. Thirdly, the more the three dimensions of mutual trust are built between Member States and their competent national authorities, the smoother cross-border cooperation becomes. The more these authorities cooperate, engage in dialogue, share experiences, expertise and data, the more likely they are to trust each other.

In this respect, cross-border cooperation is, first and foremost, built upon the social dimension of mutual trust, through interpersonal relations. Enhancing the effectiveness and sustainability of cooperation necessitated the emergence of political and, even more so, legal dimensions of mutual trust. Engaging in a regional organisation and agreeing on shared objectives constitutes the primary steps needing to be taken to reach a political level of mutual trust. Adopting norms which require Member States to cooperate in criminal matters, including the sharing of information and intelligence, has nourished the legal dimension of mutual trust. These steps have enhanced and reinforced cross-border cooperation.

Cooperation between competent national authorities can be operational with mutual trust merely being a social construct. It is then reinforced through the development of the legal dimension of mutual trust. By contrast, cooperation on a strategic level can only be achieved after developing the political dimension of mutual trust. However, this form of cooperation, as with operational cooperation,

---

[2]This series takes place in a dystopian 22nd Century Japan where it is possible to instantaneously measure and quantify a person's propensity towards criminality using a cymatic scanner. The information is recorded and analysed by the Sibyl System, a hive-mind that controls law enforcement. Sibyl's oracular judgement determines one's numerical Crime Coefficient, one's color-coded Hue over time and one's societal profile that results in an indexed Pyscho-Pass. This number determines people's value in society, as well as their right to live in freedom, under observation, in custody or not live at all.

can be strengthened and consolidated by the development of the legal dimension of mutual trust.

The virtuous circle linking mutual trust and cross-border cooperation also involves the adoption of regional platforms and actors. The more developed mutual trust is, the more likely regional platforms and actors are being established. Meanwhile, as with cooperation, their institutionalisation and their function depend on the norms which establish them as well as the level and form of trust. The development of these platforms and actors which facilitate cooperation, including the flow of data, has helped competent national authorities to strengthen—but not create—mutual trust among themselves.

In both regions, States have worked—and may further work—on the three clusters identified in the matrix (*capability building*, *capacity building* and *knowledge and experience sharing*) in order to build mutual trust along its three dimensions. They have both gone through these three clusters and made use of their respective activities in different manners and up to a certain level, which has led to different forms of mutual trust and different ways of operationalising it. By doing so, States have aimed to enhance their ability to cooperate and facilitate horizontal peer-to-peer cooperation.

Due to the Member States' historical and geopolitical proximity, the regional level is indeed the most appropriate level for building mutual trust and for fostering cooperation between competent national authorities in criminal matters.

4. Fourthly, mutual trust has a limited role in the EU-ASEAN interregional relations. As of today, a lot of work remains to be done to ensure a cohesive regional position in either the EU or ASEAN. Intra-regional mutual trust must be steady and coherent to allow inter-organisational interregionalism (regional organisation to regional organisation) to develop.

Within their own realm, the EU and ASEAN's pace for developing regional counterterrorism norms has been dictated by the lowest common denominator approach. It evidently remains the case in ASEAN due to the unanimity required to adopt any regional norms and actions. The EU was once in the same situation concerning criminal matters prior to the adoption of the Lisbon Treaty, at which point the qualified majority vote was introduced into the AFSJ. Since then, the number of instruments approximating national legislations has drastically increased and the developmental cooperation between competent national authorities continues to grow. This lowest common denominator approach has also dictated the pace of interregional relations advancements between the two regions.

The EU and ASEAN maintain multifaceted relations. However, the EU's external action tends to be more effective. Notably, the EU's approach towards ASEAN has evolved over time, moving from a one-size-fits-all approach to a tailor-made one, adapting to its interlocutor's needs, conditions, limits and objective(s). It has the ability to exert influence both actively and passively and through numerous channels of influence.

Acting upon this lowest common denominator approach, the ASEAN's capacities, willingness and level of regionalisation have determined the pace of the EU-ASEAN interregional relations development. Against their own backdrop and especially ASEAN's, the regional and national actors of the EU and ASEAN started developing social, economic and political relations, but there are very few legal considerations, and a weak normative impulse, in their interregional relations.

Regional organisations and their members have slowly worked on the three clusters identified in this study to build mutual trust, when possible along its three dimensions. They have mainly focused on the third cluster; sharing information and experience aims to ensure a development of each region's capabilities and capacities against terrorism.

In conclusion, it was demonstrated that mutual trust is intrinsic to cooperation. It has a three-fold action: a driving force for, a support to, and a consequence of the creation of regional legal architectures facilitating cross-border cooperation in criminal matters, including in terrorism-related matters. In a certain way, this study has been unable to determine the most appropriate qualifier for mutual trust. The simple fact is that mutual trust plays these three roles. Through the virtuous circle operating at different stages of the development of cross-border cooperation, especially in counterterrorism, mutual trust is indeed fostering, accompanying and emerging from the creation of the regional institutional and legal frameworks—the emergence of counterterrorism norms and the establishment and strengthening of cross-border cooperation.

II. What Way Forward?

Besides, this monograph also creates space for further legal and interdisciplinary studies in comparative regionalism and interregionalism. It demonstrated that conducting comparative regionalism and interregionalism research according to a legal methodology, complemented by a slight element of interdisciplinarity, is possible and worthwhile to provide a new perspective on international relations. By verifying the analytical matrix proposed at the outset, this study highlighted various variables (i.e. similarities and differences) that can be used as a benchmark for further regional legal studies.

Against this backdrop, new avenues of investigations can be explored. Among them, certain lines of research might fall into two main clusters.

On the one hand, these two regional organisations can be further investigated through other lines of enquiry. This study focused on criminal matters, and even more specifically on terrorism-related issues. Many criminal or non-criminal issues can be investigated with a legal or interdisciplinary perspective. Even regarding terrorism-related issues, other angles can drive further studies. For instance, a comparison between the two regions regarding the existence and role of new actors in the prevention and countering of terrorism can be of interest, as might their interregional interactions be, if there happen to be any. Indeed, citizens have increasingly contributed on this transnational issue, as well as Non-Governmental Organisations, different government ministries, such as Education Ministries, or other non-State actors. All of them can have an impact on threat reduction.

On the other hand, it would also be interesting to extend the current research question to other regional organisations, or even go further beyond the subject of this book and adopt a question that would involve investigating more regional organisations.

For instance, focusing on data sharing between competent national authorities, this monograph showed the *ASEAN Human Rights Declaration* includes a specific reference to data protection. By contrast, it is not the case in the *American Convention on Human Rights*[3] or in the *Arab Charter on Human Rights*.[4] The right to privacy is even not part of the rights protected by the *African Charter on Human and People's Rights*.[5] It may thus be asked if and how these different regional organisations have shaped cross-border cooperation.

Looking at other ways to expand this research, the African Union (AU) is also an interesting regional organisation to investigate for several reasons. The EU's influence has been greater in Africa than in Southeast Asia. This may clearly be explained by the geographical and, most importantly, by strong historical ties between the two regions, compared with ASEAN. Firstly, unlike with ASEAN, crises in Africa have even more direct impacts on the EU's security. Secondly, the 1955 Bandung Conference was a turning point in the history of decolonisation for Asian and African countries. Asian countries handed over the task of achieving full independence from all forms of colonialism to African countries that were still struggling. European countries were even more reluctant to cede ownership of their African colonies. This may thus constitute the crossing road towards this line of enquiry. As such, the EU maintains a more active voice in the region. However, with the increasing African ownership over their national policies, the EU's ability to set conditions has become restricted; as has increasingly been the case in Southeast Asia. Therefore, it can be questioned whether the AU's approach towards mutual trust and cross-border cooperation in non-traditional security matters resembles more closely that in the EU, if such initiatives exist in the AU.

Other regional organisations are also worth analysing, either because of their unique interregional links with other regional organisations or because of some dependent or independent variables. For instance, Mercosur might be considered, at first glance, to be a mix of the EU and ASEAN's approaches. Mercosur has incorporated emblematic elements from the EU such as the creation of a Mercosur Secretariat, a Parliament and a regional Permanent Appeal Court. While Mercosur Member States agreed in principle to these central bodies, their general scepticism towards ceding parts of national sovereignty to a supranational organisation remains deeply engrained. Thus, Mercosur has only adopted those institutional elements without associating them with supranational characteristics or even any binding power.

---

[3] Organisation of American States, *American Convention on Human Rights*, San José, 22 November 1969.

[4] Council of the League of Arab States, *The Arab Charter on Human Rights*, Tunis, 22 May 2004.

[5] Organisation of African Unity, *African Charter on Human and People's Rights*, Banjul, 27 June 1981.

In a nutshell, this book aimed to increase the body of knowledge by acting as a relevant piece of legal and interdisciplinary literature. This was achieved by further developing the fields of comparative regionalism and interregionalism and by providing space for future research which might extend beyond the scope of regionality in the EU.

Appendices

Appendix 1: Ratifications of the Most Relevant International and Regional Instruments by ASEAN Member States

Table established on 31 December 2022

C. C. Cocq, *Mutual Trust in Regional and Interregional Cooperation on Counterterrorism*, United Nations University Series on Regionalism 26,
https://doi.org/10.1007/978-3-031-36612-3

	Brunei Darussalam	Cambodia	Indonesia	Lao PDR	Malaysia	Myanmar	Philippines	Singapore	Thailand	Vietnam
Terrorism										
Convention on Offences and Certain Other Acts Committed on Board Aircraft (1963)	23 May 1986 (A)	22 October 1996 (A)	7 September 1976	23 October 1972 (A)	5 March 1985 (A)	23 May 1996 (A)	26 November 1965	1 March 1971 (A)	6 March 1972 (A)	10 October 1979 (A)
Convention for the Suppression of Unlawful Seizure of Aircraft (1970)	16 April 1986 (A)	8 November 1996	27 August 1976	6 April 1989	4 May 1985	22 May 1996 (A)	26 March 1973	12 April 1978	16 May 1978	17 September 1979 (A)
Convention for the Suppression of Unlawful Acts Against the Safety of Civil Aviation (1971)	16 April 1986	8 November 1996	27 August 1976	6 April 1989	4 May 1985	22 May 1996	26 March 1973	12 April 1978	16 May 1978	17 September 1979
Convention on the Prevention and Punishment of Crimes Against Internationally Protected Persons, including Diplomatic Agents (1973)	13 November 1997 (A)	27 July 2006 (A)		22 August 2002 (A)	24 September 2003 (A)	04 June 2004 (A)	26 November 1976 (A)	2 May 2008 (A)	23 February 2007 (A)	2 May 2002 (A)
International Convention Against the Taking of Hostages (1979)	18 October 1988 (A)	27 July 2006 (A)		22 August 2002 (A)	29 May 2007 (A)	4 June 2004 (A)	14 October 1980	22 October 2010 (A)	2 October 2007 (A)	9 January 2014 (A)
Convention on the Physical Protection of Nuclear Material (1980)		4 August 2006 (A)	5 November 1986	29 September 2010 (A)		6 December 2016 (A)	22 September 1981	22 September 2014 (A)	19 June 2018 (A)	4 October 2012 (A)
Protocol for the Suppression of Unlawful Acts of Violence at Airports	20 December 2000	8 November 1996	24 February 1988 (S)	7 October 2002	8 September 2006	22 May 1996	17 December 2003	22 November 1996	14 May 1996	25 August 1999

Serving International Civil Aviation, supplementary to the Convention for the Suppression of Unlawful Acts Against the Safety of Civil Aviation (1988)										
Convention for the Suppression of Unlawful Acts Against the Safety of Maritime Navigation (1988)	8 December 2003	18 August 2006		18 June 2012		19 September 2003	6 January 2004	3 February 2004		
Protocol to the Convention for the Suppression of Unlawful Acts Against the Safety of Fixed Platforms Located on the Continental Shelf (1988)										
Convention on the Marking of Plastic Explosives for the Purpose of Detection (1991)	9 July 2009 (A)			18 August 2017 (A)	27 November 2007 (A)	1 September 2004 (A)	17 December 2003 (A)	20 January 2003 (A)	25 January 2006 (A)	
Convention for the Suppression of Terrorist Bombings (1997)	14 March 2002	31 July 2006	29 June 2006	22 August 2002	24 September 2003	12 November 2001	7 January 2004	31 December 2007	12 June 2007	9 January 2014 (A)
Convention for the Suppression of the Financing of Terrorism (1999)	4 December 2002 (A)	12 December 2005	29 June 2006	29 September 2008 (A)	29 May 2007 (A)	16 August 2006	7 January 2004	30 December 2002	29 September 2004	25 September 2002 (A)

(continued)

(continued)

	Brunei Darussalam	Cambodia	Indonesia	Lao PDR	Malaysia	Myanmar	Philippines	Singapore	Thailand	Vietnam
Convention for the Suppression of Acts of Nuclear Terrorism (2005)		7 December 2006 (S)	30 September 2014 (A)		16 September 2005 (S)		15 September 2005 (S)	1 December 2006 (S)	2 May 2019	23 September 2016 (A)
Amendment to the Convention on the Physical Protection of Nuclear Material (2005)			27 May 2010			6 December 2016	16 June 2021	22 October 2014 (a)	19 June 2018	3 November 2012
Protocol of 2005 to the Convention for the Suppression of Unlawful Acts Against the Safety of Maritime Navigation								12 August 2015		
Protocol of 2005 to the Protocol for the Suppression of Unlawful Acts Against the Safety of Fixed Platforms Located on the Continental Shelf										
Convention on the Suppression of Unlawful Acts Relating to International Civil Aviation (2010)						20 March 2013 (A)				
Protocol Supplementary to the Convention for the Suppression of Unlawful Seizure of Aircraft (2010)						20 March 2013 (A)				

Protocol to amend the Convention on Offences and Certain other Acts Committed on Board Aircraft (2014)		23 January 2015 (S)			7 March 2019			25 September 2018 (a)		
Organised crime										
United Nations Convention against Transnational Organized Crime (2000)	28 March 2008 (A)	12 December 2005	20 April 2009	26 September 2003 (A)	24 September 2004	30 March 2004 (A)	28 May 2002	28 August 2007	17 October 2013	8 June 2012
Protocol to Prevent, Suppress and Punish Trafficking in Persons, Especially Women and Children, supplementing the United Nations Convention against Transnational Organized Crime (2000)	30 March 2020 (A)	2 July 2007	28 September 2009	26 September 2003 (A)	26 February 2009 (A)	30 March 2004 (A)	28 May 2002	28 September 2015 (A)	13 October 2013	8 June 2012 (A)
Protocol against the Smuggling of Migrants by Land, Sea and Air, supplementing the United Nations Convention against Transnational Organized Crime (2000)		12 December 2005	28 September 2009	26 September 2003 (A)		30 March 2004 (A)	28 May 2002		18 December 2001 (S)	
Human rights										
International Covenant on Civil and Political Rights (1966)		26 May 1992 (A)	23 February 2006 (A)	25 September 2009			23 October 1986		29 October 1996 (A)[a]	24 September 1982 (A)

(continued)

(continued)

	Brunei Darussalam	Cambodia	Indonesia	Lao PDR	Malaysia	Myanmar	Philippines	Singapore	Thailand	Vietnam
Optional Protocol to the ICCPR related to the set-up of the Human Rights Committee (1966)		27 September 2004 (S)					22 August 1989			
International Covenant on Economic, Social and Cultural Rights (1966)		26 May 1992 (A)	23 February 2006 (A)	13 February 2007		6 October 2017	7 June 1974		5 September 1999 (A)	24 September 1982 (A)
Convention against Torture and Other Cruel, Inhuman or Degrading Treatment or Punishment (1984)	22 September 2015 (S)	15 October 1992 (A)	28 October 1998	26 September 2012			18 June 1986 (A)		2 October 2007 (A)	5 February 2015
Second Optional Protocol to the ICCPR on the abolition of the death penalty (1989)							20 November 2007			
Convention on the Rights of the Child (1989)	27 December 1995 (A)	15 October 1992 (A)	5 September 1990	8 May 1991 (A)	17 February 1995 (A)	15 July 1991 (A)	21 August 1990	5 October 1995 (A)	27 March 1992 (A)	28 February 1990
Optional Protocol to the Convention on the Rights of the Child on the involvement of children in armed conflict (2000)	17 May 2016 (A)	16 July 2004	24 September 2012	20 September 2006 (A)	12 April 2012 (A)	27 September 2019	26 August 2003	11 December 2008	27 February 2006 (A)	20 December 2001
Optional Protocol to the Convention on the Rights of the Child on the sale of children, child prostitution and child pornography (2000)	21 November 2006 (A)	30 May 2002	24 September 2012	20 September 2006 (A)	12 April 2012 (A)	16 January 2012 (A)	28 May 2002		11 January 2006 (A)	20 December 2001

Optional Protocol to the Convention against Torture and Other Cruel, Inhuman or Degrading Treatment or Punishment (2002)		30 March 2007					17 April 2012 (A)			
Convention for the Protection of all Persons from Enforced Disappearance (2006)		27 June 2013 (A)	27 September 2010 (S)	29 September 2008 (S)					9 January 2012 (S)	
Optional Protocol to the IESCR (2008)										
ASEAN instruments										
Treaty on Mutual Legal Assistance in Criminal Matters (2004)	15 February 2006	8 April 2010	4 June 2008	25 June 2007	1 June 2005	22 January 2009	12 December 2008	28 April 2005	31 January 2013	25 October 2005
Convention on Counter Terrorism (2007)	4 May 2011	28 June 2010	14 May 2012	28 November 2012	11 January 2013	21 February 2012	27 April 2010	31 October 2007	21 February 2008	25 February 2011
ASEAN Charter (2007)	31 January 2008	2 April 2008	14 November 2008	14 February 2008	14 February 2008	14 July 2008	3 November 2008	17 December 2007	15 November 2008	14 March 2008
Convention against Trafficking in Persons, Especially in Women and Children (2015)	24 April 2020	25 January 2016	27 November 2017	16 May 2017	7 September 2017	16 January 2017	6 February 2017	25 January 2017	24 July 2016	5 January 2017

Note: The conventions in italics are those listed in the 2007 *ASEAN Convention on Counter Terrorism*
Date only: ratification
(S) signature, *(A)* accession, *(AA)* approval, *(a)* acceptance
[a]Thailand made eight notifications since that date

Appendix 2: National Definitions of Terrorist Offences in ASEAN

- **Main reference: International definitions**

International Convention for the Suppression of the Financing of Terrorism, New York, 9 December 1999, UNTS vol. 2178, No. 38349.

Establish the following acts as terrorist offences: directly or indirectly, unlawfully and wilfully, providing or collecting funds with the intention that they should be used or in the knowledge that they are to be used, in full or in part, whether or not it is known that the funds were actually used, in order to carry out the following acts:

- an act which constitutes an offence within the scope of and as defined in one of the treaties listed in the annex;
- any other act intended to cause death or serious bodily injury to a civilian, or to any other person not taking an active part in the hostilities in a situation of armed conflict, when the purpose of such act, by its nature or context, is to intimidate a population, or to compel a Government or an international organisation to do or to abstain from doing any act; *(NB: Inspired by the UNODC Model option C).*

attempting to commit such an offence;
participating as an accomplice or organising or directing others to commit any such offence;
wilfully contributing to the commission of such an offence by a group of persons acting with a common purpose.

- **Brunei Darussalam**

Anti-Terrorism Order, 2011, No. S 46/2011, 1 August 2011

'terrorist' means any person who [directly or indirectly, unlawfully and wilfully] [introduced with Law 48/2012]-

(a) commits, or attempts to commit, any terrorist act;
(b) prepares for any terrorist act;
(c) participates in or facilitates the commission of any terrorist act;
(d) promotes or encourages any terrorist act or
(e) is otherwise concerned in any terrorist act,

and includes any person declared in an order made under S65 to be a terrorist (S65: power to declare person or class of person a terrorist by the Minister).

'terrorist entity' means any entity owned or controlled by any terrorist or group of terrorists and includes an association of such entities.

'terrorist act' means—

1. an act or omission in or outside Brunei Darussalam which constitutes an offence within the scope of a counter-terrorism convention; or
2. the use of threat of action (whether in Brunei Darussalam or elsewhere)—

(a) where the action—

- involves serious violence against any person;
- involves serious damage to property;
- endangers any person's life;
- creates a serious risk to the health or safety of the public or a section of the public;
- involves the use of firearms or explosives;
- involves releasing into the environment or any part thereof, or distributing or otherwise exposing the public or any part thereof to—
  - any dangerous, hazardous, radioactive or harmful substance;
  - any toxic chemical;
  - any microbial or other biological agent or toxin or
  - any nuclear material;

- is designed to disrupt any public computer system or the provision of services directly related to communications infrastructure, banking or any financial services, public utilities, public transportation or public key infrastructure;
- is designed to disrupt the provision of essential emergency services; or
- involves prejudice to public security or national defence;

(b) where the use or threat is intended or reasonably regarded as intending to—

- influence of compel the Government, any other government or any international organisation to do or abstain from doing any act; or
- intimidate the public or a section of the public.

'A terrorist act does not include the activities undertaken by military forces of a State in the exercise of their official duties, to the extent that those activities are governed by other rules of international law'.

Anti-Terrorism (Amendment) Order, 2012, No. 48/2012, 2 July 2012
'terrorist group' means—

(a) any group of terrorists that—

- commits, or attempts to commit, terrorist acts by any means, directly or indirectly, unlawfully and wilfully;
- participates as an accomplice in terrorists acts (whether or not the terrorist act occurs);
- organises or directs other to commit terrorist acts (whether or not the terrorist act occurs) or
- abets, contributes, counsels or procures the commission of terrorist acts by a group of persons acting with a common purpose where the abetment, contribution, counselling or procurement is made intentionally and with the aim of furthering the terrorist act or with the knowledge of the intention of the group to commit a terrorist act (whether or not the terrorist act occurs); or

(b) any class of person declared to be a terrorist group under S65(1) by the Minister

- **Cambodia**

Law on Counter Terrorism, 20 July 2007

Articles 76 and 78: Article 76—Providing or collecting property for use in terrorist acts or in aid of terrorists

1. A penalty of imprisonment for a period between 10 years and 20 years shall be applied to a person who intentionally provides or collects property, intending or knowing that it is to be used wholly or partly in order to carry out:
   (a) an act which constitutes an offence under this Law, or under the law of a foreign State, that is within the scope of any of the treaties listed in the annex to the International Convention for the Suppression of the Financing of Terrorism; or
   (b) an act intended to cause death or serious bodily injury to a person other than a person taking an active part in armed hostilities in a situation of armed conflict if the purpose of the act, by its nature or context, is to intimidate a population, or to compel:
      - a legislative, executive or judicial institution in the Kingdom of Cambodia or in a foreign State; or
      - an international intergovernmental organisation; or
      - any other person or group of persons; to do or to refrain from doing any act.

- **Indonesia**

Government Regulation in Lieu of Legislation combating criminal acts of terrorism, No. 1/2002, 18 October 2002

Section 6: Any person who intentionally uses violence or the threat of violence to create a widespread atmosphere of terror or fear in the general population or to create mass casualties, by forcibly taking the freedom, life or property of others or causes damage or destruction to vital strategic installations or the environment or public facilities or international facilities.

This definition of terrorist has been incorporated in full in the new 2018 Law (*Undang-undang tentang Perubahan atas Undang-Undang Nomor 15 Tahun 2003 tentang Penetapan Peraturan Pemerintah Pengganti Undang Undang Nomor 1 Tahun 2002 tentang Pemberantasan Tindak Pidana Terorisme Menjadi Undang-Undang*, 21 June 2018, No. 5). The penalties have been increased in the recent legislation.

Section 5 of the Law specifies that terrorist offences shall not be considered political offences preventing any extradition

- **Lao PDR**

Law on Anti-Money Laundering and Counter-Financing of Terrorism, No. 50, 21 July 2014

Article 7: Acts of terrorism are an event in which natural persons, groups of people, organisations or terrorist organisation within or outside of the territory of the Lao PDR receive finances to conduct an act of terrorism, with the details as follow:

1. Acts that effect the national security, socio-economic foundation, foreign and international organisations, cause difficulties to international relations of the Lao PDR or chaos to people in the society;
2. Acts that affect lives, health, freedom or deemed as a physical and psychological coercion and threat;
3. Seizure, damaging properties, invasion, attack, obstruction, causing damages and chaos to computer communication and Internet systems or digital instruments of state organisations, legal persons and natural persons;
4. Processing, production, use, packaging, transportation, consolidation, and obtaining of explosives, radioactive substances, toxics, inflammables, and trading of weapons, equipment, vehicles including an offering of advice for certain act with an **intention** as defined in subparagraph 1, 2 and 3 of this article;
5. Disseminating, recruiting, encouraging, coercing, threatening, hiring or creating conditions, and aiding an act as defined in subparagraph 1, 2, 3, 4, 7 and 8 of this article;
6. Organising, financing, participating and attempting to participate in the organisation, teaching and training of selected individuals to conduct an act as defined in subparagraph 1, 2, 3, 4, 5, 7 and 8 of this article;
7. Acknowledgment of an act with objective evidence to prove that it is an act of terrorism.
8. Other offences defined as acts of terrorism as per international agreements or treaties that the Lao PDR is a party to.

- **Malaysia**

  Penal Code, Act 574 (as updated on 31 December 2014)
  'terrorist' means any person who—

(a) commits, or attempts to commit, any terrorist act; or
(b) participates in or facilitates the commission of any terrorist act

and includes a specified entity under section 66B or 66C of the Anti-Money Laundering, Anti-Terrorism Financing and Proceeds of Unlawful Activities Act 2001 [*Act 613*].

'terrorist entity' means any entity owned or controlled by any terrorist or terrorist group and includes an association of such entities;

'terrorist group' means—

(a) an entity that has as one of its activities and purposes the committing of, or the facilitation of the commission of, a terrorist act; or
(b) a specified entity under section 66B or 66C of the Anti-Money Laundering, Anti-Terrorism Financing and Proceeds of Unlawful Activities Act 2001.

'terrorist act' means an act or threat of action within or beyond Malaysia where—

(a) the act or threat falls within subsection (3) and does not fall within subsection (4);
(b) the act is done or the threat is made with the intention of advancing a political, religious or ideological cause; and
(c) the act or threat is intended or may reasonably be regarded as being **intended** to—.

- intimidate the public or a section of the public; or
- influence or compel the Government of Malaysia or the Government of any State in Malaysia, any other government, or any international organisation to do or refrain from doing any act.

An act or threat of action falls within this subsection if it—

(a) involves **serious** bodily injury to a person;
(b) endangers a person's life;
(c) causes a person's death;
(d) creates a serious risk to the health or the safety of the public or a section of the public;
(e) involves serious damage to property;
(f) involves the use of firearms, explosives or other lethal devices;
(g) involves releasing into the environment or any part of the environment or distributing or exposing the public or a section of the public to—

- any dangerous, hazardous, radioactive or harmful substance;
- any toxic chemical; or
- any microbial or other biological agent or toxin;

(h) is designed or intended to disrupt or seriously interfere with, any computer systems or the provision of any services directly related to communications infrastructure, banking or financial services, utilities, transportation or other essential infrastructure;
(i) is designed or intended to disrupt, or seriously interfere with, the provision of essential emergency services such as police, civil defence or medical services;
(j) involves prejudice to national security or public safety;
(k) involves any combination of any of the acts specified in paragraphs *(a)–(j)*,

and includes any act or omission constituting an offence under the Aviation Offences Act 1984.

An act or threat of action falls within this subsection if it—

(a) is advocacy, protest, dissent or industrial action; and
(b) is not intended—

- to cause serious bodily injury to a person;
- to endanger the life of a person;
- to cause a person's death or
- to create a serious risk to the health or safety of the public or a section of the public.

- **Myanmar**

CT Law 2014 *Counter-Terrorism Law 2014*

Section 3(b): Act of terrorism means committing or failures to commit an offence with the aim of committing terrorism as follows:

1. Intentional offence committed unlawfully against civil aviation and airport as prescribed in Chap. 4,
2. Action committed against internationally protected persons including representatives as prescribed in Chap. 5,
3. Action committed relating to taking hostage as prescribed in Chap. 6,
4. Offence concerning nuclear materials, radioactive materials and nuclear power stations as prescribed in Chap. 7,
5. Intentional offence committed unlawfully in order to harm maritime travel as prescribed in Chap. 8,
6. Intentional offence committed unlawfully in order to harm underwater resource exploration unit at offshore shelf as prescribed in Chap. 9,
7. Offence committed relating to unmarked explosives as prescribed in Chap. 10,
8. Offence committed relating to terrorist bombings as prescribed in Chap. 11,
9. Offence concerning support of money and things for terrorism as prescribed in Chap. 12,
10. Actions to severely damage the security or the life and property of the public or infrastructure which is fundamental to the public or an individual, or state-owned buildings, vehicles, equipment and facilities.
11. Act of terrorism committed against state-owned or government-owned buildings, vehicles, equipment and facilities abroad, diplomatic offices including the country's embassies and consulates.
12. Actions to produce, transfer, keep, supply or offer to supply arms and ammunition, biological, chemical and nuclear weapons, explosive weapons or nuclear materials to a terrorist or a member of a terrorist group.
13. To cause fear among the public, to cause death of or severe pain to a civilian or any other person who is not involved in fighting the battle in the midst of armed conflict with the aim of forcing the government or a local or foreign organisation to do an unlawful act or making them avoid acting lawfully, and other actions.
14. Acts of terrorism which severely damage the health and safety of the public, or the environment with the aim of terrorising.
15. Actions to insist, persuade, propagate and recruit a person to be involved in a terrorist group or in doing terrorist activities.
16. Actions to form a terrorist group, knowingly involve in a terrorist group, or to give responsibility to act.
17. Actions of concealing or knowingly allowing a terrorist or a member of a terrorist group to take refuge, hide, stay temporarily or hiding them so that they would not be arrested and taken action or so that they could escape.
18. Actions to allow a terrorist or a member of a terrorist group to use, gather, hold meeting in a building or at a place, to give terrorist training or to arrange transportation.

- **Philippines**

Human Security Act of 2007, No. 9372, 6 March 2007

Section 3. *Terrorism*—Any person who commits an act punishable under any of the following provisions of the Revised Penal Code:

1. Article 122 (Piracy in General and Mutiny in the High Seas or in the Philippine Waters);
2. Article 134 (Rebellion or Insurrection);
3. Article 134-a (Coup d' Etat), including acts committed by private persons;
4. Article 248 (Murder);
5. Article 267 (Kidnapping and Serious Illegal Detention);
6. Article 324 (Crimes Involving Destruction), or under

   (a) Presidential Decree No. 1613 (The Law on Arson);
   (b) Republic Act No. 6969 (Toxic Substances and Hazardous and Nuclear Waste Control Act of 1990);
   (c) Republic Act No. 5207, (Atomic Energy Regulatory and Liability Act of 1968);
   (d) Republic Act No. 6235 (Anti-Hijacking Law);
   (e) Presidential Decree No. 532 (Anti-Piracy and Anti-Highway Robbery Law of 1974); and,
   (f) Presidential Decree No. 1866, as amended (Decree Codifying the Laws on Illegal and Unlawful Possession, Manufacture, Dealing in, Acquisition or Disposition of Firearms, Ammunitions or Explosives)

thereby sowing and creating a condition of widespread and extraordinary fear and panic among the populace, in order to coerce the government to give in to an unlawful demand shall be guilty of the crime of terrorism and shall suffer the penalty of 40 years of imprisonment, without the benefit of parole as provided for under Act No. 4103, otherwise known as the Indeterminate Sentence Law, as amended.

The Terrorism Financing Prevention and Suppression Act of 2012, No. 10168, 20 June 2012

Section 3: 'Terrorist' refers to any natural person who:

1. commits, or attempts, or conspires to commit terrorist acts by any means, directly or indirectly, unlawfully and wilfully;
2. participates, as a principal or as an accomplice, in terrorist acts;
3. organises or directs others to commit terrorist acts or
4. contributes to the commission of terrorist acts by a group of persons acting with a common purpose where the contribution is made intentionally and with the aim of furthering the terrorist act or with the knowledge of the intention of the group to commit a terrorist act.

'Terrorist acts' refer to the following:

1. Any act in violation of Section 3 or Section 4 of the Human Security Act of 2007;
2. Any other act intended to cause death or serious bodily injury to a civilian, or to any other person not taking an active part in the hostilities in a situation of armed conflict, when the purpose of such act, by its nature or context, is to intimidate a population, or to compel a government or an international organisation to do or to abstain from doing any act;
3. Any act which constitutes an offense under this Act, that is within the scope of any of the following treaties of which the Philippines is a State party:

(a) Convention for the Suppression of Unlawful Seizure of Aircraft, 16 December 1970;
(b) Convention for the Suppression of Unlawful Acts against the Safety of Civil Aviation, 23 September 1971;
(c) Convention on the Prevention and Punishment of Crimes against Internationally Protected Persons, including Diplomatic Agents, 14 December 1973;
(d) International Convention against the Taking of Hostages, 17 December 1979;
(e) Convention on the Physical Protection of Nuclear Material 3 March 1980;
(f) Protocol for the Suppression of Unlawful Acts of Violence at Airports Serving International Civil Aviation, supplementary to the Convention for the Suppression of Unlawful Acts against the Safety of Civil Aviation, 24 February 1988;
(g) Convention for the Suppression of Unlawful Acts against the Safety of Maritime Navigation, 10 March 1988;
(h) Protocol for the Suppression of Unlawful Acts against the Safety of Fixed Platforms located on the Continental Shelf, 10 March 1988 or
(i) International Convention for the Suppression of Terrorist Bombings, 15 December 1997.

'Terrorist organisation, association or a group of persons' refers to any entity owned or controlled by any terrorist or group of terrorists that:

1. commits, or attempts to commit, terrorist acts by any means, directly or indirectly, unlawfully and wilfully;
2. participates as an accomplice in terrorist acts;
3. organises or directs others to commit terrorist acts or
4. contributes to the commission of terrorist acts by a group of persons acting with common purpose of furthering the terrorist act where the contribution is made intentionally and with the aim of furthering the terrorist act or with the knowledge of the intention of the group to commit a terrorist act.

Act to prevent, prohibit and penalise terrorism, thereby repealing Republic Act No. 9372, otherwise known as the 'Human Security Act of 2007' (also called The Anti-Terrorism Act of 2020), Republic Act No. 11579, 22 July 2020

Section 4—terrorism is committed by any person who, within or outside the Philippines, regardless of the stage of execution:

(a) Engages in acts intended to cause death or serious bodily injury to any person, or endangers a person's life;

(b) Engages in acts intended to cause extensive damage or destruction to a government or public facility, public place or private property;
(c) Engages in acts intended to cause extensive interference with, damage or destruction to critical infrastructure;
(d) Develops, manufactures, possesses, acquires, transports, supplies or uses weapons, explosives or of biological, nuclear, radiological or chemical weapons and
(e) Release of dangerous substances, or causing fire, floods or explosions

when the purpose of such act, by its nature and context, is to intimidate the general public or a segment thereof, create an atmosphere or spread a message of fear, to provoke or influence by intimidation the government or any international organisation, or seriously destabilise or destroy the fundamental political, economic or social structures of the country, or create a public emergency or seriously undermine public safety, shall be guilty of committing terrorism and shall suffer the penalty of life imprisonment without the benefit of parole and the benefits of Republic Act No. 10592, otherwise known as 'An Act Amending Articles 29, 94, 97, 98 and 99 of Act No. 3815, as amended, otherwise known as the Revised Penal Code': *Provided*, That, terrorism as defined in this section shall not include advocacy, protest, dissent, stoppage of work, industrial or mass action, and other similar exercises of civil and political rights, which are not intended to cause death or serious physical harm to a person, to endanger a person's life, or to create a serious risk to public safety.

- **Singapore**

Terrorism (Suppression of Financing) Act 2002 (Chap. 325), No. 16, Revised in 2003, 29 January 2003

'terrorist' means any person who—

(a) commits, or attempts to commit, any terrorist act; or
(b) participates in or facilitates the commission of any terrorist act, and includes any person set out in the First Schedule;

'terrorist act' means the use or threat of action—

(a) where the action—

- involves serious violence against a person;
- involves serious damage to property;
- endangers a person's life;
- creates a serious risk to the health or
- involves the use of firearms or explosives;
- involves releasing into the environment or any part thereof, or distributing or otherwise exposing the public or any part thereof to—
  - any dangerous, hazardous, radioactive or harmful substance;
  - any toxic chemical; or
  - any microbial or other biological agent, or toxin;

- disrupts, or seriously interferes with, any public computer system or the provision of any service directly related to communications infrastructure, banking and financial services, public utilities, public transportation or public key infrastructure;
- disrupts, or seriously interferes with, the provision of essential emergency services such as the police, civil defence and medical services; or
- involves prejudice to public security or national defence; and

(b) where the use or threat is intended or reasonably regarded as intending to—

- influence or compel the Government, any other government, or any international organisation to do or refrain from doing any act; or
- intimidate the public or a section of the public, and includes any action specified in the Second Schedule.

(3) Notwithstanding anything in subsection (2), a terrorist act does not include the activities undertaken by military forces of a State in the exercise of their official duties, to the extent that those activities are governed by other rules of international law.

- **Thailand**

Criminal Code, B.E. 2499 (1956), as amended until the Criminal Code (No. 17), B.E. 2547 (2003)

Section 135/1: 'Whoever, performing the Criminal Offence, as follows:

1. Commit an act of violence or exercise any act to cause a danger to life or a body harm or any person's freedom harm seriously;
2. Commit any act to cause seriously injury to transportation-system, communication-system or structure base of public interest;
3. Commit any act to cause injury to any State's property or any person's property or an envelopment to cause likely cause an important economic injury;

If such act is made by the aim to treated or enforce Thai Government, Foreign Government of International Organization make or not to make any act to cause seriously injury or for making a disorder by causing the people to be terrified, such person committing an offence of terrorisation must be punished with death, imprisonment for life or imprisonment from 3 years to 20 years and fine from six thousand Baht to one million Baht';

Anti-Terrorist Financing Act 2013, B.E. 2556, 1 February 2013

Section 3 'Terrorism' means the acts constituting an offence of terrorism under the Criminal Code or the criminal acts within the scope of a terrorism-related international convention or protocol to which Thailand is a party or which is recognised by Thailand, whether the acts are committed inside or outside the Kingdom.

- **Vietnam**

Criminal Code, No. 100/2015/QH13, 27 November 2015

Article 113: Terrorism to oppose the people's government

1. Any person who, for the purpose of opposing the people's government, infringes upon life of officials or other people shall face a penalty of 12–20 years' imprisonment, life imprisonment or death.
2. The following offences carry 10–15 years' imprisonment:

(a) Establishing, joining a terrorist organisation or an organisation sponsoring terrorism;
(b) Forcing, persuading other people to participate in terrorism; recruiting, training terrorists; manufacturing, providing weapons for terrorists;
(c) Infringing upon bodily integrity, health of officials or other people.

3. An offence that involves death threats or mental intimidation shall carry a penalty of 5–10 years' imprisonment.
4. Terrorist acts against foreign organisations, individuals, or international organisations for the purpose of destroying the Vietnam's international relationship also carry the penalties specified in this Article.
5. Any person who makes preparation for the commitment of this criminal offence shall face a penalty of 01–05 years' imprisonment.

Article 299: Terrorism

1. Any person who harms other people's life or destroy property of another organisation or individual to bring terror to the public shall face a penalty of 10–20 years' imprisonment, life imprisonment, or death.
2. This offence committed in any of the following cases shall carry a penalty of 05–15 years' imprisonment:

(a) Establishing or participating in a terrorist organisation or terrorism-financing organisation;
(b) Forcing, persuading, recruiting, training terrorists; manufacturing or providing weapons for terrorists;
(c) Infringing upon bodily integrity, health or appropriating, damaging property of another organisation or individual.

3. A person that threatens to commit any of the acts specified in Clause 1 of this Article or uses other methods to cause mental intimidation shall face a penalty of 02–07 years' imprisonment.
4. A person that prepares for the commission of this offence shall face a penalty of 01–05 years' imprisonment.
5. The offender might also have some citizenship rights deprived of, be put under mandatory supervision or prohibition from residence for 01–05 years, or have all or part of his/her property confiscated.

The Anti-Terrorism Law, No. 28/2013/QH13, 12 June 2013

Article 3: 'Terrorism' means one, several or all of the following acts committed by organisations or individuals with the aim to oppose the people's authorities, to compel the people's authorities, foreign organisations and international organisations, cause difficulties to the international relations of the Socialist Republic of Vietnam or cause panic situation in the public:

(a) Infringing upon the lives, health, and body liberty or threatening to infringe upon the lives or intimidating mental of others;
(b) Appropriating, damaging, destroying or threatening to destroy assets; attacking, infringing upon, obstructing or causing disorder to, operation of computer networks, telecommunication networks, Internet and digital equipment of agencies, organisations or individuals;
(c) Guiding the manufacture, production and use of, or manufacturing, producing, storing, transporting, trading in, weapons, explosives, radioactive materials, poison, inflammables and other instruments and means in serve of committing the acts defined at Point a and Point b, Clause 1 of this Article;
(d) Propagating, dragging into, inciting, forcing, hiring, or creating conditions for, or assisting for, the commission of the acts defined at Points a, b and c, Clause 1 of this Article;

dd/ Establishing, participating in the organisation, recruitment, training and coaching of objects with the aim to commit the acts defined at Points a, b, c and d, Clause 1 of this Article;

(e) Other acts that are considered terrorism under the anti-terrorism international treaties of which the Socialist Republic of Vietnam is a member.

'Terrorist financing' means act of mobilising, supporting with money and assets in any form for terrorist organisations and individuals.

Anti-terrorism includes activities of terrorism prevention, terrorist financing prevention, terrorism combat and terrorist financing combat.

Appendix 3: Table of the Terrorist Offences Criminalised in ASEAN Member States' Legislations

	Brunei Darussalam	Cambodia	Indonesia	Lao PDR	Malaysia	Myanmar	Philippines	Singapore	Thailand	Vietnam
Planning	X		X	X	X	X	X	X	X	X
Preparation	X	X	X	X	X	X	X	X	X	X
Perpetration	X	X	X	X	X	X	X	X	X	X
Organising	X	X	X	X	X	X	X	X	X	X
Financing of terrorist acts, organisations and individuals	X	X	X	X	X	X	X	X	X	X
Financing of the travel of foreign terrorist fighters (FTFs)	X		X		X		X	X		X
Equipping	X	X	X	X	X	X	X	X		X
Provision of training	X	X	X	X	X	X	X	X	X	X
Receiving training			X		X		X	X	X	X
Transporting	X	X			X	X	X	X		X
Travel of FTFs	X				X		X	X		X
Recruiting	X	X		X	X	X	X	X		X
Criminal association	X	X[a]		X	X		X	X	X	X
Incitement	X	X	X	X	X	X	X	X		X
Glorification	X					X		X		X

[a] Not defined as such but mentioned in Art. 78, CT Law

Appendix 4: Ratifications of the Most Relevant International Instruments by EU Member States

Table established on 31 December 2022

Terrorism						
	Convention on Offences and Certain Other Acts Committed on Board Aircraft (1963)	Convention for the Suppression of Unlawful Seizure of Aircraft (1970)	Convention for the Suppression of Unlawful Acts Against the Safety of Civil Aviation (1971)	Convention on the Prevention and Punishment of Crimes Against Internationally Protected Persons, including Diplomatic Agents (1973)	International Convention Against the Taking of Hostages (1979)	Convention on the Physical Protection of Nuclear Material (1980)
Austria	7 February 1974	11 February 1974	11 February 1974	3 August 1977 (A)	22 August 1986	21 January 1989 / obj. 12 October 2001
Belgium	6 August 1970	24 August 1973	13 August 1976	19 May 2004 (A)	16 April 1999	6 October 1991 / obj. 16 October 2001
Bulgaria	28 September 1989	19 May 1971	28 March 1973	18 July 1974	10 March 1988 (A)	11 May 1994
Croatia	5 October 1993	8 June 1993 (S)	8 June 1993 (S)	12 October 1992 (d)	23 September 2003 (d)	29 September 1992 (d)
Cyprus	31 May 1972	5 July 1972 (A)	27 July 1973	24 December 1975 (A)	13 September 1991 (A)	23 July 1998 (A)
Czech Republic	25 March 1993	14 November 1994 (S)	14 November 1994 (S)	22 February 1993 (d)	22 February 1993 (d)	1 January 1993 (d)
Denmark	17 January 1967	17 October 1972	17 January 1973	1 July 1975	11 August 1987 (A)	6 September 1991
Estonia	31 December 1993	22 December 1993 (A)	22 December 1993 (A)	21 October 1991 (A)	8 March 2002 (A)	9 May 1994 (A)
Finland	2 April 1971	15 December 1971	13 July 1973 (A)	31 October 1978	14 April 1983	22 November 1989 (A) / obj. 18 Oct 2001
France	11 September 1970	18 September 1972	30 June 1976 (A)	26 August 2003 (A)	9 June 2000 (A)	6 September 1991 (A) / obj. 12 October 2001
Germany	16 December 1969	11 October 1974	3 February 1978	25 January 1977	15 December 1980	6 September 1991 (obj. 20 September 2001)
Greece	31 May 1971	20 September 1973	15 January 1974	3 July 1984 (A)	18 June 1987	6 September 1991 (obj. 26 November 2001)
Hungary	3 December 1970	13 August 1971	27 December 1972	26 March 1975	2 September 1987 (A)	4 May 1984
Ireland	14 November 1975	24 November 1975 (A)	12 October 1976 (A)	30 June 2005 (A)	30 June 2005 (a)	6 September 1991 / obj. 28 September 2001
Italy	18 October 1968	19 February 1974	19 February 1974	30 August 1985	20 March 1986	6 September 1991 (obj.

(continued)

(continued)

Terrorism

	Convention on Offences and Certain Other Acts Committed on Board Aircraft (1963)	Convention for the Suppression of Unlawful Seizure of Aircraft (1970)	Convention for the Suppression of Unlawful Acts Against the Safety of Civil Aviation (1971)	Convention on the Prevention and Punishment of Crimes Against Internationally Protected Persons, including Diplomatic Agents (1973)	International Convention Against the Taking of Hostages (1979)	Convention on the Physical Protection of Nuclear Material (1980)
						15 October 2001)
Latvia	10 June 1997	23 October 1998 (A)	13 April 1997 (A)	14 April 1992 (A)	14 November 2002 (a)	6 November 2002 (A)
Lithuania	21 November 1996	4 December 1996 (A)	4 December 1996 (A)	23 October 2002 (A)	2 February 2001 (A)	7 December 1993
Luxembourg	21 September 1972	22 November 1978	18 May 1982	10 May 2006 (A)	29 April 1991	6 September 1991 / obj. 23 October 2001
Malta	28 June 1991	14 June 1991 (A)	14 June 1991 (A)	11 November 2001 (A)	11 November 2001 (A)	16 October 2003 (A)
Netherlands	14 November 1969	27 August 1973	27 August 1973	6 December 1988 (A)	6 December 1988	6 September 1991 / obj. 9 October 2001 / terr. app. 2 December 2005
Poland	19 March 1971	21 March 1972	28 January 1975	14 December 1982	25 May 2000 (A)	5 October 1985
Portugal	25 November 1964	27 November 1972	15 January 1973	11 September 1995 (A)	6 July 1984	6 September 1991 / obj. 18 October 2001
Romania	15 February 1974	10 July 1972	15 August 1975	15 August 1978	17 May 1990 (A)	23 November 1993
Slovakia	20 March 1995	13 December 1995 (S)	6 March 1995 (S)	28 May 1993 (d)	28 May 1993 (d)	10 February 1993 (d)
Slovenia	18 December 1992	27 May 1992 (S)	27 May 1992 (S)	6 July 1992 (d)	6 July 1992 (d)	7 July 1992 (d)
Spain	1 October 1969	30 October 1972	30 October 1972	8 August 1985 (A)	26 March 1984 (A)	6 September 1991 / obj. 4 October 2001
Sweden	17 January 1967	7 July 1971	10 July 1973 (A)	1 July 1975	15 January 1981	1 August 1980 / obj. 8 October 2001
European Union						*European Atomic Energy Community*: conf.: 6 September 1991 / obj.: 19 October 2001

	Protocol for the Suppression of Unlawful Acts of Violence at Airports Serving International Civil Aviation, supplementary to the Convention for the Suppression of Unlawful Acts Against the Safety of Civil Aviation (1988)	Convention for the Suppression of Unlawful Acts Against the Safety of Maritime Navigation (1988)	Protocol to the Convention for the Suppression of Unlawful Acts Against the Safety of Fixed Platforms Located on the Continental Shelf (1988)	Convention on the Marking of Plastic Explosives for the Purpose of Detection (1991)	International Convention for the Suppression of Terrorist Bombings (1997)	International Convention for the Suppression of the Financing of Terrorism (1999)
Austria	28 December 1989	28 December 1989	28 December 1989 (A)	31 May 1999	6 September 2000	15 April 2002
Belgium	20 April 1999			16 April 2007	20 May 2005	17 May 2004
Bulgaria	26 March 1991			8 September 1999	12 February 2002 (A)	15 April 2002
Croatia	8 June 1993			24 February 2005 (a)	2 June 2005 (A)	1 December 2003
Cyprus	23 April 2002			20 September 2002 (a)	24 January 2001	30 November 2001
Czech Republic	25 March 1993			25 Mar 1993 (S)	6 September 2000	27 December 2005
Denmark	23 November 1989	25 August 1995	25 August 1995	5 October 1998	31 August 2001	27 August 2002
Estonia	22 December 1993			5 March 1996 (a)	10 April 2002	22 May 2002
Finland	3 April 1998	12 November 1998		5 December 2001 (A)	28 May 2002 (AA)	28 June 2002 (a)
France	6 September 1989	2 December 1991 (A)	2 December 1991 (AA)	21 May 1997	19 August 1999	7 January 2002
Germany	25 April 1994	6 November 1990 (A)	6 November 1990 (a)	17 December 1998	23 April 2003	17 June 2004
Greece	25 April 1991	11 June 1993	11 June 1993	30 October 1995	27 May 2003	16 April 2004
Hungary	7 September 1988	9 November 1989	9 November 1989	11 January 1994	13 November 2001	14 October 2002
Ireland	26 July 1991			15 July 2003 (a)	30 June 2005	30 June 2005
Italy	13 March 1990	26 January 1990	26 January 1990	26 September 2002 (a)	16 April 2003	27 March 2003
Latvia	13 April 1997			17 August 1999 (a)	25 November 2002 (A)	14 November 2002
Lithuania	4 December 1996			21 November 1996 (a)	17 March 2004	20 February 2003 (A)
Luxembourg	14 November 2003			6 November 2006 (a)	6 February 2004	5 November 2003
Malta	14 June 1991			15 November 1994 (a)	11 November 2001 (A)	11 November 2001
Netherlands	11 July 1995	5 March 1992 (a)	5 March 1992 (a)	4 May 1998 (A)	7 February 2002 (A)	7 February 2002 (a)
Poland	12 August 2004	25 June 1991	25 June 1991	26 September 2006 (a)	3 February 2004	26 September 2003

(continued)

(continued)

	Protocol for the Suppression of Unlawful Acts of Violence at Airports Serving International Civil Aviation, supplementary to the Convention for the Suppression of Unlawful Acts Against the Safety of Civil Aviation (1988)	Convention for the Suppression of Unlawful Acts Against the Safety of Maritime Navigation (1988)	Protocol to the Convention for the Suppression of Unlawful Acts Against the Safety of Fixed Platforms Located on the Continental Shelf (1988)	Convention on the Marking of Plastic Explosives for the Purpose of Detection (1991)	International Convention for the Suppression of Terrorist Bombings (1997)	International Convention for the Suppression of the Financing of Terrorism (1999)
Portugal	18 December 2001	5 January 1996 (a)	5 January 1996 (a)	9 October 2002 (a)	10 November 2001	18 October 2002
Romania	3 September 1998	2 June 1993 (a)	2 June 1993 (a)	21 September 1998 (a)	29 July 2004	9 January 2003
Slovakia	20 March 1995			20 March 1995 (s)	8 December 2000	13 September 2002
Slovenia	27 May 1992			5 June 2000 (a)	25 September 2003	23 September 2004
Spain	8 May 1991	7 July 1989	7 July 1989	31 May 1994	30 April 1999	9 April 2002
Sweden	26 July 1990	13 September 1990	13 September 1990	5 April 2007	6 September 2001	6 June 2002
European Union						

	International Convention for the Suppression of Acts of Nuclear Terrorism (2005)	Amendment to the Convention on the Physical Protection of Nuclear Material (2005)	Protocol of 2005 to the Convention for the Suppression of Unlawful Acts Against the Safety of Maritime Navigation	Protocol of 2005 to the Protocol for the Suppression of Unlawful Acts Against the Safety of Fixed Platforms Located on the Continental Shelf	2010 Convention on the Suppression of Unlawful Acts Relating to International Civil Aviation	2010 Protocol Supplementary to the convention for the Suppression of Unlawful Seizure of Aircraft
Austria	14 September 2006	18 June 2006	18 June 2010	18 June 2010		
Belgium	2 October 2009	22 January 2013		2 July 2019		
Bulgaria	14 September 2005 (S)	17 March 2006	7 October 2010	7 October 2010		
Croatia	30 May 2007	11 September 2006 (AA)				
Cyprus	28 January 2008	27 February 2013 (a)			28 March 2019	28 March 2019
Czech Republic	25 July 2006	30 December 2010 (a)			2 July 2013	2 July 2013
Denmark	20 March 2007	19 May 2010 (a)		14 September 2018		
Estonia	14 September 2005 (S)	24 February 2009	16 May 2008	16 May 2008		
Finland	13 January 2009 (a)	17 June 2011 (a)				
France	11 September 2013	1 February 2013 (AA)		9 May 2018 (AA)	15 December 2016	15 December 2016
Germany						

(continued)

(continued)

	International Convention for the Suppression of Acts of Nuclear Terrorism (2005)	Amendment to the Convention on the Physical Protection of Nuclear Material (2005)	Protocol of 2005 to the Convention for the Suppression of Unlawful Acts Against the Safety of Maritime Navigation	Protocol of 2005 to the Protocol for the Suppression of Unlawful Acts Against the Safety of Fixed Platforms Located on the Continental Shelf	2010 Convention on the Suppression of Unlawful Acts Relating to International Civil Aviation	2010 Protocol Supplementary to the convention for the Suppression of Unlawful Seizure of Aircraft
	8 February 2008	21 October 2010	26 January 2016	29 January 2016 (A)	12 October 2016 (S)	12 October 2016 (S)
Greece	15 September 2005 (S)	13 December 2011	11 September 2013	11 September 2013		
Hungary	12 April 2007	4 December 2008				
Ireland	15 September 2005 (S)	22 September 2014				
Italy	21 October 2016	8 July 2015				
Latvia	25 July 2006	23 November 2010 (a)	16 November 2009	16 November 2009 (A)		
Lithuania	19 July 2007	19 May 2009				
Luxembourg	2 October 2008	24 February 2012				
Malta	26 September 2012	16 September 2013 (a)			26 September 2016	26 September 2016
Netherlands	30 June 2010 (a)	17 April 2011 (a)	1 March 2011	1 March 2011(a)	17 March 2016 (a)	17 March 2016 (a)
Poland	8 April 2010	1 June 2007				
Portugal	25 September 2014	26 November 2010	1 September 2015	1 September 2015		22 January 2019
Romania	24 January 2007	6 February 2007			22 June 2018	22 June 2018
Slovakia	23 March 2006	7 March 2013				
Slovenia	17 December 2009	1 September 2009 (a)				
Spain	22 February 2007	9 November 2007 (a)	16 April 2008	16 April 2008	10 September 2010 (S)	10 September 2010 (S)
Sweden	18 August 2014	23 March 2012	22 September 2014	22 September2014	12 July 2018 (A)	12 July 2018 (A)
European Union		Euratom: 16 December 2015 (A)				

Organised crime			
	United Nations Convention against Transnational Organized Crime (2000)	Protocol to Prevent, Suppress and Punish Trafficking in Persons, Especially Women and Children, supplementing the UNTOC (2000)	Protocol against the Smuggling of Migrants by Land, Sea and Air, supplementing the UNTOC (2000)
Austria	23 September 2004	16 September 2005	30 November 2007
Belgium	11 August 2004	11 August 2004	11 August 2004
Bulgaria	5 December 2001	5 December 2001	5 December 2001
Croatia	24 January 2003	24 January 2003	24 January 2003
Cyprus	22 April 2003	6 August 2003	6 August 2003
	24 September 2013	17 December 2014	24 September 2013

(continued)

(continued)

Organised crime			
	United Nations Convention against Transnational Organized Crime (2000)	Protocol to Prevent, Suppress and Punish Trafficking in Persons, Especially Women and Children, supplementing the UNTOC (2000)	Protocol against the Smuggling of Migrants by Land, Sea and Air, supplementing the UNTOC (2000)
Czech Republic			
Denmark	30 Sept. 2003	30 September 2003	8 December 2006
Estonia	10 February 2003	12 May 2004	12 May 2004
Finland	10 February 2004	7 September 2004 (a)	7 September 2006 (a)
France	29 October 2002	29 October 2002	29 October 2002
Germany	14 June 2006	14 June 2006	14 January 2006
Greece	11 January 2011	11 January 2011	11 January 2011
Hungary	22 December 2006	22 December 2006	22 December 2006
Ireland	17 June 2010	17 June 2010	13 December 2000 (S)
Italy	2 August 2006	2 August 2006	2 August 2006
Latvia	7 December 2001	25 May 2004	23 April 2003
Lithuania	9 May 2002	23 June 2003	12 May 2003
	Luxembourg	12 May 2008	20 April 2009
24Septe-mber 2012			
Malta	24 September 2003	24 September2003	24 September 2003
	Netherlands	26 May 2004	27 July 2005 (a)
27 July 2005 (a)			
Poland	12 November 2001	26 September2003	26 September 2003
Portugal	10 May 2004	10 May 2004	10 May 2004
Romania	4 December 2002	4 December 2002	4 December 2002
Slovakia	3 December 2003	21 September 2004	21 September 2004
Slovenia	21 May 2004	21 May 2004	21 May 2004
Spain	1 March 2002	1 March 2002	1 March 2002
Sweden	30 April 2004	1 July 2004	6 September 2006
European Union	21 May 2004 (AA)	6 September 2006 (AA)	6 September 2006 (AA)

Human rights					
	International Covenant on Civil and Political Rights (1966)	Optional Protocol to the ICCPR related to the set-up of the Human Rights Committee (1966)	International Covenant on Economic, Social and Cultural Rights (1966)	Convention against Torture and Other Cruel, Inhuman or Degrading Treatment or Punishment (1984)	Second Optional Protocol to the ICCPR on the abolition of the death penalty (1989)
Austria	10 September 1978	10 December 1987	10 September 1978	29 July 1987	2 March 1993
Belgium	21 April 1983	17 May 1994 (A)	21 April 1983	25 June 1999	8 December 1998
Bulgaria		26 March 1992 (A)	21 September1970	16 December 1986	10 August 1999

(continued)

(continued)

Human rights					
	International Covenant on Civil and Political Rights (1966)	Optional Protocol to the ICCPR related to the set-up of the Human Rights Committee (1966)	International Covenant on Economic, Social and Cultural Rights (1966)	Convention against Torture and Other Cruel, Inhuman or Degrading Treatment or Punishment (1984)	Second Optional Protocol to the ICCPR on the abolition of the death penalty (1989)
	21 September 1970				
Croatia	12 October 1992 (d)	12 October 1995 (A)	12 October 1992 (d)	12 October 1992 (d)	12 October 1995 (A)
Cyprus	2 April 1969	15 April 1992	2 April 1969	18 July 1991	10 September 1995 (A)
Czech Republic	22 February 1993 (d)	22 February 1993 (d)	22 February 1993 (d)	22 February 1993 (d)	15 June 2004 (A)
Denmark	6 January 1972	6 January 1972	6 January 1972	27 May 1987	24 February 1994
Estonia	21 October 1991 (a)	21 October 1991 (A)	21 October 1991 (A)	21 October 1991 (A)	30 January 2004 (A)
Finland	19 August 1975	19 August 1975	19 August 1975	30 August 1989	4 April 1991
France	4 November 1980 (a)	17 February 1984 (A)	4 November 1980 (A)	18 February 1986	2 October 2007 (A)
Germany	17 December 1973	25 August 1993 (A)	17 December 1973	1 October 1990	18 August 1992
Greece	5 May 1997 (a)	5 May 1997(A)	16 May 1985 (A)	6 October 1988	5 May 1997 (A)
Hungary	17 January 1974	7 September 1988 (A)	17 January 1974	15 April 1987	24 February 1994 (A)
Ireland	8 December 1989	8 December 1989 (A)	8 December 1989	11 April 2002	18 June 1993 (A)
Italy	15 September 1978	15 September 1978	15 September 1978	12 January 1989	14 February 1995
Latvia	14 April 1992 (a)	22 June 1994 (A)	14 April 1992 (A)	14 April 1992 (A)	19 April 2013 (A)
Lithuania	20 November 1991 (a)	20 November 1991 (A)	20 November 1991 (A)	1 February 1996 (A)	27 March 2002
Luxembourg	18 August 1983	18 August 1983 (A)	18 August 1983	29 September 1987	12 February 1992
Malta	13 September 1990 (a)	13 September1990 (A)	13 September 1990	13 September 1990 (A)	29 December 1994 (A)
Netherlands	11 December 1978	11 December 1978	11 December 1978	21 December 1988	26 March 1991
Poland	18 March 1977	7 November 1991 (A)	18 March 1977	26 July 1989	25 April 2014
Portugal	15 June 1978	3 May 1983	31 July 1978	9 February 1989	17 October 1990
Romania	9 December 1974	20 July 1993 (A)	9 December 1974	18 December 1990 (A)	27 February 1991
Slovakia	28 May 1993 (d)	28 May 1993 (d)	28 May 1993 (d)	28 May 1993 (d)	22 June 1999
Slovenia	6 June 1992 (d)	16 July 1993 (A)	6 July 1992 (d)	16 July 1993 (A)	10 March 1994
Spain	27 April 1977	25 January 1985 (A)	27 April 1977	21 October 1987	11 April 1991
Sweden	6 December 1971	6 December 1971	6 December 1971	8 January 1986	11 May 1990

	Convention on the Rights of the Child (1989)	Optional Protocol to the Convention on the Rights of the Child on the involvement of children in armed conflict (2000)	Optional Protocol to the Convention on the Rights of the Child on the sale of children, child prostitution and child pornography (2000)	Optional Protocol to the Convention against Torture and Other Cruel, Inhuman or Degrading Treatment or Punishment (2002)	Convention for the Protection of all Persons from Enforced Disappearance (2006)	Optional Protocol to the IESCR (2008)
Austria	6 August 1992	1 February 2002	6 May 2004	4 December 2012	7 June 2012	
Belgium	16 December 1991	6 May 2002	17 March 2006	24 October 2005 (S)	2 June 2011	20 May 2014
Bulgaria	3 June 1991	12 February 2002	12 February 2002	1 June 2011	24 September 2008 (S)	
Croatia	12 October 1992 (d)	1 November 2002	13 May 2002	25 April 2005	6 February 2007 (S)	
Cyprus	7 February 1991	2 July 2010	6 April 2006	29 April 2009	6 February 2007 (S)	29 January 2021 (S)
Czech Republic	22 February 1993 (d)	30 November 2001	26 August 2013	10 July 2006	8 February 2017	
Denmark	19 July 1991	27 August 2002	24 July 2003	25 January 2004	25 September 2007 (S)	
Estonia	21 October 1991 (A)	12 February 2014	3 August 2004	18 December 2006		
Finland	20 June 1991	10 April 2002	1 June 2012	8 October 2014	6 February 2007 (S)	31 January 2014
France	7 August 1990	5 February 2003	5 February 2003	11 November 2008	23 September 2008	18 March 2015
Germany	6 March 1992	13 December 2004	15 July 2009	4 December 2008	24 September 2009	
Greece	11 May 1993	22 Ocotber 2003	22 February 2008	11 February 2014	9 July 2015	
Hungary	7 October 1991	24 February 2010	24 February 2010	12 January 2012 (A)		
Ireland	28 September 1992	18 November 2002	7 September 2000 (S)	2 October 2007 (S)	29 March 2007 (S)	23 March 2012
Italy	5 September 1991	9 May 2002	9 May 2002	3 April 2013	3 July 2007	20 February 2015
Latvia	14 April 1992 (A)	19 December 2005	22 February 2006			
Lithuania	31 January 1992 (A)	20 February 2003	5 August 2004 (A)	20 January 2014 (A)	14 August 2013	
Luxembourg	7 March 1994	4 August 2004	2 September 2011	19 May 2010	6 February 2007 (S)	3 February 2015
Malta	30 September 1990	9 May 2002	28 September 2010	24 September 2003	27 March 2015	
Netherlands	6 February 1995 (A)	24 September 2009	23 August 2005	28 September 2010	23 March 2011	24 February 2009 (S)
Poland	7 June 1991	April 2005	4 February 2005	14 September 2005	25 June 2013 (S)	
Portugal	21 September 1990	19 August 2003	16 May 2003	15 January 2013	24 January 2014	28 January 2013
Romania	28 September 1990	10 November 2001	18 October 2001	2 July 2009	3 December 2008 (S)	
Slovakia	28 May 1993 (d)	7 July 2006	25 June 2004	14 December 2018 (S)	15 December 2014	7 March 2012

(continued)

(continued)

	Convention on the Rights of the Child (1989)	Optional Protocol to the Convention on the Rights of the Child on the involvement of children in armed conflict (2000)	Optional Protocol to the Convention on the Rights of the Child on the sale of children, child prostitution and child pornography (2000)	Optional Protocol to the Convention against Torture and Other Cruel, Inhuman or Degrading Treatment or Punishment (2002)	Convention for the Protection of all Persons from Enforced Disappearance (2006)	Optional Protocol to the IESCR (2008)
Slovenia	6 July 1992 (d)	23 September 2004	23 September 2004	23 January 2007 (A)	26 September 2007	24 September 2009 (S)
Spain	6 December 1990	8 March 2002	18 December 2001	4 April 2006	24 September 2009	23 September 2010
Sweden	29 June 1990	20 February 2003	19 January 2007	14 September 2005	6 February 2007 (S)	

Date only: ratification
(S) signature, *(A)* accession, *(AA)* approval, *(a)* acceptance, *Conf.* confirmation, *Obj.* objection

Table of Legislation (in Chronological Order)

Disclaimer—This table does not include all the sources consulted for this study, but only those who have been the most useful to it. It should be noted that if the main normative acts, publications and judgements adopted by regional and international organisations (UN, EU, ASEAN, etc.) as well as those adopted by some of the EU and ASEAN Member States are subject to a non-exhaustive enumeration, some subsidiary sources are not included in this bibliography. They appear in the footnotes.

International Instruments and Policy Documents

International Conventions, Treaties and Other International Agreements

United Nations, *Charter of the United Nations*, San Francisco, 26 June 1945.

Statute of the International Court of Justice, San Francisco, 24 October 1945.

Convention on the Privileges and Immunities of the United Nations, New York, 13 February 1946, United Nations Treaty Series (UNTS), vol. 1, No. 4, p. 15.

Convention on the Privileges and Immunities of the Specialized Agencies, New York, 21 November 1947, UNTS, vol. 33, No. 521, p. 261.

Universal Declaration of Human Rights, 10 December 1948, A/RES/217A(III), 183rd plenary meeting, UN Doc A/810, p. 71.

Geneva Convention relative to the Protection of Civilian Persons in Time of War, Geneva, 12 August 1949, UNTS, vol. 75, No. 973, p. 287.

Final Communiqué of the Bandung Conference (Afro-Asian Conference), Bandung, 18–24 April 1955.

Vienna Convention on the Diplomatic Relations, Vienna, 18 April 1961, UNTS, vol. 500, No. 7310, p. 95.

Convention on offences and certain other acts committed on board aircraft, Tokyo, 14 September 1963, *UNTS, vol. 704, No. 10106, p. 219.*

International Covenant on Civil and Political Rights, New York, 16 December 1966, UNTS, vol. 999, No. 14668, p. 171.

Optional Protocol to the International Covenant on Civil and Political Rights, New York, 16 December 1966, UNTS, vol. 999, No. 14668, p. 171.

International Covenant on Economic, Social and Cultural Rights, New York, 16 December 1966, UNTS, vol. 993, No. 14531, p. 3.

Treaty on the Non-Proliferation of Nuclear Weapons, London, Moscow and Washington, 1 July 1968, UNTS, vol. 729, No. 10485, p. 161.

Convention on the Law of Treaties, Vienna, 23 May 1969, UNTS, vol. 1155, No. 18232, p. 331.

Convention for the Suppression of Unlawful Seizure of Aircraft, The Hague, 16 December 1970, UNTS, vol. 860, No. 12325, p. 105.

Convention for the Suppression of Unlawful Acts against the Safety of Civil Aviation, Montreal, 23 September 1971, UNTS, vol. 974, No. 14118, p. 177.

Convention on the Prevention and Punishment of Crimes against Internationally Protected Persons, including Diplomatic Agents, New York, 14 December 1973, UNTS, vol. 1035, No. 15410, p. 167.

Convention on the Physical Protection of Nuclear, Vienna, 26 October 1979, UNTS, vol. 1456, No. 24631, p. 124.

International Convention against the Taking of Hostages, New York, 17 December 1979, UNTS, vol. 1316, No. 21931, p. 205.

Convention on the Elimination of All Forms of Discrimination against Women, New York, 18 December 1979, UNTS, vol. 1249, No. 20378, p. 13.

Convention against Torture and Cruel, Inhuman or Degrading Treatment or Punishment, New York, 10 December 1984, UNTS, vol. 1465, No. 24841, p. 85.

Convention on the law of treaties between States and international organisations or between international organisations, Vienna, 21 March 1986, UNTS, vol. 1155, No. 18232, p. 331.

Protocol for the Suppression of Unlawful Acts of Violence at Airports Serving International Civil Aviation, supplementary to the Convention for the suppression of Unlawful Acts against the Safety of Civil Aviation, Montreal, 24 February 1988, UNTS, vol. 1589, No. 14118, p. 474.

Convention for the Suppression of Unlawful Acts against the Safety of Maritime Navigation, Rome, 10 March 1988, UNTS, vol. 1678, No. 29004, p. 221.

Protocol for the Suppression of Unlawful Acts against the Safety of Fixed Platforms Located on the Continental Shelf, Rome, 10 March 1988, UNTS, vol. 1678, No. 29004, p. 304.

United Nations Convention against Illicit Traffic in Narcotic Drugs and Psychotropic Substances, Vienna, 20 December 1988, UNTS, vol. 1582, No. 27627, p. 95.

International Convention on the Rights of the Child, New York, 20 November 1989, UNTS, vol. 1577, No. 27531, p. 3.

Second Optional Protocol to the International Covenant on Civil and Political Rights, aiming at the abolition of the death penalty, New York, 15 December 1989, UNTS, vol. 1642, No. 14668, p. 414.

International Convention on the Protection of the Rights of All Migrant Workers and Members of their Families, New York, 18 December 1990, UNTS, vol. 2220, No. 39481, p. 3.

Convention on the Marking of Plastic for the Purpose of Detection, Montreal, 1 March 1991, UNTS, vol. 2122, No. 36984, p. 359.

Convention on the Safety of United Nations and Associated Personnel, New York, 9 December 1994, UNTS, vol. 2051, No. 35457, p. 363.

International Convention for the Suppression of Terrorist Bombings, New York, 15 December 1997, UNTS, vol. 2149, No. 37517, p. 256.

International Convention for the Suppression of the Financing of Terrorism, New York, 9 December 1999, UNTS, vol. 2178, No. 38349, p. 197.

Statute of the International Criminal Court, Rome, 17 July 1998, A/CONF.183/9, UNTS, vol. 2187, No. 38544, p. 90.

Optional Protocol to the Convention on the Elimination of All Forms of Discrimination against Women, New York, 6 October 1999, UNTS, vol. 2131, No. 20378, p. 83.

Optional Protocol to the Convention on the Rights of the Child on the Involvement of Children in Armed Conflict, New York, 25 May 2000, UNTS, vol. 2173, No. 27531, p. 222.

Optional Protocol to the Convention on the Rights of the Child on the Sale of Children, Child Prostitution and Child Pornography, New York, 25 May 2000, UNTS, vol. 2171, No. 27531, p. 227.

United Nations Convention against Transnational Organized Crime, A/RES/55/25, New York, 15 November 2000, UNTS, vol. 2225, No. 39574, p. 209.

Protocol to Prevent, Suppress and Punish Trafficking in Persons, Especially Women and Children, supplementing the United Nations Convention against Transnational Organized Crime, New York, 15 November 2000, A/RES/55/25, UNTS, vol. 2237, No. 39574, p. 319.

Protocol against the Smuggling of Migrants by Land, Sea and Air, supplementing the United Nations Convention against Transnational Organized Crime, New York, 15 November 2000, A/RES/55/25, UNTS, vol. 2241, No. 39574, p. 507.

Protocol against the Illicit Manufacturing and Trafficking in Firearms, Their Parts and Components and Ammunition, supplementing the United Nations Convention against Transnational Organized Crime, New York, 31 May 2001, A/RES/55/255, UNTS, vol. 2326, No. 39574, p. 208.

Optional Protocol to the Convention against Torture and Other Cruel, Inhuman or Degrading Treatment or Punishment, New York, 18 December 2002, UNTS, vol. 2375, No. 24841, p. 90.

United Nations Convention against Corruption, New York, 31 October 2003, UNTS, vol. 2349, No.42146, p. 41.

International Convention for the Suppression of Acts of Nuclear Terrorism, New York, 13 April 2005, UNTS, vol. 2445, No. 44004, p. 89.

Amendment to the Convention on the Physical Protection of Nuclear Material, Vienna, 8 July 2005, UNTS, vol. 1456, No. 24631, p. 1.

Protocol of 2005 to the Convention for the Suppression of Unlawful Acts against the Safety of Maritime Navigation, London, 14 October 2005, IMO Doc. LEG/CONF.15/21, UNTS, No. 29004.

Protocol of 2005 to the Protocol for the Suppression of Unlawful Acts against the Safety of Fixed Platforms Located on the Continental Shelf, London, 14 October 2005, IMO Doc. LEG/CONF.15/22, UNTS, No. 29004.

Convention on the Rights of Persons with Disabilities, New York, 13 December 2006, UNTS, vol. 2515, No. 44910, p. 3.

Optional Protocol to the Convention on the Rights of Persons with Disabilities, New York, 13 December 2006, UNTS, vol. 2518, No. 44910, p. 283.

International Convention for the Protection of All Persons from Enforced Disappearance, New York, 20 December 2006, UNTS, vol. 2717, No. 48088, p. 3.

Memorandum of understanding between the Association of Southeast Asian Nations (ASEAN) and the United Nations (UN) on ASEAN–UN cooperation, New York, 27 September 2007.

Optional Protocol to the International Covenant on Economic, Social and Cultural Rights, New York, 10 December 2008, UNTS, vol. 2922, No. 14531.

Convention on the Suppression of Unlawful Acts relating to International Civil Aviation, Beijing, 10 September 2010, DCAS Doc. No. 22.

Protocol Supplementary to the Convention for the Suppression of Unlawful Seizure of Aircraft, Beijing, 10 September 2010, ICAO Doc. No. 9959.

Optional Protocol to the Convention for the Rights of the Child on a communication procedure, New York, 19 December 2011, A/RES/66/138, vol. 2983, No. 27531.

Protocol to the Convention on Offences and Certain Other Acts Committed on Board Aircraft, Montreal, 4 April 2014, ICAO Doc. 10034.

United Nations

UN Documents: Resolutions, Decisions, Reports

Security Council Resolutions and Security Council Committee Resolutions, Declarations, Reports, Letters and Other Documents

S/RES/286(1970), *Hijacking of commercial aircraft and release of passengers and crew*, 1552nd meeting, 9 September 1970.

S/RES/579(1985), *Condemning acts of hostage-taking and abduction*, 2637th meeting, 18 December 1985.

S/RES/1267(1999), *The increase in acts of international terrorism*, 4051st meeting, 15 October 1999.

S/RES/1269(1999), *The responsibility of the Security Council in the maintenance of international peace and security*, 4053rd meeting, 19 October 1999.

S/RES/1333(2000), *The situation in Afghanistan*, 4251st meeting, 19 December 2000.

S/RES/1363(2001), *The situation in Afghanistan*, 4352nd meeting, 30 July 2001.

S/RES/1366(2001), *The role of the Security Council in the prevention of armed conflicts*, 4360th meeting, 30 August 2001.

S/RES/1368(2001), *Threats to international peace and security caused by terrorist acts*, 4370th meeting, 12 September 2001.

S/RES/1373(2001), *Threats to international peace and security caused by terrorist acts*, 4385th meeting, 28 September 2001.

S/RES/1377(2001), *Threats to international peace and security caused by terrorist acts*, 4413th meeting, 12 November 2001.

S/RES/1378(2001), *The situation in Afghanistan*, 4415th meeting, 14 November 2001.

S/PV.4734 (provisional), *Threats to international peace and security caused by terrorist acts*, 'Chairman of the Counter-Terrorism Committee established pursuant to resolution 1373(2001) concerning counter-terrorism, Sir Jeremy Greenstock', 4734th meeting, 4 April 2003.

S/PV.4752 (provisional), *Threats to international peace and security caused by terrorist acts*, 'Russia's Ambassador to the UN, Sergei Lavrov', 4752nd meeting, 6 May 2003.

S/RES/1618(2005), *Condemnation of terrorist attacks in Iraq*, 5246th meeting, 4 August 2005.

S/RES/1631(2005), *Cooperation between the United Nations and regional organizations in maintaining international peace and security*, 5282nd meeting, 17 October 2005.

Security Council Committee, Counter-Terrorism Committee, *Policy guidance on international cooperation*, S/AC.40/2010/PG.3, 14 June 2010.

S/RES/1988(2011), *Threats to international peace and security caused by terrorist acts,* 6557th meeting, 17 June 2011.

S/RES/2083(2012), *Threats to international peace and security caused by terrorist acts*, 6890th meeting, 17 December 2012.

S/RES/2129(2013), *Threats to international peace and security caused by terrorist acts*, 7086th meeting, 17 December 2013.

S/RES/2178(2014), *Condemning Violent Extremism, Underscoring Need to Prevent Travel, Support for Foreign Terrorist Fighters*, 7272nd meeting, 24 September 2014.

S/RES/2195(2014), *Threats to international peace and security*, 7351st meeting, 19 December 2014.

S/RES/2196(2015), *The situation in Central African Republic*, 7366th meeting, 22 January 2015.

S/RES/2199(2015), *Threats to international peace and security caused by terrorist acts*, 7379th meeting, 12 February 2015.

S/RES/2211(2015), *The situation in Democratic Republic of the Congo*, 7415th meeting, 26 March 2015.

S/2015/683, Letter dated 2 September 2015 from the Chair of the Security Council Committee established pursuant to resolution 1373(2001) concerning counter-terrorism addressed to the President of the Security Council, Annex 'Implementation of Security Council Resolution 2178(2014) by States affected by foreign fighters', Second report, 2 September 2015.

S/RES/2220(2015), *Non-proliferation of weapons*, 7447th meeting, 22 May 2015.

S/RES/2250(2015), *Maintenance of international peace and security*, 7573rd meeting, 9 December 2015.

S/RES/2253(2015), *Threats to international peace and security caused by terrorist acts,* 7587th meeting, 17 December 2015.

S/RES/2255(2015), *Threats to international peace and security caused by terrorist acts,* 7590th meeting, 22 December 2015.

Counter-Terrorism Committee Executive Directorate (CTED), *Implementation of Security Council 2178(2014) by States affected by foreign terrorist fighters: A compilation of three reports (S/2015/338; S/2015/683; S/2015/975)*, New York, 31 August 2016.

S/RES/2368(2017), *Threats to international peace and security caused by terrorist acts*, 8007th meeting, 20 July 2017.

S/RES/2395(2017), *Threats to international peace and security caused by terrorist acts*, 8146th meeting, 21 December 2017.

S/RES/2396(2017), *Foreign Terrorist Fighters (Returnees and Relocators)*, 8184th meeting, 21 December 2017.

S/2018/705, Letter dated 16 July 2018 from the Chair of the Security Council Committee pursuant to resolutions 1267(1999), 1989(2001) and 2253(2015) concerning Islamic State in Iraq and the Levant (Da'esh), Al-Qaida and associated individuals, groups, undertakings and entities addressed to the President of the Security Council and Twenty-second report of the Analytical Support and Sanctions Monitoring Team submitted pursuant to resolution 2368(2017) concerning ISIL (Da'esh), Al-Qaida and associated individuals and entities, 27 July 2018.

S/2018/1177, Letter dated 28 December 2018 from the Chair of the Security Council Committee established pursuant to resolution 1373(2001) concerning counter-terrorism addressed to the President of the Security Council and its Annex 'Addendum to the 2015 Madrid Guiding Principles on foreign terrorist fighters'.

S/RES/2462(2019), *Threats to international peace and security caused by terrorist acts: Preventing and combating the financing of terrorism*, 8496th meeting, 28 March 2019.

S/RES/2482(2019), *Threats to international peace and security caused by terrorist acts*, 8582nd meeting, 19 July 2019.

S/2020/95, Tenth report of the Secretary-General on the threat posed by ISIL (Da'esh) to international peace and security and the range of United Nations efforts in support of Member States in countering the threat, 4 February 2020.

S/2020/493, *Letter dated 3 June 2020 from the Chair of the Security Council Committee established pursuant to resolution 1373(2001) concerning counter-terrorism and the Chair of the Security Council Committee pursuant to resolutions 1267(1999), 1989(2011) and 2253(2015) concerning Islamic State in Iraq and the Levant (Da'esh), Al-Qaeda and associated individuals, groups, undertakings and entities addressed to the President of the Security Council*, 3 June 2020.

S/RES/2560(2020), *Threats to international peace and security caused by terrorist acts*, 29 December 2020.

General Assembly Resolutions, Declarations, Reports and Other Documents

A/RES/2(1), *Rules of Procedure Concerning Languages,* 21st plenary meeting, 1 February 1946.

A/RES/377(V), *Uniting for peace*, 302nd plenary meeting, 3 November 1950.

A/RES/2625 (XXV), *Declaration on Principles of International Law concerning Friendly Relations and Co-operation among States in accordance with the Charter of the United Nations,* 1883rd plenary session, 24 October 1970.

A/RES/3208(XXIX), *Status of the European Economic Community in the General Assembly*, 2266th plenary meeting, 11 October 1974.

A/RES/3314(XXIX), *Definition of Aggression*, 2319th plenary meeting, 14 December 1974.

A/RES/32/127, *Regional arrangements for the promotion and protection of human rights*, 105th plenary meeting, 16 December 1977.

A/RES/34/169, *Code of Conduct for Law Enforcement Officials*, 106th plenary meeting, 17 December 1979.

A/RES/40/33, *United Nations Standard Minimum Rules for the Administration of Juvenile Justice* (The 'Beijing Rules'), 96th plenary meeting, 29 November 1985.

A/RES/40/34, *Declaration of Basic Principles of Justice for Victims of Crime and Abuse of Power*, 96th plenary meeting, 29 November 1985.

A/RES/40/144, *Declaration on the human rights of individuals who are not nationals of the country in which they live*, 116th plenary meeting, 13 December 1985.

A/RES/43/173, *Body of Principles for the Protection of All Persons under Any Form of Detention or Imprisonment*, 76th plenary meeting, 9 December 1988.

A/RES/49/95, *Guidelines for the regulation of computerized personal data files,* 68th meeting, 14 December 1989.

A/RES/45/116, *Model Treaty on Extradition*, 68th plenary meeting, 14 December 1990; as amended by A/RES/52/88, 70th plenary meeting, 12 December 1997.

A/RES/45/117, *Model Treaty on Mutual Legal Assistance in criminal Matters*, 68th plenary meeting, 14 December 1990; as amended by A/RES/53/112, 53rd session, 20 January 2000.

A/46/608 and S/23177, Letter from the Permanent Representatives of France and Indonesia to the United Nations addressed to the Secretariat-General concerning the situation in Cambodia, 46th session, 30 October 1991.

A/RES/47/135, *Declaration on the rights of persons belonging to national or ethnic, religious and linguistic minorities*, 92nd plenary meeting, 18 December 1992.

A/49/748, *Crime Prevention and Criminal Justice*, Annex 'Report of the World Ministerial Conference on Organized Transnational Crime', Naples, 2 December 1994.

A/RES/49/60, *Measures to eliminate international terrorism*, 84th plenary meeting, 9 December 1994.

A/RES/49/57, *Declaration on the Enhancement of Cooperation between the United Nations and Regional Arrangements or Agencies in the Maintenance of International Peace and Security*, 84th plenary meeting, 9 December 1994.

A/RES/49/159, *Naples Political Declaration* and *Global Action Plan against Organized Transnational Crime*, 94th plenary meeting, 23 December 1994.

A/RES/50/6, *Declaration on the Occasion of the Fiftieth Anniversary of the United Nations*, 50th session, 24 October 1995.

A/RES/53/101, *Principles and guidelines for international negotiations*, 83rd plenary meeting, 8 December 1998.

A/RES/59/157, *International cooperation in the fight against transnational organized crime: Assistance to States in capacity-building with a view to facilitating the implementation of the United Nations Convention against Transnational Organized Crime and the Protocols thereto*, 74th plenary meeting, 20 December 2004.

A/59/894, Letter dated 3 August 2005 from the Chairman of the Sixth Committee addressed to the President of the General Assembly, Appendix II '*Draft Comprehensive Convention against International Terrorism*. Consolidated text prepared by the Coordinator for discussion', 59th session, 12 August 2005.

A/RES/60/1, *2005 World Summit Outcome*, 8th plenary meeting, 16 September 2005.

A/RES/60/288(2006), *United Nations Global Counter-Terrorism Strategy*, 99th plenary meeting, 8 September 2006.

A/RES/61/44, *Observer Status for the Association of Southeast Asian Nations in the General Assembly*, 64th plenary meeting, 4 December 2006.

A/RES/65/276, *Participation of the European Union in the work of the United Nations*, 65th session, 3 May 2011.

GA/L/3433, *Legal Committee Urges Conclusion of Draft Comprehensive Convention on International Terrorism*, 67th session, 6th Committee, 8 October 2012.

A/RES/68/167, *The right to privacy in the digital age*, 68th plenary meeting, 21 January 2014.

A/RES/69/166, *The right to privacy in the digital age*, 69th session, Agenda item 68(b), 18 December 2014.

A/70/328, *Cooperation between United Nations and regional and subregional organizations on mediation,* Report of the Secretary-General, 87th session, 19 August 2015.

A/RES/71/291, *Strengthening the capability of the United Nations system to assist Member States in implementing the United Nations Global Counter-Terrorism Strategy*, 87th plenary meeting, 15 June 2017.

A/74/335, *Promotion and protection of human rights and fundamental freedoms while countering terrorism,* 'Report of the Special Rapporteur on the promotion and protection of human rights and fundamental freedoms while countering terrorism', 74th session, 29 August 2019.

A/75/729, *Activities of the United Nations system in implementing the United Nations Global Counter-Terrorism Strategy*, Report of the Secretary-General, 75th session, 29 January 2021.

A/77/345, *Promotion and protection of human rights and fundamental freedoms while countering terrorism. Impact of counter-terrorism on peacemaking, peacebuilding, sustaining peace, conflict prevention and resolution*, 77th session, 16 September 2022.

UN Human Rights Council

A/HRC/13/37, *Promotion and protection of all human rights, civil, political, economic, social and cultural rights, including the right to development*, 'Report of the Special Rapporteur on the promotion and protection of human rights and fundamental freedoms while countering terrorism, Martin Scheinin', 13th session, 28 December 2008.

An Open Letter from the Coordination Committee of the Special Procedures of the Human Rights Council on the draft ASEAN Human Rights Declaration, 'ASEAN Human Rights Declaration should maintain international standards', Geneva, 16 November 2012: available at https://www.ohchr.org/EN/NewsEvents/Pages/DisplayNews.aspx?NewsID=14864&LangID=E (last accessed on 8 December 2020).

A/HRC/29/7, *Universal Periodic Review* 'Report of the Working Group on the Universal Periodic Review, Lao People's Democratic Republic', 29th session, 23 March 2015.

A/HRC/29/32, *Promotion and protection of all human rights, civil, political, economic, social and cultural rights, including the right to development*, 'Report of the Special Rapporteur on the promotion and protection of the right to freedom of opinion and expression, David Kaye', 29th session, 22 May 2015.

A/HRC/40/63, *Promotion and protection of all human rights, civil, political, economic, social and cultural rights, including the right to development*, 'Right to privacy. Report of the Special Rapporteur on the right to privacy' Fortieth session, Agenda item 3: Promotion and protection of all human rights, civil, political, economic, social and cultural rights, including the right to development, 27 February 2019.

A/HRC/42/60, *Annual report of the UN High Commissioner for Human Rights and reports of the Office of the High Commissioner and the Secretary-General. Technical assistance and capacity-building,* 'Situation of human rights in Cambodia. Report of the Special Rapporteur on the situation of human rights in Cambodia', 42nd session, 27 August 2019.

A/HRC/43/46, *Promotion and protection of all human rights, civil, political, economic, social and cultural rights, including the right to development*, 'Human rights impact of policies and practices aimed at preventing and countering violent extremism' Report of the Special Rapporteur on the promotion and protection of human rights and fundamental freedoms while countering terrorism, 43rd session, 21 February 2020.

UN Human Rights Special Procedures, 'Views of the United Nations Special Rapporteur on the promotion of and protection of human rights and fundamental freedoms while countering terrorism to the Secretariat-General's ending report pursuant to UNSCR 2482(2019) addressing the issue of linkage between terrorism and organized criminal groups (OCG)': available at https://www.ohchr.org/Documents/Issues/Terrorism/OrganizedCrimeSGReport.docx (last accessed on 8 December 2020).

UN Human Rights Special Procedures, 'ODIHR Expert consultation meetings on human rights challenges related to information gathering and sharing and new technologies in border management in the counter-terrorism and freedom of movement context. Intervention of the Special Rapporteur on the promotion and protection of human rights and fundamental freedoms while countering terrorism', 15 June 2020: available at https://www.ohchr.org/Documents/Issues/Terrorism/SR/OSCEODIHRExpertMeetingAPI_PNRdata.pdf (last accessed on 8 December 2020).

UN Human Rights Committee

CCPR/C/21/Rev.1/Add.9, *General Comment No. 27* 'Article 12: Freedom of Movement', 67th session, 2 November 1999,

CCPR/C/GC/34, *General Comment No. 34* 'Article 19: Freedoms of opinion and expression. General remarks', 102nd session, 12 September 2011.

CCPR/C/LAO/Q/1/Add.1, *Consideration of reports submitted by States parties under Article 40 of the Covenant*, 'List of issues in relation to the initial report of Lao People's Democratic Republic. Addendum. Replies of Lao People's Democratic Republic to the list of issues', 123rd session, 20 June 2018.

UN Economic and Social Council

E/CN.15/1998/5, *International Cooperation in Combating Transnational Crime*, 'Implementation of the Naples Political Declaration and global action plan against organized transnational crime: Question of the elaboration of an international Convention against organized transnational crime, and other possible instruments', Commission on Crime Prevention and Criminal Justice, 7th session, 21–30 April 1998.

E/CN.4/2002/157, Letter dated 19 March 2002 from the Permanent Representative of Singapore to the United Nations Office at Geneva addressed to the Chairperson of the Commission on Human Rights, 'Question of the violation of human rights and fundamental freedoms in any part of the world. Civil and political rights. Effective functioning of human rights mechanisms', 58th session, 25 March 2002.

E/RES/2005/17, *International cooperation in the fight against transnational organized crime*, 36th plenary meeting, 22 July 2005.

UN Documents: Meetings and Verbatim Records

A/CONF.39/26, *Final Act of the United Nations Conference on the Law of Treaties*, Vienna, 23 May 1963.

A/CONF.144/28/Rev.1, Eighth United Nations Congress on the Prevention of Crime and the Treatment of Offenders, *Guidelines on the Role of the Prosecutors*, Havana, 27 August–7 September 1990.

A/47/277-S/24111, Report of the Secretary-General pursuant to the statement adopted by Summit Meeting of the Security Council on 31 January 1992, 'An Agenda for Peace, Preventive diplomacy, peace-making and peace-keeping', 17 June 1992.

A/CONF.169/15/Add.1, Ninth United Nations Congress on the Prevention of Crime and the Treatment of Offenders, 'International Cooperation and Practical Technical Assistance for Strengthening the Rule of Law: Promoting the United Nations Crime Prevention and Criminal Justice Programme', Cairo, 29 April–8 May 1995.

A/55/383/Add.1, Report of the Ad Hoc Committee on the Elaboration of a Convention against Transnational Organized Crime on the work of its first to eleventh sessions, Addendum 'Interpretative notes for the official records (*travaux préparatoires*) of the negotiation of the United Nations Convention against Transnational Organized Crime and the Protocols thereto', 55th session, 3 November 2000.

A/CONF.222/L.6, 13th UN Congress on Crime Prevention and Criminal Justice, *Doha Declaration on integrating crime prevention and criminal justice into the wider United Nations agenda to address social and economic challenges and to promote the rule of law at the national and international levels, and public participation*, Doha, 12–19 April 2015.

GA/11639, 'Strengthened Cooperation between United Nations, Regional Organizations Vital to International Peace, Security, Speakers Stress at General Assembly', 69th General Assembly meeting, Meeting coverage, 4 May 2015.

Various Other UN Publications

A/CN.4/SER.A/1976/Add.l (Part 2), *Yearbook of the International Law Commission 1976*, Vol. II (Part II), 'Report of the International Law Commission on the work of its twenty-eighth session', 3 May–23 July 1976, Doc. A/31/10 (New York: UN publications, 1977).

A/CN.4/SER.A/2002/Add.1 (Part 2), *Yearbook of the International Law Commission 2002*, Vol. II (Part II), 'Report of the International Law Commission on the work of its fifty-fourth session', 29 April–7 June and 22 July–16 August 2002, Doc. A/57/10 (New York–Geneva: UN Publications, 2009).

UNODC/International Monetary Fund (IMF), *Model legislation on money laundering and financing of terrorism* (for civil law legal systems, 1 December 2005).

UNODC, *Model Law on Mutual Legal Assistance in Criminal Matters* (Vienna: UNODC Publications, 2007).

UNODC, Terrorism Prevention Branch, *Model legislative provisions against terrorism* (Vienna: UNODC Publications, February 2009).

UNODC, *Handbook on criminal justice responses to terrorism*, Criminal justice handbook series (New York: UN Publications, March 2009).

UNODC/Commonwealth Secretariat/IMF, *Model Provisions on Money Laundering, Terrorist Financing, Preventive Measures and Proceeds of Crime* (for common law legal systems, April 2009).

UNODC, *Manual on International Cooperation in Criminal Matters related to Terrorism* (Vienna: UNODC Publications, July 2009).

UNODC, *Criminal Intelligence. Manual for Front-line Law Enforcement* (Vienna: UNODC Publications, December 2010).

UNODC, *Criminal Intelligence. Manual for Analysts* (Vienna: UNODC Publications, April 2011).

Commission on Crime Prevention and Criminal Justice, CCPCJ/RES/22/8, *Promoting technical assistance and capacity-building to strengthen national measures and international cooperation against cybercrime*, 26 April 2013.

UNODC, 'Human Rights and Criminal Justice Responses to Terrorism' *Counter-Terrorism Legal Training Curriculum*, Module 4 (Vienna: UNODC Publications, August 2014).

Carly Nyst, 'Privacy, Protection of Personal Information and Reputation Rights' *UNICEF Discussion Paper Series: Children's Rights and Business in Digital World*, (UNICEF Publications, March 2017).

A/CN.4/SER.A/2011/Add.1 (Part 2), *Yearbook of the International Law Commission 2011*, Vol. II (Part Two), Report of the International Law Commission on the work of its sixty-third session, 26 April–3 June and 4 July–12 August 2011, Doc. A/66/10 (New York and Geneva: UN Publications, 2018).

UNODC, *Investigation, Prosecution and Adjudication of Foreign Terrorist Fighter Cases for South and South-East Asia* (Vienna: UNODC Publications, June 2018).

UNODC, *Foreign Terrorist Fighters. Manual for Judicial Training Institutes South-Eastern Europe*, updated Edition (Vienna: UNODC Publications, December 2019).

UNODC Terrorism Prevention Branch, *Menu of Services. Legislative and Capacity-Building Assistance to Prevent and Combat Terrorism*: available at https://www.unodc.org/documents/terrorism/Publications/TPB_Brochure/Menu%20of%20Services%202016/16-01352_Menu_of_Services_eBook.pdf (last accessed on 8 December 2020).

Security Council, '"Strong cooperation among counter-terrorism committees vital for combatting growing global scourge, speakers stress a subsidiary body chairs brief Security Council' SC/14716, 8915th meeting, 2 December 2021.

INTERPOL

INTERPOL Documents

AGN/20/RES/11(1951), *Request for international inquiries*, Resolution of the General Assembly, 10–15 June 1951.

I/CONS/GA/1956(2017), *Constitution of the International Criminal Police Organisation—INTERPOL*, 25th session, Vienna, 1956.

AGN/53/RES/6(1984), *Violent Crime commonly referred to as Terrorism*, 53rd session, Luxembourg, 4–11 September 1984.

AGN/53/RES/7(1984), *Application of Article 3 of the Constitution*, 53rd session, Luxembourg, 4–11 September 1984.

AG/2011/RES/07 *approving the Rules on the Processing of Data and abrogating, on 30 June 2012, the 'Rules on the Processing of Information for the Purposes of International Police Cooperation', the 'Implementing Rules for the Rules on the Processing of Information for the Purposes of International Police Cooperation', and the 'Rules Governing Access by an Intergovernmental Organization to the INTERPOL Telecommunications Network and Databases'*, 80th session, Hanoi, 31 October–November 2011.

AG/2019/RES/02 *adopting amendments to INTERPOL's Rules on the Processing of Data*, III/IRPD/GA/2011(2019) 'INTERPOL's Rules on the Processing of Data', 88th session, Santiago, 15–18 October 2019.

INTERPOL's Cooperation Agreements with National Governments and Public Authorities

Cooperation Agreement between Interpol and Europol, Brussels, 5 November 2001.

Memorandum of Understanding on the establishment of a secure communication line between Europol and Interpol, Lyon, 11 October 2011.

Cooperation Agreement between the ICPO-Interpol General Secretariat and European Police College (CEPOL), 12 December 2008.

Financial Action Task Force

International Standards on Combating Money Laundering and the Financing of Terrorism and Proliferation. FATF Recommendations, Paris, February 2012; updated in June 2019.

Organisation for Economic Cooperation and Development

Guidelines on the Protection of Privacy and Transborder Flows of Personal Data, 23 September 1980, as updated in 2013.

Council of Europe

European Convention for the Protection of Human Rights and Fundamental Freedoms, ETS No. 5, Rome, 4 November 1950.

European Convention on Extradition, ETS No. 24, Paris, 13 December 1957.

European Convention on Mutual Assistance in Criminal Matters, ETS No. 30, Strasbourg, 20 April 1959.

Additional Protocol to the European Convention on Extradition, ETS No. 86, Strasbourg, 15 October 1975.

Convention for the Suppression of Terrorism, ETS No. 90, Strasbourg, 27 January 1977.

Second Additional Protocol to the European Convention on Extradition, ETS No. 98, Strasbourg, 17 March 1978.

Additional Protocol to the European Convention on Mutual Assistance in Criminal Matters, ETS No. 99, Strasbourg, 17 March 1978.

Convention for the Protection of Individuals with regard to Automatic Processing of Personal Data, ETS No. 108, Strasbourg, 28 January 1981.

Recommendation No. R(87)3 of the Committee of Ministers to Member States on the European Prison Rules, 404th meeting, 12 February 1987.

Convention on Laundering, Search, Seizure and confiscation of the Proceeds from Crime, Strasbourg, 8 November 1990.

Second Additional Protocol to the European Convention on Mutual Assistance in Criminal Matters, ETS No. 182, Strasbourg, 1 February 2001.

Convention on Cybercrime, ETS No. 185, Budapest, 23 November 2001.

Guidelines on Human Rights and the Fight Against Terrorism, Committee of Ministers, 804th meeting, 11 July 2002.

Les Droits de l'Homme et la Lutte contre le Terrorisme. Les Lignes Directrices du Conseil de l'Europe (Strasbourg: Editions du Conseil de l'Europe, March 2005).

Protocol amending the European Convention on the Suppression of Terrorism, ETS No. 190, Strasbourg, 15 May 2003.

Committee of Ministers, *Recommendation Rec(2005)10 of the Committee of Ministers to Member States on 'special investigation techniques' in relation to serious crimes including acts of terrorism*, 924th meeting of the Ministers' Deputies, 20 April 2005.

Convention on the Prevention of Terrorism, ETS No. 196, Warsaw, 16 October 2005.

Third Additional Protocol to the European Convention on Extradition, ETS No. 209, Strasbourg, 10 November 2010.

Fourth Additional Protocol to the European Convention on Extradition, ETS No. 212, Vienna, 20 September 2012.

Ad Hoc Drafting Group on Transnational Organised Crime (PC-GR-COT), 1st meeting, Paris, 24–26 June 2013: available at https://rm.coe.int/ad-hoc-drafting-group-on-transnational-organised-crime-pc-gr-cot-1st-m/1680713dbc (last accessed on 9 December 2020).

Additional Protocol to the Council of Europe Convention on the Prevention of Terrorism, ETS No. 217, Riga, 22 October 2015.

European Committee on Crime Problems, Steering Committee, *Terms of reference,* valid from 1 January 2014 until 31 December 2015: available at http://www.coe.int/t/dghl/standardsetting/cdpc/ToR%20CDPC%202014-2015.pdf (last accessed on 9 December 2020).

Regional Sources

Association of Southeast Asian Nations

ASEAN Normative Documents

ASEAN Declaration (Bangkok Declaration), Bangkok, 8 August 1967.

Treaty of Amity and Cooperation in Southeast Asia, Bali, 24 February 1976.

Agreement on the Establishment of the ASEAN Secretariat, Bali, 24 February 1976.

Agreement Between the Government of Indonesia and ASEAN Relating to the Privileges and Immunities of the ASEAN Secretariat, Secretary-General and Foreign Minister of Indonesia, Jakarta, 20 January 1979.

The Southeast Asia Nuclear Weapon Free Zone Treaty, Bangkok, 15 December 1995.

ASEAN Declaration on Transnational Crime, Manila, 20 December 1997.

ASEAN Declaration on the Prevention and Control of Transnational Crime, Manila, 25 March 1998.

Joint Declaration for a Drug-Free ASEAN, Manila, 25 July 1998.

ASEAN Framework Agreement on Mutual Recognition Arrangements, Hanoi, 16 December 1998.

ASEAN Declaration on Joint Action to Counter Terrorism, Bandar Seri Begawan, 5 November 2001.

Agreement on Information Exchange and Establishment of Communication Procedures, adopted between the Republic of the Philippines, the Republic of Indonesia and Malaysia, Putrajaya, 7 May 2002.

Framework Agreement on Comprehensive Economic Co-operation Between ASEAN and the People's Republic of China, Phnom Penh, 5 November 2002.

Joint Declaration of ASEAN and China on Cooperation in the Field of Non-Traditional Security Issues, 6th ASEAN—China Summit, Phnom Penh, 4 November 2002.

Joint Declaration on Cooperation to Combat Terrorism, 14th ASEAN-EU Ministerial Meeting, 2003.

Declaration of ASEAN Concord II (Bali Concord II), Heads of State/Government, 9th ASEAN Summit, Bali, 7 October 2003.

Memorandum of Understanding between the Governments of the Member Countries of the Association of Southeast Asian Nations (ASEAN) and the Government of the People's Republic of China on Cooperation in the Field of Non-Traditional Security Issues, Bangkok, 10 January 2004.

Declaration on the Elimination of Violence Against Women in the ASEAN Region, Jakarta, 30 June 2004.

ASEAN Treaty on Mutual Legal Assistance in Criminal Matters, Ministers of Justice/Law Attorneys-General, Kuala Lumpur, 29 November 2004.

ASEAN Declaration against Trafficking in Persons particularly Women and Children, Vientiane, 29 November 2004.

Joint Declarations for Cooperation to Combat International Terrorism between ASEAN and:

United States of America, Bandar Seri Begawan, 1 August 2002;
India, Bali, 8 October 2003;
Australia, Jakarta, 1 July 2004;
New Zealand, Vientiane, 29 July 2005;
Canada, Kuala Lumpur, 28 July 2006.

Kuala Lumpur Declaration on the Establishment of the ASEAN Charter, Kuala Lumpur, 12 December 2005.

Declaration on the Acceleration of the Establishment of an ASEAN Community by 2015, Cebu, January 2007.

ASEAN Declaration on the Protection and Promotion of the Rights of Migrants Workers, 12th ASEAN Summit, Cebu, 13 January 2007.

ASEAN Convention on Counter-Terrorism, 12th ASEAN Summit, Cebu, Heads of State/Government, 13 April 2007.

ASEAN Charter, 13th ASEAN Summit, Singapore, 20 November 2007.

Declaration on the Inauguration of the ASEAN Intergovernmental Commission on Human Rights, 15th ASEAN Summit, Cha-Am Hua Hin, 23 October 2009.

ASEAN Intergovernmental Commission on Human Rights (Terms of reference), 15th ASEAN Summit, Cha-Am Hua Hin, 23–25 October 2009.

Agreement on the Privileges and Immunities of the Association of Southeast Asian Nations, Cha-Am, 25 October 2009.

Protocol to the ASEAN Charter on Dispute Settlement Mechanisms, Hanoi, 8 April 2010.

Bali Declaration on ASEAN Community in a Global Community of Nations (Bali Concord III), 'Plan of Action 2013-2017', 19th ASEAN Summit, Bali, 17 November 2011.

ASEAN Coordinating Council, *Rules of Procedure for the Conclusion of International Agreements by ASEAN*, 19th ASEAN Summit, Bali, 17 November 2011.

ASEAN Human Rights Declaration, 21st ASEAN Summit, Phnom Penh, 18 November 2012.

Declaration in Combating Transnational Crime, 10th ASEAN Ministerial Meeting on Transnational Crime (AMMTC), Kuala Lumpur, 30 September 2015.

ASEAN Convention against Trafficking in Persons, Especially Women and Children, 27th ASEAN Summit, Kuala Lumpur, 21 November 2015.

Kuala Lumpur Declaration on the establishment of the ASEAN Community, Kuala Lumpur, 22 November 2015.

Terms of Reference of the ASEAN Ministerial Meeting on Transnational Crime, 11th AMMTC, Manila, 20 September 2017.

Manila Declaration to Counter the Rise of Radicalisation and Violent Extremism, Manila, 20 September 2017.

Model ASEAN Extradition Treaty, adopted at 10th ASEAN Law Ministers Meeting (ALAWMM) taking place on 11–12 October 2018, Vientiane, 12 October 2018.

Other ASEAN Documents

Ten Years of ASEAN (Jakarta: ASEAN Secretariat, April 1978).

ASEAN Plan of Action, 6th ASEAN Summit, Hanoi, 15 December 1998.

ASEAN Plan of Action to Combat Transnational Crime, Yangon, 23 June 1999.

ASEAN Plan of Action for Cooperation on Immigration Matters, Davao, 18 October 2000.

Work Programme to implement the ASEAN Plan of Action to Combat Transnational Crime, Kuala Lumpur, 17 May 2002.

ACCORD Plan of Action 2005–2010, Beijing, 20 October 2005.

Report of the Eminent Persons' Group on the ASEAN Charter, December 2006: available at https://www.asean.org/wp-content/uploads/images/archive/19247.pdf (accessed on 11 February 2021).

ASEAN Defence Ministers' Meeting-Plus (ADMM-Plus), *Concept paper*, 2nd ADMM, Singapore, 13–15 November 2007.

ASEAN Senior Officials Meeting on Transnational Crime Working Group on Counter Terrorism (WG on CT)—Terms of Reference, 2nd SOMTC Working Group on Counter-Terrorism, ASEAN Secretariat Paper Agenda Item 4, Kuala Lumpur, 16 June 2008.

Roadmap for an ASEAN Community 2009–2015 (Jakarta: ASEAN Secretariat, 2009).

ASEAN Political-Security Community Blueprint (Jakarta: ASEAN Secretariat, 1 March 2009).

Cha-Am Hua Hin Declaration on the Roadmap for the ASEAN Community (2009–2015), Cha-Am, 1 March 2009.

ASEAN Comprehensive Plan of Action on Counter Terrorism, Nay Pyi Taw, 30 June 2009.

ASEAN Work Plan on Combating Illicit Drug Production, Trafficking and Use (2009–2015), Siem Reap, 17 November 2009.

'Master Plan on ASEAN Connectivity' (Jakarta: ASEAN Secretariat, 2010).

ASEAN Handbook on International Legal Cooperation in Trafficking in Persons Cases elaborated in collaboration with the UNODC (and other partners) (Jakarta: ASEAN publications, August 2010).

'Evolving Towards ASEAN 2015' *Annual Report 2011*–2012 (Jakarta: ASEAN Secretariat, June 2012).

Aseanapol Database System Technical Committee, 31st meeting, Taguig, 17–21 March 2014.

ASEAN Intergovernmental Commission on Human Rights (AICHR), 'AICHR Workshop on Regional Mechanisms: Best practices on implementation of human rights' (with partial support from UN Women and Regional EU-ASEAN Dialogue Instrument), 21 November 2014.

AICHR, 'Sharing national experience on human rights implementation in ASEAN', 23 December 2014.

Joint Communiqué, 48th ASEAN Foreign Ministers Meeting, Kuala Lumpur, 4 August 2015.

ASEAN 2025: Forging Ahead Together (Jakarta: ASEAN Secretariat, November 2015).

ASEAN Plan of Action Against Trafficking in Persons, Especially Women and Children, 27th ASEAN Summit, Kuala Lumpur, 22 November 2015.

ASEAN Political-Security Community Blueprint 2025 (Jakarta: ASEAN Secretariat, March 2016).

ASEAN, Joint Statement of the ASEAN Directors-General of Immigration Departments and Heads of Consular Affairs Divisions of the Ministries of Foreign Affairs (DGIM) on the Prevention of the Movement of Foreign Terrorist Fighters, 20th meeting of the DGIM, Bali, 23 September 2016.

Committee of Permanent Representatives to ASEAN (CPR) Handbook (Jakarta: ASEAN Secretariat, August 2017).

Revised ASEAN Comprehensive Plan of Action on Counter Terrorism, 11th AMMTC, Manila, 20 September 2017.

ASEAN Plan of Action in Combating Transnational Crime (2016–2025), 11th AMMTC, Manila, 20 September 2017.

ASEAN, Chairman's Statement of the 9th ASEAN-UN Summit, Manila, 13 November 2017.

Chairman's Statement of the 5th ASEAN-U.S. Summit to Commemorate the 40th Anniversary of ASEAN-U.S. Dialogue Relations, Manila, 13 November 2017.

Statement, 'INDONESIA: War against terrorism should respect human rights and the Rule of Law' Asian Human Rights Commission, AHRC-STM-015-2018, 6 March 2018.

ASEAN Plan of Action to Prevent and Counter the Rise of Radicalisation and Violent Extremism (2018–2025), 12th AMMTC, Nay Pyi Taw, 31 October 2018.

ASEAN Integration Report 2019 (Jakarta: ASEAN Secretariat, October 2019).

Chairman's Statement of the 10th ASEAN-UN Summit, 'Advancing Partnership for Sustainability' Bangkok/Nonthaburi, 3 November 2019.

Work Plan of the ASEAN Plan of Action to Preventing and Counter the Rise of Radicalisation and Violent Extremism (2019–2025), 13th AMMTC, Bangkok, 27 November 2019.

AICHR, Five-Year Work Plan of the AICHR (2021–2025), approved at the 53rd ASEAN Foreign Ministers' Meeting, 9 September 2020.

ASEAN, Initiative for ASEAN Integration (IAI) Work Plan IV (2021–2025*)* (Jakarta: ASEAN Secretariat, November 2020).

Chairman's Statement of the 29th ASEAN Regional Forum, Phnom Penh, 5 August 2022.

Chairman's Statement of the 12th ASEAN-United Nations Summit, 'ASEAN Addressing Challenges Together', Phnom Penh, 11 November 2022.

European Union

EU Legislative Documents

Treaty establishing the European Coal and Steel Community, Paris, 18 April 1951.

Treaty establishing the European Economic Community and related instruments (EEC Treaty) and *Treaty establishing the European Atomic Energy Community* (Euratom), Roma, 25 March 1957.

Protocol (No 36) annexed to the Treaties establishing the European Community and the European Atomic Energy Community by the Treaty establishing a single Council and a single Commission of the European Communities of 8 April 1965, O.J.E.C. L152/13, 13 July 1967.

1968 Brussels Convention on jurisdiction and the enforcement of judgments in civil and commercial matters, O.J.E.C. L299/32, 31 December 1972.

Single European Act, Luxembourg, 17 February 1986, and The Hague, 28 February 1986.

Treaty on European Union (Treaty of Maastricht), Maastricht, 7 February 1992.

Council Act of 10 March 1995 adopted on the basis of Article K.3 of the Treaty on European Union, drawing up the Convention on simplified extradition procedure between the Member States of the European Union, O.J.E.C. C78/1, 30 March 1995.

Council Act of 26 July 1995 drawing up the Convention based on Article K.3 of the Treaty on European Union on the establishment of a European Police Office (Europol Convention), O.J.E.C. C316/1, 27 November 1995.

Directive 95/46/EC of the European Parliament and of the Council of 24 October 1995 on the protection of individuals with regard to the processing of personal data and on the free movement of such data, O.J.E.C. L281/31, 23 November 1995.

Council Act of 27 September 1996 adopted on the basis of Article K.3 of the Treaty on European Union, drawing up the Convention relating to extradition between the Member States of the European Union, O.J.E.C. C313/11, 23 June 1996.

Convention determining the State responsible for examining applications for asylum lodged in one of the Member States of the European Communities (Dublin Convention), O.J. C254/1, 19 August 1997.

Treaty of Amsterdam amending the Treaty on European Union, the Treaties establishing the European Communities and certain related acts, Amsterdam, 2 October 1997.

Plan of Action of the Council and the Commission on how best to implement the provisions of the Treaty of Amsterdam on an area of freedom, security and justice, Justice and Home Affairs Council of 3 December 1998, O.J.E.C. C19/1, 23 January 1999.

Joint Action of 21 December 1998 adopted by the Council on the basis of Article K.3 of the Treaty on European Union, on making it a criminal offence to participate in a criminal organisation in the Member States of the European Union, O.J.E.C. L351/1, 29 December 1998.

Council Act of 29 May 2000 establishing in accordance with Article 34 of the Treaty on European Union the Convention on Mutual Assistance in Criminal Matters between the Member States of the European Union, O.J.E.C. C197/1, 12 July 2000.

The Schengen Acquis—Convention implementing the Schengen Agreement of 14 June 1985 between the Governments of the States of the Benelux Economic Union, the Federal Republic of Germany and the French Republic on the gradual abolition of checks at their common borders, O.J.E.C. L239/19, 22 September 2000.

Charter of fundamental rights of the European Union, O.J.E.C. C364/1, 18 December 2000.

Council Decision 2000/820/JHA of 22 December 2000 establishing a European Police College (CEPOL), O.J.E.C. L336/1, 30 December 2000.

Treaty of Nice amending the Treaty on European Union, the Treaties establishing the European Communities and certain related acts, signed at Nice, 26 February 2001, O.J.E.C. C80/1, 10 March 2001.

Directive 2001/40/EC of 28 May 2001 on the mutual recognition of decisions on the expulsion of third-country nationals, O.J.E.C. L149/34, 2 June 2001.

Protocol established by the Council in accordance with Article 34 of the Treaty on European Union to the Convention on Mutual Assistance in Criminal Matters between the Member States of the European Union, O.J.E.C. 326/2, 21 November 2001.

Council Common Position 2001/931/CFSP of 27 December 2001 on the application of specific measures to combat terrorism, O.J.E.C. L344/93, 28 December 2001.

Council Decision 2002/187/JHA of 28 February 2002 setting up Eurojust with a view to reinforcing the fight against serious crime, O.J.E.C. L62/1, 6 March 2002.

Council Framework Decision 2002/465/JHA of 13 June 2002 on Joint Investigation Teams, O.J.E.C. L162/1, 20 June 2002.

Council Framework Decision 2002/475/JHA of 13 June 2002 on combating terrorism, O.J.E.C. L164/3, 22 June 2002.

Council Framework Decision 2002/584/JHA of 13 June 2002 on the European Arrest Warrant and the Surrender Procedures between Member States, O.J.E.C. L190/1, 18 July 2002.

Treaty on European Union and Treaty establishing the European Community, O.J.E.C. C325/1, 24 December 2002.

Council Framework Decision 2003/577/JHA of 22 July 2003 on the execution in the European Union of orders freezing property or evidence, O.J.E.U. L196/45, 2 August 2003.

Council Decision 2004/191/EC of 23 February 2004 setting out the criteria and practical arrangements for the compensation of the financial imbalances resulting from the application of Directive 2001/40/EC on the mutual recognition of decisions on the expulsion of third-country nationals, O.J.E.U. L60/55, 27 February 2004.

Council Joint Action 2004/551/CFSP of 12 July 2004 on the establishment of the European Defence Agency, O.J.E.U. L245/17, 17 July 2004.

Council Regulation (EC) 2007/2004 of 26 October 2004 establishing a European Agency for the Management of Operational Cooperation at the External Borders of the Member States of the European Union, O.J.E.U. L349/1, 25 November 2004.

Council of the European Union, *The Hague Programme: Strengthening Freedom, Security and Justice in the European Union*, O.J.E.U. C53/1, 3 March 2005.

Council Framework Decision 2005/214/JHA of 24 February 2005 on the application of the principle of mutual recognition to financial penalties, O.J.E.U. L76/16, 22 March 2005.

Convention between the Kingdom of Belgium, the Federal Republic of Germany, the Kingdom of Spain, the French Republic, the Grand Duchy of Luxembourg, the Kingdom of the Netherlands and the Republic of Austria on the stepping up of cross-border cooperation, particularly in combating terrorism, cross-border crime and illegal migration (Prüm Convention), Prüm, 27 May 2005.

Council Decision 2005/671/JHA of 20 September 2005 on the exchange of information and cooperation concerning terrorist offences, O.J.E.U. L253/22, 29 September 2005.

Council Decision 2005/681/JHA of 20 September 2005 establishing the European Police College (CEPOL) and repealing Decision 2000/820/JHA, O.J.E.U. L256/63, 1 October 2005.

Council Framework Decision 2006/783/JHA of 6 October 2006 on the application of the principle of mutual recognition to confiscation orders, O.J.E.U. L328/59, 24 November 2006.

Council Framework Decision 2006/960/JHA 18 December 2006 on simplifying the exchange of information and intelligence between law enforcement authorities of the Member States of the European Union ('Swedish Framework Decision'), O.J.E.U. L386/89, 29 December 2006.

Regulation (EC) No 1986/2006 of the European Parliament and of the Council of 20 December 2006 regarding access to the Second Generation Schengen

Information System (SIS II) by the services in the Member States responsible for issuing vehicle registration certificates, O.J.E.U. L381/1, 28 December 2006.

Regulation (EC) No 1987/2006 of the European Parliament and of the Council of 20 December 2006 on the establishment, operation and use of the second generation Schengen Information System (SIS II), O.J.E.U. L381/4, 28 December 2006.

Council Decision 2007/533/JHA of 12 June 2007 on the establishment, operation and use of the second generation Schengen Information System (SIS II), O.J.E.U. L205/63, 7 August 2007.

Treaty of Lisbon Amending the Treaty on European Union and the Treaty Establishing the European Community, O.J.E.U. C306/1, 13 December 2007.

Council Decision 2008/615/JHA of 23 June 2008 on the stepping up of cross-border cooperation, particularly in combating terrorism and cross-border crime, O.J.E.U. L210/1, 6 August 2008.

Council Decision 2008/616/JHA of 23 June 2008 on the implementation of Decision 2008/615/JHA of 23 June 2008 on the stepping up of cross-border cooperation, particularly in combating terrorism and cross-border crime, O.J.E.U. L210/12, 6 August 2008.

Regulation (EC) No 764/2008 of the European Parliament and of the Council of 9 July 2008 laying down procedures relating to the application of certain national technical rules to products lawfully marketed in another Member State and repealing Decision No 3052/95/EC, O.J.E.U. L218/21, 13 August 2008.

Council Framework Decision 2008/675/JHA of 24 July 2008 on taking account of convictions in the Member States of the European Union in the course of new criminal proceedings, O.J.E.U. L220/32, 15 August 2008.

Council Framework Decision 2008/909/JHA of 27 November 2008 on the application of the principle of mutual recognition to judgments in criminal matters imposing custodial sentences or measures involving deprivation of liberty for the purposes of their enforcement in the European Union, O.J.E.U. L327/27, 5 December 2008.

Council Framework Decision 2008/919/JHA of 28 November 2008 amending the Council Framework Decision 2002/475/JHA on combating terrorism, O.J.E.U. L330/21, 9 December 2008.

Council Framework Decision 2008/947/JHA of 27 November 2008 on the application of the principle of mutual recognition to judgments and probation decisions with a view to the supervision of probation measures and alternative sanctions, O.J.E.U. L337/102, 16 December 2008.

Council Framework Decision 2008/977/JHA of 27 November 2008 on the protection of personal data processed in the framework of police and judicial cooperation in criminal matters, O.J.E.U. L350/60, 30 December 2008.

Council Framework Decision 2008/978/JHA of 18 December 2008 on the European evidence warrant for the purpose of obtaining objects, documents and data for use in proceedings in criminal matters, O.J.E.U. L350/72, 30 December 2008.

Council Framework Decision 2008/841/JHA of 24 October 2008 on the fight against organised crime, O.J.E.U. L300/42, 11 November 2008.

Council Decision 2008/976/JHA of 16 December 2008 on the European Judicial Network, O.J.E.U. L348/130, 24 December 2008.

Council Framework Decision 2009/315/JHA of 26 February 2009 on the organisation and content of the exchange of information extracted from the criminal record between Member States, O.J.E.U. L93/23, 7 April 2009.

Council Framework Decision 2009/316/JHA of 6 April 2009 on the establishment of the European Criminal Records Information System (ECRIS) in application of Article 11 of Framework Decision 2009/315/JHA, O.J.E.U. L93/33, 7 April 2009.

Council Decision 2009/426/JHA of 16 December 2008 on the strengthening of Eurojust and amending Decision 2002/187/JHA setting up Eurojust with a view to reinforcing the fight against serious crime, O.J.E.U. L138/14, 4 June 2009.

Council Decision 2009/371/JHA of 6 April 2009 establishing the European Police Office (Europol), O.J.E.U. L121/37, 15 May 2009.

Council Framework Decision 2009/829/JHA of 23 October 2009 on the application, between Member States of the European Union, of the principle of mutual recognition to decisions on supervision measures as an alternative to provisional detention, O.J.E.U. L294/20, 11 November 2009.

Resolution of the Council of 20 November 2009 on a Roadmap for strengthening procedural rights of suspected or accused persons in criminal proceedings, O.J.E.U. C295/1, 4 December 2009.

Council Decision 2009/934/JHA of 30 November 2009 adopting the implementing rules governing Europol's relations with partners, including the exchange of personal data and classified information, O.J.E.U. L325/6, 15 December 2009.

Council Decision 2009/936/JHA of 30 November 2009 adopting the implementing rules for Europol analysis work files, O.J.E.U. L325/14, 11 December 2009.

Council of the European Union, *The Stockholm Programme: An open and secure Europe serving and protecting the citizens,* O.J.E.U. C115/1, 4 May 2010.

Directive 2010/64/EU of the European Parliament and of the Council of 20 October 2010 on the right to interpretation and translation in criminal proceedings, O.J.E.U. L280/1, 26 October 2010.

Council Decision 2011/70/CFSP of 31 January 2011 updating the list of persons, groups and entities subject to Articles 2, 3 and 4 of Common Position 2001/931/CFSP on the application of specific measures to combat terrorism, O.J.E.U. L28/57, 2 February 2011.

Council Decision 2011/430/CFSP of 18 July 2011 updating the list of persons, groups and entities subject to Articles 2, 3 and 4 of Common Position 2001/931/CFSP on the application of specific measures to combat terrorism, O.J.E.U. L188/47, 19 July 2011.

Council Decision 2011/701/CFSP of 21 October 2011 amending Decision 2011/430/CFSP in order to update the list of persons, groups and entities subject to Articles 2, 3 and 4 of Common Position 2001/931/CFSP on the application of specific measures to combat terrorism, O.J.E.U. L277/18, 22 October 2011.

Regulation (EU) No 1077/2011 of the European Parliament and of the Council of 25 October 2011 establishing a European Agency for the operational management of large-scale IT systems in the area of freedom, security and justice, O.J.E.U. L286/1, 1 November 2011.

Directive 2011/99/EU of the European Parliament and of the Council of 13 December 2011 on the European protection order, O.J.E.U. L338/2, 21 December 2011.

Directive 2012/13/EU of the European Parliament and of the Council of 22 May 2012 on the right to information in criminal proceedings, O.J.E.U. L142/1, 1 June 2012.

Council Decision 2012/333/CFSP of 25 June 2012 updating the list of persons, groups and entities subject to Articles 2, 3 and 4 of Common Position 2001/931/CFSP on the application of specific measures to combat terrorism and repealing Decision 2011/872/CFSP, O.J.E.U. L165/72, 26 June 2012.

Directive 2012/29/EU of the European Parliament and of the Council of 25 October 2012 establishing minimum standards on the rights, support and protection of victims of crime, and replacing Council Framework Decision 2001/220/JHA, O.J.E.U. L315/57, 14 November 2012.

Treaty on the European Union, O.J.E.U. C326/1, 26 October 2012.

Treaty on the Functioning of the European Union, O.J.E.U. C326/1, 26 October 2012.

Protocol (No. 7) on the privileges and immunities of the European Union, O.J.E.U. C326/1, 26 October 2012.

Council Decision 2012/686/CFSP of 6 November 2012 amending Decision 2012/333/CFSP updating the list of persons, groups and entities subject to Articles 2, 3 and 4 of Common Position 2001/931/CFSP on the application of specific measures to combat terrorism, O.J.E.U. L307/80, 7 November 2012.

Regulation (EU, EURATOM) 883/2013 of the European Parliament and of the Council of 11 September 2013 concerning investigations conducted by the European Anti-Fraud Office (OLAF) and repealing Regulation (EC) No 1073/1999 of the European Parliament and of the Council and Council Regulation (Euratom) No 1074/1999, O.J.E.U. L248/1, 18 September 2013.

Directive 2013/48/EU of the European Parliament and of the Council of 22 October 2013 on the right of access to a lawyer in criminal proceedings and in European arrest warrant proceedings, and on the right to have a third party informed upon deprivation of liberty and to communicate with third persons and with consular authorities while deprived of liberty, O.J.E.U. L294/1, 6 November 2013.

Council Decision 2014/72/CFSP of 10 February 2014 updating and amending the list of persons, groups and entities subject to Articles 2, 3 and 4 of Common Position 2001/931/CFSP on the application of specific measures to combat terrorism, and repealing Decision 2013/395/CFSP, O.J.E.U. L40/56, 11 February 2014.

Directive 2014/41/EU of the European Parliament and of the Council of 3 April 2014 regarding the European Investigation Order in criminal matters, O.J.E.U. L130/1, 1 May 2014.

Council Decision (CFSP) 2015/521 of 26 March 2015 updating and amending the list of persons, groups and entities subject to Articles 2,3, and 4 of Common Position 2001/931 CFSP on the application of specific measures to combat terrorism, and repealing Decision 2014/483/CFSP, O.J.E.U. L82/107, 27 March 2015.

Council Decision (CFSP) 2015/1835 of 12 October 2015 defining the statute, seat and operational rules of the European Defence Agency, O.J.E.U. L266/55, 13 October 2015.

Regulation (EU) 2015/2219 of the European Parliament and of the Council of 25 November 2015 on the European Union Agency for Law Enforcement Training (CEPOL) and replacing and repealing Council Decision 2005/681/JHA, O.J.E.U. L319/1, 4 December 2015.

Directive (EU) 2016/343 of the European Parliament and of the Council of 9 March 2016 on the strengthening of certain aspects of the presumption of innocence and of the right to be present at the trial in criminal proceedings, O.J.E.U. L65/1, 11 March 2016.

Council Decision (CFSP) 2016/628 of 21 April 2016 updating and amending the list of persons, groups and entities subject to Articles 2, 3 and 4 of Common Position 2001/931/CFSP on the application of specific measures to combat terrorism, and amending Decision (CFSP) 2015/2430, O.J.E.U. L106/24, 22 April 2016.

Directive (EU) 2016/680 of the European Parliament and the Council of 27 April 2016 on the protection of natural persons with regard to the processing of personal data by competent authorities for the purposes of the prevention, investigation, detection or prosecution of criminal offences or the execution of criminal penalties, and on the free movement of such data, and repealing Council Framework Decision 2008/977/JHA, O.J.E.U. L119/89, 4 May 2016.

Directive (EU) 2016/681 of the European Parliament and of the Council on the use of Passenger Name Record (PNR) data for the prevention, detection, investigation and prosecution of terrorist offences and serious crime, O.J.E.U. L119/132, 27 April 2016.

Regulation (EU) 2016/679 of the European Parliament and the Council of 27 April 2016 on the protection of natural persons with regard to the processing of personal data and on the free movement of such data, and repealing Directive 95/46/EC (General Data Protection Regulation), O.J.E.U. L119/1, 4 May 2016.

Directive (EU) 2016/800 of the European Parliament and of the Council of 11 May 2016 on procedural safeguards for children who are suspects or accused persons in criminal proceedings, O.J.E.U. L132/1, 21 May 2016.

Regulation (EU) 2016/794 of the European Parliament and of the Council of 11 May 2016 on the European Union Agency for Law Enforcement Cooperation (Europol) and replacing and repealing Council Decisions 2009/371/JHA, 2009/934/JHA, 2009/935/JHA, 2009/936/JHA and 2009/968/JHA, O.J.E.U. L135/53, 24 May 2016.

Regulation (EU) 2016/1624 of the European Parliament and of the Council of 14 September 2016 on the European Border and Coast Guard and amending Regulation (EU) 2016/399 of the European Parliament and of the Council and repealing Regulation (EC) No 863/2007 of the European Parliament and of the

Council, Council Regulation (EC) No 2007/2004 and Council Decision 2005/267/ EC, O.J.E.U. L251/1, 16 September 2016.

Directive (EU) 2016/1919 of the European Parliament and of the Council of 26 October 2016 on legal aid for suspects and accused persons in criminal proceedings and for requested persons in European arrest warrant proceedings, O.J.E.U. L297/1, 4 November 2016.

Council Decision (CFSP) 2017/154 of 27 January 2017 updating the list of persons, groups and entities subject to Articles 2, 3 and 4 of Common Position 2001/931/CFSP on the application of specific measures to combat terrorism, and repealing Decision (CFSP) 2016/1136, O.J.E.U. L23/21, 28 January 2017.

Directive (EU) 2017/541 of the European Parliament and of the Council of 15 March 2017 on combating terrorism and replacing Council Framework Decision 2002/475/JHA and amending Council Decision 2005/671/JHA, O.J.E.U. L88/6, 31 March 2017.

Council Decision (CFSP) 2017/972 of 8 June 2017 updating and amending the list of persons, groups and entities subject to Articles 2, 3 and 4 of Common Position 2001/931/CFSP on the application of specific measures to combat terrorism, and amending Decision (CFSP) 2017/154, O.J.E.U. L146/139, 9 June 2017.

Council Decision (CFSP) 2017/1426 of 4 August 2017 updating the list of persons, groups and entities subject to Articles 2, 3 and 4 of Common Position 2001/931/CFSP on the application of specific measures to combat terrorism, and repealing Decision (CFSP) 2017/154, O.J.E.U. L204/95, 5 August 2017.

Council Regulation (EU) 2017/1939 of 12 October 2017 implementing enhanced cooperation on the establishment of the European Public Prosecutor's Office ('the EPPO'), O.J.E.U. L283/1, 31 October 2017.

Council Decision (CFSP) 2017/2072 of 13 November 2017 updating and amending the list of persons, groups and entities subject to Articles 2, 3 and 4 of Common Position 2001/931/CFSP on the application of specific measures to combat terrorism, and amending Decision (CFSP) 2017/1426, O.J.E.U. L295/57, 14 November 2017.

Council Decision (CFSP) 2017/20173 of 13 November 2017 amending Common Position 2001/931/CFSP on the application of specific measures to combat terrorism, O.J.E.U. L295/59, 14 November 2017.

Council Decision (CFSP) 2018/1084 of July 2018 updating the list of persons, groups and entities subject to Articles 2, 3 and 4 if Common Position 2001/931/ CFSP on the application of specific measures to combat terrorism, and repealing Decision (CSFP) 2018/475, O.J.E.U. L194/144, 31 July 2018.

Regulation (EU) 2018/1805 of the European Parliament and of the Council of 14 November 2018 on the mutual recognition of freezing orders and confiscation orders, O.J.E.U. L303/1, 28 November 2018.

Regulation (EU) 2018/1726 of the European Parliament and of the Council of 14 November 2018 on the European Union Agency for the Operational Management of Large-Scale IT Systems in the Area of Freedom, Security and Justice (eu-LISA), and amending Regulation (EC) No 1987/2006 and Council Decision

2007/533/JHA and repealing Regulation (EU) No 1077/2011, O.J.E.U. L295/99, 21 November 2018.

Regulation (EU) 2018/1727 of the European Parliament and of the Council of 14 November 2018 on the European Union Agency for Criminal Justice Cooperation (Eurojust) and replacing and repealing Council Decision 2002/187/JHA, O.J.E.U. L295/138, 21 November 2018.

Regulation (EU) 2018/1862 of the European Parliament and of the Council of 28 November 2018 on the establishment, operation and use of the Schengen Information System (SIS) in the field of police cooperation and judicial cooperation in criminal matters, amending and repealing Council Decision 2007/533/JHA, and repealing Regulation (EC) No 1986/2006 of the European Parliament and of the Council and Commission Decisions 2010/261/EU, O.J.E.U. L312/56, 7 December 2018.

Regulation (EU) 2019/816 of the European Parliament and of the Council of 17 April 2019 establishing a centralised system for the identification of Member States holding conviction information on third-country nationals and stateless persons (ECRIS-TCN) to supplement the European Criminal Records Information System and amending Regulation (EU) 2018/1726, O.J.E.U. L135/1, 22 May 2019.

Regulation (EU) 2019/817 of the European Parliament and of the Council of 20 May 2019 on establishing a framework for interoperability between EU information systems in the field of borders and visa and amending Regulations (EC) No 767/2008, (EU) 2016/399, (EU) 2017/2226, (EU) 2018/1240, (EU) 2018/1726 and (EU) 2018/1861 of the European Parliament and of the Council and Council Decisions 2004/512/EC and 2008/633/JHA, O.J.E.U. L135/27, 22 May 2019.

Regulation (EU) 2019/818 of the European Parliament and of the Council of 20 May 2019 on establishing a framework for interoperability between EU information systems in the field of police and judicial cooperation, asylum and migration and amending Regulations (EU) 2018/1726, (EU) 2018/1862 and (EU) 2019/816, O.J.E.U. L135/85, 22 May 2019.

Regulation (EU) 2019/1896 of the European Parliament and of the Council of 13 November 2019 on the European Border and Coast Guard and repealing Regulations (EU) No 1052/2013 and (EU) 2016/1624, O.J.E.U. L295/1, 14 November 2019.

European Commission, Proposal for a Regulation (EU) 2018/1862 on the establishment, operation and use of the Schengen Information System (SIS) in the field of police cooperation and judicial cooperation in criminal matters as regards the entry of alerts by Europol, COM(2020)791 final, Brussels, 9 December 2020.

European Commission, Proposal for a Regulation of the European Parliament and of the Council on automated data exchange for police cooperation ('Prüm II') amending Council Decisions 2008/615/JHA and 2008/616/JHA and Regulations (EU) 2018/1726, 2019/817 and 2019/818 of the European Parliament and of the Council, COM(2021)784 final, Brussels, 8 December 2021.

Regulation (EU) 2022/838 of the European Parliament and of the Council of 30 May 2022 amending Regulation (EU) 2018/1727 as regards the preservation, analysis and storage at Eurojust of evidence relating to genocide, crimes against humanity, war crimes and related criminal offences, O.J.E.U. L 148/1, 31 May 2022.

Regulation (EU) 2022/991 of the European Parliament and of the Council of 8 June 2022 amending Regulation (EU) 2016/794, as regards Europol's cooperation with private parties, the processing of personal data by Europol in support of criminal investigations, and Europol's role in research and innovation, O.J.E.U. L169/1, 27 June 2022.

Directive (EU) 2023/977 of the European Parliament and of the Council of 10 May 2023 on the exchange of information between the law enforcement authorities of Member States and repealing Council Framework Decision 2006/960/JHA, O.J.E.U. L134/1, 22 May 2023.

EU's External Agreements

Cooperation Agreement between Interpol and Europol, Brussels, 5 November 2001.

Agreement between the United States of America and the European Police Office, European Council, Justice, Home Affairs and Civil Protection, 14581/01, 2396th meeting, Brussels, 6 December 2001.

Supplemental Agreement between the Europol Police Office and the United States of America on the exchange of personal data and related information, Copenhagen, 20 December 2002.

Agreement between the European Union and Japan on mutual legal assistance in criminal matters, O.J.E.U. L39/20, 12 February 2010.

European Data Protection Supervisor, Opinion of 9 December 2011 on the Proposal for a Council Decision on the conclusion of the Agreement between the United States of America and the European Union on the use and transfer of Passenger Name Records to the United States Department of Homeland Security, O.J.E.U. C35/03, 9 February 2012.

Agreement between the United States of America and the European Union on the use and transfer of passenger name records to the United States Department of Homeland Security, O.J.E.U. L215/5, 11 August 2012.

Council of the European Union, *Agreement between Canada and the European Union on the transfer and processing of Passenger Name Record*, No. 12657/5/13, Brussels, 23 June 2014.

Letter of Intent between Europol and Aseanapol, 85th Interpol General Assembly, Bali, 8 November 2016.

Agreement between the United States of America and the European Union on the protection of personal information relating to the prevention, investigation, detection, and prosecution of criminal offences, O.J.E.U. L336/3, 10 December 2016.

Other EU Documents: Reports, Speeches, Press Releases and Other Documents

Amsterdam European Council, Presidency Conclusions, D/97/2, 16–17 June 1997.

Tampere European Council, Conclusions of the Presidency, SN 200/99, Brussels, 15–16 October 1999.

Tampere European Council, Annex on the body to draft a Charter of Fundamental Rights, 15–16 October 1999.

European Parliament, Resolution of 16 September 1999 on the establishment of the Charter of Fundamental Rights, O.J.E.C. C54, 25 February 2000.

Santa Maria da Feira European Council, Conclusions of the Presidency, 19–20 June 2000.

Commission of the European Communities, Communication from the Commission to the Council and the European Parliament. Biannual update of the scoreboard to review progress on the creation of an Area of 'Freedom, Security and Justice' in the European Union (second half of 2000), COM(2000) 782 final, Brussels, 30 November 2000.

European Council, Programme of measures to implement the principle of mutual recognition of recognition of decisions in criminal matters, O.J.E.C. C12/10, 15 January 2001.

Commission of the European Communities, Communication from the Commission to the Council and the European Parliament. Biannual update of the scoreboard to review progress on the creation of an Area of 'Freedom, Security and Justice' in the European Union (first half of 2001), COM(2001) 278 final, Brussels, 23 May 2001.

Declaration of the Council of the European Union, Special Council meeting, General Affairs, No. 11795/01, Brussels, 12 September 2001.

European Commission, Proposal for a Council Framework Decision on combating terrorism, COM(2001) 521 final, 19 September 2001.

European Parliament, Resolution on the extraordinary European Council meeting in Brussels on 21 September 2001, B5-0665, 0666, 0667, 0668, 0670, 0672 and 0674/2001, Brussels, 21 September 2001.

Commission of the European Communities, 'European Governance—A white paper', COM(2001) 428 final, O.J.E.C. C287/1, 12 October 2001.

Council of the European Union, 'Proposal for a Council Framework Decision on combating terrorism', doc. 12647/2/01 rev. 2, Brussels, 8 November 2001.

Commission of the European Communities, Communication from the Commission, 'European Governance: Better lawmaking', COM(2002) 275 final, Brussels, 5 June 2002.

Commission of the European Communities, Communication from the Commission, 'A new partnership with South East Asia', COM(2003) 399 final, Brussels, 9 July 2003.

European Council, 'Declaration of 25 March 2004 on combating terrorism', 2574th meeting, Brussels, 30 March 2004.

Council of the European Union, 'EU Plan of Action on Combating Terrorism', No. 10586/04, Brussels, 15 June 2004.

Council of the European Union, Conclusions of the Cologne European Council (3 and 4 June 1999), 'Extract concerning the Charter of fundamental Rights', Presidency Conclusions, SN 150/99, Brussels, 23 March 2005.

Council of the European Union, 'The European Union Counter-Terrorism Strategy', No. 14469/5/05, Brussels, 30 November 2005.

European Commission, Communication from the Commission to the European Parliament and the Council. 'The EU Counter-Terrorism Policy: main achievements and future challenges', COM(2010)386 final, Brussels, 20 July 2010.

European Commission, 'Strengthening mutual trust in the European judicial area—A Green Paper on the application of EU criminal justice legislation in the field of detention', COM(2011) 327 final, Brussels, 14 June 2011.

Council of the European Union, Presidency, Working Group on Information Exchange and Data Protection (DAPIX), '*Council Framework Decision 2006/960/ JHA*—Assessment of compliance pursuant to Article 11(2)—Draft Report', No. 13970/11, Brussels, 13 September 2011.

European Data Protection Supervisor, Opinion of 9 December 2011 on the Proposal for a Council Decision on the conclusion of the Agreement between the United States of America and the European Union on the use and transfer of Passenger Name Records to the United States Department of Homeland Security, O.J.E.U. C35/03, 9 February 2012.

European Parliament, Special Committee on Organised Crime, Corruption and Money Laundering (CRIM), 'Approche intégrée du renseignement criminel dans la lutte contre le crime organisé: dynamique locale, nationale et européenne', Hearing on 19 February 2013: available at http://www.europarl.europa.eu/document/activities/cont/201302/20130221ATT61502/20130221ATT61502EN.pdf (last accessed on 10 December 2020).

European Parliament resolution of 22 May 2012 on an EU approach to criminal law (2010/2310(INI)), O.J.E.U. C264/02E, 13 September 2013

European Parliament, Committee on Civil Liberties (LIBE Committee), Justice and Home Affairs, Draft Report on the US NSA surveillance programme, surveillance bodies in various Member States and their impact on EU citizens' fundamental rights and on transatlantic cooperation in Justice and Home Affairs, 2013/2188(INI), 8 January 2014.

European Commission, Communication from the Commission to the European Parliament, the Council, the European Economic and Social Committee and the Committee of the Regions 'The EU Justice Agenda for 2020—Strengthening Trust, Mobility and Growth within the Union', COM(2014)144 final, Strasbourg, 11 March 2014.

European Commission, Communication from the Commission to the European Parliament and the Council, 'Final implementation report of the EU Internal Security Strategy 2010-2014', COM(2014) 365 final, Brussels, 20 June 2014.

European Council, Conclusions of the European Council (26–27 June 2014), General Secretariat of the Council to Delegations, EUCO 79/14, Brussels, 27 June 2014.

European Commission, 'Report from the Commission to the European Parliament and the Council on the implementation of the Council Framework Decision 2008/919/JHA of 28 November 2008 amending Framework Decision 2002/475/JHA on combating terrorism', COM(2014) 554 final, Brussels, 5 September 2014.

EU IntCen, Intelligence Analysis Centre, Fact Sheet, 5 February 2015: available at https://www.statewatch.org/media/documents/news/2016/may/eu-intcen-factsheet.pdf (last accessed on 10 December 2020).

European Commission, Communication from the Commission to the European Parliament, the Council, the European Economic and Social Committee and the Committee of the Regions, 'The European Agenda on Security', COM(2015) 185 final, Strasbourg, 28 April 2015.

European Commission, 'EU proposes to scale up its partnership with ASEAN' *press release*, Brussels, 19 May 2015.

Council of the European Union, Presidency, Draft Council Conclusions on the Renewed European Union Internal Security Strategy 2015–2020, No. 9798/15, Brussels, 10 June 2015.

European Parliament, 'Motion for the European Parliament Resolution on the role of the EU within the UN. How better achieve EU foreign policy goals', Committee on Foreign affairs, Rapporteur: Paavo Väyrynen, 2015/2104(INI), 21 October 2015.

European Commission, Proposal for a Directive of the European Parliament and of the Council on combating terrorism and replacing Council Framework Decision 2002/475/JHA on combating terrorism, COM(2015) 625 final, Brussels, 2 December 2015.

Council of the European Union, Council conclusions on the EU Regional Strategy for Syria and Iraq as well as the Da'esh threat, General Secretariat of the Council to Delegations, Brussels, 23 May 2016.

Council of the European Union, From the Presidency to the Standing Committee on Operational Cooperation on Internal Security, Permanent Representatives Committee and the Council, 'Foreign Fighters—Enhancing the information exchange', No. 13777/16, Brussels, 4 November 2016.

European Commission, 'Security Union: Commission reports on the implementation of the EU-US TFTP and PNR Agreements' *press release*, Brussels, 19 January 2017.

European Parliament, Proposal for a Decision pursuant to Rule 197 of the Rules of Procedure on setting up a special committee on terrorism, its responsibilities, numerical strength and terms of office, 2017/2758(RSO), Plenary sitting 2014–2019, 5 July 2017.

Council of the European Union, 'SIS II—2017 Statistics' eu-LISA to Delegations, No. 8279/18, Brussels, 24 April 2018.

European Parliament, Report on the implementation of Directive 2012/29/EU establishing minimum standards on the rights, support and protection of victims of crime, 2016/2328(INI), Plenary sitting, 14 May 2018.

European Commission, Communication from the Commission to the European Parliament, the European Council, the Council, the European Economic and Social Committee and the Committee of the Regions, 'The principles of subsidiarity and proportionality: Strengthening their role in the EU's policymaking' COM(2018) 703 final, Strasbourg, 23 October 2018.

European Commission, 'Report from the Commission to the European Parliament and the Council on the implementation of Directive 2010/64/EU of the European Parliament and of the Council of 20 October 2010 on the right to interpretation and translation in criminal proceedings', COM(2018) 857 final, Brussels, 18 December 2018.

European Commission, Communication from the Commission to the European Parliament, the European Council and the Council 'Further strengthening the Rule of Law within the Union. State of play and possible next steps', COM(2019)163 final, Brussels, 3 April 2019.

European Commission, 'Rule of Law: The Commission opens a debate to strengthen the rule of law in the EU', *press release*, Brussels, 3 April 2019.

Europol, 'European Union Terrorism Situation and Trend Report (TE-SAT) 2019', *report*, 27 June 2019.

Vierstraete-Verlinde, Marc Alphonse, 'EU ACTIONPLAN on CT and P/CVE, South-East Asia PRIORITIES', EU Delegation to Indonesia and Brunei Darussalam and Mission to ASEAN, Jakarta, December 2019, 1–22.

European Parliament, Motion for a Resolution to wind up the debate on the statements by the Council and the Commission pursuant to Rule 132(2) of the Rules of Procedure on ongoing hearings under Article 7(1) of the TEU regarding Poland and Hungary (2020/2513(RSP)), plenary sitting, 9 January 2020.

Council of the European Union, Council Conclusions on EU Priorities in UN Human Rights Fora in 2020, General Secretariat of the Council to Delegations, No. 5802/20, Brussels, 17 February 2020.

Council of the European Union, 'Enlargement and Stabilisation and Association Process. The Republic of North Macedonia and the Republic of Albania—General Conclusions' General Secretariat of the Council to Delegations, No. 7002/20, Bruxelles, 25 March 2020.

European Commission, Regulatory Scrutiny Board, 'Rules of Procedure of the Regulatory Scrutiny Board' replacing the Rules of Procedure of the Regulatory Scrutiny Board of 5 October 2016, Ares(2016)5764766), Ares(2020)2060246, Bruxelles, 15 April 2020.

Council of the European Union, 'Council Conclusions on EU External Action on Preventing and Countering Terrorism and Violent Extremism' General Secretariat of the Council to Delegations, No. 8868/20, Brussels, 16 June 2020.

European Commission, 'Report from the Commission to the European Parliament and the Council on the implementation of Council Framework Decision of

13 June 2002 on the European arrest warrant and the surrender procedures between Member States', COM(2020) 270 final, Brussels, 2 July 2020.

Other Regional Organisations: Documents

Organisation of American States, *American Declaration of the Rights and Duties of Man*, 9th International Conference of American States, Bogotá, 2 May 1948.

Organisation of American States, Inter-American Commission on Human Rights, Resolution of Consultation of Ministers of Foreign Affairs, 5th meeting, Santiago, 12–18 August 1959.

Organisation of American States, *American Convention on Human Rights* (Pact of San José), San José, 22 November 1969.

Organisation of African Unity, Assembly, *African Charter on Human and People's Rights* (Banjul Charter), Banjul, 27 June 1981.

League of Arab States, *The Arab Convention for the Suppression of Terrorism*, Cairo, 22 April 1998.

Council of the League of Arab States, *The Arab Charter on Human Rights*, Tunis, 22 May 2004.

Interregional Sources

ASEAN-EU Documents

Joint Declaration, ASEAN-EC Ministerial Meeting, Brussels, 21 November 1978.

Cooperation Agreement between Member Countries of ASEAN and European Community, Kuala Lumpur, 7 March 1980.

Commission of the European Communities, 'Towards a New Asia Strategy', Communication from the Commission to the Council, COM(94) 314 final, Brussels, 13 July 1994.

Joint Declaration on co-operation to combat terrorism, 14th EU-ASEAN Ministerial Meeting, No. 5811/03, Brussels, 27–28 January 2003.

Nuremberg Declaration on an EU-ASEAN Enhanced Partnership, Nuremberg, 15 March 2007.

Phnom Penh Agenda for the Implementation of the ASEAN-EU Plan of Action (2009–2010), Phnom Penh, 28 May 2009.

ASEAN-EU Enhanced Partnership Action Plan (2013–2017), *Bandar Seri Begawan Plan of Action to strengthen the ASEAN-EU Enhanced Partnership (2013–2017)*, ASEAN-EU Ministerial Meeting, Bandar Seri Begawan, 27 April 2012.

European Union External Action, *The European Union and the Association of South East Asian Nations: Towards an Ever Stronger Natural Partnership*, Fact Sheet, No. 140722/03, Brussels, 22 July 2014.

Co-Chair's Statement of the 20th EU-ASEAN Ministerial Meeting, No. 140723/03, Brussels, 23 July 2014.

European Union External Action, *Fact sheet EU-ASEAN relations*, Brussels, 7 April 2016.

Letter of Intent between Europol and Aseanapol, 85th Interpol General Assembly, Bali, 8 November 2016.

European Union External Action—ASEAN Secretariat, *ASEAN-EU Plan of Action (2018–2022)*, Manila, 6 August 2017.

Council of the EU, 'Press statement of the ASEAN-EU commemorative summit on the occasion of the 40th anniversary of the establishment of ASEAN-EU dialogue relations', Press office—General Secretariat of the Council, Déclarations et Observations 654/17, 14 November 2017.

ASEAN-EU Work Plan to Combat Terrorism and Transnational Crime (2022–2024), referred to in 2021 Joint Statement of the 15th ASEAN Ministerial Meeting on transnational crime 'We care, we prepare, we prosper', 29 September 2021.

Plan of Action to implement the ASEAN-EU Strategic Partnership (2023–2027), Phnom Penh, 4 August 2022.

ASEAN-EU Commemorative Summit 2022, Joint Leader's Statement, 45th anniversary of ASEAN-EU Dialogue Relations, Brussels, 14 December 2022.

ASEM

Statement of ASEM Leaders on International Terrorism, Ulaanbaatar, 15 July 2016.

ASEM Foreign Ministers' Meeting (15–16 December 2019) Chair's Statement, Madrid, 16 December 2019.

'Partnership for Prosperity and Stability in the New Millennium', Final Chair Statement, 3rd ASEM Summit (ASEM3), Seoul, 20–21 October 2000.

Relevant National Legislations and Other Documents

ASEAN Member States

Brunei Darussalam

Internal Security Act 1982, No. 13/1982 (revised ed. 2002), Laws of Brunei, Chapter 133, p. 1.

Anti-Terrorism (Financial and Other Measures) (revised ed. 2008), Laws of Brunei, Chapter 197, No. S41/02, 30 November 2002, p. 1.

Anti-Terrorism Order 2011, Brunei Darussalam Government Gazette, No. S45/2011, 1 August 2011, p. 609.

Anti-Terrorism (Amendment) Order 2012, Order made under Article 83(3) of the Constitution of Brunei Darussalam, Brunei Darussalam Government Gazette, No. 48/2012, 2 July 2012, p. 657.

Cambodia

Constitution of the Kingdom of Cambodia, Constitutional Assembly, 2nd plenary session, 21 September 1993.

Law on Anti-Money Laundering and Combating the Financing of Terrorism, 24 June 2007 (revised ed. 3 June 2013).

Law on Counter Terrorism of 20 July 2007, Nation Religion King, Royal Gazette, Year 7, No. 55, week 4, 27 July 2007.

Sub-decree on Freezing of Property of Designated Terrorists and Organizations, 10 March 2014.

Law on Anti-Money Laundering and Financing of Terrorism (2020 AML-CFT Law), 27 June 2020.

Indonesia

Law No. 1/1979 of the Republic of Indonesia concerning Extradition, State Gazette of the Republic of Indonesia Year 1979 No. 2, Supplement No. 3130, 18 January 1979.

Extradition (Republic of Indonesia) Regulations 1994 No. 441 transposing the Extradition Treaty of 22 April 1992 between Government of the Republic of Indonesia and Government of Australia, Statutory Rules, Attorney-General, 24 November 1994.

Law No. 36/1999 regarding Telecommunications, State Gazette, 8 September 1999.

Government Regulation in Lieu of Legislation of the Republic of Indonesia No. 1/2002 combating criminal acts of terrorism, President of the Republic of Indonesia, State Gazette, 18 October 2002.

Law No. 15/2002 on money laundering crimes, State Gazette No. 20, Supplement No. 4191, 17 April 2002.

Law No. 25/2003 on the amendment to Law No. 15/2002 on money laundering crimes, State Gazette No. 30, Supplement No. 4191, 13 October 2003.

Law No. 12/2005 on the ratification of the International Covenant on Civil and Political Rights, State Gazette of the Republic of Indonesia Year 2005 No. 118, Supplement to State Gazette No. 4557.

Law No.1/2006 concerning mutual legal assistance in criminal matters, State Gazette Year 2006 No. 18, 3 March 2006.

Law No. 11/2008 regarding Electronic Information and Transaction (EIT Law), State Gazette Year 2008 No. 58, 21 April 2008.

Law No. 14/2008 regarding Disclosure of Public information, State Gazette Year 2008 No. 14, 30 April 2008.

Government Regulation No. 82/2012 *regarding Provision of Electronic System and Transaction* (Reg. 82), State Gazette Year 2012, No. 189, 15 October 2012.

Law No. 9/2013 on the Prevention and Eradication of Terrorism Financing Act, State Gazette Year 2013 No. 50, 13 March 2013.

Law No. 5/2018 amending the Law No. 15/2003 on Stipulation of Government Regulation in lieu of Law No. 1/2002 on Eradication of Criminal Acts of Terrorism, 21 June 2018.

Government Regulation No.77/2019 on the Prevention of the Criminal Act of Terrorism and Protection of Investigators, Public Prosecutors, Judges and Correctional Officers, 12 November 2019.

Government Regulation No. 35/2020 on Providing Compensation, Restitution, and Assistance to Witnesses and Victims (including victims of terrorism), 7 July 2020.

Lao PDR

Law on Anti-Money Laundering and Counter-Financing of Terrorism, No. 50/NA, 21 July 2014.

Malaysia

Criminal Procedure Code, Act 593, F.M.S. Cap. 6, 1935; latest amended by Act A1431.

Evidence Act, Act 56, Ordinance No. 11, 1950; latest amended by Act A1527.

Penal Code, Act 574, F.M.S. Cap. 45, 1963; latest amendment made by Act A1487.

Police Act 1967, Act 41; latest amendment made by Act 344 of 6 October 1988.

Anti-Money Laundering, Anti-Terrorism Financing and Proceeds of Unlawful Activities Act 2001, Act 613, Gazette, 4 July 2001.

Personal Data Protection Act 2010, Act 709, Gazette, 10 June 2010.

Security Offences (Special Measures) Act 2012, Act 747, Gazette, 22 June 2012; latest amended by Act A1487.

Prevention of Terrorism Act 2015 (POTA), Act 769, Gazette, 4 June 2015.

Special Measures against Terrorism in Foreign Countries 2015, Act 770, Gazette, 4 June 2015.

Myanmar

Counter-Terrorism Law 2014, No. 23/2014, 4 June 2014.

State Administration Council,*Law No. 21/2021 amending Counter-Terrorism Law*, 1 August 2021.

Philippines

Human Security Act of 2007, Republic Act No. 9372, 6 March 2007.

Data Privacy Act of 2012, Republic Act No. 10173, 25 July 2011.

The Terrorism Financing Prevention and Suppression Act of 2012, Republic Act No. 10168, 20 June 2012.

Act to prevent, prohibit and penalize terrorism, thereby repealing Republic Act No. 9372, otherwise known as the 'Human Security Act of 2007' (Anti-Terrorism Act of 2020), Republic Act No. 11579, 22 July 2020.

Singapore

Singapore's Extradition Act (Chapter 103) Act 14/1968; revised on 30 December 2000.

United Nations (Anti-terrorism measures) Regulations (Chapter 339, Section 2 (1)), Regulation 1, G.N. No. S561/2001, The Statutes of the Republic of Singapore, 13 November 2001.

Terrorism (Suppression of Financing) Act 2002 (Chapter 325), No. 16/2002, Revised in 2003, The Statutes of the Republic of Singapore, 29 January 2003.

Public Order Act (Chapter 257A), No. 15/2009, Government Gazette, 9 October 2009; revised on 31 May 2012.

Criminal Procedure Code (Chapter 68), No. 15/2010, revised in 2012, The Statutes of the Republic of Singapore, 2 January 2011.

Personal Data Protection Act 2012, No. 26/2012, Government Gazette No. 25/2012, 7 December 2012.

Organised Crime Act 2015, No. 26/2015, Government Gazette No. 27, 21 august 2015.

Public Order and Safety (Special Powers) Act 2018, No. 26/2018, Government Gazette No. 20, 20 April 2018.

Serious Crimes and Counter-Terrorism (Miscellaneous Amendments) Act 2018, Government Gazette No. 51, 31 December 2018.

Thailand

Criminal Code, B.E. 2499, 1956; amended for the Criminal Code (No. 17), B.E. 2547, 2003.

Anti-Terrorist Financing Act 2013, B.E. 2556, 1 February 2013.

Vietnam

Instructions on anti-terrorism and prevention, No. 25/2007/CT-TTg, Prime Minister of the Socialist Republic of Vietnam, 15 November 2007.

Law on Prevention of Money Laundering, No. 07/2012/QH13, National Assembly, 18 June 2012.

Anti-Terrorism Law, No. 28/2013/QH13, National Assembly, 12 June 2013.

Criminal Code, No. 100/2015/QH13, National Assembly, 27 November 2015.

EU Member States *(Sample)*

Belgium

Loi organique C-98/07272 du 30 novembre 1998 des services de renseignement et de sécurité, Moniteur Belge (M.B.) 18 December 1998, p. 40312.

Loi C-2003/09963 du 19 décembre 2003 relative aux infractions terroristes, M.B. 29 December 2003, p. 61689.

Loi C-2013/09097 du 18 février 2013 modifiant le livre II, titre I[er]ter du Code pénal, M.B. 4 March 2013, p. 13233.

Loi C-2015/09385 du 20 juillet 2015 visant à renforcer la lutte contre le terrorisme, M.B. 5 August 2015, p. 49326.

Loi C-2016/09200 du 27 avril 2016 relative à des mesures complémentaires en matière de lutte contre le terrorisme, M.B. 9 May 2016, p. 30567.

Loi C-2016/30017 du 25 décembre 2016 portant des modifications diverses au Code d'instruction criminelle et au Code pénal, en vue d'améliorer les méthodes particulières de recherche et certaines mesures d'enquête concernant Internet, les communications électroniques et les télécommunications et créant une banque de données des empreintes vocales, M.B. 17 January 2017, p. 2738.

Loi C-2017/11752 du 30 mars 2017 modifiant la loi du 30 novembre 1998 organique des services de renseignement et de sécurité et l'article 259bis du Code Pénal, M.B. 28 April 2017, p. 53768.

France

Loi du 29 juillet 1881 sur la liberté de la presse, J.O.R.F. 30 July 1881, p. 4201.

Loi No. 86-1020 du 9 septembre 1986 relative à la lute contre le terrorisme et aux atteintes à la sûreté de l'Etat, J.O.R.F. 0210, 10 September 1986, p. 10956.

Loi No. 92-686 du 22 juillet 1992 portant réforme des dispositions du code pénal relatives à la répression des crimes et délits contre la nation, l'Etat et la paix publique, J.O.R.F. 0169, 23 July 1992, p. 9893.

Loi No. 92-1336 du 16 décembre 1992 relative à l'entrée en vigueur du nouveau code pénal et à la modification de certaines dispositions de droit pénal et de procédure pénale rendue nécessaire par cette entrée en vigueur, J.O.R.F. 0298, 23 December 1992, p. 17568.

Loi No. 95-73 du 21 janvier 1995 d'orientation et de programmation relative à la sécurité, J.O.R.F. 0020, 14 January 1995, p. 1249.

Loi No. 96-647 du 22 juillet 1996 tendant à renforcer la répression du terrorisme et des atteintes aux personnes dépositaires de l'autorité publique ou charges d'une mission de service public et comportant des dispositions relatives à la police judiciaire, J.O.R.F. 0170, 23 July 1996, p. 11104.

Loi No. 96-1235 du 30 décembre 1996 relative à la détention provisoire et aux perquisitions de nuit en matière de terrorisme, J.O.R.F. 1, 1 January 1997, p. 9.

Loi No. 97-1273 du 29 décembre 1997 tendant à faciliter le jugement des actes de terrorisme, J.O.R.F. 303, 31 December 1997, p. 19312.

Assemblée Nationale (Constitution du 4 octobre 1958, 11ème législature), Débats parlementaires – Session ordinaire de 2000-2001 (195ème séance): compte-rendu intégral de la 3ème séance du mardi 5 juin 2001, J.O.R.F. Année 2001, N° 39 [2] A. N. (C.R.), 6 June 2001, pp. 3863–3906.

Loi No. 2001-1062 du 15 novembre 2001 relative à la sécurité quotidienne, J.O.R.F. 266, 16 November 2001, p. 18215.

Loi No. 2002-1094 du 29 août 2002 d'orientation et de programmation pour la sécurité intérieure, J.O.R.F. 30 August 2002, p. 14398.

Loi No. 2002-239 du 18 mars 2003 pour la sécurité intérieure, J.O.R.F. 66, 19 March 2003, p. 4761.

Loi No. 2004-204 du 9 mars 2004 portant adaptation de la justice aux évolutions de la criminalité, J.O.R.F. 59, 10 March 2004, p. 4567.

Loi No. 2006-64 du 23 janvier 2006 relative à la lutte contre le terrorisme et portant dispositions diverses relatives à la sécurité et aux contrôles frontaliers, J.O.R.F. 0020, 24 January 2006, 1129.

Loi No. 2008-1245 du 1er décembre 2008 visant à prolonger l'application des articles 3, 6 et 9 de la loi No. 2006-64 du 23 janvier 2006 relative à la lutte contre le terrorisme et portant dispositions diverses relatives à la sécurité et aux contrôles frontaliers, J.O.R.F. 0280, 2 December 2008, p. 18361.

Loi No. 2011-267 du 14 mars 2011 d'orientation et de programmation pour la performance de la sécurité intérieure, J.O.R.F. 0062, 15 March 2011, p. 4582.

Loi No. 2011-392 du 14 avril 2011 relative à la garde à vue, J.O.R.F. 0089, 15 April 2011, p. 6610.

Loi No. 2012-1432 du 21 décembre 2012 relative à la sécurité et à la lutte contre le terrorisme, J.O.R.F 0298, 22 December 2012, p. 20281.

Décret 2014-445 du 30 avril 2014 *relatif aux missions et à l'organisation de la direction générale de la sécurité intérieure*, J.O.R.F. No. 0102, 2 May 2014.

Loi No. 2014-1353 du 13 novembre 2014 renforçant les dispositions relatives à la lutte contre le terrorisme, J.O.R.F. 0263, 14 November 2014, p. 19162.

Loi No. 2015-912 du 24 juillet 2015 relative au renseignement, J.O.R.F. 0171, 26 July 2015, p. 12735.

Loi No. 2016-339 du 22 mars 2016 relative à la prévention et à la lutte contre les incivilités, contre les atteintes à la sécurité publique et contre les actes terroristes dans les transports collectifs de voyageurs, J.O.R.F. 0070, 23 March 2016, text No. 2.

Loi No. 2016-731 du 3 juin 2016 renforçant la lutte contre le crime organisé, le terrorisme et leur financement, et améliorant l'efficacité et les garanties de la procédure pénale, J.O.R.F. 0129, 4 June 2016, text No. 1.

Décret No. 2017-1095 du 14 Juin 2017 relative au coordinateur nation du renseignement et de la lutte contre le terrorisme, à la coordination nationale du renseignement et de la lutte contre le terrorisme et au centre national de contre-terrorisme, J.O.R.F. No. 0139, 15 June 2017, text No. 1.

Loi No. 2017-1510 du 30 octobre 2017 renforçant la sécurité intérieure et la lutte contre le terrorisme, J.O.R.F. 0255, 31 October 2017, text No. 1.

Loi No. 2019-222 du 23 mars 2019 de programmation 2018-2022 et de réforme pour la justice, J.O.R.F. 0071, 24 March 2019, text No. 2.

Loi No. 2020-1023 du 10 août 2020 instaurant des mesures de sûreté à l'encontre des auteurs d'infractions terroristes à l'issue de leur peine, J.O.R.F. 0196, 11 August 2020, text No. 2.

Loi No. 2021-998 du 30 juillet 2021 relative à la prévention d'actes de terrorisme et au renseignement, J.O.R.F. 0176, 31 July 2021, text No. 1.

Germany

Strafgesetzbuch (StGB) für das Deutsche Reich, 15 May 1871.

Grundgesetz für die Bundesrepublik Deutschland (German Basic Law), DEU-1949-C-39140, 23 May 1943.

Gesetz zur Änderung des Strafgesetzbuches, der Strafprozessordnung, des Gerichtsverfassungsgesetzes, der Bundesrechtanwaltsordnung und des Strafvollzugsgesetzes vom 18 August 1976 (Anti-Terror Law), Bundesgesetzblatt (BGBl) I: Seite 2181.

34 Strafrechtsänderungsgesetz vom 22 August 2002, BGBl Teil I Nr. 61, 29 August 2002: Seite 3390.

Gesetz zur Änderung der Verfolgung der Vorbereitung von schweren staatsgefährenden Gewalttaten (GVVG-Änderungsgesetz – GVVG-ÄndG), BGBl Teil I Nr. 23, 12 June 2015: Seite 926.

United Kingdom of Great Britain and Northern Ireland

Terrorism Act 2000, Chapter 11, 20 July 2000.

Terrorism Act 2006, Chapter 11, 30 March 2006.

Counter-Terrorism Act 2008, Chapter 28, 26 November 2008.

Terrorism Prevention and Investigation Measures Act 2011, Chapter 23, 14 December 2011.

Counter-Terrorism and Border Security Act 2019, Chapter 3, 12 February 2019.

Counter-Terrorism and Sentencing Act 2021, Chapter 11, 29 April 2021.

Table of Cases (Chronological Order)

International Court of Justice

Reparation for injuries suffered in the service of the United Nations, Advisory Opinion, 11 April 1949, I.C.J. Reports 1949, p. 174.

Military and Paramilitary Activities in and against Nicaragua (Nicaragua v. *United States of America), Merits, Judgment of 27 June 1986, I.C.J. Reports 1986*, p. 14.

Sovereignty over Pulau Ligitan and Pulau Sipadan (Indonesia/Malaysia), Judgement of 17 December 2002, I.C.J. Reports 2002, p. 625.

Armed Activities on the Territory of the Congo (Democratic Republic of the Congo v. *Uganda),* Judgment of 19 December 2005, *I.C.J. Reports 2005, p. 168.*

Sovereignty over Pedra Branca/Pulau Batu Puteh, Middle Rocks and South Ledge (Malaysia/Singapore), Judgment of 23 May 2008, I.C.J. Reports 2008, p. 12.

European Court of Human Rights

Klass v. *Germany*, App. No. 5029/71, judgment (merits), 2 E.H.R.R. 214, 6 September 1978.

The Sunday Times v. *the United Kingdom*, App. No. 6538/74, judgment (plenary), 2 EHRR 245, 26 April 1979.

Tarakhel v. *Switzerland*, App. No. 29217/12, judgment (Grand Chamber), ECLI: CE:ECHR:2014:1104JUD002921712, 4 November 2014.

Varga and others v. *Hungary*, App. No. 14097/12, 45135/12, 73712/12, and al., judgment (Grand Chamber), ECLI:CE:ECHR:2015:0310JUD001409712, 5 April 2016.

Avotins v. *Latvia*, App. No. 17502/07, judgment, ECLI:CE:ECHR:2016: 0523JUD001750207, 23 May 2016.

Ghoumid and others v. *France*, App. No. 52273/16, 52285/16, 52290/16 et al., judgment, ECLI:CE:ECHR:2020:0625JUD005227316, 25 June 2020.

Court of Justice of the European Union

Van Gend & Loos v. *Nederlandse Administratie der Belastingen,* C-26/62, judgment, ECLI:EU:C:1963:1, 5 February 1963.

Costa v. *Enel,* C-6/64, judgment, ECLI:EU:C:1964:66, 15 July 1964.

Internationale Handelsgesellschaft mbH v. *Einfuhr- und Vorratsstelle für Getreide und Futtermittel,* C-11/70, ECLI:EU:C:1970:114, 17 December 1970.

Opinion delivered pursuant to the second subparagraph of Article 228 (1) of the EEC Treaty—Convention N° 170 of the International Labour Organization concerning safety in the use of chemicals at work, Opinion 2/91, ECLI:EU: C:1993:106, 19 March 1993.

Opinion of the Court pursuant to Article 228 of the EC Treaty on the Accession by the Community to the European Convention for the Protection of Human Rights and Fundamental Freedoms, Opinion 2/94, ECLI:EU:1996:140, 28 March 1996.

The Queen v. *Ministry of Agriculture, Fisheries and Food, ex P Hedley Lomas*, C-5/94, judgement, ECR I-2553, ECLI:EU:C:1996:205, 23 May 1996.

Commission of the European Communities v. *Belgium*, C-471/98, judgement, ECLI:EU:C:2002:628, 5 November 2002.

Hüseyin Gözütok and Klaus Brügge, Joined Cases C-187/01 and C-385/01, judgment, ECLI:EU:C:2003:87, 11 February 2003.

Miraglia, C-469/03, judgment, ECLI:EU:C:2005:156, 10 March 2005.

Pupino, C-105/03, judgment, ECLI:EU:C:2005:386, 16 June 2005.

Commission v. *Council*, C-176/03, judgment (Grand Chamber), ECLI:EU: C:2005:542, 13 September 2005.

Giovanni dell'Orto, C-467/05, judgment, ECLI:EU:C:2007:395, 28 June 2007.

Commission v. Council, C-440/05, judgment (Grand Chamber), ECLI:EU: C:2007:625, 23 October 2007.

Kadi and Al Barakaat International Foundation v. *Council and Commission*, Joined Cases C-402/05 P and C-415/05 P, judgment, ECLI:EU:C:2008:461, 3 September 2008.

GyőrgyKatz, C-404/07, judgment, ECLI:EU:C:2008:553, 9 October 2008.

People's Mojahedin Organization of Iran v. *Council of the European Union*, T-256/07, judgment, ECLI:EU:T:2008:461, 23 October 2008.

People's Mojahedin Organization of Iran v. *Council of the European Union*, T-284/08, judgment, ECLI:EU:T:2008:593, 17 December 2008.

Turansky, C-491/07, judgment, ECLI:EU:C:2008:768, 22 December 2008.

Sison II, T-341/07, judgment (Court of First Instance), ECLI:EU:T:2011:687, 30 September 2009.

Hassan and *Ayadi*, Joined Cases C-399/06 and C-403/06, judgment, ECLI:EU: C:2009:748, 3 December 2009.

EP v. *Council of the EU*, C-130/10, judgment (action for annulment), ECLI:EU: C:2012:472, 11 March 2010.

The Queen, M. and others, C-340/08, judgment, ECLI:EU:C:2010:232, 29 April 2010.

E. and F., C-550/09, judgment, ECLI:EU:C:2010:382, 29 June 2010.

Gueye et Sameron Sanchez, Joined Cases C-483/09 and C-1/10, 15 September 2010.

Eredics and Sapi, C-205/09, judgment, ECLI:EU:C:2010:623, 21 October 2010.

N.S. and others, Joined Cases C-411/10 and C-493/10, judgment, ECLI:EU: C:2011:865, 21 December 2011.

X., C-507/10, judgment, ECLI:EU:C:2011:873, 21 December 2011.

Maurizio Giovanardi and others, C-79/11, judgment, ECLI:EU:C:2012:448, 12 July 2012.

Radu, C-396/11, judgment (Grand Chamber), ECLI:EU:C:2013:39, 29 January 2013.

Melloni v. *Ministerio Fiscal*, C-399/11, judgment (Grand Chamber), ECLI:EU: C:2013:107, 26 February 2013.

European Commission, Council of the European Union, United Kingdom of Great Britain and Northern Ireland v. *Yassin Abdullah Kadi,* Joined Cases C-584/ 10P, C-593/10 and C-595/10P, Opinion of Advocate General Bot, ECLI:EU: C:2013:176, 19 March 2013.

Commission, Council and UK v. *Yassin Abdullah Kadi*, Joined Cases C-584/ 10 P, C-593/10 P, and C-595/10 P, judgment (Grand Chamber), ECLI:EU:C:2013: 518, 18 July 2013.

Bundesrepublik Deutschland v. *Puid*, C-4/11, judgment (Grand Chamber), ECLI: EU:C:2013:740, 14 November 2013.

Abdullahi v. *Bundesasylamt,* C-394/12, judgment (Grand Chamber), ECLI:EU: C:2013:813, 10 December 2013.

Procura della Repubblica v. *M.*, C-398/12, Opinion of Advocate General Sharpston, ECLI:EU:C:2014:65, 6 February 2014.

Digital Rights Ireland Ltd et Seitlinger e.a., Joined Cases C-293/12 and C-594/ 12, judgment (Grand Chamber), ECLI:EU:C:2014:238, 8 April 2014.

Google Spain SL, Google Inc v. *Agencia Espanola de Proteccion de Datos (AEDP), Mario Costeja Gonzalez*, C-131/12, judgment (Grand Chamber), ECLI: EU:C:2014:317, 13 May 2014.

European Parliament v. *Council (Mauritius Agreement)*, C-658/11, judgment (Grand Chamber), ECLI:EU:C:2014:2025, 24 June 2014.

Opinion pursuant to Article 218(11) TFEU, Opinion 2/13 (full court), ECLI:EU: C:2014:2454, 18 December 2014.

Maximillian Schrems v. *Data Protection Commissioner*, C-362/14, judgment (Grand Chamber), ECLI:EU:C:2015:650, 6 October 2015.

Covaci, C-216/14, judgment, ECLI:EU:C:2015:686, 15 October 2015.

Aranyosi and Caldaru, Joined Cases C-404/15 and C-659/15 PPU, judgment (Grand Chamber), ECLI:EU:C:2016:198, 5 April 2016.

István Balogh, C-25/15, judgment, ECLI:EU:C:2016:423, 9 June 2016.

Milev, C-439/16 PPU, judgment, ECLI:EU:C:2016:818, 27 October 2016.

Kovalkovas, C-477/16 PPU, judgment, ECLI:EU:C:2016:861, 10 November 2016.

Tele2 Sverige AB v. *Post-och telestyrelsen* and *Secretary of State for the Home Department* v. *Tom Watson, Peter Brice, Geoffrey Lewis*, Joined Cases C-203/15 and C-698/15, judgement (Grand Chamber), ECLI:EU:C:2016:970, 21 December 2016.

C.K. and others v. *Republika Slovenija*, C-578/17 PPU, Opinion of Advocate General Tanchev, ECLI:EU:C:2017:108, 9 February 2017.

Tranca, Reiter and Opria, Joined Cases C-124/16, C-188/16 and C-213/16, judgment, ECLI:EU:C:2017:228, 22 March 2017.

Sleutjes, C-278/16, judgment, ECLI:EU:C:2017:757, 12 October 2017.

Kolev and others, C-612/15, judgement (Grand Chamber), ECLI:EU:C:2018:392, 5 June 2018.

L.M., C-216/18 PPU, judgment (Grand Chamber), ECLI:EU:C:2018:586, 28 June 2018.

Milev, C-310/18 PPU, judgment, ECLI:EU:C:2018:732, 19 September 2018.

RH, C-8/19 PPU, order, ECLI:EU:C:2019:110, 12 February 2019.

Moro, C-646/17, judgment, ECLI:EU:C:2019:489, 13 June 2019.

Gambino, C-38/18, judgment, ECLI:EU:C:2019:628, 29 July 2019.

AH and Others, C-377/18, judgment, ECLI:EU:C:2019:670, 5 September 2019.

EP, Rayonna prokuratura Lom and others, C-467/18, judgment, ECLI:EU:C:2019:765, 19 September 2019.

DK and Spetsializirana prokuratura, C-653/19 PPU, judgment, ECLI:EU:C:2019:1024, 28 November 2019.

VW, C-659/18, judgment, ECLI:EU:C:2020:201, 12 March 2020.

Data Protection Commissioner v. *Facebook Ireland Limited and Maximillian Schrems* (Shrems II), C-311/18, judgment (Grand Chamber), ECLI:EU:C:2020:559, 16 July 2020.

Bibliography

(2003). *Dictionnaire de la culture juridique* (1st ed.). PUF.
(2005). *Lexique des termes juridiques* (15th ed.). Dalloz.
Abbott, K. W., & Snidal, D. (2001). Hard and soft law in international governance. *International Organization, 54*, 421–456.
Abbott, K. W., Keohane, R., Moravcsik, A., Slaughter, A.-M., & Snidal, D. (2000). The concept of legalization. *International Organization, 54*(3), 401–420.
Abuza, Z. (2003). *Militant Islam in Southeast Asia: Crucible of terror*. Lynne Rienner.
Acharya, A. (2001). *Constructing a security community in Southeast Asia: ASEAN and the problem of regional order*. Routledge.
Acharya, A. (2004). How ideas spread: Whose norms matter? Norm localization institutional change in Asian regionalism. *International Organization, 58*(2), 239–275.
Acharya, A. (2008). *Constructing a security community in Southeast Asia. ASEAN and the problem of regional order* (2nd ed.). Routledge.
Acharya, A. (2011). Norm subsidiarity and regional orders: Sovereignty, regionalism, and rule-making in the third world. *International Studies Quarterly, 55*(1), 95–123.
Acharya, A. (2012). Comparative regionalism: A field whose time has come? *The International Spectator, 47*(1), 3–15.
Acharya, A. (2014). *Constructing a security community in Southeast Asia. ASEAN and the problem of regional order. Politics in Asia* (3rd ed.). Routledge.
Acharya, A., & Johnston, A. I. (2007a). Comparing regional institutions: An introduction. In A. Acharya & A. I. Johnston (Eds.), *Crafting cooperation: Regional international institutions in comparative perspective*. Cambridge University Press.
Acharya, A., & Johnston, A. I. (2007b). Conclusion: Institutional features, cooperation effects, and the agenda for further research on comparative regionalism. In A. Acharya & A. I. Johnston (Eds.), *Crafting cooperation: Regional international institutions in comparative perspective*. Cambridge University Press.
Adler, E., & Barnett, M. (Eds.). (1998). *Security communities*. Cambridge University Press.
Allen, D., & Smith, M. (1990). Western Europe's presence in the contemporary international arena. *Review of International Studies, 16*(1), 19–37.
Alston, P., & Goodman, R. (2007). *International human rights in context: Law, politics and morals* (3rd ed.). Oxford University Press.
Anderson, M. (2002). Trust and police co-operation. In M. Anderson & J. Apap (Eds.), *Police and justice cooperation and the new European borders. European monographs*. Kluwer Law International.

C. C. Cocq, *Mutual Trust in Regional and Interregional Cooperation on Counterterrorism*, United Nations University Series on Regionalism 26,
https://doi.org/10.1007/978-3-031-36612-3

Armada, I. (2015). The European investigation order and the lack of European standards for gathering evidence: Is a fundamental rights-based refusal the solution? *New Journal of European Criminal Law, 6*(1), 8–31.

Asp, P. (2008). Basic models of a European penal law: Mutual recognition, cooperation, harmonisation. *Europäischer Juristentag, 4*, 259–273.

Atias, C. (1985). *Epistémologie Juridique. Droit Fondamental, Droit Politique Et Théorique*. Presse Universitaires de France.

Aubrey, S. M. (2004). *The new dimension of international terrorism*. vdf Hochschulverlag AG an der ETH.

Badinter, R. (1993). Opinion no. 1: Conference on Yugoslavia, Arbitration Commission. 29 November 1991. *International Law Reports, 92*, 162–165. Cambridge: Grotius Publications Limited.

Banlaoi, R. C. (2009). *Counter terrorism measures in Southeast Asia: How effective are they?* De La Salle University, Yuchengco Center.

Barnett, M. N. (1995). The United Nations and global security: The norm is mightier than the sword. *Ethics & International Affairs, 9*, 37–54.

Barnett, M. (2008). Social constructivism. In J. Baylis, S. Smith, & P. Owens (Eds.), *The globalisation of world politics: An introduction to international politics*. Oxford University Press.

Baud, J. (1998). *Encyclopédie du renseignement et des services secrets* (2nd ed.). Lavauzelle.

Baylis, J., Smith, S., & Owens, P. (Eds.). (2008). *The globalisation of world politics: An introduction to international politics*. OUP.

Beccaria, C. *Of crimes and punishments* (originally published in Italian in 1764).

Bellamy, A. J. (2004a). *Security communities and their neighbours: Regional fortresses or global integrators*. Palgrave Macmillan.

Bellamy, A. J. (2004b). The pursuit of security in Southeast Asia: Beyond realism. In M. Beeson (Ed.), *Contemporary Southeast Asia: Regional dynamics, national differences*. Palgrave Macmillan.

Berkofsky, A. (2005). *Comparing EU and Asian integration processes. The EU a role model for Asia?* European Policy Centre.

Bessis, F. (2009). L'institution comme realisation du collectif. *Tracés: Revue de Sciences Humaines, ENS Editions*, 73–87.

Best, E., & Christiansen, T. (2008). Regionalism in international affairs. In J. Baylis, S. Smith, & P. Owens (Eds.), *The globalisation of world politics: An introduction to international politics*. Oxford University Press.

Beyer, A. C. (2010). *Counter terrorism and international power relations: The EU, ASEAN and hegemonic global governance*. I.B.Tauris & Co Ltd.

Bhanu Mehta, P. (2011). Sovereignty tradeoffs and regional integration. Theoretical and comparative reflections. In E. Sridharan (Ed.), *International relations theory and South Asia: Security political economy, domestic politics, identities, and images*. Oxford University Press.

Bigo, D. (1996). *Polices en Réseaux: L'Expérience Européenne*. Presse de Science Po.

Bilal, S. (2007). *Is the EU a model of regional integration? Risks and challenges*. Briefing for ACP-EU Joint Parliamentary Assembly's Committee on Political Affairs. Bruxelles: European Centre for Development Policy Management.

Blackstock, J. (2012). Procedural safeguards in the European Union: A road well travelled? *European Criminal Law Review, 2*(1), 20–35.

Boehm, F. (2012). *Information sharing and data protection in the area of freedom, security and justice. Towards harmonised data protection principles for information exchange at EU-level*. Springer.

Borchardt, K.-D. (2017). *The ABC of EU law*. EU Publications Office.

Born, H., & Caparini, M. (Eds.). (2013). *Democratic control of intelligence services. Containing rogue elephants*. Ashgate.

Börzel, T. A., & Risse, T. (2012). From Europeanisation to diffusion: Introduction. *West European Politics, 35*(1), 1–19.
Bossuyt, M. J. (1980). The direct applicability of international instruments on human rights. With special reference to Belgian and U.S. law. *Revue Belge de Droit International, 15*, 317–343.
Boulouis, J. (1995). *Droit institutionnel de l'Union européenne* (5th ed.). Montchrestien.
Bräutigam, T., & Miettinen, S. (Eds.). (2016). *Data protection, privacy and European regulation in the digital age*. Forum Iuris.
Breslin, S. (2007). Theorising East Asian regionalism(s): New regionalism and Asia's future(s). In M. G. Curley & N. Thomas (Eds.), *Advancing East Asian regionalism*. Routledge.
Breslin, S. (2010). The EU and Asia within an evolving global order: What is Europe? Where is Asia? *East Asia? An International Quaterly, 27*(1), 1–13.
Bretherton, C., & Vogler, J. (2005). *The European Union as a global actor. Politics & international relations* (2nd ed.). Routledge.
Bribosia, E. (2004). La Future Constitution: Point Culminant De La Constituionalisation Des Droits Fondamentaux Dans l'Union Européenne. In P. Magnette (Ed.), *La Grande Europe*. Editions de l'Université de Bruxelles.
Bribosia, E., & Weyembergh, A. (Eds.). (2002). *Lutte contre le terrorisme et droits fondamentaux*. Bruylant.
Bribosia, E., & Weyembergh, A. (2016). Confiance Mutuelle Et Droits Fondamentaux: 'Back to the Future'. *Cahiers de droit européen, 52*(2), 469–521.
Brière, C. (2019a). Cooperation of europol and eurojust with external partners in the fight against crime: A legal appraisal. In H. C. H. Hofmann, E. Vos, & M. Chamon (Eds.), *The external dimension of EU agencies and bodies. Law and policy*. Edward Elgar.
Brière, C. (2019b). Le Parquet Européen: Analyse critique d'une réussite tempérée par d'importants défis à relever. *Cahiers de droit européen, 55*(1), 149–188.
Brouwer, E. (2008). *Digital borders and real rights. Effective remedies for third-country nationals in the Schengen Information System*. Martinus, Nijhoff Publishers.
Brown, S. D. (2008). Ready, willing and enable. In S. D. Brown (Ed.), *Combating international crime. The longer arm of the law*. Routledge.
Brownlie, I. (1998). *Principles of public international law* (5th ed.). Clarendon Press.
Brunnée, J., & Toope, S. J. (2013). Constructivism and international law. In J. L. Dunoff & M. A. Pollack (Eds.), *Interdisciplinary perspectives on international law and international relations: The state of the art*. C.U.P.
Bull, H. (1982). Civilian power Europe: A contradiction in terms? *Journal of Common Market Studies, 21*(2), 149–164.
Bunyan, T. (1993). Trevi, Europol and the European state. In *Statewatching the New Europe*. Statewatch.
Bures, O. (2011). *EU counterterrorism policy. A paper tiger?* Ashgate.
Caballero-Anthony, M. (2003). *Regionalisation of peace in Asia: Experiences and prospects of ASEAN, ARF and UN partnership*. Working paper no. 42. Institute of Defence and Strategic Studies.
Caeiro, P., & Lemos, M. Â. (2013). Content and impact of approximation: The case of terrorist offences (council framework decisions of 2002 and 2008). In F. Galli & A. Weyembergh (Eds.), *Approximation of substantive criminal law in the EU. The way forward*. Editions de l'Université de Bruxelles.
Cameron-Waller, S. (2008). Interpol. A global service provider. In S. D. Brown (Ed.), *Combating international crime. The longer arm of the law*. Routledge.
Cappelletti, M., Seccombe, M., & Weiler, J. H. H. (1985). A political, legal and economic overview. In M. Cappelletti, M. Seccombe, & J. H. H. Weiler (Eds.), *Integration through law: Europe and the American federal experience*. De Gruyter.
Cappelletti, M., Seccombe, M., & Weiler, J. H. H. (Eds.). (1986). *Integration trough law. Europe and the American federal experience. Book 1 Vol. 1: Methodes, tools and institutions*. De Gruyter.

Cariat, N. (2020). Article 53. Niveau De Protection. In F. Picod, C. Rizcallah, & S. Van Drooghenbroeck (Eds.), *Charte Des Droits Fondamentaux De l'Union Européenne*. Bruylant. Droit De l'Union Européenne.

Carrera, S., Mitsilegas, V., Stefan, M., & Giuffrida, F. (2018). In P. Hustinx & M. Kennedy (Eds.), *Criminal justice and police cooperation between the EU and the UK after Brexit. Towards a principled and trust-based partnership*. CEPS & QMUL.

Cassin, R. (1951). La Déclaration Universelle Et La Mise En Oeuvre Des Droits De L'homme. *Recueil des Cours de l'Académie de Droit International, 79*, 237–367.

Cesoni, M. L. (Ed.). (2007). *Nouvelles Méthodes De Lutte Contre La Criminalité: La Normalisation De L'exception. Etude De Droit Comparé (Belgique, Etats-Unis, Italie, Pays-Bas, Allemagne, France)*. Bruylant.

Chalian, G., & Blin, A. (Eds.). (2016). *The history of terrorism from antiquity to ISIS*. University of California Press.

Chalmers, D., Davies, G., & Monti, G. (2014). *European Union law* (3rd ed.). C.U.P.

Chesterman, S. (2008). Does ASEAN exist? The association of South East Asian nations as an international legal person. *Singapore Year Book of International Law, 12*, 199–211.

Chesterman, S. (2011). *One nation under surveillance. A new social contract to defend freedom without sacrifying liberty*. Oxford University Press.

Chevallier-Govers, C. (1999). *De la coopération à l'intégration policière dans l'Union Européenne*. Bruylant.

Chow, J. T. (2005). ASEAN counterterrorism cooperation since 9/11. *Asian Survey, 45*(2), 302–321.

Clarke, G. (2012). The evolving ASEAN human rights system: The ASEAN human rights declaration of 2012. *Northwestern Journal of International Human Rights, 11*(1), 1–27.

Cocq, C. C. (2015). Development of regional legal frameworks for intelligence and information sharing in the EU and ASEAN. *Tilburg Law Review. Journal of International and European Law, Special issue: Privacy and National Security in the Digital Age, 20*(1), 58–77.

Cocq, C. C. (2016a). The EU and ASEAN approaches in fighting terrorism: Collaboration or cooperation? In *Countering Daesh extremism. European and Asian Responses*. Panorama: Insights into Asian and European affairs. Konrad Adenauer Stiftung.

Cocq, C. C. (2016b). Transposition De La Résolution 2178 (2014) Par La Belgique Et La France: Vers Une Répression Des Combattants Terroristes Étrangers Toujours Plus Préventive Et Fournie. *Les Nouveaux Problèmes Actuels de Sciences Criminelles - Lextenso, XXVI*(3), 171–191.

Cocq, C. C. (2016c). EU data protection rules applying to law enforcement activities: Towards an harmonised legal framework? *New Journal of European Criminal Law, 7*(3), 263–276.

Cocq, C. C. (2016d). Data retention regime within the EU: Reinventing a common framework after the CJEU ruling on the digital rights Ireland case? *European Journal of Policing Studies, 4*(1), 146–172.

Cocq, C. C. (2017). 'Information' and 'intelligence'. The current divergences between national legal systems and the need for common (European) notions. *New Journal of European Criminal Law, 8*(3).

Cocq, C., & Galli, F. (2013). The catalysing effect of serious crime on the use of surveillance technologies for prevention and investigation purposes. *New Journal of European Criminal Law, 4*(3), 256–289.

Cocq, C. C., & Teo, S. (2015). Countering terrorism: Challenges and opportunities in ASEAN-EU cooperation. In L. Fawcett, F. Ponjaert, & M. Telò (Eds.), *Interregionalism and the European Union. A post-revisionist approach to Europe's place in a changing world*. Ashgate.

Collins, A. (2003). *Security and Southeast Asia: Domestic, regional, and global issues*. Lynne Rienner Publishers.

Conte, P., & du Chambon, P. M. (1995). *Procédure Pénale*. Masson.

Corten, O. (2009). *Méthodologie du droit international public*. Editions de l'Université de Bruxelles.

Craig, P., & de Burca, G. (2011). *EU law: Text, cases, and materials* (5th ed.). O.U.P.
Cremona, M., Monar, J., & Poli, S. (Eds.). (2011). *The external dimension of the European Union's area of freedom, security and justice*. Peter Lang.
Croissant, A., & Barlow, D. (2007). Following the money trail: Terrorist financing and government responses in Southeast Asia. *Studies in Conflict & Terrorism, 30*(2), 131–156.
Cussac, G. (2014). Intromisión En La Intimidad Y CNI. Critica Al Modelo Español De Control Judicial Previó. *Inteligencia y Seguridad, 15*, 151–186.
Czarniawska, B. (2006). *Emerging institutions: Pyramids or anthills*. GRI-rapport no. 7. Gothenburg Research Institute.
Daillier, P., Forteau, M., & Pellet, A. (2009). *Droit international public (Nguyen Quoc Dinh †)* (8th ed.). L.G.D.J.
De Biolley, S. (2006). Collecte, échange et protection des données dans la coopération en matière pénale: le cadre légal européen en profonde mutation. *Journal de Tribunaux - Droit Européen, 131*(7), 193–199.
de Boer, N. (2013). Addressing Rights Divergences under the Charter: Melloni. Case C-399/11, Stefano Melloni V. Ministerio Fiscal, Judgment of the Court (Grand Chamber) of 26 February 2013. *Common Market Law Review, 50*(4), 1083–1103.
De Bondt, W., & Vermeulen, G. (2010). Appreciating approximation: Using common offence concepts to facilitate police and judicial cooperation in the EU. In M. Cools et al. (Eds.), *EU and international crime control: Topical issues* (Governance of security research paper series). Maklu.
De Kerchove, G., & Weyembergh, A. (Eds.). (2001). *La Reconnaissance Mutuelle Des Décisions Judiciaires Pénales Dans l'Union Européenne*. Editions de l'Université de Bruxelles.
De Kerchove, G., & Weyembergh, A. (Eds.). (2005). *La Confiance Mutuelle Dans L'espace Pénal Européen - Mutual Trust in the European Criminal Area, Études Européennes*. Éditions de l'Université de Bruxelles.
de Prado, C. (2010). Regions in the world: The EU and East Asia as foreign policy actors. *International Politics, 47*(3/4), 355–370.
Delmas-Marty, M. (1996). La preuve pénale. *Droits. Revue française de théorie juridique, 23*, 53–65.
Desierto, D. A. (2010). ASEAN's constitutionalization of international law: Challenges to evolution under the new ASEAN charter. *Columbia Journal of Transnational Law, 49*, 268–320.
Diez, T., & Manners, I. (2007). Reflecting on normative power Europe. In F. Berenskoeter & M. J. Williams (Eds.), *Power in world politics*. Routledge.
Dony, M. (2009). The EU's external relations and their evolving legal framework. In M. Teló (Ed.), *The European Union and global governance*. Routledge.
Dony, M. (2018a). *Droit De l'Union Européenne* (7th ed.). Editions de l'Université de Bruxelles.
Dony, M. (2018b). Retour sur les compétences externes implicites de l'Union. *Cahiers de droit européen, 54*(1), 109–176.
Dumitriu, E. (2004). The EU's definition of terrorism: The council framework decision on combating terrorism. *German Law Journal, 5*(5), 585–602.
Düsterhaus, D. (2015). Judicial coherence in the area of freedom, security and justice. Squaring mutual trust with effective judicial protection. *Review of European Administrative Law, 8*(2), 151–182.
Emmers, R. (2003, May). *The threat of transnational crime in Southeast Asia: Drug trafficking, human smuggling and trafficking and sea piracy*. UNISCI discussion papers.
Emmers, R. (2004). *Non-traditional security in the Asia-Pacific: The dynamics of securitization*. Marshall Cavendish.
Emmers, R. (2007). *Comprehensive security and resilience in Southeast Asia: ASEAN's approach to terrorism and piracy*. Working paper no. 132, S. Rajaratnam School of International Studies, Singapore.
Evans, P. (2015, June). *From security architecture to secure order: Prospects for cooperative security 2.0*. Asia-Pacific roundtable.

Ewers-Peters, N. M. (2018). The EU as an interorganizational influencer? *European Foreign Affairs Review, 23*(3), 365–380.
Farcy, F., & Gayraud, J.-F. (2011). *Le renseignement criminel.* CNRS Editions.
Fawcett, L. (2005). Regionalism from an historical perspective. In M. Farrell, B. Hettne, & L. Van Langenhove (Eds.), *Global politics of regionalism.* Pluto Press.
Fawcett, L., Ponjaert, F., & Telò, M. (Eds.). (2015). *Interregionalism and the European Union. A post-revisionist approach to Europe's place in a changing world.* Ashgate.
Fichera, M. (2009). *Mutual trust in European criminal law.* Working paper series no. 10, University of Edinburgh, Edinburgh.
Flassan-Yari, H. (2002). L'ASEAN ou le réveil partiel du Tiers Monde? *Etudes internationales, 33*(2), 349–360.
Flore, D. (1999). Une Justice Pénale Européenne Après Amsterdam. *Journal de Tribunaux - Droit Européen*, 121–129.
Flore, D. (2002). Le Mandat D'arrêt Européen: Première Mise En Oeuvre D'un Nouveau Paradigme De La Justice Pénale Européenne. *Journal des Tribunaux, 121*(6050), 273–281.
Flore, D. (2003). Droit Pénal Matériel Et Union Européenne. In G. De Kerchove & A. Weyembergh (Eds.), *Quelles Réformes Pour L'espace Pénal Européen?* Editions de l'Université de Bruxelles.
Flore, D. (2005). La Notion De Confiance Mutuelle: L''Alpha' Ou L''Oméga' D'une Justice Pénale Européenne. In G. De Kerchove & A. Weyembergh (Eds.), *La Confiance Mutuelle Dans L'espace Pénal Européen - Mutual trust in the European criminal area.* Editions de l'Université de Bruxelles.
Flore, D. (2009). *Droit Pénal Européen. Les Enjeux D'une Justice Pénale Européenne.* Larcier.
Frowein, J. A. (1986). Integration and the federal experience in Germany and Switzerland. In M. Cappelletti, M. Seccombe, & J. H. H. Weiler (Eds.), *Integration trough law. Europe and the American federal experience.* Walter de Gruyter.
Galli, F. (2019). *Interoperable law enforcement. Cooperation challenges in the EU area of freedom, security and justice.* EUI working paper no. 15.
Galli, F., & Weyembergh, A. (Eds.). (2012). *EU counter-terrorism offences. What impact on national legislation and case-law?* Editions de l'Université de Bruxelles.
Galli, F., & Weyembergh, A. (Eds.). (2013). *Approximation of substantive criminal law in the EU: The way forward, Etudes Européennes.* Editions de l'Université de Bruxelles.
Gamble, J. K., et al. (2005). Human-centric international law: A model and a search for empirical indicators. *Tulane Journal of International and Comparative Law, 14*, 61–80.
Gehring, T., & Oberthür, S. (2009). The causal mechanisms of interaction between international institutions. *European Journal of International Relations, 15*(1), 125–156.
Gehring, T., Oberthür, S., & Mühleck, M. (2013). European Union actorness in international institutions: Why the EU is recognized as an actor in some international institutions, but not in others. *Journal of Common Market Studies, 51*(5), 849–865.
Gershman, J. (2002). Is Southeast Asia the second front? *Foreign Affairs, 81*(4), 60–74.
Gilson, J. (2005). New interregionalism? The EU and East Asia. *Journal of European Integration, 27*(3), 307–326.
Glaser, S. (1970). *Droit international pénal conventionnel.* Bruylant.
Gless, S. (2016). Europol. In V. Mitsilegas, M. Bergström, & T. Konstadinides (Eds.), *Research handbook on EU criminal law.* Edward Elgar.
Goldsmith, J. L., & Posner, E. A.. (1998). *A theory of customary international law.* John M. Olin law economics working paper no. 63, 2nd series.
Gómez-Jara Diez, C. (2010). Models for a system of European criminal law: Unifications vs. harmonisation? *New Journal of European Criminal Law, 1*(3), 385–402.
González Cussac, J. L. (2012). El Secreto De Estado En El Proceso Penal: Denegación De Auxilio Y El Delito De Revelación. *Inteligencia y Seguridad, 12*, 141–160.
González Fuster, G. (2014). *The emergence of personal data protection as a fundamental right of the EU* (Vol. 16). Springer.

González Fuster, G., De Hert, P., & Gutwirth, S. (2011). *Privacy and data protection in the EU security continuum*. INEX policy brief no. 12.

Goold, B. J. (2011). Mind the (information) gap: Making sense of the European Union's strategic approach to transnational organised crime. In F. Allum & S. Gilmour (Eds.), *Routledge handbook of transnational organized crime*. Routledge.

Greenleaf, G. (2012). The influence of European data privacy standards outside Europe: Implications for globalisation of Convention 108. *International Data Privacy Law, 2*(1), 68–92.

Greenleaf, G. (2014a). *Asian data privacy laws: Trade and human rights perspectives*. Oxford University Press.

Greenleaf, G. (2014b). Comparisons with other Asian jurisdictions. In S. Chesterman (Ed.), *Data protection in Singapore. Privacy and sovereignty in an interconnected world*. Academy Publishing.

Griffiths, M., O'Callaghan, T., & Roach, S. C. (2008). *International relations* (2nd ed.). Routledge.

Guan, B. T. C. (2004). ASEAN's regional integration challenge: The ASEAN process. *The Copenhagen Journal of Asian Studies, 20*, 70–94.

Gunaratna, R. (2003). *Terrorism in the Asia-Pacific: Threat and response*. Times Media Pte Ltd.

Guzman, A. T. (2008). *How international law works: A rational choice theory*. Oxford University Press.

Haacke, J. (2005). *ASEAN's diplomatic and security culture: Origins, development and prospects*. Routledge.

Haas, E. (1961). International integration: The European and the universal process. *International Organization, 15*(3).

Haas, D. A. (1994). Out of others' shadows: ASEAN moves toward greater regional cooperation in the face of the EC and NAFTA. *American University International Law Review, 9*(3), 809–867.

Habermas, J. (1996). *Die Einbeziehung Des Anderen. Studien Zur Politischen Theorie*. Suhrkamp.

Hannum, H. (1996). The status of the universal declaration of human rights in national and international law. *Georgia Journal of International and Comparative Law, 25*(1), 287–397.

Harding, L. (2014). *The snowden files. The inside story of the world's most wanted man*. Vintage.

Henderson, J. (1999). *Reassessing ASEAN. International institute for strategic studies*. Routledge.

Herlin-Karnell, E. (2014). Constitutional principles in the area of freedom, security and justice. In D. A. Arcarazo & C. C. Murphy (Eds.), *EU security and justice law: After Lisbon and Stockholm*. Modern studies in European law. Hart Publishing.

Hertzberger, E. R. (2007). *Counter-terrorism intelligence cooperation in the European Union*. United Nations Interregional Crime and Justice Research Institute.

Hettne, B. (2003). The new regionalism revisited. In F. Söderbaum & T. M. Shaw (Eds.), *Theories of new regionalism* (International political economy series). Palgrave Macmillan.

Hettne, B. (2007). Interregionalism and world order: The diverging EU and US models. In M. Telò (Ed.), *European Union and new regionalism*. Ashgate.

Hettne, B. (2014). Regional actorship: A comparative approach to interregionalism. In F. Baert, T. Scaramagli, & F. Söderbaum (Eds.), *Intersecting interregionalism. Regions, global governance and the EU*. Springer.

Hettne, B. Globalization, the new regionalism and East Asia. In T. Tanaka & T. Inoguchi (Eds.), *Globalism and regionalism*. United Nations University.

Hettne, B., & Söderbaum, F. (2002). Theorizing the rise of regionness. In S. Breslin, C. W. Hughes, N. Philipps, & B. Rosamond (Eds.), *New regionalisms in the global political economy: Theories and cases*. Routledge.

Hirsch Ballin, M. F. H. (2012). *Anticipative criminal investigation. Theory and counterterrorism practice in The Netherlands and the United States*. T.M.C. Asser Press, Springer.

Hoffman, A. M. (2002). A conceptualization of trust in international relations. *European Journal of International Relations, 8*(3), 375–401.

Hoi, D. L. J. (2018, June). *Embracing change, building resilience*. ASEAN economic integration brief.

Holmes, L. (2013). Dealing with terrorism, corruption and organised crime: The EU and Asia. In T. Christiansen, E. Kirchner, & P. Murray (Eds.), *The Palgrave handbook of EU-Asia relations*. Palgrave Macmillan.

Hood, R., & Hoyle, C. (2015). *The death penalty: A worldwide perspective* (5th ed.). Oxford University Press.

Hreblay, V. (1994). *La Libre Circulation Des Personnes. Les Accords De Schengen. Politique D'aujourd'hui*. Presses Universitaires de France.

Hsu, L. (2005). Towards an ASEAN charter: Some thoughts from the legal perspective. In R. C. Severino (Ed.), *Framing the ASEAN charter*. ISEAS Publishing.

Huang, K.-B. (2008). The transformation of ASEAN as a third-party mediator in intra-regional disputes of Southeast Asia. In J. Bercovitch, K.-B. Huang, & C.-C. Teng (Eds.), *Conflict management, security and intervention in East Asia: Third party mediation in regional conflict*. Routledge.

Hufnagel, S., & McCartney, C. (Eds.). (2017). *Trust in international police and justice cooperation*. Oñati international series in law and society. Hart Publishing.

Hurd, I. (2008). Constructivism. In C. Reus-Smit & D. Snidal (Eds.), *The Oxford handbook of international relations*. O.U.P.

Huxley, T. (1993). *Insecurity in the ASEAN Region*. Royal United Services Institute for Defence Studies.

Hwee, Y. L. (2008). EU-ASEAN relations and policy learning. In R. Balme & B. Bridges (Eds.), *Europe-Asia relations: Building multilateralisms*. Studies in European Union politics. Palgrave Macmillan.

Hwee, Y. L. (2009). The EU as a security actor in Southeast Asia. In W. Hofmeister (Ed.), *Security politics in Asia and Europe*. Panorama: Insights into Asian and European affairs. Konrad-Adenauer-Stiftung.

International Bar Association's Task Force on International Terrorism. (2003). *"International terrorism: Legal challenges and responses" report*. Transnational Publishers.

Ismail, N., & Cieh, E. L. Y. (Eds.). (2013). *Beyond data protection. Strategic case studies and practical guides*. Springer.

Janssens, C. (2013). *The principle of mutual recognition in EU law*. Oxford University Press.

Kahler, M. (2000). Legalization as strategy: The Asia-Pacific case. *International Organization, 54*(3), 549–571.

Katsumata, H., Jones, D. M., & Smith, M. L. R. (2008). ASEAN, regional integration and state sovereignty. *International Security, 33*(2), 182–188.

Katzenstein, P. J. (2000). Regionalism and Asia. *New Political Economy, 5*(3), 353–368.

Keast, R., Brown, K., & Mandell, M. (2007). Getting the right mix: Unpacking integration meanings and strategies. *International Public Management Journal, 10*(1), 9–33.

Kelsen, H. (1950). *The law of the United Nations*. Stevens.

Keohane, R. O. (1988). International institutions: Two approaches. *International Studies Quarterly, 32*(4), 379–396.

Kim, M.-h. (2011). Theorizing ASEAN integration. *Asian Perspective, 35*, 407–435.

Kin Wah, C. (2004). Singapore's perspective on the Asia-Pacific security architecture. In S. Tan & A. Acharya (Eds.), *Asia-Pacific security cooperation. National interests and regional order*. An East Gate Book.

Klabbers, J. (1996). The redundancy of soft law. *Nordic Journal of International Law, 65*, 167–178.

Konstadinides, T. (2011). The Europeanisation of extradition: How many light years away to mutual confidence? In C. Eckes & T. Konstadinides (Eds.), *Crime within the area of freedom, security and justice: A European public order*. Cambridge University Press.

Koops, J. A. (2013). Inter-organisation approaches. In K. E. Jørgensen & K. V. Laatikainen (Eds.), *Routledge handbook on the European Union and international institutions*. Routledge.

Koufa, K. K. (2006). The UN, human rights and counter-terrorism. In G. Nesi (Ed.), *International cooperation in counter-terrorism. The United Nations and regional organizations in the fight against terrorism*. Law, politics & international relations. Routledge.

Krasner, S. D. (1982). Structural causes and regime consequences: Regimes as intervening variables. *International Organization, 36*(2), 185–205.

Krasner, S. (1999). *Sovereignty: Organized hypocrisy*. Princeton University Press.

Kreuzer, K. (2001). La communautarisation du droit international privé: les acquis et les perspectives. In L. Vogel (Ed.), *Unifier le droit: le rêve impossible?* Panthéon Assas Editions.

Kurus, B. (1995). The ASEAN triad: National interest, consensus-seeking, and economic co-operation. *Contemporary Southeast Asia, 16*(4), 404–420.

Labayle, H. (2014). Droit D'asile Et Confiance Mutuelle: Regard Critique Sur La Jurisprudence Européenne. *Cahiers de droit européen, 50*(3), 501–534.

Ladenburger, C. (2007). Fundamental rights and citizenship of the union. In G. Amato, H. Bribosia, & B. De Witte (Eds.), *Genèse Et Destinée De La Constitution Européenne: Commentaire Du Traité Établissant Une Constitution Pour l'Europe À La Lumiére Des Travaux Préparatoires Et Perspectives D'avenir*. Bruylant.

Lazowski, A. (2018). The sky is not the limit: Mutual trust and mutual recognition après Aranyosi and Caldararu. *Croatian Yearbook of European Law and Policy, 14*(1), 1–30.

Leboeuf, L. *Le droit européen de l'asile au défi de la confiance mutuelle*. Université Catholique de Louvain, PhD thesis, 2015.

Lemieux, F. (with the participation of Sophie Allard). (2006). *Normes et pratiques en matière de renseignement criminel. Une comparaison internationale*. Les Presses de l'Université de Laval.

Lemieux, F. (2010). The nature and structure of international police cooperation: An introduction. In F. Lemieux (Ed.), *International police cooperation. Emerging issues, theory and practice*. Willan Publishing.

Lenaerts, K. (2020). *La Charte dans L'ordre juridique de l'Union Européenne*. Opening. La Charte a 20 ans: Regards croisés pour un anniversaire. Bruxelles.

Leviter, L. (2010). The ASEAN charter: ASEAN's failure or member failure? *New York Journal of International Law and Politics, 43*(4), 159–210.

Lin, C. H. (2010). ASEAN charter: Deeper regional integration under international law? *Chinese Journal of International Law, 9*(4), 821–837.

LLobet Angli, M. (2013). What does terrorism mean? In A. Masferrer & C. Walker (Eds.), *Counter-terrorism, human rights and the rule of law: Crossing legal boundaries in defence of the state*. Edward Elgar.

Londras, F. (2010). Terrorism as an international crime. In W. A. Schabas & N. Bernaz (Eds.), *Routledge handbook of international criminal law*. Routledge.

Longo, H., Klumklomchit, T., et al. (2015). *Promoting Effective Responses to the Foreign Terrorist Fighters: Situation in Southeast Asia*. United Nations Office on Drugs and Crime.

Louis, J.-V. (1988). *L'ordre Juridique Communautaire* (4th ed.). Office des publications officielles des Communautés européennes.

Magnette, P., & Weyembergh, A. (2004). L'Espace Pénal Européen: Entre Coopération Judiciaire et Territoire Pénal Européen. In P. Magnette (Ed.), *La Grande Europe*. Editions de l'Université de Bruxelles.

Magnier, V. (1999). *Rapprochement des droits dans l'Union européenne et viabilité d'un droit commun des societies*. Librairie Générale de Droit et Jurisprudence.

Maier-Knapp, N. (2018). *How the EU promotes regional security in Southeast Asia*. Southeast Asian studies, occasional paper series, University of Freiburg, Freiburg.

Mandell, M., & Steelman, T. (2003). Understanding what can be accomplished through interorganizational innovations: The importance of typologies, context, and management strategies. *Public Management Review, 5*(2), 197–224.

Manners, I. (2002). Normative power Europe: A contradiction in terms? *Journal of Common Market Studies, 40*(2), 235–258.

Marguery, T. (2016). "Rebuttal of mutual trust and mutual recognition in criminal matters: Is 'exceptional' enough?" Special section – Mutual recognition and mutual trust: Reinforcing EU integration? (first part). *European papers, 1*(3), 943–963.

Marguery, T. (2020). Confiance mutuelle, reconnaissance mutuelle et crise de valeurs: la difficile équation entre justice pénale européenne et diversité nationale. *European papers, 5*(3), 1271–1288.

Martin Martinez, M. M. (1996). *National sovereignty and international organizations*. Kluwer Law International.

Mattheis, F., & Wunderlich, U. (2017). Regional actorness and interregional relations: ASEAN, the EU and Mercosur. *Journal of European Integration, 39*(6), 723–738.

Mattli, W. (1999). *The logic of regional integration: Europe and beyond*. Cambridge University Press.

Mattli, W. (2000). Sovereignty bargains in regional integration. *Review of International Studies, 2*(2), 149–180.

Mauzy, D. K., & Job, B. L. (2007). U.S. policy in Southeast Asia. Limited re-engagement after years of benign neglect. *Asian Survey, 47*(4), 622–641.

Mayrand, H. (2013). L'apport Mutuel Entre Constructivisme Et Théories Critiques. In R. Bachand (Ed.), *Théories Critiques Et Droit International*. Mondialisation Et Droit International. Bruylant.

McLean, D. (2007). *Transnational organized crime. A commentary on the UN convention and its protocols. Oxford commentary on international law*. Oxford University Press.

McNamara, M. (2012). Starting to untangle the web of cooperation, coordination and collaboration: A framework for public managers. *International Journal of Public Administration, 35*(6), 389–401.

Mehta, P. B. (2011). Sovereignty tradeoffs and regional integration. Theoretical and comparative reflections. In E. Sridharan (Ed.), *International relations theory and South Asia: Security, political economy, domestic politics, identities and images* (Vol. 1). Oxford University Press - India. Security, political economy, domestics politics, identities, and images.

Mette Kjær, A. (2004). *Governance. Key concepts in the social sciences*. Polity Press.

Millar, A., & Rosand, E. (2007). Implementing the UN general assembly's global counter-terrorism strategy in the Asia-Pacific. *Asian Security, 3*(3), 181–203.

Mills, J. L. (2008). *Privacy: The lost right*. O.U.P.

Mitsilegas, V. (2012). The limits of mutual trust in Europe's area of freedom, security and justice: From automatic inter-state cooperation to the slow emergence of the individual. *Yearbook of European Law, 31*(1).

Mitsilegas, V. (2015a). The European Union and the global governance of crime. In V. Mitsilegas, P. Alldridge, & L. Cheliotis (Eds.), *Globalisation, criminal law and criminal justice. Theoretical, comparative and transnational perspectives*. Hart Publishing.

Mitsilegas, V. (2015b). Judicial concepts of trust in Europe's multi-level security governance: From Melloni to Schrems via opinion 2/13. *eucrim*, 3/2015, 90–95.

Mitsilegas, V. (2016). *EU criminal law after Lisbon. Rights, trust and the transformation of justice in Europe*. Hart Publishing.

Mitsilegas, V. (2017). Internal and external dimensions of trust in Europe's area of criminal justice. In C. D. Spinellis, N. Theodorakis, E. Billis, & G. Papadimitrakopoulos (Eds.), *Europe in crisis. Crime, criminal justice and the way forward. Essays in honour of Nestor Kourakis*. Sakkoulas.

Monaco, R. (1960). Comparaison et rapprochement des législations dans le Marché commun européen. *Revue Internationale de Droit Comparé, 12*(1), 61–74.

Monnet, J. (2007). *Mémoires*. Libraire Générale Française.

Moravcsik, A. (1998). *The choice for Europe: Social purpose and state power from Messina to Maastricht*. Cornell University Press.

Morgades-Gil, S. (2015). The discretion of states in the Dublin III system for determining responsibility for examining applications for Asylum: What remains of the sovereignty and humanitarian clauses after the interpretations of the ECtHR and the CJEU? *International Journal of Refugee Law, 27*(3), 433–456.

Möstl, M. (2010). Preconditions and limits of mutual recognition. *Common Market Law Review, 47*(2), 405–436.

Müller, L. M. (2018, December). *Governing regional connectivity in Southeast Asia. The role of the ASEAN secretariat and ASEAN's external partners*. Southeast Asian studies, occasional paper series no. 42, University of Freiburg, Freiburg.

Murphy, C. C. (2012). *EU counter-terrorism law. Pre-emption and the rule of law. Modern studies in European law*. Hart Publishing.

Murray, P. J. (1997). The adequacy standard under Directive 95/46/EC: Does U.S. data protection meet this standard? *Fordham International Law Journal, 21*(3), 932–1018.

Narine, S. (2002). *Explaining ASEAN: Regionalism in Southeast Asia*. Lynne Rienner Publishers.

Naya, S., et al. (Eds.). *ASEAN economic cooperation for the 1990s: A report prepared for the ASEAN standing committee* (p. 1992). The Philippines Institute for Development Studies.

Nelles, U. (2002). Definitions of harmonisation. In A. Klip & H. van der Wilt (Eds.), *Harmonisation and harmonising measures in criminal law*. Koninklijke Nederlandse Akad. van Wetenschappen.

Nollkaemper, A. (2014). The duality of direct effect of international law. *The European Journal of International Law, 25*(1), 105–125.

Nye, J. S., Jr. (1968). *International regionalism. Readings*. Little, Brown & Company.

Nye, J. S., Jr. (2005). *Soft power: The means to success in world politics*. PublicAffairs.

Nyst, C., & Crowe, A.. (2014). *Unmasking the five eye' global surveillance practices*. Communications surveillance in the digital age. Global Information Society Watch. Privacy International.

O'Neill, M. (2012). *The evolving EU counter-terrosim legal framework. Research in EU law*. Routledge.

Oehmichen, A. (2009). *Terrorism and anti-terror legislation. The terrorised legislator?* (Vol. 34). Intersentia.

Ostropolski, T. (2015). The CJEU as a defender of mutual trust. *New Journal of European Criminal Law, 6*(2), 166–178.

Ouwerkerk, J. (2011). *Quid pro quo?: A comparative law perspective on the mutual recognition of judicial decisions in criminal matters*. Intersentia.

Paoli, L. (2008). Organized crime: New label, new phenomenon or policy expedient? *International Annals of Criminology, 46*, 37–60.

Pempel, T. J. (2005). Conclusion: Tentativeness and tensions in the construction of an Asian region. In T. J. Pempel (Ed.), *Remapping East Asia. The construction of a region*. Cornell University Press.

Pescatore, P. (1974). *The law of integration. Emergence of a new phenomenon in international relations, based on the experience of the European communities*. A.W. Sijthoff.

Phan, H. D. (2012). In R. S. Clark, B. H. Weston, R. K. Goldman, & R. B. Lillich (Eds.), *A selective approach to establishing a human rights mechanism in Southeast Asia. The case for a Southeast Asian court of human rights* (Procedural aspects of international law monograph series). Martinus Nijhoff Publishers.

Piris, J.-C., & Woon, W. (2015). *Towards a rules-based community: An ASEAN legal service*. Integrationthrough law: The role of law and the rule of law in ASEAN integration. Cambridge University Press.

Portela, C. (2013, September). *The association of Southeast Asian Nations (ASEAN): Integration, internal dynamics and external relations*. Study for the European Parliament, European Union Publications, Bruxelles.

Ramraj, V. V., Hor, M., & Roach, K. (Eds.). (2012). *Global anti-terrorism law and policy* (2nd ed.). Cambridge University Press.

Rawlinson, P. (2007). Mission impossible? Researching organized crime. In R. King & E. Wincup (Eds.), *Doing research on crime and justice* (2nd ed.). Oxford University Press.

Regilme, S. S. F., Jr. (2013). It takes two to tango: A constructivist analysis of EU-ASEAN interregional relations. In A. Boening, J.-F. Kremer, & A. van Loon (Eds.), *Global power Europe*. Springer.

Rizcallah, C. (2019). Les challenges to trust-based governance in the European Union: Assessing the use of mutual trust as a driver to EU integration. *European Law Journal, 25*(1), 37–56.

Rizcallah, C. (2022). Le principe de confiance mutuelle dans l'Union européenne: un principe en péril. *Les cahiers de la justice, 2022/3*(3), 447–460.

Roach, K. (2012). Secret evidence and its alternatives. In A. Masferrer (Ed.), *Post 9/11 and the state of permanent legal emergency. Security and human rights in countering terrorism*. Springer. Ius Gentium: Comparative perspectives on law and justice.

Roach, K. (Ed.). (2015). *Comparative counter-terrorism law. The state of the art*. Cambridge University Press.

Roberts, C. B. (2012). *ASEAN regionalism. Cooperation, values and institutionalization*. Security in Asia Pacific series. Routledge.

Rule, J. B. (2007). *Privacy in Peril*. Oxford University Press.

Samuel, T. K. (2016). *Radicalisation in Southeast Asia: A selected case study of Daesh in Indonesia, Malaysia and The Philippines*. Southeast Asia Regional Centre for Counter-Terrorism Publications.

Santori, V. (2006). The UN security council's (broad) interpretation of the notion of threat to peace in counter-terrorism. In G. Nesi (Ed.), *International cooperation in counter-terrorism. The United Nations and regional organizations in the fight against terrorism*. Ashgate Publishing.

Sapphaisal, K. (2004). *Fighting terrorism in Southeast Asia*. PhD thesis, Harvard University.

Satzger, H. (2019). Is mutual recognition a viable general path for cooperation? *New Journal of European Criminal Law, 10*(1), 44–56.

Scheinin, M., & Sorell, T. (2015, April 7). *Synthesis report from WP4, merging the ethics and law analysis and discussing their outcomes*. (D4.10) SURVEILLE project.

Schermers, H. G., & Blokker, N. M. (2003). *International institutional law: Unity within diversity* (4th ed.). Martinus Nijhoff.

Severino, R. C. (1998, 22 October). *Asia policy lecture: What ASEAN is and what it stands for*. University of Sydney, Research Institute for Asia and the Pacific.

Severino, R. C. (2006). *Southeast Asia in search of an ASEAN community: Insights from the former ASEAN Secretary-General*. ISEAS Publishing.

Severino, R. C. (2009). *The ASEAN regional forum*. Institute of Southeast Asian Studies.

Sharpe, S. (2003). An ASEAN way to security cooperation in Southeast Asia? *The Pacific Review, 16*(2).

Sim, E. W. (2008). The ASEAN charter: One of many steps towards an ASEAN economic community. *International Trade Law Review, 14*, 109–116.

Singapore Technologies Electronics Limited. (n.d.). ASEAN police forces. Develop e-community with STEE-InfoSoft solution. *STENGG, 19*(2), 14.

Snitwongse, K. (1998). Thirty years of ASEAN: Achievements through political cooperation. *The Pacific Review, 11*(2), 183–194.

Sorell, T. (leader). (2013, July 31). *Matrix of surveillance technologies*. (D2.6) SURVEILLE project.

Stessens, G. (2005). The principle of mutual confidence between judicial authorities in the area of freedom, security and justice. In G. De Kerchove & A. Weyembergh (Eds.), *L'espace Pénal Européen: Enjeux Et Perspectives*. Editions de l'Université de Bruxelles.

Sukma, R. (2004). Indonesia and regional security. The quest for cooperation security. In S. Tan & A. Acharya (Eds.), *Asia-Pacific security cooperation. National interests and regional order*. An East Gate Book.

Suominen, A. (2011). *The principle of mutual recognition in cooperation in criminal matters*. Universitas Bergensis.

Suominen, A. (2014). What role for legal certainty in criminal law within the area of freedom, security and justice in the EU? *Bergen Journal of Criminal Law and Criminal Justice, 2*(1), 1–31.

Tan, A. T. H. (Ed.). (2007). *A handbook of terrorism and insurgency in Southeast Asia*. Edward Elgar.

Teh Cheng Guan, B. (2004). Asean's regional integration challenge: The Asean process. *The Copenhagen Journal of Asian Studies, 20*, 70–94.

Telò, M. (2016). *L'Europe En Crise Et Le Monde*. Editions de l'Université de Bruxelles.

Teló, M., & Weyembergh, A. (Eds.). (2020). *Supranational governance at stake. The EU's external competences caught between complexity and fragmentation*. Routledge.

Thatcher, C. (2007). *A study of interorganizational arrangement among three regional campuses of a large land-grant university*. PhD thesis, University of Hartford.

Thibierge, C., et al. (Eds.). (2009). *La force normative. La naissance d'un concept*. Librairie Générale de Droit et de Jurisprudence.

Totaro, M. V. (2008). Positivism, constructivism, and international human rights law: The case of participatory development. *Virginia Journal of International Law, 48*(4), 719–765.

Tzanou, M. (2017). *The fundamental right to data protection. Normative value in the context of counter-terrorism surveillance*. Hart Publishing.

Van der Hilst, R. (2011, November 30). *Ranking in terms of their human rights risks, the detection technologies and uses surveyed in WP09*. DETECTER project.

Van Langenhove, L., & Thakur, R. (2006). Enhancing global governance through regional integration. *Global Governance, 12*(3), 233–240.

Vander Elst, R. (1976). Les notions de coordination, d'harmonisation, de rapprochement et d'unification du droit dans le cadre juridique de la Communauté économique européenne. In D. de Ripainsel-Landy, A. Gérard, & A. Limpens-Meinertzhagen (Eds.), *Les instruments du rapprochement des legislations dans la Communauté économique européenne*. Editions de l'Université de Bruxelles.

Vasak, K. (1982). Introduction. In K. Vasak & P. Alston (Eds.), *The international dimensions of human rights*. Greenwood Press.

Vedaschi, A. (2018). Privacy and data protection versus national security in transnational flights: The EU–Canada PNR agreement. *International Data Privacy Law, 8*(2), 124–139.

Venke, I., & Thio, L.-A. (2016). *The internal effects of ASEAN external relations. Integration through law*. Cambridge University Press.

Vervaele, J. A. E. (2014). Mutual trust in gathering of evidence at the EU level. What the past learned and the future brings? *Revista de Criminologie, Criminalistica si Penologie, 1*(2), 216–232.

Wah, C. K. (2004). Singapore's perspective on the Asia-Pacific security architecture. In S. Tan & A. Acharya (Eds.), *Asia-Pacific security cooperation: National interests and regional order*. M. E. Sharpe.

Walker, N. (2002). The problem of trust in an enlarged area of freedom, security and justice: A conceptual analysis. In M. Anderson & J. Apap (Eds.), *Police and justice cooperation and the new European borders*. Kluwer Law International. European monographs.

Wang, J. Y. (2006). International legal personality of ASEAN and the legal nature of the China-ASEAN free trade agreement. In J. Wong, Z. Keyuan, & Z. Huaqun (Eds.), *China-ASEAN relations: Economic and legal dimensions*. World Scientific.

Weatherill, S. (2007). *Cases and materials on EU Law* (8th ed.). Oxford University Press.

Weiler, J. H. H., & Haltern, U. R. (1996). The autonomy of the community legal order: Through the looking glass. *Harvard International Law Journal, 37*(2).

Westin, A. F. (1967). *Privacy and freedom*. Atheneum.

Weyembergh, A. (2002a). L'impact Du 11 Septembre Sur L'équilibre Sécurité/Liberté Dans L'espace Pénal Européen. In E. Bribosia & A. Weyembergh (Eds.), *Lutte Contre Le Terrorism Et Droits Fondamentaux*. Bruylant.

Weyembergh, A. (2002b). La Coopération Pénale Européenne Face Au Terrorisme: Rupture Ou Continuité? In K. Bannelier, T. Christakis, O. Corten, & B. Delcourt (Eds.), *Le Droit International Face Au Terrorisme*. Pedone.

Weyembergh, A. (2004a). *L'harmonisation Des Législations: Condition De L'espace Pénal Européen Et Révélateur De Ses Tensions*. Editions de l'Université de Bruxelles.

Weyembergh, A. (2004b). L'espace Pénal Européen: Entre Coopération Judiciaire Et Territoire Pénal Européen. In P. Magnette (Ed.), *La Grande Europe*. Editions de l'Université de Bruxelles.

Weyembergh, A. (2005a). Approximation of criminal laws, the constitutional treaty and the Hague programme. *Common Market Law Review, 42*(6), 1567–1597.

Weyembergh, A. (2005b). The functions of approximation of penal legislation within the EU. *Maastricht Journal of European and Comparative Law, 12*(2), 149–172.

Weyermbergh, A. (2006). Introduction. *Revue internationale de droit pénal, 77*(1), 185–192.

Weyembergh, A. (2017). Consequences of Brexit for European Union criminal law. *New Journal of European Criminal Law, 8*(3), 284–299.

Weyembergh, A. (2018). Enhanced cooperation in criminal matters: Past, present and future. In R. Kert & A. Lehner (Eds.), *Vielfalt Des Strafrechts Im Internationalen Kontext.* Neuer Wissenschaftlicher Verlag.

Weyembergh, A., & Santamaria, V. (2009). Lutte Contre Le Terrorisme Et Droits Fondamentaux Dans Le Cadre Du Troisième Pilier. La Décision-Cadre Du 13 Juin 2002 Relative À La Lutte Contre Le Terrorisme Et Le Principe De La Légalité. In J. Rideau (Ed.), *Les Droits Fondamentaux Dans l'Union Européenne. Dans Le Sillage De La Constitution Européenne.* Bruylant.

Weyembergh, A., Armada, I., & Brière, C. (2014a, January). E*uropean added value assessment: The EU arrest warrant. Annex I: Critical assessment of the existing European arrest warrant framework decision.* Study for the European parliament, European Parliament, Bruxelles.

Weyembergh, A., Armada, I., & Brière, C. (2014b). *The inter-agency cooperation and future architecture of the EU criminal justice and law enforcement area.* Study for the European parliament, European Union Publications, Bruxelles.

Weyembergh, A., & Cocq, C. C. (Eds.), (2023). Foreign terrorist fighters: Enhancing the synergies between the EU's internal and external strategies, special issue, *New Journal of European Criminal Law*. 14(2).

Wiener, A., & Diez, T. (Eds.). (2004). *European integration theory*. Oxford University Press.

Willems, A. (2016). Mutual trust as a term of art in EU criminal law: Revealing its hybrid character. *European Journal of Legal Studies, 9*(1), 211–249.

Willems, A. (2017). *Demystifying the trust problem in EU criminal law: Enhancing mutual trust by harmonising criminal procedural rights?* PhD thesis, Vrije Universiteit Brussel & Université libre de Bruxelles.

Willems, A. (2021). *The principle of mutual trust in EU criminal law. Hart studies in European criminal law*. Hart Publishing.

Wilson, G. (2014). *The United Nations and collective security Routledge research in international law*. Routledge.

Woods, M. J. (2005). Counterintelligence and access to transactional records: A practical history of USA patriot Act Section 215. *Journal of National Security, Law & Policy, 1*(1), 37–71.

Wunderlich, J.-U. (2012a). Comparing regional organisations in global multilateral institutions: ASEAN, the EU and the UN. *Asia Europe Journal, 10*(2–3), 127–143.

Wunderlich, J.-U. (2012b). The EU an actor *Sui Generis*? A comparison of EU and ASEAN actorness. *Journal of Common Market Studies, 50*(4), 653–669.

Xanthopoulou, E. (2020). *Fundamental rights and mutual trust in the area of freedom, security and justice. A role for proportionality? Modern studies in European law*. Hart Publishing.

Printed by Printforce, the Netherlands